Microsoft on Trial

NEW HORIZONS IN COMPETITION LAW AND ECONOMICS

Series Editors: Steven D. Anderman, *Department of Law, University of Essex, UK* and Rudolph J.R. Peritz, *New York Law School, USA*

This series has been created to provide research based analysis and discussion of the appropriate role for economic thinking in the formulation of competition law and policy. The books in the series will move beyond studies of the traditional role of economics – that of helping to define markets and assess market power – to explore the extent to which economic thinking can play a role in the formulation of legal norms, such as abuse of a dominant position, restriction of competition and substantial impediments to or lessening of competition. This in many ways is the *new horizon* of competition law policy.

US antitrust policy, influenced in its formative years by the Chicago School, has already experienced an expansion of the role of economic thinking in its competition rules. Now the EU is committed to a greater role for economic thinking in its Block Exemption Regulations and Modernisation package as well as possibly in its reform of Article 102. Yet these developments still raise the issue of the *extent* to which economics should be adopted in defining the public interest in competition policy and what role economists should play in legal argument. The series will provide a forum for research perspectives that are critical of an unduly-expanded role for economics as well as those that support its greater use.

Titles in the series include:

Competition Law and Patents
A Follow-on Innovation Perspective in the Biopharmaceutical Industry
Irina Haracoglou

Antitrust and Regulation in the EU and US
Legal and Economic Perspectives
Edited by François Lévêque and Howard Shelanski

Competition Law, Innovation and Antitrust
An Analysis of Tying and Technological Integration
Hedvig Schmidt

Intellectual Property and the Limits of Antitrust
A Comparative Study of US and EU Approaches
Katarzyna Czapracka

Microsoft on Trial
Legal and Economic Analysis of a Transatlantic Antitrust Case
Edited by Luca Rubini

Microsoft on Trial

Legal and Economic Analysis of a Transatlantic Antitrust Case

Edited by

Luca Rubini

Lecturer and Deputy Director of the Institute of European Law, Birmingham Law School, UK

NEW HORIZONS IN COMPETITION LAW AND ECONOMICS

Edward Elgar

Cheltenham, UK • Northampton, MA, USA

Published by
Edward Elgar Publishing Limited
The Lypiatts
15 Lansdown Road
Cheltenham
Glos GL50 2JA
UK

Edward Elgar Publishing, Inc.
William Pratt House
9 Dewey Court
Northampton
Massachusetts 01060
USA

A catalogue record for this book
is available from the British Library

Library of Congress Control Number: 2009941150

Mixed Sources
Product group from well-managed
forests and other controlled sources
www.fsc.org Cert no. SA-COC-1565
© 1996 Forest Stewardship Council
FSC

ISBN 978 1 84844 244 3

Printed and bound by MPG Books Group, UK

‘Far-off, most secret, and inviolate Rose,
Enfold me in my hour of hours’
(W.B. Yeats, *The Wind Among the Reeds*, 1896)

To Barbara

Contents

Contributors

Steven Anderman, Professor of Law, University of Essex.

Arianna Andreangeli, Lecturer in Law, Liverpool Law School, University of Liverpool.

Markus Baldauf, Senior Associate, RBB Economics, London.

Nicholas Banasevic, Deputy Head of Unit, Mergers – Task Force Financial Crisis, DG Competition, European Commission. Formerly member of the DG Competition Microsoft case-team.

Jean-François Bellis, partner at the law firm Van Bael & Bellis, Brussels, Professor, Institute of European Studies, University of Brussels (VUB). He has represented Microsoft in the EC case on the tying issue and the imposition of the monitoring mechanism.

Nicholas Economides, Professor of Economics, Stern Business School, New York University; Executive Director, NET Institute.

Jens Fejø, Professor, Dr.jur., Copenhagen Business School.

Ian S. Forrester, Queen's Counsel at the Scots Bar, Visiting Professor, University of Glasgow; partner at White & Case, Brussels. He has represented Microsoft in the EC case on the interoperability issue.

Eleanor M. Fox, Walter J. Derenberg Professor of Trade Regulation at New York University School of Law.

Maria J. Gil-Moltó, Lecturer, Department of Economics, University of Leicester.

Per Hellström, Head of Unit, Antitrust: IT, Internet and Consumer Electronics Unit, DG Competition, European Commission. Formerly member of the Legal Service team representing the European Commission in the Microsoft case, including before the Court of First Instance.

Colin Jackson, PhD, independent advisor in information technologies. He led the team of technical experts appointed by the European Commission to support the case team investigating Microsoft and its behaviour in the server and media player markets in Case T-201/04 and the interim measures part of the case. Trained as a physicist, he moved into information technology. He was a founder and managing director of OTR until 2005 when he sold his interest in the company.

Tim Kasten, partner at the law firm Van Bael & Bellis, Brussels. He has assisted Jean-François Bellis in the EC case on the tying issue and the imposition of the monitoring mechanism.

Ioannis Lianos, Reader in Competition Law and Economics, Faculty of Laws, University College London (UCL); co-Director Centre for Law and Economics; Jevons Institute of Competition Law and Economics, UCL; Emile Noel Fellow, New York University Law School.

Rudolph J.R. Peritz, Professor of Law and Director, IProgress Project, New York Law School.

Carlo Petrucci, Ph.D candidate and Postgraduate Teaching Assistant, School of Law, University of Birmingham.

Derek Ridyard, Partner, RBB Economics, London.

Luca Rubini, Lecturer in Law and Deputy Director of the Institute of European Law, School of Law, University of Birmingham.

Bo Vesterdorf, Dr.iur. hc; consultant to the law firms of Herbert Smith LLP, UK, and Plesner, Denmark; former judge of the Court of First Instance from 1989 to 2007 and its President from 1998 to 2007.

Ann Walsh, University Tutor, School of Law, University of Leicester.

Acknowledgements

Many people have made this publication possible. I need to thank immediately the School of Law, University of Birmingham, and the Institute of European Law for having supported in many ways the organization of the research workshop of March 2008 and the conference of May 2008 on which this book is based. The research assistance of Paul Mora has been invaluable in the final steps towards the conclusion of the manuscript. The kind and efficient people at Edward Elgar must also be mentioned and particularly Rudolph Peritz and Steven Anderman, editors of the series, that have trusted in this project from its beginning. Finally, a special thought goes to Ian Forrester and Colin Jackson, who were involved in the EC case on opposite sides, for their kind, honest and illuminating advice at various stages of the project. This book is dedicated to my wife Barbara for her support but mostly for tolerating the intruding presence of this project in our early family life.

Luca Rubini
Birmingham, 20 July 2010

Abbreviations

AD	analogue-to-digital
API	applications programming interface
CD	compact disc
CFI	Court of First Instance
CIFS	Common Internet File System
CODEC	coder/decoder or compressor/decompressor
COM	component object model
CORBA	Common Object Request Broker Architecture
DA	digital-to-analogue
DAP	Directory Access Protocol
DCE	distributed computing environment
DCOM	distributed component object model
Dfs	Distributed file system
DG Comp	Directorate General for Competition, European Commission
DLL	dynamic-link library
DOJ	US Department of Justice
DRM	digital rights management
DVD	digital versatile disc
EC	European Communities
ECJ	European Court of Justice
EEA	European Economic Area
EU	European Union
FTC	US Federal Trade Commission
GUI	graphical user interface
HTML	HyperText Markup Language
IDL	Interface Definition Language
IE	Internet Explorer
IETF	Internet Engineering Task Force
IP	intellectual property
IPR	intellectual property right
IPv4	Internet Protocol version 4
IT	information technology
JVM	Java Virtual Machine
KCC	knowledge consistency checker

KDC	key distribution centre
LAN	local area network
LDAP	Lightweight Directory Access Protocol
LINFO	Linux Information Project
MS-DOS	Microsoft Disc Operating System
NTLM	New Technology Lan Manager
OECD	Organisation for Economic Co-operation and Development
OEM	original equipment manufacturer
OSF	Open Software Foundation
OSI	open systems interconnection
PAC	privilege access certificate
PC	personal computer
PDA	personal digital assistant
R&D	research and development
RAM	Random Access Memory
RMI	remote message invocation
RNI	Raw Native Interface
RPC	remote procedure call
SAM	security accounts manager
SASL	Simple Authentication and Security Layer
SDK	software developer kit
SMB	Server Message Block
SSO	standard setting organization
TCP	Transport Control Protocol
TCP/IP	Transport Control Protocol/Internet Protocol
TRIPS	Agreement on Trade-Related Aspects of Intellectual Property Rights
UN	United Nations
UNCTAD	United Nations Conference for Trade and Development
US	United States
WMP	Windows Media Player
WSPP	Work Group Server Protocol Programme
WTO	World Trade Organization

Preface

A little elephant is very keen on skating. She practises on and on, improves and begins participating in various contests taking place on the little village lake in winter time. With age (and practice) our little elephant grows and grows and becomes quite a physical presence on the little lake and in the speed and free skating competitions. In the local rural community, skating is a very much practised and extremely dreamed of activity. Worries and complaints about the weight and size of the elephant are increasingly voiced by contenders and viewers. Although big she is very fast and agile in both speed and free racing and often outclasses her competitors. Her magnitude, however, is often seen as a serious obstacle to contenders and a danger to the solidity of the ice level. Local villagers have mixed views. They enjoy the muscular and confident style of the elephant to which they are very much accustomed. At the same time, they seem to share the same worries about the fairness of the races and the overall condition of their lake. They want to keep enjoying this old, good sport. What shall be done? Should the elephant be prohibited to participate in skating sports altogether or, less drastically, should the rules of the game be reviewed to allow a fairer and less perilous sporting activity that is appreciated by so many? And, if so, how should the skating sports in this mountain lake be regulated? Is there a dramatic choice between punishing the elephant because it is ultimately an elephant and safeguarding the sport that is so dear to all involved? Or (following a more or less magical intervention) shall we, and our once little elephant, hope in her transformation into a little, less menacing mouse? In fairy-tale style, this story and its ensuing questions sum up the main antitrust issues raised by the transatlantic legal review of Microsoft's conduct.

This book offers the opportunity to analyse one of the most difficult topics in antitrust laws: the regulation of unilateral conduct of dominant players. The legal disputes that saw Microsoft, its products and commercial strategies subject to competition law scrutiny represent a paradigmatic example of the difficulties raised by unilateral conduct and the economic and legal assessment of its impact on competition and society's welfare, particularly in the context of a complex technical scenario.

In simple terms, the various strands of litigation on both sides of the Atlantic concerned two issues: on the one hand, the extent to which

Microsoft should be obliged to supply details of how to reproduce certain features of its server technology so that other servers could function smoothly within a Windows network (EC case); on the other hand, to what extent the bundling of (depending on the views) extra products or features, like a web-browser (US case) or a media player (EC case), with the Windows operating system significantly restricted the commercial opportunities of producers of competing products or features.

After reading both the US and EC cases that involved Microsoft, it could be argued that the title of the book is not really appropriate. In fact it could easily be rephrased as 'unilateral conduct on trial' or better 'anti-trust regulation of unilateral conduct on trial'. In other words, for several reasons the Microsoft cases represent excellent *test-cases* of the 'anti-trust' and 'efficiency' paradoxes highlighted by Robert Bork[1] and Eleanor Fox[2] respectively. Their interest is certainly not confined to the specific facts of the litigation, or to the vicissitudes of a major company. The real interest derives from the economic and legal issues raised, and their treatment under (EC and US) antitrust laws. As we try to sketch in these brief introductory notes, the extraordinary commercial position of Microsoft and the characteristics of a crucial sector like information technology may help in explaining the case. Most crucially, however, one is left to wonder as to the broader implications of these cases, and particularly the EC one, on the future development of competition law and policy. Further, despite turning on a previously unreached level of technical difficulty, these cases (like any important one) raise grander questions as to the attitude and purpose of competition policy in both the European Union and the United States.[3]

This book has its origin in two events (a research workshop and a conference) organized by the Institute of European Law of the Law School of the University of Birmingham in 2008. This 'Microsoft initiative' provided the opportunity to bring to Birmingham high-profile speakers, often directly involved in the EC case. This represents the core of the project underlying this book which attempts to build and expand on this solid base and make available to the wider public the interesting debate that took place in the West Midlands.

What the editor has attempted to do is to gather various experts who could each provide their own perspective on the EC and US cases and cover all the

---

1 R.H. Bork, The Antitrust Paradox (2nd edition, New York: Free Press, 1993).

2 E.M. Fox, 'The Efficiency Paradox' in R. Pitofsky (ed.), *How the Chicago School Overshot the Mark: The Effect of Conservative Economic Analysis on US Antitrust* (Oxford: Oxford University Press, 2008, p. 77).

3 Ibid.

major issues raised by them. The background of the contributors is varied, ranging from information technology to law and economics. They come from both sides of the Atlantic, from practice and academia, and some of them are immediately associated with the European dispute. Although the emphasis lies particularly on the more recent EC case, US litigation is analysed as well, for its own significance and as representing a necessary basis for comparison of the EC case. Indeed, the US and EC cases can be seen as steps in one single *saga*. Although they obviously involved different authorities applying different laws, and with different approaches, both cases were confronted not only with similar claims but also with similar issues. This is clearly exemplified by the European investigation into the bundling of the Windows Operating System with Internet Explorer which intriguingly echoes the subject of the US case of ten years ago. This recently closed (and final?) chapter in the saga thus seems to rehearse its starting point.[4]

Both the US and EC cases have been highly controversial, politically charged, dramatic (with judges being replaced), even theatrical (with robes worn even when this is not usually done) – and for various reasons. Before briefly presenting the various contributions to this book, and showing their place within its scheme, we thus outline five factors which in our view define the 'Microsoft case'.

First, Microsoft is not like any other company. It is a very successful and powerful enterprise, created and led for many years by one of the true gurus of this age, and operating in a crucial and sensitive sector affecting every aspect of everyday life of the large majority of the world population. It is fair to say that virtually anyone who uses a personal computer at the beginning of the twenty-first century is conversant with one or more Microsoft products. Windows, its PC operating system, is omnipresent. Hence, the commercial decisions of this company affect virtually everyone. Indeed, modern literacy is defined by the familiarity with software, and more generally information technology.

Secondly, beneath user-friendly graphic interfaces and (more or less) intuitive functions, software is extremely complex. This is a key element of the Microsoft case, and more generally of any economic/legal assessment of information technology scenarios. The motto for a sound approach to the analysis of the various issues of the Microsoft case is therefore

---

[4] In fact, the European saga is not completely closed. The EUR 899 million fine imposed on Microsoft with Commission Decision C(2008) 764 final of 27 February 2008, for failure to comply with the obligation to supply the required interoperability information, is currently subject to judicial review before the General Court (formerly the Court of First Instance). See *Microsoft* v *Commission* (case T-167/08) action brought on 9 May 2008 [2008] OJ C171/41.

'technical issues first'. If the technicalities are not properly understood, one seriously risks raising up a fine castle built on very shaky foundations. It could be grand and beautiful in appearance but it would lead to wrong legal and economic conclusions. Eventually, it would not resist the effects of a close and comprehensive scrutiny. The reader is therefore advised of the importance of properly understanding the basic technology aspects of the case.

Thirdly, economics is not always univocal in the determination of the welfare effects of behaviour in markets such as information technology, denoted by complex dynamics and resting on network effects, standardization and integration, fast pace of innovation and obsolescence. As a consequence, an economic-informed antitrust law may be affected by different readings of the efficiency of the scenario under scrutiny.

Fourthly, fluidity (if not lack of clarity) of the law is another important factor. Antitrust is a powerful tool that allows governments to interfere with market functioning. By its own nature, however, its normative framework is far from elaborate and precise. In both the United States and the European Union, the fundamental provisions, including those regulating unilateral conduct, are basic, even skeletal. The old language of Article 82 EC (1957) and sections 1 and 2 of the Sherman Act (1890) is general and broad. It simply outlines the unclear boundaries within which lawyers and economists must operate. Further, antitrust rules are often, and increasingly, based more on 'standards' requiring a case-by-case analysis rather than on predetermined 'rules' of immediate, almost automatic application. And this is particularly so with respect to the most controversial cases of commercial behaviour – and those at issue in the Microsoft cases are paradigmatic in this respect – which are very often unilateral. This open nature, together with the changing attitude towards antitrust policy, has meant that through decades and years, the interpretation and application of the same provisions have changed, often dramatically, to reflect the prevailing antitrust philosophy. More specifically, both the EC and US antitrust systems are currently undertaking a review of the treatment of unilateral behaviour.

Fifthly, as hinted at the end of the previous paragraph (and even before), attitudes towards a more or less interventionist use of antitrust law may develop and change. This ultimately depends on the *conceptions* of competition law prevailing in a certain society, on the *goals* that are assigned to it. It is interesting to ask whether the US and/or EC cases represented a shift towards a more robust antitrust intervention, or otherwise. What is in any case clear is that the competition policy visions underpinning the parties' positions in the case were different and informed by different views of what antitrust law should be about.

These are, in our view, the main keys to interpretation of the Microsoft saga.

We can now proceed with a brief presentation of the contents of the book. Part I, containing the chapter by Colin Jackson, sets forth the technical background of the two cases in an accessible and concise way. The proper understanding of the basic technology issues is of crucial importance to properly comprehend the case. The reader is therefore advised to ponder and treasure this primer. Part II includes contributions by those who were directly involved and litigated the EC case, on the side of the Commission and Microsoft. Although the authors speak in a personal capacity, it is clear that no-one else could have a more direct knowledge of the case. In various respects, therefore, Chapters 2 by Nicholas Banasevic and Per Hellström, 3 by Ian Forrester and 4 by Jean-François Bellis and Tim Kasten offer the reader an invaluable insight into the case. The full flavour of the litigation before the Court of First Instance (CFI) is captured by the documents that accompany this book and can easily be downloaded from the book's webpage (see below). As a conclusion of this review of the EC case, in Chapter 5, Jens Fejø provides a brief but systematic summary of the findings of the ruling of the CFI, as well as a few initial reflections.

The nine contributions to Part III are devoted to the full analysis of the EC case and also of the US one, with recurring parallels between the two. The examination is not only legal but also economic. Rudolph Peritz begins with a thorough analysis of the US case, providing also a comparison between US and EC approaches to interoperability in Chapter 6. This provides a good bridge to the following three chapters which concentrate on the interoperability issue. While Steven Anderman in Chapter 7 assesses the legal criteria used by the CFI, Eleanor Fox briefly scrutinizes them from an American perspective, intriguingly enquiring how a US court would have approached a similar question. Ann Walsh's Chapter 9 builds upon the analysis of interoperability with a comprehensive examination of its links with the two crucial aspects of standardization and innovation. Chapter 10 by Arianna Andreangeli shifts the focus towards the tying aspect of the EC case. The importance of technological integration is underlined and, again, a parallel is drawn with the approach of US antitrust law to these cases. In the following two chapters, the three contributors (Maria Gil-Molto, Derek Ridyard and Markus Baldauf) examine the two sides of the EC case from the economic perspective. The various schools of thought are set forth and discussed, and an ingenious reading of tying is offered. Chapter 13 by Nicholas Economides and Ioannis Lianos, is devoted to the crucial issues raised by remedies. The focus of this detailed contribution is mainly on the EC case but ample reference and parallels are made to the US counterpart too. Carlo Petrucci's Chapter 14 closes Part III, exploring the case for an international competition agreement regulating unilateral behaviour. This provides a timely opportunity to reconsider the 'conceptions' and 'purposes' of antitrust, that normative element which is of paramount importance to understanding the actual interpretation and application of positive antitrust laws. An Epilogue of Bo Vesterdorf, who presided over the CFI in the EC case, constitutes a fitting conclusion to the book.

The reader should be aware that during the production of this book the Treaty of Lisbon entered into force (1 December 2009). While introducing important amendments in many areas of European law, it has virtually left unchanged the main competition provisions (with the possible exception of a succulent but probably moot debate on whether competition policy has been upgraded to one of the 'objectives' of the European Union: see Article 3.2 of the Treaty on the European Union and its linked Protocol on the Internal Market and Competition). The numbering of the provisions of the now Treaty on the Functioning of the European Union (TFEU, previously European Community Treaty or EC Treaty or Treaty of Rome) has changed. For our purposes the former Articles 81 and 82 EC have become Articles 101 and 102 TFEU. Similarly, the names of the two main European Courts have changed (the Court of First Instance is now the General Court, while the European Court of Justice becomes the Court of Justice of the European Union). Since these changes are merely cosmetic, and not of substance, it has been decided not to amend the various chapters with the new numbering and nomenclature. The so far familiar jargon of European lawyers has been kept and the effort to adjust it to the current new cloth will be minimal.

To pay homage to information technology, as mentioned above, the book's webpage includes various documents concerning the US and EC litigation (and beyond), which can be downloaded and represent invaluable reference to a full understanding of the various arguments put forward in the two cases and their contexts.[5] Some of these documents are not easily (if at all) accessible to the public – an additional motive to make them available to the eager and inquisitive reader.

LUCA RUBINI
Birmingham, 20 July 2010

---

[5] See http://www.e-elgar.co.uk/pdfs/rubini.pdf.

Cases

EUROPEAN COURT OF JUSTICE AND COURT OF FIRST INSTANCE CASES

US CASES

PERMANENT COURT OF INTERNATIONAL JUSTICE CASE

Legislation

EC LAW

Treaties

Directives

Regulations

Decisions

Other Documents

US LAW

Other documents

WTO

OTHER INTERNATIONAL LEGISLATION

PART I

Technical background

1. The basic technology issues at stake

Colin Jackson*

1. INTRODUCTION

Both sides of the European Microsoft case involved a debate over whether it was appropriate to impose an obligation on a very large player in order to achieve compensating advantages for other players. Thus, with respect to interoperability, the case concerned whether Microsoft should be compelled to deliver details of how to reproduce certain features of its server technology so that other manufacturers could guarantee that their servers would function seamlessly as a part of a Windows network. This involved documenting and sharing technical information to assist in building those features only – but not duplicating the software code involved. As to tying, the case concerned whether Microsoft, having launched a new version of Windows with extra products built into it such that other suppliers of such products might be threatened, could be obliged to redesign Windows to deliver an operating system without those products. In both sides of the case the obligation imposed was balanced against the advantage for others.

From the viewpoint of a participant in the EC case, its technical basis was significantly more complex than its US counterpart. This chapter concentrates on the former. However, a brief comparison with the latter is included later that builds upon the explanations of the technology concerning the EC case.

Many of the articles written about the Microsoft proceedings fail to convey the technical complexity of the issues at stake. The almost byzantine complication of these topics, combined with the unavoidability of dealing with the ferocious, technical details, made it a most remarkable case. The latter conveniently broke down into two parts: interoperability/refusal to supply and tying. It is the former that requires an unusually detailed level of technical understanding, even beyond that normally possessed by

* The views expressed in this chapter are the author's personal views and do not necessarily represent the position of any other party.

a typical employee in an organisation's information technology department. Unfortunately, without an understanding of the technology, it is impossible to follow the case. Furthermore, since the technical concepts are complex, they have tended to be oversimplified or even avoided in the course of the commentary and debate about the legal principles.

Key issues that could be superficially expressed in a few, high-level sentences frequently involved a colossal amount of effort and almost incomprehensible, technical arguments. Examples where such intense debate took place included: the extent to which there were serious problems of interoperability between different software products; defining precisely which protocols had to be released for interoperability; the potential revelation of secrets; the necessary documentation describing how to build software having the crucial features for adequate interoperability; the technical difficulties experienced by SAMBA (represented in the 2006 hearing by intervener, Free Software Foundation Europe); the functioning of media players and the extent to which they were technically linked to operating systems.

This chapter provides the reader with a simplified but comprehensive overview of the technical issues over which much argument took place. It should be noted, at the outset, that these were subsequently elaborated by all the parties, going considerably beyond what is written here. However, no person trying to understand this case properly can avoid getting to grips with these basic, yet hard-to-grasp, technical matters. This includes being able to interpret what was meant in Sun's original request to Microsoft in 1998 for 'the complete information required to allow Sun . . . to provide native support for the complete set of Active Directory technologies on Solaris' and information 'necessary to provide native support for COM objects on Solaris'. It also includes being able to understand the Remedies proposed in the Decision.

Information technology, like any other technically-based subject, consists of a very wide range of complex minutiae and developments. Such subjects are typically founded on basic facts and hypotheses, on top of which slightly more advanced concepts follow logically. These, in turn, lead to further advances, and so on. The whole edifice can be envisaged as a form of woodland canopy. The basic facts and hypotheses form the tree trunks and everything else follows, in the form of the trees' main branches leading to sub-branches, continuing on ultimately to a myriad of twigs. Within all this complex structure, to make matters worse, there are interconnections between some of the branches and twigs of the different trees. The purpose of this chapter is to enable the reader to understand the fundamental technology issues involved in the Microsoft case – but not to argue their merits, which is the role of other chapters. This means guiding the reader from the ground to the ends of the particular twigs on which this particular case was fought. This, in turn, implies some inevitable simplification in order to 'stick to the essentials'. It also means that this is not an attempt to cover the whole of information technology in a few pages. It assumes that the reader has almost no technical knowledge but has, at least, a passing acquaintance with a PC. From time to time, remarks indicate what parts of the case turned on particular technology questions. These references have no special, legal authority and are merely pointers.

2. INTEROPERABILITY

What is an Operating System?

In simple terms, a computer consists of an assembly of hardware modules such as processors, memory, disk-drives and other peripherals. These all intercommunicate via various data-buses. A processor, as a function of its fabrication, will only execute its manufacturer's predetermined set of instructions. An instruction is an item of data held in memory in the form of zeros and ones that a processor reads and translates as a command to perform an operation, such as, for example, arithmetic, modification of memory contents or jumping to another memory location for the next instruction. Instructions in this form, which a processor can understand immediately, are called machine code. A package of instructions has to be constructed so that the computer can perform some form of useful task. Such packages are known, interchangeably, as software, software programs or just simply programs. These can consist of machine code instructions. They can also take the form of other higher-level instructions, which require translation into machine code. This is explained shortly.

In the early days, programmers not only had to create software that would enable a computer to undertake some form of calculation or data manipulation but they also had to deal with issues such as where to place results in memory in order to initiate printing, or whereabouts on a disk to record data. This quickly became tedious. It eventually became clear that it would be more productive if special, common software could be written that did nothing more than deal with the 'housekeeping'. It would be separate from the software doing useful tasks. In fact, it would make the running of the computer hardware entirely invisible to the software performing useful work. The special software that performed the 'housekeeping' involved in managing a computer's resources became known as an operating system. Any other software wanting to do something useful would periodically request the operating system to perform a task such as printing a result. The quite separate software that produced the useful result became known as an application.

One of an operating system's most important housekeeping tasks was the storing, loading and supervision of an application program.

In the early days of computing, almost all computers were large devices occupying entire rooms. Each computer had an operating system. Jumping ahead to more modern times, computers have significantly reduced in size. Nevertheless, unless they are dedicated to highly-specialized functions, as a general rule, each will still have an operating system.

At first, operating systems were supplied by computer hardware manufacturers, since each vendor's processors had quite different instruction sets. Because the operating system had to deal with the underlying hardware in minute detail, each manufacturer's operating system was 'hand-built' to match. Later, operating systems were programmed more abstractly in high-level languages (explained below), leaving only a small fraction of an operating system to be written in the machine code of the particular processor on which it was running. This enabled some operating systems to be developed that were able to function on quite different hardware.

Different Levels of Software

Although computer processors can only operate by obeying the machine code instructions described above, this is not a particularly convenient form for the large-scale production of software. Instead of having to refer to processors' register contents, memory-location addresses, and the like, and also having to remember what they represent at the time, it is much easier to deal with items that have normal names and where familiar operations are involved, such as 'subtract tax from gross pay to give net pay'. This idea gave birth to so-called high-level languages. Here the software instructions are written in statements that use recognizable names and operations. Special computer programs called compilers translate programs written in such languages into machine code. The completely-translated, machine-code version is then able to be run by a processor. Another approach is to use a special program called an interpreter. This works its way through each high-level statement in turn, presenting the processor with machine code to execute as it goes along.

Programs written in high-level languages are often called source code. Their machine code 'translations' are frequently referred to as binary code. There is a further connotation to the term 'source code'. It can sometimes be taken to mean the confidential, high-level language program that is not publicly available. It may have considerable value.

On the other hand, some source code is made available by developers at no charge, although specific licensing agreements apply concerning its subsequent use or modification. This is known as 'Open Source' software.

Systems versus Applications Software

The simple separation of software between operating systems and applications did not last long. In order to make programmers' use of computers more productive, computer manufacturers provided a series of specialized programs along with their operating systems. These performed basic functions such as copying files, formatting disks and sorting data. These system utilities eventually came to be accepted as forming part of the operating system collection of programs. They were collectively called systems software. They were not referred to as applications.

Operating System Libraries

An operating system enables much software to function by providing shared libraries of commonly used routines, but where some will be used potentially 'on the fly' by programs. This particular type of library is interchangeably called a 'run-time library' or a 'dynamic-link library' (DLL). This consists of a collection of precompiled sub-programs that are loaded into memory dynamically and linked to application programs as required so that they can function.

How Operating System Suppliers Bundle in System Utilities and Applications

The lines between systems software and applications can be blurred by operating system suppliers. This can take place when an application that would normally be supplied by an independent third party is provided instead by the operating system supplier as part of the systems software bundle. In a further step, which links it technically to the operating system, the latter can be made to use the application on a routine basis to provide support for an operating system task. In a step of significantly deeper integration, the application can even be split up and parts of it integrated into the operating system and its libraries. This means that what is left of the application will not work at all unless that particular operating system is present. This is what occurred with Windows Media Player and is explained later. It also took place with Internet Explorer. The consequences of the latter formed part of the US proceedings under US antitrust law.

What is an API?

Applications programs frequently need to request the underlying operating system to supply them with a service. An example of this would be obtaining the time of day and the date. The software interface that is used is called an applications programming interface (API). To enable an API to be used, the operating system's supplier has to provide thorough documentation to an applications developer. This must describe unambiguously how a particular API is to be used and how it works in terms of what to put in and what will be returned.

This procedure has important implications for a process known as porting. An application may be developed to run on one operating system, use the APIs supplied and become commercially successful. The applications developer may then wish to make the program more widely available by getting it to run on a different operating system (porting it). If this is attempted, the requests to the new operating system via the old APIs will fail, unless the new operating system provides APIs which, as far as the application is concerned, operate identically. To make this possible, documentation called a specification needs to be supplied to the new operating system supplier so that the APIs can be accurately implemented. Without such a specification, the new operating system supplier would be obliged to undertake a slow process of educated guesswork and trial and error, known as reverse-engineering, in order to try and work out how each API works. There is no guarantee that such a process would succeed.

Networked Computers and the Concept of Client and Server

In the 1970s, commercial computing was predominantly undertaken by large, so-called mainframe computers. Desktop access to these was provided by simple terminals that consisted essentially of screens, keyboards and some simple electronics. The greater the number of terminals to be connected, the more powerful the computers had to be. This arrangement had obvious limitations and did not scale well – more terminals added meant that more computing power was needed.

At the end of the 1970s, the personal computer (PC) appeared. At first it was considered to be a novelty or hobbyist device. However, personnel in some companies began to buy them, sometimes clandestinely, to provide an independent means of performing simple computations at their workplace and without interference from the information technology departments that managed the mainframe computers. Although initially ignored, once IBM launched its PC, information technology departments took this to be a seal of approval for the concept. The IBM PC was supported by a substantial marketing campaign and early customers could choose between three different operating systems, of which one was Microsoft's MS-DOS. IBM's hardware was also imitated by several other manufacturers. These took licences to load their own version of the hardware with the same Microsoft operating system as IBM used. As a result, such devices were purchased in increasingly large numbers by commercial and government organizations, thus achieving for Microsoft an exceptionally broad base.

Thus, with the advent of PCs, individual computers became scattered throughout organizations, each machine having substantial processing ability. There was also a parallel development in which data networks and communications technologies advanced, enabling these PCs to be attached to high-speed networks. Information technology departments then faced two problems: first, how to connect the PCs to their networks and regain 'order and control' over all corporate computing; secondly, how to accomplish this in a way that would not, once again, be limited by the scaling problems described above. The solution turned out to be client/server computing. In this model, one computer, the client, makes a request to another, the server. The server undertakes the operation requested and returns the answer to the client. If, in the process of providing the response, the server needs to make a request to a further computer, it turns itself into a client for that particular operation and makes a further request to another server, and so on. This client/server model ultimately revolutionized computing and enabled very large networks to operate without major bottlenecks building up. The best example of such an arrangement is the World Wide Web over the Internet. Through common usage, desktop computers became colloquially referred to as clients and the computers to which they were connected known in a similarly loose fashion as servers. Communication between such servers was thus frequently referred to as being server-to-server. All this contrasted starkly with the old 1970s computing technology where a large, central computer was connected to a substantial number of 'dumb' terminals. It also contrasted with the massive numbers of PCs that became owned by private individuals and were located in their homes.

Some networks connected together different types of computer that ran different operating systems and that sometimes interoperated using different protocols (protocols are explained shortly). Such networks were said to be heterogeneous – for obvious reasons. An example of such would be a network supporting computers running Windows, UNIX and Linux, which are different operating systems (also described below). By contrast, other networks just connected computers that ran the same operating systems and used the same protocols. These were said to be homogeneous. An example of the latter would be a network connecting an all-Windows environment.

Operating System Examples and Brief History of Microsoft's Relevant Products

For PC-based machines, apart from Microsoft's products, operating systems that were available at the time included Mac OS X for Apple's computers and Solaris for Sun's machines. Solaris was based on UNIX, an operating system originally developed in the 1970s by Bell Laboratories and from which several different versions were subsequently created by various parties. UNIX and another operating system called Linux were designed so that they could be made to work on different computer processors.

Microsoft's operating system, Windows, was developed primarily for the microprocessors developed by hardware manufacturer, Intel. However, even some later versions of Windows were initially designed to run on DEC's Alpha processors as well as Intel's hardware. The relevant history of Microsoft's operating systems is now briefly explained. These were developed over several years, with improvements being added to successive generations.

Most people will be familiar with Microsoft's PC client products which, in broad terms, evolved as follows. Its earliest operating system was MS-DOS, which appeared in the early 1980s. This was followed by Windows 3.0 and then 3.1, the Microsoft operating system versions that introduced the now familiar graphical user interface. This was, in turn, followed in chronological order by Windows 95, Windows 98, Windows 98 SE, Windows NT 4.0, Windows 2000 and Windows XP – all successive versions being released between 1995 and 2001. Microsoft also continued its programme of operating system enhancements beyond Windows XP.

The server operating system products will be less familiar. Windows NT was developed to be suitable for both clients and servers, NT standing for New Technology. Prior to this, the Microsoft operating systems were widely felt to be insufficiently reliable to be used as servers in networked computing environments. Windows NT was intended to address this shortcoming. It was released between 1993 and 1996, evolving through several versions from NT 3.1 and culminating in NT 4.0. Its successor server product consisted of three special versions: Windows 2000 Server, Windows 2000 Advanced Server and Windows 2000 Datacenter Server.

Each of these was aimed at different levels of server performance. The successors to these were called Windows 2003 Server and originally consisted of four versions: Standard edition, Enterprise edition, Datacenter edition and Web edition. Microsoft also continued its release of improved server operating systems beyond these.

Distributed Systems and Transparency

In the preceding explanations, it has been implied that a program is an item of software that runs on a single computer, with help being provided by the underlying operating system. However, in a networked environment this could mean that some resources were underutilised whilst others, running at maximum capacity, acted as bottlenecks.

To overcome this, some programs can be designed in the form of components such that some of the latter may run on different computers on a network. To shield programmers from having to deal with the potentially ferocious complexity of managing all this, special systems software has to be provided. This makes the running of such distributed systems invisible to the programmer. This transparent distribution of resources across a network is an important facet of the Microsoft case.

What are Protocols?

It is, therefore, evident that, in a networked environment, different software components or even entire programs will sometimes need to communicate with each other, often across the network. To do this, they interchange packets of data in a structured way according to a predetermined set of rules. These rules are known as protocols. Protocols define the format, sequence, timing and error checking involved in these exchanges. Very many different protocols exist, each having being designed to fulfil a specific purpose.

For example, one could be used simply to convey basic packets of data over a wireless network. Another could operate at a much higher level and be used to exchange an e-mail. In this way, once a basic data transportation mechanism had been established with one protocol, another could take advantage of this and provide a higher-level service. Thus protocols can run within protocols. Some protocols form a coherent layer of services, the top one requiring the presence of the protocol immediately underneath, and so on. This is unsurprisingly known as a protocol 'stack'.

The concept of protocols is fundamental to a proper understanding of the Microsoft Decision and its Remedy.

Distribution, Object-oriented Programming and the (Brief) Role of Microsoft's COM/DCOM

To proceed further, it is necessary to understand a little about a particular programming technique known as object-oriented programming. The term 'object' was used extensively throughout the Commission's Decision, and ensuing arguments, and related to this concept.

Originally, programs were written as a set of programming steps that precisely worked through the computation to be undertaken. The individual, computational steps could also, as appropriate, perform operations on data. The data was accessible to the entire program and was stored separately from it. High-level languages such as Basic or C are examples of this so-called procedural approach. Within such a sequence of steps, a program could call, whenever required, for a common procedure (sometimes called a subroutine) to be performed. It is only a small step to realize that these procedures could also be distributed around a computing network, rather than remaining on one computer. Specialized systems software was developed that would enable a program to call a procedure that could, potentially, be executed on a remote computer but which, most importantly, shielded the complexity involved from the programmer. This was termed a remote procedure call or RPC.

Object-oriented programming is different from the above procedural form. Its ultimate aim was to permit the creation of reusable software components. The idea behind such an approach is as follows. A so-called software object combines in a single entity both processing (these operations are more formally known as methods) and data (known formally as attributes). As stated above, in traditional programming approaches these are normally kept quite separate. In short, an object encapsulates a data structure, the data it contains and the code that operates on it in such a way that its inner workings and data layout are hidden from the outside world. If the face that it presents externally remains unchanged, then its internal efficiency can be safely improved without compromising any software that uses it. These characteristics alone make software more manageable. Software objects having the same common operations and attributes are bundled together in what are known as classes. In this way, any object which is declared to be a member of a particular class automatically inherits the common operations and attributes of that class. When programs are run, whole structures of objects are created (and destroyed) dynamically. Each individual executing structure is known as an instance. By using these concepts, a program can be constructed as a collection of cooperating objects. Smalltalk and Java are object-oriented languages.

Once again, objects can also be distributed around a computing network, as opposed to remaining on one computer. The communication between objects, no matter where they are, corresponds to one object making a request (more formally called invoking a method) to execute an operation on another. Again, specialized systems software has to provide this service for the objects. In this way, with the appropriate network and systems-software infrastructure in the background, an application programmer could be entirely unaware that a computer on the other side of the world was performing part of the work.

In practice, it turned out to be difficult to achieve this in a world of assorted computers and operating systems. Getting different manufacturers' operating systems, libraries of standard software routines and network protocols to interwork efficiently was a daunting task. An early attempt to provide a public standard for such software, that would be independent of operating systems, was called CORBA (Common Object Request Broker Architecture) developed by the Object Management Group, an industry-wide standards organization. With CORBA, objects written in different languages and distributed around a network could work together as though they formed a single program on a single computer. To make this possible, CORBA required software objects to 'publish' the interfaces that they presented to the object-managing software system. This was done by means of what was called an Interface Definition Language (IDL).

Microsoft developed its own proprietary, distributed, object-management system that used IDL to specify the interfaces. This specialized system software was called COM/DCOM. COM stands for component object model and DCOM for distributed component object model. DCOM extended COM and enabled objects to be located on different computers within a network. A further development, COM+, expanded the services offered. Interestingly, as part of its internal functioning, and hidden from the programmer, this Microsoft software made use of RPCs to support the complex, inter-system linkages required. Microsoft's RPC was based on that of the OSF (Open Software Foundation) DCE/RPC (distributed computing environment/remote procedure call).

This Microsoft RPC facility was, of course, available to be used by programmers writing software in the traditional way. Furthermore, it is important to underline that any program, no matter how it is constructed, may wish to request the operating system to perform some specific service. To do this, the software code simply makes the request by using the appropriate API. In reality, unbeknown to the programmer, this might involve procedures resident on remote computers.

The COM/DCOM facility, RPCs and IDL play an important part in the server-to-server protocols that lie at the heart of the documentation remedy in the Microsoft case. COM information was specifically requested in Sun's 1998 letter.

Standards and Documentation

Many protocols are used by a great number of different computer systems across the world. Self-evidently, this implies that many of the protocols have had to be agreed in advance by accepted industry bodies. Furthermore, these protocols have had to be clearly and unambiguously documented so that different parties in different locations could build computer systems that used them correctly. Examples of two protocols pre-agreed by an industry body are Internet Protocol Version 4 (IPv4) and Transport Control Protocol (TCP), both ratified by the Internet Engineering Task Force (IETF). Most people will at some time have come across the term TCP/IP, reflecting the combined use of these two protocols by communications networks, including the Internet.

In contrast to such public protocols, some have been developed privately by operating system suppliers, for example. In either case, where an operating system has become very widely used, these protocols can become a de facto standard. If such a protocol is proprietary, it then falls on the supplier to produce adequate and accurate documentation for its users. An example of a proprietary de facto standard in the past was Systems Network Architecture (SNA), a collection of networking protocols, which was originally developed by IBM in the early 1970s.

Software developers who use protocols created by others rely almost entirely on the quality of the documentation made available to them in order that their implementations work correctly in all circumstances. If a protocol turns out to operate in an unexpected manner in some circumstances, this needs to be recorded too. Such idiosyncrasies can be very important. Thus, in a similar way to APIs, programmers need complete, clear and unambiguous specifications of protocols in order to be able to implement them accurately.

Documentation may also include what is called a reference implementation. This is an example of the code that could be written for the implementation of a protocol. It represents a fictitious example and is one of the potentially infinite ways in which such computer instructions could be expressed. It helps programmers understand what the documentation intends that they do. It does not reveal any party's actual source code.

Extensions to Standard Protocols

Standardized protocols developed by accepted public organizations often incorporate places where some extra information can be added and interchanged between parties. The extra information may be well-defined or it may be unspecified, it being left to an implementer to add a desired extra feature. Sometimes a standard protocol may be unofficially modified for proprietary use. In either case, such modifications are usually referred to as protocol extensions.

What are Work Group Servers?

Work group servers are inexpensive computers that provide basic services to office workers' client PCs in the form of the sharing of printers, files and other resources, and the administration of the access to these or other services by either users or groups of users linked to the work group network. Such work groups are frequently made up of small to medium-sized networks. Many office workers will be familiar with such servers, which are found scattered around their places of work. They will also be familiar with the ability to be able to share files with other users on the same network. In the Windows environment, this file-sharing involves two services called CIFS and Dfs. This is explained below.

Work group servers frequently run other small, shared applications as well.

The Microsoft case focuses on work group server operating systems.

File Services

As stated above, one of the core services provided by work group server operating systems is the provision of file services.

So-called network file systems allow users to share files over a network. An important feature of such services is that they hide from users the complexity relating to where individual files are stored. The approach is to make it appear to users that the files that they are accessing are located on a locally-attached disk, whereas, in reality, they reside on different servers spread across the network. This provides a logical view of the files rather than an exact physical view. Microsoft's basic system was called Common Internet File System (CIFS). The protocol used was also sometimes referred to as CIFS. This was developed out of an earlier protocol called Server Message Block (SMB), originally created by IBM in the early 1980s. In fact, apart from a few small changes, CIFS and SMB are basically the same protocol. It is thus common to see references to CIFS/SMB. The word 'Internet' in CIFS originates from Microsoft's application to the IETF in 1996/1997. The application time expired but the term 'Internet' remained in the name.

Microsoft's Distributed File System (Dfs), which used CIFS, was a further 'add-on' development in the late 1990s for Windows NT 4.0 servers and clients. Enhancements continued with later versions of Windows operating systems. As stated above, with CIFS/SMB, a user can access a file on another computer that has been declared to be 'shared'. The file appears to the user as though it is resident on that user's hard disk. With Dfs, an administrator takes a group of files that are located on different servers and, with this facility, enables a user to view them as a set of files contained within a newly-named common folder that also appears to be resident on a user's hard disk. In this way, the complexities of accessing various files on different remote servers are completely hidden from users. The purpose of this service is to simplify the sharing of groups of distributed files. Users are spared having to perform laborious searches using 'My Network Places' on their Windows-based computers.

The adequacy of documentation available for the Dfs protocols formed part of the Microsoft case.

Security and User and Group Administration Services

An important element of the services provided by a work group server operating system is ensuring that access to the resources available is controlled in a secure fashion. This means that single or groups of users must only be able to use the services for which they have been given permission. There are two aspects to the achievement of this: authentication and authorization. The operating system has to handle both. Authentication is the act of verifying that a user really is who he or she purports to be. Authorization is the process of checking just precisely what a user is permitted to do and either providing or blocking access accordingly.

The Microsoft case involves some of the specific details of how this was achieved in practice. However, before proceeding with the explanation, it is necessary to understand the notion of directories.

What is a Directory?

It takes very little imagination to realize that, in a network of clients and servers, resources such as printers, disk drives, scanners and the like could be spread out amongst the various computers in a very complicated way. Furthermore, the information concerning the user and group administration services relating to all this would need to be stored and then either accessed or updated by the various computers concerned. This conveniently leads to the concept of what is known as a directory.

This is effectively a collection of information concerning all the resources contained within the network. This even covers program files, including those connected with operating systems. It also includes user and group administration services information. A directory can be thought of as a form of 'Yellow Pages' and 'White Pages'. In the former, resources can be located according to their properties. In the latter, they can be looked up by name. Each item in a directory can be envisaged as having an account that contains a description of all its properties, including its name. The concept of directories is used in many contexts and is not just limited to work group server operating systems. However, the concept of directories was particularly important in the Microsoft case.

In a collection of networked computers, the directory resides on a designated server or even servers.

Over the years, a whole specialized area of technology has grown up around directories. This is concerned with issues such as how to store and retrieve the information efficiently and how to update a directory when the networks of computers involved are very large and can even be spread across different time zones in different parts of the world. Directories became so important that international standards (called 'X.500') were even developed in the 1980s in the hope that they would be widely used. These standards related to subjects such as common ways of accessing directory data and the organization of the latter. They also defined a protocol for accessing a directory. Given the information technology world's penchant for using acronyms, this was, unsurprisingly, called DAP (Directory Access Protocol).

What is LDAP and What was it Intended to be Used For?

When DAP was first designed, it was assumed that the exchange of data over computer networks would take place in a particular way, known as the 'OSI model'. DAP was designed to be able to operate in this environment and dealt with a lot of the complexity that was involved in the communications model envisaged, such as connection set-up. However, the advent of the Internet and the protocols that were employed there meant that data communications evolved in a simpler way than the full 'OSI model'. This meant that a lot of the complexity involved in writing programs that used DAP became an unnecessary overhead, as well as the substantial computing load imposed on the processors then available. As a result, a simpler tool than DAP was developed that would operate directly over the Internet protocols involved and that omitted the unwanted or rarely-used complications. This became known as LDAP (Lightweight Directory Access Protocol). It also eliminated a lot of the unnecessary DAP complications such as its complex way of referring to the names of directory items. Although simpler to use, LDAP is not a universal panacea. It is effective where rapid directory queries are involved or infrequent directory updates are required. It is thus suitable for looking up a user's password but not for a bulk update of a large amount of directory data.

It is important to note that programs can be designed in very many ways and they can simply use LDAP to communicate with the server or servers that hold the directory information. As such, LDAP communication may be thought of as a kind of 'language'. Directory servers can be designed to 'talk' only LDAP, for example. However, and this is important, they can also be designed to use other, different means to receive and send data, particularly when larges amounts are involved. In such cases, LDAP may be just an added-on form of directory communication.

This point is also important for the understanding of the Microsoft case.

Role of Domains in the Microsoft World plus Domain Controllers

Although the idea of having a directory of all the resources, hardware and software making up a networked environment can seem to be logically appealing, it can be readily imagined that administering a gigantic register of everything could very quickly become a nightmare. For this reason, in a Windows environment, collections of client and server computers that share user account and security information can be broken down into separate groups called domains. It should be noted that, as a matter of principle, this is a logical grouping for administrative purposes. It is not a physical one. In other words, individual members of a domain could be scattered around different locations. Nevertheless, a member of a particular domain can 'log on' to it and, depending on the various authorizations stored, have access to the different resources also registered in that domain. A domain is therefore a key administrative concept and forms an integral part of the user and group administration services described earlier. The person who supervises and controls the workings of a particular domain is known as its administrator. All Windows operating systems from NT 3.1 to later versions use domains.

In its simplest form, a domain could be used to include all the users for a single company. However, in large organizations, it could, for example, be much more convenient to have different domains for each country, state or even city location. Furthermore, if one company purchased another, given the ubiquity of Microsoft operating systems, it would be more than likely that the new company had already implemented its own particular domain structure. In a further twist, personnel could be relocated to different geographical locations but still remain members of their original domains. In short, an organization could have several domains, each containing members that were spread around different geographical locations, with each user being limited to his or her domain. It is self-evident that in such circumstances, users in one domain might need to use or access resources contained in others.

To overcome the problem of users being locked into and limited to their own domain, the concept of trust relationships was eventually implemented by Microsoft. A trust relationship is a form of administration link between two domains that concerns authentication. One domain is declared to be the trusting domain and the other the trusted domain. The trusting domain simply trusts the other to accurately authenticate the trusted domain's own users. Note that it does not allow the trusted domain to authorize anything on its behalf. Trust is a one-way, authentication relationship. The trusted domain does not accord the trusting domain the same privilege. For this to happen, a second relationship has to be established the other way around. Such a mutually reciprocal arrangement is, unsurprisingly, called a two-way trust relationship. It is important to note that trusting another domain does not give the trusted domain's users the right to access the trusting domain's resources. For this to happen, the trusting domain still has to assign authorization permissions to individuals in the other domain in exactly the same way as it would for its own members.

There is a further complication to the concept of trust relationships and this is the notion of a so-called transitive relationship. Suppose that domain A establishes a two-way trust with domain B. Suppose also that domain B establishes a separate, two-way trust relationship with domain C. If the trust relationships are transitive, the trust relationship granted by A to B is automatically extended to C, i.e. A also has a two-way trust relationship with C. One-way, two-way and transitive trusts became possible with Windows. The significance of this is explained below.

This notion of trust relationships between domains leads to hierarchies and other linkages of trust relationships that eventually became features of Windows. This gave rise, first of all, to the concept of 'trees'. A tree is a hierarchy of domains linked by transitive, two-way trust relationships. This can be thought of as a form of family tree. At the top of the tree is the 'parent', called a root domain. Immediately under that are its 'children'. Immediately under each 'child' are the 'grandchildren', and so on. Of course, although the root domain will be there, the tree underneath is not obliged to be symmetrical. Some 'children' will not have any 'grandchildren', and so on down the hierarchy. Instead of several 'children and grandchildren' there may be only one, in a similar way. Thankfully, as the Windows environment uses a standard way of naming domains (that used by websites), understanding a tree becomes straightforward because it uses a form with which most people will be unconsciously familiar. Tree names must be contiguous in the following way. Suppose that the root domain is called bigcompany.com. In this case, the names of the domains immediately below it must prepend this name, e.g. hq.bigcompany.com or milanoffice.bigcompany.com. These two examples suppose that it was convenient to create a separate domain for the HQ and the Milan offices of the organization called bigcompany. In the same vein, at the Milan office, it might be considered worthwhile to have separate domains for sales and finance, giving rise to two further domains called sales.milanoffice.bigcompany.com and finance.milanoffice.bigcompany.com. It can thus be envisaged how a tree is formed.

In a significant organization, it is nevertheless possible for several, independent tree structures to coexist, each having a tree root that has a completely different name, but where the names in the hierarchies under each root having names are contiguous according to the prepending process, described above. This conveniently brings up Microsoft's notion of a 'forest'. This is simply where the root domain of one tree with a different name is connected by a transitive, two-way trust relationship to the root domain of another tree. The combination of all these is called a forest. It is easy to imagine how a forest can be generated when companies are taken over or merged. Most importantly, the default trust relationship in a Microsoft forest is two-way and transitive. This creates a large simplification in the management of trust relationships within a forest. This is because authentication in one domain is promulgated throughout the rest of the forest of which it forms part.

In a Windows environment, some servers manage the administration of domains and are known as domain controllers. Depending on the workload, these may perform other functions but are usually dedicated to this task. This contrasts with ordinary servers, which may routinely perform several tasks.

Each domain controller maintains a directory of all the objects within its domain. However, a form of summary list that covers an entire forest can be generated in addition. This is called a global catalog. Although the latter lists all a forest's objects, only a small number of preselected properties for each object are stored there. A copy of the global catalog is maintained on each of the domain controllers that have been set up to perform this additional role. The global catalog allows users in their specific domains to quickly locate resources that are contained in others.

Just exactly how domain controllers work and manage the functioning of a directory depends on the version of the Windows operating system that is being used. This is explained later. However, the role and functioning of domains and domain controllers are crucial concepts for the understanding of the Microsoft case. By way of example, a great deal of the technical argument in the 2006 hearing required a detailed knowledge of these concepts.

Work Group Servers and Heterogeneous Networks

Within a corporate environment, computer services can be applied to run several different parts of a business, e.g. manufacturing systems, accounting systems and product design systems. In addition, computer services are also provided for general administrative tasks at the desktop and include file, print and other services. All of these systems may use the same corporate network, although they may have very limited interoperability. For example, the manufacturing system might make certain status reports available by publishing them on an internal web-server. Permitted desktops would then view such content via their browsers. The network is said to be heterogeneous because it is supporting all the intercommunications between the disparate systems. In this sense, heterogeneous networks are very common.

A sub-set of the above is the provision of computer services for general administrative tasks. As explained earlier, this is known as work group computing. Within this sub-set, the problem is to connect seamlessly at all levels the servers that support the administrative services delivered to the desktop. The case describes the obstacles that stood in the way of achieving this. Taking the work group sub-set of corporate computer services, a heterogeneous network of servers within the same domain became increasingly difficult to achieve with the introduction of a Microsoft product called Active Directory. The reason for this is quite complex and is explained in detail in the sections that follow. As such, heterogeneity became reduced in this sub-set of corporate computer services. Various proposals were put forward that only achieved limited interoperability similar to that described in the preceding paragraph. This was insufficient to provide the interoperability required between work group servers in the same domain. In that sense, heterogeneous networks became relatively rare.

Microsoft's Directory Products Leading to Active Directory

Domains are clearly a particular concern of Microsoft's server operating systems. Microsoft originally introduced the concept of domains with Windows NT. However, at this point, domains were effectively self-contained, unrelated entities, although trust relationships could be set up between them. Trees and forests did not exist. With Windows NT, each domain's management was controlled by a server called a 'primary domain controller'. It was given this name because, in the event of it failing, another server, designated as a 'backup domain controller', could take over. There could be more than one backup domain controller or even none. The management of a domain involved the primary domain controller managing a master collection of records called a security accounts manager registry. With the usual propensity for acronyms, this was known as the SAM registry. Interestingly, this did not support the X.500 directory standards or LDAP. Data had to be accessed via a special Microsoft API. The primary domain controller periodically sent copies of its SAM registry to the backup domain controller(s). Apart from being able to take over if the primary controller failed, the backup domain controllers could also share the workload in a busy network environment. Servers not involved with any of these activities were simply known as member servers of a domain, their resources being recorded in the SAM registry. As mentioned earlier, a person called an administrator had to set up and maintain the primary and backup domain controllers.

With the launch of Windows 2000, a radically different approach was taken to the organization and the management of domains with the advent of a significantly improved service named 'Active Directory'. The reader will recall that Sun's letter requested information concerning Active Directory technologies.

In brief, Active Directory introduced the concept of trees and forests, allowed the use of LDAP, employed different security techniques and allowed many more users to be managed. Active Directory also introduced a new user and group administration service named Group Policy. This applied a standard set of security options and controls to users designated to be part of a particular group. Group Policy thus simplified the administration of users and computers. Thus when a user logged in, if the Group Policy feature was enabled, Active Directory would check which policy applied and then provide the requisite desktop configuration and permissions for that user. One of Active Directory's most important changes, however, was the totally different way that domain controllers worked. Here, it used a technique called multi-master replication. This is another key concept in understanding the Microsoft case and is explained later.

First, though, it is necessary to understand the security technique changes as these, too, are crucial to following the case.

Security Within the Operating System Environment and the Role of Kerberos in the Microsoft Environment

With Windows NT, the authentication protocol that was used was called NTLM. This was proprietary to Microsoft. It was basically used in the processes between a PC client, a domain controller and a server where authentication of the client was involved. This ultimately allowed a server to provide the authorized services for a particular user, the details of which had been stored in the SAM registry in the domain controller.

With Active Directory, there was a major change made in the protocol used. Authentication was based on a protocol called Kerberos. For various technical reasons, this was a significant improvement on NTLM. Kerberos, though, had not been developed by Microsoft but by MIT. The specification for this protocol was in the public domain (it was specifically so-called version 5 and documented by the IETF, mentioned earlier). However, Microsoft took this public standard but added a proprietary extension to it. To understand the significance of this, it is necessary to have at least a basic understanding of how Kerberos works in the authentication process.

This operates through the issuing and exchange of so-called tickets. Starting at the beginning, a user's password is stored on an Active Directory domain controller in an encrypted form. When a user logs on at his or her PC client, a process familiar to most people, an encoded version of the password is passed to the domain controller. This compares the user's password to the stored version. If it matches, the user is deemed to be authenticated. At this point a so-called 'ticket' is generated. This contains the name of the Windows user and the time that the ticket is to remain valid. A good analogy is an entrance ticket for a country fair. This ticket is sent to the PC client. However, this ticket is special and can be thought of as a master ticket or a 'ticket-granting ticket' in that it is going to be used to generate further tickets. When the user's PC client needs to access particular resources on another server, it sends this master ticket to a domain controller. This transmitted ticket consists of two parts: one that is in clear text and the other that is protected by strong encryption. The domain controller then generates a second so-called service ticket which only remains valid for a given time period and for that particular purpose. A good analogy for a service ticket is a voucher for an individual ride at a country fair. This service ticket, which in Microsoft's version also contains authorization data (see shortly below), is presented to the server that will provide the service and access to the required resource is then granted. Provided that the user remains logged on, tickets that expire are renewed.

The Kerberos system requires that tickets are issued by a software function called a key distribution centre (KDC). In Active Directory, this KDC function is incorporated in every domain controller.

The objective of Kerberos is to provide a secure authentication mechanism. However, in the tickets, the IETF standard does allow some authorization data to be carried in a specially-defined area of the Kerberos protocol called the 'authorization data' field. Microsoft uses this to carry a proprietary structure called a privilege access certificate (PAC, a further acronym and sometimes referred to as a privilege *attribute* certificate). This is carried within the encrypted part of the Kerberos ticket. Microsoft uses this PAC to include authorization data in each Kerberos ticket-granting ticket and ticket. Furthermore, the encrypted part of a ticket also contains an additional, security-check item which is, itself, further encrypted. It is important to underline that the content and structure of this PAC information is specific to Microsoft. It is not defined in the IETF standard, apart from the fact that the 'authorization data' field is available for use.

Thus, in summary, in the Kerberos process, a KDC will initially generate a ticket that includes Microsoft-specific authorization information carried as a PAC in the 'authorization data' area. This PAC will be inherited and carried along by subsequent ticket requests or renewals. There is a fundamental consequence of this. Any external party managing to observe a totally-decrypted Kerberos transaction generated by Active Directory would be able to recognize the information being transferred because it would correspond to the standard format specified by the IETF. However, they would not be able to interpret the information contained in the PAC. This is also crucial to understanding the Microsoft case.

A corollary is that any Windows 2000 computer within a domain, including a work group server, would reject tickets that contained PACs that did not comply with Microsoft's standard. This is also a crucial issue as it fundamentally affects the acceptance of a non-Microsoft server within a group of Microsoft servers

How Does This Affect LDAP?

The following short section forms a particularly dense 'acronym soup'. However, it has particular relevance because it provides the background as to why some of the technical solutions proposed during the course of the case would or would not work. It also explains the relevance of Sun's allegation that Microsoft had made undocumented extensions to something called 'SASL'.

The Windows 2000 generation and later operating systems in this case used the international standard LDAP version 3. This was designed to use as an option an authentication framework called Simple Authentication and Security Layer (SASL). The idea behind its use is as follows. Instead of an LDAP information exchange just taking place in the open over the basic communications protocols, TCP/IP, referred to earlier, an authentication protocol is first 'negotiated' by SASL and then a security protocol is inserted between LDAP and TCP/IP. This means that, following authentication, the subsequent LDAP information exchanges will be carried securely across the network connections.

To make this clearer, SASL is a special authentication framework that first finds out what secure authentication protocols are available, secondly performs the necessary work to 'fire up' a selected authentication protocol plus subsequent security protocol, and then finally drops out, letting the now-secured communication continue. In order to do this SASL uses a series of 'mechanisms' that consist of the patterns of information exchanges that are required to initiate a whole series of authentication protocol exchanges. Thus, SASL mechanisms are defined for several authentication exchanges. One of these mechanisms 'fires up' Kerberos version 5, explained above. When a PC client that wishes to make a series of LDAP transactions successfully initiates a SASL process that will start up the various exchanges involved in authentication, this is technically known as a 'SASL binding operation'.

As a function of the selected protocol, various messages will then be interchanged between the PC client and the relevant domain controller. In the case of Active Directory, Kerberos version 5 is selected and is initially used by LDAP.

It should be noted that the Kerberos interchanges conveyed contain the proprietary PAC, described above, although this is independent of SASL. If a secure authentication protocol exchange such as Kerberos fails, a PC client can make a so-called 'anonymous' LDAP request. An 'anonymous' authentication is a standard mechanism used by LDAP but provides extremely limited, read-only access to directory resources.

Part of the dispute concerned as to whether or not the SASL binding operation had also had proprietary extensions added to it by Microsoft. It also concerned the extent to which LDAP could be used to access and update Active Directory information.

To summarize with respect to both of these issues, when LDAP is used it 'fires up' SASL. Sun alleged that Microsoft had made undocumented extensions to SASL. In any case, when either SASL or Kerberos (which it initiates) fail, LDAP is reduced to being able to provide only very limited information.

This results in a significant handicap to a non-Microsoft server.

Key Distributed Feature of Active Directory's Functioning

In contrast to the workings of the directory service available in Windows NT, Active Directory uses a technique called multi-master replication. The essential elements of this will now be explained.

In Windows NT, each domain has a primary domain controller and, potentially, other backup domain controllers. Self-evidently, the primary domain controller is 'in charge', unless it fails. From time to time, the master information on the primary device is copied to the backups. With Active Directory, the situation is different. All the domain controllers within a domain are peers. With such a system, if any change is made to one of these domain controllers, the modification is propagated to the others through a special process. This means that there is no master copy of a directory. The name given to the propagation process is multi-master replication. The process for propagating changes in Active Directory is very efficient. It only passes on data changes and, even then, the net result of several changes to the same object. Although this may sound simple, the process is quite complex. An example of the latter is how to handle the accessing of a directory object on one domain controller, where the object has been updated but the update propagation has not yet been received. It has to be remembered that with the concept of forests and trees, the span of such interchanges could be very large and even involve multiple domains spread over different continents. The entire replication process takes place using special, Microsoft-specific RPCs and even a standard e-mail protocol.

With Active Directory, it is necessary to create and maintain a topology of physical network connections to enable the domain controllers to intercommunicate efficiently during replication. For this, Active Directory uses what are termed 'sites'. A site is a physical network covering a particular location that has good physical communication between all parts of that network. It is usually a local area network, the 'LAN' with which most people are familiar. The topology of connections within (and between) sites is independent of the forest/tree domains structure. An administrator also has to set up the topology of these interconnections. This ultimately determines how domain controllers' replication takes place. This is worked out in the following way. Each domain controller regularly runs a software component called a knowledge consistency checker (KCC). This creates the replication schedule and the links to be used within a site for domain controllers to propagate their replication data between each other. The KCC can dynamically adjust these every time it runs. If a new domain controller is added somewhere, the KCC automatically amends the links and replication schedule accordingly. Sites may also have to have connections between them. These inter-site connections are also set up by an administrator. Once again the KCC works out the best way to use all the available connections, including taking account of unavailable connections. A domain controller's KCC normally runs every 15 minutes.

It can thus be seen that Active Directory consists of many domain controllers, none of which is the master, potentially spread over a large geographic area and all periodically propagating directory-change information to each other as appropriate. It thus forms a genuinely distributed system.

The Active Directory protocols used for transactions within a domain are considerably more varied than those relating to exchanges between domains. That is a consequence of the replication traffic.

The distinction between intra- and inter-domain interoperability played an important part in the Microsoft case. In the April 2006 hearing, Microsoft presented a boundary to what it believed it should disclose and termed this 'off limits' environment the 'Blue Bubble'. This appeared to include the intra-domain and inter-site protocols, amongst others.

Upgrade Migration Path for Microsoft Operating Systems Leading to Active Directory Native Mode and the Technical Consequences

When all the domain controllers within a domain are running the Windows 2000 (or later) operating systems and the full functionality of Active Directory is available to users, Active Directory is said to be operating in 'native' mode. In other words, the system is operating fully without constraint and users are able to make use of the features that it was designed to provide.

However, it can be readily imagined that, following its introduction, as new computers running the Windows 2000 operating system were introduced to networks or as operating systems were simply upgraded on existing computers, some domain controllers would still be running Windows NT whilst others would be using Windows 2000. To allow for this, Active Directory was able to operate in what was termed 'mixed mode'. This allowed domain controllers using Windows NT to coexist in a domain with those running Windows 2000. This mixed-mode operation was the default setting for Active Directory. Its purpose was to provide a gradual way of migrating a domain from the old Windows NT directory system to Active Directory, provided with Windows 2000, without requiring an immediate, all-or-nothing conversion. So that Active Directory could provide services to servers in a domain that was running the old, Windows NT operating system, a single, Active Directory domain controller had to be nominated to act as the primary domain controller that the old system required.

Mixed mode, however, came at a price. The full services of Active Directory (in particular Group Policy, described earlier) were not available. To be able to take advantage of the complete range, native mode had to be selected for a domain. This required that all its domain controllers (including the old backup domain controllers) had to be upgraded to Windows 2000. Furthermore, conversion to native mode was a one-way process.

A corollary of this is that conversion to native mode in a domain locked out the addition of any potential, additional or replacement domain controllers for that domain if they ran the old Windows NT operating system. This is also fundamental to the understanding of the Microsoft case.

Sometimes, organizations that were running native mode Active Directory acquired new companies that were still running the old NT systems. There was thus a requirement to link an NT domain to a native mode system. This was done through the concept of defining a so-called external-trust relationship. It had, however, a limitation. An external-trust relationship had to be specifically set up between two named domains, the NT newcomer domain and a named domain within the native mode system. However, an external trust is two-way but not transitive. That meant that the NT domain was only trusted by the named native-mode domain. The trust relationship was not propagated throughout the native-mode forest. For other domains in the latter to share trust with the new NT domain, separate, parallel, external-trust relationships had to be established with each of them on an individual basis.

SAMBA's Problem

Now that the consequences of a Windows NT domain controller faced with Windows 2000 and Active Directory have been understood, this is the point at which to introduce the intervening party, SAMBA. It confronted significant challenges.

SAMBA is the name given to a collection of software programs that enable a server using a non-Microsoft operating system to provide file and print services to Windows PC clients by means of the CIFS/SMB protocol. The development of this began informally in 1992 when an Australian, Andrew Tridgell, succeeded in connecting a computer running a Unix operating system to another in his home running a Microsoft operating system and which made the Unix-running computer appear as if it were a file server to the Microsoft machine. He made this possible by reverse-engineering the SMB protocol. Since then, the SAMBA group and its software have grown. SAMBA runs on other operating systems, including Linux. The software is an Open Source product and is licensed freely under the terms of the GNU General Public Licence. Participants in the SAMBA project provide their services at no charge to the group. SAMBA 'advanced' from the SMB protocol to implementing the CIFS/SMB protocol.

At the time of the case, by using SAMBA, a server running a UNIX-based operating system could provide file and print services, including Dfs interoperability, and was also even able to act as a primary domain controller in a Windows NT environment. It could not act as a backup domain controller in the latter.

With the advent of Active Directory with the Windows 2000 operating system, as explainer earlier, networks of computers running both systems had to coexist. In particular, some domain controllers would be running Windows NT whilst others used Windows 2000. In this situation, Active Directory ran in its default mixed mode. Here, in a domain running the old, NT operating system, a single Active Directory domain controller had to be nominated to act as the primary domain controller, which the NT system required. However, a server running SAMBA was not able to act in this Active Directory role. As it was also not able to act as a backup domain controller, the jump to Active Directory with Windows 2000 meant that SAMBA's ability to be a domain controller had ceased. However, a SAMBA server could still be a member server in a domain.

SAMBA's situation was described in the Commission's Decision. It also provided a key battleground for the interoperability argument that took place at the 2006 CFI hearing.

Problem of a Non-Microsoft Server/Operating System Becoming Part of a Group of Microsoft Servers/Operating Systems

If a server running a Microsoft operating system is added to an existing Windows environment, as described above, it will efficiently interoperate with all the existing computers: PC clients, domain controllers and member servers. If a server running a competing operating system is added, it will have to perform equally well; otherwise users will ultimately perceive that the expected, 'behind-the-scenes', technical transparency no longer exists. This could create unacceptable overheads, inconveniences, or even failure. An example of inconvenience could be a systems administrator having to create a new domain and a user having to log on twice, once to access the normal Microsoft available resources and again for the resources of the non-Microsoft server in that domain. During the case, there was debate over whether such inconveniences had a significant effect on customer behaviour or purchase decisions.

A first requirement to enable technical transparency to be maintained is that the non-Microsoft server operating system has to interoperate in exactly the same way as a Microsoft server. This means it must be able to use all the relevant protocols and APIs in a conformant manner. This, in turn, means the new operating system's supplier would need to have access to complete and accurate documentation concerning the use of the requisite protocols as well as the necessary APIs. The latter is necessary because Microsoft computers will be trying to access the new server, expecting it also to be a Windows-based device.

With Active Directory, there is also a second and deeper problem and this concerns domain controllers. It was explained earlier that Active Directory's domain controllers are all peers. In fact, they are all operating independently, each deciding what directory synchronizing data needs to be interchanged with others and each running their own KCCs at regular intervals. The Active Directory model is a distributed system that requires each independent domain controller to operate according to identical rules and to come to identical decisions in identical circumstances. This means that a form of group behaviour is involved.

A good analogy to this situation is a hive of bees. Each bee has a preprogrammed behaviour where intercommunication between the bees is such that an independent movement by one insect, with its body for example, is immediately understood and potentially acted upon by others. In this way a whole hive intercommunicates and ultimately behaves as a corporate body. However, if an artificial bee is introduced that has an incomplete or faulty set of movements, then its seemingly innocent scratching of a leg might, for example, be propagated throughout the colony and inadvertently send the entire hive off to a non-existent flower grove. Similarly, if a non-Microsoft domain controller did not make exactly the same assumptions, perform exactly the same replication calculations and decisions, and behave as its interconnecting Microsoft peers, the propagation of replication information across the correct links could be fatally compromised. This could lead to chaos and an irretrievably broken directory system. This means that a really complete description and explanation for the use of protocols and APIs, and which covered any detailed implicit assumptions, would have to be available and be faithfully followed by the developer of the non-Microsoft operating system.

It is important to note that the last sentence does not mean that a non-Microsoft domain controller would have to behave in an identical fashion for every other conceivable activity that it could undertake, for example the way that it stored its files.

It should now be evident that just providing any communications protocol would not solve this particular problem, it would have to include the directory replication protocols.

Problem of Documenting the Interfaces to Permit Interworking Without Revealing Secrets Concerning How the Rest of Windows Works

Because of the absolute requirement to include any implicit assumptions made in producing the necessarily complete documentation required, it might be argued that revealing some of these assumptions would automatically mean revealing confidential information that concerned the inner workings of the Windows operating system.

Returning to the bee analogy, suppose that two bees each discovered two flower gardens that were each a major, new source of nectar but where both gardens were identically attractive. If one bee decided that one garden was to be exploited first while the other made the opposite decision, both bees would enter the hive, make their requisite 'body movements' and end up by circulating conflicting information to the rest of the hive. Suppose, however, that bees had been preprogrammed through evolution to always break the tie in exactly the same way and that the tie-breaking mechanism involved using the altitude of the flower gardens: in case of a tie the lowest altitude is always the winner. This way, both bees would return to the hive, exhibit the same 'body movement' behaviour and harmony would be preserved.

In a complete description of each bee's communications behaviour, it would, however, be necessary to reveal the altitude tie-breaking mechanism. Immediately, an observer would know that part of a bee's internal workings involved altitude measurement.

The above analogy refers to the Active Directory mechanism used to propagate directory change information. Domain controllers do this by using identical decision-making mechanisms, even in tie-breaking situations, although they operate independently. This produces the cooperative group behaviour that successfully propagates the changes without making errors or creating inconsistencies. Microsoft claimed that if they revealed the details of these protocols, they would reveal hidden, internal workings of other parts of the Windows operating system. These were said to be valuable trade secrets.

This was a 'front-line' issue, fundamental to the case, which was argued strongly by both sides. This will be elaborated in the following chapters.

Technical Points and Competition

The competition choice involved balancing Microsoft's interest in exploiting its server technology for itself and the interest of the wider community in being able to create new server products by being able to interoperate adequately with Microsoft's server technology.

The function of this chapter has not been to reach any conclusion about the application of the competition rules, and none are expressed. However, three technical comments may help readers to reflect on this.

First, the technology underlying Active Directory was complex and its development had almost certainly required considerable effort. The product was successfully implemented in many organizations and could scale to accommodate large numbers of users, employing a multi-master replication technique to achieve a distributed service.

Secondly, in an existing Windows environment, setting up a server running a Windows operating system was a relatively simple process compared to setting up a server running a non-Microsoft operating system in the Windows environment and that was subject to the limitations described.

Thirdly, while there was a great debate about interoperability, it was not true that Microsoft had to tolerate any copying of its source code. The remedy was intended to require Microsoft to provide sufficient protocol documentation to enable a potential competitor to make a server that could be inserted into a network of Windows work group servers and perform on an equal footing with them.

3. TYING: WINDOWS MEDIA PLAYER

Necessary Background

The reader will be relieved to know that the technological aspects of this second aspect of the case, tying, are very much easier to grasp than interoperability. Furthermore, much (but not all) of the basic, technical 'vocabulary' has already been covered. Before tackling the media player, it is therefore necessary to provide a little background knowledge in the form of a simplified description of the basic media technologies involved. This needs to be supplemented with a brief explanation of the remaining concepts, such as codecs, container files, streaming protocols and digital rights management.

What are Digital Media?

The process of recording images and sound in a digital form involves sampling. When sound waves impinge upon a traditional microphone, they create an electrical signal that changes over time as a function of the minute air-pressure variations involved. This signal is an analogue form of the sound experienced. The reverse process can be readily imagined.

In this, a loud-speaker or iPod earpiece, for example, will take such a signal and vibrate the air as a function of its time variation, thus recreating something close to the original sound. In simple terms, devices like old-fashioned tape-recorders effectively recorded the signal from a microphone. On playback, the tape-recorder's loud-speakers converted the recorded signal into sound.

In the digital world, a different approach is taken to capturing a microphone's output. Here, the process involves sampling. At regular but extremely short intervals, fractions of a second, the analogue signal from the microphone is measured. These measurements are then recorded and, self-evidently, form a sequence of numbers. For this technique to work in practice, it is important that the measurements are made sufficiently accurately and quickly. This entire process is called, unsurprisingly analogue-to-digital (AD) conversion. The opposite process, digital-to-analogue (DA) turns the numbers back into a time-varying signal again. For this to work perfectly, the measurements have to be delivered to the DA converter at exactly the same rate as they were collected.

It turns out that, by sampling at a rate that is greater than twice the highest frequency of the analogue signal, no information is lost. The basic, standard sampling rate for an audio signal is 44.1 kHz. If each sample takes up 16 bits (0s and 1s that can represent 65,536 different signal levels), a quick calculation shows that an hour of stereo music for two independent left and right signals will generate 635 Mbytes of data.

The same line of argument works for video, except that the numbers are much larger. To understand this conceptually, think of a video-camera's focal plane as being three rectangular arrays of light sensors instead of microphones, the array being 1,920 wide by 1,080 high. There are three arrays because there is one for each colour: red, green and blue. Now imagine each sensor collecting 10-bit samples (representing 1,024 different levels) 60 times per second for each of the colours. Another quick calculation shows that this will generate 1.7 terabytes of data for an hour of video. If this were transmitted over a 1 Mbit/sec Internet connection, it would take more than 11 weeks to download a single half-hour television show.

What is a Codec?

Clearly all of the above volumes of sampling measurements are neither an economical nor a practical way of distributing media. To overcome this problem, a large number of data-compression schemes have been invented. These reduce the large volumes of data to a manageable size and yet lose almost none of the original information. They compress the data using specially-designed algorithms and then store it. Some have been agreed by standards bodies, others are proprietary schemes. Each compression technique also pairs with the reverse process, decompression. These schemes have been given the generic name of 'codecs'. This stands for coder/decoder or compressor/decompressor. Some codecs are able to recreate exactly the original list of signal measurements. These are known as 'lossless codecs'. Others perform less well, but recreate a set of samples such that, following conversion into audio or video, the imperfections generated are barely perceptible to the human ear or eye. These are known as 'lossy codecs'. The latter achieve significant compression rates. Audio and video require separate codecs for greatest efficiency because of their very different spatial and temporal compression requirements.

Files, Formats and Media File Standards

Before proceeding further, it is necessary to understand a little bit about one of computing's basic concepts: files. In simple terms, a file is simply a collection of data that is given a name. It can consist of a collection of records, each of which conforms to a predetermined, common format. It can also contain an arbitrarily structured set of 0 and 1 bits corresponding to an image, for example. The file format can be specified in an arbitrary manner by a programmer for the convenience of a particular program. However, the format can also have been predetermined by an industry body so that files can be freely exchanged between parties and so that specific, pre-agreed data representing particular functionality can be carried. A file is the computer equivalent of the familiar, paper file used in offices. A file can also hold other files. Operating systems have to deal with a large number of files coming from various sources and, of course, files are listed in the directories described earlier.

Some file formats have been designed for a particular type of data such as a photograph or image. The well-known JPEG is an example of this. Others have been designed for different purposes, such as text files for word-processing. In order that a computer can deal with a file in an appropriate manner, there has to be a way of indicating in advance what the file format is. A popular way of doing this is to append the file type as a so-called 'file extension' after the file name and to place a full stop before the extension. Thus a photograph file might be called 'Washington' and be in the JPEG format, leading to Washington.JPEG.

Thus, a file that contains data to be handled by a specific codec such as WMA will have .WMA appended to its file name.

A special file format has also been designed that can be used to hold several types of compressed data produced by codecs. This is called a 'container' file. These containers can each contain several different files within them. Some container file formats are confined to audio, some to single images, whereas others are specifically for multi-media content. Thus, a container holding a movie might contain several separate files intended to be played together such as video, audio and titles. Examples of container file formats are WAV for audio only, TIFF for still images only and AVI for multimedia. Container files are a frequent source of confusion. For example, an AVI container could hold several files to deliver a simple media experience. However, one particular AVI container could well hold files compressed with quite different video and audio codecs to those contained in another. This is because the AVI container has been designed to be able to hold, as part of its constituents, different types of compressed files. By contrast, a non-container format such as a WMA file only holds data compressed by a WMA codec.

In summary, standard formats come from two main sources. Some, such as MPEG, were developed by industry bodies (MPEG stands for Moving Picture Experts Group). Others, such as AVI, were created by private companies, in this particular case Microsoft. There are many different formats and all have various advantages and disadvantages. Different file formats each need their own, specific codec.

This conveniently brings us to the media player.

What is a Media Player?

A media player is an application program. Its basic purpose is to read files of audio and video information, to process these and to output instructions via the operating system that will ultimately be understood by a computer's loud-speakers and displays. A media player runs on a PC client. A key function is to take compressed files and to decompress them in order to play the content.

A fully-featured media player must be able to handle different containers and codecs in order to be able to do this. Without having the necessary codecs installed, a media player will be unable to play files recorded in a particular format.

A media player, like any application program, makes use of the 'infrastructure' provided by the operating system. It expects that the media containers supported by the operating system will have run-time library support. It expects that the most common codecs will be supported, either being provided with the operating system or being installed later, probably through downloading. The codecs and container libraries (software modules designed to deal with container files) will have had to be written to use general graphics and audio software components of the operating system that ultimately use the device drivers that operate the specific display and audio hardware.

Streaming and Downloading

Basically, audio-visual files can be played in two ways: from a previously downloaded file or from a continuous stream of file data.

With the first possibility, a file is transferred over a network onto a user's PC. This is called a download. Once the download has been completed, a media player then takes the file and plays the content to the user. Since only the transfer of a file from one computer to another takes place before the media player begins its work, no special audio-visual protocols are involved with the transfer.

With the second possibility, the media player takes the data as it is transmitted and plays it back 'on the fly'. Effectively, the file is sent to the media player in a nearly constant stream. This usually involves a specialized streaming-server sending the data in the first place. Streamed data may be sent over a network using special streaming protocols, where the Internet is involved. A streaming protocol trades timeliness for accuracy. The explanation for this is the following. Ordinary file copying is handled by protocols that involve copious acknowledgement of receipt of the data that is transferred, coupled with the retransmission of corrupted blocks of data. However, if a user were viewing a live event, the delays and corresponding 'jerks' provoked by retransmission of any error blocks could easily become unacceptable. Streaming protocols fix such problems. They can, for example, contain so-called 'forward error correction data', which can be used to correct some errors without any retransmission, and for which the sender will not be expecting to receive any acknowledgement. A sender might also receive back and be expected to comply with requests to change the streaming-rate when a particular network connection is unable to keep up. As a result, a media player needs to have streaming capability built in; otherwise, it will be unable to perform the streaming form of playback that uses special protocols. The live streaming of such content (which may be prerecorded) over the Internet is known as webcasting.

APIs Again

Software developers often write programs that request an installed media player to provide a particular service. An example of this would be calling a media player API in order to play streamed audio. By doing this, developers avoid having to write new software to create the specific functionality required.

This means that an installed media player has to make APIs available for the programmers and they, in turn, need to have an accurate description of how to use them. To make this easier, suppliers often provide so-called software development kits (SDKs). These are a form of programming tool-box that is used to create software that will automatically use the correct APIs in the appropriate way.

What is DRM?

Digitally stored media can be easily copied or transferred from one computer to another. The copying process is accurate and audio-visual content is thus not degraded. This means that such media could be unlawfully copied and widely distributed without any loss of quality occurring. To prevent this, a technological development called digital rights management (DRM) came about. The idea in principle is that special software converts audio-visual content into a protected form before it is made available for distribution. Only media players that support a particular DRM technology are able to convert such protected content into a readable form. Furthermore, media players can only read media-file content if users provide the correct DRM permissions.

Content providers can thus package their material in a DRM-protected form. To this end, suppliers' DRM capability is added to their SDKs. For example, where Microsoft media formats were involved at the time, content providers could use Windows Media Rights Manager for this purpose. The latter was one of the components of the Windows Media SDK.

Media Player Examples at the Time of the Case

Media players were produced by several suppliers. They included RealOne Player by RealNetworks, Winamp by Nullsoft, Apple's QuickTime player and Microsoft's Windows Media Player. There were several others. Many depended on codecs supplied by third parties to enable them to process particular file formats. Not all media players supported all formats.

At the time of the case, Microsoft's latest player was Windows Media Player 9. This, for example, did not support Apple's or RealNetworks' formats. Similarly, it did not support the MPEG-4 file format for video content. It did have Microsoft's DRM technology built in as part of a service called Windows Media Rights Manager, mentioned above.

At the server end, streaming content was delivered in the case of Microsoft by software called Windows Media Services 9 Series. This would only run on servers running Windows operating systems.

Incorporation of Windows Media Player in the Operating System

At the time of the complaint about conduct in 1999, with one exception, users' media players had been installed on their PC clients in either or both of two main ways: non-Microsoft players had already been pre-installed on their computers by the time of purchase or users subsequently downloaded players over the Internet, paying the appropriate fee where necessary.

The exception was Windows Media Player where a PC ran a Windows operating system. Beginning with Windows 98, Microsoft provided its media player along with the operating system as part of a 'bundle' (bundle is the competition term for tying together separate items). Thereafter, Windows Media Player was always provided with the operating system. As time went by, parts of the Windows Media Player software were effectively removed from the application and became internal components of the Windows operating system. Thus, instead of the operating system having to request the media player to perform some services, the software components for this already resided there. In this way, when users looked up files containing photographs, for example, and requested a so-called 'thumbnails' view that displayed tiny images of the visual content stored within them, these absorbed media player components were used by the operating system to generate the images.

This meant that the remaining Windows Media Player application could not run without an underlying Windows operating system.

This characteristic of the close relationship between the Windows Media Player and the Windows operating system is important to the understanding of the Microsoft case.

By contrast, at the time, Microsoft had released a self-contained version of Windows Media Player 9 that would run on Mac OS, Apple's operating system, which was, in turn, based on UNIX. Self-evidently, the underlying Apple operating system did not already incorporate parts of the Windows Media Player code. This Apple version of the latter effectively reverted it to a standalone application.

Windows Media Player Redistributable Code

At the time of the case, a downloadable form of Windows Media Player 9 was made available by Microsoft. This consisted of a media player in modular form and was called Windows Media Player Redistributable.

The idea for having this was as follows. For some specialized purposes, Microsoft would supply an operating system that was stripped down to its bare essentials. This could involve the Windows Media Player not being present. In such circumstances, should a software developer need to introduce parts of or even the entire media player functionality, he or she could download and then incorporate the necessary components available from Windows Media Player Redistributable. This also made it possible for content providers to include Windows Media Player 9 in their webpages or for software developers to integrate it into their applications programs. Clearly, to exploit the latter, developers would make use of the media player APIs that the various components exposed.

All this meant that if a version of the Windows operating system had to be produced without the Windows Media Player, the latter could quickly be reintroduced, even by applications programs or webpages.

In the Microsoft case, arguments relating to the removal or not of Windows Media Player 9 were also considered to cover implicitly the redistributable code version. The role of the redistributable code is, therefore, important to the understanding of the Microsoft case.

Technical Point Summary: Relevance to Tying

To bring this section to a close, it is worthwhile summarizing the preceding explanations.

First, it was possible to create a standalone version of Windows Media Player 9 that was independent of the Windows operating system.

Secondly, it was also possible to have a version of the Windows operating system without Windows Media Player 9.

Thirdly, in such a case, it was even possible to reinstall modules of Windows Media Player 9 from Windows Media Player Redistributable.

4. BRIEF COMPARISON WITH THE TECHNOLOGY ISSUES INVOLVED IN THE US MICROSOFT CASE

Having understood the basic technology issues involved in the EC case, this is now a convenient point at which to compare briefly what was involved in the US proceedings.

Use of the Term 'Middleware'

The US case concerns a category of software to which the label 'middleware' was attributed. This was an unusual use of this term. In simple terms, middleware is normally used in the information technology world to describe the unseen software 'glue' that enables distributed applications to work. Parts of these may be running on one or more computers connected via a network. Middleware can be thought of as a set of services which are accessed by programmers through programming interfaces. Middleware services enable the information processing functions of an application to be transparently distributed across a network. Programmers can access such services by using their appropriate APIs without needing to know where the services will be performed. Thus COM/DCOM mentioned earlier is an example of conventional middleware.

The US case concentrates on browsers (specifically Internet Explorer and Netscape Navigator) and on a machine-independent language, Java. Both the Internet Explorer application and the Java language can be used as platforms by other applications to provide their desired results. As such, in the US case, the term 'middleware' has been somewhat unconventionally used to describe both collectively. In fact, in the Final Judgment, the term is used to cover specifically the functionality provided by Internet Explorer, Microsoft's Java Virtual Machine, Windows Media Player, Windows Messenger, Outlook Express and their successors or software having similar functionality.

Navigator and Java Provided Potential, Operating-System-Independent Platforms

In simple terms, a browser is a program that is used to locate and display webpages. The primary use of a browser is to perform this function for material available on the World Wide Web. It is also used to access information on web servers connected to private networks, as well as files stored in an appropriate manner within file systems.

As part of its functioning, a browser takes HTML (HyperText Markup Language), and renders it into the corresponding characters and format within the browser window. Browser functionality is also frequently enhanced by so-called 'plug-ins'. These are software components that usually do not work in a standalone fashion but rely on the services provided by the application to which they 'plug in'. These allow an application to display in a browser window content that is much richer than could be obtained from the browser alone. Flash is an example of a plug-in.

Netscape was originally developing versions of its Navigator browser to run on different operating systems. If a software developer were to create an application that entirely relied on the APIs provided by Navigator, then in a networked environment, that application would be able to provide its results, through Navigator, on many different operating systems.

Java consists of the following and was originally developed by Sun:

- programs are written in the Java language;
- the Java instructions are translated by a program called a compiler into an intermediate language called Java bytecode;
- another programme called a Java Virtual Machine (JVM) converts the bytecode into machine code, which is then executed.

A JVM is created that is specific to an operating system and the processor on which it is running. There are thus several JVMs, each one corresponding to a different operating system/processor. Part of this Java environment includes a set of shared libraries of commonly used routines accessed via APIs. It can thus be seen that if a Java program could be entirely supported by a Java library, it would be able to run on any machine and also be independent of the underlying operating system.

In 1995, Netscape agreed to provide a copy of the Java environment with each copy of its Navigator browser.

Integration of Internet Explorer into the Windows Operating System

Originally, Internet Explorer was provided in 1995 as a standalone application for Windows 95. Standalone versions were also created for other operating systems, including Mac OS.

Subsequently, Microsoft placed part of Internet Explorer's specific code into the operating system, in particular into the libraries providing operating system functions. In this way, Internet Explorer would not function without an underlying Windows operating system. This is an analogous process to that described in detail previously concerning Windows Media Player. It also worked the other way around. For example, if a software developer decided to use Microsoft's HTMLHELP function to implement an application's help function, he or she would invoke the requisite API. However, this was only available through Internet Explorer.

Java Developers Obliged to Depend on the Windows Environment

Sun's original intention was that software developers would be able to create programs that would run on any computer and irrespective of the operating system. There was, however, a problem. The Java libraries were somewhat limited and did not expose sufficient APIs to enable a normally featured program to work. As a result, programmers had to make up this deficiency by relying on APIs exposed by the specific operating system on top of which the Java environment was functioning. This meant that the original purpose of Java was not being achieved.

To overcome this, Sun sponsored the development of a mechanism that would make it possible to use these operating-system-specific APIs but which hid this from a Java programmer. This would then make Java programs truly portable between different operating systems. The mechanism was called Java Native Interface (JNI).

The Java environment supplied by Netscape along with Navigator complied with Sun's mechanism.

Microsoft developed its own version of Sun's mechanism and which executed more rapidly. This was called Raw Native Interface (RNI). However, there was an incompatibility. A developer who produced software using Microsoft's mechanism rather than Sun's would find that the software would not run on Sun's Windows version of the JVM. This incompatibility was removed in 1998, when a court order required Microsoft to implement Sun's process.

Subsequent to this, Sun developed a technique called Java Remote Method Invocation (RMI). However, Java RMI was not provided with Microsoft's Java environment. This created a problem for programmers who would normally call communications interfaces that certainly had to be available on end-users' Windows client PCs. To get around this, they were obliged to rely on Microsoft-specific interfaces.

In 1998, Netscape ceased to distribute Java with its latest version 5 of Navigator. By contrast, a standalone version of Microsoft's Java environment was made available to independent software developers. It was provided independently of Internet Explorer.

Eventually, the only effective way of being absolutely sure that a developed application would be compatible with Microsoft's Java environment was to use Microsoft's development tools.

The US Remedy

The Final Judgment in the United States required that Microsoft document the Windows APIs and communications protocols that were used between client and server operating systems. The reason for this is obvious from the above brief description of the technical aspects of the US case. The browsers and the Java environment – the middleware – were running on client PCs. The applications serving them were running on servers. It contrasts with the EC case requiring that server-to-server protocols be documented also.

As opposed to the Commission's Decision concerning the Windows Media Player, it only required the means of access, in whatever form, to the offending 'middleware' product to be removed. It did not require removal of the code from the Windows operating system.

5. CONCLUSIONS

We, therefore, arrive at a state of knowledge that enables this chapter to draw to a close.

At this point, the reader is well-equipped to follow the numerous arguments made by the parties involved in this case. Many of the technical points explained by the various participants during its course went considerably beyond what has been provided here. However, with the foundations provided by this chapter, the essentials of what is at stake should be comprehensible.

Sun's original request for 'the complete information required to allow Sun . . . to provide native support for the complete set of Active Directory technologies on Solaris' and information 'necessary to provide native support for COM objects on Solaris' should now be understandable as should the limitations of the various solutions that were proposed. The manner in which Windows Media Player had become linked to the Windows operating system should also be clear.

Furthermore, the terminology of Remedies laid out in the Decision should now be understandable. For example, in the case of interoperability, 'Microsoft should be ordered to disclose complete and accurate specifications for the protocols used by Windows work group servers in order to provide file, print and group and user administration services to Windows work group networks . . .. Microsoft should not be required to disclose its own implementation of these specifications, that is to say, its own source code.' In the case of tying, 'Microsoft will have to offer a version of Windows for client PCs which does not include Windows Media Player . . .. Microsoft must refrain from using any technological . . . means which would have the equivalent effect of tying WMP to Windows. The unbundled version of Windows must in particular not be less performing than the version of Windows which comes bundled with WMP, regard being had to WMP's functionality which, by definition, will not be part of the unbundled version of Windows.'

In summary, the technical background has been laid down for the chapters that follow.

As a final comment, it should now be clear why the technical complexity inherent to this dispute strained the abilities of judges, advocates and experts to unprecedented limits as they struggled to understand, explain and articulate the issues in what is, perhaps, one of the most unusual competition cases ever.

PART II

From Brussels to Luxembourg: a European story

2. Windows into the world of abuse of dominance: An analysis of the Commission's 2004 Microsoft Decision and the CFI's 2007 judgment

Nicholas Banasevic and Per Hellström*

1. INTRODUCTION

On 24 March 2004, the European Commission concluded by way of Decision that Microsoft had violated Article 82 of the EC Treaty by abusing its dominant position in client PC operating systems in two ways. First, it had illegally refused to supply interoperability information which was indispensable for rival vendors to compete in the work group server operating systems market. Secondly, it had illegally tied its Windows Media Player product to its Windows PC operating system. The Commission also imposed a fine of €497,196 million for what it found to be a very serious infringement of Article 82 EC.[1]

On 7 June 2004, Microsoft appealed this Decision to the second highest Court in Europe, the European Court of First Instance (CFI). On 17 September 2007, sitting as a Grand Chamber of 13 judges, the CFI upheld the substance of the Commission's Decision as regards both abuses, as well as the fine that the Commission had imposed.[2] Microsoft chose not to appeal the CFI's judgment to the European Court of Justice.

---

* The views expressed in this chapter are the authors' personal views, and do not necessarily represent the position of the European Commission. We are grateful to Friedrich Wenzel Bulst, Kevin Coates, Vittorio di Bucci, Ryan Gordon Heath and Thomas Kramler for their comments on and input to this chapter.

[1] Commission Decision 2007/53/EC of 24 March 2004 [2007] OJ L32/23 (hereinafter 'The Decision').

[2] Case T-201/04 *Microsoft* v *Commission* [2007] ECR II-3601 ('the CFI judgment'). The CFI did not uphold the Decision's provision relating to the monitoring

This chapter provides an analysis of both the Commission's Decision and the CFI's judgment. It is structured as follows. Section 2 outlines some general aspects which are of key importance to the case. Section 3 then describes the refusal to supply abuse. Section 4 outlines the tying abuse, whilst section 5 concludes.

2. SOME KEY ASPECTS

Introduction

Before examining each of the abuses in more detail, we believe that two important issues of context should be highlighted. These are (1) the CFI's standard of review in its judgment; and (2) the nature and extent of Microsoft's market power in PC operating systems.

Standard of Judicial Review

As with any judgment, the CFI ruling must be read and understood in its context and interpreted against the background of the specific circumstances of the case. As regards the CFI's general standard of review, the CFI restated established case law that 'insofar as the Commission's decision is the result of complex technical appraisals, those appraisals are in principle subject to only limited review by the Court, which means that the Community Courts cannot substitute their own assessment of matters of fact for the Commission's'.[3]

However, in the following paragraph, the CFI went on to state that:

> However, while the Community Courts recognise that the Commission has a margin of appreciation in economic or technical matters, that does not mean that they must decline to review the Commission's interpretation of economic or technical data. The Community Courts must not only establish whether the evidence put forward is factually accurate, reliable and consistent but must also determine whether that evidence contains all the relevant data that must be taken into consideration in appraising a complex situation and whether it is capable of substantiating the conclusions drawn from it.[4]

---

of Microsoft's compliance to the extent that such a provision (i) required Microsoft to pay for such a monitoring mechanism; and (ii) allowed any monitoring trustee to access Microsoft information independently of the Commission.

3 CFI judgment, para. 88.

4 CFI judgment, para. 89.

It is therefore clear that the CFI conducted a detailed and thorough review of the entirety of the Commission's case, and indeed, an examination of the judgment confirms the depth of the CFI's analysis. Certain commentators have attempted to characterize the CFI's review as rather cursory, as if the CFI had almost waved the Decision through without more than a token look. However, in light of the above, we find such a characterization unjustified.

We also believe that because of this detailed factual analysis by the CFI, one should be careful in drawing general conclusions about the implications of the judgment. Although the judgment is, of course, based on certain principles (and indeed on previous case law), the findings very much turn on the specific and in many respects exceptional circumstances of the case (not least the enduring degree of market power that Microsoft has held, and which we now turn to briefly).

Microsoft's Dominance

Naturally, there is no issue with the possession of dominance by an undertaking. However, in particular in sectors such as the IT sector, where products have to interoperate with other products (the interoperability case), or where certain software products may be combined with other software products (the tying case), the possession of an enduring degree of monopoly power may provide the dominant company with the opportunity to abuse its monopoly position by extending it into adjacent markets.[5] This is what the Commission found in its Decision, and what the CFI confirmed. Indeed, looking beyond the two abuses covered by the Decision, the CFI stated that 'since Microsoft is very likely to maintain its dominant position on the client PC operating systems market, at least over the coming years, it cannot be precluded that it will have other opportunities to use leveraging vis-à-vis other adjacent markets'.[6]

In our view, in the Microsoft case, one of the specific characteristics that

---

5 This chapter does not focus on the economic theories of the case. However, it is worth noting that the Decision fully addressed Microsoft's argument that there was no economic incentive for Microsoft to anti-competitively 'leverage' from PC operating systems into adjacent, complementary markets because of the 'one monopoly profit' theory (according to which there is only one monopoly profit to be gained in separate markets with complementary products). The Decision found that when a dynamic analysis is undertaken, there were in fact a number of incentives for Microsoft to engage in such practices, not least the commercial motive to move into adjacent markets as a means of protecting its primary PC operating system monopoly.

6 CFI judgment, para. 1363.

has to be borne in mind is the overwhelming degree of market power that Microsoft has held in the market for PC operating systems, and the enduring nature of such market power. As the Decision outlined,[7] Microsoft has held very high market shares in the PC operating systems market for many years (in excess of 90 per cent since 2000), and throughout that period, its market position has been protected by what is known as the applications barrier to entry, namely the fact that the vast majority of applications are written to the Windows platform. In this regard, the CFI confirmed that:

> the Commission was correct to find . . . that the quasi-monopoly that Microsoft has held on the client PC operating systems market for many years enables it to 'determine to a large extent and independently of its competitors the set of coherent communications rules that will govern the de facto standard for interoperability in work group networks'.[8]

We believe that the nature of this market power plays an important role in the analysis of the case. Indeed, it has implications for both abuses. For example, as regards refusal to supply, the fact that Microsoft is the de facto standard in the market has important implications for the findings relating to the indispensability of the interoperability information that was refused. As regards tying, Microsoft's near monopoly similarly has important implications for the findings relating to the ubiquity of the Windows Media Player. We will examine these points in more detail in the analysis of the individual abuse sections, which now follows.

3. THE REFUSAL TO SUPPLY ABUSE

Introduction

The key to understanding the refusal to supply abuse is the fact that it relates to a refusal to supply *interoperability information*. Naturally, interoperability between different software products is a matter of degree, and here, the Decision relied on the EC Software Directive for the definition of interoperability to be used. It defined interoperability as 'the ability to exchange information and mutually to use the information which has been exchanged'.[9] Particularly in the IT sector, the ability for different

---

7 For example, see Decision, recital 436.

8 CFI judgment, para. 392.

9 See Decision, recital 36, referring to recital 12 to the Software Directive (Council Directive 91/250/EEC of 14 May 1991 [1991] OJ L122/42, 17 May 1991).

products to interoperate is a crucial factor for them to be able to function properly, and hence to compete on their individual merits.

Microsoft has over the years made significant interoperability disclosures in certain areas, not least via its Microsoft Developer Network, whereby Microsoft publishes interoperability information to ensure that complementary applications can run smoothly on top of its Windows operating system. In contrast, the Decision observed that Microsoft no longer supplied interoperability information in a market where its own products faced competition.[10] Therefore, for work group server operating systems, which are operating systems which are designed to interoperate with PC operating systems and provide them with basic network services such as file and print sharing and user authentication, whilst Microsoft allowed for the necessary interoperability with its PCs for its own work group server operating system, it did not for rival products.

The remainder of this section will go over the specifics of the case, first by introducing the case law that was applied, and then by going through the relevant criteria.

Case Law

For the refusal to supply abuse, the Commission undertook the strictest legal test and hence the one most favourable to Microsoft by assuming that the interoperability information that was refused was protected by intellectual property rights.[11] It therefore applied the exceptional circumstances test that had first been outlined by the Court of Justice in *Magill*.[12]

Following the Commission's Decision, the Court of Justice issued its judgment in *IMS Health*.[13] This closely followed *Magill*, and confirmed that in exceptional circumstances, a refusal to license intellectual property may be abusive. These exceptional circumstances were again outlined by the CFI in paragraphs 332–333 of the judgment, and are as follows:

---

10 Microsoft had initially supplied such information when it had entered the market, and hence when it was in its interests to do so.

11 Although it did not conclude that the information was indeed covered by intellectual property rights. In this regard, it is interesting to note that Microsoft did not invoke intellectual property rights in its initial refusal to supply vis-à-vis Sun Microsystems, and remained non-specific on its claims about the scope and nature of the alleged intellectual property right until very late in the Commission's proceedings.

12 Joined Cases C-241/91 P and C-242/91 P, *RTE and ITP* v *Commission* [1995] ECR I-743 ('*Magill*').

13 Case C-418/01 *IMS Health GmbH* v *NDC Health* [2004] ECR I-5039.

- the refusal relates to a product or service indispensable to the exercise of a particular activity on a neighbouring market; . . .
- the refusal is of such a kind as to exclude any effective competition on that neighbouring market; . . .
- the refusal prevents the appearance of a new product for which there is potential consumer demand.

  Once it is established that such circumstances are present, the refusal by the holder of a dominant position to grant a license may infringe Article 82 EC unless the refusal is objectively justified.

Two other points are worth mentioning here.

First, the CFI confirmed that parties were generally free to choose their business partners, and hence to refuse to deal with (or in this case license intellectual property to) others in the market.[14] Although this may seem obvious, we believe that it is often drowned out of the debate, particularly by those who argue, mistakenly in our view, that the Microsoft case will somehow lead to the floodgates opening, and companies having to be wary of wholesale expropriation of their intellectual property by the Commission. We should not forget, after all, that Microsoft is one of the extremely rare cases in the history of EC competition law of a company being ordered to supply information which is (or indeed might be) covered by intellectual property rights.

Secondly, the Commission had argued that it was appropriate to look at the entirety of the circumstances, and hence that exceptional circumstances other than those listed in *IMS* should also be considered (such as the extraordinary nature of Microsoft's market power, the fact that the refusal concerned interoperability information and the fact that Microsoft had previously supplied the same type of interoperability information but had then cut off this supply). The CFI did not go into this question, essentially concluding that it was sufficient that the *IMS Health* criteria were met.[15] Nevertheless, we submit that the Commission's argumentation about Microsoft's extraordinary market power is implicitly taken into account in the CFI's consideration of some of the *IMS Helath* criteria, not least on indispensability. Similarly, the fact that the information that was refused is interoperability information is an important part of the CFI's analysis, but within the framework of the established *IMS Health* criteria.

Let us now turn to these criteria.

---

[14] CFI judgment, para. 319.
[15] CFI judgment, para. 336.

Indispensability

The core of the analysis on indispensability is the notion of interoperability. The point of departure here was the EC Software Directive, which outlined the notion of 'two-way interoperability'. Here, the CFI confirmed:

> that the concept of interoperability employed in the contested decision – according to which interoperability between two software products means the capacity for them to exchange information and to use that information mutually in order to allow each of those software products to function in all the ways envisaged – is consistent with that envisaged in Directive 91/250.[16]

With this in mind, the reason why the interoperability information which Microsoft refused to disclose was indispensable to be able to compete in the work group server operating systems market is Microsoft's monopoly power in PC operating systems. As specified above, work group server operating systems need to interoperate with PC operating systems in order to be able to provide PC users with the basic set of work group services (file and print sharing, and group and user administration). Indeed, here, the CFI found that:

> as the Windows operating system is thus present on virtually all client PCs installed within organisations, non-Windows work group server operating systems cannot continue to be marketed if they are incapable of achieving a high degree of interoperability with Windows.[17]

The CFI went on to find that:

> in light of the very narrow technological and privileged links that Microsoft has established between its Windows client PC and work group server operating systems, and of the fact that Windows is present on virtually all client PCs installed within organisations, the Commission was correct to find, at recital 697 to the contested decision, that Microsoft was able to impose the Windows domain architecture as the 'de facto standard for work group computing'.[18]

The CFI also confirmed that it was important that non-Windows work group server operating systems were able to interoperate with Windows client PCs on an equal footing with Windows work group server operating

---

16 CFI judgment, para. 225.
17 CFI judgment, para. 388.
18 CFI judgment, para. 392.

systems.[19] In our view, in the specific context of the case, this reflects the established EC competition law notion of competition on the merits. In the present case, products in the work group server operating systems market are differentiated according to many different criteria relating to their core functionality, such as reliability, security and speed. Therefore, if they are unable to interoperate with Windows client PCs on an equal footing, i.e. in the same way that Windows work group server operating systems do, then there will be no competition on the merits on the basis of the core functionalities of Windows and non-Windows work group server operating systems products because of Microsoft's artificial interoperability advantage.

The CFI's conclusion on this point is telling:

> The Court also concludes from those considerations that the absence of such interoperability with the Windows domain architecture has the effect of reinforcing Microsoft's competitive position on the work group server operating systems market, particularly because it induces consumers to use its work group server operating system in preference to its competitors', although its competitors' operating systems offer features to which consumers attach great importance.[20]

This finding comes after a detailed review by the CFI of a range of evidence in the Decision which outlined that on the core functionalities of work group server operating systems valued by consumers, non-Windows work group server operating systems were generally rated higher than Windows work group server operating systems. As such, the reason why Windows work group server operating systems were gaining market share was the privileged interoperability connection which Microsoft had reserved for itself. Indeed, we believe that this is, in a nutshell, why the Commission felt obliged to pursue the case.

Elimination of Competition

The Decision found that there was a risk of elimination of competition in the work group server operating systems market as a result of Microsoft's refusal to supply, and the judgment confirmed the Commission's findings. A number of points are noteworthy in this respect.

It has been argued in some quarters, including at the time by Microsoft,

---

19 See in particular CFI judgment, paras 230 and 374. More precisely, the findings relate to the Windows domain architecture.

20 CFI judgment, para. 422.

that there is a difference between the notions of 'risk of elimination of competition' and 'likelihood to eliminate competition' and that the latter, 'more stringent' notion is what must be demonstrated by the Commission. However, the CFI was very clear on this point:

> The expressions 'risk of elimination of competition' and 'likely to eliminate competition' are used without distinction by the Community judicature to reflect the same idea, namely that Article 82 EC does not apply only from the time when there is no more, or practically no more, competition on the market.[21]

The CFI then highlighted the importance of safeguarding effective enforcement of Article 82 EC:

> If the Commission were required to wait until competitors were eliminated from the market, or until their elimination was sufficiently imminent, before being able to take action under Article 82 EC, that would clearly run counter to the objective of that provision, which is to maintain undistorted competition in the common market and, in particular, to safeguard the competition that still exists on the relevant market.[22]

Indeed, this is illustrated in the specific context of the case. It is clear that as a result of Microsoft's refusal, the Commission had identified a clear trend in favour of Microsoft's products in the secondary market which was not due to any inherent quality advantage of Microsoft's products, but due to the artificial interoperability advantage resulting from the refusal. By the time of the Decision, Microsoft's position in this secondary market had reached at least 60 per cent and continued to grow in a market that was characterized by network effects and where the interoperability information in question was indispensable.[23]

Moreover, due to the reality of the market under consideration, it is only logical that the prospect of elimination of competition would not be immediate. Servers are expensive products with a life-cycle of several years and are hence not replaced regularly. There will therefore be a constituency of legacy products which will not disappear overnight as a result

---

[21] CFI judgment, para. 561.

[22] CFI judgment, para. 561.

[23] In this sense, the finding relating to elimination of competition is the logical extension of the finding that the interoperability information which Microsoft refused to disclose was indispensable to compete in the work group server operating systems market. If the information is indispensable, then without it, you cannot compete on the merits, and you will be forced (ultimately) to exit the market.

of Microsoft's refusal, and the trend in the market in Microsoft's favour would be played out over time. Against this background, to attempt to reduce the debate to a semantic one is, as the CFI put it, an argument which is 'purely one of terminology and is wholly irrelevant',[24] and which attempts to side-step the reality of the actual developments in the market.

The CFI also made clear, in paragraph 563 of the judgment, that it was not necessary:

> to demonstrate that all competition on the market would be eliminated. What matters, for the purpose of establishing an infringement of Article 82 EC, is that the refusal at issue is liable to, or is likely to, eliminate all effective competition on the market. It must be made clear that the fact that the competitors of the dominant undertaking retain a marginal presence in certain niches on the market cannot suffice to substantiate the existence of such competition.

We submit that this again is an illustration of a logical, real-world application to the case. For there to be an elimination of competition should not, of course, mean that there cannot be a single copy of a rival work group server operating system to Microsoft's on the market. What matters is effective competition. As the CFI put it:

> Microsoft's refusal has the consequence that its competitors' products are confined to marginal positions or even made unprofitable. The fact that there may be marginal competition between operators on the market cannot therefore invalidate the Commission's argument that all effective competition was at risk of being eliminated on that market.[25]

New Product

The application of the new product criterion by the CFI has perhaps been the subject of greatest debate for the refusal to supply abuse following the judgment. The CFI made clear that this criterion should be 'considered under Article 82(b) EC, which prohibits abusive practices which consist in "limiting production, markets or technical developments to the . . . prejudice of consumers"',[26] and it made reference to both the *IMS Health* and *Magill* judgments which had considered prejudice to consumers under this heading.[27]

Then, in paragraph 647 of the judgment, the CFI went on to state that:

---

24 CFI judgment, para. 561.
25 CFI judgment, para. 593.
26 CFI judgment, para. 643.
27 CFI judgment, paras 644–6.

> the circumstance relating to the appearance of a new product, as envisaged in Magill and IMS Health . . . cannot be the only parameter which determines whether a refusal to license an intellectual property right is capable of causing prejudice to consumers within the meaning of Article 82(b) EC. As that provision states, such prejudice may arise where there is a limitation not only of production or markets, but also of technical development.

We have heard it argued that this represents a departure from the existing jurisprudence in the sense that it widens the notion of harm to consumers under a refusal to license intellectual property abuse. This is held to be the case because the CFI adds 'limitation of technical development' as a relevant notion under the 'new product' criterion to the notions of 'limitations to production or markets'.[28] If this is a departure, then we believe that its scope should not be exaggerated, since all three concepts (i.e. limitation of production, markets and technical development, all to the prejudice of consumers) are part of the specific wording of Article 82(b) EC, which is the prism through which the case law sets out that the new product criterion should be viewed.

In any case, we would submit that when the specifics of the Microsoft case are examined, the notion of limitation of technical development applied by the CFI makes eminent sense. What the Commission found, and what the CFI confirmed, was that as a result of Microsoft's refusal, innovative products, which could be differentiated from one another on key features, were prevented from coming to the market:

> the contested decision rests on the concept that, once the obstacle represented for Microsoft's competitors by the insufficient degree of interoperability with the Windows domain architecture has been removed, those competitors will be able to offer work group server operating systems which, far from merely reproducing the Windows systems already on the market, will be distinguished from those systems with respect to parameters which consumers consider important (see, to that effect, recital 699 to the contested decision).[29]

What is more, the evidence demonstrated that for these key features, consumers generally preferred third-party products to those of Microsoft. As a result, the consumer suffered because these products could not reach him because of the artificial interoperability advantage engendered by Microsoft's refusal:

---

28 Which might be said to be encapsulated in Cases C-241 and 242/91 P *Magill* and Case C-418/01 *IMS Health* in this context.

29 CFI judgment, para. 656.

> the limitation thus placed on consumer choice is all the more damaging to consumers because, as already observed at paragraphs 407 to 412 above, they consider that non-Microsoft work group server operating systems are better than Windows work group server operating systems with respect to a series of features to which they attach great importance.[30]

In this context, it would not make any sense if, to apply the case law, it were deemed necessary for there to be a predeveloped product ready and waiting to enter the secondary market absent the refusal, as was the case in *Magill*, and as we have heard some argue should have been the case in the Microsoft case. This is because the development of a work group server operating system involves the deployment of significant resources over a period of several years. Given this, a work group server operating system vendor will most likely not even start to develop his product until he knows that he will have access to the interoperability information to connect with the Windows PC monopoly, precisely because that information is indispensable to compete in the market. To argue that he must have a new product ready and waiting to justify the very disclosure of this information therefore does not make sense in a real-world application of the facts.

In any case, we do not believe that it is an implied requirement of the case law for the 'new product' to be 'ready and waiting' to be put on the secondary market. In paragraph 49 of *IMS Health*, the Court of Justice qualified what it meant by 'new product' when it stated that the situation would only be potentially abusive where 'the undertaking which requested the licence does not intend to limit itself essentially to duplicating the goods or services already offered on the secondary market by the owner of the intellectual property right'.

By analogy with the Microsoft case, therefore, this means that the third-party products which are prevented from emerging as a result of the refusal cannot be copies of Microsoft's own product in the secondary market, namely Microsoft's work group server operating system.[31] Therefore, the notion of third-party products which can be differentiated from those of the dominant firm in the secondary market (and which are not 'pre-developed') and for which there is potential consumer demand is in our view consistent with the notion of a new product as defined by the case law.[32]

All in all, therefore, we believe that given the facts at hand, the CFI

---

30 CFI judgment, para. 652.

31 In this instance, this mirrors the analysis on objective justification, which is addressed in the next sub-section.

32 The secondary market is of course where, according to the jurisprudence, these products must be prevented from emerging, since this is where the risk of elimination of competition must manifest itself.

applied the existing case law in the most logical manner. We also find it noteworthy that the CFI examined in significant detail notions such as consumer choice, customer lock-in and innovation in the market.[33] In our view therefore, the CFI's application of the case law had a strong real-world resonance.

Objective Justification

The CFI confirmed that even if the above-mentioned exceptional circumstances were fulfilled, a company could objectively justify its refusal. As regards the burden of proof, the CFI made clear that while it was of course necessary for the Commission to discharge its burden to demonstrate an infringement of Article 82 EC, it was for the dominant company to substantiate any claims of objective justification (and for the Commission to then, as appropriate, show that these claims could not be accepted).[34]

In the present case, Microsoft essentially made two claims according to which its refusal was objectively justified. First, it claimed that the information which it had refused to disclose was covered by intellectual property rights. The CFI pointed out, as the Commission had done, that this could not as a matter of principle be an objective justification because it would contradict and render meaningless the concept that the case law had established that refusals to license intellectual property could, in exceptional circumstances, constitute an abuse of a dominant position.[35]

Microsoft's more specific argument relating to objective justification was that disclosure of the information which it had refused to disclose would harm its incentives to innovate, essentially because it would allow the undertakings to which the information had been disclosed to copy/clone its products. Here again, the analysis must turn on the specifics of the case. This means examining the nature of the information that Microsoft had refused to disclose.

In this regard, the CFI confirmed the Commission's analysis which was that since the information was interface information which was designed to allow two different products (PC operating systems and work group server operating systems) to interoperate with each other, it would not be possible for rivals to copy/clone the core functionality of the Microsoft products themselves as a result of the disclosure.[36] It could not therefore

---

33 As the Commission had done in the Decision.

34 CFI judgment, para. 688.

35 CFI judgment, para. 690.

36 CFI judgment, para. 697 *et seq.*

be claimed by Microsoft that disclosure of the interoperability information would reduce its incentives to innovate. In this sense, the information that was refused is different in nature to the source code of either the PC operating system or the work group server operating system, disclosure of which could indeed reveal the core functionality of Microsoft's products. Had this been what was at stake during the Commission's procedure, one imagines that the analysis would have been different.

The CFI illustrated its findings further. It noted, amongst other things, that it was:

> normal practice for operators in the industry to disclose to third parties the information which will facilitate interoperability with their products and Microsoft itself had followed that practice until it was sufficiently established on the work group server operating systems market. Such disclosure allows the operators concerned to make their own products more attractive and therefore more valuable. In fact, none of the parties has claimed in the present case that such disclosure had had any negative impact on those operators' incentives to innovate. It is common in the industry to freely share such information, since it enhances the value of one's own product.[37]

The CFI also confirmed the Commission's findings as regards Microsoft's settlement with the US Department of Justice. During the Commission's administrative procedure, Microsoft had acknowledged that the interoperability disclosures which it had made pursuant to this settlement[38] had not negatively impacted its incentives to innovate.[39] As a result, the CFI found that:

> if the disclosures made under the United States settlement . . . as regards server-to-client protocols had no negative impact on Microsoft's incentives to innovate (recital 728 to the contested decision), there is no obvious reason to believe that the consequences should be any different in the case of disclosure relating to server/server protocols.[40]

We would also add that just one week after the Commission's 2004 Decision, Microsoft and Sun entered into a far-reaching settlement which included provisions for more extensive interoperability disclosures by Microsoft than those covered by the Decision. This settlement had, in

---

37 CFI judgment, para. 702.

38 These were interoperability disclosures of the same type as those covered by the Decision, although because of the different scope of the US case, they did not include server to server disclosures.

39 Decision, recital 728.

40 CFI judgment, para. 703.

Microsoft's own view, no negative impact on Microsoft's incentives to innovate. In fact, at a joint press conference with Sun following the settlement, Microsoft stated that both companies would continue to compete and innovate and that 'the impact of the settlement [would] not be less innovation, but more innovation'.[41]

More recently, in February 2008, Microsoft made another press announcement that the company was undertaking 'strategic changes in technology and business practices to expand interoperability', *inter alia*, by making the interoperability information covered by the Commission's Decision and other information available free of charge on its website.[42] Commenting on this initiative, Microsoft's CEO stated that 'Essentially what we are permitting is more innovation around our products, more interoperability . . . but it's a path that we commit ourselves to because it's good for customers, and it's consistent with our legal obligation'.[43] If Microsoft delivers in the way it has said it will, we cannot agree more.

4. THE TYING ABUSE

Introduction

The second abusive conduct in which Microsoft was found to have engaged consisted in the fact that Microsoft made the availability of the Windows client PC operating system conditional on the simultaneous acquisition of the Windows Media Player product, i.e. it tied Windows Media Player to its monopoly product, Windows. Before examining the criteria outlined in the Decision, and which were confirmed by the CFI, it is worth saying a few words of introduction about how Microsoft had attempted to portray Windows Media Player, and what the CFI found in this regard.

During the court proceedings, Microsoft went to great lengths in an attempt to deny the existence of a separate application called Windows Media Player. Microsoft instead referred to what it called 'media functionality' in Windows, and argued that the inclusion of such functionality was simply 'a normal and necessary step in the evolution of [Windows]'.[44]

By way of preliminary observation, the CFI critically noted that

---

41 See CFI judgment, para. 687, referring to the Commission's position.

42 See www.microsoft.com/presspass/press/2008/feb08/02-21expandinteroperabilitypr.mspx.

43 See www.iht.com/articles/2008/03/03/business/msft.php.

44 See CFI judgment, para. 935.

Microsoft's argument 'relies to a large extent on the vague concept of media functionality',[45] but that it was clear from the Decision that the tying behaviour in question related to the distinct application software that is Windows Media Player.[46]

The CFI also noted that the inclusion of Windows Media Player together with Windows was in fact not the result of a 'necessary step in the evolution' of Windows, but rather a strategic decision involving the highest executive level of Microsoft.[47] In fact, in the period 1998–1999, RealNetworks' RealPlayer product was the clear market leader in the streaming media player market, and was recognized, even by Microsoft itself, as the better product. Microsoft's own stand-alone player, then called NetShow and later renamed Windows Media Player, was struggling based on competition on the merits.[48]

Indeed, the CFI noted that Microsoft itself had acknowledged in the hearing that its decision to tie its stand-alone product to Windows was not dictated by technical constraints or efficiencies.[49] Moreover, the CFI considered that arguing that the tie was dictated by technical reasons 'is scarcely credible in the light of the content of certain of its own internal communications'.[50] This is in particular a reference to an e-mail sent from a Microsoft executive to Microsoft's Chairman in 1997, in which he proposed to 'reposition [the] streaming media battle from NetShow vs. Real to Windows vs. Real', and to 'follow the [Internet Explorer] strategy wherever appropriate'.[51] In light of this, the CFI concluded 'that the integration of Windows Media Player in Windows was primarily designed to make Windows Media Player more competitive with RealPlayer by

---

45 CFI judgment, para. 916.

46 The CFI pointed out that 'Microsoft itself differentiates, in its technical documentation, the files which constitute Windows Media Player from the other media files, in particular those relating to the basic media infrastructure of the operating system': CFI judgment, para. 916.

47 'Microsoft's argument that the integration of Windows Media Player in the Windows operating system was dictated by technical reasons is scarcely credible in the light of the content of certain of its own internal communications. Thus, it follows from Mr Bay's email of 3 January 1999 to Mr Gates . . . that the integration of Windows Media Player in Windows was primarily designed to make Windows Media Player more competitive with RealPlayer by presenting it as a constituent part of Windows and not as application software that might be compared with RealPlayer': CFI judgment, para. 937.

48 See in particular CFI judgment, paras 1046 and 1080.

49 CFI judgment, para. 936.

50 CFI judgment, para. 937.

51 CFI judgment, para. 911.

presenting it as a constituent part of Windows and not as application software that might be compared with RealPlayer'.[52]

In a nutshell therefore, as the CFI identified, the case related to the fact that rather than competing head to head with RealPlayer, Microsoft tied Windows Media Player to Windows, thereby relying on the ubiquity of its PC operating system (which was installed on 90 per cent + of all PCs in the world). Customers and consumers would have no choice but to pay for the bundle, and there would be no way of uninstalling the Windows Media Player. Let us now look at how the Commission and the CFI approached the case from a legal perspective.

Case Law

In its Decision, the Commission had referred to consistent case law on tying, such as *Hilti* and *Tetra Pak II*,[53] setting out the legal conditions to be met as regards tying. Essentially, there are four such conditions, which are as follows:

- the undertaking concerned is dominant in the tying product (in this case, PC operating systems);
- the tying and tied products are two separate products;
- customers are not given a choice to obtain the tying product without the tied product; and
- the practice is liable to foreclose competition.

On top of these conditions, the undertaking concerned may provide an objective justification for its tie, such as in the form of efficiencies in its conduct (which would then have to outweigh the anti-competitive effects of the tying for the conduct not to be deemed abusive).

Microsoft argued before the CFI[54] that the Commission had in this case applied 'a new and highly speculative theory' based on some future and indirect effects of the behaviour, and also questioned the reliance on Article 82(d) EC. The CFI rejected Microsoft's argument on this point as '*purely semantic*',[55] and confirmed the Commission's analysis of the

---

[52] CFI judgment, para. 937.

[53] Case T-30/89 *Hilti* v *Commission* [1991] ECR II-1439; Case T-83/91 *Tetra Pak* v *Commission* [1994] ECR II-755, upheld on appeal in Case C-333/94 P *Tetra Pak* v *Commission* [1996] ECR I-5951.

[54] See CFI judgment, para. 846.

[55] CFI judgment, para. 850.

constituent elements of tying as 'correct and . . . consistent both with Article 82 EC and with the case-law'.[56]

The remainder of this section will therefore examine the constituent elements of tying in turn (with the exception of dominance in the tying product, PC operating systems, which has already been discussed), as well as the question of objective justification: the separate products point, the issue of coercion (i.e. not being able to obtain the tying product without the tied product), the question of foreclosure, and finally objective justification.

Separate Products

The issue of what constitutes a separate product was one of the central questions of the tying case. As noted above, Microsoft went to great lengths to avoid recognizing the existence of the Windows Media Player as a distinct application, but consistently referred to the, as noted by the CFI, 'vague concept' of media functionality.

The CFI first noted that the relevant moment in time for the separate product assessment 'is by reference to the factual and technical situation that existed at the time when, according to the Commission, the impugned conduct became harmful, and therefore the period after May 1999'.[57] The CFI then went on to confirm the existing jurisprudence that the distinctness of products must be assessed by reference to customer demand, in other words, whether there existed a separate consumer demand for the tied product, in this case, streaming media players.[58] In this particular instance, this was demonstrated by a number of factors, namely:

- A PC operating system is systems software while a media player is applications software. These are clearly different in terms of the functionalities they offer consumers (CFI judgment, paragraph 926).
- There are suppliers of stand-alone streaming media players (paragraph 927), and 'a not insignificant number of customers' obtain media players from these companies separately from their PC operating system, which shows that they regard the two products as separate (paragraph 932).

---

[56] CFI judgment, paras 859 and 869. See also para. 862, where the CFI confirmed that as well as the Commission's analysis being consistent with the general provisions of Article 82 EC, 'the constituent elements of abusive tying identified by the Commission at recital 794 to the contested decision coincide effectively with the conditions laid down in Article 82(d) EC'.

[57] CFI judgment, para. 914.

[58] CFI judgment, paras 917, 920.

- Microsoft itself designed its own Windows Media Player for other operating systems, namely Apple Mac and Solaris (paragraph 928).
- Microsoft's own practices vis-à-vis Windows Media Player, including (i) the fact that it could be downloaded independently of Windows from Microsoft's website, and that Windows Media Player upgrades were released independently of Windows (paragraph 929); (ii) the fact that Microsoft promotes Windows Media Player separately (paragraph 930); and (iii) the fact that there is a specific software development kit licence for Windows Media Player separate from the one for Windows (paragraph 931).

The CFI therefore rejected Microsoft's suggested separate product test which was whether there was a demand for the tying product without the tied product, in other words whether customers wanted 'Windows without media functionality'.[59] This, the CFI said, amounts to a claim that complementary products (such as PC operating systems and media players) 'cannot constitute separate products for the purposes of Article 82 EC, which is contrary to the Community case-law on bundling'.[60] With respect to the products under consideration, the CFI went on to note that 'in the case of complementary products, such as client PC operating systems and application software, it is quite possible that customers will wish to obtain the products together, but from different sources'.[61]

The CFI's analysis is rooted in the realities of the products in question. Here again, as was the case with the refusal to supply abuse, an examination of the specifics of the market is important. It is obvious that PC operating systems and streaming media players are products which are closely related. Indeed, they are complementary. Both are software products that are installed on a PC, and the latter will only work if the former is present. But that does not mean that they are not separate products in economic, commercial and, indeed, legal terms.

In this market, consumers generally do not purchase PC operating systems as stand-alone products. Rather, they generally buy PCs from PC manufacturers (such as HP, Dell, Lenovo, Acer, etc.) which assemble a range of hardware and software products on a consumer's behalf. There

---

[59] It should be noted that Microsoft had also argued that media players are somehow linked, by nature or according to commercial usage, to PC operating systems, but this did not impress the CFI. The CFI remarked that 'it is difficult to speak of commercial usage in an industry that is 95% controlled by Microsoft' (see CFI judgment, para. 940).

[60] CFI judgment, para. 921.

[61] CFI judgment, para. 922.

is therefore almost always a PC operating system pre-installed on a PC when it is purchased by a consumer (and it is almost always Windows). It is therefore misleading to ask whether consumers want an operating system without a media player when they do not in fact buy an operating system directly. Rather, and we would be the first to acknowledge this, when consumers buy a PC, they want to have a range of software products pre-installed on it, including an operating system and a media player.[62] However, this does not mean that the PC operating system and the media player, which are separate products, must be from the same source.[63]

In this respect, the CFI confirmed that Microsoft had ignored the particular intermediary role played by PC manufacturers in the market, and noted that:

> if OEMs [original equipment manufacturers] and consumers were able to obtain Windows without Windows Media Player, that would not mean that they would choose to obtain Windows without a streaming media player. OEMs follow consumer demand for a pre-installed media player on the operating system and offer a software package including a streaming media player that works with Windows, the difference being that that player would not necessarily be Windows Media Player.[64]

This captures the essence of the Commission's case. It was not about putting on the market an operating system such that consumers would not get a media player (we have heard this argued on occasion, but we find such caricatures disappointing). This is because, as noted above, given the role that PC manufacturers play in this market, a PC will generally come pre-installed with both a PC operating system and a media player. As such, the Commission's case was about seeking to ensure that there was competition on the merits for the media player, such that a company should not be able de facto to impose its own media player product on PC manufacturers, and therefore on consumers simply by virtue of its monopoly in an adjacent, complementary market, that of PC operating systems.

---

62 Similarly, as the CFI noted at para. 922, 'the fact that most client PC users want their client PC operating system to come with word-processing software does not transform those separate products into a single product for the purposes of Article 82 EC'.

63 A logical extension of Microsoft's argument would mean that the moment it deems it necessary to bundle a new application with Windows, then that application is no longer a separate product on the grounds that there is no demand for Windows without it.

64 CFI judgment, para. 923.

It is true that the Decision's remedy has not met with significant success. In our view, however, for the reasons we have described above, this is unrelated to the 'red-herring' issue of whether there is a demand for a PC operating system without a media player. Rather, our view is that by the time the Commission's remedy took effect (which was only in 2005 following the President of the CFI's interim measures order), Windows Media Player had effectively been tied with Windows for around six years. As the Decision highlighted, it had already become a market leader as a result of the tie, and given this and the network effects in the market, by the time the remedy took effect, we believe that it is likely that because of the tie, it had become a 'must-have' product for PC manufacturers. These factors have led some to criticize the Commission's remedy as not going far enough, and that it should therefore have either: (i) obliged Microsoft to only offer the unbundled version of Windows (as opposed to being able still also to offer the bundled version); or (ii) obliged there to be a price differential between the bundled and unbundled versions of Windows; or (iii) obliged Microsoft to carry a range of other media players together with Windows.

Coercion

The CFI confirmed that it was not possible for either PC manufacturers or consumers, for contractual and technical reasons, to obtain Windows without Windows Media Player.[65] Therefore, the CFI stated that the relevant condition relating to supplementary obligations in Article 82(d) EC was fulfilled:

> consumers are unable to acquire the Windows client PC operating system without simultaneously acquiring Windows Media Player, which means . . . that the condition that the conclusion of contracts is made subject to acceptance of supplementary obligations must be considered to be satisfied.[66]

Microsoft had made arguments that customers were not obliged to use the Windows Media Player, and that they could also download and use other media players. However, the CFI confirmed that this was not relevant to the issue of whether Windows could be *obtained* without Windows Media Player:

> nor . . . is it relevant for the purposes of the examination of the present condition that, as Microsoft claims, consumers are not obliged to use the Windows

---

65 See CFI judgment, paras 962–5.
66 CFI judgment, para. 961.

> Media Player which they find pre-installed on their client PC and that they can install and use other undertakings' media players on their PCs. Again, neither Article 82(d) EC nor the case-law on bundling requires that consumers must be forced to use the tied product or prevented from using the same product supplied by a competitor of the dominant undertaking in order for the condition that the conclusion of contracts is made subject to acceptance of supplementary obligations to be capable of being regarded as satisfied.[67]

On this point, we are not saying, and neither did the CFI, that the fact that customers are not obliged to use Windows Media Player or that other media players could be downloaded for free is irrelevant in the overall analysis of the tie. Far from it, particularly in an effects-based examination of the market at hand. The Commission considered these points in detail in the next stage of its analysis, namely foreclosure, and we will hence outline the relevant considerations below.

Before moving on, however, it is worth noting that Microsoft had also argued that there could not be any coercion since customers are not required to pay anything extra for Windows Media Player within Windows. However, we believe that the CFI rightly rejected this argument, *inter alia*, because Microsoft itself acknowledged that the price of Windows Media Player was included in the price of the bundled Windows. As the CFI stated, referring to Microsoft's own argumentation: 'as is evident from paragraph 232 of Microsoft's application, the price of Windows Media Player is included in the total price of the Windows client PC operating system'.[68]

Foreclosure

The Commission had made clear in the Decision that in previous tying cases (which it called 'classical tying cases'), 'the Commission and the Courts considered the foreclosure effect for competing vendors to be demonstrated by the bundling of a separate product with the dominant product'.[69] However, the Commission noted that in the case of Windows Media Player, such foreclosure could not be automatically assumed because:

> users can and do to a certain extent obtain third party media players through the Internet, sometimes for free. There are therefore indeed good reasons not to assume without further analysis that tying WMP [Windows Media Player] con-

---

[67] CFI judgment, para. 970.
[68] CFI judgment, para. 968.
[69] Decision, recital 841.

> stitutes conduct which by its very nature is liable to foreclose competition'.[70] As such, 'there are indeed circumstances relating to the tying of WMP which warrant a closer examination of the effects that tying has on competition in this case.'[71]

Microsoft frequently attempted to portray the Commission's statement referring to 'classical tying cases' as an indication that the Commission was somehow departing from the previous case law. However, this was not the case. As the quotes from the Decision referred to in the previous paragraph demonstrate, the Commission simply made clear that given the specificities of the market, it would go further in its analysis than in previous cases to demonstrate liability of foreclosure. We are surprised, particularly in an era where it is increasingly generally accepted that an effects-based analysis needs to be conducted for single-firm conduct, that the Commission was reproached for its endeavour to move beyond the simple assumption that tying in itself in all cases equated to foreclosure, and instead analysed the specificities of the case at hand.[72]

As regards the substance of the foreclosure analysis, the Commission had included three separate elements in the Decision. First, it had highlighted that tying Windows Media Player afforded Microsoft unmatched ubiquity on client PCs worldwide. In this respect, the Decision included a detailed analysis of the workings of the market and found that the advantage that the ubiquity which Windows Media Player attained as a result of the tie could not be fully offset (i) by rival media player vendors concluding installation agreements with PC manufacturers; (ii) through downloading by consumers; or (iii) via alternative distribution channels.[73]

The second stage of the Commission's foreclosure analysis examined the effects of Microsoft's tie on content providers and software developers in the market (in other words, those who write media content and develop media-based applications) on the basis of a detailed market enquiry which the Commission had carried out. In a nutshell, the Commission found that because Microsoft's tie ensured virtual ubiquity on PCs for Windows Media Player, content providers and software developers were guaranteed to reach virtually the entire population of users if they wrote content for and developed to the Windows Media format. Given the fact that writing content or applications for additional media formats entailed

---

[70] Decision, recital 841.

[71] Decision, recital 841.

[72] In this respect, see paras 868–9 and 1035 of the judgment, where the CFI approved of the Commission's endeavour to look into the effects of the tying and confirmed that it did not amount to a new legal theory.

[73] See Decision, section 5.3.2.1.4.1.

significant additional costs but provided little in the way of being able to reach additional users, Microsoft's tie provided artificial incentives to content providers and software developers to write content for/develop to the Windows Media format (irrespective of the quality of other media players/formats). There was therefore an artificial self-reinforcing snowball effect/feedback loop in favour of Windows Media Player, because the more content or applications that were developed for the Windows Media format, the more users would be attracted to that format, which would in turn attract more content providers and software developers to it, etc.[74]

The third stage of the Commission's foreclosure analysis examined, *inter alia*, a range of market data, which outlined that, despite the fact that a range of product surveys concluded that Windows Media Player did not have a quality advantage over other media players,[75] the market trend since Microsoft had begun its tying, both in terms of media player and media format usage, was significantly in Microsoft's favour.[76]

Microsoft claimed that the Commission had applied a 'new and highly speculative theory, relying on a prospective analysis'[77] of the likely future effects. However, the CFI stated that Microsoft's argument was 'based on a selective and inaccurate reading of the contested decision',[78] since Microsoft's arguments essentially related only to the second of the three stages of the Commission's foreclosure analysis referred to above. In any event, the CFI upheld all three stages of the Commission's foreclosure analysis, but specified that only the first was necessary to demonstrate liability of foreclosure, as we shall now outline.

In this respect, the CFI confirmed that Microsoft had distorted competition on the merits in the market through its tying because it had created a disincentive for consumers and PC manufacturers to use and install alternative media players (see paragraphs 1041–8 of the CFI judgment). As such the CFI noted that 'no third-party media player could achieve such a level of market penetration without having the advantage in terms of distribution that Windows Media Player enjoys as a result of Microsoft's use of its Windows client PC operating system'.[79]

---

74 See Decision, section 5.3.2.1.4.2.

75 Indeed, the majority of product surveys considered in the Decision, including those provided by Microsoft, in fact held that RealNetworks' Real Player was a superior product to the Windows Media Player.

76 See Decision, section 5.3.2.1.4.3.

77 See CFI judgment, para. 1032.

78 CFI judgment, para. 1033.

79 CFI judgment, para. 1039. See also in this regard para. 1088, where the CFI stated that 'because of the bundling, Microsoft's competitors are *a priori* at

The CFI therefore found that such a distortion of the competitive process was sufficient to establish liability of foreclosure under Article 82. It stated that as regards:

> the first stage of its reasoning [relating to foreclosure], the Commission demonstrated to the requisite legal standard that the bundling of Windows and Windows Media Player . . . inevitably had significant consequences for the structure of competition. That practice allowed Microsoft to obtain an unparalleled advantage with respect to the distribution of its product and to ensure the ubiquity of Windows Media Player on client PCs throughout the world, thus providing a disincentive for users to make use of third-party media players and for OEMs to pre-install such players on client PCs.[80]

The CFI therefore confirmed 'that the Commission's findings in the first stage of its reasoning are in themselves sufficient to establish that the fourth constituent element of abusive bundling is present in this case'.[81]

We have heard this element of the judgment criticized on the grounds that it is 'too *per se*' in its conclusion about foreclosure/harm to competition, and is not effects-based. We disagree with such a characterization. We submit that the CFI examined in detail the nature of Microsoft's conduct and then analysed whether this would be liable to have a detrimental effect in the market.

Of course, what such an analysis will entail will differ in every case. In our view, a coherent effects-based analysis does not in itself therefore imply the need for detailed mathematical calculations or the like, although such tools can certainly provide a valuable input where appropriate. We believe that the foundations of a coherent effects-based approach therefore lie in a logical examination of the specific facts under consideration, and an analysis of the likely effect in the market through a coherent theory of harm. We believe that the CFI endorsed such an approach when it concluded for the first element of the Commission's foreclosure analysis that:

> those findings are not based on any new or speculative theory, but on the nature of the impugned conduct, on the conditions of the market and on the essential features of the relevant products. They are based on accurate, reliable and consistent evidence which Microsoft, by merely contending that it is pure conjecture, has not succeeded in showing to be incorrect.[82]

---

a disadvantage even if their products are inherently better than Windows Media Player'.

80 CFI judgment, para. 1054.

81 CFI judgment, para. 1058.

82 CFI judgment, para. 1058.

The CFI did nevertheless go on to examine the second and third stages of the Commission's foreclosure analysis. It first confirmed that Microsoft's tying directly affected the incentives of content providers and software developers. Because of the tie, and the ubiquity this afforded Windows Media Player, content providers and software developers had a strong incentive to develop their solutions on the basis of Windows Media technology only (remember that supporting several technologies incurs significant additional costs), and this reinforced the foreclosure effect of the tying practice.[83] The CFI also confirmed the Commission's analysis of the evolution of the market, which consistently pointed to a trend in favour of usage of the Windows Media Player and Windows Media formats.[84]

Overall therefore, we submit that both the Decision and the judgment contained an extensive analysis of the workings of the market in the analysis of foreclosure, which included detailed findings about the effects of Microsoft's practice on both consumers and innovation in the market. That is only right given the specific circumstances of the case and the need, in our view, for Article 82 EC cases to exhibit an effects-based analysis. Although the CFI stated that only the first of the Commission's three elements was necessary to fulfil the conditions of the case law as regards foreclosure, we believe that the fact that it also considered the other two elements shows that it agreed that these were also relevant considerations.

Objective Justification

Microsoft's main argument under objective justification was the 'platform benefit' argument: namely that bundling Windows Media Player was indispensable in order to achieve the platform efficiencies which were a core part of Microsoft's business model. In this regard, as the CFI noted, Microsoft 'claims . . . that the integration of media functionality in Windows is indispensable in order for software developers and Internet site creators to be able to continue to benefit from the significant advantages offered by the "stable and well-defined" Windows platform'.

As we have outlined above on foreclosure, it is indeed the case that content providers and applications developers would be attracted to the Windows Media platform as a result of the tie, but not because Windows Media Player was necessarily a better product than other products, but because the tie with Windows afforded it the same ubiquity as Windows

[83] CFI judgment, paras 1063–76.
[84] CFI judgment, paras 1080–87.

itself. In other words, the tie allowed Windows Media Player to 'piggy-back' on the ubiquity of Windows and hence artificially affect the incentives of content providers and applications developers in favour of Windows Media Player.

The only advantage or benefit which this therefore offered was not to the process of competition, but to Microsoft itself, in that it provided Microsoft the opportunity to extend its monopoly to a separate market without having to compete on the merits of its product. Therefore, what Microsoft presented as a fundamental part of its business model was in fact precisely one of the foreclosure mechanisms which the Commission had identified and which the CFI confirmed. We believe that it is only natural that such a claim of objective justification should be rejected. Indeed, a logical extension of Microsoft's argument would imply that Microsoft potentially should be allowed to extend its monopoly to any separate application which it might choose to bundle with Windows in the name of a so-called 'platform benefit'. What Microsoft calls a 'platform benefit' is in fact the very mechanism through which foreclosure in the adjacent market occurs. As the CFI noted:

> the fact that that tying enables software developers and Internet site creators to be sure that Windows Media Player is present on virtually all client PCs in the world is precisely one of the main reasons why the Commission correctly took the view that the bundling led to the foreclosure of competing media players from the market.[85]

The CFI also confirmed that the other benefits or efficiencies which Microsoft claimed resulted from the tie either did not exist, or to the extent that they did, had nothing to do with the tie.[86] One such claimed benefit was that consumers attach value to having both an operating system and a

---

[85] CFI judgment, para. 1151. In the same vein, in para. 1152, the CFI noted that 'by such an argument Microsoft is in fact claiming that the integration of Windows Media Player in Windows and the marketing of Windows in that form alone lead to the de facto standardisation of the Windows Media Player platform, which has beneficial effects on the market. Although, generally, standardisation may effectively present certain advantages, it cannot be allowed to be imposed unilaterally by an undertaking in a dominant position by means of tying.'

[86] See CFI judgment, para. 1054. It is noteworthy that during the Commission procedure, Microsoft had not claimed that there were any technical efficiencies deriving from the tie, in other words, that as a result of the tie, Windows and Windows Media Player worked technically better than without the tie. In para. 1160, the CFI noted that 'Microsoft asserts, for the first time, that "Windows . . . operate[s] faster when media functionality is integrated". In that regard, it is sufficient to state that that assertion is unsupported.'

media player pre-installed when they purchase a PC – it facilitates a more convenient 'out-of-the-box' experience which means that consumers do not need to spend time and effort on having to install products which they will need or want to use.[87] We would be the first to recognize that there is indeed such consumer utility to be derived from users obtaining a PC with both an operating system and a media player pre-installed (as well as most likely a variety of other applications). But again, it is clear that such a benefit is not related to or dependent on the dominant company in PC operating systems tying its media player. As the CFI noted, 'consumer demand for an "out-of-the-box" client PC incorporating a streaming media player can be fully satisfied by OEMs, who are in the business of assembling such PCs and combining, *inter alia*, a client PC operating system with the applications desired by consumers'.[88]

Microsoft made other such claims which were essentially of the same nature. For example, Microsoft argued that media players were a platform for complementary applications and that PC manufacturers 'depend on the addition of functionality to Windows to create PCs that will appeal to customers and that will support the creation of interesting new applications'.[89] However, this again confused what Microsoft claimed to be a general benefit or efficiency with what was in fact an artificial competitive advantage for its own media player as a result of the tie. As the CFI confirmed, the efficiency in question had nothing to do with the tie and could therefore be achieved without it. As such, the CFI noted that PC manufacturers could offer PCs with 'interesting new applications' themselves by obtaining them from software developers,[90] and that 'it is wholly unnecessary for a streaming media player to be integrated in a client PC operating system in order to be able to provide such platform service'.[91]

5. CONCLUSION

The Microsoft case was clearly significant in the development of EC competition law, and naturally, it is underpinned by important principles, which in themselves are based on a consistent line of case law.

At the same time, however, we believe that the case turned on the

[87] In a sense, this issue is linked to the 'separate products' analysis outlined above.

[88] CFI judgment, para. 1155.

[89] CFI judgment, para. 1156.

[90] CFI judgment, para. 1156.

[91] CFI judgment, para. 1158.

specifics of the facts under consideration. In this respect, we submit that the nature of Microsoft's market power in terms of its scope, duration and potential to affect other markets is truly exceptional. As such, overgeneralization about what the judgment will mean is dangerous.[92] Claims that the refusal to supply abuse will lead to more widespread 'expropriation' of intellectual property rights in Europe and that the tying abuse will prevent dominant companies from innovating ignore the facts of the case and are wide of the mark.[93]

What happened in the refusal to supply case was that in order to monopolize an adjacent market and to avoid having to compete on the merits of its product, Microsoft refused to disclose interface information that it had previously disclosed and which other companies routinely disclose. As regards tying, Microsoft attached a separate product to its monopoly product in order to monopolize an adjacent market, again without having to compete on the merits of its own product.

Naturally, dominant companies should be allowed to compete aggressively on the merits of their own products. However, as the CFI confirmed, Microsoft's practices did not constitute such competition and were detrimental to consumer choice and to innovation in the market. We submit that in circumstances where dominant companies act in such a way, the Commission should always be prepared to act.

---

[92] Of course, it may mean more for Microsoft itself. As the CFI noted in para. 1363, 'since Microsoft is very likely to maintain its dominant position on the client PC operating systems market, at least over the coming years, it cannot be precluded that it will have other opportunities to use leveraging vis-à-vis other adjacent markets. Furthermore, Microsoft had already faced proceedings in the United States for a practice similar to the abusive tying at issue, namely the tying of its Internet Explorer browser and its Windows client PC operating system, and the possibility cannot be precluded that it might commit the same type of infringement in future with other application software.'

[93] Referring to the judgment, one commentator even stated, on the day of the judgment itself, that '[t]he signal it sends to the international community is that Europe is closed for business, that competition is about cloning products as opposed to adding value – which Microsoft is trying to do'. See comments of Philip Marsden at http://uk.reuters.com/article/UKNews1/idUKL1731018220070917?pageNumber=1&virtualBrandChannel=0.

3. Victa placet mihi causa: the compulsory licensing part of the Microsoft case

Ian S. Forrester QC*

1. INTRODUCTION

On 17 September 2007, the 13 judges of the Grand Chamber of the European Court of First Instance (CFI) rendered judgment in Case T-201/04 *Microsoft* v *Commission*.[1] A few days before the judgment, a number of the advocate protagonists in the case who, at that moment, had no idea what the CFI would do, gathered at a conference organized under the auspices of the International Bar Association in the European University Institute, Fiesole. The paper which I presented on that occasion set forth the principal themes presented by that portion of the case as to which I had the honour of serving as the advocate of Microsoft. Jean-François Bellis, with whom I argued the case, is addressing the 'product integration' part of the case in Chapter 4 (with Tim Kasten).

The Microsoft Decision[2] involved two alleged abuses. One related to the design of the Windows operating system which drives the great majority of personal computers, and the lawfulness of incorporating additional functionalities therein. The other related to the nature and extent of Microsoft's duty to reveal details of how its server products interact, notably as regards client-to-server and server-to-server communications. Each alleged infringement in a sense concerned whether Microsoft, as an

* The opinions expressed are wholly personal. The remark in the title is found in Lucan's literary work *Pharsalia*, adapting a remark made by Marcus Porcius Cato, which may be translated as 'even though my case was defeated, I found it persuasive'.

1 [2007] ECR II-3601.

2 Commission Decision 2007/53/EC of 24 March 2004 [2007] OJ L32/23 (hereinafter 'the Decision'). Author's note: the decision was adopted by the Commission on 24 March 2004, but there was a typographical error three years later when the publication in the Official Journal occurred.

industry leader, was obliged to pursue policies which assisted its competitors. Each involved new theories of infringement. Despite the newness of these theories, the largest fine in antitrust history was imposed. The case has been widely discussed and written about.[3]

I will address the 'interoperability' or 'compulsory licensing' part of the case. After considering the fine, I shall describe the continuing controversy over whether Microsoft must license without remuneration and without confidentiality protections. To focus the discussion of a case presenting a large number of separate points, I list in boxes a number of specific questions which were presented to the judges.

2. SOME PRELIMINARY REMARKS

Various factors rendered the case challenging:

- The size, fame, name, prominence and success of Microsoft and Microsoft's celebrated antitrust encounters in the United States: past battles between Microsoft and its rivals certainly cast a shadow over the EC proceedings. It must have been tempting for commentators to take at face value the proposition that the company had done something controversial or reprehensible.
- A US battle being re-run in Europe: the complainants in Europe were largely US companies which had not prevailed in domestic US litigation. European complainants were largely absent. Not one

[3] See e.g. M. Dolmans and T. Graf, 'Analysis of Tying under Article 82 EC: The European Commission's Microsoft Decision in Perspective' (2004) *World Competition* 225; I. Forrester, 'Article 82: Remedies in Search of Theories?' (2004) *Fordham Corporate Law Institute* 167; D. Ridyard 'Compulsory Access under EC Competition Law: A New Doctrine of "Convenient Facilities" and the Case for Price Regulation' (2004) *European Competition Law Review* 669; D. Geradin, 'Limiting the Scope of Article 82 EC: What Can the EU Learn from the U.S. Supreme Court's Judgment in *Trinko* in the Wake of *Microsoft*, *IMS*, and *Deutsche Telekom*?' (2005) *Common Market Law Review* 1519; H. Leupold and S. Pautke, '*IMS Health* vs. *Microsoft*: Befindet sich die Kommission bei Kartellrechtlichen Zwangslizenzen (erneut) auf Konfrontationskurs mit dem EuGH?' (2005) *EWS* 108; T. Körber, 'Geistiges Eigentum, essential facilities und "Innovationsmissbrauch": Überlegungen zum *Microsoft*-Fall im Lichte der EuGH-Entscheidung *IMS Health GmbH*' (2004) *RIW* 881; J. Drexl, 'Intellectual Property and Antitrust Law: *IMS Health* and *Trinko* – Antitrust Placebo for Consumers Instead of Sound Economics in Refusal-to-Deal Cases' (2004) *IIC* 788; P. Thyri, 'Immaterialgüterrechte und Zugang zur wesentlichen Einrichtund: Der Fall *Microsoft* im Licht von *IMS-Health*' (2005) *WuW* 388.

end-user customer had complained about the alleged infringing acts.

- Establishing what was factually at stake given the complexity of the technology: was the material at stake banal, trivial or significantly creative? Was access to it indispensable to survive or prosper, or a mere convenience or advantage? The legal issues are much easier to understand for lawyers than the technical ones, so it is tempting not to consider the facts and to assume the validity of the proposition that, for example, the company had refused to deliver 'interoperability information'. For that reason, this chapter begins by recalling the factual context.
- The implementation of 'distributed' technologies at stake in a competing operating system depended in important part upon perfect identity of performance across all operating systems in a network. Thus achieving 'interoperability' involved endowing competitors' products with unique characteristics (such as a distributed directory service running on multiple servers simultaneously) they did not otherwise possess.
- Was the duty of the dominant player to empower rivals to supply perfect interoperability, even if this involved identical functionality? Must Microsoft enable what is generally accepted to be 'interoperability' between two *different* software systems or must it enable a competitor to create a 'drop-in' replacement for the Windows server when it is functioning 'as one' with *other* Windows servers in a network to provide a single service?
- The substantial gap between US jurisprudence and the European Commission's position on single firm conduct both in richness of the law and the substantive rules. Only a few European judicial authorities concern compulsory licensing under Article 82 EC. *Volvo/Veng*,[4] *Magill*,[5] and *IMS Health*[6] were the main authorities;

---

[4] Case 238/87 *Volvo* v *Veng (UK) Ltd* [1988] ECR 6211.

[5] Commission Decision 89/205/EC of 21 December 1988 (*Magill TV Guide/ITP, BBC and RTE*), [1989] OJ L78/43, upheld by the CFI in Case T-69/89 *Radio Telefis Eireann* v *Commission* [1991] ECR II-485, upheld on appeal by the ECJ in Joined Cases C-241/91 P and C-242/91 P *Radio Telefis Eireann (RTE) and Independent Television Publications Ltd (ITP)* v *Commission* [1995] ECR I-743.

[6] Commission Decision 2002/165/EC of 3 July 2001 (*NDC Health/IMS Health: Interim Measures*) [2002] OJ L59/18, withdrawn by Commission Decision 2003/741/EC of 13 August 2003 (*NDC Health/IMS Health: Interim Measures*) [2003] OJ L268/69; Case C-418/01 *IMS Health GmbH & Co. OHG* v *NDC Health GmbH & Co. KG* [2004] ECR I-5039.

Bronner[7] and *Commercial Solvents*[8] were referred to on refusals to deal in general. These EC cases seem to align with US jurisprudence, including the recent *Trinko*[9] case before the US Supreme Court. Was *IMS Health*, decided just after the Microsoft Decision, the authoritative word, or should it be rewritten? Was interoperability such an important goal that the *IMS Health* criteria on compulsory licensing had to be radically adapted?

- The applicable and not easy principles of patent and copyright and trade secret law applicable to computer software. Could Microsoft's arguments about patents, copyright and trade secrets be dismissed as irrelevant? Were there no intellectual property (IP) constraints on competition law enforcement? For example, was it correct that competition law owed no deference to trade secrets, as these are private interests not conferred by public law? Could the Commission properly defend itself by doubting whether some of Microsoft's patents had been properly granted? What was the effect of the Copyright Directive?[10]

The Challenge of the Name 'Microsoft'

Microsoft is a company which has made extraordinary technological and commercial achievements in only 30 years. Its products have great importance for our daily lives at home and at work. A litigation or a controversy involving Microsoft frequently proceeds in a unique manner, with a lot of technology to understand as background and a lot of passion in the foreground. Other IT companies may be very large and may even be dominant, but somehow Microsoft arouses a unique level of concern. Indeed, one intervening party made the assertion that 'de facto Microsoft enjoys a position that resembles more that of a sovereign state than of a market player'. There may well have been a sense that it is necessary to apply special standards to Microsoft because of its wealth and the importance of its influence over computers. The argument is that because Microsoft

---

[7] Case C-7/97 *Oscar Bronner GmbH & Co. KG* v *Mediaprint Zeitungs- und Zeitschriftenverlag GmbH & Co. KG and others* [1998] ECR I-7791.

[8] Joined Cases 6/73 and 7/73 *Commercial Solvents and others* v *Commission* [1974] ECR 223.

[9] *Verizon Communications, Inc.* v *Law Offices of Curtis Trinko*, 540 U.S. 398 (2004). See also the *Verizon* v *Trinko* roundtable discussion in (2004) *Global Competition Review* 16.

[10] Directive 2001/29/EC on the harmonization of certain aspects of copyright and related rights in the information society [2001] OJ L167/10.

is 'special', normal rules are ineffective; and that a Microsoft precedent need not trouble other high technology companies, since it will only affect Microsoft.

To this concern, one could respond that Microsoft's activities are neither unregulated nor unsupervised by government agencies. This applies to the scope of IP and copyright protection for software and inventions associated with computers, including provisions to promote reverse-engineering. It applies to public procurement: governments sometimes choose to prescribe that as a policy matter they will procure software only if it meets certain requirements, including interoperability developments. The public sector in most European countries accounts for between 10 and 25 per cent of all software purchases. When governments say what they wish to buy, vendors listen. Government regulation applies in a variety of other ways as well, whether the rules relate to software security, privacy, features for the disabled or the use of local languages.

It is not the case that only novel invocations of Article 82 EC can regulate or constrain the influence of Microsoft. To put it plainly, if the concern of the European Commission was how to control the market power of Microsoft, governments and international organizations have the resources, and use those resources, to do this in a variety of ways.

That policy observation leads to a legal one. Distorting normal legal principles to reach the desired result creates its own subsequent distortions, difficulties and injustices. Article 82 EC is not designed to regulate the market but to remedy abuses of market power. A rule compelling divulgation of secret technology or penalizing the improvement of a richly-featured product cannot be limited to the special situation of Microsoft. The principles adopted in the judgment must be capable of being applied in a predictable and rational manner in other high-technology controversies. We must be able to formulate permanently valid principles by reference to which the Microsoft Decision can convincingly be defended. For competition law to help competition, new cases should challenge clearly identifiable abuses, the blocking of unexploited markets, affirmative hindering of competitive opportunity, demonstrated consumer harm.

It would be foolish to argue that the Commission lacks the power to create new offences or that the holders of IP rights are immune from Article 82 EC. Microsoft argued that the Decision was an attempt to reconfigure how the marketplace works, by handicapping the leading player in two respects. It condemns a company for not offering a product which no rational person would want to buy. It sees the offering of extra functionalities in a richly-featured product not as the delivery of something better, more useful and more enjoyable, but as an unlawful tying by reference to a fear of what other people might do in response to the launch.

And it condemns a company for not saying 'yes' to a competitor who asks for a huge amount of disclosure to enable it to use valuable and secret future technology. It is not easy to see what general principles dominant players should extract from the Decision. But without clear principles, enforcement becomes unforeseeable and potentially arbitrary.

The 'interoperability information' was not a readily measurable physical specification like a map of a city or a simple encoded number or password. Microsoft's first duty was not to grant a compulsory licence, but instead to describe in detail, in writing, how some of its server technology works. This required hundreds of people observing how the software functions and recording that in thousands of pages of documentation to be licensed.

The infringement giving rise to the compulsory licensing remedy was that Microsoft did not – but should have – supplied its competitors with this technological insight when it was being developed. This would have allowed them to deploy in their own products a directory service which was otherwise unique to Microsoft and thus technically to emulate how an important part of the Windows server operating system would function once launched. They would at the same time gain access to the Windows server world in which Microsoft might otherwise become dominant.

Such obligatory divulgation of sophisticated technical secrets differentiates this case from all its supposed predecessor cases in European law. The encroachment upon the rightholder's interests in each of those earlier cases was limited to not being able to impose contractually an exclusion of unwelcome competition.

3. TECHNICAL BACKGROUND

It is necessary to put the alleged infringement in technical context. The PC revolution in the 1980s with which Microsoft in particular is associated has changed within an astonishingly short time the way we work, how we amuse ourselves, and how we communicate with others.

In the early days of the computer industry in the 1960s, mainframe computers were the norm for companies which could afford them. Offered by IBM, Fujitsu, Nixdorf and others, they were powerful and costly, calling for skilled installation, set-up and maintenance. There was little interoperability among mainframes from different vendors. Users commonly went to a single firm for their computing needs. (Antitrust controversies touched the use of peripheral equipment, like printers made by 'outside' suppliers, for mainframes.) In the 1970s, Digital Equipment achieved considerable success with a line of less expensive computers (called minicomputers) that were well-suited to engineering and scientific tasks. There was little or no interoperability between them and mainframes. Computers were still far too expensive to be purchased by consumers or most small businesses.

The PC Revolution

By 1980, a number of companies (Amstrad, Apple and others) had started offering microcomputers that were the precursors to what are now called PCs. Products such as the Tandy TRS-80, the Apple II (the first to offer the 'mouse'), the Commodore PET and the Atari 800 ran their own operating systems. As a result, applications programs written for one brand of PC would not run on any other brand. Users could not share information between PCs, nor could they easily transfer their computing skills from one PC to another.

In 1980, IBM announced plans to introduce what it called the 'personal computer'. The first IBM PC was offered with a choice of three operating systems: CP/M-86 from Digital Research, UCSD-P System and MS-DOS from Microsoft. Over time, MS-DOS became the most popular of the three. A number of companies launched PCs using similar hardware to that of IBM, and using the MS-DOS operating system under licence from Microsoft. Microsoft continually added new functionality to that operating system and its successors.

Microsoft was fortunate to recognize early the potential of a common 'platform', a single operating system which could run on many different brands of PCs with the same basic architecture. This stimulated software developers to create applications which could run on any brand of PC.

The user interfaces of Microsoft operating systems provided a consistent means for users to interact with their computers and thus to use their computing skills on different machines. Microsoft made efforts to convince software developers and manufacturers of the merits of Microsoft operating systems as easy-to-use, attractively-priced and flexible. The company encountered extraordinary success in a short time. That success has engendered intense competition law scrutiny during the past 15 years.

The Server Revolution

The PC revolution revealed a remarkably high demand for accessible, convenient, inexpensive, easy-to-use computers which would serve the domestic or professional needs of non-technical people. This in turn created a demand for software which could coordinate networks of PCs in using printers, exchanging documents, filing, authenticating users logging on to a network, authorizing particular users to do particular tasks, storing data, and many other tasks as technology evolved. The first, primitive, software for these server functionalities, such as LAN Manager, a layer of code developed with IBM as part of the software of the PC, emerged in the late 1980s. By the 1990s these tasks were performed by dedicated 'server computers', commonly called servers. The interoperability half of the Microsoft case related to operating systems for such servers.[11] Microsoft launched its basic Windows NT 3.5 server software in 1992, which was then updated in 1997 and completely reconfigured in 2000 as Windows Server 2000. Microsoft concentrated on developing server operating systems which were easy to configure, easy to use and relatively inexpensive. Those who were familiar with the design of Windows for PCs would find the design of the Windows server operating system user-friendly. Windows Server 2000 and its subsequent versions have been very successful.

Server vendors like Sun and IBM already offered mature versions of UNIX server operating systems in 1992, when the first Windows operating system emerged. In addition, Novell had developed NetWare into the leading server operating system for providing 'file and print' services and 'user and group administration' services to millions of PCs running Windows. The rise of open source software for PCs was matched by the arrival of 'Linux' open source server operating systems. These emerged on the market in 1998 and rapidly progressed, such that by 2004 work group servers running Linux accounted for 11 per cent of the market for operating systems on 'work group' servers. This share of a valuable market was attained without special access to any Windows technology.

Although servers usually perform a number of functions, the Decision concentrates only on the server when executing a few specific tasks: 'file and print' and 'user and group administration' or directory services. The Decision called these 'work group services'.

PC operating systems communicate with server operating systems (client-to-server), and server operating systems communicate among

---

[11] The operating system of a computer schedules its execution of tasks and controls the flow of information within the computer and between the computer and peripheral devices. Operating systems perform two other related functions. First, they provide a 'user interface', the means by which a user interacts with his computer. User interfaces for computers have evolved over the last 30 years from punch card readers, to teletype terminals, to character-based user interfaces, to graphical user interfaces. Secondly, operating systems enable users to find and use information contained in various storage devices which can be 'local', such as a CD-ROM drive, or 'remote', such as 'networks' that connect computers in geographically separated offices.

themselves (server-to-server), by means of communications protocols. Communications protocols can be thought of as software techniques used by server operating systems to communicate information across a network. They can be quite routine or very complex.

Microsoft's directory service, given the trade name 'Active Directory', was distinctive or even unique in several respects when launched in 2000. When running Active Directory, individual servers functioned as exact replicas of each other. If a problem arose, each directory server was programmed to make its own decision on how to react without 'consulting' other servers. Thus the system collectively delivered a single outcome. A number of patents covered the technology. Microsoft claimed that its directory service was superior to those of its rivals. Microsoft's server software could scale to 10,000 while rivals could scale to less than 100. It was suggested that the technology involved was not particularly complex, and that the protocols to be divulged were straightforward. These contentions were contested by Microsoft.

A Sun or IBM server not running Active Directory could perform the Active Directory function in a Windows network only if, for directory purposes, it behaved identically to the Windows servers. (There was dispute over whether this capacity to act identically needs duplication of portions of the software, or merely imitation.) Thus, while there was no doubt that divulging the details of how servers performing the Active Directory collectively function would assist a new entrant to penetrate the Windows server world, it was technically necessary to replicate functionality in order to achieve this end.

Reality of Interoperability Across Mixed Networks

Microsoft observed that in many companies, government departments and universities, it is routine to find a wide range of software products from different vendors working together and with Windows. Although a great majority of PC 'clients' run Windows operating systems, they must interact with many other software and hardware products. Client operating systems, server operating systems, applications programs and the associated hardware must all work together. Thus, interoperability was and is a daily reality in business life.

Microsoft also submitted surveys conducted by Mercer Management Consulting, which indicated that businesses do not choose server operating systems based on concerns about interoperability with Windows client and server operating systems. They assume such interoperability exists, and make their choices by reference to ease of set-up, price, ease of maintenance, and the like. The routine existence of 'heterogeneous' computing networks in Europe demonstrated, argued Microsoft, that it was readily possible to achieve efficient interoperability between rival server operating systems and Windows client and server operating systems. Microsoft's server technology enjoyed a considerable distribution advantage: the Windows format was familiar to any user of a PC running Windows, Windows servers were easy to set up and install, and Active Directory was an important asset. There was no doubt that sharing the techniques of Active Directory with rivals would confer advantage on them if they could make it work reliably.

The Commission acknowledged that 'interoperability is a matter of degree and that various software products in a system 'interoperate' (at least partially) when they are able to exchange information and mutually to use the information which has been exchanged'.[12] Accordingly, it conceded, interoperability occurs along a continuum; it is not an absolute standard. However, it suggested that although rival server operating systems could compete, they could not compete 'viably' unless given access to Microsoft communications protocols.

Microsoft described five or six well-recognized techniques to achieve efficient interoperability between different software products in a network. The Decision recognizes that a number of methods exist to enable interoperability in heterogeneous networks containing non-Microsoft server operating systems and Windows client and server operating systems. Indeed, many of these methods were developed without access to the communications protocols that the Decision would force Microsoft to license to its competitors. The availability of such interoperability solutions further suggested that interoperability was feasible without compulsory licensing.

Microsoft also pointed to the success of Linux servers without access to the protocols. It argued that two server operating systems can interoperate in the sense of exchanging information with one another or providing services to one another without the need for the two products to be exactly the same. It also observed that to make a 'plug replacement' to permit competitors to replicate features of Microsoft's products was an immensely burdensome remedy. By contrast, the Decision identified a rather modest specific inconvenience: the user might, in some configurations, have to 'log on' twice, when accessing multiple networks inside one company (there were solutions to this supposed problem, also).

Understanding these concepts presented formidable difficulties for those involved in the case. Most outside observers have had even greater

---

12 Microsoft Decision, recital 33.

difficulty thoroughly grasping the conflicting factual claims. Yet this technical history is indispensable to an understanding of the controversy. Was interoperability between server and server perfect, or adequate, or poor? Did the extensive evidence of functioning networks using many different brands of software and hardware prove that there was no significant problem, although there might be intermittent, solvable ones? Or was the Commission right to say that Microsoft's rivals could not compete 'viably' unless they were given access to Microsoft's server technology?

Even if as to these technological questions the Commission had been right in every detail, that would merely reveal a factual problem in how the market functioned. There remained the legal question of whether the compulsory divulgation was lawful and proportionate.

4. THE REQUEST AND THE COMPLAINT

In September 1998, Sun Microsystems, a supplier of both operating systems for servers and the server hardware itself, requested from Microsoft a reference implementation (access to the source code) of a large part of what would later be launched as Windows Server 2000, as well as access to a large volume of other secret material. Sun's request was for detailed information about how Windows server operating systems functioned. The letter sent by Sun read as follows (my emphasis):[13]

> We are writing to you to request that Microsoft provide [Sun] with the complete information required to allow Sun to provide native support for *COM objects* on Solaris.
>
> We also request that Microsoft provide [Sun] with the *complete information* required to allow [Sun] to provide native support for the *complete set of Active Directory technologies on Solaris*.
>
> We believe it is in the industry's best interest that applications written to execute on Solaris be able to seamlessly communicate via COM and/or Active Directory with the Windows operating systems and/or with Windows-based software.
>
> We believe that Microsoft should include a reference implementation and such other information as is necessary to insure, without reverse engineering, that COM objects and the complete set of Active Directory technologies will run in full compatible fashion on Solaris. We think it necessary that such information be provided for the full range of COM objects as well as for the full set of Active Directory technologies currently on the market. We also think it

[13] Case T-201/04 R *Microsoft Corporation* v *Commission*, Order of 22 December 2004 [2004] ECR II-4463, para. 4.

> necessary that such information be provided in a timely manner and on a continuing basis for COM objects and Active Directory technologies which are to be released to the market in the future.

The material requested collectively represented a considerable portion of the innovation contained in the Windows server operating system then under development. It did not mention communications protocols. Thus, assuming Microsoft's response was a refusal, Microsoft did not refuse to provide communications protocols. (Nor were communications protocols mentioned in Sun's complaint to the Commission.) The Commission says that a request for a licence to Microsoft's communications protocols was 'implicit' in Sun's letter.

Sun's request called for a wider divulgation than the Decision compels. The Commission took the position that it was wise to demand from Microsoft, which was likely to be reluctant, a broad range of material (thus leaving the addressee of an excessive request for help to decide what help is legally obligatory).

Microsoft replied with an invitation to talk face-to-face, and suggested that there were technical alternatives to the disclosures requested. It did not say 'no' to Sun's request but did not say 'yes'. Its response did not mention that its software was protected by IP rights, a fact the Commission regarded as significant (the refusal did not invoke a reason much invoked thereafter) and Microsoft regarded as normal (the material's secrecy and value were obvious).

QUESTIONS CONCERNING THE EXISTENCE OF A REFUSAL TO LICENSE

- Did a refusal to license occur in autumn 1998 following the request to Microsoft?
- What relevance is to be attributed to the fact that Microsoft's response was not an outright refusal, but a proposal to discuss the matter and a reminder of already available means of interoperating?
- Was the request (which demanded wider and different divulgation than the Decision called for as to abuse and as to remedy) adequate to engage any responsibility to reply on the part of Microsoft?
- What is the duty of a dominant company when receiving an overly broad request to supply information or grant access?

Must it assess the request and grant access to what it considers to be required under the law; or may it refuse such requests outright?

- What relevance is to be attributed to the fact that the licensee wished to make a directly competing product (as opposed to a new product in a separate market)?
- What was the relevance of the fact that the technology requested was secret, was still under development, and had not yet been launched commercially?
- Is it relevant that no royalty was proposed by Sun to Microsoft?
- Is it relevant that Microsoft in its response to Sun did not expressly mention the fact that the technology was covered by IP rights?

The Statements of Objections

The Commission issued a First Statement of Objections in August 2000 in which it alleged that Microsoft had abused its dominant position in client operating systems by depriving other server operating system vendors of Microsoft technology they needed to enable their products to interoperate with those client operating systems (client-to-server interoperability).

The Second Statement of Objections in August 2001 reiterated earlier allegations about client-to-server interoperability. It added that Microsoft deprived other server operating system vendors of technology they needed to enable their products to interoperate with the Windows server operating system ('server-to-server interoperability'). (Separately, it asserted for the first time that the design of Windows to include media functionality amounted to a violation of Article 82(b) and (d) EC.)

By the time Microsoft responded to the Second Statement of Objections, it had (in November 2001) entered into a settlement with the US Department of Justice and certain US states of an antitrust lawsuit they had brought in 1998.[14] Microsoft urged the Commission to consider the settlement as a

[14] That lawsuit focused on Microsoft's inclusion of Web browsing software, called Internet Explorer, in Windows 98. The District Court found that Microsoft unlawfully 'tied' Internet Explorer to Windows in violation of sections 1 and 2 of the Sherman Act. The Court of Appeals, however, reversed on the finding on tying under section 1 and limited its objection under section 2 to limited aspects of the manner in which Microsoft had integrated Web browsing functionality

change in factual circumstances. Specifically, with regard to interoperability, Microsoft noted that the settlement (now embodied in a court order) required Microsoft to make available licences to all of the communications protocols that Windows server operating systems use to interoperate with PCs running Windows client operating systems. So client-to-server advantages, if they had ever existed for Microsoft, had been eliminated by the settlement.[15] Extensive discussions between the Commission and Microsoft now began and continued until the taking of the Decision in March 2004.

In a typical Article 82 EC decision, the dominance, the abuse and the remedy relate to the same relevant market. In the interoperability half of the Microsoft case, the alleged abuse related to the market for PC operating systems, while the effect and the remedy related to the server market. When the Commission issued a Third Statement of Objections in August 2003, it sharply narrowed the market definition. The Commission said that

---

into Windows, but not integration of that functionality generally (*United States* v *Microsoft Corp.*, 253 F.3d 34, 47, 58 (D.C. Cir. 2001)). Noting the risk of 'deterring welfare-enhancing innovation' (at 90), the Court of Appeals remanded the tying claim, instructing the District Court to analyse it under a 'rule of reason' analysis in which the pro-competitive justifications for including Web browsing functionality in Windows were fully considered (at 74). In that regard, the Court of Appeals noted that Windows serves as a 'platform for third-party applications' (at 74). As the Court of Appeals observed, adding new functionality to Windows, such as Web browsing, may benefit not only consumers but also software developers who can draw upon that functionality in creating their own applications (at 90). The Court also noted that using 'the very same lines of code' to perform multiple functions may provide efficiencies (at 87). While not passing on these potential efficiencies in the absence of appropriate fact finding by the District Court, the Court of Appeals concluded that 'integration of new functionality into platform software is a common practice and that wooden application of per se rules in this litigation may cast a cloud over platform innovation in the market for PCs' (at 95).

15 The settlement was approved by the US District Court for the District of Columbia (*United States* v *Microsoft Corp.*, 231 F. Supp. 2d 76, 144 (D.D.C. 2002), hereinafter 'US Final Judgment') in November 2002. At the same time, the court rejected additional relief sought by various states at the urging of Microsoft's competitors (*New York* v *Microsoft Corp.*, 224 F. Supp. 2d 76, 197 n.85 (D.D.C. 2002), noting 'the substantial involvement of Microsoft's competitors' in drafting the requested relief. That relief included provisions similar to those contained in what emerged 16 months later as articles 5(a) and 6(a) of the European Commission's Microsoft Decision (compare *New York* v *Microsoft Corp.*, 224 F. Supp. 2d at 226–33 with art. 5(a) of the Decision; and compare *New York* v *Microsoft Corp.*, 224 F. Supp. 2d at 245–55 with art. 6(a) of the Decision). Before rejecting that relief, the court heard testimony, subject to cross-examination, from 34 witnesses in a 32-day trial, including witnesses from Sun, Novell and RealNetworks. In a 324-page opinion, the court found that the relief sought was likely to retard rather than to promote competition and threatened to harm consumers and other industry participants.

the relevant market where the abuse was felt was for 'work group server operating systems' running on servers costing less than US$25,000 (as opposed to the US$100,000 figure in the Second Statement of Objections) and only when the (multipurpose) server is being used to provide two types of services to Windows client operating systems: 'file and print' services and 'user and group administration' (that is directory) services.

This narrowing of the relevant market (which Microsoft called gerrymandering, the less-than-honourable drawing of artificial lines to achieve a desired result) was necessary for the Commission's theory. Microsoft was dominant in the market for PCs and was using this dominance to eliminate all competition on another market, a server market. Now, it was obvious that servers made by Sun and IBM were not at risk of disappearance. So as to exclude them from consideration, the Commission focused on what it called work group servers. This reduced the technologies at stake to file and print (desired by SAMBA, one of Microsoft's open source rivals) and directory services (desired, among other things, in the Sun complaint). In that market (albeit disregarding the majority of such servers' functions, and trying to capture them only while performing the two selected functions), for inexpensive and easy-to-use servers, Microsoft was growing fast, as was Linux.

QUESTION CONCERNING THE RELEVANT MARKET

- Was the relevant market correctly defined or had it been 'gerrymandered' to create the impression of relevant market effects?

Microsoft's negotiations with the Commission intensified in the early months of 2004 and ultimately involved face-to-face discussions between Commissioner Mario Monti and Microsoft CEO Steve Ballmer. However, they did not lead to a settlement. Commissioner Monti stated that consumers would be 'better served with a decision that creates a strong precedent', and noted that it was 'essential to have a precedent which will establish clear principles for the future conduct of a company with such a strong dominant position in the market'.[16] Accordingly, on 24 March

[16] Commission Memorandum MEMO/04/70 of 24 March 2004, Microsoft – Questions and Answers on Commission Decision.

2004, the Commission adopted a Decision against Microsoft. In article 2, the Decision provides that:

> Microsoft Corporation has infringed Article 82 of the Treaty and Article 54 of the EEA Agreement by:
> (a) refusing to supply the Interoperability Information and allow its use for the purpose of developing and distributing work group server operating system products, from October 1998 until the date of this Decision.

In article 3 of the Decision, the Commission imposed a fine of €497,196,304 (worth, on the date of the CFI judgment about US$690 million) on Microsoft. In article 4 of the Decision, the Commission ordered Microsoft to bring to an end the infringement by drawing up a description of:

> the complete and accurate specifications for all the Protocols implemented in Windows Work Group Server Operating Systems and that are used by Windows Work Group Servers to deliver file and print services and group and user administration services, including the Windows Domain Controller services, Active Directory services and Group Policy services, to Windows Work Group Networks.[17]

Microsoft appealed, and also filed an application requesting interim measures suspending the remedies pending the Court's judgment on the merits. This application was dismissed on 22 December 2004 on the ground that Microsoft had failed to show it would suffer serious and irreparable harm if the Decision was implemented immediately.[18] The outcome was largely determined by considerations relevant to interim measures: in particular, the President of the CFI considered that Microsoft could protect itself contractually against the risks of disclosure of its technology pursuant to the Decision. However, the Order contains a number of comments on the merits of the case, as it concluded that Microsoft had shown a *prima facie* case that the Decision might be considered illegal. The President did acknowledge that 'Microsoft's argument is likely to raise one or more important questions of principle which may affect the legality of the Commission's analysis'.[19]

In the main action, a hearing took place before the 13 judges of the CFI on 24–28 April 2006. The Report for the Hearing was the best this

---

[17] Decision, article 1(1).

[18] Case T-201/04 R, *Microsoft Corporation* v *Commission*, Order of 22 December 2004 [2004] ECR II-4463.

[19] Order of the President, para. 398.

advocate had ever read: a very thorough, clear and fair description of the questions at stake, explaining the case much better than most articles. The Court was evidently well-prepared, reflected in the large number of questions asked by the judges.

5. THE FACTS AND THE LAW

The Debate About Interoperability

It was agreed that Microsoft enjoyed a position of dominance as to operating systems for PCs. ('Super-dominance', whatever that means, was mentioned as a concept in the CFI proceedings.) At the time of the alleged refusal, Microsoft did not enjoy a dominant position as to operating systems for servers to coordinate networks of PCs. A number of companies supplied servers, including Sun, Novell, IBM and others, and had done so for longer than Microsoft. The Commission also conceded that interoperability between servers of different brands did exist[20] but not well enough for Microsoft's competitors. It claimed that practical interoperability was imperfect, so as to prevent competitors from competing 'viably', and Microsoft's conduct put others at a competitive disadvantage. The degree of interoperability in force was 'insufficient to enable competitors to viably stay in the market'.[21]

A key topic in the case was obviously the meaning of 'interoperability' necessary to 'compete viably'. Before getting to the legal question of whether the legal criteria for compulsory licensing could be expanded by reference to the important goal of enhancing interoperability, it was necessary to consider the factual question of whether in actual practice existing levels of interoperability were good, adequate but could be improved, or were inadequate to sustain long-term viable competition.

Microsoft demonstrated that in actual practice, heterogeneous networks were common: inside large users of computing resources they were routine, almost universal. Customers may use an IBM directory server with Windows file servers or other servers, or vice versa; or use two separate directory services for separate parts of the business, with the engineering department using UNIX servers and the sales department using Windows servers. Customers who used the new Windows directory service, Active Directory, also used other servers in separate networks from Linux, IBM, Novell and Sun. There were plenty of examples showing how big

20 Decision, para. 690.
21 Decision, para. 589 and n. 712.

organizations use different server operating systems for different functions or for different parts of the organization. They worked together.

Microsoft supplied the Commission with about 50 statements from large users of computing power, describing how they resolved the challenge of having a heterogeneous network. The Commission sent out Article 11 EC letters to a number of others. Details came from one European army, a navy, two national police forces, six government agencies, NATO, a large city, three other international organizations and 31 large companies, most of them household names.[22] They used a wide variety of hardware and software. So Microsoft argued that interoperability problems of having different servers were solvable, whether the servers perform only 'work group' tasks or perform 20 tasks simultaneously. Problems do arise but are capable of solution. So in the real world every hour of every day in every city in Europe, hundreds of thousands of servers and millions of client PCs interoperate successfully.

Competing suppliers of server operating systems stress in their publicity material how interoperable their products are in a Windows environment. This combination of heterogeneity and interoperability did not emerge by accident but because Microsoft and other companies helped accomplish it. Without interoperability few customers would buy servers or server operating systems.

Alternative solutions to the actual imperfections as to interoperability were rejected by the Decision. It said reverse-engineering of the characteristics of Microsoft operating systems was too slow, that disclosures by Microsoft were not enough, and that customers were worried about interoperability. But there was only one single example given of a concrete problem for users identified in the Decision in paragraph 183, that users *may* have to log on twice when using the services of two networks in their organization. The word 'may' was used, not 'will', because technical solutions exist to remove the need to log on twice.

Microsoft argued that interoperability already exists as customers and as computer scientists understand it. The word 'interoperability' should not be used as an attractive slogan (with which no person of goodwill can disagree) to justify a major antitrust incursion on private property. Microsoft noted the absence of any complaint from customers, and suggested that the possible inconvenience of having to log on twice did not justify imposing the biggest disclosure of technical secrets in competition law history.

---

22 Among others: Akzo Nobel, Alitalia, Carrefour, the City of Vienna, Nokia, Novo Nordisk A/S, Royal Dutch/Shell Group, the UK Inland Revenue.

There was a subsidiary question presented by the technical characteristics of a key part of the Windows server operating system, namely Active Directory. A distinction was drawn by Microsoft between communications between servers with a view to communicating data back and forth, and communications between multiple servers working as one to provide a single network service, in this case directory or file and print. These communications are of a 'closely-coupled' kind 'within the service boundary' or within a 'bubble' (alternative synonyms used to describe the special nature of the communications between servers running Active Directory). Servers performing the Active Directory function act as a team of identical entities doing a single job collectively such that for the user the group functions in the same way as a traditional mainframe computer operating a single directory. Because each server must act in exactly the same way ('thinks alike', to use a human analogy), whenever the network encounters a problem there is no need to issue instructions, no need to consult; the server which is best placed to act self-selects and addresses the problem. These servers exhibit 'crowd behaviour' in such a manner that only an identically-programmed server can participate in delivering their functionality collectively.

For a server from one vendor to replace seamlessly another vendor's server confronts the physical fact that equivalent functionality and identical logic producing identical behaviours are necessary for certain purposes. The technology which Microsoft must disclose and should allegedly have revealed is intended to enable that functional equivalence. The Decision's effect, though not its primary goal, was to enable a licensee to build a product which accurately imitates the functionality of a Windows server when executing certain key network functions, directory services and file and print services (though not when it is executing any other services). Over the three years since the adoption of the Decision various synonyms have been used for the exact goal of what the licensee should be enabled to create, including 'clone' (which was discarded as confusing), 'drop-in replacement', 'functional equivalent' or 'replacement'.

Participating in this internal functioning of the various servers (within the service boundary or within the 'bubble' in which these complex functions take place) does not involve what the computer world regards as interoperability.[23] In ordinary life, two companies never independently

[23] An analogy can be made to the IBM undertaking from 1984. IBM, which was then a dominant enterprise, agreed to reveal details of the external interfaces of its mainframe computers. The Commission emphasized that it would not reveal the internal secrets of how the mainframe performed its calculations. So a distinction was made between 'inside the service boundary' (the 'internals') and 'the outside', the printers and disk drives (the 'external' equipment).

develop products with identical logic and identical functionality.[24] Yet the only way in which the goal of the Decision can be achieved inside the service boundary is if the licensee servers behave identically to the Windows server.

It must have been very difficult for non-technical judges to master these conflicting factual questions via the pleadings. No one could deny that interoperability was an important policy goal. There was little common ground on what sort of interoperability or the supposed lack thereof justified creating radically new competition law offences.

QUESTIONS ABOUT INTEROPERABILITY

- Is interoperability in and of itself a relevant goal under EC competition law justifying or helping to justify a special duty to deal?
- Is commercially efficient or adequate (but less-than-perfect) interoperability a sufficiently serious problem to justify a compulsory licence? What level of adequacy will exclude the necessity of such a licence?
- What is the significance of the fact that many users of computing power use servers and PCs from competing suppliers, which routinely work together?
- What is the relevance of the fact that for certain complex products, total interoperability can only be achieved by allowing the requesting party to make a functional copy of the dominant company's product?

The Question of Interruption of Previous Supply

We should at this stage remember another debate, about interruption of supply. *Commercial Solvents*[25] was the first case where the Commission accused a supplier of abusing its dominant position by cutting off supplies (of a chemical vital to a customer as retaliation for a disagreement).

---

[24] One notable exception is the open source SAMBA project under which a handful of devotees are striving not to create a new server operating system product for sale in the market, but to create an open source and free functional replica or 'clone' of the Windows server operating system for use in Windows networks.

[25] See above.

The question arose of whether Microsoft's behaviour fitted into the *Commercial Solvents* pattern.

In the early days, Microsoft licensed server technology to AT&T that was used to create a product called AS/U (Advanced Services for UNIX). Beginning in 1991, Microsoft had agreed to license AT&T with technology for the early networking product called LAN Manager. In 1992, Microsoft also provided AT&T with the corresponding code in Windows NT server. In 1998, Microsoft and AT&T agreed that although AT&T could continue to use the technology and software it had received for NT, Microsoft was not bound to license software and technology relating to future releases of Windows servers. The contract expired in 2000.

A number of products based on AS/U were created by leading UNIX vendors, including Sun Microsystem's PC NetLink. The Commission contended that Microsoft's conduct vis-à-vis Sun involved a disruption of previous levels of supply.[26] It is agreed that Microsoft was not supplying communications protocols to Sun before Sun made its request in September 1998. Sun Microsystems and several other vendors which sold servers with their own server operating systems did license AS/U from AT&T. However, their sales of 'work group' servers were modest. There was no evidence that those sales declined after Microsoft and AT&T agreed not to extend their licence agreement to include new technology embodied in Windows Server 2000. Novell never made any use of AS/U, so Microsoft's dealings with AT&T had no effect on Novell. The same of course applies to open source Linux operating systems, which were making strong headway from 1999.

A decision by Microsoft to license software code and technology (then basic) to AT&T in the early 1990s ought not, said Microsoft, to oblige Microsoft to license for the indefinite future. Declining to assume a perpetual obligation to license all new advances and all new generations of technology is not a disruption of supply. It would seem strange if licensing current technology to one person implied a continuing duty to other persons to supply new technology.

Nevertheless, according to the Decision, Microsoft interrupted supply:

> Microsoft has diminished the level of disclosures that it makes concerning information necessary to achieve such interoperability. Microsoft has turned down a formal request by Sun concerning such interoperability information.[27]

---

[26] Decision, section 5.3.1.1.3.2.
[27] Decision, para. 780.

QUESTIONS CONCERNING THE SUPPOSED INTERRUPTION OF SUPPLY

- What was the relevance of the fact that during the 1990s Microsoft supplied to AT&T (with rights to sub-license) software code and technology as to the early version of Microsoft's server operating systems?
- Does the making available of technology by licence to one licensee compel subsequent licences to other licensees of subsequent technology?
- Does the sophistication of the later technology, or its coverage by IP rights, affect any duty to supply?
- Does the termination of a contract with a licensee on agreed terms constitute an interruption of supply to sub-licensees of the licensee?

The Remedy

Pursuant to article 4 of the Decision, Microsoft had to prepare 'a complete and accurate specification'. Thus Microsoft must first research; then describe; then divulge to its competitors; then license them to use it and Microsoft's IP rights in the process. In addition, Microsoft must make the specially written description easy enough for a person without deep expertise of Windows to use. This was a first in competition law history anywhere on earth. At stake were the protocols and technology governing client-to-server and server-to-server communications in the sense of interoperability as the word is commonly understood, and server-to-server communications within the service boundaries ('inside' Active Directory).

More specifically, from the summer of 2004, 210 software engineers in three countries at different times were studying over 6.69 million lines of source code (2.39 million for directory, and 4.30 million for file and print) to identify how their communications protocols functioned. Because the task was large and difficult, and because parts of the code go back to the early 1990s, Microsoft recruited retired Microsoft engineers who worked for the company at that time. Team members studied the source code, read the preparatory design material, chased down the engineers who wrote it and clarified why they had done things in a particular way. With that understanding, a description of functionality could be prepared and the pages fitted into a comprehensible whole. Little of the material was already in existence because the software was designed as proprietary code, not intended for the public domain. Accordingly, the kind of 'specification' years later demanded by the Decision had to be written specially. It then had to be tested. Teams in India and China helped at this stage. Some of the tests involved harnessing together hundreds of computers simultaneously to check what had been done. Tens of thousands of working hours were spent on creating this 'specification'. Microsoft also offered to give expert help to would-be licensees, and to show them the actual source code of Windows. As described below, there have been a number of disagreements over what format was best for the specification, and over the presence of errors. After an immense amount of discussion between the company and the Monitoring Trustee, these are now for the most part concluded.

The Court was shown a sample of the original source code, a combination of text and symbols which is understandable by an engineer and which, when turned mechanically into zeros and ones by a compiler, is the operating system which controls a Windows server. That was the embodiment of the technology: the original text written by Microsoft engineers and adapted over the years to increase functionality, improve performance, make corrections, enable scaleability, and so forth.

Armed with the specification, the licensee can make a software product which will be identical in the sense that a server using it will be a functional equivalent, with identical behaviour and identical logic, doing the same thing as the functions being imitated. The licensee's code will have different zeros and ones to the original Microsoft code. In that limited sense they may differ. But from the customer's viewpoint they will functionally be the same (and technically for certain purposes they must be identical).

QUESTIONS AS TO THE FACTS

- Was the Commission's appraisal of the facts as to interoperability vitiated by error?
- Were the abuse identified by the Decision and its remedy, the divulgation, proportionate to the identified interoperability problem?

On the Principle of Divulgation

In any Article 82 EC controversy, the allegedly dominant rightholder will rely on his right to enjoy private property; the skill, money and time invested in creative effort, and the value attributed by society to encouraging innovation and investment via IP rights; and claim that any encroachment puts in danger all other persons similarly situated. Such enrichment and detriment respectively would not be remedied by royalties.[28] On the other hand, the 'infringer' will rely on the foreclosure of competition due to the invoked right, the lack of research and development involved, the improbable nature of the right, the unreasonable or capricious behaviour of the dominant player, the peripheral impact upon the dominant player contrasted with the victim's vital need, and the very moderate nature of the contemplated compulsion. The challenge for the antitrust enforcer is to identify the relevant circumstances and to decide wisely.

Microsoft was accused of having refused to supply 'interoperability information' to enable competitors to develop their own technology for making operating systems for server computers performing so-called work group functions.[29] Microsoft's incentive to innovate receded before the need to protect innovation in general, according to the Commission:

---

[28] In *IMS Health* the Commission had argued that IMS's temporary loss of its IPR would be compensated by reasonable royalties (Case T-184/01 R *IMS Health Inc.* v *Commission* [2001] ECR II-3193, para. 142). This argument, however, did not impress the Court, which in the following paragraph (para. 143) stressed: [i]t is important initially to recall that the *public interest in respect of property rights in general and of intellectual property rights in particular* is expressly reflected in Articles 30 EC and 295 EC. The mere fact that the applicant has invoked and sought to enforce its copyright in the 1,860 brick structure for economic reasons does not lessen its entitlement to rely upon the exclusive right granted by national law for *the very purpose of rewarding innovation*' (emphasis added).

[29] 'Microsoft has been enjoying a dominant (quasi-monopoly) position on the client PC operating system market for many years. This position of market strength enables Microsoft to determine to a large extent and independently of its competitors the set of coherent communications rules that will govern the de facto standard for interoperability in work group networks. As such, interoperability with the Windows domain architecture is necessary for a work group server operating system vendor in order to viably stay on the market.' Decision, para. 779.

'The data collected by the Commission show that there is a risk of elimination of competition in the work group server operating system market. Microsoft's market share has increased swiftly. The company has reached a dominant position in the relevant market. This position continues to be reinforced. Technologies that will lead to a further lock-in into Microsoft's products at the work group server and client PC level are quickly gaining traction in the market. The Commission's investigation has also produced evidence that establishes a causal link between the market evolution and the interoperability advantage enjoyed by Microsoft. Furthermore, there is no actual or potential substitute to disclosures by Microsoft of interoperability information.' Decision, para. 781.

> Microsoft's refusal to supply has the consequence of stifling innovation in the impacted market and of diminishing consumers' choices by locking them into a homogeneous Microsoft solution. As such, it is in particular inconsistent with the provisions of Article 82(b) of the Treaty.[30]

Microsoft's view was that, as to client-server communications, Microsoft had eliminated any advantage it enjoyed through making available the communications protocols used by Windows 'client' PCs and Windows servers as part of the US settlement; and that as to server-to-server communications, there was no need for action since in actual practice servers communicated effectively with other servers. The success in a short time of Linux servers without access to the 'refused' technology further demonstrated the lack of the acute problem alleged by the Commission.

The so-called 'interoperability information' was not in the public domain (unlike the material at stake in *Magill* or the alleged industry standard in *IMS Health*); it was future technology when requested in September 1998, and would be launched only in 2000; the specifications derived from the software code were hugely voluminous (thousands of pages of electronic text once written specially); the technology was the fruit of hundreds of person years of development effort; it was covered by a number of patents issued by European and other agencies, whose issuance confirmed the complexity and novelty; it was copyright; and there was neither practical need nor legal obligation to deliver it to a competitor to make a replica incorporating or imitating what Microsoft effort had created. The Commission did not identify any specific new product that might come from the compulsory licence, but it expressed the hope that disclosure would lead to the emergence of new or innovative products. Microsoft observed that if a licensee wanted merely to imitate the Microsoft product, he would be free to do so.

The Commission applied a so-called balancing test, which weighed Microsoft's incentives to innovate against the incentives of the whole industry to innovate were Microsoft required to make its technology available for licence:[31]

---

30 Decision, para. 782.

31 The test used in the Decision entails an ad hoc balancing of the 'general public good' against a dominant undertaking's right to deal with whom it pleases. 'The central function of intellectual property rights is to protect the moral rights in a right-holder's work and ensure a reward for the creative effort. But it is also an essential objective of intellectual property law that creativity should be stimulated for the general public good. A refusal by an undertaking to grant a licence may, under exceptional circumstances, be contrary to the general public good by consti-

> a detailed examination of the scope of the disclosure at stake leads to the conclusion that, on balance, the possible negative impact of an order to supply on Microsoft's incentives to innovate is outweighed by its positive impact on the level of innovation of the whole industry (including Microsoft). As such, the need to protect Microsoft's incentives to innovate cannot constitute an objective justification that would offset the exceptional circumstances identified.[32]

Commission officials spoke of the likelihood that the degree of innovation in the market would *increase* as a result of the Commission's intervention. Rival server vendors would be able to focus development efforts on innovations in their products, since they would now be able to compete on the merits of these products, without an 'artificial interoperability obstacle'. Rivals which could deploy Active Directory would certainly have an advantage and could focus on other kinds of creativity. Furthermore, as rivals' products improved, this would spur Microsoft's own incentives to innovate, as it would 'no longer be able to simply rely on the artificial interoperability advantage to win in the market'.[33] Microsoft called this a horticultural approach: to stimulate growth, prune the roses – dubious for technology.

The Commission, as noted above, stated that it expected the divulgation of the technology would lead to the emergence of new products, but it identified no specific new products; and there was no limiting principle in the Decision whereby a licensee would be obliged to make a new product. Indeed, there seems to be a tension between the duty to help competitors create a functionally equivalent substitute product and the expression of a hope that 'new' products will emerge. When a dominant company receives a request for help of a technological kind from a competitor, it is at risk of abusing Article 82 EC if its refusal seems likely to damage the public good. Whether it is obliged to license or not will be decided only after the refusal has occurred by comparing its incentives to innovate with others' interests in enjoying the licensed technology.

---

tuting an abuse of a dominant position with harmful effects on innovation and on consumers.' Decision, para. 711.

'The major objective justification put forward by Microsoft relates to Microsoft's intellectual property over Windows. However, a detailed examination of the scope of the disclosure at stake leads to the conclusion that, on balance, the possible negative impact of an order to supply on Microsoft's incentives to innovate is outweighed by its positive impact on the level of innovation of the whole industry (including Microsoft). As such, the need to protect Microsoft's incentives to innovate cannot constitute an objective justification that would offset the exceptional circumstances identified.' Decision, para. 783.

32 Decision, para. 783.

33 Former Commission official Jürgen Mensching, speaking at the Fourth Sweet & Maxwell Annual Competition Law Review Conference, 22 October 2004.

It seems difficult to create an infringement based upon an *ex post facto* appraisal of whether a licence would enhance innovation. On this basis, there is *always* the chance that opening up the treasure chest of technology might lead to advantage for society. But that is a very speculative justification for a huge encroachment on the interests of the rightholder.

CONCERNING THE DECISION TO COMPEL DIVULGATION

- Was it correct to dismiss as insignificant the emergence and rise of Linux when analysing the effective market?
- Was the new balancing test economically wise and legally sound, and was it appropriately performed?
- Is it relevant that the Decision did not identify any specific new product that would emerge through the divulgation?
- Is the Decision right to find that a compulsory licence will encourage the licensor to be more creative?

Intellectual Property Rights and the IMS Health Criteria

The interrelationship between intellectual property rights (IPRs) and competition law has been a recurrent theme for antitrust enforcers, practitioners and academics in recent years.[34] The standard theory is that, generally, the two are not in conflict, but that they converge in the pursuit of the same objective, the creation of a competitive market led by technological innovation for the benefit of consumers.[35]

[34] For example, the Joint Hearings of the DOJ and the FTC: 'Competition and Intellectual Property Law and Policy in the Knowledge-Based Economy' (2002), see www.ftc.gov/opp/intellect/index.htm; FTC Report, *To Promote Innovation: The Proper Balance of Competition and Patent Law and Policy* (October 2003), available at www.ftc.gov/opp/intellect/index.htm; and the Comments received by the European Commission in relation to the Draft new block exemption regulation and draft guidelines on the application of Article 81 to technology transfer agreements, available at europa.eu.int/comm/competition/antitrust/technology_transfer_2/.

[35] See e.g. L. Peeperkorn, 'IP Licences and Competition Rules: Striking the Right Balance' (2003) *World Competition* 527, 528. Judging by the US example, this has not always been the case; see e.g. W. Bowman, *Patent and Antitrust Law: Legal and Economic Appraisal* (Chicago and London: Chicago University Press, 1973).

The purpose of IP protection is to provide all firms with incentives to innovate, including the ability to use their innovations to their own competitive advantage and prevent competitors from misappropriating the benefits of their investments in research and development. The mere invocation by a dominant company of IPRs cannot, as a matter of principle, constitute an abuse.

Introduction

2004 saw two remarkable events, almost simultaneously. In April 2004, the European Court of Justice rendered a judgment in *IMS Health* which seemed to prescribe fresh and updated judicial criteria for compulsory licensing. In March 2004, the Commission's Decision in the Microsoft case imposed a compulsory licence of a description of part of Microsoft's software code in the operating system for its servers.

If the *IMS Health* judgment had been pronounced in February 2004, the Commission Decision in the Microsoft case must necessarily have been different. Is the Microsoft Decision the first word of a new compulsory licensing era, so that the *IMS Health* test must be adapted immediately after it was adopted?

The *IMS Health* judgment

In *IMS Health* (as in *Magill*) the Commission was requested to intervene in order to palliate the anti-competitive consequences of the successful invocation of a national IPR. The complainants[36] said there was no possibility for companies wishing to offer pharmaceutical sales data in Germany to employ any convention for ascribing sales data geographically other than the convention used by IMS, the map known as the 1860 brick structure. To supply usable marketing data to customers, that data had to be useful to pharmaceutical customers. There were no substitutes or alternatives to reporting sales along the same geographic lines as the map of postcodes drawn up by IMS. IMS was successfully claiming that use of this format constituted a breach of its copyright. The Commission found that IMS's bringing of copyright infringement actions was an abuse of its dominant position. The Commission considered that the litigation was likely to eliminate all competition, and that the refusal to grant a licence lacked 'objective justification'.[37]

---

[36] The author represented the complainant NDC in the interim measures proceedings; and represented the Commission in *Magill* before the CFI and the ECJ.

[37] The Commission did not base its attack on the possibility that IMS had hijacked an industry standard. I share the view of my colleague, James Killick, that the Commission could have looked at the case from the basis that the brick

As in *Magill*, the Commission's Decision in *IMS Health* was criticized on intellectual property grounds, since it was thought contrary to 'well-established legal principles' and because it risked to 'discourage investment in intellectual property'.[38] As in *Magill*, the Commission's Decision in *IMS Health* was suspended by the President of the CFI.[39] National litigation in Germany culminated in a preliminary reference ruling of the Court of Justice on 29 April 2004, which constitutes the most authoritative pronouncement of the European judicature to this date on compulsory licensing of IPRs.[40]

The ruling of the Court of Justice, drawing from *Magill* and *Bronner*, stated or recapitulated the four conditions under which a dominant undertaking may be ordered to license its intellectual property rights:

(1) The product or service protected by copyright must be *indispensable* for carrying on a particular business. The test is one of an 'equally efficient competitor'. There is no indispensability if there are 'alternative solutions, even if they are less advantageous'. A company wishing to receive a licence must 'intend to offer new goods or services not offered by the owner of the right and for which there is potential consumer demand'.[41]

(2) The refusal must *prevent the emergence of a new product for which there is potential unmet consumer demand*. The requesting party must 'not intend to limit itself essentially to duplicating the goods or services already offered on the secondary market by the owner of the copyright, but intends to produce new goods or services not offered by the owner of the right'. Microsoft asserted that a licensee product replicating the functionality of say, Active Directory, would not be a 'new product' which was being denied to consum-

---

structure was originally an open industry standard and argued that IMS was claiming IPRs over that standard for the abusive purpose of excluding competition by preventing its competitors from using the standard. See J. Killick, 'IMS and Microsoft Judged in the Cold Light of *IMS*' (2004) *Competition Law Review* 23, 30, available at www.clasf.org/CompLRev/assets/Vol1Issue2Article2.pdf.

38 See e.g. J. Temple Lang, 'European Community Competition Policy: How Far Does it Benefit Consumers?' (2004) *Boletín Latinoamericano de competencia* (February), 128, 129, available at europa.eu.int/comm/competition/international/others. See also J. Temple Lang, 'Anticompetitive Non-Pricing Abuses under European and National Antitrust Law' (2003) *Fordham Corp. L Inst.* 303.

39 Case T-184/01 R *IMS Health*.

40 Case C-418/01 *IMS Health*.

41 Case C-418/01 *IMS Health*.

ers, and would merely offer the same functionality albeit under a different name.

(3) The refusal must not *be objectively justified.*

(4) The refusal must be such as to *exclude all competition* on the secondary market.

These conditions are cumulative.[42] One may assume (like members of the Court of Justice) that they are likely to be interpreted restrictively and applied with much caution.[43]

The Advocate General's Opinion and the Court of Justice's judgment in *IMS Health* diverge. Advocate General Tizzano started his analysis[44] from *Commercial Solvents* and *Télémarketing*[45] (which are 'true' refusal-to-deal cases) before going on to the IP cases *Volvo/Veng* and *Magill* (refusals to license), as well as to *Bronner*. The Court of Justice chose to start its analysis[46] directly from *Volvo/Veng* and *Magill.* This implies that the encroachment on IPRs by compulsory licensing is to be examined separately from the general refusal-to-deal cases.

Nature of the licensed material and the rights covering it

Before considering the *IMS Health* tests, there are two preliminary questions. Do different IPRs 'deserve' different levels of respect when compulsory licensing is under consideration? Can the nature of the *material* to be licensed affect the outcome?

Article 295 EC does not confer immunity from the competition rules upon holders of IPRs: it may be said to confirm the proposition that Community policies must be pursued giving proper respect to private

---

42 See Advocate General Poiares Maduro's Opinion of 14 July 2004 in Case C-109/03 *KPN Telecom BV* v *Onafhankelijke Post en Telecommunicatie Autoriteit (OPTA)* [2004] ECR I-1127, para. 35.

43 As acknowledged by Advocate General Poiares Maduro, '*a duty under Article 82 EC for a dominant undertaking to aid its competitors should not be assumed too lightly and refusal to supply a competitor is not automatically considered abusive just because the inputs in question are necessary to compete on a secondary market. A balance should be kept between the interest in preserving or creating free competition in a particular market and the interest in not deterring investment and innovation by demanding that the fruits of commercial success be shared with competitors*', *KPN Telecom BV*, para. 39.

44 Advocate General Tizzano's Opinion, paras. 48, 49 in Case C-418/01 *IMS Health*.

45 Case 311/84 *Télémarketing* v *CLT and IPB* [1985] ECR 3261.

46 Case C-418/01 *IMS Health*, para. 34 *et seq.*

property interests.[47] Any encroachment upon it has to be capable of being analysed, justified and defended without embarrassment and without violence to international treaty obligations.

Volvo/Veng, *Magill* and *IMS Health* concerned rights whose subject-matter was rather 'thin' and not covered by secrecy (design of a spare part, copyright over a public list of forthcoming TV programmes, or the map of 1,860 districts following German postal code boundaries). I have described the compulsory licences in *Magill* and *IMS Health* as capable of being regarded as very rare correctives for the consequences of invoking rights upon such subject matters in a manner which foreclosed competition.[48] The doubts over the *IMS Health* and *Magill* judgments, which involved debated (even doubtful) rights to control the use of non-secret information, should confirm that the tests there deployed are minima. In other words, it is arguable that 'mainstream' IPRs in innovation-driven industries should be subject to more demanding criteria and proof before compulsory licensing can be contemplated.

There is little conclusive authority. Having been involved in *Magill*, *IMS Health* and the *Microsoft* case, I can voice a personal opinion which is that the nature of the material and its public or secret status is relevant; that compulsory licences are more likely in the case of 'thin' rights such as those at stake in *Volvo/Veng*, *Magill* and *IMS Health*; and that rights existing under patent or under copyright or trade secret law are equally worthy of protection, respect and deference in the eyes of competition law.

Must competition law treat certain categories of human effort and the law which protects that effort more deferentially than other categories? In *Magill*, the Commission argued that the fact that 'programme listings are not in themselves secret, innovative or related to research' was relevant to its decision to condemn the refusal to license.[49] Similar arguments were

---

47 As well as Article 295, Article 30 EC refers to 'the protection of industrial and commercial property'.

48 See I. Forrester, 'EC Competition Law as a Limitation on the Use of IP Rights in Europe: Is there a Reason to Panic?' in C.D. Ehlermann and I. Atanasiu (eds.), *European Competition Law Annual 2003: What is an Abuse of a Dominant Position?* (Oxford: Hart Publishing, 2006), pp. 503–21, available at www.iue.it/RSCAS/Research/Competition/2003(papers).shtml; I. Forrester, 'Compulsory Licensing in Europe: A Rare Cure to Aberrant National Intellectual Property', presentation at the Department of Justice/Federal Trade Commission Hearings on Competition and Intellectual Property Law and Policy in the Knowledge-Based Economy: Comparative Law Topics, 22 may 2002, Washington, DC, available at www.ftc.gov/opp/intellect/020522forrester.pdf.

49 See Case T-69/89 *Radio Telefis Eireann* v *Commission* [1991] ECR II-485, para. 46.

made in *IMS Health*. However, in both *Magill* and *IMS Health*, the courts did not comment on the assertion, although Advocate General Jacobs did in *Bronner*.[50] The *Magill* and *IMS Health* material was public domain material protected by a debated (or 'thin') right: the status of what some call 'five star' material (secret, future technology, the fruit of ongoing research, manifestly very complex) protected by 'five star' legal rights (patents, copyright and trade secrets), as opposed to 'two star' material protected by 'two star' rights, was examined in the *Microsoft* case.

The President of the CFI noted the question in his Order of 22 December 2004, but decided that it had to be resolved in the main action. He did say, however, that:

> the hitherto secret specifications for the communications protocols which the Decision requires Microsoft to draw up and disclose are clearly fundamentally different from the information at issue in Magill and IMS Health. In those cases the information at issue was widely known in the sector: the television programme listings were sent free of charge to newspapers every week and the map of Germany was in reality an industry standard for the presentation of sales figures. However, the question whether, and if so to what extent, a distinction must be drawn according to whether the information is known or secret is even less amenable to determination at this stage because account must be taken more generally of parameters such as the value of the underlying investment, the value of the information concerned for the organisation of the dominant undertaking and the value transferred to competitors in the event of disclosure.[51]

It is not by accident that the first compulsory licence under Article 82 EC (*Magill*) was imposed in a case involving no secrecy, no research, a disputed copyright and consumer prejudice; nor that the second case, *IMS Health*, also involved a modest level of innovation. In cases like *Ladbroke* and *Bronner*, the complainant lost, and deservedly. The Court of Justice's judgment in *IMS Health* offers a set of four criteria which make sense in a large number of different circumstances. They seem capable of being applied to 'five star' innovation protected by 'five star' IPRs. Applying them will give rise to difficulty in particular circumstances, but they are rational. They may not be the last word, but they are well crafted and are capable of being reconciled with the protection of innovation. The *IMS Health* tests could have sufficed to decide the *Microsoft* case. There are two tests which could equally be regarded as of prime relevance in the case.

---

50 Case C-7/97 *Oscar Bronner*.

51 Case T-201/04 R *Microsoft Corporation* v *Commission*, Order of 22 December 2004, para. 207.

One involves the blocking of an innovation to the detriment of customers, and the other is the blocking of all competition. Following the judgment of the CFI the criteria for compulsory licensing have been sharply relaxed.

The *IMS Health* tests

The First of the IMS Health Tests: New Product Denied to Customers

The Magill TV Guide was a product Irish consumers desired. It was something new. Those who were involved in Magill will recollect the interest shown by the CFI in the physical demonstration of the new product: dozens of multichannel guides in other Member States, and none in Ireland after the extinction of the Magill TV Guide.

One of the challenges in establishing a compulsory licensing regime is to avoid an arbitrary standard-less test. Every IPR is likely to be used to prevent competition, by preventing the replication of copyright material, the manufacture of a patented object or the exploitation of a trade secret. It is pointless to say that such a refusal is anti-competitive, since blocking competition is one of the entitlements conferred by the right. In *Magill*, the result made obviously good sense: it was foolish (to the ordinary consumer) that advertising schedules of forthcoming television programmes could not be reproduced as Magill proposed. But what was the limiting principle? What was the distinguishing feature by which the BBC could be challenged, without creating gross uncertainty for other rightholders? The Court of Justice's answer was: a new product for which there was unmet consumer demand. The three broadcasters were using their Irish copyright to prevent the replication of their works to launch a new kind of publication which consumers demanded but were not getting. There was consumer harm.

The new product test will be an easy way of filtering out meritless complaints about refusals to license. It also makes logical sense. Any IPR involves some blocking of product differentiation. Making a blue version of a red product would not satisfy the test. According to *IMS Health*, essentially 'duplicating the goods or services already offered on the secondary market by the owner of the copyright' is not sufficient.[52]

Making a completely new product which consumers want would satisfy the test. Duplication with some differentiation ('mine would be better') will not on its own suffice. It will often be debatable whether the 'infringing' product is really new or merely incrementally superior. Whether a much better product is new will be a common subject of discussion. What is new may need verification of the facts, as in the case of *IMS Health* where the

---

[52] Case C-418/01 *IMS Health*, para. 49.

German courts were given the task of investigating the question of whether the 'infringing' party was indeed offering something different to IMS.

In the Microsoft case, the test is said to be satisfied by the possible emergence of unspecified products. Now, whenever technology is released via licences, products will *probably* emerge that were not previously on the market. But is this really enough to satisfy the 'new product' test? Is it necessary for the test to be satisfied that the 'new' products can be identified before the licence? No specific new product had been identified by the Commission; and of course, the licences which Microsoft grants do not limit the licensee's freedom to make a non-innovative product.

Moreover, Microsoft is not denying any product to consumers, unlike the broadcasters in *Magill*. It is offering server operating systems which are in its eyes superior to others. It is preventing other companies from duplicating such functionalities, not from creating alternatives which are superior or cheaper, or otherwise different. Microsoft denies that endowing its competitors with the capacity to make a directory service which is of identical functionality to its own directory service will lead to the making of a new product for which there is unmet consumer demand.

The Second IMS Health Test

On the next condition, elimination of competition, the Court of Justice's test in *IMS Health* (29 April 2004) speaks of 'elimination of all competition'.[53] By contrast, the test in the *Microsoft* case (24 March 2004), is the 'risk of elimination of competition', a test based on probabilities. The contested behaviour did not eliminate all competition. It hindered, so said the Commission, viable competition.

According to the Commission, 'the degree of interoperability that can be achieved on the basis of Microsoft's disclosures is insufficient to enable competitors to viably stay in the market'.[54] Thus, the goal of the Decision is delivering a 'sufficient' degree of supply of interoperability, and thus, by implication, a 'sufficient' degree of competition. Microsoft argued that absolute elimination is the legal test, and that if Novell and Linux server operating systems never used the controversial communications technology, that test was not and could not be satisfied.

The Third IMS Health Test

As to indispensability, courts must ask whether the protected IPRs are indeed indispensable for competitors to carry on their business activities.

---

53 Case C-418/01 *IMS Health*, para. 52.

54 Decision, para. 589, n. 712.

Bronner (not an IP case) and *Ladbroke* indicate that access is not indispensable if a dominant undertaking's competitors can develop and market their products without access, even if it would be more convenient for them to have it. The existence of several types of server operating system confirmed that competing products existed without having had access to the technology at issue, one of them (Linux) having emerged during the period of the alleged abuse.

Particular debate concerned whether the technology was meant to assist the competing servers more perfectly to communicate with Microsoft servers or to act in a network of Microsoft servers which necessarily involves replicating how a Microsoft server acts. The Decision states[55] that Microsoft's specifications are indispensable because no other alternative was available by which Microsoft's competitors could interoperate with servers using the Windows operating system.

The Fourth IMS Health Test

The fourth condition was objective justification. Any dominant company would say it is objectively justified in not disclosing its intellectual property to a major competitor wishing to help to displace the dominant player's products. There may be cases where the refusal would indeed block all competition, where a licence is indispensable and where a new product would be made by the licensee. The rightholder might reasonably refer to the heavy research and development expenditure, the limited period of available patent protection, and to the firm's own view of the best way of exploiting its own invention. (Advocate General Jacobs in *Bronner* reviews US case law and points out there three categories of objective justification: technical, commercial and efficiencies.)[56]

---

[55] Decision, para. 669: 'As regards the use of open industry standards implemented in Windows, interoperability within a Windows work group network largely depends on specifications that are proprietary or are extended versions of standard protocols. Therefore, open industry standards fall short of *enabling competitors to achieve the same degree of interoperability with the Windows domain architecture as Windows work group server operating systems do*. Since all major work group server operating system vendors already support most of the open industry standards supported in Windows, it can be concluded that this degree of interoperability proves to be insufficient for them to viably compete in the market. Therefore, reliance on open industry standards cannot be considered to be at present a realistic substitute to disclosures by Microsoft'. (Emphasis added.)

[56] See Advocate General's Opinion in Case C-7/97 *Oscar Bronner*, para. 47:

The US essential facilities doctrine has developed to require a company with monopoly power to contract with a competitor where five conditions are met. First, an essential facility is controlled by a monopolist. A facility will be regarded

> ## QUESTIONS ABOUT COMPULSORY LICENSING
>
> - Are the *IMS Health* tests the relevant ones? Can they be supplemented?
> - Is the investment of money and time by the dominant company in creating the material to be licensed a relevant factor? If so, does one look at the investment in the relevant product, or more widely to the investments in other products (failure and successes) on which the licensor worked?
> - Is it relevant that the request was made to enable the licensee to make a directly competing product?
> - Is there a difference in the legal test depending on whether the information is covered by IPRs or not?
> - If interoperability is a policy goal of such importance that enhancing interoperability has become a new criterion for compelling a licence, do the other *IMS Health* tests such as total elimination of competition and new product for which there is unmet consumer demand still apply?

Different intellectual property rights

The Commission has advanced novel theories about trade secret law, which are of wider interest. It argued in the Microsoft case that antitrust owes little deference to trade secrets, as the reasons and motives for keeping the material secret should be considered first. The Commission has expressed the view that trade secrets should therefore be treated differently from

---

as essential when access to it is indispensable in order to compete on the market with the company that controls it. The following have for example been held to be essential facilities: railroad bridges serving the town of St Louis; a local telecommunications network; a local electricity network. Secondly, a competitor is unable practically or reasonably to duplicate the essential facility. It is not sufficient that duplication would be difficult or expensive, but absolute impossibility is not required. Thirdly, the use of the facility is denied to a competitor. That condition would appear to include the refusal to contract on reasonable terms. Fourthly, it is feasible for the facility to be provided. Fifthly, there is no legitimate business reason for refusing access to the facility. A company in a dominant position which controls an essential facility can justify the refusal to enter a contract for legitimate technical or commercial reasons. It may also be possible to justify a refusal to contract on grounds of efficiency. (References omitted.)

IPRs affirmatively 'created by law' such as patents. This approach[57] seems to differentiate between 'good' and 'bad' IPRs in a manner similar to that adopted by the Court of Justice in its early cases such as *Sirena*[58] and *Café Hag I*.[59] Microsoft disagrees: trade secrets constitute valuable property and are an IPR, just like patents and copyright, and are protected under TRIPS.

Indeed, the Commission argues that the rules on compulsory licensing of IPRs should not apply to knowhow licensing, on the grounds that the act of not licensing an IPR affirmatively created by IP law is fundamentally different to that of 'not revealing' a 'secret', the existence of which merely results from a unilateral business decision. So one question to be settled is whether competition law may more readily compel a licence in a case involving trade secrets than in a case involving other IP interests.

Even though the Commission doubts the existence of IPRs relevant to the controversy, it has still ordered Microsoft to license the IP:

> The order to supply is therefore not limited to disclosing specifications but also encompasses authorising the implementation of such specifications in work group server operating system products . . . to the extent that this Decision might require Microsoft to refrain from fully enforcing any of its intellectual property rights, this would be justified by the need to put an end to the abuse.[60]

Microsoft stated that many patents cover the technology. The Commission's response was that the patents may have been wrongly granted or that it may be possible for a licensee to engineer around the software inventions over which Microsoft held patent protection. Microsoft responded that there was no reason for a licensee to seek an alternative means of exploiting the licence, and that it was not for the Commission to second-guess the decisions of national or European patent authorities. Subsequently, the Commission has suggested that all or nearly all of the licensed material should be licensed royalty-free on a worldwide basis. Royalties might be demanded only for 'innovative' technology, but not for innovation in the commonly understood sense. This topic is addressed further below.

Microsoft notes it has copyright in the source code and in the

---

[57] See R. Milgrim, 'Commission Proposed Capital Punishment – by Definition – for Trade Secrets, a Uniquely Valuable IP Right' (2006) *Journal of Patent and Trademark Office Society* 911.

[58] Case 40/70 *Sirena S.r.l.* v *Eda S.r.l. and others* [1971] ECR 69.

[59] Case 192/73 *Van Zuylen frères* v *Hag AG* [1974] ECR 731.

[60] Decision, paras 1003, 1004.

specifications painfully drawn up by its engineers; and that any implementation of those specifications must infringe its copyright interests. The Commission denies any encroachment of copyright. It says that Microsoft must deliver a specially written, detailed description of the functionality implemented by its own source code, rather than licensing the source code as such: so the source code of the licensee's program would be different from the Microsoft original, even if the functionality were the same. Microsoft replies that this functional replication of how software performs is entirely inconsistent with the goals and terms of the Software Directive.[61]

QUESTIONS ABOUT INTELLECTUAL PROPERTY

- What relevance is to be attributed to the fact that the information requested was subject to IPRs?
- Is any distinction to be made between these various rights? Does it matter if a licensor possesses patents, or copyright or trade secret rights, or believes it does, over the material requested?
- Should any distinction be made between the different types of IPRs (patents, copyright, trademark and know how)?
- Is knowhow and the law which protects it eligible only for a lesser degree of respect than other rights in the face of antitrust concerns?
- Did the Decision lawfully reconcile the long-term incentives to innovate (given by IPRs) with the shorter-term incentives of competition law?
- May the Commission defend a compulsory patent licence by doubting the validity of the issued patents?

Need for legal certainty

Establishing constraints on compulsory licensing creates legal certainty for market operators, at the cost of limiting the enforcer's freedom to condemn. Any *ex post* regime based on condemnation, such as the prohibition of abuses, needs predictability to be lawful. While legal uncertainty

[61] Council Directive 91/250/EC on the legal protection of computer programs [1991] OJ L211/42.

is, indeed, inherent in antitrust,[62] stability in enforcement patterns is necessary for business's growth and prosperity. Business needs reasonably clear guidance. A 'standardless' test risks being applied in an arbitrary manner.

Everyone would agree that duties to license should be imposed only in the rarest cases, the categories of which should be defined. Predictable rules should always be the basis for a legal regime based on condemnation. Legal principles applied to one dominant player should be capable of being applied in the future to other dominant players.

If the Decision were well-founded in condemning Microsoft's behaviour, considerable practical difficulties would arise for future addressees of requests to license. Consider the situation of the dominant holder of an important technological advantage who receives a broadly-formulated request for access to the technology from a competitor who wishes to use that technology to build a competing product. The rightholder will normally prefer not to grant such a licence, but will surely not wish to risk being condemned and heavily fined for abuse of a dominant position. If the request for technical assistance is very broad, is there really a duty to deliver as opposed to a duty to discuss what is appropriate? The dominant player should not be obliged to identify what lesser disclosure might satisfy its legal duty.

Moreover, the application of the test poses numerous questions. It appears difficult enough for the enforcers to ensure a consistent and objective application of such a test. It would be even more difficult for the Court of Justice to question the Commission's findings. Other unanswered questions remain. Do judges and competition authorities have the right background for setting the appropriate terms of access? Since the owner refuses to license, someone else would have to assess and set the amount of compensation. This could be anything between the licensing cost and the opportunity cost of licensing (i.e. the income taken away by the additional rightholder). This is difficult enough for a regulator and, as noted by others, very difficult indeed for a general enforcer.[63]

---

[62] See R. Hawk and N. Denaeijer, 'The Development of Articles 81 and 82 EC Treaty: Legal Certainty' in C.-D. Ehlermann and I. Atanasiu (eds.), *European Competition Law Annual 2000: The Modernisation of EC Antitrust Policy* (Oxford: Hart Publishing, 2001), pp.130, 137, 140.

[63] See also V. Korah, 'Refusals to License Contrary to Article 82 EC – IMS – When are the Circumstances Special?' Fordham IP Conference Papers (2005).

QUESTIONS ABOUT ISSUES OF GENERAL PRINCIPLE

- Was Microsoft correct to say that the Commission Decision was intended to change how the market operates rather than to condemn recognizably infringing conduct?
- Are the criteria established by the Decision adequately clear and capable of being applied in future cases?

6. FINES

I have now described the principal points which were debated as to the merits of the interoperability half of the case. I add some thoughts on the fine of €497,196,304. The imposition of the largest fine in history presented an obvious financial concern even for a company which is prosperous. It also presented a moral element: Microsoft was accused not just of a technical offence but a wilful breach of the law. Although the huge fine is almost always referred to in press accounts of the case, the fine and its amount received only a few paragraphs in the Commission Decision.

Supposed Absence of Novelty of the Infringements

Paragraph 1057 of the Decision states:

> The Commission is not applying any new rule of law; . . . this case is based on a constant practice . . . expressed and developed in previous cases . . . in the absence of the application of any novel concept of competition law . . . Microsoft should have known it was acting unlawfully.

The relevant legal precedents on the interoperability side of the case (*Volvo/Veng*, *Magill*, *Ladbroke*, *Bronner* and *IMS Health*) suggest that in March 2004 the only judicial authority upholding a compulsory licence was *Magill*. The alleged abuse in the *Microsoft* case was not hindering exports; it was not a cartel; it was not blocking parallel trade; it was no hard-core infringement. It was failing to draw up a detailed and lengthy description of secret technology not yet on the market, information necessary to ensure that Microsoft's Active Directory technology could work perfectly on competitors' products. The core of the alleged infringement was not agreeing to an obviously unreasonable request. Microsoft argued that if the Commission truly believed its assertions in the Decision at paragraph 1057 about the relevant law, that *Magill* and the *Microsoft* case were completely consistent, then the relevant law was manifestly misunderstood by the Commission. Who could imagine that failure to create a detailed description of an immense quantity of secret future technology for a competitor could constitute an infringement of Article 82 EC? Who would have thought that in September 1998 there was a duty to say 'yes' to such a request by reference to a completely new set of exceptional circumstances? The same surprise could be voiced, with equal force, as to the suggestion that it was an obviously unlawful tie to bring out a more richly configured product while not leaving on the market the unimproved version of that product. Microsoft said that if the Commission were really of that opinion, then the Commission had completely misunderstood the applicable precedents.

Legal Precedents on How to Set the Fine in Case of an Antitrust Novelty

Fines in a regime of law are imposed for recognized offences. Penalties should not be visited on those who had at least good grounds to trust their conduct was lawful. Competition law is not a static science. Sometimes the boundaries of offensive conduct are well defined. Going over the boundary if detected is likely to attract a fine, even a severe fine, as in the case of cartel agreements.

Sometimes the boundary is not clear. When a new line is drawn, the penalty is either non-existent or modest. In past cases where the Commission has elected to establish a new offence, it has commonly imposed a symbolic fine or even no fine. In *Magill* no fines were imposed even though the three broadcasters had acted simultaneously and identically to put out of business the Magill TV Guide, and even though in that case there was clear customer harm (for example, Irish television addicts had to buy three magazines instead of one).

Arithmetic by which the Fine was Calculated

The starting amount was €165,732,101. The Decision proceeded from the proposition that Microsoft engaged in a very serious infringement. The very serious designation has historically been confined to conduct that is plainly an infringement of the competition rules, such as hard-core price fixing or explicit market allocation schemes, conduct especially repugnant to Europe's competition culture, conduct worthy of an exemplary fine.

The Commission set the initial amount of the fine at 7.5 per cent of Microsoft's combined EEA turnover for client PC operating systems and server operating systems. After having laid such stress on the relevant market being 'operating systems for work group servers costing less than US$25,000' the fine is based on 'all servers'. The Commission did not explain why it took into account Microsoft's turnover for its Windows 2000 Server Standard Edition when the alleged abuse related to work group server operating systems. Most income was earned from servers acting outside the alleged relevant market. Did the Commission depart from its own market definition?

Increase for Deterrence

Then there was a doubling of the initial amount, justified by Microsoft's significant economic capacity and the need to ensure a sufficient deterrent effect. It was not clear what it is that Microsoft should be deterred from doing. Was it disallowing access to new technology (Active Directory) or was it adding new technology (Windows Media Player with streaming capacity)?

Increase for Long Duration

The Commission increased the amount of the fine by 50 per cent for what it described as the long duration of the infringements. It says Microsoft made two acts of supposed procedural misconduct: 'systematically requesting significant extensions to the deadlines granted' and 'using part of the limited resources of the Commission in settlement discussions during the procedure'. The proceedings indeed lasted five years. The Commission can reject any request for an unreasonable extension of time to reply to a Statement of Objections and it did so during the proceedings. The theories of the Commission went through several cycles in the Statements of Objections in August 2000, August 2001 and August 2003. It seems severe that the length of the Commission's reflections on the case justified imposing additional financial penalties.

In March 2004, after 15 months of settlement negotiations, the Commissioner announced the need for 'a precedent which will establish clear principles for . . . future conduct'. At that moment he praised the company which had looked for a creative solution: 'I would like to stress the constructive and cooperative spirit displayed by Microsoft in the last few weeks. I also want to acknowledge the high degree of professionalism of the members of the Microsoft team at all levels.' Microsoft's reward fr manifesting that constructiveness and cooperativeness was an incre fine. If a company asks for better conditions for the exercise of it to be heard and is granted more time, the company ought not heavier fine later. Likewise, if it elects to come forward with settlement proposals, it ought not to risk receiving a bigger fine.

One must suspect that the Decision to impose any fine upon Microsoft was coloured by what people would think. The biggest fine in history might reinforce the impression of guilt and distract from the implications of the creation of the new abuse theories. If this were true, the fine served to justify the finding of the abuse, rather than as a calibrated sanction to punish an abuse.

QUESTIONS ABOUT THE FINE

- Was the imposition of any fine lawful?
- Were the infringements novel?
- Was the Commission entitled to increase the fine because Microsoft had sought and obtained extensions of time to reply to its Statements of Objections?
- Was the Commission entitled to increase the fine because Microsoft had engaged in settlement negotiations?

7. SUBSEQUENT DEVELOPMENTS

Agreements to Enhance Interoperability Between Microsoft and Competitors

Microsoft has made a series of public announcements confirming or reinforcing its efforts regarding interoperability. In December 2003, Marshall Phelps announced that 'Microsoft is open for business when it comes to IP licensing'.[64] Microsoft thus committed to license its patents to interested

[64] On 3 December 2003, Microsoft Deputy General Counsel Marshall Phelps announced an updated intellectual property policy aimed at 'convey[ing] that Microsoft is open for business when it comes to IP licensing'. See Q&A: Microsoft Unveils New Policy on Intellectual Property: Microsoft Deputy General Counsel Marshall Phelps explains how today's announcement of an updated intellectual property policy will boost access to innovation across the IT industry', www.microsoft.com/presspass/features/2003/dec03/12-03ExpandIPQA.mspx. Microsoft's IP Licensing Program includes programs for licensing source code for Microsoft Windows, Microsoft Office and other software, hundreds of Microsoft-designed communications protocols, the Office XML schemas and file formats, and Microsoft's diverse IP portfolio. More information about Microsoft's IP

parties in a commercially reasonable manner under terms standard in the industry. Numerous licensing programmes are listed on Microsoft's website (including the 2001 United States Consent Decree). If a company wants to use existing protocol documentation outside the scope of the current licence, Microsoft states that it is prepared to discuss licensing terms. Microsoft has also stated that it is open to requests from any bona fide company for documentation and licensing terms for protocols that are not currently documented or offered for licence. Respect for Microsoft's intellectual property will be a condition of any such licence.

In July 2006 Microsoft announced the 'Windows Principles: Twelve Tenets to Promote Competition'.[65] Under the Principles, Microsoft commits to make available, on commercially reasonable terms, all of the communications protocols that it has built into Windows and that are used to facilitate communication with Windows Server. A parallel initiative is the notion of 'Interoperability by design', another aspect of Microsoft's interoperability strategy reflected in its development efforts.[66]

At least 50 examples can be noted of active interoperability collaboration in which Microsoft has engaged recently, including collaboration with Microsoft's direct competitors. Agreements were reached with Apple,[67] EMC,[68] Novell,[69] Sun,[70] Oracle and Symbian,[71] and also with the Interop Vendor Alliance (IVA), a global industry group of software and hardware

---

Licensing Program is available at www.microsoft.com/about/legal/intellectual-property/default.mspx.

[65] See http://www.microsoft.com/presspass/newsroom/winxp/windowsprinciples.mspx.

[66] See http://www.microsoft.com/presspass/newsroom/winxp/windowsprinciples.mspx.

[67] See http://www.microsoft.com/presspass/press/2006/jan06/01-10Macworld2006PR.mspx.

[68] See http://www.microsoft.com/presspass/press/2006/oct06/10-03MSEMCPR.mspx.

[69] See http://www.microsoft.com/presspass/press/2006/nov06/11-02MSNovellPR.mspx.

[70] See Web Single Sign-On Metadata Exchange Protocol, available at developers.sun.com/techtopics/identity/interop/web_sso_mex_may2005.pdf.

[71] See e.g. the following Press Releases: '*Microsoft announces exchange ActiveSync licensing agreement with Sony Ericsson*,' available at www.microsoft.com/presspass/press/2006/feb06/02-06SonyExchangePR.mspx?pf=true; '*Microsoft and Motorola form strategic alliance to extend unified communications to mobile devices*', www.microsoft.com/presspass/press/2006/jun06/06-25UCGMotorolaPR.mspx?pf=true; and *palmOne licenses Microsoft exchange server Synchronization Protocol for integration with next-generation Treo Smartphones*', www.microsoft.com/presspass/press/2004/oct04/10-05PalmOnePR.mspx?pf=true.

vendors that works together to enhance the way that diverse products interoperate with Microsoft's operating systems and applications. The IVA was founded in November 2006 by Microsoft and includes members like BEA Systems, Citrix, NEC, Novell, Siemens, Sun Microsystems and more than a dozen others. Its activities include interoperability testing, sharing of relevant technical information, and communicating about interoperability solutions to customers.[72]

8. LICENSING CASES AND FOLLOW-UP

The reaching of these various understandings and initiatives has not eliminated interoperability controversies arising from the Commission Decision of March 2004. In order to put in perspective the history I am about to tell regarding the implementation of the remedy on the interoperability half of the case, we may usefully recall the 'tying' half of the case. There Microsoft received a succession of precise instructions concerning what files should be removed to create the reduced version of Windows, what the product should be called and even how it should be packaged. The launch of the new product Windows XP-N was therefore accomplished smoothly because the Commission's instructions implementing the remedy were precise and detailed.

Concerning interoperability, the Decision called for licensing on reasonable and non-discriminatory terms, such that royalties should 'not reflect the "strategic value" stemming from Microsoft's market power'. Just after Christmas 2004, upon the rejection of its application for interim measures, Microsoft activated a website giving access to the licence terms governing access to the technology.

There have been serious controversies about how the material should be compiled and presented; whether royalties could be charged; and whether licensees could be obliged to keep confidential the licensed material.

Controversies about Confidentiality

I begin with the debate which is easiest to comprehend. The question is whether Microsoft would be following reasonable and non-discriminatory terms if it were to compel its licensees to keep confidential the licensed material. An appeal (Case T-313/05) was filed on 10 August 2005 against a Decision of the Commission according to which, if the CFI ruled in

[72] *See* www.microsoft.com/presspass/press/2006/nov06/11-14IVA07PR.mspx.

favour of the Commission in the main case (Case T-201/04), Microsoft would immediately be required to permit its licensed technology to be disseminated on an 'open source' basis: that means without being allowed to impose confidentiality constraints upon the licensee. Open source software is shared freely among members of the open source community, who must allow its unlimited exploitation. Such terms would permit a licensee to disclose all the details of an implementation of Microsoft's technology, thus placing Microsoft's trade secrets in the public domain.

The Commission's Decision was being challenged on a variety of grounds, including public international law, on the ground that the Commission lacked jurisdiction to destroy valuable intellectual property created in a third country and principally exploited there. The case was abandoned in the autumn of 2007.

Controversies about Scope and Adequacy

As noted above, after the President's Order of 22 December 2004 rejecting Microsoft's request for suspension, Microsoft activated a website revealing its licence terms and announcing the availability for inspection of the documentation. In June 2005, the Commission sent to Microsoft a technical report about difficulties of using and accessing the data, to which Microsoft replied, in effect promising the same process of continual polishing of the documentation as applies under the US (client-to-server) program, and pointing out various errors and misunderstandings. This debate about the completeness and ease of use of the material was overshadowed by a quite separate controversy which arose in October 2005, as to the *scope* of disclosure called for. The debate related to whether Microsoft had to deliver such level of detail as would permit licensees to emulate server-to-server communications 'over the wire' or whether it was to deliver at a more detailed standard, that of drop-in or 'plug replaceability' of the function delivered through the relevant protocol. This was a sensitive topic as it presented the issue of whether a licensee would need to duplicate perfectly certain algorithms (computing formulae) in order to achieve the desired result. Obviously, the wider the scope, the greater the encroachment on Microsoft's interests; the narrower the scope, the less the technological advantage to the licensees.[73] There was an exchange,

[73] This matter had arisen even during the hearing on interim measures, when it was suggested that only the narrower scope of disclosure would be necessary. There was no explicit clarification during the hearing of the main action in April 2006.

during which Microsoft noted that these two scopes were obviously different, and stating that it would execute either, so long as the Commission would specify which it was to be. The Commission declined to give such written confirmation, but Microsoft recorded in writing its understanding of the oral discussions with the Commission, and stated that it would supply the broader scope, including where necessary algorithms and other internal details so as to enable drop-in replaceability of a Windows server by a licensee's server. Microsoft submitted further documentation in November 2005, and continued to deliver ever more detailed documentation more or less continuously thereafter for about seven months, with a particular burst of effort after the Monitoring Trustee's work plan was adopted in April 2006, specifying in detail the format required.

In November 2005, the Commission took a Decision under Article 24 (1) of Regulation 1/2003 threatening the company with a fine for not having complied with its obligations under the March 2004 Decision. The Decision gave Microsoft until 15 December 2005 to remedy the alleged deficiencies. Without studying what was delivered on that date, the Commission moved to the next stage, a Statement of Objections, claiming that the deficiencies identified had not been remedied.

By contrast, Microsoft's independent experts stated that what Microsoft had produced in December 2005 was 'complete and accurate'. Microsoft stated that it would do whatever was explicitly required of it, and as an aid to licensees offered them further help in using the technology, as well as a sight of its source code.

In April 2006, the Trustee and Microsoft's engineers agreed on a detailed work plan in the format favoured by the Trustee. By 18 July 2006, Microsoft had executed the documentation (thousands of electronic pages long) in that format and was praised for having done a good job. Nevertheless, on 12 July 2006, the Commission imposed a fine of €280,500,000 on Microsoft. That Decision was challenged in Case T-271/06, which was abandoned in 2007 after the judgment of the CFI.

Price Controversies

The Decision allowed Microsoft to apply reasonable and non-discriminatory royalties. The Commission has claimed that Microsoft's proposed licensing terms are unsatisfactory in that Microsoft has not proved to the Commission that its licensing terms are reasonable and non-discriminatory. The pricing controversy has given special prominence to a set of 'pricing principles' developed by the Commission and Microsoft. These were intended for use by the Trustee in resolving any dispute that might arise with a prospective licensee about appropriate level of royalties for the specification.[74] In the event of dispute, the Trustee could consider four factors:

- whether the protocols represent Microsoft's own creation;
- whether the creations by Microsoft constitute innovation;
- a market valuation of comparable technologies; and
- other factors that he deems appropriate.

The pricing principles were intended to guide the Trustee in the event of a specific dispute about what would be a reasonable royalty. No such dispute has arisen. Some ten licensees have agreed on the royalties they will pay without recourse to dispute resolution procedures. However, the principles were being used as an overarching standard against which to judge the royalty rates put up for negotiation by the company.

Even though there have not been any disputes with actual licensees about royalty rates, the principles have given rise to a number of points of debate with the Commission. For example, the Commission holds that it need consider market comparators only if the technology has been found to be innovative in the sense that it is superior to all other technologies on the market. In addition, it has been argued that no royalty should be paid for technology which solved problems particular to Microsoft software as opposed to problems of general applicability.

Further, the Commission has argued that the price should be set at a level which permits viable competition between the licensee and Microsoft. On this theory, since the licensees by the Commission's estimation could need as long as two years to implement the specification by building their own software and might have to spend well over US$100 million in the process, the price of the licence should, it is argued, be set low enough to make that effort worthwhile. It seems curious that although the Commission is claiming that the technology lacks any innovation and is rather trivial, it also claims that Microsoft must take into account in its pricing the very substantial efforts and costs of competitors to implement the technology.

There was sharp debate over the level of innovation reflected in the licensed technology. The company said it had dozens of granted or pending patents which read on the licensed technology. The Commission's experts, TAEUS, and the Trustee concluded that Microsoft had not proved the point to their satisfaction, and that accordingly only a few pieces of the

---

74 The WSSP Pricing Principles are available from the Microsoft website at www.microsoft.com/downloads/details.aspx?FamilyId=5A9CACB3-E823-4522-967C-A6EE3CD3995D&displaylang=en.

specification merited any compensation at all.[75] Indeed, the Commission's current position is that the technology should be made available free of charge or for a nominal fee, on a worldwide basis. According to the Trustee 'all of the described features were considered either to have been Microsoft implementations of prior developments by others, or to have been anticipated by prior developments and to be immediately obvious minor extensions to that prior work'. PricewaterhouseCoopers supplied evidence to the effect that the royalty rates proposed by Microsoft were at least 30 per cent below market norms for similar technology. Microsoft recalled that the proposed royalty programmes could be negotiated to meet the individual requirements of the licensee, and that it was 'open for business' in dealing with prospective licensees; and that it had concluded licences with several companies. The Commission nonetheless took the view that the proposed maximum royalty rate of 5 per cent was not 'reasonable' since, according to the Commission, there was no 'significant innovation' in the licensed material. The Commission contends that it is entitled to examine the question of innovation because the Decision forbids the exploitation by Microsoft of the 'strategic' value of the technology. Thus, the asserted infringing conduct consisted of proposing as a basis for negotiation a royalty rate of 5 per cent of the licensee's selling price for whatever product the licensee made based upon the licensed technology.[76]

The Commission, rather than trying to prove Microsoft's terms are unreasonable, claimed that Microsoft had not proved to the Commission's satisfaction certain key points (the comparable transactions are comparable, the innovations are innovative). The Commission in effect argued

---

[75] On 1 March 2007, the Commission issued a Press Release (IP/07/269) 'Competition: Commission warns Microsoft of further penalties over unreasonable pricing as interoperability information lacks significant innovation'.

[76] In August 2006 Microsoft submitted a proposal on licensing terms for the protocol specifications after several discussions, stating that Microsoft was 'willing to entertain any reasonable price offer from any potential licensee, and that we are willing to be flexible to meet any unique business needs of potential licensees'. See Microsoft Statement on European Commission Action on Protocol Pricing, available at www.microsoft.com/presspass/press/2007/mar07/03-01PricingProtocolPR.mspx. The licensing arrangement may simplistically be outlined as follows. The four options are (i) a licence for all intellectual property rights in the WSPP protocols and the protocol specifications ('All IP'); (ii) a licence limited to Microsoft's patents on the WSPP protocols ('Patent Only'); (iii) a licence limited to Microsoft's trade secrets disclosed in the protocol specifications ('Trade Secret Only'); and (iv) a licence limited to the IDL files ('IDL Only'). Microsoft further divided the protocols into Gold, Silver and Bronze price categories based on the degree of innovation. (A fourth category includes protocols, not necessarily innovative, for which there will be no royalty.)

that Microsoft has a burden under the 2004 Decision to prove to the Commission that its prices are 'reasonable'.

The company disagreed with these factual conclusions, pointing to the amount of time and effort deployed in creating the technology whose characteristics must be divulged in the licensed specification. However, the company said it was willing to charge lower royalties so as to avoid being penalized, and accordingly asked what lower figures would be acceptable and not unreasonable or excessive. The Commission was unwilling to prescribe a figure, on the grounds that it is not a price regulator.

On 1 March 2007 the Commission issued a Statement of Objections pursuant to Article 24 of Regulation 1/2003, threatening a daily penalty, backdated to 16 December 2005, in an amount which was initially €500,000 per day, then €2,000,000 per day during 40 days ending on 30 July 2006, then €3,000,000 per day after 31 July 2006. On 27 February 2008, the Commission imposed a fine of €899,000,000. That fine is under appeal in Case T-167/08.

The company was thus subjected to the largest penalty in world competition law history for proposing as a basis for commercial negotiations a royalty rate higher than the public authority deemed appropriate.

9. CONCLUSION

Compulsory licensing is a particularly hot antitrust topic. There is a clear divergence (noted by Hew Pate, former head of the Antitrust Division, among other commentators) between the liberal or minimalist[77] approach which prevails in the United States, celebrated by the US Supreme Court in *Trinko*,[78] and more recent cases, and the more formalistic or maximalist approach of the European Commission.[79] In the *Microsoft* case, the Commission ordered a company to draw up a detailed description of its own technology for the purpose of delivering to competitors the means of incorporating that technology in their own products.[80] The link between

---

77 W. Kolasky, General Counsel of the FTC, speaking in Brussels at a conference on The Article 82 EC Abuse Concept, 30 September 2004, referred approvingly to the 'modesty' of the US authorities in their approach of antitrust enforcement, as opposed to the European Commission's policy.

78 *Verizon Communications, Inc.* v *Law Offices of Curtis Trinko*.

79 I. Forrester, 'Article 82: Remedies in Search of Theories?' (2004) *Fordham Corp. L Inst.* 167.

80 S. Scotchmer, 'Standing on the Shoulders of Giants: Cumulative Research and the Patent Law' (1991) *Journal of Economic Perspectives* 29.

the compelled conduct and the infringing act was rather distant. The compelled conduct had great political and industrial symbolism.

Of course, every Article 82 EC case is likely to create new ground, and perfectly compelling precedents are rare. In a democratic society, the law must be sufficiently predictable for individuals to plan their affairs. This is especially true in the case of laws which condemn or which inflict punishment. The balancing test involves comparing the dominant player's own interests and incentives to innovate with those of society as a whole. There are formidable challenges in being subject to a standard which is difficult to apply and difficult to foresee. There are not less significant challenges for judicial review of decisions based upon policy choices and broad balancings of public and private advantage. The judgment was the subject of intense media interest, rumour and speculation. It was exceptionally long and to some extent case-specific. Unfortunately, the judgment has not definitively clarified the limits of the possible duty of a dominant player to grant a licence.

The judgment of the CFI was not appealed, so that there is now a clear discrepancy between the standards prescribed in *IMS Health* by the Court of Justice and those prescribed by the CFI in the *Microsoft* case. We will see the law better once more judicial authority exists, via challenges to refusals by competition agencies to order a licence, challenges to the ordering of a licence by competition agencies, and references to the European Court. In ten years' time, I predict that there will be a doctrine in Europe broadly parallel to that in the United States.

European law on compulsory licensing is today sharply at odds with US law. Major legal discrepancies between friendly jurisdictions commonly drift back to alignment after a while, in which case the Microsoft case would be a second *Sirena*,[81] an eccentricity born of overenthusiasm.

---

81 Case 40/70 *Sirena S.r.l.* v *Eda S.r.l. and others* [1971] ECR 69.

4. The Microsoft Windows Media Player tying case

Jean-François Bellis and Tim Kasten*

1. INTRODUCTION

The ability to engage in product innovation by incorporating new features demanded by consumers, and by continually improving these features, is a key engine of economic progress. Indeed, this innovation is so common that it is often taken for granted. For example, consumers of high-technology products (such as mobile telephones, MP3 players and video game consoles) simply expect that current models will build on previous advances and offer new features. This trend is also seen in many low-technology products as well (e.g. consumers expect newspapers and magazines to add new sections and features over time). Software products are, of course, no different, and consumers have come to expect that their programs and operating systems will continuously provide updates with newer features. For example, every new version of the Windows and Apple Macintosh operating systems include features that were not present in the previous versions. Similarly, Internet search engines such as Google have improved their capabilities, and are now capable of searching news stories, images and maps in addition to merely searching websites.

In its 2004 Microsoft Decision, the European Commission (the 'Commission') set forth its views on when such integration and improvement can constitute an infringement of EC competition law, at least when carried out by undertakings with market power. In its judgment of 17 September 2007, the Court of First Instance ('CFI') upheld the Commission's Decision. This chapter addresses the current state of EC competition law[1] in view of these developments.

---

* Jean-François Bellis and Tim Kasten represented Microsoft on issues related to the tying infringement and the imposition of the monitoring mechanism throughout the proceedings discussed in this paper.

[1] Although the Microsoft Decision involved an infringement of Article 82 EC (which prohibits the abuse of a dominant position), tying can also constitute

2. THE COMMISSION'S DECISION

On 24 March 2004, the Commission adopted a Decision against Microsoft in Case COMP/C-3/37.792 – *Microsoft* (the 'Decision').[2] This Decision concluded that Microsoft committed two substantive infringements of Article 82 EC and Article 54 of the EEA Agreement (hereafter collectively 'Article 82 EC'), namely by (i) refusing to supply so-called 'Interoperability Information' and (ii) tying Windows Media Player with its client PC operating systems. This chapter focuses on the latter of these two infringements.

It is important to bear in mind that the Commission's Decision followed an own-initiative investigation.[3] The Commission never received a single complaint from third-party developers of media players or from any Microsoft customer regarding the event that triggered the abuse, namely Microsoft's decision to improve the media functionality already present in Windows by adding support to view digital content streamed over the Internet.[4] Further to its own-initiative investigation, the Commission adopted a Statement of Objections in August 2001, where, in the space of just over four pages, it accused Microsoft of infringing Article 82(b) and Article 82(d) EC by bundling Windows Media Player in Windows. Notably, the Statement of Objections did not cite to any market evidence to support its allegations, and there was no other indication that the

---

an infringement of Article 81 EC (which prohibits agreements that restrict competition by both dominant and non-dominant undertakings). See Commission Guidelines on Vertical Restraints [2000] OJ C291/1, para. 215.

2 A non-confidential copy of the Decision (as well as many other Commission materials related to the case) is available at http://ec.europa.eu/comm/competition/antitrust/cases/index/by_nr_75.html#i37_792.

3 See 'Commission concludes on Microsoft investigation, imposes conduct remedies and a fine', 24 March 2004, IP/04/382 ('In 2000, the Commission enlarged its investigation, on its own initiative, to study the effects of the tying of Microsoft's Windows Media Player with the company's Windows 2000 PC operating system').

4 See Decision, recitals 985-6, which note that the harm being addressed by the Commission was the fact that the functionality in Windows 'matched competitors' products'. Although this is not clearly stated in the Decision, the media functionality that was already uniformly present in Windows before Microsoft 'matched competitors' products' included the ability to play digital content on CDs or downloaded over the Internet, and the ability to stream digital content over high-bandwidth connections (support for Internet streaming consisted of the additional ability to stream digital content over the low-bandwidth connections available on dial-up Internet connections).

Commission carried out a market investigation before reaching its preliminary conclusion.

The case stalled throughout 2002,[5] a year which saw the CFI overturn three Commission decisions in concentration cases.[6] Following these setbacks, the Commission instituted a number of procedural reforms, including the creation of a 'Devil's advocate' panel to double-check its analysis.[7] Although the purpose of this panel was intended to improve the Commission's review of concentration cases, a panel was also created to double-check the Commission's analysis in the Microsoft proceedings, reflecting the importance of the case.

There is no public information available on the conclusions drawn by the Devil's advocate panel in the Microsoft case. Nevertheless, it is interesting to note that following the creation of this panel, the Commission carried out its first (and only) market investigation of the issues underlying the alleged tying infringement in the spring of 2003, following which it adopted a Supplementary Statement of Objections in August 2003.[8]

The full details of the Commission's market investigation are not identified in the Decision. Thus, there is no public information available to identify (i) all of the questions asked by the Commission,[9] or (ii) the results of this investigation. This information was, however, made available to Microsoft as part of its rights of access to the Commission's file. In addition, the Decision selectively quotes from some of the questions and responses received, providing further information.

One significant issue that was missing from the Commission's market investigation was whether there was demand for a version of Windows without the media functionality at issue. For example, the Commission

---

5 Although the Commission did begin to carry out a market investigation with respect to its allegations regarding Microsoft's refusal to supply 'interoperability information', no such investigation took place regarding its allegations of tying during this time. See Decision, recital 7.

6 Case T-342/99 *Airtours* v *Commission* [2002] ECR II-2585; Case T-301/01 *Schneider Electric* v *Commission* [2002] ECR II-4071; and Case T-5/02 *Tetra Laval* v *Commission* [2002] ECR II-4381.

7 See 'Last Stand for Mario Monti?', *BusinessWeek*, 17 November 2003, available at www.businessweek.com/magazine/content/03_46/b3858093_mz054.htm.

8 See Decision, recitals 9–10.

9 The Commission's request for information to content providers consisted of 62 questions, the request for information to content owners consisted of 61 questions, the request for information to trade associations consisted of 11 questions and the request for information to software developers consisted of 22 questions. Some, but not all, of these questions overlapped.

never asked original equipment manufacturers (OEMs) such as HP or Dell whether they had any interest in obtaining a version of Windows without this functionality, or whether they believed that end-users would have such an interest. The Commission also never asked business customers (who license Windows directly from Microsoft) whether they had an interest in such a product. Instead, as the Decision notes, the only questions asked were directed to 'content owners, content providers, software developers and associations of such companies'.[10]

The Commission's questionnaires involved a number of issues, including the choices made by content providers, content owners and software developers regarding the digital format(s) they support, the reasons for those choices, and whether the companies expected future changes. A particular focus was on why these companies chose Microsoft; questions about why these companies may have chosen another company were generally not asked. Although many of these questions were relevant to the Commission's analysis, however, it appears that the Commission never tabulated the results of all of its questions.[11]

Key responses that supported Microsoft's arguments were generally ignored in the August 2003 Statement of Objections and the Decision. For example, Microsoft had argued in response to the August 2001 Statement of Objections that the alleged tie did not lead to foreclosure because content providers and software developers remained free to rely on media formats and technologies other than those provided by Microsoft. Microsoft also submitted current evidence of numerous content owners and content providers who relied on RealNetworks' formats, and pointed out that usage of all formats (including those of Microsoft, RealNetworks and others) continued to increase despite the alleged infringement. The importance of this issue led the Commission to ask about the formats and technologies used by the respondents to its 2003 market enquiry. The responses received by the Commission revealed that the content owners and content providers who responded made

---

[10] See Decision, recital 9. It is not clear how the Commission chose the 46 companies who received these requests for information, of which 33 responded. Surprisingly, one of the 46 addressees of the request for information (and one of the 33 respondents) was RealNetworks, which had at this time already intervened in the proceedings in support of the Commission.

[11] As part of its rights of access to the Commission's file, Microsoft requested that the Commission provide it with any machine-readable tabulation of the results of the market enquiry (Microsoft routinely provided the Commission with tabulated results of its own surveys). The Commission informed Microsoft that it did not prepare a tabulation of its results.

such content available in, on average, three of the four major formats identified by the Commission. The market investigation also revealed that 11 of the 14 software developers who responded relied on at least two media technologies, with five supporting three (of the three that supported only one technology, one supported only Apple's QuickTime). These results, however, were not disclosed in the 2003 Statement of Objections (or elsewhere). They only became known to Microsoft after Microsoft was given access to the Commission's file at the time the 2003 Statement of Objections was issued and could independently tabulate the responses.[12]

In addition to providing a very selective reading of the results of its market investigation, the 2003 Statement of Objections also identified two alternative proposed remedies on which the Commission was seeking Microsoft's views. The first involved the 'untying' of Windows Media Player from Windows, whereby Microsoft would be required to offer a version of Windows without Windows Media Player included.[13] In the Commission's view, '[t]his is the normal remedy for a tying infringement'. The second remedy involved a 'must-carry' provision, whereby Microsoft would be obliged to offer competing media players with Windows. Ultimately, the Commission abandoned the 'must-carry' approach after Microsoft argued (i) that this remedy implied the existence of an infringement based on an essential facilities theory, the elements of which the Commission did not and could not establish, and (ii) that remedying a tying infringement with an obligation to engage in still more tying would involve numerous practical problems.[14]

After granting Microsoft the right to a hearing, which took place in November 2003, and after sending a 'letter of facts' to Microsoft in January 2004, the Commission adopted its Decision. The Decision, *inter alia*, confirmed the position taken in its August 2001 and August 2003 Statements of Objections that Microsoft infringed Article 82 EC by engaging in tying. In this regard, the Commission applied the following test, which is set out in recital 794 to the Decision:

---

12 In responding to the 2003 Statement of Objections, Microsoft also raised a number of other objections about the way in which the Commission reported on its market survey. For example, Microsoft identified that a number of statements supported its views and also pointed out that some quotations used by the Commission were taken out of context.

13 See 'Commission gives Microsoft last opportunity to comment before concluding its antitrust probe', 6 August 2003, IP/03/1150.

14 Among other problems, Microsoft noted that it may prove difficult to identify which media players should be carried without engaging in discrimination.

> Tying prohibited under Article 82 of the Treaty requires the presence of the following elements: (i) the tying and tied goods are two separate products; (ii) the undertaking concerned is dominant in the tying product market; (iii) the undertaking concerned does not give customers a choice to obtain the tying product without the tied product; and (iv) tying forecloses competition.

In addition to the above, a fifth element was recognized by the Commission in recital 961 to the Decision, namely the absence of an objective justification.

In recital 984, the Commission concluded that the tie 'violates the prohibition to abuse a dominant position enshrined in Article 82 of the Treaty and in particular point (d) of the second paragraph thereof' (recital 984). The reason that the Commission based its infringement on Article 82(d) 'in particular' appears to be because the Commission's August 2001 Statement of Objections alleged an infringement of that specific provision (the August 2003 Statement of Objections did 'not purport to cover abusive practices different from' the previous Statement of Objections), and the Commission cannot of course introduce a new legal basis in a Decision that was not identified in a previous Statement of Objections. Nevertheless, Article 2(b) of the operative part of the Decision created some confusion on this point, as it indicated that the Commission based its finding of an infringement on Article 82 generally, and not Article 82(d) in particular.

3. THE REMEDY

As a result of Microsoft's infringement, the Decision imposed as a remedy on Microsoft a requirement to develop a version of Windows without Windows Media Player. Microsoft was, however, expressly allowed to continue to offer the full-featured version which remained on the market. Thus, Article 6(a) of the 2004 Decision provided that 'Microsoft Corporation shall, within 90 days of the date of notification of this Decision, offer a full-functioning version of the Windows Client PC Operating System which does not incorporate Windows Media Player; Microsoft Corporation retains the right to offer a bundle of the Windows Client PC Operating System and Windows Media Player'.

Following the dismissal of Microsoft's application to suspend this requirement in Case T-201/04 R, Microsoft and the Commission engaged in a series of meetings and exchanged numerous letters to help clarify this requirement. The Commission ultimately provided very specific guidance to Microsoft, not only identifying which precise files were to be removed from this unbundled version, but also providing specific advice and recommendations on the name to be used (ultimately 'N')[15] and the language for the warning labels to be included on the retail box.

As reported in various news articles, this version of Windows has been completely rejected by the market.[16] This confirmed Microsoft's argument throughout the administrative proceedings that OEMs and end-users did not want a version of Windows that offered fewer features.

It has been argued that the failure of the remedy was predictable due to the fact that the Commission did not require Microsoft to impose a price difference between the full-featured version and the 'N' version of its operating systems. This criticism is based on a mistaken view of the record before the Commission. Rather than carrying out a market investigation to determine the views of Microsoft's customers (namely, OEMs, corporate customers and end-users), the Commission instead chose to rely exclusively on statements made by RealNetworks, which had separately brought litigation against Microsoft in the United States. RealNetworks claimed to the Commission that it had an interest in reaching exclusive agreements with OEMs.[17] Although Microsoft pointed out to the Commission that RealNetworks had elsewhere publicly stated that such agreements were not a high priority for the company, the Commission accepted RealNetworks' views without subjecting them to any independent critical review.[18]

It was therefore the Commission's view that third party media player

---

15 For example, the Commission criticized the names 'Windows XP Reduced Media Edition' and 'Windows XP without Windows Media Player', believing these names focused too much on the absence of this feature. Instead, the Commission suggested that Microsoft name the product with a neutral letter. Ultimately, the letter 'N' was offered and accepted, with an explanation on the package explaining that 'N' stands for 'not with Windows Media Player'.

16 See e.g. 'Microsoft says "EU version" of Windows Vista a dud', www.informationweek.com/news/internet/showArticle.jhtml?articleID=199700301.

17 RealNetworks could already reach non-exclusive agreements with OEMs to pre-install its media player during the relevant time.

18 In a March 2001 interview, Rob Glaser, the founder and CEO of RealNetworks, was asked: 'Were there things you thought were important starting out that turned out not to be?'. In response, Mr Glaser stated: 'I thought that [software] bundles with hardware for operating systems would be more important than they turned out to be. We did four or five deals with IBM, Gateway, Compaq – and these were hard deals to do – and they just didn't matter that much. No matter how many distribution deals like that we do, probably more than 90 percent of our users will come in and get our products and updates electronically'. See 'If I Knew Then What I Know Now: Rob Glaser vs. Goliath', *Business 2.0*, May 2001. Microsoft submitted this evidence to the Commission during its investigation, but it was not addressed in the Decision.

vendors such as RealNetworks would be interested in reaching agreements with OEMs. Since the Commission also understood that third-party media player vendors must generally pay OEMs for pre-installation agreements (whether exclusive or not), as it noted in recital 856 to the Decision, the Commission therefore assumed that the OEMs could derive additional income from the 'N' version of Windows because third-party media player vendors would pay them to enter into exclusive agreements. This assumption has turned out to be wrong.

Microsoft and RealNetworks ultimately negotiated a settlement to the US lawsuit prior to the CFI's judgment. Ironically, the agreement did not require Microsoft to offer the 'N' edition of Windows, but rather required Microsoft to further enhance its Windows Media platform such that RealNetworks could develop richer media experiences.

4. THE COURT OF FIRST INSTANCE'S JUDGMENT

Following the adoption of the Decision, Microsoft lodged an appeal before the CFI in an application dated 7 June 2004. This section of the chapter summarizes some of the key arguments raised by Microsoft, identifies the way in which the CFI assessed these arguments and highlights some important consequences of the CFI's judgment.

Legal Basis of the Tying Infringement

Microsoft's arguments

An initial claim raised by Microsoft was that the Commission failed to meet the specific requirements of Article 82(d) EC, on which it based its finding of an infringement. Among other arguments, Microsoft noted that Article 82(d) EC expressly required a showing that the alleged 'tying' and 'tied' product had no connection by their 'nature or according to commercial usage'.[19]

Microsoft pointed out that the Decision, however, did not even try to

---

[19] The CFI's summary of Microsoft's argument in this regard is capable of creating confusion. In paras 846 and 867 of the judgment, the CFI suggests that Microsoft was criticizing the Commission for adding a foreclosure requirement not expressly provided for in Article 82(d) EC. This was not Microsoft's argument. Microsoft's argument was that the Commission's need to separately identify the element of foreclosure in its new test demonstrated that it was not applying Article 82(d) EC because that provision does not require an independent finding of foreclosure.

meet this requirement, but simply concluded that an undertaking could be found to have infringed Article 82 EC even if the tie was in accordance with commercial usage, relying for support on the judgment in *Tetra Pak II*[20] (see recital 961).

Microsoft did not dispute the Commission's argument that the Court of Justice concluded in *Tetra Pak II* that an undertaking could be found to have engaged in a tie under Article 82 even if the tie was in accordance with commercial usage. Microsoft noted, however, that *Tetra Pak II* involved an infringement that was based on Article 82 generally, and not Article 82(d) in particular. Thus, in the paragraph cited by the Commission, the Court of Justice was merely rejecting Tetra Pak's attempt to reclassify the case as an infringement under Article 82(d) specifically, noting that the Commission could properly rely on a theory based on Article 82 generally:

> It must, moreover, be stressed that the list of abusive practices set out in the second paragraph of Article [82] of the Treaty is not exhaustive. Consequently, even where tied sales of two products are in accordance with commercial usage or there is a natural link between the two products in question, such sales may still constitute abuse within the meaning of Article [82] unless they are objectively justified. The reasoning of the Court of First Instance in paragraph 137 of its judgment is not therefore in any way defective.

In other words, Microsoft pointed out that the Court of Justice rejected Tetra Pak's argument on the ground that the Commission was entitled to find a tying infringement outside the specific circumstances identified in Article 82(d). However, the Court of Justice did not address whether the Commission could disregard some of the elements of Article 82(d) when the Commission expressly based the finding of an infringement on that specific provision.

The CFI judgment

In its judgment, the CFI concluded that Microsoft's claim was '*purely semantic*' (CFI judgment, paragraph 850). Generally repeating the Commission's arguments without addressing Microsoft's response, the CFI noted that the abusive practices set out in Article 82 EC do not provide an exhaustive list (CFI judgment, paragraph 860), a point that Microsoft did not dispute. The CFI also accepted the Commission's claim that it had based its finding of infringement on Article 82 generally as well

---

20 Case C-333/94 P *Tetra Pak* v *Commission* [1996] ECR I-5951, para. 37.

as Article 82(d) specifically, concluding that the Commission was correct to do so (CFI judgment, paragraph 861).[21]

The CFI next addressed Microsoft's argument that the Commission failed to meet all of the elements of Article 82(d). The CFI's assessment of this issue was very brief, and it simply noted that the elements of the tying test actually applied by the Commission 'coincide effectively with the conditions laid down in Article 82(d) EC' (CFI judgment, paragraph 862).

Accordingly, regardless of whether the Commission applies Article 82(d) in particular, or Article 82 generally, the CFI's judgment makes it clear that an undertaking will be found to have engaged in illegal tying where the following elements are met:

(i) the tying and tied goods are two separate products;
(ii) the undertaking concerned is dominant in the tying product market;[22]
(iii) the undertaking concerned does not give customers a choice to obtain the tying product without the tied product;
(iv) tying forecloses competition; and
(v) the tie is not objectively justified.

Broader consequences of the CFI judgment

The way in which the CFI addressed Microsoft's arguments is interesting insofar as it suggests that a finding of an infringement of Article 82 EC can be upheld even where the Commission does not strictly meet all the requisite elements of the legal tests it purports to apply. Although the CFI accepted the Commission's argument that it based the finding on an infringement on Article 82 generally, it was not disputed that the Commission also based its finding on Article 82(d) specifically. Nevertheless, the CFI upheld this separate finding as well, despite the fact that the Commission had taken the view that it did not need to meet one of the express conditions set out in Article 82(d).

Accordingly, where the Commission does base a finding of an infringement on a specific provision of the Treaty, 'semantic' arguments based on a literal reading of the elements identified in that provision would seem unlikely to prevail if the CFI's judgment is to be followed in future cases.

---

[21] Despite having concluded that the Commission changed its legal basis to Article 82 generally as well as Article 82(d) specifically in the Decision, the CFI did not consider whether such a change was appropriate in light of the fact that the Statements of Objections relied exclusively on Article 82(b) and (d).

[22] Microsoft did not challenge the finding of dominance in the client PC operating system market, and therefore this element is not discussed further in this chapter.

The Existence of Two Products

Microsoft's arguments

Microsoft argued that the Commission failed to establish the existence of two products because the alleged tying product (the Windows PC operating system) and alleged tied product (Windows Media Player) constitute a single, integrated product. According to Microsoft, Windows Media Player is one of many integrated features in Windows.

Microsoft pointed out that this requirement obliged the Commission to properly define two distinct product markets. Accordingly, Microsoft argued that the Commission must establish a distinct product market for the tied product (Internet streaming media players) and a distinct product market for the tying product without the tied product (client PC operating systems without this functionality).[23] Although Microsoft did not dispute the existence of a distinct market for the tied product, it argued that the Commission failed to establish the existence of a distinct market for the tying product without the tied product.

In this respect, Microsoft referred to the sale of shoes with laces, an example used by the Commission itself in its Vertical Restraints Guidelines. It is undeniably true that there is a distinct market for laces without shoes. However, one cannot infer from this the existence of a distinct market for shoes without laces. Instead, one must carry out a normal market definition analysis, which looks primarily to customer demand. Since an inappreciable number of customers (if any) want to buy shoes without laces, one cannot properly define a relevant market for such a product. Instead, the market must be defined in accordance with customer demand, which shows that the market is properly defined as shoes with laces. Thus, even

---

[23] In fact, even this test may be unduly restrictive, as it focuses on historic demand and could force dominant undertakings to freeze products in their current state. Thus, this test should arguably also include a factor requiring the Commission to take into account whether, in the foreseeable future, there is likely to be demand for the alleged tying product without the alleged tied product. Indeed, the Commission itself acknowledged in recital 808 to the Decision that its test could risk 'ignoring efficiency benefits from new product integration', but went on to note that this is not a concern here because in 'the case of WMP, however, there is non-insignificant consumer demand for alternative players some four years after Microsoft started tying its streaming media players with Windows'. It is also notable that, in n. 938 of the Decision, the Commission suggests that integration which causes complete foreclosure (as the Commission claims occurred after Microsoft included support for the mouse-driven interface in Windows) would demonstrate that the foreclosed functionality is part of Windows, and thus there is no tying.

though there is distinct demand for laces without shoes, and even though producers of laces would undoubtedly prefer that shoes are sold with laces separately, it would be absurd to treat the sale of shoes with laces as a tying practice. The Commission expressly embraced that view in its Vertical Restraints Guidelines,[24] where it stated:

> What is to be considered as a distinct product is determined, first of all, by the demand of the buyers. Two products are distinct if, in the absence of tying, from the buyers' perspective the products are purchased by them on two different markets. For instance, since customers want to buy shoes with laces, it has become commercial usage for shoe manufacturers to supply shoes with laces. Therefore, the sale of shoes with laces is not a tying practice.

Microsoft repeatedly pointed out during both the administrative and judicial proceedings that there is no evidence that any of its customers (home users, corporate customers or OEMs)[25] want to obtain PC operating systems without the streaming media functionality at issue. The Commission simply refused to investigate this issue by making enquiries of such customers.[26] Accordingly, in Microsoft's view, the Commission could not properly conclude that there is a distinct tying market for client PC operating systems without this streaming media functionality.

The Commission's primary response to Microsoft's argument was to slightly amend this element of the tying test. Rather than seeking to establish that 'the tying and tied goods are two separate products', as it initially set out in its test in recital 794, the Commission instead looked exclusively at whether there is a distinct market for the 'tied' product, reasoning that

---

24 See Commission Guidelines on Vertical Restraints [2000] OJ C291/1, para. 216.

25 Microsoft's Windows is licensed directly to end-users (home users via retail and corporate customers) and licensed to original equipment manufacturers (OEMs) such as Dell and HP for sale in the EEA (see Decision, recital 1011).

26 Instead, in recital 807 to the Decision, the Commission limited itself to hypothesizing that such demand might exist on the basis of two factors. First, it identified a program that allegedly allowed end-users to remove Windows Media Player. Notwithstanding the fact that this argument directly contradicted the Commission's separate finding that Windows Media Player could not be removed (see e.g. recital 824), there was no evidence that the program worked in the way the Commission believed and there was no evidence that it was ever used. Secondly, the Commission claimed that some corporate customers would not want the 'bundled' version because they do not want their employees to use media players at work. However, it provided no support for this claim (e.g. it did not identify any particular company with such an interest), nor did it assess whether such demand was significant enough to justify defining a distinct market for such a product.

one can infer from this a distinct market for the 'tying' product without the 'tied' product. In support of its interpretation, the Commission tried to draw on the judgments of the CFI in *Hilti*[27] and *Tetra Pak II*.[28] According to the Commission, the CFI rejected similar '*integrative*' arguments raised by Hilti and Tetra Pak, concluding that tying existed under Article 82 EC simply because 'there existed independent manufacturers who specialised in the manufacture of the tied product, a fact which indicated that there was separate consumer demand and hence a distinct market for the tied product' (Decision, recital 802).

In reply to this claim, Microsoft noted that the Commission's analysis failed to appreciate the fundamental differences between the Microsoft case, on the one hand, and *Hilti* and *Tetra Pak II*, on the other hand. In *Hilti* and *Tetra Pak II*, it was commonly accepted that there was distinct demand for the 'tying' product without the 'tied' product. The fact that customers purchased third-party consumables for use with Hilti's and Tetra Pak's primary products (nail guns/nail cartridges and liquid packaging machines) necessarily demonstrated that customers wanted to obtain the primary products without the consumables (nails and drinks cartons), because the consumables were homogenous[29] products purchased separately. In contrast, the media functionality in Windows and third-party media players are not homogeneous,[30] are not consumables and are offered for free. Thus, customers can, and frequently do, use multiple media players. Accordingly, unlike the situations in *Hilti* and *Tetra Pak II*, consumer demand for the 'tied' product from a third party in the Microsoft case does not logically demonstrate that consumers do not want the alleged 'tying' product with the alleged 'tied' product. It is not a 'zero-sum' situation in which an increase in demand for one media player

---

[27] Case T-30/89 *Hilti AG* v *Commission* [1991] ECR II-1439.

[28] Case T-83/91 *Tetra Pak International SA* v *Commission* [1994] ECR II-755.

[29] In this context, 'homogenous' products are products that do not vary in their essential characteristics. While there may be differences in quality, nails and cartons are essentially identical to other nails and cartons, respectively, as they serve the same purpose.

[30] For example, different media players support different media formats. Thus, an end-user wanting to play a file encoded in RealNetworks' format must have RealNetworks' media player installed because RealNetworks has no commercial interest in licensing its formats for use with other media players. End-users interested in playing the widest number of formats will therefore want more media players. In addition, end-users will prefer the 'look and feel' of certain media players more than others depending on the use to which the media player is put.

necessarily results in a corresponding loss of demand for another media player. Instead, consumers generally will want both.

The Commission also argued that, to the extent that end-users do want PC operating systems with streaming media functionality, such demand can be met by OEMs. According to recital 959 to the Decision, 'OEMs act as purchasing agents for consumers in providing such bundles', and thus the choice of whether to include the media functionality in Windows or a third-party media player should be left to the OEMs.

Microsoft argued that the Commission's conclusion is based on two fundamental mistakes. First, the Commission's argument is factually incorrect because it is based on the notion that third-party media players can easily replace the media functionality in Windows. In actuality, however, even if third-party media players provide comparable end-user functionality, they cannot replace the platform functionality in Windows. Every developer designs software to work in a slightly different way, which means that the programming interfaces available to third parties will differ depending on the developer. Thus, third-party programs and websites that rely on the media functionality in Windows would not work correctly if this media functionality was removed and replaced with a third-party media player—programs and websites that rely specifically on Windows programming interfaces require the presence of that specific functionality in Windows. Indeed, the Commission itself acknowledged this point in recital 454 to the Decision, where it recognized that third-party programs that rely on the functionality in Windows require the presence of Microsoft-specific functionality.

Secondly, Microsoft also claimed that the Commission's argument is wrong as a matter of principle. Even dominant companies must be allowed to design their products to meet customer demand and match the offerings of competitors. They should not be required to rely on independent third parties to build the final product out of a series of different components from different sources. If customers demand operating systems with media functionality and all significant competitors offer operating systems with media functionality, nothing in Article 82 EC should restrict Microsoft's freedom to meet this demand itself.

Finally, Microsoft pointed out that the failure of the remedy confirmed its arguments about the lack of demand for Windows without this media functionality. To comply with the requirements of Article 6 of the Decision, Microsoft had made available a version of Windows without the media functionality at issue. In response to this offer, no OEMs expressed an interest, and there was a similar lack of demand for this product in the retail channel.

The CFI judgment

In its judgment, the CFI began by recognizing that what initially appear to be separate products may be regarded as forming a single product over time (CFI judgment, paragraph 913). However, since the CFI also concluded that the issue of whether products were distinct had to be assessed at the time the infringement began (CFI judgment, paragraph 914), the ability to apply such a forward-looking analysis would seem very limited in practice.

The CFI also agreed that the distinctness of products for the purpose of Article 82 EC 'has to be assessed by reference to customer demand' (CFI judgment, paragraph 917). For these purposes, however, the CFI agreed with the Commission that the reference to 'customer demand' in tying cases simply meant that there must be separate demand for the tied product (thus, it is irrelevant whether there is also demand for the tying product without the tied product). The CFI supported this view with three arguments.

First, the CFI stated that the Commission's approach was supported by the *Hilti* and *Tetra Pak II* cases (CFI judgment, paragraph 920). Notably, the CFI did not address Microsoft's arguments distinguishing these cases.

Secondly, the CFI argued that accepting Microsoft's position that there must be distinct demand for the tying product without the tied product would be tantamount to 'contending that complementary products cannot constitute separate products' (CFI judgment, paragraph 921). In this regard, the CFI noted that '[i]n the case of complementary products, such as client PC operating systems and application software, it is quite possible that customers will wish to obtain the products together, but from different sources' (CFI judgment, paragraph 921). In addition, the CFI argued that regard should be had to 'the particular intermediary role played by OEMs', which would themselves be able to meet any consumer demand for client PC operating systems with pre-installed media players (CFI judgment, paragraph 923).

Thirdly, the CFI argued that, in any event, the Commission rightly observed in recital 807 to the Decision that 'there exists a demand for client PC operating systems without streaming media players'. According to the CFI, such demand exists 'for example by companies afraid that their staff might use [streaming media players] for non-work-related purposes', a point it claimed that Microsoft did not dispute (CFI judgment, paragraph 924).[31]

---

[31] In fact, and as summarized above, Microsoft did dispute this point in its submissions to the CFI. The CFI even seemed to acknowledge this argument

Finally, the CFI rejected Microsoft's attempt to introduce new evidence regarding the ineffectiveness of the remedy. The CFI reasoned that such evidence could not be relied on because, *inter alia*, the lawfulness of a Community measure must be assessed on the basis of the facts existing at the time the measure was adopted (CFI judgment, paragraph 943).

Broader consequences of the CFI judgment

The CFI's reasoning on the 'two products' element is particularly noteworthy insofar as it concludes for the first time that there are circumstances in which the Commission is entitled to define relevant product markets with no regard to whether there is customer demand for those products.[32] Thus, the CFI concluded that the Commission could define the 'tying' product even in the absence of a specific finding that this 'tying' product constituted a relevant product market.

This is a very broad-reaching conclusion, as it would seem to apply to any number of products. For example, to return to the example used in the Commission's Vertical Restraints Guidelines, it no longer seems correct to conclude that the sale of shoes without laces is not a tying practice on the grounds that there is insufficient demand for shoes without laces. Instead, the relevant issue would seem to be that, since shoes and laces are complementary products, and since there is distinct demand for laces apart from shoes, shoes without laces can be deemed to constitute a relevant product market for purposes of tying. The same conclusion can be reached to define a relevant market for mobile telephones without integrated features such as novelty ring tones, games and cameras, or for newspapers without classified advertisements and crossword puzzles.

It is also noteworthy that the CFI rejected Microsoft's test based on the potential precedent that it alleged would be created. Thus, the CFI concluded that Microsoft's test must be rejected because it would mean

---

(albeit very briefly) in para. 892 of the judgment, where it summarized one of Microsoft's arguments as follows: 'In the present case, moreover, the Commission has never identified a customer wishing to obtain what is alleged to be the tying product without what is alleged to be the tied product'. Given its statement that Microsoft did not dispute this fact, it is unsurprising that the CFI failed to address Microsoft's arguments on this point.

32 It should be noted that the Commission also identified a number of other factors to support its finding that Windows and Windows Media Player constituted distinct products, the relevance of which were challenged by Microsoft. The CFI accepted the Commission's argument that these other factors 'demonstrate the existence of separate consumer demand for streaming media players' (CFI judgment, para. 925).

that complementary products could never constitute distinct products. It should be noted that Microsoft disputed this interpretation of its argument when it was first raised by the Commission in its Defence. Microsoft argued that its interpretation of the customer demand test (which involved the assessment of demand for the tying product without the tied product) was capable of distinguishing between complementary products, as had been done in *Hilti* and *Tetra Pak II*. However, the CFI did not address these arguments, and instead merely endorsed the concerns expressed by the Commission. Interestingly, however, while the CFI was willing to accept this precedent-based argument by the Commission, it regarded an attempt to raise a similar precedent-based argument as 'hypothetical' and 'speculative' when raised by Microsoft (see below).

Finally, the Microsoft judgment raises the interesting issue of whether and when new evidence can be relied on to either challenge or defend a Commission Decision. At the time of the Decision, the Commission's file did not contain any evidence about the existence of potential demand for a version of Windows without Windows Media Player. This was because, first, Microsoft did not offer such a product and, secondly, the Commission did not carry out any investigation by which it asked Microsoft's customers about their interest in such a product. For its part, the Commission did not appear to have any concerns about the use of evidence that post-dated its Decision, at least when it favoured its case. Indeed, it was the Commission and not Microsoft that initially raised the issue about potential demand for Windows XP N, the version that Microsoft created to comply with the Decision. Thus, in footnote 230 of its Rejoinder, the Commission cited to press reports and claimed that OEMs HP and Toshiba were planning to offer this version.[33] Accordingly, the Commission had obviously taken the view that such evidence was relevant to the case.[34]

It also appears that the CFI itself accepted that there are occasions where developments that post-date the Decision can be relied on, at least for purposes of defending a Decision. For example, the CFI relied

[33] Microsoft did not have the right to respond to this argument in writing. Nevertheless, during the oral hearing (which took place about ten months later), Microsoft rebutted this argument by noting that no OEM had offered, or was offering, Windows XP N. In addition, Microsoft noted that demand through the retail channel was also virtually non-existent.

[34] The Commission also referred to other post-Decision developments to defend against claims that Microsoft raised in its application for annulment. For example, in response to Microsoft's claim that there was no clear meaning of Windows Media Player, the Commission referred to correspondence that Microsoft and the Commission exchanged on this topic in the period following the Decision.

on post-Decision developments to reject Microsoft's argument that the removal of Windows Media Player from Windows would entail the degrading of the operating system. Thus, in paragraph 1165 of its judgment, the CFI stated 'The Court further notes that, pursuant to the remedy prescribed in Article 6(a) of the contested decision, Microsoft placed on the market a version of Windows without Windows Media Player and that that version is fully functional'.

Lack of Customer Choice/Coercion

Microsoft's arguments

Microsoft also argued that the third element of the Commission's test (i.e. that the undertaking concerned does not give customers a choice to obtain the tying product without the tied product) was incorrectly applied by the Commission. In Microsoft's view, this element is intended to reflect whether there is consumer harm, of which there was none because end-users are not required to pay anything extra for the media functionality in Windows, are not required to use the media functionality in Windows, and are not restricted from using third-party media players instead of, or in addition to, the media functionality in Windows.

The CFI judgment

In its judgment, the CFI concluded that it was irrelevant that Microsoft did not charge a separate price (CFI judgment, paragraphs 968–9) or force customers to use the functionality (CFI judgment, paragraph 970). Instead, all that mattered was that customers were unable to acquire the Windows client PC operating system without the Windows Media Player (CFI judgment, paragraph 961).

Broader consequences of the CFI judgment

This aspect of the test for tying would appear to be readily fulfilled. In virtually all products that incorporate different features, customers are not given the choice to obtain the 'tying' product without the 'tied' product.

Foreclosure

Microsoft's arguments

Microsoft argued that its case was unlike all previous tying cases in that the conduct at issue did not directly foreclose any third parties. Thus, the existence of the media functionality in Windows did not prevent users from obtaining, installing and using any third-party media player of their choosing, nor did it prevent OEMs from pre-installing as many third-party media players as they wished to install. In contrast, the tying at issue in *Tetra Pak II* involved a contractual provision that required buyers of carton-filling equipment sold by Tetra Pak to buy all their requirements of cartons from Tetra Pak. As already discussed above, this directly foreclosed third parties because every carton that Tetra Pak forced a customer to take was one carton less for Tetra Pak's competitors to sell to that customer.

As Microsoft pointed out, it was not alone in seeing the uniqueness of this case. The Commission itself candidly admitted that the case differed from what it referred to as 'classical' tying cases like *Hilti* and *Tetra Pak II*. Thus, in recital 841 to the Decision, the Commission noted:

> While in classical tying cases, the Commission and Courts considered the foreclosure effect for competing vendors to be demonstrated by the bundling of a separate product with the dominant product, in the case at issue, users can and do to a certain extent obtain third party media players through the Internet, sometimes for free. There are therefore indeed good reasons not to assume without further analysis that tying WMP constitutes conduct which by its very nature is liable to foreclose competition. (Emphasis in original.)

Thus, the Commission's foreclosure theory in the Microsoft case was not based on the same type of direct foreclosure found in cases like *Hilti* and *Tetra Pak II*. Given that Microsoft's conduct had no obvious consequences on the ability of end-users to acquire and use third-party media players, a further analysis of the market context was necessary to determine whether the conduct was liable to foreclose third-party media players. The Commission explained its theory in recital 842 to the Decision as follows:

> In the following sections, it will be explained why tying in this specific case has the potential to foreclose competition so that the maintenance of an effective competitive structure is put at risk. In a nutshell, tying WMP with the dominant Windows makes WMP the platform of choice for complementary content and applications which in turn risks foreclosing competition in the market for media players.

In other words, the Commission believed that Microsoft's tie did not lead to foreclosure *per se* because of its direct effects on customers and end-users. Instead, the Commission believed that Microsoft's tie led to foreclosure because of its effects on independent developers of content and applications, who would make Windows Media Player the 'platform of choice'.

The Commission believed that Windows Media Player would become the platform of choice based on the premises that it costs more to rely on multiple formats and technologies (recitals 883, 893–4) and that a technology's reach is an important factor in deciding whether to rely on that technology (recitals 886, 895–6). In other words, given the assumption that independent developers of content and applications will want to maximize their distribution at the lowest possible cost, and given Microsoft's ubiquity, developers of content and applications will choose Microsoft's formats and technologies (recital 892). Finally, as more developers of content and applications choose Microsoft's formats and technologies, the possibility of market entry will become difficult (recital 891).

As noted above, the Commission tested this hypothesis in the market investigation it carried out in 2003. This investigation revealed, however, that independent developers of content and applications were not making Windows Media Player the 'platform of choice', despite the passage of four years from the start of the alleged infringement. Instead, as also noted above, content owners and content providers supported on average three of the four major formats identified by the Commission, and 11 of 14 software developers supported at least two media technologies (with five supporting three, and one supporting only Apple's QuickTime).

Microsoft argued that these results undermined the premises of the Commission's reasoning. For example, with respect to the issue of costs, Microsoft argued that the Commission focused on the wrong question. The question was not simply whether it costs more to rely on multiple formats and technologies, but rather whether the benefits of doing so offset the costs.[35]

Instead of further investigating this issue, however, the Commission stuck by its theory. Although the Commission accepted that Windows Media Player had not yet become the platform of choice, it nevertheless concluded that this did not invalidate its assumption that it might at some indeterminate point in the future. This prospective analysis was set forth in recital 890 to its Decision as follows:

> This trend [in favour of encoding in Windows Media formats] is not invalidated by Microsoft's reference to the fact that the majority of content owners and content developers presently still support multiple formats. As long as third party media players' usage is still significant, the trade-off of supporting

---

[35] As Microsoft explained, focusing only on costs would lead one to conclude that retail stores should only stock one model and brand of each product, since it obviously costs more to stock additional models and brands. However, the fact that retail stores stock multiple versions of many products demonstrates that the benefits of doing so outweigh the costs. Similarly, the fact that the Commission's own market surveys showed that content providers, content owners and software developers relied on multiple formats and technologies must indicate that the benefits of doing so outweigh the costs.

> additional formats may indeed be positive for providers of complementary content and software. The same holds true for software developers. Entity T25 states that '[w]e are willing to incur these additional costs to offer consumers a media player software that plays a large variety of file formats as long as it is necessary to reach the overall majority of consumers. This might change if one Technology will have gained such a strong position that additional Technologies will have become more or less irrelevant'. Furthermore, some respondents further qualify their support of other formats than Windows Media: '[Company] currently only offers support for Windows Media formats in a prominent way. Some but not all services still offer some support for Real formats'. When asked whether the additional costs of multiple format support are in the future likely to influence companies' decisions on whether to develop applications for Technologies other than Windows Media, 12 out of 13 software developers state that this is the case. (Internal footnotes omitted.)

Microsoft argued that the Commission should be subject to a particularly high burden of proof if it was allowed to apply such a prospective theory under Article 82 EC, given that it is inherently difficult to predict the future (as recognized in *Tetra Laval*)[36] and violations of Article 82 are sanctioned by potentially very large fines. Microsoft also argued that the Commission committed serious errors in making its predictions by failing to consider all the relevant factors necessary to support them (e.g. the Commission did not assess in its Decision whether the costs of relying on multiple formats and technologies outweighed the benefits of doing so).

In addition, Microsoft pointed out that the Commission's theory of how the market operated was undermined by its own analysis in the *AOL/TimeWarner* merger case. In that case (which was decided in 2000, one year after Microsoft's alleged tying abuse began), the Commission analysed whether AOL/TimeWarner could become dominant in the market for media players given that AOL owned the media player Winamp and TimeWarner had a large music catalogue. In assessing this issue, the Commission considered what would result if the merged entity exclusively encoded TimeWarner's content in a format supported only by Winamp. Based on the reasoning underlying the Commission's foreclosure theory

---

[36] See Case C-12/03 P *Commission* v *Tetra Laval* [2005] ECR I-987, para. 44, where the Court noted that predictions about events supposed to occur over a lengthy period of time in the future were difficult to make because they rely on 'chains of cause and effect [which] are dimly discernible, uncertain and difficult to establish'. Notably, the predictions at issue in that case were to take place within four years, the same amount of time as that which elapsed between the starting date of the tying infringement in Microsoft and the Commission's market investigation. Since no changes had yet occurred, the Commission's prediction was therefore meant to cover a period much longer than four years.

against Microsoft, one would have expected the Commission to conclude that such a prospect was unlikely because AOL/TimeWarner, like other content providers, would be inexorably led to encode its content in a media format supported by Windows given its reach. This is not, however, what the Commission concluded. Instead, the Commission concluded that AOL/TimeWarner could successfully adopt a strategy of encoding its content exclusively in a format supported by Winamp, leading Winamp, rather than Windows Media Player, to 'shortly become the most popular player in the world'.[37] Notably, the AOL/TimeWarner Decision makes no mention of the so-called 'ubiquity of Windows Media Player' as a factor that could impede this process. The Commission apparently dismissed this concern on the grounds that 'music players can be freely and easily downloaded on a PC, which may support more than one player'.[38]

As events have unfolded, the Commission's market analysis in *AOL/TimeWarner* has proven to be more accurate than that in the Microsoft case. The ease with which media players can be downloaded means that even those content providers who encode in a single format are not necessarily driven to Windows Media formats. Indeed, since the time of the Decision, Adobe's Flash Player, which the Commission did not even include in its market analysis, has increased its market share at a rapid rate, and, according to a study commissioned by Adobe, has overtaken Windows Media Player.[39] According to Adobe's website, 'Adobe® Flash® Player is the world's most pervasive software platform, used by over 2 million professionals and reaching 99% of Internet-enabled desktops in mature markets as well as a wide range of devices'.[40] Adobe's success is consistent with the Commission's conclusion in *AOL/TimeWarner* that the widespread distribution of media functionality in Windows would not drive content providers to use Windows Media formats. Indeed, as Microsoft pointed out, the Commission itself exclusively encoded its video streaming content in RealNetworks' format at the time of the Decision, despite its obvious interest in ensuring the widest possible dissemination of information on its activities (the Commission has now also created

37 Case COMP/M.1845 – *AOL/TimeWarner*, 11 October 2000, para. 63.

38 *AOL/TimeWarner*, para. 63

39 This undermines the Commission's claim that 'Microsoft's media player format has, as a result of its conduct, come to dominate the market'. See Introductory Remarks on Court of First Instance Ruling on Microsoft's Abuse of Dominant Market Position, SPEECH/07/539.

40 This is based on a survey conducted by Millward Brown in September 2008, available at www.adobe.com/products/player_census/flashplayer/.

a YouTube channel, which, like all content available on YouTube, is encoded exclusively in Flash formats).

Finally, Microsoft challenged the Commission's conclusion that any supposed standardization on the Windows Media format would cause a reduction in the usage of third-party media players. The Commission argued that '[o]nce complementary software is encoded in the proprietary Windows media formats, it can only be played back on independent vendors' media players if Microsoft chooses to license its technology' (recital 881). In fact, Microsoft did license this technology at no cost, something the Commission acknowledged in its Decision (see e.g. recital 892). Thus, third parties can and do develop alternative media player applications that can play all content encoded in the Windows Media formats. Accordingly, even if the Windows Media format became an industry standard, *quod non*, third parties such as RealNetworks could still develop their own media players capable of playing such content.

The CFI judgment

The CFI largely rejected Microsoft's arguments, concluding that most were based on an incorrect interpretation of the Commission's foreclosure theory (CFI judgment, paragraph 1033). According to the CFI, the Commission's foreclosure theory consists of three stages (CFI judgment, paragraphs 978, 979, 983, 988):

> In the first stage, [the Commission] establishes that the tied sale ensures that Windows Media Player is ubiquitous on client PCs worldwide (recitals 843 to 878 to the contested decision) . . .
>
> In the second stage, the Commission examines the effects of that bundling on content providers and software developers, and on certain adjacent markets (recitals 879 to 899 to the contested decision). The Commission considers, in substance, that in view of the indirect network effects that obtain in the media player market, the 'ubiquitous presence of the [Windows Media Player] code provides [that media player] with a significant competitive advantage, which is liable to have a harmful effect on the structure of competition in that market' (recital 878 to the contested decision) . . .
>
> Last, in the third stage, the Commission examines market development in the light of market surveys carried out by Media Metrix, Synovate and Nielsen/NetRatings (recitals 900 to 944 to the contested decision). In substance, the data obtained in those surveys 'consistently point to a trend in favour of usage of [Windows Media Player] and Windows Media formats to the detriment of the main competing media players (and media player technologies)' (recital 944 to the contested decision).

According to the CFI, Microsoft's arguments are based on a 'selective and inaccurate reading of the contested decision' because they 'essentially focus on the second of the three stages of the Commission's reasoning'

(CFI judgment, paragraph 1033). Thus, the CFI concludes that the second stage of the Commission's test is superfluous, and that Microsoft's arguments are largely irrelevant because they essentially focus on that stage of the analysis.[41]

According to the CFI, the Commission could correctly conclude that Microsoft's bundling had the inevitable consequence of altering the balance of competition in favour of Microsoft (CFI judgment, paragraph 1034). While Microsoft had argued that the Commission itself accepted that the effects of any tie did not lead to foreclosure *per se* because customers and end-users could obtain and use multiple media players, the CFI reached the opposite conclusion. According to the CFI, 'the Commission's findings in the first stage of its reasoning are in themselves sufficient to establish that the fourth constituent element of abusive bundling is present in this case' (CFI judgment, paragraph 1058).

This was because the CFI concluded that the tie afforded Microsoft ubiquity 'which cannot be counterbalanced by the other methods of distributing media players' (CFI judgment, paragraph 1036). The CFI disagreed with Microsoft's argument that any initial ubiquity it enjoyed would not matter, as customers could easily obtain and use third-party media players. In this regard, the CFI argued that 'it is clear that, as the Commission correctly states at recital 845 to the contested decision, "[u]sers who find [Windows Media Player] pre-installed on their client PCs are indeed in general less likely to use alternative media players as they already have an application which delivers media streaming and playback functionality"' (CFI judgment, paragraph 1041).[42]

The CFI noted that 'the Commission was correct to state, at recital 857

---

41 Notably, President Vesterdorf reached the opposite conclusion in his Order in Case T-201/04 R, which addressed Microsoft's request for the suspension of the Decision. In para. 399 of that Order, President Vesterdorf summarized the Commission's foreclosure theory as follows: 'In the present case, the Commission considered, essentially, that the anti-competitive effect of the tying was the result of "indirect network effects". Those effects related to the fact that the presence of Windows Media Player in all the operating systems distributed by Windows gives content providers and applications manufacturers an incentive to design their products on the basis of Windows Media Player (recital 842). For the purpose of demonstrating that fact, the Commission relied largely on present or past factual material relating to the incentives for content providers and software developers (recitals 879 to 896). None the less, as may be seen in particular from recitals 842 and 984 to the Decision, that material supports what is at least in part a prospective analysis of the risks for competition resulting from the impugned practice'.

42 The CFI did not address Microsoft's argument that, as the Commission itself acknowledged elsewhere in the Decision, third-party media players cannot replace the functionality in Windows, as these products are not homogenous (the

to the contested decision, that the impugned conduct created disincentives for OEMs to ship third-party media players on their client PCs' (CFI judgment, paragraph 1043). In this regard, the CFI argued that 'OEMs are reluctant to add a second media player to the package which they offer consumers, as a second media player uses hard-disk capacity on the client PC while offering functionality similar, in essence, to that of Windows Media Player and when it is unlikely that consumers will be prepared to pay a higher price for such a bundle' (CFI judgment, paragraph 1044).[43] In addition, the CFI argued that 'the presence of several media players on the same client PC creates a risk of confusion on the part of users and an increase in customer support and testing costs', and 'Microsoft itself emphasised that OEMs generally operate on thin profit margins and that they would therefore prefer to avoid having to bear such costs' (CFI judgment, paragraph 1045).[44]

Significantly, the CFI did accept Microsoft's arguments that 'a number of OEMs continue to add third-party media players', and also noted that it was 'also common ground that the number of media players and the extent of the use of multiple players are continually increasing' (CFI judgment, paragraph 1055). The CFI, however, did not address Microsoft's claim that this demonstrated that OEMs were interested in installing more, not fewer, media players, and that third-party media player vendors themselves had no interest in reaching 'exclusivity' arrangements of the type that the Decision was meant to allow.

Instead, the CFI reasoned that this evidence did 'not invalidate the Commission's conclusion that the impugned conduct was likely to weaken competition within the meaning of the case-law' (CFI judgment, paragraph

---

Commission's concession of this point is reproduced briefly in para. 1132 of the judgment). This issue is discussed further below.

[43] The CFI did not address Microsoft's argument that there are no such hard disk problems. As Microsoft pointed out in its submissions, there are no hard disk capacity problems involved in installing third-party media players because, at a size of approximately 10 megabytes, third party media players constitute only .025% of the size of a normal modern-sized hard disk (which was 40 gigabytes at the time of the proceedings, and has since continually increased). The Court also did not address Microsoft's claim that the Commission did not itself investigate this point, but instead simply referred to findings made in the US proceedings regarding other functionality (see Decision, recital 851 and n.1000).

[44] While Microsoft did not dispute the claim that OEMs face increased customer support and testing costs by adding additional software, it did argue that these same costs would have to be borne by OEMs regardless of whether they chose the full-featured version of Windows or a version without Windows Media Player.

1055). In this regard, the CFI pointed out that 'the data mentioned at recitals 905 to 926 to the contested decision show a clear tendency in favour of using Windows Media Player to the detriment of competing media players' (CFI judgment, paragraph 1056).[45] In addition, the CFI noted that 'Microsoft itself' submitted information showing 'that the significant growth in the use of Windows Media Player has not come about because that player is of better quality than competing media players or because those media players, and particularly RealPlayer, have certain defects' (CFI Judgment, para 1057).[46]

Having reached this conclusion, the CFI noted that it was 'not necessary to examine the arguments which Microsoft puts forward against the findings made by the Commission in the other two stages of its reasoning', but went on to 'examine them briefly' (CFI judgment, paragraph 1059).

With respect to the second stage of the Commission's reasoning, the CFI concluded that the Commission correctly considered that the market was characterized by indirect network effects, and that content providers and software developers tended primarily to use Windows Media Player as that provided a greater reach (CFI judgment, paragraph 1062). More particularly, the CFI concluded that 'the Commission was quite correct to find that the provision of several different technologies give rise to additional development, infrastructure and administrative costs for content providers, who were therefore inclined to use only one technology' (CFI judgment, paragraph 1064). The CFI also accepted that the Commission's market enquiry demonstrated that 'encoding streamed content in several formats is expensive and time consuming' (CFI judgment, paragraph 1065).

Turning to Microsoft's argument that the Commission failed to assess

---

[45] The CFI did not address Microsoft's argument that, since all third-party media player vendors were experiencing remarkable growth during the relevant period, Microsoft's growth was not shown to have come to 'the detriment of' third-party media players. While RealNetworks' usage shares *relative* to those of Windows Media Player and third-party media players declined, this was inevitable since RealNetworks originally had a 100% share.

[46] As Microsoft argued, the information provided in recitals 948 to 951 to the Decision, which consisted of a series of reviews of various media players, was not provided as a scientific sample of the ratings of various media players. Instead, this information was submitted to the Commission to show that its market definition was unduly limited. Once the Commission used this evidence to suggest that Windows Media Player was 'inferior', Microsoft immediately responded to this claim, and some of Microsoft's arguments are referenced (albeit briefly) in n. 1206 of the Decision (e.g. Microsoft pointed out that respondents to the Commission's questionnaires did not view Windows Media Player as inferior to RealNetworks).

whether the costs of encoding in several formats outweighed the benefits, the CFI rejected this view, stating that '[t]he Commission had questioned content providers about that point in the 2003 market enquiry and the content providers expressed their views on the subject (see recitals 884, 887, 889 and 890 to the contested decision)' (CFI judgment, paragraph 1066).[47] The CFI also concluded that 'the more widely distributed a media player is, the more content providers are inclined to create content for the technology implemented in that media player' (CFI judgment, paragraph 1067).

The CFI also concluded that the same factors were true with respect to software developers. Since, it believed, the Commission correctly concluded that 'the development of software for several media technologies entails additional costs' (CFI judgment, paragraph 1073), and since this was 'likely to influence their decision on whether to develop applications for additional technologies' (CFI judgment, paragraph 1074), the Commission could correctly conclude that 'software developers who wrote applications that relied on a media player had incentives to write foremost to Windows Media Player'.

The CFI did not address Microsoft's argument that the results of the Commission's market surveys about the actual practice of content providers, content owners and software developers undermined the inferences drawn by the Commission with respect to its selective reading of some of the answers to its market enquiry. Thus, for example, the CFI did not explain how the Commission could rely on such findings when they were disputed by results showing that the vast majority of content

---

[47] Notably, the CFI does not identify the views of the content providers on these issues. This is because, while the Commission did ask several questions relevant to the cost-benefit trade-off, these were among the questions the Commission ignored in its Decision. Thus, the Commission's market enquiry asked the following questions of content providers and content owners: 'Do any of the above additional costs [i.e., the additional costs of making content available in other formats] influence your decisions on how many Technologies you use to provide content? If so, which costs influence such decisions?'; 'In your view, what are the benefits of supporting multiple Technologies?'; 'If applicable, are these additional costs (see previous question) [i.e., if the company is planning to offer digital content in Microsoft's formats, any additional costs of doing so] likely in the future to influence your company's decision whether to offer content based on Technologies other than Microsoft's? If so, please explain'; and 'If one Technology were to become the clear leader would it still be worthwhile to support other formats and at what point would the costs outweigh the benefits?'. The only question identified in the Decision is the last question (see n. 1088), and it is only identified because it was referenced in a quote provided by one of the respondents. Not one answer to any of these questions is identified in the Decision.

owners, content providers and applications developers all relied on multiple formats and technologies. Finally, the CFI also did not address Microsoft's argument that the Commission failed to explain the inconsistencies between its analysis in *AOL/TimeWarner* and that applied in the Microsoft case.

Broader consequences of the CFI judgment

The CFI's conclusions on foreclosure are significant, not least because they would seem to reduce the scope for an effects-based analysis under Article 82 EC in some situations. In the Commission's view, the mere fact that Microsoft made available Windows Media Player only with Windows was not sufficient to cause foreclosure, as, in contrast to 'classical' tying cases, third parties remained free to obtain and use third-party media players. This is clear from recitals 877–8 to the Decision, where, having concluded that third-party media player vendors cannot match the distribution of Windows, the Commission stated that it would demonstrate the existence of foreclosure based on the combination of Microsoft's ubiquity with the specific features of the market, including the existence of indirect network effects (instead of relying solely on Microsoft's 'ubiquity'):

> From the above, it follows that alternative distribution channels do not enable media players competing with WMP to match the ubiquitous and guaranteed presence of the pre-installed WMP code on client PCs worldwide. This situation is not altered by the US Final Judgment as WMP binary code continues to be pre-installed together with Windows on every Windows client PC shipped to customers.
>
> It will be shown in the following that, in view of the indirect network effects obtaining in the media player market, the ubiquitous presence of the WMP code provides it with a significant competitive advantage, which is liable to have a harmful effect on the structure of competition in that market.[48]

The special nature of the Commission's foreclosure theory against Windows Media Player was also demonstrated in its Observations of 21 July 2004 on Microsoft's application for suspension in Case T-201/04 R. In paragraph 183 of that pleading (the Commission's first pleading after its Decision was adopted) the Commission confirmed the novelty of its foreclosure theory by noting that the mere act of distributing streaming media

---

[48] The Commission's reference to provisions of the US Final Judgment in this context concerned section III.H, under which Microsoft developed a mechanism that allowed end-users and OEMs to easily disable functionality such as Windows Media Player through a variety of ways, all without removing the underlying functionality (which remained available for use in third-party software).

functionality with Windows was not conduct from which the Commission could infer foreclosure *per se*:

> It is correct that the Decision, unlike previous cases such as *Hilti* and *Tetra Pak II*, does not infer foreclosure *per se* (cf. recitals 841 et seq.), but takes into consideration the specific circumstances of the present case, i.e. that media players can be downloaded via the Internet and some media players come for free. (Internal citations omitted.)

The CFI, however, effectively concluded that the Commission tried to prove too much: 'the Court concludes that the Commission's findings in the first stage of its reasoning are in themselves sufficient to establish that the fourth constituent element of abusive bundling is present in this case' (CFI judgment, paragraph 1058). In other words, the Court seemed to conclude that the mere fact that Microsoft gave itself a distribution advantage for Windows Media Player was sufficient to establish an infringement of Article 82 EC under the specific facts of the case. Although this advantage had no appreciable effects on end-users, who remained free to download and use as many media players as they wanted, and although it was 'common ground' that the evidence showed end-users were increasing their usage of multiple media players, the CFI rejected this evidence and instead focused more on the possibility that Microsoft's distribution advantage might make it more difficult for developers of third-party media players to convince OEMs to pre-install their products.[49]

Although it deemed the Commission's 'second stage' to be unnecessary, and therefore only addressed Microsoft's arguments 'briefly', the CFI's review of the Commission's arguments in this stage of its analysis is also interesting insofar as it shows a high degree of deference to the Commission's findings. As recital 890 to the Decision makes clear, at the time of the Decision (and five years after the start of the infringement) the Commission believed that content providers still had incentives to encode in multiple formats, and software developers still had incentives to write to multiple technologies.[50] Instead of using this data to question its premises about how the market operated, however, the Commission

---

[49] Under the approach adopted by the CFI, it would seem that the Commission did not need to carry out any market investigation into the likely effects of the conduct on content providers, content owners and software developers.

[50] This did not, however, prevent the Commission from warning that the '[e]vidence described in this Decision suggests that the market may already be tipping in favour of WMP' (Decision, recital 1071). As time continued to pass without any significant changes, however, the Commission ultimately stopped making such dire predictions in its submissions to the CFI.

simply concluded that enough time had not yet passed for its predictions to come true. Significantly, the CFI accepted the Commission's explanation without subjecting it to a particularly stringent review. The CFI did not, for example, require the Commission to provide a satisfactory explanation for why its analysis differed so markedly from *AOL/TimeWarner*. Nor did the CFI inquire into why the Commission failed to report its findings on several issues raised in its questionnaires.

Objective Justification

Microsoft's arguments

In Microsoft's view, the Decision directly challenges Microsoft's ability to engage in beneficial and pro-competitive conduct. Thus, the Decision imposes limits on Microsoft's ability to meet consumer and industry demand for new and improved functionality with each new release of the Windows PC operating system, thereby preventing Microsoft from matching the ever-improving offerings of operating systems of competitors like Apple or Linux. End-users expect operating systems to offer new functionality as technology develops, much in the same way that they expect other consumer products to incorporate new functionality over time. Similarly, third-party developers of software applications and websites, who frequently rely on functionality present in an operating system instead of duplicating this functionality in their own programs and services,[51] also look to developers of operating systems to increase the platform functionality present in the operating system.

Microsoft also argued that integrating new functionality in Windows enables it to create cross-dependencies and reduce the amount of redundant code. If Microsoft is unable to depend on the existence of such functionality in its operating system, as is currently the case with respect to Internet streaming functionality, Microsoft argued that Windows would no longer be able to rely on the existence of such functionality when

[51] To encourage third-party software developers to develop programs for Windows, and thereby increase the value of Windows, Microsoft freely exposes this functionality through publicly-available applications programming interfaces, or APIs. By calling on these APIs, third-party software developers can seamlessly integrate this functionality in their own programs without having to devote time and resources to developing and testing alternative functionality. One example of an API exposed by Windows is the Create Menu API. This API allows a software developer to insert the familiar pull-down menus that are common in software applications such as a word-processing program. Before this menu functionality was included in Windows, every third-party software developer who wanted to use menus had to write their own software code to display menus.

developing other aspects of its operating system. In essence, Microsoft claimed, this would freeze the development of such functionality. None of these points was ever disputed by the Commission.

Although the Decision did not directly challenge Microsoft's ability to offer new and improved functionality, insofar as it allows Microsoft to add new functionality provided it makes available versions of its operating system without such functionality, Microsoft argued that it indirectly threatens this ability by preventing it from offering such improved functionality on a uniform basis. Microsoft noted that the primary consumer and industry benefits provided by the Windows PC operating system required the existence of a *uniform* platform for third-party software applications and websites, and noted how its policy of offering a uniform platform has been an essential element of its success. According to Microsoft, providing a uniform platform allows third-party software and website developers to be sure that programs and websites designed to run on Windows will in fact work on all PCs running Windows. Microsoft noted that this makes it significantly easier for third-party developers to write programs and design websites for Windows, explaining why so many third-party programs and services are available for Windows today. Microsoft also noted that end-users benefit from the uniform platform because this made available a large number of inexpensive software programs and content-rich websites, and also because end-users could be sure that third party software and services designed for Windows will work on their system.

Microsoft argued that these benefits would be lost if it could no longer offer a uniform platform because third-party developers would need to separately develop, test and market different versions of their products for each different version of Windows. This would increase the costs of such software and make it more difficult for end-users to know whether a given third-party program works on their specific PC. Although this is already a problem when one specific functionality must be removed, Microsoft noted that this issue would become increasingly problematic to the extent that the Commission carried through with its threat to use the Decision as a precedent to require the removal of other functionality.[52]

Thus, Microsoft argued that whereas the competitive harm identified in

---

[52] See 'Commissioner Monti's Statement on Microsoft', 18 March 2004, IP/04/365 ('It is essential to have a precedent which will establish clear principles for the future conduct of a company with such a strong dominant position in the market'); 'Commission concludes on Microsoft investigation, imposes conduct remedies and a fine', 24 March 2004, IP/04/382 ('The Commission believes the remedies will bring the antitrust violations to an end, that they are proportionate, and that they establish clear principles for the future conduct of the company').

the Decision was highly speculative, the benefits flowing from Microsoft's business model, which entails integration of new functionality into Windows over time, are substantial and should have been given more weight by the Commission. Indeed, as Microsoft pointed out, in 2002 the US District Court for the District of Columbia expressly weighed the benefits of integrating new functionality in Windows when deciding whether to accept the code removal remedy ultimately adopted by the Commission in its Decision. In assessing this issue, the District Court heard testimony, subject to cross-examination, from 34 witnesses in a 32-day trial, including witnesses that were also active in the Commission proceedings. In a 324-page opinion, the District Court found that breaking the uniformity of the Windows platform was likely to retard rather than to promote competition and threatened to harm consumers and other industry participants. In a unanimous judgment, sitting *en banc* (i.e. in plenary session), the US Court of Appeals upheld the District Court's conclusion. Indeed, the Court of Appeals congratulated the District Court for accepting a solution 'without intruding itself into the design and engineering of the Windows operating system'.

In contrast, the Commission dismissed Microsoft's arguments about the efficiencies generated by a uniform platform in a mere 15 paragraphs in its 2004 Decision. Instead of carrying out a thorough investigation of these issues, the Commission chose to rely on the statements of a single competitor, US company RealNetworks, whose testimony had already been rejected in the US proceedings. Although the Commission expressly wanted to create a precedent with its Decision, the Commission never considered the broader implications of its Decision, such as by considering the efficiencies generated by Microsoft's conduct for third parties. Mischaracterizing Microsoft's argument for a uniform Windows platform as a demand for standardization across the industry (Decision, recital 969), the Commission simply concluded that this justification could not be taken into account. Microsoft therefore argued that the Commission failed properly to assess this issue.

The CFI judgment

In reviewing Microsoft's arguments, the CFI first noted that the dominant undertaking faced the initial burden to raise a plea of an objective justification during the administrative procedure and support it with arguments and evidence (CFI judgment, paragraph 1144). Once this was done, the burden fell on the Commission to show that the arguments and evidence relied on cannot prevail, and, accordingly, that the justification put forward cannot be accepted (CFI judgment, paragraph 1144).

In assessing Microsoft's arguments, the CFI first concluded that the

Commission did not interfere with Microsoft's ability to integrate and improve new functionality in Windows as such, since Microsoft could still do so as long as it offered an 'unbundled' version (CFI judgment, paragraphs 1149–50).

With respect to Microsoft's argument about the need to preserve uniformity, the CFI noted that this 'may' have advantages, but concluded that 'Microsoft is not entitled to rely on the fact that the bundling ensures the uniform presence of media functionality in Windows' because this 'is precisely one of the main reasons why the Commission correctly took the view that the bundling led to the foreclosure of competing media players' (CFI judgment, paragraph 1151). In other words, the CFI appears to have concluded that the Commission need not, when assessing an objective justification, consider the positive effects of conduct that it determines brings about negative effects.

The CFI also concluded that Microsoft had not shown how integration was 'essential to enable software developers and Internet site creators to use the Windows platform effectively' (CFI judgment, paragraph 1157). In this regard, the CFI noted that 'integration' as such was unnecessary for purposes of providing platform services, referring to the fact that third parties can, and do, write applications for third party media players and also for new updates of Windows Media Player that are not necessarily pre-installed (CFI judgment, paragraph 1158). Moreover, the CFI noted that Microsoft had not shown that the 'integration of Windows Media Player in Windows creates technical efficiencies or, in other words, that it "lead[s] to superior technical product performance"' (CFI judgment, paragraph 1159).[53]

The CFI also argued that Microsoft failed to demonstrate 'to the

---

[53] In fact, Microsoft did argue that there were technical efficiencies, some of which the Commission itself identifies in recital 962 to the Decision. Subsequently, the Commission stated in para. 235 of its Defence that 'it is striking that Microsoft, throughout the administrative procedure, has not argued that there are any "technical efficiencies" relating to the integration of Windows Media Player with Windows (in other words, that the integrated product offers superior technical product performance)'. In making this claim, the Commission now equated 'technical efficiencies' only with 'superior product performance'. In response to the Commission's claim, Microsoft informed the CFI that it in fact had provided evidence during the administrative procedure showing that programs that rely on common functionality (instead of each providing its own functionality) use less of a PC's random access memory and microprocessor capacity (this evidence was provided in the paper identified in n. 1221 of the Decision). The CFI rejected Microsoft's claim, noting that this was a 'new argument' and 'unsupported' (CFI judgment, paragraph 1160).

requisite legal standard' its claims that applications will no longer work correctly when implemented on a version of Windows without Windows Media Player (CFI judgment, paragraph 1163), and rejected as 'unfounded' Microsoft's argument that the removal of Windows Media Player will affect the functioning of other parts of Windows (CFI judgment, paragraph 1164).[54]

Finally, the CFI rejected Microsoft's argument that the Decision would bring about the fragmentation of the platform, as it could require Microsoft to offer multiple versions of Windows. In this regard, the CFI agreed with the Commission that such arguments were 'hypothetical and speculative' (CFI judgment, paragraph 1166).

Broader consequences of the CFI judgment

The CFI's suggestion that certain benefits can be ignored when assessing whether conduct amounts to an abuse would seem very far-reaching, particularly with regard to tying cases. Thus, in the Microsoft case, the CFI suggested that the benefits of uniformity could be disregarded because they led to the claimed foreclosure effect (CFI judgment, paragraph 1151). If this rule was confirmed in future tying cases, it would seem to mean that a tie can never be justified. No matter how beneficial the tie may be, it will always be seen as contributing to the claimed foreclosure effect.

In other cases, however, the European Courts have taken a less strict view about what justifications may be considered. For example, in reviewing the bonus scheme at issue in *British Airways*, the Court of Justice did not conclude that the efficiencies generated by the bonus scheme should be disregarded because they were found to have resulted in anti-competitive effects. Instead, the Court of Justice determined that the assessment should take account of these benefits:

---

54 Part of the problem that Microsoft encountered in identifying such dependencies was that the Commission had never clearly identified what it meant by Windows Media Player during the administrative proceedings, and thus Microsoft could not identify with certainty what files had to be removed by the time its application for annulment was due. Assuming that the Commission was identifying Windows Media Player as the components that were distributed to end-users who downloaded new versions of Windows Media Player updates, Microsoft created a version of Windows without such components and showed how it created a number of problems (including those identified in para. 1164 of the judgment). Subsequently, the Commission clarified that some of these components should be considered 'basic media infrastructure' and not Windows Media Player, and ultimately identified to Microsoft the precise files to be removed from Windows XP. Once this issue was resolved, Microsoft provided a new list of functionality that was affected.

> Assessment of the economic justification for a system of discounts or bonuses established by an undertaking in a dominant position is to be made on the basis of the whole of the circumstances of the case (see, to that effect, *Michelin*, paragraph 73). It has to be determined whether the exclusionary effect arising from such a system, which is disadvantageous for competition, may be counterbalanced, or outweighed, by advantages in terms of efficiency which also benefit the consumer. If the exclusionary effect of that system bears no relation to advantages for the market and consumers, or if it goes beyond what is necessary in order to attain those advantages, that system must be regarded as an abuse.[55]

In the Microsoft case, however, the CFI seems to have adopted a new rule in which certain benefits may be disregarded when carrying out this balancing test. The circumstances in which this will occur remain to be seen. Given that the Microsoft case is rare in that the CFI accepted that the conduct gave rise to efficiencies, however, it may be some time before the European Courts are asked to reconsider this precise issue.

The CFI's decision to allow the Commission to regard as 'hypothetical' and 'speculative' the future application of the Decision against other functionality in Windows is also notable. Indeed, the Commission alone is responsible for any uncertainty that results about the potential application of the Decision to other functionality in Windows. If the Commission intended to apply the Decision as a precedent against other functionality in Windows (as it claimed it would do), it could simply have acknowledged this point and thereby removed the hypothetical, speculative aspect of Microsoft's claim. Perhaps unsurprisingly, the day the judgment was announced the Commission seemingly removed the 'hypothetical' and 'speculative' nature of this issue, noting that the case was 'an important precedent, not just for this particular product on this particular market'.[56]

5. CONCLUSION

After the judgment, the Commission has sent mixed signals about its relevance for other companies. On the one hand, the Commission has embraced the case as setting a very broad precedent. Thus, Commissioner Kroes stated in her initial comments on the judgment that 'The 2004

---

55 Case C-95/04 P *British Airways* v *Commission* [2007] ECRI-2331, judgment of 15 March 2007, para. 86.

56 See Introductory Remarks on Court of First Instance Ruling on Microsoft's Abuse of Dominant Market Position, SPEECH/07/539.

Decision set an important precedent in terms of the obligations of dominant companies to allow competition, in particular in high tech industries' (a statement intended to cover both infringements), and 'This is an important precedent, not just for this particular product on this particular market'[57] (a statement limited to the tying infringement).

However, towards the end of these initial comments, the Commissioner appeared to take a large step back from these statements, indicating that the case was specific only to Microsoft. First, the Commissioner stated the following:

> You may hear scare stories about the supposed negative consequences of this ruling for other companies and for innovation on the market. The Commission notes that the Court itself has concluded that Microsoft failed to show that the decision would have a significant negative effect on its incentives to innovate. Let me be clear – there is one company that will have to change its illegal behaviour as a result of this ruling: Microsoft.

Arguably, this statement was limited to the refusal to supply claim, as it was in this section of its judgment that the CFI drew conclusions about Microsoft's incentives to innovate. However, this statement was followed by a similar statement that apparently covers both infringements:

> The Commission decision made clear that this was in many ways an exceptional case. Super-dominance like Microsoft's is rare. The Court has confirmed that.

This language was then repeated in the Commission's press release of that day. In that press release, the Commission again indicated that its case may be very limited:

> The Commission will carefully analyse the judgment and will consider its implications for future antitrust enforcement in these sectors and in others. It is clear, however, that this is an exceptional case with extremely harmful abuses by a company in a quasi-monopolistic position on the market.[58]

---

[57] See Introductory Remarks on Court of First Instance Ruling on Microsoft's Abuse of Dominant Market Position, SPEECH/07/539.

[58] See 'Antitrust: Commission welcomes CFI ruling upholding Commission's decision on Microsoft's abuse of dominant position', 17 September 2007, MEMO/07/359. The Commission also had previously suggested that its Microsoft Decision would be applied in a limited way after Airbus applied to intervene in support of Microsoft (Airbus reportedly was concerned that the Microsoft Decision would affect its ability to choose providers for parts such as plane seats and galleys). Thus, in an article written after Airbus withdrew its application to intervene, a Commission spokesperson was reported to have stated that 'the

For purposes of clarity, it should be noted that neither the Commission's Decision nor the CFI's judgment suggests that they applied different rules because Microsoft had either a 'super-dominant' or 'quasi-monopolistic' position. Both the Decision and the judgment found a violation of Article 82 EC, which prohibits the abuse of a 'dominant' position. Accordingly, it is difficult to see how the broad legal principles established by the Commission and CFI (such as those discussed above regarding the necessary elements of tying) would differ if applied to a company that is 'merely' dominant. Moreover, given that an abuse is an 'objective' concept,[59] it clearly cannot be the situation that Microsoft is held out for special treatment under EC competition law.

A striking aspect of the CFI's judgment in the Microsoft case is its reliance on a strictly form-based and *per se* approach to Article 82 EC. As discussed in this chapter, however, the Decision itself is premised on an effects-based theory. Thus, the Commission took into account the direct effects of the tie, noting that end-users were not directly harmed as they remained free to obtain and use multiple media players. Instead, the Commission established harm to end-users on the basis of what it found to be the likely effects of Microsoft's conduct on content owners, content providers and software developers, which it believed would ultimately affect the position of third-party media player vendors and therefore indirectly harm end-users.

The CFI, however, rejected most of the Commission's analysis as being superfluous. Instead, the CFI concluded that all the Commission needed to establish was that Microsoft gave itself an advantage that third-party media player vendors could not match. Thus, according to the CFI, it was sufficient that third-party media player vendors could not enter into agreements with OEMs providing for the exclusive distribution of their media players, even though end-users could (and, as the CFI acknowledged, did) obtain and use other media players. In other words, the harm to the competitive process caused by Microsoft's refusal to allow OEMs to supply Windows exclusively with third-party media players was sufficient to establish harm to end-users. In reaching this conclusion, the CFI therefore determined that the effects of Microsoft's conduct were irrelevant.

In addition to reflecting a *per se* approach, the CFI's judgment (like the Decision itself) was also largely form-based. To assess whether Microsoft had engaged in tying, the Commission and CFI began by identifying

---

Commission couldn't see how its decision on Microsoft would have a direct effect on Airbus'. See www.macworld.com/news/2004/09/24/airbus/index.php.

[59] Case 85/76 *Hoffmann-La Roche* v *Commission* [1979] ECR 461, para. 91.

the elements of a tying infringement, and subsequently tried to establish each element separately. This approach can be classified as 'form-based' because it did not permit the Commission or CFI to consider the interplay of the various elements.

For example, this approach allowed both the Commission and the CFI to treat the justification for the practice put forward by Microsoft as an attempt to defend a practice that had already been determined to constitute an abusive tie. Notably, this was not the way that Microsoft presented its argument. Instead, Microsoft began its pleading by explaining the benefits of incorporating new functionality, and improving this functionality over time, and demonstrating that this was a common practice. This was intended to support Microsoft's argument that the conduct at issue could not constitute an abuse, as it constituted normal competition on the merits.[60] Microsoft's pleading then contrasted the Commission's emphasis on the speculative aspects of its foreclosure theory with its failure to give sufficient weight to the substantial, proven benefits of its conduct. By adopting the form-based approach set out in the Decision and judgment, however, the Commission and the CFI did not have to address these specific concerns, making it much easier to reject Microsoft's arguments. After reaching the preliminary conclusion that there was an abuse without having to consider the benefits of Microsoft's conduct, the Commission and the CFI set an impossible task for Microsoft to justify its conduct.[61]

Before the CFI had issued its judgment, some of Microsoft's critics suggested that a loss by the Commission would result in a significant blow to the Commission's ability to enforce the competition rules.[62] Such exaggerated claims hide the true importance of the case, which concerns

---

[60] See Case 85/76 *Hoffmann-La Roche* v *Commission* [1979] ECR 461, para. 91: 'The concept of abuse is an objective concept relating to the behaviour of an undertaking in a dominant position which is such as to influence the structure of a market where, as a result of the very presence of the undertaking in question, the degree of competition is weakened *and which, through recourse to methods different from those which condition normal competition* in products or services on the basis of the transactions of commercial operators, has the effect of hindering the maintenance of the degree of competition still existing in the market or the growth of that competition'. (Emphasis added.)

[61] See Joined Cases T-191/98, T-212–214/98 *Atlantic Container Line and others* v *Commission* [2003] ECR II-3275, para. 1112 ('However, because Article [82] of the Treaty does not provide for any exemption, abusive practices are prohibited regardless of the advantages which may accrue to the perpetrators of such practices or to third parties').

[62] See e.g. 'All sides await verdict in Microsoft–EU case', *International Herald Tribune*, 9 September 2007, available at www.iht.com/articles/2007/09/09/business/msft10.php.

the critical issue of when product integration and product improvement, which are common and normally beneficial practices, can constitute an infringement of EC competition law.[63]

When all is said and done, the conduct for which Microsoft has been condemned essentially consists in having failed to offer to OEMs and end-customers the choice to take a version of Windows in which they appear to have no interest whatsoever, as clearly shown by the failure of the N version of Windows which Microsoft was ordered to offer in Europe. It is difficult to see what consumer harm could have been inflicted by this most paradoxical abuse. Compared to the situation before the infringement started, and despite the failure of the remedy imposed by the Commisssion, there is more consumer choice today and, as the CFI itself has recognized, consumers are increasing their usage of multiple media players. Was this a case requiring intervention by the Commission?

63 Similarly, critics of Microsoft erroneously suggested that Microsoft was arguing that it should be permitted to bundle anything with an operating system, including a 'ham sandwich'. However, Microsoft did not dispute that there were limits on its ability to include functionality in Windows. Instead, Microsoft argued that such limitations should not prevent it from adding and improving functionality that customers expected in a modern client PC operating system, including media functionality (the improvement of which had not been criticized in the seven years prior to the addition of support for Internet streaming technology).

5. The Microsoft case: you reap what you sow?

Jens Fejø

1. INTRODUCTION

When Bill Gates, President of Microsoft, declared to members of Microsoft's sales force in February 1997: 'What we are trying to do is use our server control to do new protocols and lock out Sun and Oracle specifically . . . Now, I don't know if we'll get to that or not, but that's what we are trying to do', he was entering a dangerous area of business. This statement was held against Microsoft by the Commission in its Decision,[1] and by the Court of First Instance (CFI) in its later judgment,[2] both finding Microsoft to have violated Article 82 of the EC Treaty. How this information was leaked is not completely clear, but it certainly deserves to be highlighted in view of the many arguments Microsoft's advocates put forward in its defence. These arguments, however, failed to convince the CFI, which confirmed the Commission's Decision to impose on Microsoft a fine of more than €497,000,000. This followed the CFI's affirmation of the Commission's finding that Microsoft abused its dominant position on two counts. First, by illegally *refusing to supply* to competing producers of non-Windows operating systems for certain servers the protocols necessary to grant interoperability with Windows operating systems for the same servers and client PCs. Secondly, by *tying or bundling* Windows Media Player (WMP) with Windows operating system. Only the part of the Decision appointing a monitoring trustee was annulled.

Before we venture into a more detailed study of the case, there should be room for a few short observations. First, it is clear that the company involved in the case was no ordinary company (and not a European

1 Commission Decision 2007/53/EC of 24 March 2004 [2007] OJ 2007 L32/23 ('the Decision') recital 778.

2 Case T-201/04 *Microsoft Corporation* v *Commission* [2007] ECR II-3601 ('CFI judgement'), para. 771 and again in paras 1349–50.

company). As has been stated, we are faced with an undertaking with an 'immense worldwide market power'.[3] Secondly, the company was no stranger to antitrust legislation, as it had been through US courts on similar charges.[4]

It is also clear that the Commission put great importance on the case.[5] The CFI, for its part, showed a remarkable degree of deference towards the Commission's assessment and limited its scrutiny to whether the latter had made 'manifest errors'. At the same time it must be said that not all arguments in relation to interoperability and tying were dismissed right away. Thus, in the interim relief procedure, the President of the CFI held that Microsoft's application for annulment of the interoperability part of the Decision was not at first sight unfounded and that Microsoft had established a *prima facie* case. Similarly, with regard to the tying part of the Decision, it was held that Microsoft's arguments raised complex questions and that here too a *prima facie* case had been established.[6] Therefore, although the petition for interim measures was rejected – mainly due to lack of serious and irreparable harm to Microsoft – the President seems at the beginning to have accepted, at least to a certain extent, the arguments pleaded by Microsoft. But, as mentioned, the outcome of the case was different. The CFI thoroughly demolished Microsoft's defences and largely confirmed the Commission's conclusions.

---

[3] See Bo Vesterdorf, former President of the CFI and presiding in the case, 'Article 82 EC: Where Do We Stand after the *Microsoft* Judgment?' (2008) *Global Antitrust Review* 1, 14.

[4] CFI judgment, paras 51–8. See also e.g. D. Evans, A. Nichols and R. Schmalensee, 'United States v. Microsoft: Did Consumers Win?' (2005) *Journal of Competition Law and Economics* 497; J. Gstalter, 'L'arrêt Microsoft et la mise en œuvre de l'article 82 CE. Quels enseignements pour l'analyse fondée sur les effets?' (2007) *Revue Trimesterielle de Droit Européen* 742; and R. Moldén, 'Mandatory Supply of Interoperability Information: The *Microsoft* Judgment' (2008) *European Business Organization Law Review* 305, 308 and 313 *et seq.*

[5] See e.g. A. Andreangeli 'Case Note on T-201/04, Microsoft v Commission, Judgment of 17 September 2007' (2008) *Common Market Law Review* 863, 864 *et seq.*, who talks about a 'watchful eye' on Microsoft.

[6] Order of the President, 22 December 2004, Proceedings for Interim Relief – Article 82 EC [2004] ECR II-4463.

2. THE MICROSOFT CASE

Background to the Case: the Commission's Decision

Microsoft designed, developed and marketed a wide variety of software products for different kinds of computing devices including, in particular, operating systems for client PCs, operating systems for work group servers and streaming media players. Microsoft also provided technical assistance for its various products.

The previous chapters and other contributions in this book have already analysed the Commission's Decision. For the purposes of this chapter, which focuses on the CFI judgment, it is sufficient to mention that the Commission found that Microsoft had committed an illegal refusal to license in violation of Article 82 EC by not giving a clear confirmation to a request by Sun Microsystems, Inc. ('Sun') of the complete information required to allow Sun to provide native support for COM objects on Solaris and of Active Directory technologies on Solaris. Modern office computers are often linked together in a network controlled by a 'server'. When linked to such a network, a personal computer is a 'client PC'. An operating system is the software controlling the basic functions of a server or a client PC. The network is labelled a Windows work group network or a Windows domain when running on a Microsoft operating system.[7] The Commission also found that Microsoft's tying of WMP with Windows client PC operating systems in the period from May 1999 to the date of notification of the Decision was abusive. Finally, as mentioned, the Commission imposed fines and other remedies which are not dealt with in this chapter.

The CFI Judgement

Microsoft sought the annulment of the Decision of the Commission, and the CFI made a thorough assessment of the two central elements of the Decision. In this respect, the CFI also dealt with intellectual property rights (IPRs).

Although the previous chapters already set out and comment on the findings of the CFI, they do not always do so systematically. It is thus thought useful to provide the reader with a brief and orderly summary,

---

7 Several important issues of a highly technical character are dealt with in the case but are not explained in this chapter. See Chapter 1 for a thorough exposition.

concluding with a few comments on the main findings of the CFI. Any reader already sufficiently familiar with the judgement can therefore skip the summary and proceed immediately to this author's reflections.

The specific IPR element: refusal to supply interoperability information
In the substantial part of the judgment, the CFI dealt first with the refusal to supply the element that was closely linked to the IPRs. Microsoft put forward three pleas:

(i) that the criteria which permits an undertaking in a dominant position to be compelled to grant a licence, as defined by the Community judicature, were not satisfied in the present case;
(ii) that Sun did not request access to the 'technology' that the Commission had ordered Microsoft to disclose and that its letter of 6 October 1998 could not in any event be interpreted as containing a refusal on its part;
(iii) that the Commission did not properly take account of the obligations imposed on the European Community by the TRIPS Agreement.[8]

We now analyse these three claims in turn.

Criteria for Imposing a Compulsory Licence
After a thorough examination, the CFI first found that there was no inconsistency between the scope of the Decision[9] and the 'interoperability standard' required by the Commission in that Decision.[10] Secondly, it found that the Commission had adopted the Decision on the assumption that Microsoft had been able to rely on IPRs in the case.[11]

The central issue to be resolved in this part was therefore whether, as the Commission claimed and Microsoft denied, the conditions on which an undertaking in a dominant position may be required to grant a licence covering its IPRs were satisfied in the present case.[12]

When dealing with the circumstances by reference to which the abusive conduct had to be analysed, the CFI started by making it clear that

---

[8] The Agreement on Trade-Related Aspects of Intellectual Property Rights (TRIPS) of 15 April 1994. Annex 1 C to the Agreement Establishing the World Trade Organization.
[9] Decision, article 5(a).
[10] CFI judgment, paras 151–266.
[11] CFI judgment, paras 283–84.
[12] CFI judgment, para. 290.

Microsoft and the Commission disagreed as to the criteria established in the case law that were applicable in an IPR situation.[13]

To this, the CFI added that although undertakings are, as a rule, free to choose their business partners, in certain circumstances a refusal to supply on the part of a dominant undertaking may constitute an abuse of a dominant position within the meaning of Article 82 EC unless it is objectively justified.[14] The CFI then recalled five judgments handed down by the Court of Justice dealing with related issues. The CFI then gave an account of these cases. They were *Commercial Solvents*,[15] *Volvo*,[16] *Magill*,[17] *Bronner*[18] and *IMS Health*.[19] In this respect it might be noted that the CFI mentioned, with reference to *Bronner*, that the Court of Justice had recited the exceptional circumstances which it had established in *Magill* and stated:

> [E]ven if that case-law on the exercise of an intellectual property right were applicable to the exercise of any property right whatever, it would still be necessary, for [that] judgment to be effectively relied upon in order to plead the existence of an abuse within the meaning of Article [82 EC] in a situation such as that which forms the subject-matter of the . . . question, not only that the refusal of the service comprised in home delivery be likely to eliminate all competition in the daily newspaper market on the part of the person requesting the service and that such refusal be incapable of being objectively justified, but also that the service in itself be indispensable to carrying on that person's business, inasmuch as there is no actual or potential substitute in existence for that home-delivery scheme.[20]

From its consideration of the judgments of the Court of Justice, the CFI drew the conclusion[21] that it followed from the case law so cited that the refusal by an undertaking holding a dominant position to license a third party to use a product covered by an IPR cannot in itself constitute an abuse of a dominant position within the meaning of Article 82 EC. Only in exceptional circumstances can the exercise of the exclusive right by the owner of the IPR give rise to such an abuse.

---

13 CFI judgment, paras. 312 *et seq.*

14 CFI judgment, para. 319.

15 Joined Cases 6/73 and 7/73 *Commercial Solvents* v *Commission* [1974] ECR 223. In addition, the CFI here also pointed to a case concerning a refusal to supply a service: Case 311/84 *CBEM* [1985] ECR 3261.

16 Case 238/87 *Volvo* v *Veng (UK) Ltd* [1988] ECR 6211.

17 Joined Cases C-241/91 P and C-242/91 P *RTE and ITP* v *Commission* [1995] ECR I-743 ('*Magill*').

18 Case C-7/97 *Oscar Bronner* [1998] ECR I-7791.

19 Case C-418/01 *IMS Health* [2004] ECR I-5039.

20 Case C-7/97 Oscar *Bronner*, para. 41.

21 CFI judgment, para. 331.

It also followed from that case law[22] that the following circumstances, in particular, must be considered to be exceptional:

(i) the refusal relates to a product or service indispensable to the exercise of a particular activity on a neighbouring market;
(ii) the refusal is of such a kind as to exclude any effective competition on that neighbouring market;
(iii) the refusal prevents the appearance of a new product for which there is potential consumer demand.

The CFI went on to state[23] that once it had been established that such circumstances are present, the refusal by the holder of a dominant position to grant a licence might infringe Article 82 EC unless the refusal is objectively justified.

The CFI noted that the circumstance that the refusal prevents the appearance of a new product for which there was potential consumer demand is found only in the case law on the exercise of an IPR.[24]

Finally, the CFI expressed that it was appropriate to add that it was necessary to distinguish two markets: namely, a market constituted by that product or service, and on which the undertaking refusing to supply holds a dominant position, and a neighbouring market on which the product or service is used in the manufacture of another product or for the supply of another service. The fact that the indispensable product or service is not marketed separately does not exclude from the outset the possibility of identifying a separate market.[25] Thus, the CFI expressed the view that the Court of Justice previously had held[26] that it was sufficient that a potential market or even a hypothetical market could be identified and that such was the case where the products or services were indispensable to the conduct of a particular business activity and where there was an actual demand for them on the part of undertakings which sought to carry on that business. The Court of Justice had concluded in the following paragraph of the judgment that it was decisive that two different stages of production were identified and that they were interconnected in that the upstream product was indispensable for supply of the downstream product.[27]

The CFI thereafter spelled out that it considered, in the light of the

---

22 CFI judgment, para. 332.
23 CFI judgment, para. 333.
24 CFI judgment, para. 334.
25 With reference here to Case C-418/01 *IMS Health*, para. 43.
26 With reference to Case C-418/01 *IMS Health*, para. 44.
27 CFI judgment, para. 335.

foregoing factors, that it was appropriate in the Microsoft case, first of all, to decide whether the circumstances identified in *Magill* and *IMS Health*, as described by the CFI, were also present in this case. Only if it found that one or more of those circumstances were absent would the CFI proceed to assess the particular circumstances invoked by the Commission.[28]

The CFI then went into the various elements outlined in its account of the Court of Justice cases on the duty to license a third party based on Article 82 EC.

The first point in the CFI's investigation was the issue of the *indispensable nature* of the interoperability information.[29] The CFI pointed to the fact that the Commission had adopted a two-stage approach in determining whether the information at issue was indispensable, in that, first of all, the Commission had considered what degree of interoperability with the Windows domain architecture non-Microsoft work group server operating systems must achieve in order for its competitors to be able to remain viably on the market, and, secondly, it appraised whether the interoperability that Microsoft refused to disclose was indispensable to the attainment of that degree of interoperability. Microsoft had claimed that this reasoning was incorrect in law and in fact. Microsoft´s assertions, however, were rejected by the CFI.[30] Microsoft had not demonstrated that the Commission´s analysis was manifestly incorrect. Part of the CFI's rejection was a reference to Microsoft´s dominant position on the client PC operating systems market, which exhibited 'extraordinary features', since, notably, its market share on that market was more than 90 per cent and since Windows represented the 'quasi-standard' for those operating systems.[31] It followed that Microsoft had failed to demonstrate that the interoperability information did not quality as indispensable.[32]

The next point to assess was the issue of *elimination of competition*.[33] The CFI here examined the four categories of arguments put forward by Microsoft in support of its contention that the criterion relating to the elimination of competition was not present in this case: first, the definition of the relevant product market; secondly, the method used to calculate market shares; thirdly, the applicable criterion; and, fourthly, the assessment of the market data and the competitive situation.[34] As to

28 CFI judgment, para. 336.
29 CFI judgment, para. 337 *et seq*.
30 CFI judgment, paras 369–436.
31 CFI judgment, para. 387.
32 CFI judgment, para. 436.
33 CFI judgment, para. 437 *et seq*.
34 CFI judgment, para. 479.

all four points, the CFI rejected Microsoft's arguments.[35] The CFI drew the conclusion that the refusal at issue entailed the risk of elimination of competition.[36]

The CFI also rejected the arguments by Microsoft that it had not been established that its refusal prevented the appearance of a new product for which there was unsatisfied consumer demand.[37] It emphasized that the fact that Microsoft's conduct prevented the appearance of a new product on the market should be considered under Article 82(b), which prohibits abusive practices that consist in 'limiting production, markets or technical developments to the . . . prejudice of consumers'. Interestingly, the CFI here pointed to the fact that in both *Magill* and *IMS Health*, it had, more specifically, been considered that by their refusal the companies involved had limited production or markets *to the prejudice of consumers*.[38] However, the CFI went on to state that the appearance of a new product could not be the only parameter which determines whether a refusal to license an IPR is capable of causing prejudice to consumers within the meaning of Article 82(b). As that provision states, such prejudice may arise where there is a limitation not only of production or markets, but also of technical development. And it was on that last hypothesis that the Commission had based its finding in the Microsoft Decision. Thus, the Commission had considered that Microsoft's refusal to supply the relevant information *limited technical development* to the prejudice of consumers within the meaning of Article 82(b), and it had rejected Microsoft's assertion that it had not been demonstrated that its refusal caused prejudice to consumers.[39]

The CFI found that the Commission′s findings were not manifestly incorrect.[40] Thus, owing to the lack of interoperability that competing work group server operating systems products could achieve with the Windows domain architecture, an increasing number of consumers were locked into a homogeneous Windows solution at the level of work group server operating systems. Consumers' purchasing decisions in respect of work group server operating systems were channelled towards Microsoft's products. The limitation thus placed on consumer choice was all the more damaging to consumers because they considered that non-Microsoft work group server operating systems were better than Windows work group

---

35 CFI judgment, paras 480–619.
36 CFI judgment, para. 620.
37 CFI judgment, paras 621–65.
38 CFI judgment, paras 644–6.
39 CFI judgment, paras 644–8.
40 CFI judgment, para. 649.

server operating systems with respect to a series of features to which they attached great importance, such as 'reliability/availability of the . . . system' and 'security included with the server operating system'.[41] The CFI concluded from its considerations that the Commission's finding to the effect that Microsoft's refusal limited technical development to the prejudice of consumers within the meaning of Article 82(b) EC was not manifestly incorrect. The CFI therefore found that the criterion relating to the appearance of a new product was present in the case.[42]

This led the CFI to take up the question of the absence of *objective justification*.[43] Microsoft had claimed that the refusal to supply the information was objectively justified by the IPRs which it held over the 'technology' concerned.[44] The CFI noted that. as justification for its conduct, Microsoft had relied solely on the fact that the technology concerned was covered by IPRs. Microsoft had made clear that if it were required to grant third parties access to that technology that 'would . . . eliminate future incentives to invest in the creation of more intellectual property'. It had also relied on that fact that the technology was secret and valuable and that it contained important innovations.

The CFI considered that, even on the assumption that all this was correct, the fact that the communication protocols covered by the Decision, or the specifications for those protocols, were covered by IPRs could not constitute objective justification within the meaning of *Magill* and *IMS Health*. Microsoft's argument was inconsistent with the *raison d'être* of the exception which that case law recognized in favour of free competition, since if the mere fact of holding IPRs could in itself constitute objective justification for the refusal to grant a licence, the exception established by the case law could never apply. In other words, a refusal to license an IPR could never be considered to constitute an infringement of Article 82 EC even though in *Magill* and *IMS Health* the Court of Justice specifically stated the contrary.[45]

It might be said here, as an interruption, that in my view the Court of Justice did not – as the CFI here seems to argue – make reference to IPRs and Article 82 EC. The Court of Justice restricted its statements as close to the cases at hand as possible in order to express the rule of law. And in those previous cases, there had in fact been IPRs, etc. However,

---

[41] CFI judgment, paras 650–2 with reference to an investigation made by Mercer Management Consulting.

[42] CFI judgment, para. 665.

[43] CFI judgment, para. 666 *et seq*.

[44] CFI judgment, para. 666.

[45] CFI judgment, para. 690.

the CFI went on to accept that the Community judicature considers that the ability of the holder of an IPR to exploit that right solely for his own benefit constitutes the very substance of his exclusive right. Accordingly, a simple refusal, even on the part of an undertaking in a dominant position, to grant a licence to a third party cannot in itself constitute an abuse of a dominant position within the meaning of Article 82 EC. It is only when it is accompanied by exceptional circumstances such as those hitherto envisaged in the case law that such a refusal can be characterized as abusive and that, accordingly, it is permissible, in the public interest in maintaining effective competition on the market, to encroach upon the exclusive right of the holder of the IPR by requiring him to grant licences to third parties seeking to enter or remain on that market. Such exceptional circumstances were present in this case.[46]

The CFI further found that the argument which Microsoft had put forward, namely that the technology concerned was secret and of great value to the licensees and contained important innovations, also could not succeed.[47]

First, the fact that the technology concerned was secret was the consequence of a unilateral business decision on Microsoft's part. Furthermore, Microsoft could not rely on the argument that the interoperability information was secret as a ground for not being required to disclose it unless the exceptional circumstances identified by the Court of Justice in *Magill* and *IMS Health* were present and, at the same time, justify its refusal by what it alleged to be the secret nature of the information. There was no reason why secret technology should enjoy a higher level of protection than, for example, technology which had necessarily been disclosed to the public by its inventor in a patent application procedure.

Secondly, from the moment at which it was established (as in this case) that the interoperability information was *indispensable*, that information was necessarily of great value to the competitors who wished to have access to it.

Thirdly, it was inherent in the fact that the undertaking concerned held an IPR that the subject matter of that right was innovative or original. There can be no patent without an invention and no copyright without an original work. In its Decision the Commission had not simply rejected Microsoft's assertion that the fact that the technology concerned was covered by IPRs justified its refusal to disclose the relevant information. The Commission had also examined Microsoft's argument that, if it

46 CFI judgment, para. 691.
47 CFI judgment, paras 692–712.

were required to give third parties access to that technology, there would be a negative impact on its incentives to innovate. The CFI found that Microsoft, which bore the initial burden of proof, did not sufficiently establish that if it were required to disclose the interoperability information, that would have a significant negative impact on its incentives to innovate. Microsoft had merely put forward vague, general and theoretical arguments on that point. Thus, Microsoft had merely stated that '[d]isclosure would . . . eliminate future incentives to invest in the creation of more intellectual property', without specifying the technologies or products to which it thus referred. In certain passages Microsoft envisaged a negative impact on its incentives to innovate by reference to its operating systems in general, namely both those for client PCs and those for servers. In that regard, the CFI found it sufficient to note that the Commission quite correctly had refuted Microsoft's arguments relating to the fear that its products would be cloned. And the CFI found that it must be borne in mind, in particular, that the remedy prescribed in the Decision to make available within 120 days the interoperability information to any undertaking having an interest in developing and distributing work group server operating systems products does not, and was not designed to, allow Microsoft's competitors to copy its products. It followed that it had not been demonstrated that the disclosure of the information to which that remedy related would significantly reduce – still less eliminate – Microsoft's incentives to innovate. In that context, the CFI observed that it is normal practice for operators in the industry to disclose to third parties the information which will facilitate interoperability with their products and Microsoft itself had followed that practice until it was sufficiently established on the work group server operating systems market. Such disclosure would allow the operators concerned to make their own products more attractive and therefore more valuable. In fact, none of the parties had claimed that such disclosure had had any negative impact on those operators' incentives to innovate in the present case. The CFI further considered that if the disclosures made under the US settlement had no negative impact on Microsoft's incentives to innovate, there was no obvious reason to believe that the consequences should be any different in the case of disclosure relating to server/server protocols.

Lastly, the CFI found that Microsoft's assertion that, in the Decision, the Commission applied a new evaluation test when rejecting the objective justification which Microsoft had submitted was based on a misreading of that Decision. That assertion was based on a single sentence in the Decision, which was in a part of the Decision containing the findings of the Commission's analysis of the refusal at issue. That sentence read as follows:

> [A] detailed examination of the scope of the disclosure at stake leads to the conclusion that, on balance, the possible negative impact of an order to supply on Microsoft's incentives to innovate is outweighed by its positive impact on the level of innovation of the whole industry (including Microsoft).

The CFI said that the sentence had to be read in conjunction with the one coming immediately afterwards in the same recital, which stated that:

> the need to protect Microsoft's incentives to innovate cannot constitute an objective justification that would offset the exceptional circumstances identified.

It also had to be compared with another recital to the Decision, where the Commission set out the following considerations:

> It has been established above . . . that Microsoft's refusal to supply [creates a risk of elimination of] competition in the relevant market for work group server operating systems, that this is due to the fact that the refused input is indispensable to carry on business in that market and that Microsoft's refusal has a negative impact on technical development to the prejudice of consumers. In view of these exceptional circumstances, Microsoft's refusal cannot be objectively justified merely by the fact that it constitutes a refusal to license intellectual property. It is therefore necessary to assess whether Microsoft's arguments regarding its incentives to innovate outweigh these exceptional circumstances.[48]

The CFI concluded from this that, in accordance with the principles laid down in the case law,[49] the Commission, after establishing that the exceptional circumstances identified by the Court of Justice in *Magill* and *IMS Health* were present in this case, proceeded to consider whether the justification put forward by Microsoft on the basis of the alleged impact on its incentives to innovate might prevail over those exceptional circumstances, including the circumstance that the refusal at issue limited technical development to the prejudice of consumers within the meaning of Article 82(b) EC.

The CFI referred to the fact that the Commission came to a negative conclusion, not by balancing the negative impact which the imposition of a requirement to supply the information at issue might have on Microsoft's incentives to innovate against the positive impact of that obligation on innovation in the industry as a whole, but after refuting Microsoft's

---

48 Decision, recital 712.
49 As described in CFI judgement, paras 331–3.

arguments relating to the fear that its products might be cloned,[50] establishing that the disclosure of interoperability was widespread in the industry concerned[51] and showing that a commitment to the Commission made by IBM in 1984 was not substantially different from what Microsoft was ordered to do in the Decision[52] and that its approach was consistent with the Software Directive.[53]

It followed from all of these considerations that Microsoft had not demonstrated the existence of any objective justification for its refusal to disclose the interoperability at issue.[54] As the exceptional circumstances identified by the Court of Justice in *Magill* and *IMS Health* were also present in this case, this first part of the plea was rejected as wholly unfounded.[55]

Sun's 'Request'

As the second part of Microsoft's argument, it was held that Sun had not requested to be supplied by Microsoft with the technology which the Commission ordered it to disclose. This, however, was easily rejected by the CFI.[56]

The TRIPS Agreement

As the third part of Microsoft's argument, it was argued that the Commission did not take proper account of the obligations imposed on the European Communities by the TRIPS Agreement. That was also rejected by the CFI.[57]

It thus followed that the single plea put forward in connection with the first issue on the duty to grant a licence was rejected in its entirety as unfounded.[58]

The tying/bundling element

The next part of the judgment dealt with Microsoft's argument against the finding of the Commission's Decision on the bundling of Windows Media

---

[50] Decision, recitals 713–29.
[51] Decision, recitals 730–5.
[52] Decision, recitals 736–42.
[53] Decision, recitals 743–63. Directive 91/250 IEC on the legal protection of computer programs [1991] OJ L122/42.
[54] CFI judgment, para. 711.
[55] CFI judgment, paras 692–712.
[56] CFI judgment, paras 713–76.
[57] CFI judgment, paras 777–812.
[58] CFI judgment, para. 813.

Player with the Windows client PC operating system.[59] The Commission had stated that tying prohibited under Article 82 EC requires the presence of five factors:[60]

(i) that the tying and tied products are two separate products;
(ii) that the concerned undertaking is dominant in the market for the tying product;
(iii) that the undertaking concerned does not give customers a choice to obtain the tying product without the tied product;
(vi) that the practice in question forecloses competition; and
(v) that there is an absence of an objective justification.

Before going into these requirements (in the following called factors 1 to 5), a number of factual and technical findings in the Commission's Decision forming the background of the conduct in question were summarized. The CFI noted that these findings were not in effect disputed by Microsoft.[61] A number of introductory assertions, however, which Microsoft had put forward concerning the conditions necessary to establish the existence of abusive bundling[62] were examined by the CFI. Having referred to these arguments, the CFI expressed the view that Microsoft's arguments were purely semantic and that they could not be accepted. The CFI pointed to the way in which the Commission had structured its argument relating to bundling in the Decision with reference to the five factors.

Next, the CFI dealt with Microsoft's two pleas. The first related to infringement of Article 82 EC, where the Commission had found that Microsoft's conduct in making the availability of the Windows client PC operating system conditional on the simultaneous acquisition of Windows Media Player constituted an abusive tied sale.[63] The second plea related to the remedy,[64] whereby Microsoft were required to offer a version of its operating system which did not incorporate Windows Media Player. Microsoft found this remedy to be a breach of the principle of proportionality.

---

59 CFI judgment, para. 814 *et seq*.
60 Decision, recitals 794 and 795.
61 CFI judgment, paras 815–38.
62 The CFI uses the phrases tying and bundling without a clear distinction between them. In the French version of the judgment, the wording '*vente liée*' is mostly used, but '*groupage*' or '*couplage*' are also seen.
63 Decision, article 2(b).
64 Prescribed in Decision, article 6.

As to the first plea, the CFI pointed out that the Commission had examined Microsoft's conduct in light of the first four factors.[65]

The Commission had first observed that Microsoft had a dominant position (factor 2) on the client PC operating systems market.[66] The CFI noted that Microsoft had not disputed that fact. The Commission had thereafter said that streaming media players and client PC operating systems were two separate products (factor 1).[67] Thirdly, the Commission had stated that Microsoft did not give customers the choice of obtaining Windows without Windows Media Player (factor 3).[68] And fourthly, the Commission had claimed that the tying of Windows Media Player foreclosed competition in the media players market (factor 4).[69] The Commission had in particular observed that in 'classical' tying cases, both the Commission and the European Courts had 'considered the foreclosure effect for competing vendors to be demonstrated by the bundling of a separate product with the dominant product'.[70]

But the Commission had concurrently stated that, in the present case, there were good reasons not to assume without further analysis that tying Windows Media Player constituted conduct which by its very nature was liable to foreclose competition. The Commission had considered, in essence, that tying Windows Media Player with the dominant Windows made Windows Media Player the platform of choice for *complementary content* and applications which in turn created a risk of foreclosing competition in the market for media players.[71] Furthermore, this had spill-over effects on competition in related products such as media encoding and management software (often server-side) and also in client PC operating systems for which media players compatible with quality content were an important application.[72] As a last point, the Commission had examined the basis on which Microsoft had relied in its attempt to demonstrate that the abusive conduct imputed to it was objectively justified (factor 5).[73]

The CFI considered that the Commission's analysis of the constituent elements of bundling was correct and that it was consistent both with

65 CFI judgment, para. 853 referring to Decision, recitals 799–954.
66 Decision, recital 799.
67 CFI judgment, para. 853 referring to Decision, recitals 800–25.
68 CFI judgment, para. 856 referring to Decision, recitals 826–34.
69 CFI judgment, para. 857 referring to Decision, recitals 835–954.
70 CFI judgment, para. 857 referring to Decision, recital 841.
71 Decision, recital 842.
72 Decision, recital 842.
73 CFI judgment, para. 858 referring to Decision, recitals 955–70.

Article 82 EC and with the case law. The Commission was correct to rely on the five factors set out in the Decision in deciding whether Microsoft's conduct constituted abusive tying. Those factors could be deduced both from the very concept of bundling and from the case law.[74] Explicitly, the CFI pointed to the fact that bundling by an undertaking in a dominant position may also infringe Article 82 where it does not correspond to the example given in Article 82(d). Accordingly, in order to establish the existence of abusive bundling, the Commission had been correct to rely in its Decision on Article 82 in its entirety and not exclusively on Article 82(d).[75] And in any event, the CFI held that the constituent elements of abusive tying identified by the Commission coincided effectively with the conditions laid down in Article 82(d) and thereby rejected Microsoft's argument that in the present case the Commission had applied conditions which differed, from two perspectives, from those laid down in Article 82(d).[76] The CFI observed that, while neither that provision nor, more generally, Article 82 as a whole contains any reference to the anti-competitive effect of bundling, the fact remained that, in principle, conduct would be regarded as abusive only if it was capable of restricting competition.[77]

Against this background, the CFI considered that the question of the bundling had to be assessed by reference to the five factors set out in the Decision. The CFI expressed the view that the requirement of a dominant position (factor 2) must be considered to be met, because it was common ground that Microsoft had a dominant position on the market for the tying product, namely client PC operating systems.[78]

As to the existence of two separate products (factor 1), the CFI stated that the Commission had been correct to find that client PC operating systems and streaming media players constituted separate products.[79] Although the CFI, by way of preliminary observation, noted that the IT and communications industry is an industry in constant and rapid evolution, so that what initially appear to be separate products may subsequently be regarded as forming a single product both from the tech-

---

74 CFI judgment, para. 859 where the CFI referred, in particular, to Case T-30/89 *Hilti* v *Commission* [1991] ECR II-1439, upheld in Case C-53/92 P *Hilti* v *Commission* [1994] ECR I-667, and judgments of the CFI and the Court of Justice in Case T-83/91 *Tetra Pak* v *Commission* [1994] ECR 11-755; Case C-333/94 P *Tetra Park* v *Commission* [1996] ECR I-5951.

75 CFI judgment, para. 861.

76 CFI judgment, paras 862–3.

77 CFI judgment, para. 867 with reference to Case T-203/01 *Michelin* v *Commission* [2003] ECR II-4071, para. 237.

78 CFI judgment, paras 869–70.

79 CFI judgment, paras 872–944.

nological aspect and from the perspective of the competition rules, it was by reference to the factual and technical situation that existed at the time when the impugned conduct became harmful that the CFI had to assess whether the Commission was correct to find that streaming media players and client PC operating systems constituted two separate products. And that was the period after May 1999 where Microsoft released the version of Windows incorporating Windows Media Player.[80] The CFI further noted that Microsoft had relied to a large extent on the vague concept of media functionality in its arguments concerning the bundling of Windows and Windows Media Player. Furthermore, the CFI stated that Microsoft's argument, based on the contention that there was no demand for a Windows client PC operating system without a streaming media player, amounted to contending that complementary products could not constitute separate products for the purposes of Article 82 EC. But this was found by the CFI to be contrary to the Community case law on bundling.[81] In addition, in the case of complementary products, such as client PC operating systems and applications software, it was quite possible that customers would wish to obtain the products together, but from different sources.[82] In any event, there existed a demand for client PC operating systems without streaming media players, for example by companies afraid that their staff might use them for non-work-related purposes, a fact that had not been disputed by Microsoft.[83] In addition, the CFI found that a series of factors based on the nature and technical features of the products concerned, the facts observed on the market, the history of the development of the products concerned and Microsoft's commercial practice demonstrated the existence of separate consumer demand for streaming media players.[84]

This conclusion was not undermined by Microsoft's other arguments. Among them was the argument that the integration of Windows Media Player in the Windows operating system was dictated by technical reasons. The CFI found this to be scarcely credible in light of the content of certain of Microsoft's own internal communications. Thus, it followed from, *inter alia*, Bill Gates' remarks referred to at the beginning of this chapter that the integration of Windows Media Player in Windows was primarily designed to make Windows Media Player more competitive

---

80 CFI judgment, paras 913–5.

81 CFI judgment, paras 919–21 with reference to the judgments in Case T-30/89 *Hilti* and Case C-53/92 *Hilti*.

82 CFI judgment, para. 922.

83 CFI judgment, para. 924.

84 CFI judgment, paras 925–32.

with RealPlayer by presenting it as a constituent part of Windows and not as applications software that might be compared with RealPlayer.[85] Among the arguments was also Microsoft's claim that the Commission had failed to show that media functionality was not linked to client PC operating systems according to commercial usage. It was difficult to speak of commercial usage in an industry that was 95 per cent controlled by Microsoft.[86] In any event, it was settled case law that even when the tying of two products is consistent with commercial usage or when there is a natural link between the two products in question, it may nonetheless constitute abuse within the meaning of Article 82, unless it was objectively justified[87] (factor 5). A final argument put forward by Microsoft was also rejected, namely that the unbundled version of Windows which Microsoft had placed on the market pursuant to the remedy issued by the Commission had had no success. The CFI reacted to this by pointing to the fact that the lawfulness of a Community measure must be assessed on the basis of the matters of fact and of law existing at the time when the measure was adopted. Furthermore, any doubts as to the effectiveness of the remedy ordered by the Commission did not in themselves prove that its finding as to the existence of two separate products was wrong.[88]

The next point that the CFI had to assess was that consumers were unable to choose to obtain the tying product without the tied product (factor 3).[89] The CFI here described Microsoft's contention to be, in essence, that the fact that Microsoft integrated Windows Media Player in the Windows client PC operating system did not entail any coercion or supplementary obligation within the meaning of Article 82(d). Microsoft thus emphasized that customers paid nothing extra for the media functionality of Windows; in the second place, they were not obliged to use that functionality; and, in the third place, they were not prevented from installing and using competitors' media players. But the CFI observed that it could not be disputed that consumers were unable to acquire the Windows client PC operating system without simultaneously acquiring Windows Media Player. That meant that the conclusion of contracts was made subject to acceptance of supplementary obligations.[90] Under Microsoft's licensing

---

85 CFI judgment, para. 937.
86 CFI judgment, para. 940.
87 CFI judgment, para. 942 with reference to Case C-333/94 P *Tetra Pak II*, para. 37.
88 CFI judgment, para. 943.
89 CFI judgment, paras 945–75.
90 CFI judgment, para. 961.

system, it was not possible to obtain a licence to the Windows operating system without Windows Media Player.[91] The coercion thus applied was not just contractual in nature but also technical. In effect, it was not technically possible to uninstall Windows Media Player. Furthermore, Microsoft could not rely on the fact that customers were not required to pay anything extra for Windows Media Player.[92] First, it could not be inferred that the media player was provided free of charge since the price of Windows Media Player was included in the total price of the Windows client PC operating system. In any event, it did not follow from either Article 82(d) or the case law on bundling that consumers must necessarily pay a certain price for the tied product in order for it to be concluded that they are subject to supplementary obligations within the meaning of that provision.[93] It was also not relevant for the purposes of the examination of the present condition that, as Microsoft had claimed, consumers were not obliged to use the Windows Media Player which they found pre-installed on their client PC and that they could install and use other undertakings' media players on their PCs. Again, neither Article 82(d) nor the case law on bundling required that consumers must be forced to use the tied product or must be prevented from using the same product supplied by a competitor of the dominant undertaking in order for the condition that the conclusion of contracts is made subject to acceptance of supplementary obligations to be capable of being regarded as satisfied. For example, as the Commission had correctly observed in *Hilti,* users were not forced to use the Hilti branded nails which they obtained with the Hilti branded nail gun.[94] The CFI hereby observed that original equipment manufacturers (OEMs) were deterred from pre-installing a second streaming media player on client PCs and that consumers had an incentive to use Windows Media Player at the expense of competing media players, notwithstanding that the latter were of better quality. The CFI also rejected Microsoft's argument which was based on certain measures which it adopted pursuant to the US settlement.[95]

The conclusion by the CFI was thus that the Commission was correct to find that the condition relating to the imposition of supplementary obligations was satisfied in the present case.[96]

The next point was the foreclosure of competition (factor 4). After

---

[91] CFI judgment, para. 962.
[92] CFI judgment, para. 967.
[93] CFI judgment, paras 968–9.
[94] CFI judgment, para. 970.
[95] CFI judgment, paras 972–4.
[96] CFI judgment, para. 975.

a comprehensive analysis, the CFI found[97] that the final conclusion which the Commission had set out in its Decision concerning the anti-competitive effects of the bundling was well founded. The Commission was thus correct to make the findings that Microsoft had used Windows as a distribution channel to ensure for itself a significant competitive advantage on the media players market; because of the bundling, Microsoft's competitors were *a priori* at a disadvantage even if their products were inherently better than Windows Media Player. Microsoft interfered with the normal competitive process, which would benefit users by ensuring quicker cycles of innovation as a consequence of unfettered competition on the merits. The bundling increased the content and applications barriers to entry, which protected Windows, and facilitated the erection of such barriers for Windows Media Player. Microsoft shielded itself from effective competition from vendors of potentially more efficient media players who could challenge its position, and thus reduced the talent and capital invested in innovation of media players. By means of the bundling, Microsoft might expand its position in adjacent media-related software markets and weaken effective competition, to the detriment of consumers; by means of the bundling, Microsoft sent signals which deterred innovation in any technologies in which it might conceivably take an interest and which it might tie with Windows in the future. So the CFI concluded[98] that the Commission therefore had had ground to state in its Decision[99] that there was a reasonable likelihood that tying Windows and Windows Media Player would lead to a lessening of competition so that the maintenance of an effective competition structure would not be ensured in the foreseeable future. The CFI went on to state[100] that it must be made clear that the Commission did not find that the tying would lead to the elimination of all competition on the market for streaming media players. Microsoft's argument that, several years after the beginning of the abuse at issue, a number of third-party media players were still present on the market did not therefore invalidate the Commission's argument.

It followed from all of these considerations that Microsoft had put forward no argument capable of vitiating the merits of the findings made by the Commission in its Decision concerning factor 4 relating to the foreclosure of competition. The CFI therefore had to conclude that the

---

97 CFI judgment, para. 1088 *et seq*.
98 CFI judgment, para. 1089.
99 Decision, recital 984.
100 CFI judgment, para. 1089.

Commission had demonstrated to the requisite legal standard that the condition was satisfied in the present case.[101]

The last point to consider in this connection was the Commission's examination of the argument whereby Microsoft had sought to show that the bundling produced *efficiency gains* that would outweigh the anti-competitive effects identified. This point was studied under the title of absence of objective justification (factor 5). The CFI found, however, that Microsoft had not demonstrated the existence of any objective justification for the abusive bundling of Windows Media Player with the Windows client PC operating system.[102]

Finally, Microsoft argued that the Commission had failed to comply with the obligations imposed on the Communities by various provisions of the TRIPS Agreement.[103] However, the CFI pointed to the fact that it was settled case law that, given their nature and structure, WTO Agreements are not in principle among the rules by reference to which the Community judicature will review the legality of measures adopted by the Community institutions. It is only where the Community intended to implement a particular obligation assumed under the WTO, or where the Community measure refers expressly to specific provisions of the WTO Agreements, that the Community judicature must review the legality of the Community measure in question in the light of the WTO rules. As the circumstances of the present case clearly did not correspond to either of those two situations, Microsoft could not rely on the TRIPS Agreement. The Commission had furthermore correctly observed that it followed expressly from Article 40(2) of the TRIPS Agreement that the members of the WTO are entitled to regulate the abusive use of such rights in order to avoid effects which harm competition.[104]

It followed that the first plea was to be rejected as unfounded in its entirety.

The second plea – related to an alleged breach of the *principle of proportionality*. The Commission's Decision had, by way of remedy for the

---

101 CFI judgment, para. 1090.

102 CFI judgment, paras 1091–167.

103 CFI judgment, paras 1188–92

104 Article 40(2) TRIPS provides as follows: 'Nothing in this Agreement shall prevent Members from specifying in their legislation licensing practices or conditions that may in particular cases constitute an abuse of intellectual property rights having an adverse effect on competition in the relevant market. As provided above, a Member may adopt, consistently with the other provisions of this Agreement, appropriate measures to prevent or control such practices, which may include for example exclusive grantback conditions, conditions preventing challenges to validity and coercive package licensing, in the light of the relevant laws and regulations of that Member.'

abusive tying, ordered Microsoft to offer, within 90 days of the date of notification of that Decision, a full-functioning version of its Windows client PC operating system which did not incorporate Windows Media Player. Microsoft was to retain the right to offer a bundle of its Windows client PC operating system and Windows Media Player. The decision also provided that Microsoft was to communicate to the Commission, within the same period, all the measures which it had taken to comply with that obligation. The Decision had, in addition, provided details of that remedy. Microsoft thought this to be in breach of the principle of proportionality.

The CFI, however, found that this plea had to be rejected as unfounded. It pointed to the fact that, far from being disproportionate, the remedy prescribed in the Decision was an appropriate means of putting an end to the abuse in question and of resolving the competition issues identified, while causing the least possible inconvenience to Microsoft and its business model. Thus, the implementation of that measure did not entail any change in Microsoft's current technical practice other than the development of the version of Windows imposed by the decision. And, in particular, Microsoft retained the right to continue to offer the bundle of Windows and Windows Media Player while the Commission's sole intention had been to make it possible for consumers to obtain Windows without Windows Media Player. The remedy did not affect Microsoft′s ability to market its media player and, in particular, to offer it for downloading from the Internet. The Commission was, furthermore, correct to consider that the measures taken by Microsoft pursuant to the US settlement were not sufficient to put an end to the abuse and to resolve the competition issues identified.[105]

The conclusion of all this was that the claims relating to the annulment of the contested decision had to be rejected insofar as they concerned the bundling of Windows and Windows Media Player.[106]

3. REFLECTIONS ON THE CFI JUDGMENT

The CFI judgment in the Microsoft case is interesting for a variety of reasons.[107] One is that the judgment deals with difficult issues concerning

---

[105] CFI judgment, paras 1194–228.

[106] CFI judgment, para. 1229.

[107] See also P. Arhel, 'L'affaire Microsoft: à propos de la decision du TPICE de 17 septembre 2007', *Les Petites Affiches*, Doctrine, 21 November 2007, 3; H.C. Hausmann, 'Das Microsoft-Urteil: Zwischen Kartellrecht und gewerblichen Schutzrechten' (2008) *Multimedia und Recht* 381.

the interpretation of the requirements necessary to conclude that a refusal to grant a licence to competitors of an IPR covering information is an infringement of Article 82 EC. Another reason is the immense importance and energy put into the case by the Commission, and by the CFI.[108] In the same vein, it should not be forgotten that, at the same time, the Commission was reviewing the law and policy relating to Article 82 EC, dealing with a series of general questions as to its interpretation and application.[109] It is hardly surprising that the judgment provoked many comments in Europe and abroad.[110]

It must be noted at the outset that the CFI made it clear that its judicial scrutiny of the Commission's decision did not involve a comprehensive review of all questions decided by the Commission. As the CFI put it: the European Courts' review of complex economic appraisals made by the Commission was necessarily limited to checking whether the relevant rules on procedure and on stating reasons had been complied with, whether the facts had been accurately stated, and whether there has been any manifest error of assessment or a misuse of powers.[111] Likewise, insofar as the Commission's Decision was the result of complex technical appraisals, those appraisals were in principle subject to only limited review by the CFI, which meant that the latter could not substitute its own assessment of matters of fact for that of the Commission.[112] Despite these statements it is clear that the CFI went far in its assessment of the Decision. This may be seen, *inter alia*, also from critical comments, such as those issued by the US Assistant Attorney General after the CFI judgment. In a press release issued immediately after the judgment, he said:

> In the United States, the antitrust laws are enforced to protect consumers by protecting competition, not competitors. In the absence of demonstrable consumer harm, all companies, including dominant firms, are encouraged to compete vigorously. U.S. courts recognize the potential benefits to consumers

---

[108] See B. Vesterdorf, 'Article 82 EC: Where Do We Stand after the *Microsoft* Judgment?' (2008) *Global Antitrust Review* 1, 2.

[109] See especially Commission Discussion Paper on the Application of Article 82 to Exclusionary Abuses, December 2005. See also the follow-up from December 2008 in 'Communication from the Commission – Guidance on the Commission's Enforcement Priorities in Applying Article 82 of the EC Treaty to Abusive Exclusionary Conduct by Dominant Undertakings', OJ [2009] C45/7, 24.2.2009.

[110] See e.g. L. Idot, 'Comment mettre fin à une superdominance?' in (2007) *Europe*, October, Focus, 2, and M. Debroux, 'Vers une banalisation de la propiété intellectuelle dans l'analyse d'abus de dominance?' (2007) *Contrats Concurrence Consommation*, October, Focus, 2.

[111] CFI judgment, para. 87.

[112] CFI judgment, para. 88.

> when a company, including a dominant company, makes unilateral business decisions, for example to add features to its popular products or license its intellectual property to rivals, or to refuse to do so.[113]

This press release has been characterized as generating a 'war of words' between the Commission and the United States.[114]

Another factor which may give rise to some hesitation is the way in which the CFI presented the requirements found in Court of Justice case law. The CFI proceeded on the basis of general statements which cannot be said to be the approach usually adopted by the Court of Justice. When reading the Court of Justice's judgments, it is clear that the Court relies heavily on the precise factual circumstances of the case before reaching its conclusions. Thus, for instance, in *IMS Health*[115] the Court of Justice very precisely recalled the circumstances that were present in *Magill* when coming to its conclusion about the consequences of that Decision for the case at hand. Similarly, in *Volvo*[116] the Court of Justice was very precise whenever it referred to the 'protected design' and, furthermore, when it noted that the situation dealt with was a 'design right covering car body panels'. The recent Court of Justice judgment in *Bertelsmann*[117] where the CFI's general scheme from the *Airtours* judgment[118] for assessing collective dominance was commented upon with some hesitation by the Court of Justice, might even be seen as an indirect critique of the CFI's judgment in the Microsoft case. It might thus be seen as a well-placed signal from the Court of Justice to the CFI not to be too theoretical. In *Bertelsmann*, the Court of Justice thus expressed the view that:

> In applying those criteria, it is *necessary to avoid a mechanical approach involving the separate verification of each of those criteria taken in isolation*, while taking no account of the overall economic mechanism of a hypothetical tacit coordination.
>
> In that regard, the assessment of, for example, the transparency of a particular market *should not be undertaken in an isolated and abstract manner*, but

---

113 'Assistant Attorney General for antitrust, Thomas O. Barnett, issues statement on European Microsoft decision', 17 September 2007, available at www.usdoj.gov/atr/public/press_releases/2007/226070.htm.

114 See S. Howarth and K. McMahon, '"Windows has Performed an Illegal Operation": The Court of First Instance's Judgment in *Microsoft* v *Commission*' (2008) *European Competition Law Review* 117.

115 Case C-418/01 *IMS Health* [2004] ECR I-5039.

116 Case 238/87 *Volvo* [1988] ECR 6211.

117 Case C-413/06 P *Bertelsmann and Sony* v *Impala and others* [2008] ECR I-4951.

118 Case T-342/99 *Airtours* v *Commission* [2002] ECR II-2585.

> should be carried out using the mechanism of a hypothetical tacit coordination as a basis.[119]

One might easily construe these words of the Court of Justice as a warning against the 'general approach' of the CFI in the Microsoft case.

The Refusal to License Issue

As can be seen from the foregoing, the starting point for the CFI, based on the Court of Justice's finding in *Volvo* and later judgments,[120] was the fact that the refusal by an undertaking holding a dominant position to license a third party to use a product covered by an IPR *cannot in itself* constitute an abuse of a dominant position within the meaning of Article 82 EC. It is only in *exceptional circumstances* that the exercise of the exclusive right by the owner of the IPR may give rise to such an abuse. The Court of Justice case law required situations (a product or service indispensable to the exercise of a particular activity on a neighbouring market, that the refusal excludes any effective competition on that neighbouring market, the refusal prevents the appearance of a new product for which there is potential consumer demand) to be present in order to characterize the circumstances to be exceptional. Even when it has been established that such circumstances are present, the refusal may be *objectively justified.*

The CFI, however, noted that the criterion that the refusal prevents the appearance of a new product for which there is potential consumer demand is found only in the case law on the exercise of an IPR.[121] The CFI observed that it was appropriate to add that it was necessary to distinguish two markets: namely, a market constituted by that product or service and on which the undertaking refusing to supply holds a dominant position, and a neighbouring market on which the product or service is used in the manufacture of another product or for the supply of another service. The fact that the indispensable product or service was not marketed separately did not exclude from the outset the possibility of identifying a separate market.[122] Thus, the CFI confirmed the view that the Court of Justice had

---

119 Case C-413/06 *Bertelsmann*, paras. 124–6 (emphasis added).

120 Interestingly, the CFI in its judgment presents the circumstances from the Court of Justice's judgment in Joined Cases 6/73 and 7/73 *Commercial Solvents* v *Commission* [1974] ECR 223. But the CFI does not apply this judgment in its subsequent reasoning.

121 CFI judgment, para. 334.

122 With reference to Case C-418/01 *IMS Health*, para. 43.

held[123] that it was sufficient that a potential market or even a hypothetical market could be identified and that such was the case where the products or services were indispensable to the conduct of a particular business activity and where there was an actual demand for them on the part of undertakings which sought to carry on that business. The Court of Justice had concluded in the following paragraph of the judgment that it was decisive that two different stages of production were identified and that they were interconnected, in that the upstream product was indispensable for supply of the downstream product.[124]

One should take note of the specific references to the IPRs in relation to new products. The CFI here points to the Court of Justice's requirement in this regard, but there is no mention in the judgment of the content of these rights. However, Bo Vesterdorf, the former president of the CFI in the Microsoft case, highlights this issue by stating that it is important that the substantive criteria for acquiring the exclusive right do not become too easy to fulfil, especially as regards patents. In a footnote to this statement, he expresses the following view: 'One may for example wonder how the compilation of television programme listings in *Magill* could represent creativity worthy of copyright protection. The same applies to the *IMS Health* case.'[125] This seems to be a hidden critique of the Court of Justice's handling of IPRs, but at the same time it might be seen as an acceptance of the worthiness of protection of the IPRs in the Microsoft case. In any event, the CFI based its judgment on the most favourable position for Microsoft by assuming that the information at issue was covered by IPRs.[126]

As to the issue of elimination of any effective competition on the neighbouring market, it seems fair to claim that the Commission and the CFI were right in their conclusion, and that in light of the complex economic appraisals, the CFI should not and could not substitute its own assessment of matters of fact for that of the Commission. On the other hand, the Commission's finding to this point seems to me convincing and unquestionable.

The necessity or 'indispensability' of the information is the first issue to address. Thus, as shown above, the CFI accepted the Commission's approach without really questioning the alternative ways to achieve the

---

[123] With reference to Case C-418/01 *IMS Health*, para. 44.

[124] CFI judgment, para. 335.

[125] B. Vesterdorf, 'Article 82 EC: Where Do We Stand after the *Microsoft* Judgment?' (2008) *Global Antitrust Review* 1, 41.

[126] As to the relation to IPRs, see e.g. D. Eklöf, 'Microsofts licensvägran i skottlinjen' (2007–08) *Juridisk Tidsskrift* 681, 684.

desired interoperability. Thus, the CFI can be said to have made a rather superficial assessment of the issue when it limited itself only to point to the 'valuable' nature of the protocols for Microsoft as well as for its competitors. This appears to be a broadening of the previous case law of the Court of Justice, especially when looking at *Bronner*, since in that case the Court of Justice spelled out, as quoted by the CFI, that 'the service in itself be indispensable to carrying on that person's business, inasmuch as there is no actual or potential substitute in existence for that home-delivery scheme'.[127]

As has been noted by Vesterdorf,[128] with the CFI's acceptance of the Commission's approach, the concept of indispensability has now been broadened to also cover 'economic indispensability'. It is especially argued that the criterion based on objective, almost physical indispensability (the so-called concept of 'essential facility') has been broadened to include an economic assessment.

This is a questionable broadening. It seems to be highly debatable whether this new approach taken by the CFI would have been able to survive had its judgment been appealed to the Court of Justice. Despite the enormous differences between the factual circumstances in *Bronner* and the Microsoft case, I consider the fact that the judgment in *Bronner* referred to 'no actual or potential substitute in existence' to be very important. In accordance with *Bronner*, even a potential substitute would have been sufficient. Although the judgment in *Bronner* did not specifically refer to the statements of Advocate General Jacobs in this regard, the explanation in his Opinion must be seen as the necessary background of that judgment. Advocate General Jacobs explained that access:

> can be justified in terms of competition policy only in cases in which the dominant undertaking has a genuine stranglehold on the related market. That might be the case for example where duplication of the facility is impossible or extremely difficult owing to physical, geographical or legal constraints or is highly undesirable for reasons of public policy. It is not sufficient that the undertaking's control over a facility should give it a competitive advantage.

He continued by saying that:

> I do not rule out the possibility that the cost of duplicating a facility might alone constitute an insuperable barrier to entry. That might be so particularly

127 Case C-7/97 *Oscar Bronner*, para. 41.

128 B. Vesterdorf, 'Article 82 EC: Where Do We Stand after the *Microsoft* Judgment?' (2008) *Global Antitrust Review* 1, 7.

> in cases in which the creation of the facility took place under non-competitive conditions, for example, partly through public funding. However, the test in my view must be an objective one: in other words, in order for refusal of access to amount to an abuse, it must be extremely difficult not merely for the undertaking demanding access but for any other undertaking to compete. Thus, if the cost of duplicating the facility alone is the barrier to entry, it must be such as to deter any prudent undertaking from entering the market.[129]

One might wonder whether Vesterdorf's statement is an intriguing indication of a divided CFI on the indispensability requirement, since no express indication of a broadening from previous Court of Justice judgments is given in the CFI judgment read on its own.

Several authors have seen the concept of 'new product' as interpreted by the CFI as far-reaching and controversial.[130] From the Court of Justice's judgment in *IMS Health*, it could be deduced that the function of the requirement of the emergence of a 'new product' relates to the consideration that, in the balancing of the interest in protection of the IPR and the economic freedom of its owner against the interest in protection of free competition, the latter can prevail *only* where refusal to grant a licence prevents the development of the secondary market to the detriment of consumers.[131] From this, the Court of Justice had drawn the conclusion that the refusal to license an IPR would only be abusive where the undertaking requesting it did not simply intend essentially to duplicate the goods or services already offered on the secondary market by the owner of the IPR, but intended to produce 'new goods or services' not offered by the owner of the right for which there was a potential consumer demand.[132]

The CFI position in the Microsoft case is ambivalent. On the one hand, it recognized that the requirement that the refusal prevents the appearance of a new product for which there is potential consumer demand had only been found in the case law on the exercise of an IPR.[133] This statement may be interpreted as meaning that the 'new product' element is not required when a dominating company is asked to give access to an important (essential) facility *not covered by IPR*. On the other hand, the CFI went further and brought in the notion of 'technical development'.[134] That

---

[129] Advocate General Jacobs in Case C-7/97 *Oscar Bronner*, paras. 65 *et seq.*

[130] See e.g. A. Andreangeli, 'Case Note on T-201/04, Microsoft v Commission, Judgment of 17 September 2007' (2008) *Common Market Law Review* 863, 882 *et seq*, and Moldén, n. 4 above, 328.

[131] Case C-418/01 *IMS Health*, para. 48, and CFI judgment, para. 646.

[132] Case C-418/01 *IMS Health*, para. 49.

[133] CFI judgment, para. 334.

[134] CFI judgment, para. 647.

had been the thesis on which the Commission had based its finding in its Decision. The Commission considered that Microsoft's refusal to supply the relevant information limited technical development to the prejudice of consumers within the meaning of Article 82(b). The CFI did not find these findings of the Commission to be manifestly incorrect. On the contrary, it accepted the view of the Commission that, owing to the lack of interoperability which competing work group server operating system products could achieve with the Windows domain architecture, an increasing number of consumers were locked into a homogeneous Windows solution at the level of work group server operating systems. And Microsoft's refusal prevented its competitors from developing work group server operating systems capable of attaining a sufficient degree of interoperability with the Windows domain architecture. That had the consequence that consumers' purchasing decisions in respect of work group server operating systems were channelled in the direction of Microsoft's products. Added to this, in the view of the CFI, was that the limitation thus placed on choice was all the more damaging to consumers because they considered that non-Microsoft work group server operating systems were better than Windows work group server operating systems with respect to a series of features to which they attached great importance, such as 'reliability/availability of the . . . system' and 'security included with the server operating system'. This artificial advantage in terms of interoperability that Microsoft retained by its refusal would discourage its competitors from developing and marketing work group server operating systems with innovative features, to the prejudice, notably, of consumers.[135]

It can be argued that the CFI was too much taken in by the Commission's Decision in relation to this 'technical development'. The Decision rested on the concept that, once the obstacles represented for Microsoft′s competitors by the insufficient degree of interoperability with the Windows domain architecture were removed, those competitors would be able to offer work group server operating systems which, far from merely reproducing the Windows systems already on the market, would be distinguished from those systems with respect to parameters which consumers consider important.[136] The likelihood of such an outcome, however, might be seen as somewhat hypothetical when viewed in light of the actual case. This is despite the fact that, on the one hand, the Court of Justice has been very specific and precise in relation to the background and the factual circumstances of cases such as *Magill* and *IMS Health*, and especially in

---

135 CFI judgment, paras 650–3.
136 CFI judgment, para. 656.

pointing to the requirement that the dominating company should not be able to reserve for itself a dominating position over a 'secondary market' by hindering the emergence of *totally new* products or services for which there was a consumer demand not being satisfied,[137] and, on the other hand, in *IMS Health* seems to have acknowledged that there are great difficulties in assessing what constitutes a 'new product'.[138]

The CFI appeared to be far less demanding than the Court of Justice. It could thus easily be argued that a much deeper scrutiny into the effects on the market of denial of access to the information as to interoperability would have been more in line with the demanding case law of the Court of Justice on this point. By relying on the concept of 'technical development' (which it should be recalled, is present in the wording of Article 82(b) EC) instead of 'new product', the CFI seems undoubtedly to have opened a much broader door for requiring access to IPRs than what has been the policy of the Court of Justice.[139] An impact to 'technical development' may easily be found to exist. It is a concept of a very broad scope. One may even go so far as to say that every refusal to license would satisfy the conditions set up by the CFI, as every product manufactured with the licence would arguably constitute 'technical development'.[140]

Consequently, Vesterdorf notes:

> Simply put: in order to find an abusive refusal to grant a licence, it is no longer a *conditio sine qua non* that the refusal prevents the emergence of a new product in a strict sense: also the prevention of technical development may be abusive. . . . Since the conditions under which a refusal to license a product must remain *exceptional,* this definition or broadening of the, 'new product' criterion must, like any other exception, be interpreted restrictively.[141]

If one looks at the possible consequences for competition of the finding on 'technical development' in the long run, one criticism is that the Commission and the CFI have opened the way for competitors to manufacture software that would match Microsoft's dominant software. Competitors might, instead of striving at better results for their development of new products, remain dependent on Microsoft's software,

---

137 As to this, see Joined Cases C-241 and 242/91 *Magill*, para. 53 *et seq*.

138 Case C-418/01 *IMS Health*, para. 48 *et seq*. (twice using the word 'only'). See also Andreangeli, n. 5 above, 883–4.

139 See also Andreangeli, n. 5 above, 883 *et seq*.

140 See also J. Langer, 'The Court of First Instance´s Microsoft Decision: Just an Orthodox Ruling in an Un-Orthodox Case' (2008) *Legal Issues of Economic Integration* 183, 192.

141 B. Vesterdorf, 'Article 82 EC: Where Do We Stand after the *Microsoft* Judgment?' (2008) *Global Antitrust Review* 1, 9.

resulting in a stiffening of competition rather than an encouragement of innovation. The CFI approach was based on the assumption that high-tech markets are strongly characterized by network effects because computer operating systems and computer programs by nature are built up to work in connection with other hardware and software. As is clear from the arguments of the Commission in the case, their value increases along with the number of users that choose them. From that consequence it follows that more end-users will prefer the strong and well-established software, while intermediaries will direct their supplies towards the well-established program and software. All kinds of users will naturally invest energy, time and other forms of resources to acquaint themselves with the dominant system. When that has been done, it will be difficult to persuade them to switch to new or competing systems or programs since they have already invested in this system. That investment would to a large extent be lost if they were to shift to another system, and in turning to a competing system, they would again have to invest the same amount of energy, time and other resources. Therefore, there will be a strong preference to stay with the chosen system standard, which would cause great difficulties for competing newcomers on the market.

The competitive situation established when ordering the dominating company to disclose information to its competitors might bring an additional consideration into the picture. As pointed out from several sides, this might lead to the establishment of a platform for talks between competitors. When the CFI requires Microsoft to give its competitors access to software that will match Microsoft´s dominant software perfectly, meetings between the licensor and the licensees are inevitable. This might turn out to be a good opportunity for making approaches for coordination of market behaviour.[142] For instance, Ian Forrester refers to the reply given by Microsoft to Sun´s request for access as being an invitation to talk face-to face.[143]

Of course, this does not in itself constitute a cartel. There are also arguments in the opposite direction. First of all, a general approach can be taken by pointing to the overall idea that even though high-tech industries are heavily dependent on innovation and R&D, which therefore should be protected as much as possible, the reaction to that is that a society based on a liberal system must require that the competitive climate and process is preserved to the highest possible degree in order to avoid the negative effects of a deviation through preservation of protective measures. With the opening up of the possibilities for applying the Microsoft standard

---

142 See e.g. Moldén, n. 4 above, 331.

143 See Chapter 4.

by competitors, there might be a very strong incentive for them to strive towards developing new and competing standards. But again, one could be sceptical as to the approach of the dominating company. There could be several means whereby the dominating company creates solutions or connections specifically designed to lock-in other companies, as well as the end-users, into dependence. However, as the Court of Justice and the CFI have recognized, it is only under exceptional circumstances that Article 82 EC is applicable towards holders of IPRs.[144]

One thing not to overlook is the approach taken by the Court of Justice in the *Bronner* judgment, where it was clear that the concern of the Court was the competitive situation of the *specific* undertaking seeking to obtain access to the service comprised in home delivery. That can be seen not only from the wording of the *Bronner* judgement at paragraph 41, quoted above,[145] but also from paragraph 37 (not referred to by the CFI in its presentation of the Microsoft case) where the Court of Justice spelled out that it needs to be determined whether the refusal constituted an abuse of a dominant position within the meaning of Article 82 on the ground that such refusal deprives 'that competitor' of a means of distribution judged essential for the sale of its newspaper. The words highlight that the Court of Justice was referring to the competitive situation of a specific competitor (the complainant), not all competitors of the dominating company. The CFI, however, in the Microsoft case seems to have been more concerned with the possibilities for competitors of Microsoft on the market, not with the specific company requiring access.[146]

The last point assessed by the CFI was whether the refusal of disclosure of the interoperability information was 'objectively justified'. The CFI concluded that such a justification was not present in the actual case. This appears to be well in accordance with the signals of the Court of Justice (and with the Commission in its Article 82 Discussion Paper).[147]

---

144 These last points have been inspired by Andreangeli, n. 5 above, 878 *et seq*. See also C. Bergqvist, 'Konkurrencesagen mod Microsoft' (2008) *Ugeskrift for Retsvaesen* 103, 110.

145 See text to n. 20 above.

146 See also e.g. Langer, n. 140 above, 192.

147 See e.g. the Court of Justice in Cases T-191 and 212–214/98) *Atlantic Container Line AB and others* v *Commission* [2003] ECR II-3275, para. 1111 *et seq*. And see European Commission, DG Competition Discussion Paper on the Application of Article 82 EC Treaty to Exclusionary Abuses, Brussels, December 2005, para. 78. See also the follow-up from December 2008 in '*Communication from the Commission – Guidance on the Commission's Enforcement Priorities in Applying Article 82 of the EC Treaty to Abusive Exclusionary Conduct by Dominant Undertakings*', OJ [2009] C45/7, 24/2/2009.

As mentioned, the CFI thus found that the mere fact of holding IPRs could not in itself constitute objective justification for the refusal to grant a licence when the exceptional circumstances necessary for a finding of abuse of a dominant position had been satisfied.[148] This must mean that something more is necessary in order to bring the situation of refusal outside the scope of Article 82. And that could not, in the Microsoft case, be the argument that the requirement to give access to the information might lead Microsoft to withhold its innovation process. Simply, it is not likely that Microsoft might decide not to create new innovations or to slow down on existing innovations.

The Tying/Bundling Issue

The finding of the CFI as to the tying/bundling issue does not require extensive comments. It seems to be well in line with former case law of the Court of Justice, and in the present context the arguments presented by Microsoft do not have a convincing character.

In their comments on to the Commission's Decision in Chapter 4, Jean-François Bellis and Tim Kasten state that the tying part of the decision 'directly challenges Microsoft's ability to engage in beneficial and pro-competitive conduct'.[149] That, in my view, is a clear misinterpretation of EU competition law, at least if one believes that tying can be accepted under the circumstances present in the Microsoft case. The example of what consumers expect from new mobile telephones given in the comment thus directly overlooks the fact that Microsoft was in a very dominant position, whereas that is not the situation or only very seldom the situation with the companies offering mobile telephones. The same rejection can be made of the point of view in the said comments which gives as an example selling shoes with laces, which is said to amount to tying only if there is a demand for shoes without laces. This overlooks the difference from the Microsoft case where the dominant position was manifest.

The point could, however, have been raised whether the CFI's relying on 'technological development' and not only as in previous case law on tying and ordinary products could have other implications. One could thus in principle argue that the tying not only brings together two separable products or solutions into one. It might also have a positive effect on the combined solution, for example as to functionality, that would otherwise not be reached. This would probably be a more acceptable point of

---

[148] CFI judgment, paras 689 and 691.
[149] See Chapter 4.

view when dealing with complex IT solutions. But the fact that Microsoft had not bundled the two products together from the very beginning contradicts this combined solution argument under the actual circumstances.

Another point might be brought forward. When Microsoft claimed that it had not been shown that media functionality was not linked according to commercial usage to client PC operating systems, the CFI not only rejected this argument by pointing to the fact that it was difficult to speak of commercial usage in an industry that was 95 per cent controlled by Microsoft, but it also pointed to settled case law showing that even when the tying of two products has been consistent with commercial usage, or when there is a natural link between the two products in question, it might constitute an abuse within the meaning of Article 82 EC, unless it is objectively justified.[150] On the other hand, against the criticism that could be raised on the basis of commercial usage, reference must be made to the explicit reference by the CFI to issues of fact and law *existing at the time when the measure was adopted.* This demonstrates that competition law does not restrict the development of future technical solutions where different parts are put together and sold in a bundle. What today might seem natural in connection with an operating system may not have been so at the time of its introduction into the market. For instance, many applications of today that are components of a modern PDA (personal digital assistant) might have been within the area of abuse if originally marketed by a dominating firm not as a supplementary item.

The argument used in *Tetra Pak II*, where the Court of Justice rejected the dominating company's reliance on protecting consumers against, *inter alia*, harm from unauthorized additional products in order to justify a tying[151] could also have been used here by the CFI to support its conclusion. The dominating company cannot substitute for the tasks of the legislator without thereby violating the competition rules.

The fact that consumers could download other media players free of charge in addition to Windows Media Player included in the operating system did not take away the excluding effect of Microsoft's tying, and it seems fair to concentrate especially on this effect of Microsoft's bundling. In the short run, consumers might thus benefit from the tying, even in the way that they could be said not to be charged for the Windows Media Player included in the operating system. But as soon as this bundling

---

150 CFI judgment, para. 942 with reference to Case C-333/94 P *Tetra Pak II*, para. 37.

151 Case C-333/94 *Tetra Pak II,* paras 79–84.

produced negative effects on Microsoft's competitors that must be seen as a negative effect also directly impacting the consumers.

It must be noted that the market situation with an extremely dominant Microsoft tying together its media player with its operating system must be viewed as the core element in the assessment of this part of the judgment. So I do not concur with a critique saying that the CFI appears somewhat short-sighted, since it did not sufficiently take into account the competition dynamics of the relevant market and especially the circumstance that in high-tech industries there is a strong trend toward the emergence of products based on technological integration of new features which should therefore warrant a more 'realistic' and flexible attitude to those forms of conduct.[152] In my view, the CFI correctly relied on the 'classical' tying schemes in order to assess whether Microsoft had committed an abuse, and the overriding arguments put forward by the CFI appear to have been fair and to the point under the actual circumstances.

4. CONCLUDING REMARKS

It has been said that the Microsoft judgment may have far-reaching consequences.[153] However, the special circumstances surrounding the case (a very dominant company, special need for licence, tying after having sold the same products without tying, etc.) and the fact that the company itself through its leading person had directly expressed the intent of forcing competitors out of the market may lead one to view this conclusion with a little scepticism. The case might not have been as clear had the circumstances in respect of these facts been different. However, it is to be expected from the outcome of the Microsoft case that the Commission will now proceed with full force with its considerations concerning the reform of Article 82 EC.[154]

Perhaps what Microsoft received from the CFI was no more than could be expected after its bold statement, and indeed its forceful defence during the proceedings before the CFI. It does not happen every day that a US company of such a high calibre is accused of abusing its market power to squeeze out its competitors serving their European customers to the detriment of the final consumers, without being able to show a valid docu-

---

152 Andreangeli, n. 5 above, 893 with further references.

153 See e.g. B. Vesterdorf, 'Article 82 EC: Where Do We Stand after the *Microsoft* Judgment?' (2008) *Global Antitrust Review* 1, 14.

154 See also T. Körber, 'Wettbewerb in dynamischen Märkten zwischen Innovationsschutz und Machtmissbrauch' (2007) *Wirtschaft und Wettbewerb* 1209, 1210.

mentation of a technically viable development. There remains a strong need for scrutiny by the Court of Justice of the CFI's judgment. In the end, the question can be raised whether the solution as regards interoperability chosen by the Commission and accepted by the CFI may in reality turn out to have negative effects on competition. Would the outcome of the case have been the same had Bill Gates not made the quoted, and for competition authorities very provocative, declaration, or – put another way – could the outcome be seen as a confirmation of the proverb that 'you reap what you sow'?

PART III

Innovation, competition and welfare in the IT sector: transatlantic perspectives, international horizons

6. The Microsoft chronicles

Rudolph J.R. Peritz

1. INTRODUCTION

If there is a twentieth century icon, if there is a symbol for the information economy in the United States, it is Bill Gates and his Microsoft Corporation – a symbol for the best and worst of that century's economic transformation into a networked domain of knowledge bases and communication protocols. At best Bill Gates symbolized the possibility of success beyond the wildest dreams of a software geek, a college drop-out who left Harvard and went home to the buzz culture of Seattle with its coffee bars, its software garages, and its grunge rock cellars. Everyone, it seemed, wanted to be like Bill. Again, in its best light, Microsoft developed a software platform that helped lift personal computing into a worldwide technology for the information economy. But there was the dark side: At its worst, Microsoft abused the power of its Windows monopoly in a succession of predatory excesses not seen since the heyday of John D. Rockefeller and his Standard Oil Company. Both Rockefeller and Gates created networks for national distribution, one the first physical network for nationwide petroleum transport and the other the first virtual network of worldwide software standards for PCs. And, according to the Justice Departments and federal courts of their eras, both violated the antitrust laws to gain and maintain the dominance of those networks.

But similar means did not lead to similar ends. Standard Oil was broken up into 33 companies; Microsoft remains intact. Why was Microsoft not broken up into two firms, one with the intellectual property rights (IPRs) to Windows and the other to the applications software, as the Justice Department and 20 states demanded? Or three firms, each with all of Microsoft's IPRs – three Baby Bills – as called for by laissez-faire advocate turned Netscape counsel Robert Bork?

Adherents of *réal politique* would respond that the 2001 installation of George W. Bush as President seated a new administration whose corporatist ideology hid behind the rhetoric of laissez-faire. In this view, Microsoft was left intact as the national champion to maintain US global dominance of the information technology sector. That is an easy answer and, it can be forcefully argued, the right one.

Nonetheless, that answer proves too much because it does not take into account the Justice Department Antitrust Division's approach to the Microsoft case and the implications of its limitations. Those limitations took a strong case on the facts and made it a hard case on the law and, finally, a disappointing one on the remedy. The European Commission case against Microsoft provides a useful contrast to the US approach and its limitations, although it must be kept in mind that the US case struck at the core of Microsoft's business – the Windows operating system and web-browser – while the EC case focused on closely tied but ancillary lines of business – media players and low-end network servers.[1] The chapter is divided into three major sections.

The first section takes a close look at the fully litigated US case, the findings of fact regarding Microsoft's course of predatory conduct as well as the legal arguments that framed them. The section focuses on the opinions of trial court Judge Thomas Penfield Jackson.

The second section continues with the US case by exploring the issues of technological bundling and its antitrust corollary, technological tying. After close attention to the Court of Appeals' opinions,[2] the section analyses the reasons for current US rejection of the leverage theory that underlies traditional antitrust treatment of tying, a rejection expressed in most US court opinions following two decades of questionable economic criticism. The underlying conduct at issue is Microsoft's integration of

---

1 The European Commission has recently launched an investigation into Microsoft's bundling of Internet Explorer with its operating system, according to EC spokesman Jonathon Todd. Report available from Dow Jones Newswire at www.borsaitaliana.it/borsa/area-news/news/mf-dow-jones/internazionali-dettaglio.html?newsId=563524&lang=en.

2 The opinions in the case are referenced as follows: *United States* v *Microsoft Corp.*, 980 F.Supp. 537 (D.D.C. 1998) (contempt proceeding) (hereinafter *Microsoft I*), rev'd, 147 F.3d 935 (D.C. Cir. 1998) (contempt appeal) (hereinafter *Microsoft II*); *United States* v *Microsoft Corp.*, 1998 WL 614485 (D.D.C. 1998) (memo and decree on Microsoft's motions for summary judgment) (hereinafter *Microsoft III*); *United States* v *Microsoft Corp.*, 84 F.Supp.2d 9 (D.D.C. 1999) (findings of fact) (hereinafter *Microsoft IVa*); *United States* v *Microsoft Corp.*, 87 F.Supp.2d 30 (D.D.C. 2000) (conclusions of law) (hereinafter *Microsoft IVb*), aff'd in part and rev'd in part, *United States* v *Microsoft Corp.*, 253 F.3d 34 (D.C. Cir. 2001) (*en banc*) (merits appeal) (hereinafter *Microsoft V*), cert. denied, 534 U.S. 952 (2001); *United States* v *Microsoft Corp.*, 231 F.Supp.2d 144 (D.D.C. 2002) (Justice Department settlement approval) (hereinafter Microsoft *VI*). The references are adapted from D. McGowan, 'Between Logic and Experience, Error Costs and the U.S. v. Microsoft Corp.' (2005) *Berkeley Technology Law Journal* 1185 at n. 1.

applications software into the Windows operating system, both Internet Explorer and Windows Media Player.

The third section contrasts US and European Commission approaches to determining the obligations of dominant firms to provide information for software interoperability. On both sides of the Atlantic, the liability issues and to some extent the remedies reflect differing attitudes toward Microsoft's obligations to license and to provide information to competitors who produce software that must work efficiently within the industry technical standards defined by Microsoft Windows. Here, both antitrust and intellectual property policies about compulsory cooperation and compulsory licensing come into play. The context for this section is Microsoft's strategic conduct in the operating system market for low-end network servers.

The US court opinions address an array of liability issues that emerge from Microsoft's long-standing strategy of software integration, issues including its purposes and its effects, particularly its effects on software developers. The integration strategy was crucial to Microsoft's attaining dominance as early as the integration of DOS and Windows 3.11 to form Windows 95, and more recently in the integration of Internet Explorer and Windows Media Player into later versions of Windows. At the core of Microsoft's commercial strategies at least since Windows 95 have been software integration and the control over the industry-standard information that resulted.

In 2007, three years after the European Commission published its findings, the European Court of First Instance (CFI) affirmed in an opinion that gave surprising deference to Commission findings. The CFI decision was quickly followed by trans-Atlantic sabre-rattling in an exchange of public statements from the directors of the US Department of Justice Antitrust Division and the European Commission. The CFI judgment together with the rhetorical encounter present an opportunity to investigate, first of all, contrasting approaches taken to the relationship between antitrust and IPRs, and secondly, a largely ignored competition policy situated within the US patent regime.

The chapter concludes with some observations about the innovation and competition policies expressed in the bundle of opinions in the Microsoft case.

2. FACTUAL CONTEXT AND BACKGROUND

Antitrust scrutiny of Microsoft in the United States began with an extensive but inconsequential Federal Trade Commission (FTC) investigation in 1990, proceeded to the Justice Department's monopolization suits in 1994 and 1998, and continued in private suits until settlement of the RealNetworks case in 2004. Most attention has been paid to the fully litigated 1998 case, which 20 state Attorneys General joined as plaintiffs. In that litigation, the trial court phase concluded with Judge Thomas Penfield Jackson's holding that Microsoft had violated the Sherman Anti-Trust Act by monopolizing the market for Intel-compatible operating systems, by attempting to monopolize the market for web-browsers, and by tying Internet Explorer to the Windows operating system. Judge Jackson adopted the plaintiffs' proffered remedy and decreed that, thenceforth, there would be two Microsofts, one of them with ownership rights to Windows and the other with the rights to Microsoft applications software, including Internet Explorer. The decree also imposed restrictions and mandates regarding Microsoft's business practices and required external oversight as well as public reporting. The United States Circuit Court for the District of Columbia (Circuit) Court of Appeals reversed Judge Jackson's decision in significant part, affirmed only the monopolization holding, and remanded to another trial court judge for further proceedings, including reconsideration of remedies. The structural remedies fell and Microsoft remained intact.[3]

In the beginning, which was 1975, Bill Gates and friends created Microsoft. But it was five years later that IBM put Microsoft into the new economy's catbird seat. Not only did IBM choose Microsoft's version of DOS (Disc Operating System) as the only operating system distributed with its PCs, but in one of the great commercial blunders of the twentieth century, IBM disdained any equity interest in Microsoft and any rights

---

[3] See n. 2 above for listing and designation of *Microsoft* opinions. It is useful to note that the Windows software systems, and DOS before it, were written for PCs designed around processor chips once produced only by Intel and later by several additional companies. IBM chose Intel for its PC processor chips just as it chose Microsoft for its PC operating system. The PC market would split into two sub-markets based on two incompatible processor chip technologies, one consisting of IBM and its clones, and the other of Apple Computer systems, which used an incompatible processor chip. Although the Apple technology was considered to be more efficient and stable, and easier to use, its market share eventually fell to single digit percentages because, it is generally believed, Apple refused to license its technology. In consequence, no Apple clones developed and prices did not fall as they did in the IBM clone market because Apple was unable to match the economies of scale and the network effects resulting from the massive numbers of PCs produced and distributed in the IBM-compatible market. By the 1990s, Windows had monopolized the much larger IBM clone sub-market, which had come to be known as the Intel-compatible PC operating system market, a change no doubt resulting from IBM's decline and Intel's continued dominance.

in the software. Microsoft's MS-DOS would soon become the dominant operating system in the exploding market for IBM and IBM-compatible PCs. In the mid-1980s, Microsoft introduced the first Windows operating system and was promptly sued by Apple for infringing its copyrights for mouse-and-icon, point-and-click operating system design. Microsoft prevailed in what can best be understood as decisions reflecting the old economy mindset of unfamiliarity with computer software and narrow conceptions of their intellectual property protection.[4] With both MS-DOS and Windows, Microsoft adapted others' innovation and, by both fortune and design, found itself in a position to dominate an industry driven by the lemming logic of network economics. The question of whether Microsoft engaged in predatory practices to tip and maintain the market in its favour by reinforcing network market propensities toward all-or-nothing equilibria would occupy the antitrust enforcement agencies for the next decade.[5]

On 20 August 1993, the FTC informed Microsoft that it was closing its three-year investigation after the Commissioners twice deadlocked on staff recommendations to issue an administrative complaint and consider

---

4 *Apple Computer, Inc.* v *Microsoft Corp.*, 35 F.3d 1435 (9th Cir. 1994).

5 *See* R.J.R. Peritz, 'Tipping and Network Effects' in D. Moss (ed.), *Network Access: Lessons Learned in Regulation and Antitrust* (New York: Routledge Press, 2004). Cf. 'Microsoft sees software "agent" as way to avoid distractions', 17 July 2000, *New York Times*, C1 (remarking on Microsoft's 'longstanding industry reputation as a mere imitator, not an innovator').

Strictly speaking, Windows 3.1, introduced in 1986, was not an operating system. Rather it was a platform designed to run on DOS software, allowing users to issue the equivalent to DOS commands by pointing-and-clicking screen icons instead of typing arcane codes. Windows 3.1 was GUI (graphical user interface) software to simplify communication between the user and DOS. Windows 95 would combine Microsoft's MS-DOS and the Windows 3.1 layer into an integrated platform almost ten years later.

Perhaps the clearest sight-line into the earlier architecture comes from the US$155,000,000 settlement of Caldera's antitrust case against Microsoft. As reported by the Associated Press, Caldera charged that Microsoft included false error messages in Windows 3.1 that appeared whenever it detected Caldera's DOS, in order to deceive and unnerve users into switching to Microsoft DOS. Caldera charged further that Microsoft later built needless incompatibilities into Windows 3.1 simply to assure that it would run properly only with Microsoft's MS-DOS. 'Caldera, Microsoft settle suit', 10 January 2000, available at http://wire.ap.org/APnews/center_story.html; 'Microsoft and Caldera settle antitrust suit', *New York Times*, 11 January 2000, C2; *Caldera, Inc.* v *Microsoft Corp.*, 72 F. Supp.2d. 1295 (D.Utah 1999). See also *Aldridge* v *Microsoft Corp.*, 995 F.Supp. 728 (S.D.Tex. 1998) (antitrust and common law claims based on claims of misleading error messages).

a cease and desist order, the agency's equivalent to an injunction. On the same day, the Justice Department confirmed that it would initiate its own investigation of Microsoft and make use of the FTC materials. Less than a year later, Microsoft signed a consent judgment with the Justice Department, agreeing to eliminate certain contract restrictions on PC manufacturers, including a provision that conditioned the licensing of Windows on installation of Internet Explorer.[6] Those manufacturers included Compaq, Gateway and IBM. Microsoft intended, according to findings of fact in the Justice Department's subsequent 1998 case, to block access to distribution channels for products perceived as threats to Windows' continuing dominance – that is, to raise entry barriers to stop web-browsers and other competing products from reaching end-users.

By 1995, Microsoft had shifted corporate strategy to take account of the Internet's growing importance by shipping Internet Explorer (IE) as an applications program to run on the Windows 95 platform. Microsoft soon began to give away rather than sell IE. Netscape was forced to follow suit with its Navigator software, then the leading web-browser. Users would presumably have a choice between two strong browsers, both available at no direct cost. In 1996, Microsoft changed IE's software architecture from a stand-alone applications program to a group of modules that was shipped as part of Windows 95. The change benefited applications software programmers to the extent the change would ease compliance with interoperability protocols to IE. The harm was that the new software architecture in effect did the work of earlier contractual provisions, in apparent violation of the 1994 consent decree, provisions that required IBM, Gateway, Compaq and other PC manufacturers to install IE but not Netscape Navigator – still the industry leader. PC manufacturers were left with little choice but to accede, in practical terms denying Navigator the main access channel to new users. Indeed, Microsoft was aware of market

---

[6] 'In July 1994, officials at the Department of Justice (DOJ), on behalf of the U.S., filed suit against Microsoft, charging the company with, among other things, unlawfully maintaining a monopoly in the operating system market through anti-competitive terms in its licensing and software developer agreements. The parties subsequently entered into a consent decree, thus avoiding a trial on the merits.' See *United States* v *Microsoft Corp.*, 56 F.3d 1448 (D.C.Cir.1995), rev'ing, 159 F.R.D. 318 (D.D.C. 1995) (Tunney Act appeal of 1994 consent decree). Three years later, the Justice Department filed a civil contempt action against Microsoft for allegedly violating one of the decree's provisions. On appeal from a grant of a preliminary injunction, this court held that Microsoft's technological bundling of IE 3.0 and 4.0 with Windows 95 did not violate the relevant provision of the consent decree. See *Microsoft II*.

studies showing that few users would have the technical knowledge to uninstall IE, find a copy of Navigator and install it.

Moreover, Microsoft's revised licensing agreement also required PC manufacturers to pay royalties for Windows OS whenever a PC was shipped, whether or not it was shipped with Windows. The intent, of course, was to coerce PC manufacturers into shipping all PCs with Windows. When IBM refused to accede to all conditions, particularly because it did not want to abandon its billion dollar investment in its own OS/2 operating system, Microsoft withheld pre-release access to necessary information about the new Windows 95, costing IBM millions of dollars in PC sales. As a general matter, Microsoft charged lower royalties to PC manufacturers who cooperated more whole-heartedly, giving them a competitive advantage in a market where price competition was fierce.[7]

The effects of Microsoft's strategies were three: in the operating systems market for PCs, Microsoft was maintaining its monopoly. In the browser market, Microsoft was denying access to IE's only significant rival, Netscape Navigator. In a more expansive definition of the operating systems market for PCs, Microsoft was denying access to Java, the potential 'middleware' software that was shipped with Navigator and threatened to commodify Windows and all operating systems as fungible substitutes, not unlike disk drives, RAM and other PC components.

In late 1997, the Justice Department and the European Commission filed a civil contempt action, alleging that Microsoft's architectural bundling of IE with Windows 95 violated the 1994 consent decree. While Microsoft agreed to eliminate some of the challenged practices, the suit proved to be an embarrassment to the enforcement agencies. It was an embarrassment because the agencies had intended to keep Microsoft from tying Windows 95 to IE, and argued that the architectural change was functionally a tie-in that violated the consent decree. Microsoft argued that Windows 95 and IE were not two separate products tied together but part of one integrated operating system, and that, according to the consent decree section IV(E)(i), their agreement not to tie-in 'shall not be construed to prohibit Microsoft from developing integrated products'. Judge Thomas Penfield Jackson rejected the argument and issued a temporary injunction requiring Microsoft to offer Windows 95 and IE separately. The District of Columbia Circuit Court of Appeals reversed, however, holding that Judge Jackson had misconstrued the consent decree. Further, in a sweeping opinion that went beyond the consent decree, the Court of Appeals afforded enormous discretion to Microsoft and to others when they

[7] *Microsoft IVb*, Conclusions of Law.

engaged in what it called 'technological tying'. As a result, even if IE's new architecture did amount to tying under the antitrust laws, it was apparently legal, at least according to two judges in the Court of Appeals.[8]

Adding to the embarrassment, the entire proceeding was irrelevant in practical effect because, a month earlier, the Court of Appeals had already ruled that the consent decree did not apply to Windows 98 and, thus, that Microsoft could ship the new software, which extended the architectural integration of IE into Windows even more deeply. In consequence, by the time the Court of Appeals dissolved the temporary injunction in the Windows 95 matter, Windows 98 was already on retailers' shelves and in PCs awaiting shipment. Windows 95 was obsolete.

Two events, one of them public and the other behind closed doors, added new twists to the saga. First, without public announcement, Microsoft had again changed the IE software architecture. In later releases of Windows 95 and in Windows 98, Microsoft disingenuously redefined as IE components some modules used by both Windows and IE. In short, some Windows functions were treated as 'outsourced' to IE. The feigned outsourcing was designed in such a way that disabling IE would also disable the outsourced modules and, with them, Windows itself.[9] Of course, this particular design was not necessary technologically but rather an artifact of the particular linkage logics that Microsoft chose. Moreover, although there was some benefit to applications software programmers in the deeper integration, the harms were multiple. Users could not delete IE because of the architecture and, in some applications, Windows forced users to employ IE as the web-browser. Finally, evidence at trial would include studies finding that the new architecture resulted in a less stable, less efficient operating system. That is, with the newest architecture, Windows 98 was slower and crashed more frequently than its predecessors.

The second event, with great public fanfare, was the Justice Department's second antitrust suit, filed on precisely the day Windows 98 was shipped for sale. Twenty state Attorneys General joined the case, which was assigned to the same Judge Jackson because he was already deeply knowledgeable in the case. The government plaintiffs alleged that Microsoft used predatory tactics to maintain its Windows monopoly, attempted

---

[8] *Microsoft II*, 147 F.3d at 945–52 (three-judge panel splitting 2–1), reversing *Microsoft I* ('the Final Judgment').

[9] 'A Government expert, Glenn Weadock, testified that Microsoft "design[ed] [IE] so that some of the code that it uses co-resides in the same library files as other code needed for Windows".' *Microsoft V*, 253 F.3d at 66; see, generally, Brief of Prof. Lawrence Lessig as *Amicus Curiae* (1 February 2000), available at http://www.lessig.org/content/testimony/ab/ab.pdf.

to monopolize the web-browser market, and engaged in sundry conduct in restraint of competition. The governments' approach promised a case study of exclusionary conduct in the new economy.

Through the lens of network economics, Microsoft's dominance can be explained as resulting from factors other than the quality and price of its Windows products. To begin, its early success resulted directly from IBM's fortuitous choice of MS-DOS as the operating system for its PCs, giving Microsoft the enormous first-mover advantage of a large customer base in an expanding market. Further, because IBM was the industry leader in PC manufacturing, its choice set the industry standard and others followed even though there were not significant technological incompatibilities among the various versions of DOS available. With IBM's success, the market quickly moved toward Microsoft DOS as the standard operating system. Still, other versions of DOS were compatible and, as a result, Microsoft's dominance was not secure. Even the introduction of Windows as a user-friendly layer of software did not tip the entire market inexorably toward Microsoft because Windows 3.1 was not itself an operating system but a graphical user interface that worked with rivals' DOS software. Indeed, Microsoft apparently sought to exclude DOS rivals by engaging in various anti-competitive practices, including the screen posting of false error messages when Windows detected a competing DOS program.[10]

What shifted the dynamics of network economics into high gear were Microsoft's introduction, marketing and distribution of Windows 95, which integrated DOS operating system functions and the Windows 3.1 point-and-click layer into one software package, eliminating the need for separate DOS software. The entire market for separate DOS software would disappear. As part of an apparent strategy to hasten DOS's demise, Microsoft Windows 95 was designed to be incompatible with earlier versions of DOS-plus-Windows 3.1. In consequence, applications programs (for example, word-processing or spreadsheet software) running on the old DOS-plus-Windows 3.1 platform either did not run well on Windows 95, or caused intermittent system crashes, or simply did not run at all. At the same time, Microsoft gave PC manufacturers strong financial incentives to ship Windows 95 to new customers, despite inventories of DOS and Windows 3.1, and increased the price of the older software. At retail, new users paid less for Windows 95 than for its predecessor.

Microsoft's business strategy effected a perfect understanding of network economics insofar as it was designed to increase the pressures of technological compatibility that were driving the market's inclination

---

10 See *Caldera*, n. 5 above.

toward tipping to Windows as the industry standard. PC manufacturers shipped only Windows 95 because Microsoft not only gave them financial incentives but also threatened sanctions including higher royalties and withholding of crucial technical information about new software. Actual substitutes were not shipped and potential ones not developed. New PC users had little choice but to accept Windows 95. After some initial concern about available applications software for Windows 95, which was not backward-compatible with prior versions of Windows, PC users saw that the entire industry of applications software was shifting. It was shifting because applications software companies realized they would have to revise their software to meet Windows 95 protocols or face a disappearing customer base. At the same time, Microsoft was giving financial incentives to applications software companies to turn their resources toward (re)writing software for Windows 95. Old PC users felt compelled to switch to Windows 95 because their current applications would no longer be supported and new versions would run only on Windows 95. New applications were being written for Windows 95, not its 3.1 predecessor. At each phase in this positive feedback cycle, each switch to Windows 95 by a user or a software provider increased the incentives of others in the cycle to switch for fear of abandonment to unsupported technical standards and a declining user base. Soon Windows 95 pushed Microsoft's market share of PC operating systems past 90 per cent and DOS was eliminated entirely as a separate market. Would Microsoft have locked-in the market to Windows 95 as global standard for PC operating systems absent the sticks-and-carrots strategy of reinforcing the positive feedback mechanism's tendency to produce a winner-take-all outcome in this network market?[11]

Although opinions differed on how much of Microsoft's success resulted from its predatory course of conduct and how much from the winner-take-all dynamics of new economy markets, the Justice Department and 20 state Attorneys General were convinced that it was Microsoft's illegal conduct that assured continued dominance in the market for PC operating system software and threatened monopolization of the browser market. In particular, they asserted that Microsoft acted with the singular purpose of protecting its Windows monopoly. Microsoft's campaign to coerce IBM into dropping its Windows-compatible OS/2 Warp operating system was obviously predatory. Potential developers of new operating systems channelled their innovation energies elsewhere because they became more and more convinced it would remain the industry standard, even if more

[11] *Microsoft IVa*, Findings of Fact, available at www.usdoj.gov/atr/cases/f3800/msjudgex.htm.

expensive and less efficient than its competitors old and new, because users were locked into applications programs that ran only on the Windows 95 platform. And everyone understood that it made economic sense for applications software developers to write new programs or revise old ones for the massive Windows 95 customer base rather than for older Windows or marginal operating systems with few customers and thus with dim prospects for displacing Windows 95. Microsoft recognized its monopoly depended on maintaining this applications barrier to entry. That much was straightforward.

But what was surprising to many outside the software industry and the venture capital markets serving it was the government's assertion that the same motivation – to maintain the operating systems market's applications barrier to entry – drove Microsoft to develop IE and to pursue its relentless campaign against Netscape Navigator and Sun Microsystems's Java platform. The plaintiffs would ultimately persuade Judge Jackson that Microsoft was responding to another kind of threat to the Windows monopoly. It was the threat of 'middleware', of software that stood between Windows and the user. Middleware threatened to make Windows 95 invisible to the user, just as Windows 3.1 had lowered the curtain on DOS. No one would care about the underlying operating system, just as no-one cared about the brand of RAM or disk drive running under the skin of the PC.

Middleware is yet another layer of software, one that sits atop the operating system (whether Windows, Apple's Mac OS, IBM's OS/2, Linux or others) and thus is 'multi-platform'. That is, applications program developers could write their software to run on the top layer of Java (the multi-platform middleware) and ignore the particular operating system below. As a result, an applications software package written to run on Java would be compatible with any underlying operating system. Users and software developers would no longer be locked-in to Windows. Indeed, they would be locked into Java. The positive feedback loop benefiting Windows would be broken and, even worse, Java middleware would provoke a new feedback loop. Windows would become just another operating system.

Judge Jackson determined that Microsoft saw Netscape Navigator as the most dangerous middleware threat to Windows. The Navigator threat was so great, it turns out, because it was distributed with the Java package. The Java package included a programming language and associated programs that generated middleware allowing applications program developers to create programs that would run on the Java platform and thus with Navigator. At bottom, when Microsoft restrained distribution of Navigator, it was primarily concerned with excluding Java and, with it, the threat of burying Windows in an unseen software layer.

Microsoft's concern with middleware included other software as well. Judge Jackson's findings of fact recite evidence of Microsoft's success at excluding other perceived middleware threats, including small pieces of software written by Apple and by Intel to enhance Windows' multimedia capabilities.

But it was Navigator and Java that grabbed Microsoft's corporate attention. Bill Gates's worst nightmare was a new library of Java-driven applications programs, running on any operating system and using Navigator to access an Internet full of data, entertainment and remote applications.[12] There would be no need for a large and cumbersome operating system like Windows. PCs would be smaller and cheaper. It was Microsoft's intention to stifle software development for middleware, especially for Navigator and Java. In this light, Judge Jackson would conclude, Microsoft attempted to monopolize the browser market as the means to maintain its Windows monopoly.

Nevertheless, it is likely that Microsoft's purposes were multiple – not only to maintain the Windows monopoly but also to dominate a browser market that would become important in its own right. As part of its effort to dominate the browser market, Microsoft engaged in what might be called predatory innovation. Microsoft licensed Java from Sun Microsystems in order to develop an IE that offered the same capabilities as Navigator. But its programmers altered the Java technology shipped with Windows/IE, according to Microsoft, to improve performance. As a by-product of the changes, however, the Windows version of Java could no longer run on other operating systems. As a result, its value as a multi-platform technology was destroyed. Sun Microsystems sued Microsoft, claiming copyright and trademark infringements as well as breach of contract. Ultimately, the trial judge ruled in Sun's favour to the extent of enjoining Microsoft from shipping altered versions of Java.[13]

As for the public spectacle, Judge Jackson concluded a 76-day bench

---

[12] That approach, now called 'cloud computing', has only recently begun to inspire adherents and attract investment. See e.g. S. Lohr, 'Google and I.B.M. join in "cloud computing" research', *New York Times*, 7 October 2007, available at www.nytimes.com/2007/10/08/technology/08cloud.html.

[13] *Sun Microsystems, Inc.* v *Microsoft Corp.*, 999 F.Supp. 1301 (D.C.N.D. Cal. 1998); 'Microsoft is told to abide by Sun on JAVA', *New York Times*, 26 January 2000, C2. Of course, Microsoft's corporate strategy was not limited to a holding pattern. In addition to recognizing the importance of IE as a web-browser, Microsoft engaged in significant efforts to increase its market shares in operating systems for large Internet 'server' computers and for small hand-held devices. As well, it invested in cable and satellite television products, both by purchase and by product development.

trial in five months amidst intense media attention. The parties spent the spring of 1999 in fruitless settlement negotiations. Some weeks after announcing that he would publish his findings of fact on an unspecified Friday evening,[14] Judge Jackson did indeed post on the court's website findings that were 412 paragraphs in length. One month later, in December 1999, he appointed Judge Richard A. Posner as mediator but the meetings ended in April 2000 without settlement. Judge Jackson quickly issued his conclusions of law. The court held that Microsoft violated Sherman Act sections 1 and 2 by engaging in a predatory course of conduct to maintain the applications barrier to entering the market for Intel-compatible operating systems for PCs, the market dominated by its Windows software. As well, the court held that Microsoft attempted to monopolize the market for web-browser software and illegally tied IE and Windows.

As it moved through the appeals process, the case against Microsoft remained difficult even though the evidence clearly supported the government's claims that Bill Gates and cohorts engaged in an anti-competitive course of conduct, bullying strong companies such as IBM and Intel, and weak ones like Apple. It was a difficult case even though Microsoft abused its monopoly power by effectively restraining Java's and Netscape Navigator's access to markets, by stifling innovation that threatened Windows, and by discriminating in price among PC manufacturers in a market driven by intense price competition. It was difficult even though Bill Gates treated the 1994 consent decree and the 1999 trial with an arrogance not seen since John D. Rockefeller ignored the judgment of the Ohio Supreme Court and carried his corporate baggage to New Jersey and the laissez-faire regime created by his attorneys.[15] Bill Gates told Intel executives in a 1995 meeting that 'This antitrust thing will blow over'. Flouting the 1994 consent decree, he went on to boast, 'We haven't changed our business practices at all'. After the 1999 trial, Gates refused to acknowledge that Microsoft's conduct was anti-competitive.[16]

The remedy phase began with an air of efficiency. But the trial court's approach and remedies themselves raised controversy. To begin, Judge Jackson ordered Microsoft to submit a plan of divestiture within 60 days. The plan was to provide for separation of the operating systems business

---

14 Judge Jackson chose Friday evening to give the stock market the weekend to digest the implications for Microsoft shares.

15 *See* R.J.R. Peritz, 'The "Rule of Reason" in Antitrust Law: Property Logic in Restraint of Competition' (1989) *Hastings Law Journal* 285.

16 S. Lohr, 'Gates quoted as seeing case "blow over"', *New York Times*, 11 November 1998, available at http://query.nytimes.com/gst/fullpage.html?res=9C0CE6D61F3EF932A25752C1A96E958260.

from the applications business, the latter defined as including IE. In addition, the decree ordered a series of conduct remedies to remain in effect for three years. The two new Microsofts were enjoined, for example, from giving favourable terms to any PC manufacturers, from withholding product information from hardware or software developers, and from engaging in tying or exclusive contracts. The overall purpose was not to punish Microsoft but rather to assure equal access to information about what was and still is, after all, the industry-standard operating system, to bring down entry barriers to software markets and, over all, to promote innovation in the information technology sector. Certainly, the intent was praiseworthy.

The difficulties, however, were numerous and provoked intense public debate. First of all, some critics argued that this particular break-up would simply create two monopolies with no incentive to compete with one another. The applications business would include Microsoft Office, which already dominated its product market, and IE, which, according to Judge Jackson, was dangerously close to monopolizing the browser market. Even then, IE's market share approached 60 per cent, a likely tipping point to set in motion the winner-take-almost-all logic of network industries that ensued. Nonetheless, network economics would suggest that the separation of the Windows platform from applications software would break a powerful positive feedback loop based on the very theory underlying the litigation – the applications barrier to entry. Yet Microsoft's strategic history of software integration would arguably survive the decree; the dominant question underlying future controversies over the decree would likely be whether integrating a new application into Windows would for legal purposes transform any application into an operating system module. This view would be consistent with the D.C. Circuit's approach to the 1994 consent decree, an approach which granted Microsoft discretion to engage in 'technological tying' by software integration, notwithstanding the consent decree's prohibition of contractual tying.

On the other side of the remedy debate, Microsoft and its allies argued that the dissolution would destroy the intra-corporate synergy that fuelled its innovation and, moreover, that the conduct remedies would intrude on Microsoft's entrepreneurial prerogatives in products that were protected by IPRs. Most troubling of all, what if the remedies destroyed the world's most successful company and, in crucial ways, dissipated the United States' greatest asset, its national champion, in the new economy?

There was a second difficulty raised by Judge Jackson's remedies. Some argued that several of the conduct remedies (the ban against exclusive contracts, for example) were not supported by the conclusions of law. Indeed, Judge Jackson had concluded that Microsoft's exclusive contracts did not violate the antitrust laws. Even the Findings of Fact raised questions about remedies. For instance, the judge's timeframe throughout was relatively short: 'the next few years . . . several years distant . . . a few years'. If the duration and effect of the Windows monopoly or harm to consumers could not be gauged beyond that short timeframe, then corporate dissolution seemed too harsh a remedy. Didn't the short timeframe acknowledge the speed of change in the new economy and, with it, the potential folly of breaking up a monopoly that innovation would unseat in relatively short order?

The Microsoft case was the monopolization case of the new economy just as *Standard Oil* had been the icon of the old. It began as an easy case on the facts, devolved into a difficult case on the law, and floated atop roiling cross-currents of intense debate over remedies.

It was no surprise that Judge Jackson stayed the decree pending appeal of the liability case. On appeal, the D.C. Circuit left unchanged the findings of fact, affirmed in part and reversed in part the conclusions of law, and vacated the decree for remedy. In short, only the holding of monopolization was affirmed and the case was remanded – but not to Judge Jackson because the Court of Appeals agreed with Microsoft's claims of judicial misconduct and the appearance of partiality.[17]

As for the remedies, on remand, there were extensive hearings before the newly assigned Judge Colleen Kollar-Kotelly. Thereafter, Microsoft and the Justice Department, recently staffed with appointments by the new Bush Administration, quickly agreed to a settlement, joined immediately by 11 states. Adopting the settlement, the judge's new decree retained district court oversight for five years and included behavioural constraints and imperatives. Microsoft remained intact.

In particular, Microsoft was required to disclose the information necessary to foster interoperation between Windows and third-party 'middleware' software products, including server operating systems. The decree limited Microsoft's ability to enter into agreements that excluded competitors from the marketplace. Moreover, Microsoft was explicitly prohibited from retaliating or threatening to retaliate against licensees for supporting competing products. In this regard, the decree paid special attention to the competitive importance of 'non-Microsoft middleware', which certainly included Sun Microsystems's Java technology. Moreover, original equipment manufacturers (OEMs) were permitted flexibility in configuring icons, shortcuts and menu items on desktop screens, including automatic launching of software programs, so long as the programs

---

[17] See *Microsoft V*.

did not 'drastically alter the Windows user interface'. As a general matter, Microsoft was required to license Windows under the same terms to all PC makers, although quantity discounts were permitted. Pricing terms had to be published on the website established for those purposes. Finally, Microsoft was to appoint an internal compliance officer to assure that its officers and managers read and comprehended the settlement. A committee was appointed by the plaintiffs to supervise compliance with the decree.

It should be noted that Judge Kollar-Kotelly issued an extensive opinion accompanying the remedial decree that approved the settlement. The opinion characterized the settlement as a consent decree and declared that 'Nothing in this Final Judgment is intended to confer upon any other persons any rights or remedies of any nature whatsoever hereunder or by reason of this Final Judgment'. Much criticized, this language negated Sherman Act section 5(a), which gives *prima facie* effect in follow-on private cases to findings of antitrust liability in fully litigated government actions.[18]

According to a *New York Times* report, the early court-ordered status reports 'suggest that the November 2002 consent decree . . . has neither fostered significant competition nor changed Microsoft's anticompetitive behavior'.[19] The very first report had objected that the licence contained anti-competitive terms, including a requirement that licensees sign non-disclosure agreements even before reading the licence terms, a stipulation deterring use and development of free software like Linux, as well as a blanket provision prohibiting licensees from suing Microsoft. Linux, of course, is a significant competitor in the market for network server operating systems.[20] The second report stated that in addition to six substantive reports of continuing violations, Microsoft's licensing program resulted in only three new licensees. Separately, Microsoft agreed with the Justice Department to offer a software update to Windows XP so that it would no

---

[18] See *Microsoft* VI, n. 2 above, for the opinions regarding approval of the settlement under the Tunney Act. The opinion addressing the remedies sought by the non-settling states is reported at *New York* v. *Microsoft Corp.*, 224 F. Supp. 2d 76 (D.D.C. 2002) (Final Judgment), also available at www.usdoj.gov/art/cases/f200400/200457.htm (12 November 2002).

[19] *New York Times*, 17 January 2002, C2.

[20] Cf. *Microsoft Corp.* v *Lindows.com, Inc.*, 2002 WL 32085605 (W.D. Wash. 2002) (denying plaintiff's motion for preliminary injunction on grounds of evidence raising substantial question of fact whether 'Windows' term was generic); the case was settled for $20 million in exchange for defendant's stopping use of Lindows name. See http://www.pcworld.com/article/116947/microsoft_lindows_make_a_deal.html.

longer force users searching for music online to use Internet Explorer.[21] In 2006, continuing difficulties led the parties to agree to a five-year extension of Microsoft's licensing obligations. In 2008, the district judge extended the other provisions for at least two years.[22]

By June 2004, all state plaintiffs had agreed to join the settlement. West Virginia, for example, joined as part of settling for US$21,000,000 in an associated suit accusing Microsoft of overcharging consumers in that state for Windows. California had earlier joined as part of a similar US$1.1 billion settlement. In all, Microsoft established a reserve of US$1.55 billion to cover state settlements.[23]

There have also been a number of private lawsuits. In 2000, Microsoft paid Caldera US$155,000,000 in settlement of an antitrust suit claiming predatory use of Windows 3.1 to monopolize the DOS platform. In 2003, Microsoft paid US$23,300,000 to settle an antitrust lawsuit with Be Inc., a software company no longer in business. Microsoft recently agreed to pay US$750,000,000 to AOL/Time Warner, the current owner of Netscape software, to settle its suit. The agreement included a long-term licence wherein AOL agreed to use Microsoft's Windows Media Player for distributing and playing digital media content.[24]

Sun Microsystems filed suit for antitrust violations and copyright infringement seeking at least US$1 billion in damages as well as injunctive relief. The Fourth Circuit Court of Appeals dissolved a district court injunction ordering Microsoft to distribute Java software as originally received but upheld a second preliminary injunction that prohibited Microsoft from distributing its own version of Java technology because it likely violated Sun's copyright. Microsoft had customized Java to run more

---

21 S. Lohr, 'Microsoft eases licensing under pressure from U.S.', *New York Times*, 4 July 2003, C3.

22 See e.g. W.H. Page and S.J. Childers, 'Measuring Compliance with Compulsory Licensing Remedies in the American Microsoft Case', 6 November 2008, available at http://ssrn.com/abstract=1149862.

23 L.J. Flynn, 'Microsoft settles 6 more suits', *New York Times*, 29 October 2003, C6. Massachusetts was the last state to settle, with Microsoft agreeing to distribute up to US$34,000,000 in vouchers to state consumers as well as vouchers to school districts in the amount of half the difference between US$34,000,000 and the value of the vouchers actually distributed. 'Microsoft and Massachusetts Plaintiffs Settle Massachusetts Class Action Lawsuit', available at www.microsoft.com/presspass/press/2004/jun04/06-29masettlementpr.mspx.

24 *Caldera*, n. 4 above; 'Caldera, Microsoft settle suit', 10 January 2000, http://wire.ap.org/APnews/center—story.html (AP wire); 'Microsoft settles antitrust suit with Be Inc.', *New York Times*, 8 September 2003, C5; S. Lohr, 'Digital media becomes focus as Microsoft and AOL settle', *New York Times*, 2 June 2003, C1.

efficiently with Windows, with the result that Java would not run at all on other platforms. In April 2004, Microsoft and Sun Microsystems, Inc. announced that they had 'entered into a broad technology collaboration arrangement to enable their products to work better together and to settle all pending litigation between the two companies. The companies have also entered into agreements on patents and other issues.'[25]

Windows Media Player was in a worldwide competitive battle with RealNetworks' Real One Player, with each having in excess of 300,000,000 registered users. In December 2003, RealNetworks filed a US$1 billion antitrust suit claiming that Microsoft was using its monopoly power to restrain competition and limit consumer choice in digital media markets by bundling Windows Media Player with Windows. While bundling has been a successful marketing strategy for Microsoft since Windows first arrived as a middleware interface for DOS, it should be noted that in the Justice Department's second *Microsoft* suit, the court rejected Microsoft's claim that web-browsers were integral components of PC operating systems. It would be even more difficult to persuade a federal court that a media player is integral to an operating system.

Two years later, the case settled. Microsoft paid RealNetworks US$761,000,000 in cash and services. Microsoft agreed to promote Rhapsody, a subscription service for online music that competes with iTunes, throughout Microsoft's MSN network; moreover, the parties agreed to work together to assure RealPlayer's seamless interoperability with Windows. The settlement brought to US$4.6 billion Microsoft's cost of settling private lawsuits stemming from the Justice Department's case.[26]

3. JUDICIAL DEFERENCE TO MICROSOFT'S STRATEGY OF SOFTWARE INTEGRATION

This section begins by chronicling Microsoft's long-standing strategy of software integration – its purposes and its effects on both PC users and software developers. Attention then shifts to the approaches taken toward

---

25 'Microsoft and Sun Microsystems enter broad cooperation agreement; settle outstanding litigation', www.microsoft.com/presspass/press/2004/apr04/04-02SunAgreementPR.mspx; S. Lohr, 'Court lifts order that required Windows to include Java', *New York Times*, 27 June 2003, C3; A. Harmon, 'Microsoft loses a round to rival Sun', *New York Times*, 24 December 2002, C1.

26 J. Krim, 'Real Networks, Microsoft settle suit', *Washington Post*, 12 October 2005, D1; J. Markoff, 'Real Networks accuse Microsoft of restricting competition', *New York Times*, 19 December 2003, C1.

technological bundling and tying by the D.C. Circuit in its two *Microsoft* opinions. The section concludes with an analysis of what the Microsoft case suggests about leverage theory, which US courts and commentators largely reject, and their European counterparts embrace, as a plausible economic logic for the practice of bundling.

Microsoft's Strategy of Software Integration

Software integration has long been a winning strategy for Microsoft. The introduction of the Windows 95 operating system in particular was a huge success. Earlier versions of Windows software, including the immediately prior 3.11, were not actually operating systems. They did not manage the PC environment. Rather, they were similar in function to the current Java software – multi-platform middleware designed to present themselves as user-friendly liaisons to the underlying PC operating systems that actually did the management work. In the era of Windows 3.11, the most popular PC operating systems comprised a highly compatible group of DOS (Disc Operating System) software. Microsoft's version was called MS-DOS. Taking ideas and iconography from its Apple OS predecessors, which evolved from still earlier work by Xerox, Microsoft Windows allowed users to issue DOS commands by mouse-pointing-and-clicking screen icons instead of typing strings of characters and punctuation marks. Introduced in 1986, Windows 3.1 was such a graphical user interface (GUI), designed to translate mouse clicks into DOS operating system commands. It was almost ten years later that Windows 95 would combine Microsoft's MS-DOS and the Windows 3.11 GUI middleware layer into an integrated platform. It was not long before Microsoft's integration would eliminate all DOS software under its various brands as a separate product market entirely.

One sight-line into Microsoft's early integration strategy emerges from Caldera's antitrust case against Microsoft, which settled before trial for US$155,000,000. Caldera is the successor in interest to Digital Research, Inc. (DR), which developed DR-DOS. Caldera charged that Microsoft included false error messages in Windows 3.1 that appeared on-screen whenever Windows detected DR-DOS, in order to deceive and unnerve users into switching to Microsoft's MS-DOS. Caldera charged further that Microsoft later made needless changes to MS-DOS and Windows 3.1 simply to create incompatibilities between 3.1 and rivals of MS-DOS software, including DR-DOS.[27]

Microsoft established a pattern of integrating applications software into

---

[27] *Caldera*, n. 5 above.

Windows 95, including file compression programs and other disk utilities, usually by copycatting them or simply buying the software or their developers. The next antitrust-provoking episode of software integration emerged a few years later out of the browser wars between Netscape Navigator and Internet Explorer (IE).[28] IE began as a separate applications program and ended up as a partially integrated complement to later versions of Windows 95 and its successors. Windows Media Player has gone through a similar life-cycle. Although Microsoft's coercion of Intel and Apple to drop development of multimedia modules was portrayed in *Microsoft IV* as intimidation of middleware rivals to protect Windows, the pressure was more specifically intended to protect its Media Player. Bill Gates and his advisors saw third-party multimedia software as alternative platforms to support applications functions that required multimedia resources, applications including popular computer games and audio-visual content such as DVDs and streaming media. Microsoft strategists were unnerved that software developers would have attractive platform alternatives to Media Player, alternatives with incompatible formats in markets inclined toward a winner-take-all equilibrium. Yet because the US case ultimately succeeded only on the claim that Microsoft monopolized the market for Intel-compatible operating systems software, the remedies were addressed to third-party multimedia software rivals only to the extent they function as middleware. Thus, Microsoft was required to enter into licences for interoperability information with Netscape Navigator and Sun Microsystems' Java but also Apple QuickTime only to the limited extent they perform what are defined as operating system functions.

And so the remedies were limited. For example, third-party media players are included in the remedy decree only to the extent of their inclusion in the definition of middleware, without regard to consumer choice in the media player market. In this regard, Microsoft must 'disclose those APIs, along with related technical information, which [Windows Media Player] utilizes to interoperate with the Windows platform'.[29] The limited purpose is to restrain Microsoft from eliminating multimedia software only as middleware threats to Windows by technological lock-out. Similarly, Microsoft is not required to remedy the harm to Navigator in the web-browser market or QuickTime in the multimedia software market by distributing them with Windows because the government did not show how Microsoft's exclusionary conduct caused harm to competition in

---

[28] *See generally*, *Amicus Curiae* Brief of Lawrence Lessig, n. 9 above; Note, 'Rethinking Software Tying' (2000) 17 *Yale J. Reg.* 367.

[29] See *Microsoft VI*.

browser or media player markets. Nor must Microsoft segregate IE from Windows for the purpose of opening competition in the browser market.

By contrast, the EC complaint proceeded on the view that there was something different involved than a middleware threat to Windows' dominance. The bundling, the integration of Windows Media Player and Windows, would harm consumers and rivals by 'undermin[ing] the competitive structure in the market for media players and risk[ing] . . . spill-over effects in adjacent markets [such as] . . . handhelds where streaming media is going to play an increasingly important role'.[30] Microsoft is a powerful if not the dominant player in those markets, which threaten, when dominated, monopoly prices and fewer choices to consumers. Thus, must-carry provisions or segregating Windows Media Player from Windows were rightly evaluated in light of concerns about dominance in those adjacent markets for Windows-compatible applications software.

According to the D.C. Circuit Court of Appeals, Microsoft's integration of IE (and presumably Windows Media Player) into Windows was a technical decision that should be granted some measure of deference. It is the measure that changed between the D.C. Circuit's two *Microsoft* opinions. The next two sections examine their differing deference doctrines. The final section concludes with a discussion of US attitudes toward leverage theory, the traditional framework now broadly criticized and rejected, for understanding tying doctrine and the underlying commercial conduct of bundling and integration. The criticism is found to be largely unwarranted.

Microsoft I and *II*: Judicial Deference to 'Technological Tying'

The opinions by Judge Jackson in *Microsoft I* and the D.C. Circuit in *Microsoft II* do not purport to apply antitrust law to an agreement to determine its competitive effects. They engage instead in judicial interpretation of the parties' agreement to settle their antitrust litigation over Windows 95. The procedural context was a civil contempt hearing commenced by the Justice Department, based on the claim that Microsoft had breached the terms of the settlement agreement. In particular, the courts focused on the contract question of the parties' intentions with respect to section IV(E) of the settlement agreement, which was embodied in Judge Jackson's decree:

---

[30] On 24 March 2004, the Commission issued Decision 2007/53/EC relating to a proceeding pursuant to Article 82 [EC] and Article 54 of the EEA Agreement against Microsoft Corporation (Case COMP/C-3.37.792 – *Microsoft*) [2007] OJ L32/23; Case T-201/04 *Microsoft Corporation* v *Commission* [2007] ECRII-3601, judgment 17 September 2007, Court of First Instance.

> Microsoft shall not enter into any License Agreement in which the terms of that agreement are expressly or impliedly conditioned upon:
>
> (i) the licensing of any other Covered Product, Operating System Software product or other product (provided, however, that this provision in and of itself shall not be construed to prohibit Microsoft from developing integrated products);[31]

The question joined was the distinction to be made between prohibited tying and the parenthetical permission to develop integrated software products. The context, of course, included the well-known fact that Windows 95 itself was the product of integrating Windows 3.11 and MS-DOS. Rephrased, the contract question before the courts can be understood as asking whether the tying prohibition imposed any limits on future software integration involving Windows 95.

The D.C. Circuit's opinion focused on determining the parties' intentions for entering the agreement, a determination that must be 'consistent with the antitrust laws and accomplishes the parties' evident desires on entering the decree'. The court resolved the issues of private intention and public law by defining the governments' intentions in terms of antitrust law: on one side of the settlement negotiations, the 'Department and DG IV were concerned with the alleged anticompetitive effects of tie-ins'.[32] On the other side, 'Microsoft's goal was to preserve its freedom to design products that consumers would like'.[33]

It was in this bargain contract scenario that the court situated the line between permissible integration and prohibited tying of software products. Integration was permissible if it was 'genuine', if it was 'beneficial when compared to a purchaser combination'. In determining the level of proof required to establish permissible integration, the court proceeded from the assumption that '[a]ntitrust scholars have long recognized the undesirability of having courts oversee product design, and any dampening of technological innovation would be at cross-purposes with antitrust law'. In consequence, a 'court's evaluation of a claim of integration must be narrow and deferential'. Proper deference to Microsoft's decision to integrate was expressed in the following standard: 'The question is not whether the integration is a *net* plus but merely whether there is a plausible claim that it brings some advantage.'[34] The rejected 'net plus' approach

---

31 *Microsoft II*, 147 F.3d at 939.

32 'The Department' and 'DG IV' refer to the Justice Department and the 'European competition authorities', which negotiated the settlement agreement with Microsoft. *Microsoft II*, 147 F.3d at 939.

33 *Microsoft II*, 147 F.3d at 949.

34 *Microsoft II*, 147 F.3d at 949–50.

would have approximated a standard rule of reason inquiry into the net competitive effects of the restraint.

The court was easily satisfied that Microsoft's claims of benefits met the standard of plausible advantage. The court concluded:

> The test for the integration of Windows 95 then comes down to the question of whether its integrated design offers benefits when compared to a purchaser's combination of corresponding stand-alone functionalities. The decree's evident embrace of Windows 95 as a permissible single product can be taken as manifesting the parties' agreement that it met this test.[35]

The D.C. Circuit adverted to opinions by other circuit courts to support its view that the parties' apparent agreement regarding 'plausible advantage' fell within the perimeter of antitrust legality. The support derived from a doctrine of judicial deference to product integration in the information technology sector: other federal appeals courts had already recognized 'the limits of their institutional competence', which provided their ground for 'reject[ing] theories of "technological tying"'.[36] In short, Microsoft's strategy of software integration was given judicial deference that fell just short of *per se* legality.

Microsoft II and *V*: Judicial Deference to Technological Bundling

Although the D.C. Circuit in *Microsoft II* was careful to state that it was construing the settlement agreement rather than articulating antitrust law, the distinction was difficult to maintain because the court defined the Justice Department's contractual intent as carrying out antitrust

---

35 *Microsoft II*, 147 F.3d at 950. 'On the facts before us, Microsoft has clearly met the burden of ascribing facially plausible benefits to its integrated design as compared to an operating system combined with a stand-alone browser such as Netscape's Navigator. Incorporating browsing functionality into the operating system allows applications to avail themselves of that functionality without starting up a separate browser application. J.A. paras 944, 965. Further, components of IE 3.0 and even more IE 4 – especially the HTML reader – provide system services not directly related to Web browsing, enhancing the functionality of a wide variety of applications. J.A. paras 607–22, 1646–48. Finally, IE 4 technologies are used to upgrade some aspects of the operating system unrelated to Web browsing. For example, they are used to let users customize their "Start" menus, making favored applications more readily available. J.A. paras 490–95; 1662–64. They also make possible "thumbnail" previews of files on the computer's hard drive, using the HTML reader to display a richer view of the files' contents. J.A. paras 1664-69.' *Microsoft II*, 147 F.3d at 950–1.

36 *Microsoft II*, 147 F.3d at 950 (citations omitted).

policy.[37] The practical irrelevancy of the Circuit's fine distinction can be seen in Judge Jackson's memorandum opinion in *Microsoft III*. Although he expressed 'misgivings' about treating technological integration as a special category of tying, he nonetheless treated the D.C. Circuit's contractual intent analysis as controlling law on the tying issue.[38] In consequence, Judge Jackson adopted the Court of Appeals' extreme view of judicial deference to deny the government plaintiffs' motion for summary judgment. The motion asked the court to conclude before trial that Microsoft's integration of IE and Windows was *per se* illegal under *Jefferson Parrish,* then the prevailing US Supreme Court precedent for tying doctrine.[39] But the court's extreme deference not only led to rejecting *Jefferson Parrish's* doctrine that tying provisions were *per se* illegal when forced by a firm with market power, but also to rushing past the traditional rule of reason inquiry to a shortened quick-look analysis.[40] This strict judicial deference was satisfied by easily carried assertions of 'plausible advantage', which directed courts to conclusions of antitrust legality.

Three years later, the second D.C. Circuit opinion, *Microsoft V*, took a different view of judicial deference, this time deference to Microsoft's decision to integrate IE into Windows 98. At first sight, the two views can be understood as products of their procedural contexts: the first was a contempt proceeding to determine contract intentions behind a settlement agreement and the other a review on the merits of Sherman Act liability. But there was substantive similarity that transcended the procedural difference insofar as both opinions ultimately relied on antitrust law and policy to support their differing views of judicial deference. Indeed, the latter court *en banc* seemed to recognize that the three-judge panel's earlier opinion applied an extremely deferential approach that was not only treated as antitrust precedent by Judge Jackson and but prone to similar treatment by other courts: 'To the extent that [*Microsoft II*] completely disclaimed judicial capacity to evaluate "high-tech product design", it cannot be said to conform to prevailing antitrust doctrine.'[41]

---

37 There is also the nice question of whether DG IV intended or even had the power to enter into an agreement whose obligations were governed by US antitrust policy.

38 *Microsoft III*, at *10.

39 *Microsoft III*, at *10; *Jefferson Parish Hosp. Dist. No. 2* v *Hyde*, 466 U.S. 2 (1984).

40 For the 'quick-look' doctrine, see *California Dental Ass'n* v *FTC*, 526 U.S. 756 (1999); *Broadcast Music, Inc.* v *Columbia Broadcasting System*, 441 U.S. 1 (1979).

41 *Microsoft V*, 253 F.3d at 92.

Microsoft V was an unanimous *per curiam* opinion from the entire court sitting *en banc*, an unsigned opinion that reformulated the earlier panel's judicial deference doctrine to accord with well-settled antitrust doctrine. In contrast to the three-judge panel whose *Microsoft II* opinion turned to the very broadly stated policies of encouraging innovation and asserting judicial incompetence in evaluating claims of innovation, the court *en banc* in *Microsoft V* neither turned to general policy prescriptions nor ascribed to such broad protestations of institutional incompetence. Rather, it assumed the traditional judicial role of applying legal doctrine to the facts at hand: here, applying Sherman Act doctrine to two tying claims that were both based on Microsoft's technological integration of IE into Windows 98. The first claim, under Sherman Act, section 2, was that Microsoft's integration was predatory conduct whose purpose and effect were to maintain its Windows' monopoly of the market for Intel-compatible operating systems. The second claim was that the very same integration amounted to an agreement in restraint of trade prohibited under Sherman Act, section 1. Ultimately, the court concluded that both tying claims were to be adjudicated under the rule of reason, the customary ad hoc approach intended to determine the competitive effects of the tying restraint in the particular circumstances of the case at hand.

Still, the legal doctrine presented a perplexing context for the case. Under Sherman Act, section 2, tying provisions imposed by a dominant firm are evaluated under a full-blown rule of reason that calls for scrutiny of actual effects on competition. But under Sherman Act, section 1, tying provisions forced on buyers by a less-than-dominant firm can be illegal *per se* – that is, without regard to competitive effects.[42] The D.C. Circuit ignored this awkward disparity and addressed each claim separately.

Under section 1 of the Sherman Act, the standard question was whether the technological tying amounted to a 'contract, combination, or conspiracy in restraint of trade'. The D.C. Circuit did not reach the ultimate question because it determined as a preliminary matter that the district court took an improper approach to the inquiry by applying the doctrine of *per se* illegality. Although tying by a firm with substantial market power

---

[42] If there is any justification for the difference, it would be that the potential remedy of divestiture under Sherman Act, s. 2 should call for more measured analysis of the conduct and its anti-competitive effects. Forced tying under s. 1 remains the only vertical restraint that is illegal *per se* after the recent *Leegin* decision moved minimum resale price maintenance inquiry to the rule of reason. In this light, the Supreme Court seems poised to eliminate the need for the special category of technological tying that the D.C. Circuit carved out of the *per se* treatment of forced tying.

would generally call for *per se* treatment, the D.C. Circuit declared that a special category of technological tying called for rule of reason analysis in this case because:

> we cannot comfortably say that bundling in platform software markets has so little 'redeeming virtue', . . . and that there would be so 'very little loss to society' from its ban, that 'an inquiry into its costs in the individual case [can be] considered . . . unnecessary.[43]

The case was thus remanded to the trial court for further proceedings with the caveat that '[i]n light of the monopoly maintenance section, obviously, we do not find that Microsoft's integration is welfare-enhancing or that it should be absolved of tying liability'.[44]

In the monopoly maintenance section of the opinion, the court applied the standard rule of reason analysis. Monopolization doctrine under Sherman Act, section 2 broadly involved two elements: first, whether Microsoft possessed monopoly power in the market for Intel-compatible operating systems; secondly, whether Microsoft abused that dominance by engaging in predatory conduct. Folded into the inquiry was the standard third element of determining competitive effects. Microsoft appealed the conclusions of law on the first and second elements. The court forcefully affirmed the trial court's conclusion that Microsoft possessed monopoly power. As for the conduct element, tying was but one of the six asserted forms of predatory behaviour.[45] This section's discussion is limited to the court's treatment of Microsoft's integration of IE and Windows as a form of anti-competitive tying.

The tying claim involved:

> three specific actions Microsoft took to weld IE to Windows: excluding IE from the 'Add/Remove Programs' utility; designing Windows so as in certain circumstances to override the user's choice of a default browser other than IE; and commingling code related to browsing and other code in the same files.[46]

Each action was a conscious software design decision. In the first and second design decisions, Microsoft blocked removal of IE and sometimes even required its use. Regarding the third, 'the District Court . . . found that Microsoft commingled operating system-only and browser-only routines in the same library files'. In consequence, 'any attempt to delete

43 *Microsoft V*, 253 F.3d at 94 (citations omitted).
44 *Microsoft V*, 253 F.3d at 89.
45 *Microsoft V*, 253 F.3d at 58–78.
46 *Microsoft V*, 253 F.3d at 64–5.

the files containing IE would, at the same time, cripple the operating system'.[47]

None of these design decisions was necessitated by an innovation logic of software integration intended to bring even plausible advantage to users. Perhaps the strongest instance of anti-competitive purpose is the commingling of code, which involved nothing more than the organization of separate software modules in a common library. Some of the modules were accessed only by Windows, some only by IE, others by both, and still others by entirely different applications software.

Such library organization is not unusual in the industry. It is important to understand that a modular library structure does not itself necessitate that module removal 'cripple the operating system'. The crippling effect in the case at hand was a conscious design choice. Each module could easily have been flagged to identify its uses; the identifying flags would have allowed software removal routines to recognize shared modules and allow them to remain in the library upon removal of IE or, for that matter, any other applications software. Indeed, current versions of Windows flag shared files in applications software. Thus it was more Microsoft's design choice not to flag library modules than the commingling itself that was predatory. Nonetheless, neither the court nor the plaintiffs recognized the distinction between the technological design decision to create a modular library and the strategic commercial decision not to flag modules.

If the court had identified the issue as predatory commercial design, it would undoubtedly have concluded that the decision not to flag shared modules lacked any benefit to users. Just like blocking removal of IE and requiring its use, the purpose of failing to flag shared modules was locking-in users and creating barriers to entry for rivals. Indeed, if the court had distinguished the design question from the broader issue of software integration, a rule of reason analysis of the issue of library design likely would have tilted toward Microsoft. Would the court have concluded that commingled code was itself unlawful tying by a dominant firm? That remains to be seen in the United States.

In Europe, of course, software integration of Windows Media Player even short of commingling code was found to be an abuse of dominance. Moreover, with regard to the European complaint about network server software, there arises the interesting question whether Microsoft's withholding of interoperability information from rivals can be understood as a looser form of technological tying or software integration of the Windows

---

47 *Microsoft V*, 253 F.3d at 85, 65.

PC operating system and Microsoft's network server software. Close scrutiny of the interoperability question is taken up below.

In the US case as litigated, the D.C. Circuit's entire discussion of commingling code and technological integration more generally was confined to the claim under Sherman Act, section 2 that Microsoft monopolized the operating systems market.[48] Under the rule of reason, the lawfulness of product design decisions depended on their competitive effects, informed by their purpose. And so the court framed its analysis of competitive effects with the trial court finding that:

> Microsoft's executives believed . . . its contractual restrictions placed on OEMs would not be sufficient in themselves to reverse the direction of Navigator's usage share. Consequently, in late 1995 or early 1996, Microsoft set out to bind [IE] more tightly to Windows 95 as a technical matter.[49]

In that light, the D.C. Circuit concluded that the integration had the following anti-competitive effects. First, because blocking the removal of IE is 'something other than competition on the merits, has the effect of significantly reducing usage of rivals' products and hence protecting its own operating system monopoly, it is anticompetitive'. Secondly, overriding consumer choice of a browser with IE was also found to be anticompetitive. Both actions 'reduce the usage share of rival browsers not by making Microsoft's own browser more attractive to consumers but, rather, by discouraging OEMs from distributing rival products'. Finally, commingling code had the similar effect of 'reducing rivals' usage share' and thus diminishing software developers' interest in writing programs for rival browsers.[50]

As for pro-competitive effects, the court evaluated Microsoft's justifications for the software integration. The court began:

> Microsoft proffers no justification for two of the three challenged actions that it took in integrating IE into Windows – excluding IE from the Add/Remove Programs utility and commingling browser and operating system code.[51]

---

48 In the discussion of tying under Sherman Act, s. 1, the Circuit stated: 'Although the District Court also found that Microsoft commingled operating system-only and browser-only routines in the same library files . . . it did not include this as a basis for tying liability despite plaintiffs' request that it do so'. *Microsoft V*, 253 F.3d at 85 (citations omitted).

49 *Microsoft V*, 253 F.3d at 64 (citing Findings of Fact, para. 160).

50 *Microsoft V*, 253 F.3d at 66.

51 *Microsoft V*, 253 F.3d. In another section of the opinion, however, the court recognized that 'the "shared" library files that perform OS and browser functions

Although Microsoft made some broad claims about the benefits of integrating IE and the operating system, the court dismissed them as too general. But Microsoft did assert that overriding consumer choice in some circumstances increased ease of use.

Given both anti-competitive and pro-competitive effects, the court determined that Microsoft would prevail on this particular issue because the government failed to carry the burden of demonstrating that the anti-competitive effects outweighed the asserted benefit of overriding consumer choice.[52]

In formal approach, the court treated software integration or technological tying under the rule of reason much as it would any putatively predatory conduct with unpredictable competitive effects. Yet there remained exceptional judicial deference in the court's treatment of Microsoft's asserted benefit as a pro-competitive effect insofar as it was based on facts that seem to evidence nothing more than *Microsoft II*'s earlier standard of 'plausible advantage'. That is, the court in *Microsoft V* allowed a 'plausible advantage' of increased ease of use to trump all evidence of anti-competitive effects and shift to the government the burden of establishing the net competitive effect. Although shifting burdens of proof follow the form of the structured rule of reason that has become mainstream doctrine in the United States, the minimal burden of proof satisfied by slight evidence of ease of use is not as different as it might appear from *Microsoft II*'s standard of 'plausible advantage'. Judicial deference to software integration decisions remains a powerful doctrine in the D.C. Circuit's antitrust jurisprudence.

Leverage Theory as the Logic for Tying

In the Sherman Act case on the merits, the government plaintiffs initially won three claims; but after the D.C. Circuit's *en banc* review in *Microsoft V*, victory survived only in the monopolization claim. Even that victory was less than convincing insofar as the government plaintiffs offered no theory of causation. The Circuit acknowledged Microsoft's argument that the determination of illegality should be reversed because the plaintiffs proved no causation element. But the argument failed because the court was willing to infer causation from the predatory conduct: 'To some

with the very same lines of code . . . may save drive space from the clutter of redundant routines and memory when consumers use both the OS and browser simultaneously'. *Microsoft V*, 253 F.3d at 87.

52 *Microsoft V*, 253 F.3d at 67.

degree, "the defendant is made to suffer the uncertain consequences of its own undesirable conduct"'.[53] Still, the lapse did have consequences later in the remedy stage of the proceedings. The D.C. Circuit instructed the lower court on remand:

> Microsoft's concerns over causation have more purchase in connection with the appropriate remedy issue, i.e., whether the court should impose a structural remedy or merely enjoin the offensive conduct at issue. As we point out later in this opinion, divestiture is a remedy that is imposed only with great caution, in part because its long-term efficacy is rarely certain . . . Absent some measure of confidence that there has been an actual loss to competition that needs to be restored, wisdom counsels against adopting radical structural relief.[54]

The missing theory of causation was leverage theory. Judge Jackson had earlier rejected the theory, observing that 'monopoly leveraging theory is in serious doubt', not only amongst commentators but also in opinions from a number of appeals courts, including the D.C. Circuit, which had noted 'substantial academic criticism' some 20 years earlier.[55]

In sharp contrast, the European Commission put 'technological leveraging' centre stage as its theory of causation. The Commission determined that Microsoft, aided by the tailwind of network effects, abused its dominant position in the operating systems market by using it as leverage in markets for two complementary products, media players and low-end network server software. But the US courts have abjured leverage theory. Indeed, leverage theory does not appear even once in the Court of Appeals' opinion. Why did the government fail to appeal the district court's rejection of leverage theory in the US case?

In the physical sciences (biology, chemistry, physics) new paradigms displace older ones. To burn paper, we are taught, requires oxygen, not phlogiston. To understand supernovas, astrophysicists turn to Einstein, not Newton. But in antitrust economics, old paradigms continue to

---

53 *Microsoft V*, 253 F.3d at 79 (citing Phillip E. Areeda *et al.*, *Antitrust Law* (1995), vol. 3, para. 651c, at 78).

54 *Microsoft V*, 253 F.3d at 80.

55 *Microsoft III*, 1998 WL 614485, at *27 (citations omitted). See also *Jefferson Parish Hosp. Dist. No. 2* v *Hyde*, 466 U.S. 2, 36 (1984) (O'Connor J concurring) ('The existence of a tied product normally does not increase the profit that the seller with market power can extract from sales of the tying product'). But see *Eastman Kodak Co.* v *Image Technical Services*, 504 U.S. 451, 479 n. 29 (1992) (observing that the court had 'held many times that power gained through some natural and legal advantage such as a patent, copyright, or business acumen can give rise to liability if a seller exploits his dominant position in one market to expand his empire into the next').

flourish despite the emergence of new ones. Thus, *static* price theory (particularly the Chicago School approach) still has great purchase among federal judges despite the widespread acceptance among economists of *dynamic* theories derived from information economics and game theory.

The static and dynamic paradigms differ in two important respects. First, they proceed from different assumptions about market conditions. Chicago School theorists assume that market conditions remain static, allowing them to attribute changes in price to changes in output. Economists in the mainstream dynamic paradigms examine changes in market conditions resulting from innovation, strategic conduct and other exogenous factors – the very changes held constant in static price theory. Secondly, static and dynamic methodologies look to different time horizons: neo-classical price theory deals with snapshots of short-term price and output changes. Dynamic approaches, in contrast, deal with moving pictures of changed conditions resulting from innovation and strategic behaviour over the longer term. The methodological difference persists even when the Chicago School analyst recognizes innovation and strategic behaviour because the conduct is still analysed in the snapshots of a short-term, statics analysis.

Tying doctrine offers a good example of the gap between policies to further static and dynamic efficiencies. The traditional antitrust concern underlying tying is leverage – using power in one product market as a lever to gain power in a second market. The theory is dynamic insofar as it recognizes the strategy as working over time to achieve a future result. Chicago Schoolers following Robert Bork have persuaded federal judges that a leverage theory of tying makes no economic sense because a monopolist can already obtain the profit-maximizing price in the monopolized market for the tying product.[56] For example, if Microsoft announced it would license Windows only on the condition that customers also purchase all of their rewritable CDs and printer paper from Microsoft, gaining second and third monopolies would not yield greater profits to Microsoft. These tying conditions would not yield greater profits, according to statics logic, because a triple monopolist can charge no more for the bundle of three products without losing customers who refuse to pay more for the bundle than they paid for them separately. In short, statics analysis holds that the profit-maximizing price for the bundle equals the sum of the prices for the separate products.

[56] For example, Judge Richard Posner, perhaps the most thoughtful of the first-generation Chicago Schoolers, maintained a 'fixed sum' view of tying in a relatively recent patent licensing opinion, *Scheiber* v *Dolby Laboratories, Inc.*, 293 F.3d 1014, 1020–21 (7th Cir. 2002).

At first blush, this view seems correct within the static, short-run model of price theory. But even on its own terms, this 'fixed sum' theory is limited by rigid and typically counterfactual assumptions: first, as in the example above, Microsoft is assumed to be charging the perfect monopoly price in the Windows market and therefore has nothing to gain. But if the price is not profit-maximizing, either because the monopoly is not perfect or not perfectly executed, then there is something to gain. Perfect execution requires perfect (and thus costless) information. Secondly, as in the example with CDs and printer paper, perfect competition is assumed in the tied product markets. When real markets do not reflect such conditions of perfection, and they rarely do, the 'fixed sum' theory simply does not apply because the monopolist has something to gain. These conditions of imperfection go largely unrecognized by judges and scholars who reject leverage theory based on the 'fixed sum' critique.[57]

Within the statics approach, price theorists and their judicial acolytes nonetheless assert that tying has real economic consequences only as a strategy to price discriminate. For example, the technological tying of a printer and replacement print cartridges is seen as a costless measure of the customer's intensity of use that provides the information for charging different prices to different users, prices that depend on their intensity of use. Low printer prices help sellers lock-in both high- and low-intensity users; sellers make supra-competitive profits from high-cost replacement ink cartridges, increasingly more as intensity of use increases. Overall, sellers' revenues are higher than they would be under a single profit-maximizing price. Sellers are better off. At the same time, users who would not pay the higher price for printers stay in the market; they are not worse off in the sense that they pay no more for the bundle than their intensity of use can support. In this view, the prices paid for the bundle remain the fixed

---

[57] See e.g. *Eastman Kodak Co.* v *Image Technical Services, Inc.*, 504 U.S. 451, 495 n.2 (1992) (Scalia, J dissenting); an article by Chicago School economist Ward Bowman is the classic reference for this view. But the article has been misunderstood insofar as the limiting assumptions described therein and rehearsed in the text above are either misunderstood or ignored. In consequence, the 'fixed sum' thesis is vastly overextended. Bowman wrote: 'The term "leverage", in this article, specifically describes the establishment of a new or second monopoly. The existence of such leverage depends upon the effect of the tying arrangement on the output of the tied product. *If the tying seller is maximizing his return* [i.e. if there is a perfect monopoly] on the tying product and the same output of the tied product can still be produced under circumstances *consistent with competitive production* [i.e. if there is a perfect competition] of the tied product, no additional or new monopoly effect should be assumed': W. Bowman, 'Tying Arrangements and the Leverage Problem' (1957) *Yale Law Journal* 19, 20 (emphasis added).

sums individual users would pay for the individual items. In terms of static efficiency, everyone is better off – that is, the dreaded deadweight welfare loss is lessened.[58]

But the price discrimination theory for tying has its own conditions of possibility. First, perfect price discrimination requires perfect (and costless) information about intensity of demand for the monopolized product. In markets with imperfect information, the efficiency results vary. As imperfections grow, deadweight loss increases and output declines from competitive to single-price monopoly levels. Secondly, there must be supra-competitive profits available in the second market to make the price discrimination worthwhile; at the same time, the fixed-sum critique of leverage theory requires perfect competition in the second market. In short, either both leverage theory and price discrimination can provide plausible explanations for tying, or neither one can. Thirdly, price discrimination cannot explain proportional ties, that is, ties such as nuts and bolts, computers and operating systems, or peanut butter and jelly. There, intensity of demand for the tying product cannot be measured by the sales quantity of the tied product because the quantity does not vary with use. Regardless of the use profile, one nut goes with one bolt, one computer with one operating system, and so on. If leverage theory is rejected as an explanation for proportional ties, price theorists are left without a statics theory to explain the practice.

Moreover, when a dynamic long-run view is taken, the economic logic changes drastically from the statics analysis of neo-classical price theory. Indeed, Harvard law professor Louis Kaplow gave a preliminary explanation some 20 years ago of how the traditional leverage theory seen in judicial tying doctrine reflected concerns that we now term dynamic effects such as market foreclosure, reputation effects, strategic positioning and increasing market share, effects that are invisible to the static model of neo-classical price theory which has influenced so many antitrust decisions in the last 30 years.[59]

Moreover, in the context of innovation economics, the dynamic long-run view also requires another look at the claim that perfect price discrimination is a social good. In the short-run, output moves toward competitive

---

58 Wealth transfers are not considered, though in strictest economic terms they should be because allocative efficiency is a function of the given distribution of wealth. As wealth changes, so do tastes, then demand, and with them, allocative efficiency.

59 L. Kaplow, 'Extension of Monopoly Power through Leverage' (1985) *Columbia Law Review* 515, 523–4; R. Bork, *The Antitrust Paradox* (New York: Free Press, 1978), pp. 373–4 (fixed sum conjecture).

levels and, with it, approaches an efficient allocation of society's resources. But there is a price to be paid: differential pricing redistributes wealth from inventors and other users to producers. With perfect information, users who value the product more pay more for it. When the users are inventors, their costs of production increase. Simple marginal economics tells us that as the price of inputs for invention increases, the demand for those inputs weakens. The production of invention will be costlier and will decline from levels reached under competitive markets for input factors, precisely because of the transfer of wealth ignored by price theorists. In short, future inventive activity will recede.

Finally, a dynamic long-run view has the added value of recognizing the increasing gains to tying in markets that exhibit system effects. In such markets, an expanding customer base shifts the demand curve outward, increases the value of the bundle, and therefore permits a higher price at every output level. Microsoft's strategy of tying IE to Windows and coercing business partners to drop Navigator is a good example of a successful long-run strategy whose costs to Microsoft can be understood as investments reflected in the zero price of IE and the short-run costs of coercion to maintain in the long run the applications software barrier to entering the market for Intel-compatible operating systems.[60] A leverage theory of the case offers the dynamic explanation that Microsoft adopted a strategy to forego current profits in pursuit of future gains in markets for complementary products.

As for the US monopolization case against Microsoft, the government's reticence regarding leverage theory had wide-ranging consequences. Most obviously, it weakened the tying and attempt to monopolize claims in two ways. First, it deprived them of a theory of causation. Secondly, it allowed them to ignore the importance of defining the secondary markets involved; the failure to define relevant markets was the basis for the D.C. Circuit's reversal of the tying and attempt to monopolize claims in *Microsoft V*. Less visibly but equally important, the reticence undermined the government's request for injunctive relief – for dissolution – in the monopolization claim. The D.C. Circuit explicitly instructed the lower court on remand to take the absence of causation theory into account in assessing remedies.

In the EC case, however, the leverage theory of causation logically pointed toward remedies more broadly drawn to ameliorate the anti-competitive effects of Microsoft's abusive leveraging of its dominance into the secondary markets of media players and low-end network servers.

---

60 See e.g. *Microsoft V*, 253 F.3d at 55.

4. THE TRANS-ATLANTIC DEBATE: INFORMATION, COMPETITION AND INNOVATION

The nimbic[61] question of information access and interoperability looms over the trans-Atlantic expanse of the Microsoft case. In the US case, the monopolization claim succeeded by characterizing Microsoft's predatory conduct as maintaining a software applications barrier to entering the market for Intel-compatible operating systems. In the rhetoric of competition law, Microsoft would remain dominant as long as its users were locked into Windows as the only Gate(s)way to the largest-by-far software library of compatible applications. The D.C. Circuit dismissed out-of-hand Microsoft's claim that intellectual property rights authorized its restraints. Economists modelled Microsoft's strategy in purely competition terms according to a theory of two-sided markets.[62] But in the EC case, the question of interoperability was addressed in broader terms that explicitly addressed the interplay of competition policy and intellectual property rights. In consequence, the decision treated information access and interoperability as issues that brought into focus the tension between market access and exclusionary rights as alternative means of promoting innovation.

The two sections that follow investigate the competitive effects of Microsoft's course of denying an array of rivals access to information needed to achieve compatibility with the Windows platform for PCs. The first section discusses private ownership of technical industry standards and its implications for interoperability. The second section then turns to the trans-Atlantic debate that erupted following the European Court of First Instance decision, the debate over consumer welfare and its relationships to competition policy and intellectual property rights.

61 The neological reference is to nimbus, both its traditional meaning of storm clouds and its information technological allusion to cloud or distributed computing. The conjunction of two meanings suggests the threat of cloud computing to Microsoft's dominance. Cloud computing requires interoperability. See e.g. S. Lohr, 'Google and I.B.M. join in "cloud computing" research', *New York Times*, 8 October 2007, available at www.nytimes.com/2007/10/08/technology/08cloud.html?emc=eta1.

62 See e.g. J.C. Rochet and J. Tirole, 'Two-Sided Markets: A Progress Report', 12 March 2004, available at http://faculty.haas.berkeley.edu/hermalin/rochet_tirole.pdf.

Industry Standards, Information and Interoperability

This section takes up the compound topic of information access and interoperability to investigate its antitrust implications for technical industry standards in the Microsoft case. Of course, Microsoft's dominance has made Windows the technical industry standard worldwide for PC software developers. In consequence, Windows raises compatibility barriers to market entry whenever Microsoft chooses to withhold technical information, particularly APIs[63] or other protocols. The breadth and depth of Windows' many technological protocols have resulted in a complex standard that is highly differentiated from alternative platforms, whether for hardware designers, applications developers or software platform rivals.

Through the antitrust lens of the US case, Microsoft can be understood as having monopolized the Intel-compatible PC platform market by using impermissible means to strengthen ties between software developers and software users. What tied these two sides of the market together was Windows' set of standard technical protocols. The strategy, now well-modelled by economists, followed from Microsoft's brilliant early recognition that network effects were functioning at two levels. The Windows protocols established PC-system-wide interoperability not only on the developer and user sides but also between them – what economists call both one-sided and two-sided network effects.

First, on each side of the Windows platform, the value of network membership increased as membership expanded. On one side, each new PC user increased the value of membership simply by expanding the size of the user network that communicated through compatible file formats

[63] API is the acronym for 'applications programming interface'. All applications programs require information to function in platform environments such as Windows. The APIs can be understood as the keys that unlock the doors to enter the correct module in the operating system to perform the standard function that is called for. Whether games, spreadsheets or web-browsers, applications software depends upon the platform to perform basic functions and manage the computer environment. In this context, not only media players but network server operating systems can be seen as having the same need for entry keys as applications programs. The value of a platform to applications programmers is that it relieves them from writing code in every piece of software to perform standard functions involving the use of the keyboard, mouse and a wide variety of other hardware such as random access memory (RAM), the processor chip, the hard drive, or external components such as printers and wifi networks. Each platform has its own APIs, and so writing for Windows, for example, requires APIs that have nothing to do with APIs for Linux. Each platform has its own set of keys to unlock the modules that perform standard functions.

and other standard protocols. On the other side, more software developers using the Windows protocol set produced similar effects for similar reasons. Secondly, the Windows platform linked the two sides to produce two-sided network effects as well. As the network on one side grew, membership on the other side grew: more PC users attracted more software developers, who produced more software, which then attracted more PC users. Sheer network size on each side was a magnetic draw for the other, a draw that grew more powerful as each side grew because increasing size strengthened member expectations of longevity, improvement and further expansion of networks with stable protocols for compatibility.[64] The same dynamics rendered alternative networks built around other platforms less attractive and less threatening to the Windows monopoly.

These intra- and inter-network effects reinforced one another to produce a kind of multiplier effect which was powered by the de facto industry standards embodied in the dominant Windows platform. At the same time, the multiplier effect produced a by-product that was actually Microsoft's primary interest: the ever-increasing indispensability of Windows as the standard platform. In the US case, Microsoft monopolized the operating systems market for Intel-compatible PCs by controlling distribution of information about the Windows platform and thereby managing the multiplier effect that intensified the platform power of Windows. These mutually reinforcing network effects locked-in customers while technical incompatibility simultaneously locked-out rival platforms. Integrating a web-browser, media player, or another complementary product into Windows would heighten entry barriers to those product markets because their zero direct price and familiarity to users would require competing software to be better enough to overcome costs of switching to the rival. Scholars of strategic marketing have shown that switching costs need not be great; their effectiveness in sustaining customer lock-in is notoriously out of proportion to actual costs.[65]

---

64 These expectations were not met when subsequent versions of Windows were not backwardly compatible; Microsoft strategies to promote migration to new versions is beyond the scope of this chapter, although it should be said that they began with migration incentives to software developers and ended largely with PC users who either followed the revised software trail or remained with abandoned and unsupported earlier software versions. Microsoft has recognized the widespread disaffection with Windows Vista, at least to the extent of offering business customers the option of purchasing new PCs with a Windows XP 'downgrade'.

65 See e.g. R.J.R. Peritz, 'Antitrust Policy and Aggressive Business Strategy: A Historical Perspective on Understanding Commercial Purposes and Effects' in 'Workshop and Conference on Marketing, Competitive Conduct and Antitrust Policy' (2002) *Journal of Public Policy and Marketing* 237.

Still, the well-recognized benefits associated with industry standard platforms should not be overlooked. At the price of opportunity costs, an industry standard platform lowers use costs and thus encourages continued investment in learning and innovation. For user networks on all sides of the dominant Windows platform, the issue for intra-systemic competition is access to technical information and, with it, platform compatibility. Moreover, rival platform developers require information to meet technical protocols as well – whether Linux to compete directly, Java to build cross-platform middleware, or media players to carve out sub-market niches. Hence, access to interoperability information is the competition issue that lies at the core of both the US case about middleware (extra-systemic competition) and the EC case about media players and network servers (intra-systemic competition). In sum, both cases can be understood as seeking to enjoin Microsoft from harming or internalizing the public benefits of industry standards.

In the US case, the evidence showed that Microsoft's strategies reflected an early and unmatched understanding of these two-sided markets: in sub-markets where Microsoft did not develop its own applications software, it made interoperability information universally available in order to strengthen the positive feedback loops within and across the developer and user networks. Indeed, key software developers received from Microsoft not only interoperability information but also financial incentives to write for Windows. In sharp contrast, Microsoft refused to provide interoperability information to IBM, for example, unless it agreed to stop marketing its OS/2 Warp operating system for PCs. The strategy lingered even after the case was concluded. Status reports to the court supervising the conduct remedies describe the ongoing difficulty of obtaining licences from Microsoft that provide interoperability information. In the first 18 months, over 100 companies approached Microsoft for licences under the remedial decree. Seven were granted. Moreover, only after much delay did Microsoft eliminate provisions that prohibited licensees from dealing with Linux (then a start-up rival) and from suing Microsoft.[66]

Armed with insight into one-sided and two-sided network effects, Microsoft's strategy was simple, though the tactics were varied and complex. The strategy was to maintain Windows' technological incompatibility with other platforms and to control its interoperability with

---

[66] A listing of all status reports is available at www.usdoj.gov/atr/cases/ms_index.htm. For commentary, see R.J.R. Peritz, 'Competition Policy and its Implications for Intellectual Property Rights in the United States' in Steven D. Anderman (ed.), *The Interface Between Intellectual Property Rights and Competition Policy* (Cambridge: Cambridge University Press, 2007).

networked complements on all sides of the market. Controlling access to the Windows platform allowed Microsoft to favour its own course of software and content development: For developers whose software did not compete with a Microsoft product, interoperability information was provided and, when deemed advantageous, signing bonuses were paid in order to maintain or expand the software library. But to seek dominance for Internet Explorer, Microsoft Office, Windows Media Player, Windows work group server software, and other complementary products, Microsoft would deny interoperability information to rivals. It is the latter strategy of denying interoperability information that attracted the attention of the European Commission.

Both the First and Second Statements of Objections of the European Commission asserted that Microsoft withheld information in order to hinder third parties from making their operating systems for work group servers compatible with Windows, the de facto industry standard for PCs. In this network environment of interoperating systems, Microsoft licenses both competing and complementary operating systems software. But it is not clear whether to define the PC or the network operating system as the primary platform. If it is a matter of scope, then the server network is primary insofar as it defines the set of PCs and their components, including their individual operating systems. But if it is a matter of scale, then Windows for PCs is primary because it is the dominant platform both within and without virtually every work group worldwide. In either view, however, the economic logic is unassailable: inelastic demand for the globally dominant Windows for PCs identifies it as the primary platform because it embodies inescapable technical standards to which work group networks must adhere. This economic logic defines work group server software as the complementary product and, of course, brings us back to the EC case. It was control of interoperability information about Windows protocols that gave Microsoft the monopoly power to apply a leverage strategy to gain special advantage over rivals in the work group server software market for its NT version of Windows for work groups. The advantage was that Windows NT and Windows for PCs were designed and written from the same set of specifications and, indeed, used much of the same code. Where they differed, they nonetheless adhered to the same set of technical standards, and so their communication protocols are naturally compatible.

Designers of competing software for work group servers must have access to the very same protocols, the same Windows vocabulary and syntax, to achieve compatibility. Should Microsoft as the dominant firm have an obligation to give public access to the technical standards for Windows compatibility? In the United States, when an industry standard is owned by a single firm, antitrust questions have been posed about that firm's duty to disclose information to market participants. In the landmark *Berkey Photo* v *Eastman Kodak* decision, decided some 25 years ago, the influential Second Circuit Court of Appeals rejected a competitor's claim that Eastman Kodak, the dominant firm, owed competitors a duty to predisclose new products in order to permit them to learn how to make their complementary products or services compatible with the new Kodak product line. The court concluded that Eastman Kodak had a right to its competitive advantages and, moreover, that a disclosure rule would be unworkable.[67] Still, unlike cameras and photographic equipment, information technology provides the central nervous system for the economic and social networks that have become essential facilities of everyday life. Should that be enough to distinguish Microsoft from Eastman Kodak?

Some years later, the Federal Trade Commission challenged the conduct of Intel Corporation, which is the dominant producer of the microprocessing chip at the heart of PCs as well as many other devices. Intel refused to provide technical information necessary for customers to produce complementary products compatible with Intel's microprocessor chips, which were the de facto industry standard. Intel stopped sharing the information with customers who asserted intellectual property rights against Intel. The case was settled with a consent decree in which Intel agreed not to withhold information in such circumstances.[68] But in a related private case, the Federal Circuit refused to apply the essential facilities doctrine because the complaining party was not a competitor (as US law requires) but only a customer of Intel.[69] In consequence, an essential facilities doctrine imposed no obligation on Intel to disclose the information. As a general matter, the antitrust laws do not prohibit a firm from withholding information for a legitimate business reason. And maintaining market advantage that amounts to dominance is a legitimate business reason.

More recently, the Federal Court in one of the *Rambus* cases held that a patent 'holder's breach of its alleged duty to disclose its patents under an industry [standard-setting] committee's patent disclosure policy was

---

67 *Berkey Photo, Inc.* v *Eastman Kodak Co.*, 603 F.2d 263 (2d. Cir 1979), cert. denied, 444 U.S. 1093 (1980).

68 *In re Intel Corp.*, 1999 F.T.C. Lexis 145 (3 August 1999) (complaint, Dkt. No. 9288); FTC Decision and Order available at www.ftc.gov/os/1999/08/intel.do.htm.

69 *Intergraph Corp.* v *Intel Corp.*, 3 F.Supp.2d 1255 (N.D.Ala. 1998), reversed, 195 F.3d 1346 (Fed. Cir. 1999).

not, by itself, sufficient to give rise to antitrust liability', even though the committee's action unknowingly made the Rambus patent the technological standard for the industry and thus made Rambus the dominant firm.[70] However, the court did note that the plaintiff was 'not barred from asserting that Rambus's overall course of conduct, which may include the circumstances and intent behind its decision to not disclose its patents and patent applications, violated antitrust laws'.[71] The standard-setting cases, however, must be understood as addressing an extended duty to disclose under special circumstances where silence may be tantamount to fraud.

In the Microsoft case, Judge Jackson found that 'Microsoft tried to convince IBM to move its business away from products that themselves competed directly with Windows and Office . . . When IBM refused . . . Microsoft punished IBM . . . with higher prices, a late license for Windows 95, and the withholding of technical and marketing support.'[72] Without pre-release access to the technical information needed for compatibility with Windows 95, IBM was unable to conform its products in time to compete with its rivals until the crucial initial selling season had passed. The trial court determined that those coercive refusals to provide information were part of Microsoft's monopolizing course of conduct.[73]

As a general matter, US antitrust laws do not impose on individual firms, even on monopolies, an affirmative duty to share information or otherwise do business with anyone. Nonetheless, there have been a good number of decisions over the years (sometimes termed essential facility cases) that imposed remedial duties to deal in decrees embodying compulsory licences. On a few occasions, the Supreme Court has imposed on dominant firms a duty to deal with competitors. The earliest instance was the decision in *Terminal Railroad Association* (1912), a joint venture of railroads

---

70 *Hynix Semiconductor, Inc.* v *Rambus, Inc.*, 441 F.Supp.2d 1066 (N.D.Cal. 2006).

71 441 F.Supp.2d at 1081. See also *Broadcom Corp.* v *Qualcomm, Inc.*, 501 F.3d 297, 312 n.7 (3d Cir. 2007) (distinguishing *Hynix*).

72 *Microsoft IVa*, 84 F.Supp.2d at 116.

73 Two courts have disagreed over an essential facilities doctrine's application to Microsoft Windows. Compare *Aldridge* v *Microsoft Corp.*, 995 F.Supp. 728 (S.D.Tex. 1998) (concluding that essential facilities doctrine does apply to some portions of Windows software but not to the PC hardware manufacturer) with *In re Microsoft Corp. Antitrust Litigation*, 274 F.Supp.2d 743 (D.Md. 2003) (concluding essential facilities doctrine does not apply and so does not require information disclosure to independent software developers about interoperability protocols, not discussed in any subsequent court decision).

that owned the only railroad switching yard across the Mississippi River at the important City of St. Louis hub. The Court required the joint venture to provide access to non-members at non-discriminatory rates. The Court determined that, 'in view of the inherent physical conditions', no practical alternative was available. In *Lorain Journal* (1951), the Court enjoined the only daily newspaper, termed an 'indispensable medium', in a region of northern Ohio from refusing to sell advertising space to customers of a competing radio station. Despite regulatory oversight by the Federal Power Commission, the Court in *Otter Tail Power* (1973) required an electrical utility to make available its transmission lines to wheel electrical power from competing utilities to its former customers. Through the course of such decisions was born the 'essential facilities' doctrine and the accompanying remedy of compulsory access.[74]

It should be noted that while the term 'essential facility' has long been used by federal courts and antitrust scholars, it has never been explicitly adopted by the Supreme Court.[75] Regardless of the nomenclature, these decisions have been called into doubt by the decision in *Verizon Communications* v *Trinko*,[76] which defined quite narrowly the defendant monopolist's duty to deal with competitors. In particular, the Supreme Court concluded that 'deficient assistance to rivals' in providing access to Verizon's regional telephone network did not amount to monopolization since it satisfied the Federal Communication Commission's standard for access requirements under the 1996 Telecommunications Act. The Court adopted the FCC's view despite a provision in the statute that explicitly reserved pre-existing antitrust standards.

Writing for the Court, Justice Scalia observed in passing that a monopolist's duty would be just as narrow for an essential facility, should the Court ever explicitly adopt the doctrine. Justice Scalia's observation was clearly no more than *obiter dictum*. Nonetheless, his opinion has fertilized a new growth of scholarly commentary, which has divided into two stands. One takes the view that the observation and the opinion more broadly should be read in the limiting circumstance of a statute specifically focused on the FCC and the telecommunications industry. The problem with this

---

74 *United States* v *Terminal RR Assn*, 212 U.S. 1 (1912); *Lorain Journal Co.* v *United States*, 342 U.S. 143 (1951); *Otter Tail Power Co.* v *United States*, 410 U.S. 366 (1973); see also *Aspen Skiing Co.* v *Aspen Highlands Skiing Corp.*, 472 U.S. 585 (1985).

75 *AT&T Corp.* v *Iowa Utilities Bd.*, 525 U.S. 366, 428 (1999) (Breyer J concurring in part and dissenting in part) (observing that Court never explicitly adopted essential facilities doctrine).

76 540 U.S. 398 (2004).

view is that the statute in *Trinko* has a clear antitrust 'savings clause' that was given short shrift. The other stand takes the opinion as a prestatement of the Court's attitude toward the essential facilities doctrine more broadly. Given the Court's antitrust track record of non-linear jurisprudence, prestatements cannot earn the rank of precedent unless and until they are later adopted. Which view is right will only be seen in retrospect, if at all.[77] After *Trinko*, whether a dominant firm has an antitrust duty to disclose information remains an open question, but a question influentially answered in the affirmative by both the district and circuit courts in the Microsoft case.

Innovation, Competition and Consumer Harm

The preceding section discussed private ownership of technical industry standards and its antitrust implications for information access and interoperability in those circumstances. This section proceeds from a broadened vision of competition policy as comprising not only antitrust but intellectual property rights (IPRs). Inquiry into issues of consumer welfare, information access and interoperability begins with the European Court of First Instance's analysis of Microsoft's conduct in the work group server market, then considers the likely US treatment, and concludes with an alternative approach.

A trans-Atlantic debate erupted following the CFI decision[78] upholding the Commission, a debate over consumer welfare and its relationships to antitrust and IPRs. The CFI decision was still fresh when directors of the US Antitrust Division and the European Competition Commission crossed rhetorical swords. The *New York Times* printed front page news of this sharp exchange between Brussels and Washington, this clash over who really protects consumers.

In praising the CFI decision, European Commissioner for Competition Neelie Kroes stated, 'the Court has confirmed the Commission's view that consumers are suffering at the hands of Microsoft'. But Thomas Barnett, Antitrust Division Chief of the US Justice Department, brandished a conflicting view of consumer effects. He charged that the CFI decision, 'rather than helping consumers, may have the unfortunate consequence of harming consumers by chilling innovation and discouraging

---

[77] For a more recent opinion that seems to reflect *Trinko*'s view of the relationship between antitrust and regulatory regimes, see *Credit Suisse Securities* v *Billing*, 127 S. Ct. 2383 (2007).

[78] Case T-201/04 *Microsoft* v *Commission* [2007] ECRII-3601.

competition'.[79] Before turning to the US and EC cases, this section goes in search of suffering consumers, some of Kroes's and some of Barnett's. What of Kroes's consumers who suffered at the hands of Microsoft? And how has the European Commission chilled innovation and discouraged competition to harm Barnett's consumers? Who understands the true interests of consumers here – Kroes or Barnett?

Of course, Kroes does: Microsoft engaged in a course of conduct to restrain competition in two markets for complementary products, media players and work group server software. As a result, consumers are harmed by costs of dominance, including restricted choice, lower quality and higher prices.

In the server market, Microsoft refused to supply the information rivals need to make their server software compatible with networked PCs running Windows – and almost all of them do. Think of this incompatibility as trying to order dinner from a menu written in an entirely foreign language. You would need a dictionary if not an interpreter. But Microsoft owns IPRs to the dictionary and the interpreter. Kroes's consumers are harmed by Microsoft's patent and trade secret claims of protection for Windows protocols because, without a menu of those protocols, Linux, Solaris and other non-Microsoft operating systems for servers lack the vocabulary and syntax needed to communicate with all those PCs running Windows. The protocols are vital and perhaps indispensable information for network servers to communicate with Windows PCs. The CFI opinion rightly concluded that in such exceptional circumstances, the access called for by competition policy properly trumps Microsoft's exclusionary rights in its intellectual property.

On the other hand, it appears that Barnett is right: requiring Microsoft to share its intellectual property with competitors – with rival server software companies – chills innovation.[80]

In this view, the CFI decision discourages not only Microsoft but every software company from developing communication protocols if they have to share them with competitors. Competitors should be required to solve their own problems rather than demand access to Microsoft's intellectual property. Barnett's consumers are harmed insofar as compulsory licensing takes control and profits from software companies like Microsoft

---

[79] K.J. O'Brien and S. Lohr, 'Microsoft ruling may bode ill for other companies', *New York Times*, 18 September 2007, A1; D. Lawsky, 'E.U. official lambasts U.S. Justice Dept. on Microsoft', *Reuters*, 19 September 2007.

[80] On incentive theory, see R.J.R. Peritz, 'Patents and Progress: The Incentive Conundrum', paper presented at ATRIP Annual Conference, Max-Planck Institute, Munich, Germany, 21 July 2008.

that have used their ingenuity and resources to develop new and better products. Future innovators will turn their attentions to products that promise stronger intellectual property protection and higher profits. In sum, the CFI judgment threatens to chill innovation in the development of communication protocols and, in consequence, threatens to abandon Barnett's consumers to the inefficiencies of slower and less stable computer networks.

So, who's right here? This question is addressed first in the familiar terms of the competition policies we Americans call antitrust and, then, in alternative terms of a neglected competition policy working within the patent regime.

Could it be that both Kroes and Barnett are right? Certainly they agree that consumers benefit from innovation. Where they disagree is on the choice of policy for encouraging innovation. For Kroes, innovation requires open competition on the merits, and that can call for limits on IPRs that exclude rivals. For Barnett, innovation depends on an expansive attitude toward those IPRs because they encourage innovation by stopping free-riding competitors from profiting from the innovator's work. In short, Kroes and Barnett have different views of what it means to compete by innovation.

It is a policy stand-off, an innovation paradox. The paradox is that innovation is understood as resulting from both open competition and IPRs, from policies calling for both access to and exclusion from the information embodied in intellectual property.

What's to be done about the innovation paradox that stands between Kroes and Barnett? This section begins its inquiry with a quick comparison of the US and EC approaches to the question of interoperability, the question of access to protected information about the products of innovation. This is a useful point of convergence because, of course, Microsoft is in the business of information flow. The very purpose of an operating system is to create an environment for smooth and reliable information flow, whether between PC components (for example, between computer screen and mouse) or between local area network components (for example, between PCs and work group servers). Microsoft sells operating systems for both PCs and networks. It controls the market for the first and seeks control of the other. In both markets Microsoft products and business strategies are based on control of information flows.

The US case involved Microsoft's strategy to maintain its Windows monopoly in the intra-PC environment by controlling access to information. Developers of key applications software were given full information access to protocols for interoperability with Windows. But firms whose products included competing software (IBM's OS/Warp and Apple

QuickTime, for example) were denied such information unless they promised to withdraw them.[81]

Moreover, Microsoft blocked access to and information flow about Java in order to protect the interoperability barrier to competition and thereby maintain Windows' brand identity and functional importance. The library of applications software for the Windows platform continues to provide an effective entry barrier because PC users adopt Windows not for its own sake but rather for access to the largest and most stable library of software for work and play, a library bound together by Windows protocols as the set of industry technical standards. If developers were to revise their applications software to run on the Java platform and thus with any underlying operating system, the interoperability barrier would dissolve and Windows would no longer be needed as the industry standard. Other operating systems could compete on price and quality.

The EC case involved what might be called an 'information squeeze' strategy to raise an interoperability barrier to adjacent markets. Microsoft's purpose was to dominate the server software market by blocking the flow of information to developers of rival server operating systems software, by denying access to the very protocol specifications that makes Windows for PCs compatible with Windows for servers. Here, Microsoft's course of withholding compatibility information from rival server software developers was intended to support its campaign to hamstring effective competition in the market for network server software, a market whose product is one among many complementary modules of the larger system of network components, both hardware and software.

In both the EC and US cases, Microsoft lost and, in both, it was ordered to license the interoperability information that rivals need – the protocols for middleware in the US case and, in the EC case, the protocols for server compatibility with Windows PCs. In the United States, Microsoft issued less than a handful of middleware protocol licences in 18 months following the final court decree. About the same time, Microsoft entered into a series of bilateral agreements to settle antitrust cases described in the preceding section, together with more patent development and pooling. Will that strategic shift from withstanding government attacks on exclusionary conduct to pursuing government grants of exclusionary rights lead to information access beyond the bilateralism of strategic joint ventures?

---

81 See also *Novel* v *Microsoft* (D.Utah 2004) (complaint alleging WordPerfect software object of monopolizing conduct), available at www.novell.com/news/press/archive/2004/11/complaint.pdf; *In re Microsoft Corp. Antitrust Litigation*, 2005 WL 1398643 (D.Md. 2005) (in a consolidated case, Microsoft's motions for summary judgment granted in part and denied in part).

Whether Microsoft remains committed to closed source strategies or more open conditions for interoperability remains to be seen.

But in the trans-Atlantic debate after the CFI judgment, Kroes and Barnett disagreed over the proper resolution of the innovation paradox, the tension between competition policy and IPRs as the proper means to foster innovation. Does the resolution make any practical difference? There is evidence that it does.

In the EC case, the conflict was resolved as follows. First, the CFI simply assumed that Microsoft has patent and trade secret protection of the protocols in question, despite some hesitation over the strength of the claims. Secondly, the CFI confirmed the Commission's determination that, under exceptional circumstances, competition policy can trump IPRs. The exceptional circumstances turn on the question of access to an indispensable asset controlled by a dominant firm, here Windows protocols controlled by Microsoft. The protocols amounted to an essential facility for entry into the adjacent server market.

In the US case, the issue was resolved differently. First, the court dismissed Microsoft's intellectual property claims as 'border[ing] on the frivolous'.[82] Thus, there was no need to confront the paradox. Yet in another part of the decision, the court did recognize as a special case 'technological tying' with software platforms, that is, integrating Internet Explorer into Windows. As a result, Microsoft was given broad discretion to integrate software into Windows even when consumers received only a slight benefit, even when the level of innovation was trivial.

Two other US Courts of Appeals, however, have addressed the innovation paradox directly, with the result a conflict of views. The Federal Circuit Court, which has exclusive jurisdiction over all appeals in patents and trademarks, declared that IPRs trump antitrust, the court stating that a simple refusal to license a patent can never violate the antitrust laws because patents are essentially exclusionary rights.[83] However, the Ninth Circuit Court, sitting not far from Silicon Valley in California, took a very different approach, an approach favouring antitrust, consistent with the European Commission in attitude and outcome, though somewhat different in analysis.[84] And so one powerful US court gave priority to IPRs, the other to antitrust limitations.

But these two US cases were decided almost ten years ago and, since

---

82 *Microsoft V*, 22 F.3d at 63.

83 *In re Independent Service Organizations Antitrust Litigation*, 203 F.3d 1322 (Fed. Cir. 2000).

84 *Image Tech. Serv.* v *Eastman Kodak*, 125 F.3d 1195, 1218 (9th Cir. 1997).

then, there has been a continuing contraction of antitrust law that includes greater deference to IPRs.[85] And so, in practical terms, if a US court were to decide the EC Microsoft case today, the decision would likely reflect the Federal Circuit's approach and Tom Barnett's strong support of expansive IPRs as the preferred means of encouraging innovation.

In a US antitrust court, the EC Microsoft case would likely face two formidable obstacles to compulsory licensing of Windows protocol information. The first obstacle is the policy, found in both antitrust doctrine and patent legislation, that a patentholder cannot be compelled to license her invention for the sake of promoting competition or encouraging innovation. The second obstacle is the broader doctrine that exceptional circumstances themselves do not trump a dominant firm's right to refuse to deal. It is highly unlikely that an antitrust court in the United States today would compel Microsoft to license protocol information to rival server software companies.

In the United States, the land where IPRs trump antitrust and dominant firms are free to refuse access to indispensable information, is there any alternative competition policy to correct a market failure of information asymmetry? Indeed there is. Patent policy provides a prescription if not a cure for this market failure when the product is a patented invention. Perhaps more than any other intellectual property regime, the patent system is intended to provide open access to the information needed for

---

[85] The most recent examples include three opinions of the Supreme Court since the appointment of Chief Justice John Roberts. The first was a unanimous decision in which the Roberts Court overruled long-standing antitrust doctrine to declare that 'the mere fact that a tying product is patented does not support . . . a presumption . . . of market power'. *Illinois Tool Works, Inc.* v *Independent Ink, Inc.*, 547 U.S. 28, 31 (2006) (citing 102 Stat. 4674, Nov. 19, 1988, codified at 35 U.S.C. s. 271(d)), overruling *Jefferson Parish Hospital Dist. No. 2* v *Hyde,* 466 U.S. 2 (1984). As a result, contracts conditioning the sale of patented inventions on the purchase of complementary staple products no longer fall into the category of *per se* illegality. In two other cases, the Roberts Court's antitrust doctrine was channelled by the logic of trademark rights. In *Leegin Creative Leather Products, Inc.* v *PSKS, Inc.*, 127 S.Ct. 2705 (2007), a deeply divided Court overruled a venerable doctrine of *per se* illegality in holding that resale price maintenance is to be judged by the rule of reason. In *Texaco, Inc.* v *Dagher*, 547 U.S. 1 (2006), a unanimous Court held that the decision by Equilon Enterprises, a joint venture between Texaco and Shell Oil – to sell gasoline at the same price to their separate chains of branded service station owners was not *per se* illegal as a horizontal price fixing agreement. See R.J.R. Peritz, 'The Roberts Court after Two Years: Antitrust, Intellectual Property Rights, and Competition Policy' (2008) *Antitrust Bulletin* 153 (symposium on the Supreme Court's antitrust jurisprudence under Chief Justice John Roberts), also available at http://ssrn.com/author=75649.

competition by innovation. This is not a new view; it is only a shift in emphasis.[86]

The remainder of this section takes a quick look at how the US patent regime can be understood as addressing competition problems, in particular the market failure of information asymmetry.[87] My example derives from the facts of the EC Microsoft case. The key to the analysis remains information flow. The inquiry raises two questions for US patent policy. First, precisely what obligations for information access accompany patent rights as they are currently understood, particularly patent protection of computer software? Secondly, what changes in US patent doctrine would improve its internal competition policy of promoting information flow? These questions involve the patent regime's publication requirement, which is intended to promote information flow and thereby improve the conditions for producing further inventions

In the EC case, Microsoft insisted that patent rights in some Windows protocols (and trade secret rights in others) protected it from antitrust liability for its refusal to disclose them.[88] But would that argument make sense in the United States? Wouldn't there already be public access to the Windows protocols in the US Patent Office database, making unnecessary an antitrust remedy of compulsory licensing simply to gain access? After all, every patent application folder must include a description that is clear enough to enable any person having ordinary skill in the art to make or use the invention. Although files traditionally were kept secret during the patent application process, since 1999 any applicant intending to file outside the United States must make the application public within 18 months.[89] The Windows patents, even if still pending, would likely be public knowledge.

What then should we expect to find if we were to search the US Patent Office database? We should not expect to find the actual protocols because Microsoft is not required to disclose them. Indeed, Microsoft characterized some of them as trade secrets. Ten years ago the Federal Circuit

---

86 *See* R.J.R. Peritz, 'Patents and Progress: The Incentive Conundrum', paper presented at ATRIP Annual Conference, Max-Planck Institute, Munich, Germany, 21 July 2008.

87 The section does not look to copyright misuse because copyright has become relatively unimportant since software has become so easily patentable, in part because copyright doctrine allows broad access to software through its fair use and misuse doctrines. *See* Peritz, n. 65 above.

88 Of course a question might be raised about whether such protocols even merit patent protection; the Commission made that argument.

89 Patent Act, 35 U.S.C. s. 122(b) (2000).

Court declared that a general functional description usually satisfies the so-called description and enablement requirement[90] for software patents. But in practical terms, there is no real enablement. Enabling a skilled programmer to make or use the Windows patents would require flow charts, source code and the detailed descriptions that annotate modules, descriptions that computer programmers always include as documentation for others who subsequently need to understand, change or fix the source code. Both protocols and programmer comments are embedded in source code listings, while protocols also appear in software documentation. Why is a general functional description usually enough for the Federal Circuit Court and, thus, for the Patent Office? Because, according to the court, conversion of functional description into source code is 'a mere clerical function to a skilled programmer'.[91]

This proposition rings hollow for anyone who has actually designed or written operating systems or complex applications software. Indeed, no judge sitting on the Federal Circuit could have taken such a view after having any actual experience in the field. The author of this chapter spent some years designing and writing such software, and the experience testifies to the reality that conversion of systems design specifications to programming language source code is often challenging work that involves much more than mere clerical function. Nonetheless, the Federal Circuit in its nescience requires only a general description of the software process.

While general information about software function has some limited use value, its satisfaction of the patent disclosure requirement creates two kinds of problems. First, general claims and descriptions produce software patents that are too broad and, as a result, foreclose too much competition. Secondly, and more to the point in this chapter, there is insufficient information flow for subsequent inventors. The combination is deadly: broad patent rights and little public information about them.

If the patent regime is intended to encourage learning from prior art and thereby foster competition by invention, the level and quality of information must be improved. The current requirement of a general process description requires only a low level of information and, in consequence, erects an interoperability barrier to further invention, a barrier that benefits the patentholder by keeping rivals out, rather than an information flow that benefits society by enabling competitors to improve and surpass the invention.

---

90 Patent Act, s. 112.

91 *Northern Telecom, Inc.* v *Datapoint Corp.*, 908 F.2d 931, 942 (Fed. Cir. 1990) (citing *In re Sherwood*, 613 F.2d 809, 817 n.6 (C.C.P.A. 1980)).

The current requirement actually raises an information barrier to entry in two directions. First, it blocks the flow of information that the patent regime promises as a public benefit in exchange for the private right to practice the invention. Secondly, it allows the patentholder to assert trade secrecy for particular elements of the software patent, as Microsoft did for the protocols embedded in patented software.[92]

And so a conflict arises deep within the patent regime: on one side sits the patent requirement of disclosure, and on the other, the trade secret-like privilege of non-disclosure. They coexist only because the Federal Circuit's description requirement mistakenly permits secrecy in its midst. The patent regime, properly implemented, would call for a change in the software description and enablement standard, a change that recognizes the information value of source code and system documentation, a change that requires their publication. Moreover, in the broader view of innovation policy, a proper patent obligation to disclose would promote competition and obviate the need for antitrust litigation over issues of interoperability and compulsory disclosure with patented software.

What impact would a proper patent disclosure requirement have on a case resulting in a compulsory licence like that decreed in the EC Microsoft case? While patent law should require complete disclosure of the software protocols embedded in Microsoft's server software, the disclosure should not be understood as defining the scope of a compulsory licence issued by an antitrust court. To be more specific, the US patent requirement of description and enablement should include disclosure of the protocols themselves, as well as their configuration and use in the 'Active Directory' process module described in the EC case. That is part of the software source code and documentation that should be disclosed to the world.

Nonetheless, such disclosure, which properly falls under the US requirement of describing an invention's 'best mode',[93] should not define the antitrust terms of the compulsory licence. A distinction should be made between the protocols themselves and their configuration and use in the 'Active Directory'. The raw protocols are simply information devoid of invention; they provide the vocabulary and syntax that server software needs to communicate with Windows PCs and, thus, are properly within the scope of the compulsory licence. But the 'Active Directory' comes from creative use of the protocols; it is the poetry written with the vocabulary

---

[92] See e.g. *Lockwood* v *American Airlines, Inc.*, 107 F.3d 1565 (Fed. Cir. 1997).

[93] Patent Act, s. 112 also includes the 'best mode' requirement.

and syntax.[94] A properly written compulsory licence should cure the information asymmetry by providing only the raw protocols, thereby promoting competition in the invention of other directories, competition in the invention of other configurations of the protocols and associated data that servers need to regulate their Windows PC networks.

5. CONCLUDING REMARKS

There is little disagreement that US antitrust enforcement has declined over the past 30 years, particularly during Republican administrations whose appointments to the enforcement agencies and the Federal Courts have typically reflected a radical laissez-faire ideology reminiscent of the early twentieth century. At the same time, while the Federal Circuit for the most part has been expanding IPRs over the past 20 years, recent Supreme Court decisions and scholarly activity have given rise to a countercurrent of open competition.[95] This disparity raises serious questions about the public benefit of having the Federal Circuit as a specialty court with institutional competency in patent and trademark matters but without authority or competency for the broader policy questions of promoting progress, particularly in view of Supreme Court oversight as a scarce resource.

Nonetheless, we in the United States need not and should not confine ourselves to antitrust law as the sole expression of competition policy. The patent and copyright laws are not composed entirely of exclusionary rights. They also express their own competition policies, policies that predate the Sherman Anti-Trust Act by exactly 100 years. They promote progress through invention and innovation, progress that is served by both competition and cooperation, with competition depending on public access to and use of the new ideas and information embodied in patented inventions.[96] As described in the example of software patents, improved information flow and more open competition would result from the simple step of imposing more rigorous disclosure requirements. Moreover, the recognition of patent law as a competition regime would ease the pressure on antitrust policy to do work done more efficiently by intellectual

---

[94] The poetry metaphor makes patent sense in light of computer software's textual character despite the metaphor's copyright aroma.

[95] R.J.R. Peritz, 'The Roberts Court after Two Years: Antitrust, Intellectual Property Rights, and Competition Policy' (2008) *Antitrust Bulletin* 153.

[96] 'Freedom to Experiment: Toward a Concept of Inventor Welfare' (2008) *Journal of the Patent and Trademark Office Society* 245, also available at http://ssrn.com/author=75649.

property policy. Finally, antitrust and IPRs would be better understood as intertwined approaches to promoting progress. One result would be a better informed set of public policy alternatives and regulatory tools for mediating between the legitimate expectations of private right holders and public beneficiaries regarding the rewards from invention and innovation. Simply put, US innovation policy would profit from recognition that competition policy encompasses not only antitrust law but the patent regime and its neighbours in the domain of IPRs as well.

7. *Microsoft* v *Commission* and the interoperability issue

Steven Anderman

1. INTRODUCTION

The judgment of the Court of First Instance (CFI) in *Microsoft* v *Commission*[1] offers the latest judicial pronouncement on the relationship between competition law and the exercise of intellectual property rights (IPRs). The CFI continues to stress that only in 'exceptional' circumstances will an IPR owner be subject to a competition law remedy of compulsory licensing because a refusal to license infringes Article 82 EC. It maintains that in 'normal' cases the owner of an IPR is entitled to refuse to license because exclusivity is the very substance of the intellectual property right. However, the case has undoubtedly modified and extended the test of exceptional circumstances. Prior to the Microsoft case, the test of 'exceptional circumstances' tended to be defined by the criteria established by the Court of Justice in its *Magill*[2] and *IMS Health*[3] judgments. After the Microsoft case, it appears that the test of exceptional circumstances may have been widened to include another parameter which extends the test under Article 82(b) EC to certain forms of conduct limiting the technical development of secondary markets. This means that even where an IPR is exploited in a manner that is lawful under the intellectual property (IP) laws, the practice adopted to exploit the IP may, in certain circumstances, be found to be unlawful under the competition rules. It also means that the basis upon which competition law finds a refusal to share IPRs abusive is less clearly articulated. The main purpose of this chapter is look more closely at what is left of the exceptional circumstances test after the Microsoft case; or, to put it another way, how much room is left for

1 Case T-201/04 *Microsoft* v *Commission* [2007] ECR II-3601.

2 Joined Cases C-241 and 242/91 P *RTE and ITV* v *Commission* [1995] ECR I-743 ('*Magill*').

3 Case C-418/01 *IMS Health GmbH* v *NDC Health GmbH & Co. KG* [2004] ECR I-5039.

owners of IPRs to exercise their normal exclusivity rights without infringing Article 82 EC? However, to answer this properly, it will be necessary to take a closer look at three other features of the case: the significance of the findings of 'indispensability' of the interface protocols of Microsoft Windows to interoperability in the 'second market'; the significance of the finding that it was enough to show that there was a 'risk' of elimination of competition in the second market; and the finding of an absence of objective justification

2. THE FACTS OF THE MICROSOFT CASE

The facts of the Microsoft case are located firmly in the information technology sector. In 2000 and 2001, the European Commission investigated Microsoft after a complaint by Sun Microsystems, one of Microsoft's most important competitors in the work group server market. Sun complained that Microsoft provided inadequate information about interface codes for Sun to equip its Solaris servers to interoperate smoothly with Microsoft's 'integrated' package of Windows 2000, Office Suite and work group server operating system because it refused to disclose how the integration between Windows and Office Suite and its server operating system worked. This refusal had the effect of preventing Sun from offering certain services to Windows-based users of its high quality Solaris work group server. The Commission in a decision issued on 24 March 2004 found that Microsoft had abused its near monopoly in the Windows operating system under Article 82 EC by deliberately restricting interoperability between the Windows operating system (OS) and non-Microsoft work group servers such as those operated by Sun Microsystems. The Commission found that by refusing to disclose interface protocols to other work group server makers to allow them to continue to interoperate with MS Windows Microsoft was attempting to lever its dominant position in the Windows PC operating systems market to obtain dominance in the work group server operating systems market and media player markets.[4] There was a separate abuse relating to the bundling or tying of the Windows Media Player with the Windows PC operating system with Microsoft's media player but this article concentrates solely on the interoperability issue.

The remedies imposed by the Commission for the refusal to supply interface information included a fine of €497,200,000 for its infringements of Article 82 and an order that Microsoft must divulge all necessary

---

4 Commission Decision 2007/53/EC of 24 March 2004 [2007] OJ L32/23.

interface information to allow non-MS work group server operating systems to achieve full interoperability with Windows PCs and MS work group servers within 120 days. This was to enable rival vendors to compete on a level playing field in the work group server operating systems market. Insofar as this information was copyright protected, the Commission indicated that it would require a compulsory copyright licence to be given to competitors in the work group server market in order to bring the infringement of Article 82 to an end. Microsoft was to receive remuneration that was reasonable and was based on non-discriminatory terms. The Commission also required Microsoft to update the disclosed information each time it brings to the market new versions of its relevant products. The Commission also indicated that it planned to appoint a monitoring trustee to oversee that Microsoft's interface disclosures were complete and accurate. This remedy of compulsory disclosure of interface information was reminiscent of the remedy agreed in the IBM undertaking of 1984.[5] It was noteworthy too that the remedy of compulsory disclosure was not restricted to any one particular complainant but appeared to be aimed at all participants in the work server market.

Microsoft appealed to the CFI against the fine and remedies imposed by the Commission. Before the appeal was heard, and following an adverse report by the monitoring trustee and its own experts, the Commission adopted a further decision in 2006 to penalize Microsoft another €280,500,000 million for continued non-compliance with its 2004 decision.

3. COURT OF FIRST INSTANCE JUDGMENT

The starting point in analysing the CFI judgment is to understand that the Court determined that its review of the Commission's findings of fact was to be a limited one. Early on, the CFI made it clear that insofar as the Commission's findings of fact were based on complex economic and technical assessments, it would undertake only a limited review, as opposed to its normal general review of the Commission's decisions. By restricting itself to a limited review, the CFI accepted that it could not substitute its own assessment of matters of fact for that of the Commission. It was limited to checking the accuracy of the facts, whether the evidence contained all the relevant data, and whether the data were capable of substantiating the

---

[5] See European Commission, *XIVth Report on Competition Policy* (1984), paras 94–5.

conclusions drawn, i.e. it would not overturn the Commission's findings unless it could find manifestly incorrect findings of fact or errors of assessment of law. This respected the Commission's margin of appreciation in economic and technical matters. As mentioned, this chapter will focus on the issue of interoperability by analysing the 'exceptional circumstances' in which competition law will find that a refusal to license an IPR will be an infringement of Article 82 EC. This requires three other preliminary issues to be examined: (i) the significance of the findings of 'indispensability' of the interface protocols to interoperability in the 'second market'; (ii) the significance of the finding that there was a 'risk' of elimination of competition in the second market; and (iii) the significance of the finding of an absence of objective justification.

The 'Indispensability' of the Interface Protocols to Interoperability

The increased width of the definition of 'exceptional circumstances' in defining the concept of abuse in the CFI's judgment[6] must be seen first of all in the context of its treatment of the concept of dominance. The CFI accepted the Commission's findings that Microsoft's Windows OS was the de facto standard infrastructure for work group servers[7] and that work group servers were a separate market.[8] These findings invoke 'essential facilities' reasoning, i.e. that Windows was not only a monopoly in its own market of operating systems but also an indispensable input for the second market for work group servers. The CFI found no error in the Commission's finding that access to MS Windows OS was 'necessary to maintain viability in the market for work servers'.[9] The CFI accepted that the interface information was essential to viability on the market.[10] Thus far, the Court's judgment was consistent with previous case law of the Court of Justice that held that an IP owner with a monopoly in a 'primary' market may have certain special responsibilities under Article 82 EC towards competitors in 'secondary' and dependent markets.[11]

However, it was also consistent with the view of the courts that the abuse itself rested on the foundations of a finding of a special form of dominance, an 'essential facility' type of dominance. This finding is itself an indispensable precondition for a finding that there are 'exceptional'

6 Case T-201/04 *Microsoft* v *Commission*.
7 CFI judgment, para. 392.
8 CFI judgment, paras 480–530.
9 CFI judgment, paras 392–3.
10 CFI judgment, paras 421–2.
11 Case 238/87 *Volvo* v *Veng (UK) Ltd* [1988] ECR 1.

circumstances in which a compulsory licence of an IPR may be granted under Article 82 EC.

For many, if not most, forms of abuse, the concept of dominance in Article 82 EC is viewed as a separate finding before the concept of abuse is considered. Once an undertaking is found to be dominant, the investigation moves on to determine whether the undertaking's conduct amounts to an abuse. In most cases, the degree of dominance seems to be relatively unimportant as long as the market power of the undertaking exceeds the legal definitional threshold of dominance. The actual degree of dominance in the cases has varied from market shares of 39 to 100 per cent.[12]

In certain refusals to supply cases, however, particularly those involving compulsory licenses of IPRs, there is a closer link between the nature of the degree of dominance and the concept of abuse. The nature of the dominance required to be found is that the product protected by an IPR must be an 'essential facility' or rather, as the Court of Justice has chosen to define it, both a de facto monopoly, with no available substitutes, and an indispensable input into a second market.[13] If the product is a monopoly but is not an indispensable input into a second market, its owner has no obligation to supply or license unless there is an abuse of the *United Brands* type.[14] The reasons for the linkage with a particular finding of dominance is that once a product reaches the stage that its market power or degree of dominance amounts to an essential facility, a refusal to supply or license can be abusive because it will result in the exclusion of access or elimination of competition in the markets dependent upon the input.

Yet at the same time, the imposition of a stringent definition of dominance in such cases ensures that regulation is kept to the margins of business conduct. The more demanding definition of dominance creates a wide scope for lawful refusals to supply or license. Anyone reading Advocate General Jacob's opinion, or the judgment of the Court of Justice, in *Bronner*[15] can see evidence of a desire to limit the scope of essential facilities reasoning to truly egregious cases of misuse of market power. The twin requirements of monopoly (for which there is no substitute) and 'indispensable' input will ensure that the issue of refusal to license an IPR will

---

12 See e.g. Case T-219/99 *British Airways* v *Commission* [2003] ECR II-5917 (BA found dominant with a 40–46 per cent market share). Case COMP/38.233 *Wanadoo Interactive* (dominant with only a market share of 39 per cent).

13 Joined Cases C-241 and 242/91 P *Magill*.

14 Case 27/96 *United Brands* v *Commission* [1978] ECR 207.

15 Case C-7/97 *Oscar Bronner GmbH & Co. KG* v *Mediaprint* [1998] ECR I-7791.

only surface in the most exceptional cases under Article 82 EC even with a wider definition of 'exceptional circumstances'.

The foundations for this type of dominance as the basis of an exclusionary abuse were established in *Commercial Solvents*,[16] where a refusal to supply by a firm enjoying an essential facilities type of dominance was found to infringe Article 82 EC because it eliminated competition in a secondary dependent market, and elimination of competition was held to be *a fortiori* a distortion of competition. The abuse applies where (i) there are two well-defined markets (often defined narrowly), and (ii) the owner of an asset in the first market enjoys a monopoly which is indispensable to competitors in a secondary dependent market (or to another level of economic activity). Its essence is the concern that the refusal will be used as a means to leverage a monopolist's power in one market to exclude competitors and competition in a second market.

Whether the owner's asset is a privatized nationalized monopoly or a product developed from the start by private investment in research and development and IP protection and risk-taking seems not to be relevant; what counts is the nature of its market power. As long as the product is found to enjoy both a monopoly in an economic sense, i.e. that there is no substitute available, and to be an indispensable input into a secondary dependent market, it meets the definition. The evidence for indispensability consists of proof of a lack of available substitutes and a finding that the competitor cannot itself invest and replicate the facility of the incumbent firm. In *Bronner*, Advocate General Jacobs was concerned to ensure that the definition of indispensability was sufficiently tight to prevent opportunistic conduct by competitors. The Court of Justice agreed and offered a test of indispensability that meant that only if it were impossible to replicate the 'essential' product by an undertaking *with the resources of the incumbent* would the product be viewed as indispensable.[17] This suggested either a physical impossibility or a legal barrier (IPRs or regulation). In *Magill*, the Court of Justice found that the TV companies enjoyed a de facto monopoly over the listings which was an indispensable input into the TV guide market. The existence of a copyright in the programme listings operated as a barrier to the competitor Magill obtaining access to the listings and required a remedy of compulsory licence rather than a simple order to supply. In the Microsoft case, a further factor proving indispensability was the finding of a network effects barrier to entry. This

---

16 Joined Cases 6 and 7/73 *ICI and Commercial Solvents* v *Commission* [1974] ECR 223.

17 Case C-7/97 *Oscar Bronner*.

factor meant that any competitor attempting to replicate the Windows product would fail unless it could win over the tens of thousands of applications makers to interoperate with it. One significance of the Microsoft case was that the monopoly enjoyed by Microsoft was an economic one underpinned not only by the owner's IP in the Windows OS but also by the applications barrier to entry that prevented substitution by competitors.

In the Microsoft case, the CFI confirmed the Commission's theory of a 'leveraging' abuse, that is to say that the Court found that Microsoft was guilty of leveraging its exceptional dominant power in the operating systems market to achieve dominance in the work group server market.[18] The indispensable infrastructure in the first market (Windows OS) was used as a springboard to mount a campaign to obtain significant market power in (or eliminate competition) the second market, the work group server market.

Significance of the Finding that there was a 'Risk' of Elimination of Competition in the Second Market

The influence of the finding of essential facilities dominance was not confined to the CFI's acceptance of the finding of a leveraging exclusionary abuse; it also underpinned the Court's acceptance of the Commission's argument that it was enough to prove that the refusal to supply gave rise to 'a risk of' elimination of competition in the second market in order to establish an abuse under Article 82 EC. The Court held that the test did not require the Commission to establish that competition had been eliminated or that its elimination was imminent.[19] Microsoft had argued that in IP cases, following the case law, there must be a stricter test: it must be shown that the conduct was 'likely to eliminate' all competition or that the conduct of the dominant undertaking had a 'high probability' of elimination of all competition.

The CFI, however, agreed with the Commission, saying that Microsoft's complaint was purely one of terminology and wholly irrelevant.[20] For the Community courts, the CFI said, the two tests 'reflect the same idea, namely that Article 82 EC does not apply only when there is no more competition in the market or that elimination is imminent'. This would be counter to the objective of the provision which is to maintain undistorted competition in the market and safeguard the competition that still exists.

---

18 CFI judgment, para. 1344.
19 CFI judgment, para. 457.
20 CFI judgment, para. 561.

The Court also noted that 'network effects' would make it harder for competitors once ejected to come back into the market. The CFI emphasized that under Article 82 EC, what matters to establish an infringement is that the refusal *is liable to or likely to eliminate all effective competition on the market*. The fact that some competitors 'retain a marginal presence in some niches of the market' does not constitute the existence of such competition.[21]

Of course, there is a considerable difference between the two standards of proof: 'liable to' and 'likely to' eliminate competition. The CFI's judgment, however, appeared to wish to emphasize that the test in Article 82 EC is not concerned with establishing a particular standard of proof of effects. Rather, it wanted to stress that it was enough to show conduct that *could possibly* produce such effects, and this is in line with previous Court of Justice case law on Article 82 EC. For example, in *Commercial Solvents* v *Commission*,[22] the Court of Justice referred to the test as 'risks eliminating competition'. In *Telemarketing*,[23] the Court used the standard of 'possibility of eliminating all competition'.

Yet, this part of the decision must be read in the light of the fact that the existence of essential facilities dominance itself actually offered strong evidence that the *likely* effect of the abuse would have been to eliminate competition. The Commission had found that access to MS Windows OS was 'necessary to maintain viability in the market for work servers'[24] and that such information was essential to viability on the market.[25] Indeed, insofar as the interface information was indispensable to a continued presence on the work group server market, it was in fact not only likely that competitors would be eliminated from the market, but also that once ejected, competitors would find it impossible to return to the market because of the existence of the 'network effects' barrier to entry.

To economists as well as lawyers, one implication of this judgment is that the CFI appears not to be particularly impressed by the concept of reforming Article 82 EC to add a stronger test of effects as a constituent element of this particular abuse. The judgment reiterates that the test of abuse under Article 82 EC is conduct to which objectively abusive intent could be attributed and which creates a plausible risk of the harm of elimination of effective competition. Consequently, once essential facilities

---

21 CFI judgment, para. 563.
22 Joined Cases 6 and 7/73 *ICI and Commercial Solvents v Commission*.
23 Case 311/84 *CBEM Telemarketing* v *CLT* [1985] ECR 3261.
24 CFI judgment, paras 392–3.
25 CFI judgment, paras 421–2.

dominance is established, it will not be difficult for the Commission to prove the probable exclusionary effects of a refusal to license.

The 'Exceptional Circumstances' in which a Refusal to License an IPR will be an Infringement of Article 82 EC

Owners of essential facilities of tangible products such as ports or railway lines may have special responsibilities that extend to offering access to competitors whether new or old.[26] The existence of their exceptional form of dominance dictates their exceptional form of special responsibility under Article 82 EC. In the case of IPRs, however, there must be a further finding of 'exceptional circumstances'. This added constituent element to the abuse reflects the accommodation with IPRs incorporated in the Article 82 case law. Article 82 recognizes both the legitimacy of the 'existence' of IPRs, i.e. the criteria chosen by Member States for the grant of such rights, and certain features of their 'exercise'. The Court of Justice in *Volvo* v *Veng* indicated that the 'normal exercise' of exclusivity associated with IPRs would be respected under Article 82 EC in its primary market but might be curbed in a secondary dependent market, for example where there was an arbitrary refusal of the dominant owner of IP protected spare parts to supply independent repairers in the maintenance market.[27] In *Magill*[28] and *IMS Health*,[29] the Court of Justice went on to maintain that where an IP was involved, it was necessary to show that there must be 'exceptional circumstances' present before Article 82 EC could be used to override the free exercise of an IPR. The 'exceptional circumstances' test as expounded in these two cases consisted of three cumulative conditions. (This, of course, was in addition to the requirement that the nature of dominance in the first market was a monopoly which was an indispensable input into the second market.) The first condition was that the undertaking asking for a compulsory licence must offer a new product for which there was potential or demonstrable consumer demand. Secondly, the Commission needed to show that the refusal to license would lead to an elimination of all competition on the secondary market. Thirdly, it had to

---

[26] See *Sea Containers Ltd/ Stena Sealink* [1994] OJ L15/8; *Port of Rodby* [1994] OJ L55/52. See J. Temple Lang, 'Defining Legitimate Competition: Companies Duties to Supply Competitors and Access to Essential Facilities' (1994) *Fordham International Law Journal* 437; D. Ridyard, 'Essential Facilities and the Obligation to Supply Competitors' (1996) *ECLR* 438.

[27] Case 238/87 *Volvo* v *Veng (UK) Ltd.*

[28] Case C-241/91 P *Magill.*

[29] Case C-418/01 *IMS Health GmbH.*

be shown that the dominant undertaking had no objective justification for refusing to license.

Microsoft argued that in this case too there should be a strict test based on the 'new product' rule as set out in the *IMS Health* case.[30] This argument was not entirely convincing since the Court of Justice in *IMS Health* said that the facts of *Magill* were 'sufficient' to meet the exceptional circumstances test, implying that other categories of exceptional circumstances could exist.[31]

Microsoft also attempted to establish that competitors would not be providing a new product but replicating MS Windows server operating systems, 'mimicking their functionality' and that therefore consumers would not be harmed by its refusal to share interface information. Had Microsoft succeeded in proving this assertion, the case may have been otherwise decided but the Commission argued somewhat more successfully that MS's competitors could use the interface disclosures to develop the advanced features of their own products[32] and liven up the competitive landscape.[33] It argued therefore that the refusal to continue to supply interface information stopped 'follow-on' innovation. The facts as found supported this point since the Solaris work group server offered more functions, e.g. reliability/availability of the network and security than the Microsoft work group servers.[34]

In its argument on appeal, the Commission reiterated its position but in the process of responding to the CFI's questioning, it seemed to achieve a clearer focus.

(i) The Commission refined the new product argument by arguing that the definition of 'new product' is one that doesn't duplicate existing products but adds substantial elements arising from competitor's own research efforts.

(ii) It took a far more effective line on the crucial issue of adapting the exceptional circumstances categories to the facts of the case, partly in response to the questioning of the Court.[35] It reiterated the point that *IMS Health* did not establish an exhaustive list of exceptional circumstances. But this time it seemed to be more strategic by making the point

---

30 At one point, Microsoft also argued that none of the criteria in Case C-7/97 *Oscar Bronner* were satisfied but this was on the basis that *Bronner* should apply if there were no IPRs at stake. See CFI judgment, para. 301.

31 Case C-418/01 *IMS Health*, para. 107.

32 CFI judgment, para. 695.

33 See CFI judgment, para. 725.

34 See e.g. CFI judgment, para. 652.

35 CFI judgment, para. 317.

that the framework for analysing the test of refusal to supply was provided by Article 82(b), which declares it an abuse to *limit technical development* to the prejudice of consumers. It argued that the refusal to provide the indispensable interface information amounted to a blockage of interoperability in the specific sector of information technology and a blow to 'follow-on' innovation in the secondary market. It also explained that this factor differentiated the facts of the case from the *IMS Health* and *Magill*-type cases.[36] This was more focused than its earlier insistence that the framework could be established simply by looking at the entirety or totality of the circumstances.

(iii) Finally, it also drew attention to the fact that Microsoft was disrupting an existing pattern of a history of supply of interface information to the sector and the discontinuation of supply had occurred after Microsoft had made use of interoperability in the sector to build up its market for Windows operating systems.[37] This point also reminds us that on this point, too, the facts of Microsoft can be significantly distinguished from a refusal to supply a new entrant to the sector (as was the case in the facts of *Magill* and *IMS Health*).[38]

The CFI accepted almost all of the Commission's arguments, and indeed developed them in certain respects. The Court emphasized that the test of new product must be considered under Article 82 EC which makes it an abuse to limit technical developments to the prejudice of consumers.

It pointed out that the new product rule in *Magill* was meant to protect consumers from the harm of preventing the appearance of a totally new product, one not offered by the dominant firm and one for which there was a potential consumer demand.

It also stressed that in *IMS Health*, the Court of Justice had emphasized the damage to consumer interests that can arise where the refusal to grant a licence *prevents the development of a secondary market* to the detriment of consumers.

It then concluded that the *Magill* and *IMS Health* new product rule cannot be the only parameter which determines whether a refusal to license an IPR is capable of causing prejudice to consumers within the meaning of Article 82(b) EC. That provision refers to limiting not only production or markets, but also a limitation of technical development.[39]

---

36 CFI judgment, para. 305.

37 CFI judgment, para. 307.

38 See S. Anderman, 'Does the Microsoft Case Offer a New Paradigm for the 'Exceptional Circumstances' Test and Compulsory Licenses under EC Competition Law' (2004) *Competition Law Review* 7, 13–14.

39 CFI judgment, para. 647.

The Court went on to find that the Commission had evidence for its finding that the refusal to supply would prevent the competitors from 'developing the advanced features of their own products available in the web of interoperability relationships that underpin the Windows domain architecture' and evidence for its finding that 'the refusal caused prejudice to consumers'.[40]

Hence the Court concluded that the Commission's findings were not manifestly incorrect.[41]

What are the implications of this judgment for future cases? In the first place we must recognize that this judgment is one that is explicitly rooted in its findings of facts: interoperability issues in the information technology sector; obstruction to innovative competitors by an owner of a de facto industrial standard after a history of a continued relationship of sharing code information.

Nevertheless, it is clear that after the CFI judgment, the 'exceptional circumstances' test has wider parameters than the 'new product' rule in *Magill.* We had an intimation of this possibility in *IMS Health* but now we have a confirmation. The only issue is how wide are the parameters?

The parameters are probably not as wide as suggested by a literal reading of paragraph 664 which states that Article 82 covers not only those practices which may prejudice consumers directly but also those which indirectly prejudice them by impairing an effective competitive structure.

It is wise to remind ourselves first of all that the test of exceptional circumstances set out in Court of Justice judgments presupposes that the IP protected product in the first market must be both a monopoly and an indispensable input into the second market. Secondly, a constituent element of the abuse must be that there is strong evidence that the practice of the IP owner will give rise to the risk of 'eliminating effective competition' in the market. This probably places limits on the definition of impairment of 'an effective competitive structure'.

The crucial test of 'exceptional circumstances' after the Microsoft judgment is to discern how the new product test been redefined. In this case there were two factors that seemed to be influential in the CFI's judgment: first, this was a case concerning the need to maintain interoperability in the information technology sector to ensure the continuation of demonstrable plural sources of innovation, sources which were also demonstrably satisfying consumer needs that were not satisfied by Microsoft. Sun had

---

40 CFI judgment, paras 651–6.

41 CFI judgment, para. 665.

demonstrated that it was a real source of innovation and promised to continue to be so. This case did not concern a new entrant seeking access. Sun and other work server makers had enjoyed a long period of interoperability with Windows based on its willing supply of interface information, albeit to a predecessor of Sun. Microsoft's decision to discontinue this practice after receiving the letter from Sun, whatever their obvious irritation at the scope of the request, could objectively be viewed as an abuse comparable to the definition of abuse in a line of cases since *Commercial Solvents.* Moreover, the refusal in such circumstances could legitimately be construed as exceptional circumstances satisfying a modified new product test owing to its limitation of technical development in the sector to the prejudice of consumers.[42]

After the Microsoft case, the category of exceptional circumstances when applied to *new entrants* will continue to require that the new entrant offers a new product for which these is potential or demonstrable consumer demand, however that is defined by the case law. As we know, the definition of new product continues to be opaque. All we know is that the new entrant may not offer a replica or clone of the product already offered by the owner of an IP protected industrial standard. What is less clear is the extent to which and way in which the new product must be different than the old. In the Microsoft case, a close look at the facts of work group servers indicated a recognizable difference in the functionalities of the Solaris servers from those of Microsoft.

But of course, the Microsoft case was not a case of a new entrant similar to *Magill* and *IMS Health.* It was a case of a dominant firm disrupting an existing relationship of interoperability on grounds which could be found to be anti-competitive. Following the Microsoft case, we can assume that where an incumbent has already been dealing with undertakings operating in a dependent secondary market and the competitor in the secondary market (i) already has advanced features in their own products, and (ii) requires access to the interface information in order to continue viably to develop such advanced features, Article 82(b) will apply. Innovators will get such protection because a refusal in such circumstances will limit the 'technical development' of the market.

Yet will it stop there? In the Microsoft case, the Commission did not seem to consider the distinction between new entrant and established relationship particularly significant.[43] It merely drew attention to the fact that this was the case here. The CFI thought it more significant but only as an

42 CFI judgment, para. 665.
43 CFI judgment, para. 307.

added factor. Yet the CFI judgment in the Microsoft case drew attention to the fact that the language and purpose of Article 82(b) EC now guides us in defining the outer limits of the competition rules. And, in respect of monopoly undertakings with an indispensable product which have historically provided access to competitors in secondary markets, the test of exceptional circumstances may be even wider and possibly moving closer to cases of essential facilities which are not IP protected. *Commercial Solvents* continues to provide possible authority for the interpretation of Article 82(b) EC and that provision refers to limiting 'markets', as well as 'technical development', to the prejudice of consumers. Where a monopolist with an indispensable input disrupts a relationship of previous supply for reasons that could be viewed as anti-competitive, it may be sufficiently egregious behaviour to bypass the established exceptional circumstances test for IP owners.[44]

Finding of an Absence of Objective Justification

The CFI firmly held that Microsoft's assertion that it would have less incentive to develop a given technology if it is required to make that technology available to its competitors could only be raised under the head of objective justification.[45]

The CFI also held that once the constituent elements of the abuse have been established, the burden shifts to the dominant firm to raise any plea of objective justification and support it with arguments and evidence.[46] In this case Microsoft did not meet its burden. Its arguments were vague, general and theoretical. It merely stated that '[d]isclosure would . . . eliminate future incentives to invest in the creation of more intellectual property', without specifying the technologies or products to which it thus referred.[47]

The CFI made it clear that what was called for was not a balancing exercise of the two theories of innovation but a more legalistic assessment of Microsoft's arguments. The Court concluded that the Commission's conclusion was not based on a balancing of the two conflicting views of innovation but its findings: that there was no basis to Microsoft's claims that its products would be cloned; that disclosure of interoperability was

---

44 See discussion in S.D. Anderman and J. Kallaugher, *Technology Transfers and the New EU Competition Rules: IP Licensing after Modernisation* (Oxford: Oxford University Press, 2006), pp. 280–89.

45 CFI judgment, para. 659.

46 CFI judgment, para. 688.

47 CFI judgment, para. 698.

widespread in the industry – IBM had already committed to this course in the 1980s; and that Directive 91/250 was consistent with this policy.

So the Court did not engage with the Commission's attempt to balance the possible negative impact of an order to supply on Microsoft's incentives to innovate and the positive impact on the whole industry including Microsoft.[48] It contented itself with the conclusion that Microsoft had not made out an adequate case for objective justification. This suggests that the CFI will in future deal with arguments about pro-consumer efficiencies and incentives to innovate as an attempted objective justification. They will be dealt with not as a simple balancing test, along the lines of a US style rule of reason analysis, but more as a legal claim that can be overridden if the practice also deprives consumers of a new product or creates a risk of elimination of effective competition.

4. CONCLUSIONS

(i) The relationship of EC competition law as a 'second tier' of regulation of the exercise of IPRs is reinforced by this judgment. There will continue to be an internal balance between exclusivity and access within the law relating to IPRs and the possibility of an external limit created by the competition law rules. A feature of this is the treatment of the decompilation issue under Article 6 of the Software Directive.[49] Even where the rules of IP law may provide an alternative method of resolving the dispute, if the conduct of the IP owner transgresses the prohibition of Article 82 EC, competition law will provide a remedy to ensure access. This raises the interesting issue whether IP laws should reform themselves to minimize intervention by competition law or should leave it to competition law to intervene whenever its rules are contravened by the exercise of an IPR.

(ii) While the category of 'exceptional circumstances' has been opened up to meet the purposes of Article 82(b) EC, little new light has been thrown on the nature of the 'reasonable and non-discriminatory' terms which are meant to govern compulsory access. Indeed, the CFI's reversal of the Commission's appointment of an independent monitoring trustee to oversee the issue of fair pricing of compulsory access raises new questions.

---

48 See discussion in C. Ritter, 'Refusal to Deal and Essential Facilities: Does Intellectual Property Require Special Deference compared to Tangible Property?' (2005) *World Competition* 281, 298.

49 Directive 91/250/EC on the legal protection of computer programs [1991] OJ L122/42.

(iii) By emphatically limiting the standard of proof of risk of elimination of effective competition, the judgment suggests a lesser role for economic argument in the legal rules defining the concept of effects of abuse under Article 82 EC and may affect the current discussion of reform of Article 82.

8. The EC Microsoft case and duty to deal: the transatlantic divide

Eleanor M. Fox*

1. INTRODUCTION

This chapter examines Microsoft's offence in refusing to give full information to its work group server operating systems rivals so that they could interoperate as seamlessly with Microsoft's PC and work group server operating systems as Microsoft could.[1] It is well known that firms, even monopolists, have no general duty to deal, and this is especially true when a claim is made that the firm must share its intellectual property (IP). A dominant firm has a duty to deal only in the event of exceptional circumstances. The question is: Did the facts of the Microsoft case involve 'exceptional circumstances'?

The Microsoft case was preceded by two important precedents on duty to license IP: *Magill*[2] and *IMS Health*.[3] The Court of First Instance (CFI) in the Microsoft case purported to apply the criteria laid down in *Magill* and *IMS Health*, but pushed the round peg of the Microsoft facts into the square boxes of *Magill* and *IMS Health*. This chapter proposes abandoning the square boxes and resorting to concept rather than rules to determine when circumstances are so exceptionally important to consumers and the market that a duty to deal should arise. Resorting to concept, and given the general perspective of EC competition law, the European courts would probably find a duty. But is there a transatlantic divide?

---

* The author thanks John Vickers for helpful comments on an earlier draft of this chapter. A form of the essay originally appeared in (2008) *Competition Policy International* (Spring). It is reprinted, as revised, with permission of Competition Policy International.

1 Case T-201/04 *Microsoft* v *Commission* [2007] ECR II-3601 (hereinafter 'CFI judgment').

2 Joined Cases C-241 and 242/91P *RTE, ITP and BBC* v *Commission* [1995] ECR I-743 ('*Magill*').

3 Case C-418/01 *IMS Health* v *NDC Health* [2004] ECR I-5039.

2. THE PRECEDENTS AND THEIR LIMIT

The European Court of Justice charted refusal-to-deal territory in two important cases: *IMS Health* and *Magill*. In *Magill*, the Court found that owners of copyrights in their TV schedules had a duty to license the schedules to a consolidated TV guide because consumers wanted a consolidated TV guide and the refusals blocked its emergence. In *IMS Health*, the Court found that the owners of copyrights in a grid system demarking geographic boundaries for the collection of pharmaceutical sales data would have a duty to license the grid system if (reciting the *Magill* factors):

(i) the access was indispensible to enable an undertaking to carry on business on a market;
(ii) the refusal prevented the emergence of a product for which there is a potential consumer demand; and
(iii) the refusal excluded any competition on a secondary market.

The three criteria were, said the Court, 'sufficient' to trigger the exceptional circumstances exception from the general principle that a firm can choose to deal with whom it likes. If the three factors exist and a dominant firm has no objective justification for refusing to deal, it must deal.

IMS Health and *Magill* are formalistic judgments. The *Magill* case was special because people wanted a consolidated TV guide and could not get one unless the three broadcasters provided the necessary inputs. The refusal blocked the market. The controlling three factors set forth in *Magill* simply describe the facts of the case. In *IMS Health*, the Court simply held that it was for the national court to apply the *Magill* factors.

Then along came the Microsoft case. The problem before the European Commission and then the Court of First Instance (CFI) was whether, under the circumstances, Microsoft was obliged to give seamless interoperability information to the work group server rivals who needed access to the standard operating system. The CFI held the problem up to the light of the *IMS Health* and *Magill* criteria, and gave an expansive construction to each of the three *Magill* factors:

(i) The CFI found (or rather upheld the Commission finding) that rivals' access to complete interoperability information was indispensable to their business. The CFI, however, seemed to discount the fact that much (although not all) of the information was already provided by Microsoft; the withheld information seemed not indispensible to enable the undertakings to carry on their business, but it did handicap them.

(ii) The CFI found that the refusal prevented the emergence of a new product that consumers demanded. Microsoft's withholding of protocols did not prevent the emergence of a new product in the sense that BBC's and ITP's refusals to Magill precluded the emergence of a TV guide; although it did significantly undermine the rivals' incentives to innovate, and it sounded the death knell to some of their products.

(iii) The CFI found that the refusal excluded any competition on a secondary market. But Microsoft's refusal did not exclude all work group server operating systems competition; rather, it created a risk that competition would be excluded in the future. More accurately, it seriously undermined competition on the merits.

The CFI concluded that the facts of the Microsoft case fit the three *Magill* criteria and therefore qualified as 'exceptional circumstances', and, finding that Microsoft had no objective justification such as efficiencies, it ordered Microsoft to provide seamless interoperability information.

3. THE FACTS OF THE MICROSOFT CASE

In the Microsoft case, the Commission's story was simple (even while factually complex). It began some years before the investigation was initiated. Microsoft controlled the PC operating systems, occupying more than 95 per cent of the market. It had great power; it was the world standard. Its operating system hosted many applications, and some were potential platforms for challenging Microsoft's operating system power. Microsoft developed strategies to use its leverage to protect its power. For example:

- Netscape pioneered the web-browser. Before Microsoft had a browser of its own, it welcomed Netscape on its desktop. Microsoft then made its own browser and took actions to 'cut off Netscape's air supply'.[4]
- RealNetworks pioneered the media player. Before Microsoft had a media player of its own, Microsoft shared the desktop with RealNetworks. Microsoft then made a media player of its own and bundled its media player with its operating system.

---

4 See M. France, 'Decoding the Trial: Microsoft Misses its First Shot', *BusinessWeek Online*, 29 January 1998, www.businessweek.com/microsoft/updates/up90129a.htm.

- Novell and Sun Microsystems pioneered work group server operating systems. Microsoft provided the information they needed to interoperate seamlessly with Microsoft's Windows. Microsoft then made its own work group server operating software and turned the spigot to cut back the information flow to what were now their rivals.

In its investigation, the Commission conducted a survey. The survey results showed that, over a wide range of products, users rated the rivals' work group systems more favourably than they rated Microsoft's on the qualities of reliability, availability, security, ease of use and speed; but Microsoft (of course) surpassed all others on interoperability because it held the knob to the faucet and seamless interoperability was the one quality that many users could not do without. As a result, products of rivals that users liked dropped from the market.[5]

The Commission's ammunition also included the Computer Software Directive.[6] In this Directive, the Community legislature attached high importance to the interoperability of computer software. By the Commission's account, the Directive regarded interoperability as of the essence for effective computer use. This suggests that, in the context of Community policy, computer interoperability may be valued more highly than exclusive proprietary rights in interface protocols.

Did Microsoft have a duty not to turn off the faucet?

4. THE SAFE APPROACH, THE IRONY, AND THE OTHER PATH

Applying the *IMS Health* and *Magill* factors was undoubtedly a safe approach for the CFI to take if the facts of the Microsoft case fit the factors. If so, the CFI could simply apply the rules as established by the Court of Justice.

The Microsoft facts did not fit the factors very snugly; but they fit the concept of essentiality much better than the facts of either *IMS Health* or *Magill*. *Magill* was only about a consolidated TV guide in Ireland and whether it would be available a week before programmes aired. *IMS Health* was only about boundaries of territories in Germany used by

---

5 CFI judgment, paras 572, 573.

6 Council Directive on the legal protection of computer programs 91/250/EEC of 14 May 1991, [1991] OJ L122/42.

pharmaceutical companies for assembling their sales data. What great power over the lives of people did the BBC or IMS wield by trying to keep their proprietary information to themselves? The Microsoft case, on the other hand, is about people's access, worldwide, to the best computing systems possible. The irony is that a literal applier of the rules and categories of *IMS Health* and *Magill* would have held that Microsoft's refusal was not an abuse of dominance, even though so much more was at stake in the Microsoft case than in the two paradigm Court of Justice cases decreeing a duty to deal.[7]

How much more satisfying it would have been for the CFI to have asked the important questions:

(1) Are consumers and the market seriously disadvantaged by denial of full access to interoperability information? If the answer is 'yes':
(2) Would the respondent and the market be seriously disadvantaged by a duty to grant access?

In deference to the principle that there is generally no duty to share one's property, it may and should be assumed that no access would be ordered, in any event, unless the disadvantage to consumers and the market is qualitatively of a very serious order; thus, a weak form of 'essentiality'.

We turn to question one. Were the users disadvantaged by denial of full access? According to the Commission's fact-finding in the Microsoft case, computer users were seriously disadvantaged by lack of full interoperability. Microsoft was *the* standard in a network market. Rival providers were subject to the power and incentive of Microsoft to throw noise into their interconnections. The Commission's evidence that users preferred certain rivals' products on all qualities except interoperability, and had to forego first choices because interoperability problems were serious, was powerful testimony.

Secondly, would Microsoft and the market be disadvantaged by an antitrust duty of Microsoft to provide seamless interoperability information? According to the facts, they would not be. Recall that Microsoft provided complete information under conditions of competition and changed its course only after it integrated. This is a telling indication that Microsoft was happy to provide the information when a strategy of exclusion would

---

[7] *See* E.M. Fox, 'Monopolization, Abuse of Dominance, and Refusal to License Intellectual Property to Competitors—Do Antitrust Duties Help or Hurt Competition and Innovation? How Do We Know?' in Claus-Dieter Ehlermann and Isabela. Atanasiu (eds), *European Competition Law Annual 2005: What is an Abuse of a Dominant Position?* (Oxford: Hart Publishing, 2006).

hurt it, and that the flow of information was optimal for the market.[8] Would a duty to provide full interoperability information undermine Microsoft's incentives to invent? Under EC law, Microsoft had the burden to prove it would, and Microsoft did not carry its burden. The interface was a by-product that Microsoft had to create in any event for its own internal operability.

5. ACROSS THE OCEAN

The structure of analysis set out above aligns with the values and perspectives of EC law, but it is not the only plausible approach. US law takes a different tack. The US perspective may be derived from the US Supreme Court's opinion in *Verizon* v *Trinko*.[9]

In *Trinko*, Bell Atlantic (later acquired by Verizon), was the incumbent telephone service provider in north-eastern United States. Bell Atlantic owned the elements of the local loop – bottleneck elements connecting long-distance service to the local market. For many years, it did so under conditions of legal monopoly in local service areas. Technology changed, making local service competition feasible. The US Congress passed the 1996 Telecommunications Act, easing the way for new entry into local service and requiring incumbents to give their rivals non-discriminatory access to the local loop. Bell Atlantic, wanting to keep its customers to itself, gave its new rivals access to the local loop and undertook to serve them in this regard, as required by the new Act, but then it disrupted the service. The rivals complained to the Federal Communications Commission. The FCC agreed with their claims, penalized Bell Atlantic, and ordered Bell Atlantic to compensate the rivals. In an ensuing private antitrust suit, the question was whether Bell Atlantic's conduct was also an antitrust violation, which it might have been because the 1996 Act declared that it did not pre-empt the antitrust laws. The US Supreme Court held in the negative. In doing so it set forth principles for analysis in Sherman Act duty-to-deal cases.

According to the US Supreme Court, the first strong principle is: no duty

---

[8] The importance of this circumstance has been highlighted by Judge Robert Bork in the *Aspen* case (see nn. 10 and 11 below), and by Justice Antonin Scalia in *Trinko* (see n. 9 below).

[9] *Verizon Communications* v *Law Offices of Curtis V. Trinko*, 540 U.S. 398 (2004) ('*Trinko*'). *Trinko* is not an IP case. Recent IP case law underscores the principle of IP exclusivity. See e.g. *In re Independent Service Organizations Antitrust Litigation*, 203 F.3d 1322 (Fed. Cir. 2000), cert. denied, 531 U.S. 1143 (2001).

to deal. The Court expressed antipathy to 'sharing duties', stating that such duties undermine investment and inventiveness. The Court recognized an exception for 'exceptional circumstances' but treated it as very rare. It stated that the Supreme Court had never recognized an essential facilities doctrine (which is normally regarded as the paradigm 'exceptional circumstance'). It ruled that even if such a doctrine exists it cannot be invoked where either the defendant has engaged in some dealing, as opposed to a total refusal, or where a regulatory agency (as distinct from an antitrust authority) has the power to order a course of dealing. In putting forth its argument, plaintiff Trinko had relied on an important Supreme Court case called *Aspen Skiing*.[10] The Court acknowledged *Aspen* as the exception to the no-duty rule. In *Aspen,* the dominant three-mountain ski resort had joined with the plaintiff ski mountain in offering a four-mountain ski ticket for many years, but then changed its course, sacrificing the revenues it would have received from the four-mountain ticket. The *Aspen* Court found a monopoly violation, based on the defendant's exclusionary conduct that had no efficiency justification. The *Trinko* Court called *Aspen* the outer limits of the exception from the no-duty rule, and in fact implicitly overruled the approach and perspective of *Aspen* while purporting to respect it.[11] Indeed, extolling the principle of freedom to choose not to deal, the *Trinko* Court stated that antitrust does not impose affirmative duties just because it can be argued that consumers would be better off.[12]

Any analyst applying the law and spirit of *Trinko* to the EC Microsoft facts would not start the analysis with the question posed above: Are consumers seriously disadvantaged by work group suppliers' lack of seamless access to the standard operating-system network? Analysis would start with quite a different question: Why should Microsoft be ordered to share its property with anyone, let alone rivals? US courts generally presume that a duty to deal will seriously impair a monopoly firm's incentives – to the harm of the market and innovation.[13] Microsoft would not have the burden to prove that a duty to deal would impair its incentives. The presumption in favour of Microsoft's freedom of action would be difficult to overcome.[14]

---

10 *Aspen Skiing Co.* v *Aspen Highlands Skiing Corp.*, 472 U.S. 585 (1985).

11 *See* E.M. Fox, 'Is there Life in *Aspen* after *Trinko*? The Silent Revolution of Section 2 of the Sherman Act' (2005) *Antitrust Law Journal* 153.

12 *Trinko*, 540 U.S. at 414.

13 See *Massachusetts* v *Microsoft Corp.*, 373 F.3d 1199, 1215–25 (D.C. Cir. 2004).

14 *See* E.M. Fox, 'The Efficiency Paradox' in Robert Pitofsky (eds), *How the Chicago School Overshot the Mark: The Effect of Conservative Economic Analysis*

This, then, is the great transatlantic divide, even if and when a European court rises above rules to principles and asks the important question: What is the effect of the challenged behaviour on consumers and the market?

---

on US Antitrust (Oxford: Oxford University Press, 2008), arguing that the current US perspective tends to protect dominance at the expense of consumers.

9. *Microsoft* v *Commission*: interoperability, emerging standards and innovation in the software industry

Ann Walsh

1. INTRODUCTION

In September 2007 the Court of First Instance (CFI) delivered its judgment[1] on Microsoft's appeal of the European Commission's 2004 Decision. Following a long investigation, Microsoft was found guilty of infringing Article 82 EC,[2] by abusing its dominant position in two ways 'first by refusing to supply work group server interoperability information to its rivals, and secondly by tying its streamed media player Windows Media Player (WMP) to its Windows PC operating system. The remedy imposed involved a record fine[3] on Microsoft and an order to end the abuses within specified timescales[4] by supplying the required interoperability information[5] and a version of Windows without WMP.[6]

After a controversial Commission Decision, the competition, intellectual property (IP) and software worlds awaited the CFI's Microsoft judgment with great excitement, aware of its potential to reshape the thorny area defined by this intersection. Many factors contributed to this controversy, including the uncertainties surrounding Article 82 EC, the unparal-

1 Case T-201/04 *Microsoft* v *Commission* [2007] ECR II-3601 (hereinafter 'CFI judgment').

2 Commission Decision 2007/53/EC of 24 March 2004 [2007] OJ L32/23 (hereinafter 'the Decision').

3 Decision, para. 1080.

4 Decision, paras 1010, 1017.

5 Decision, para. 999.

6 Decision, para. 1011.

leled power of Microsoft, and the differing US[7] and European perspectives on the abuse of dominance.[8] Since the judgment, controversies have mounted with concerns about the extent of CFI review of such complex technical and economic assessments.[9] Generally attracting lesser attention were the underlying property rights at issue. While the Microsoft case was heard as though IP protection existed, the actual extent of that protection, especially of software standards and interoperability information, was left unresolved.[10] The open source sector is associated with less restrictive IP. The volume and perceived quality of much open source potentially undermines the traditional IP protection of software, by challenging its necessity and helpfulness.

The aim of this chapter is to examine three issues which have previously had relatively little *jurisprudential* attention, namely software interoperability, standardization and innovation. First, at its core, Microsoft's interoperability problem centres on the threshold for indispensability for enforced access in terms of quantity and quality of access to interoperability information. These issues will be explored particularly in relation to the availability of password information for rivals' work group servers.

The second issue concerns the interplay between standards, IP and competition law. The economic and technical benefits of standards will be explored, together with Microsoft's conduct in both preventing the appearance of standard interfaces to its own products, and undermining emerging independent or open standards. Its strategy of adding private unilateral extensions to previously open standards raises the spectre of over-aggressive protection of monopolistic platforms.

A third issue explores innovation, *Magill*'s need for a new product and the specific difficulties of assessing newness in software products, and some concerns surrounding the test for limiting technical development. Additionally Microsoft tried to justify its refusal on the grounds that undermining its IP by enforcing access to its interoperability information undermined its motivation to innovate.[11] This was rejected by the

---

7 Cf US District Court for the District of Columbia, Memorandum Opinion with Findings of Fact and Final Judgment of 1 November 2002 *In re State of New York et al.* v *Microsoft Corporation*, Civil Action No. 98-1233 (CKK) and *In re United States of America* v *Microsoft Corporation*, Civil Action No. 98-1233 (CKK).

8 J. Winterscheid, 'The EC Decision Against Microsoft: Windows on the World, Glass Houses, or Through the Looking Glass?', available at www.abanet.org/antitrust/source/09-04/Sep04MSBB.pdf.

9 CFI judgment, paras 86–7.

10 CFI judgment, para. 288.

11 CFI judgment, paras 659, 670.

Commission, and ultimately the CFI, convinced that Microsoft would continue to innovate regardless. While the judgment may indeed lead to a *general* overall increase in innovation, and Microsoft may indeed continue to innovate despite the judgment, the potential for the judgment to diminish incentives to innovate in particular areas like infrastructure and interoperability should also be considered.

This chapter will look at the extent to which interoperability can be controlled, either by dominant undertakings or competition regulation. It will examine the dependence of both innovation and competition on accessible standards, and question whether some types of conduct relating to standards should become new tests for abuse. It will explore the Microsoft case's focus on limiting technical development, and some difficulties inherent in this test.

2. BACKGROUND: COMPETITION LAW

Article 82 EC condemns 'Any abuse by . . . undertakings of a dominant position . . . in so far as it may affect trade between Member States'. Following this strikingly general statement is a non-exhaustive list of examples, including that most relevant for our discussion, Article 82 (b) EC 'limiting production, markets or technical development to the prejudice of consumers'.

Despite a significant volume of case law expanding, refining, clarifying and apparently applying the law, there is still considerable uncertainty about the exact conditions amounting to abuse.[12] Distinguishing between 'normal competition' and 'abuse'[13] can be almost impossible, with each having elements of the other. Importantly the non-dominant cannot offend Article 82 EC, and conduct acceptable in an undertaking's earlier growth stages can become unacceptable on attaining dominance.[14] Super-dominance, as acquired by Microsoft, may further deepen[15] the

---

[12] See e.g. E. Derclaye, 'Abuse of a Dominant Position and Intellectual Property Rights: A Suggestion to Reconcile the Community Courts' Case Law' (2003) *World Competition* 685.

[13] See e.g. R. Whish, *Competition Law* (5th edn, London: Butterworths, 2003), p. 197. (6th edn, Oxford: Oxford University Press, 2009), pp. 188–206.

[14] K. Krechmer and E. Baskin, *Microsoft Anti-Trust Litigation-The Case for Standards* (Boulder: University of Colorado, 2000), p. 3, available at www.csrstds.com/WSD2000.html.

[15] Case C-395/96 P, *Compagnie Maritime Belge* [2000] ECR I-1365, Advocate General Opinion, paras 132, 137.

special responsibility not to further weaken competition. One common route to abuse is the refusal to deal in a desired raw material.

Refusal to Deal

Despite the significant volume of cases, including *Commercial Solvents*,[16] *Volvo*,[17] *Magill*,[18] *Ladbroke*,[19] *Bronner*[20] and *IMS Health*,[21] the necessary triggering conditions for abuse are still unclear, as evidenced by the considerable academic discussion available.[22]

As the CFI confirmed in the Microsoft Case,[23] two competing sets of conditions seem to arise depending on the involvement of IP.[24] *Magill* concerned access to copyrighted television listings, and found refusal to license abusive if (i) the refusal blocked the emergence of a new product,[25] (ii) the raw material requested was indispensable,[26] (iii) the refusal was likely to exclude competition in the downstream market,[27] and (iv) the refusal was unjustified.[28] In contrast, *Bronner* concerned access to a home-delivery facility rather than IP. Excluding the new product criterion, its abuse requirements were similar to *Magill.*

Despite *IMS Health's* clarification that the *Magill* conditions were cumulative, considerable uncertainties remain. The exact threshold for indispensability is uncertain, particularly after the shadowy arrival of an essential facilities doctrine.[29] Both *Bronner* and *IMS Health* suggested

---

16 Cases C-6 and 7/73 *Commercial Solvents* v *Commission* [1974] ECR 223.

17 Case C-238/87 *Volvo* v *Veng (UK) Ltd* [1988] ECR 6211.

18 Cases C-241 and 242/91 P *Radio Telefis Eireann and Independent Television Publications Ltd (ITP)* v *Commission* [1995] ECR I-743 ('*Magill*').

19 Case T-504/93 *Tiercé Ladbroke SA* v *Commission* [1997] ECR II-923 ('*Ladbroke*').

20 Case C-7/97 *Oscar Bronner GmbH & Co. KG* v *Mediaprint* [1998] ECR I-7791.

21 Case C-418/01 *IMS Health Gmbh & Co KG* v *NDC Health* [2004] ECR-I-5039.

22 See e.g. Derclaye, n. 12 above.

23 CFI judgment para. 334.

24 See e.g. F. Lévêque, 'Innovation, Leveraging and Essential Facilities: Interoperability Licensing in the EU Microsoft Case' (2005) *World Competition* 71.

25 Joined Cases C-241 and 242/91 P *Magill*, para. 54.

26 *Magill*, para. 53.

27 *Magill*, para. 56.

28 *Magill* para. 55.

29 See e.g. C. Reimann, 'Essential Function vs Essential Facility: Defining the Amount of R&D Protection in High-tech Industries after *IMS* and *Microsoft*' (2004) *Competition Law Review* 49.

a high threshold, but the CFI in the Microsoft case accepted a test of remaining 'viably on the market'.[30] The extent of the elimination of competition is also unclear as shown by the debate on how strong or likely the risk had to be.[31] This uncertainty is especially apparent in situations where competition is marginal but durable. There is also very little guidance on what could amount to objective justification,[32] highlighting real concerns about legal certainty and predictability for the undertakings concerned.[33] Unfortunately the CFI appears to have provided little clarification here. Another issue is the quality of the IP. Both *Magill* and *IMS Health* involved material with dubious copyright status, and some question whether their rules are appropriate for more 'worthy' copyright[34] like *Microsoft*'s.[35] Yet it is said some of Microsoft's IP may have originated in the public domain, raising interesting issues about the ownership of derived works. The new product requirement invokes considerable debate,[36] especially for software products which are regularly revised or enhanced, and arguably requires a different understanding of 'new'.

It is also worth considering why Article 82 EC was drafted in the way it was. What exactly was meant by 'limiting technical development', and how was it meant to differ from limiting production or markets? The 'classic' Article 82 EC cases like *Magill*, *Bronner* and *IMS Health* do not really explore limiting technical development, and it is interesting to speculate why this element has had so little jurisprudential attention. How should the courts' criteria for abuse be expanded to accommodate this element appropriately?

In summary, the Microsoft case involves uncertain requirements for finding abuse in the context of unparalleled dominance and very little guidance on assessing the limiting of technical development in the high-tech software sector.

---

30 CFI judgment, para. 229.

31 See e.g. CFI judgment, paras 456, 560.

32 For example bad debts in *BBI/Boosey & Hawkes* [1987] OJ L286/36.

33 Lévêque, n. 24 above, 80.

34 Alternatively one could suggest that interoperability specifications were non-creative derivatives from Microsoft's creative work in Windows, much as the TV listings in *Magill* were non-creative derivatives of RTE's creative programming work.

35 Reimann, n. 29 above, 61.

36 S.D. Anderman, 'Does the Microsoft Case Offer a New Paradigm for the "Exceptional Circumstances" Test and Compulsory Licenses under EC Competition Law' (2004) *Competition Law Review* 7, 13, and Lévêque, n. 24 above, 73 and 75.

Background: the Software Sector

The software sector brings its own peculiarities relevant to our discussion, and can be significantly distinguished from capacity-bound resources like ports, chemicals or home-delivery systems. It is non-exhaustive, infinitely reproducible and easily distributed. Software is protected by intellectual property rights as a literary work under the EC Software Directive.[37] Patent protection is also available, albeit more contentiously.

Usually, purchasing software involves the supply of non-human readable executables, libraries and object code. The source code, that all-important core dictating the software's behaviour, is largely hidden because it is usually not provided to users. The user buys the means to access a type of behaviour or functional performance, rather than access to the human-readable elements (source code) *causing* that behaviour. Ironically, software is protected mainly by copyright as a literary work, but in this respect it is unlike many other literary copyright works like novels.

Software also brings an overwhelming need for interoperability, complicated by the tradition for continually improving, repairing and releasing software. Version dependence brings an inherent fragility to interoperability.[38] What worked for Windows NT did not with Windows 2000.

Network effects are deeply significant in the software sector. The unparalleled dominance of Windows makes porting to other platforms uneconomic for many software vendors, resulting in many applications programs being made available only for Windows.[39] Known as the applications barrier to entry,[40] a positive feedback loop effectively increases the dominance of Windows and induces de facto standard status for it. This tendency towards tipping makes challenge difficult, even by those with *superior technology*, and highlights the Commission's desire for anticipatory action.[41]

---

37 Council Directive 91/250/EC on the legal protection of computer programs [1991] OJ L122/42 ('Software Directive').

38 Decision, para. 282.

39 Decision, para. 452; CFI judgment, para. 31.

40 B. Rotenberg, *The Legal Regulation of Software Interoperability in the EU*, Jean Monnet Working Paper No. 7 (New York: NYU School of Law, 2005), pp. 10–12, available at www.jeanmonnetprogram.org/papers/05/050701.rtf.

41 V. Korah, *An Introduction to EC Competition Law and Practice* (Oxford: Hart Publishing, 2004), p. 175.

Background: Microsoft

Two Microsoft products are relevant to the interoperability discussion, the Windows PC operating system, and the Windows work group server operating system. With market shares of 93 per cent and 60 per cent respectively, Microsoft were considered super-dominant in the first,[42] and dominant in the second.[43] Server operating systems were also developed by companies like Sun, increasingly concerned by the reduction in the interoperability information available for communication between their servers and Windows PCs.

While the existence of some interoperability was acknowledged by both sides, there was disagreement on the exact threshold required.[44] The Commission argued that Microsoft refused to supply the interface information which was indispensable for external severs to interoperate with Windows.[45] This limited innovation[46] and risked the elimination of competition[47] to the detriment of consumers.[48]

Microsoft's various arguments – that the presence of alternative routes for interoperability defeated indispensability,[49] that competing servers in the market proved competition was not being eliminated,[50] that refusal was justified on the grounds of protecting valuable IP[51] and that forced disclosure would encourage copying and reduce incentives to innovate,[52] both at Microsoft and indirectly across the industry – were each in turn rejected by the CFI.

Outline

Interoperability in the Microsoft case encompassed a variety of interesting elements such as distinguishing between indispensable and desirable

---

42 Decision, para. 843; CFI judgment, para. 31.
43 Decision, paras 514, 541; CFI judgment, para. 33.
44 Decision, para. 589 and n. 712; CFI judgment, paras 109, 110, 139 and 211.
45 Case T-201/04 R *Microsoft* v *Commission* [2004] ECR II-4463, Report for the Hearing, paras 28–9.
46 Decision, paras 693–701.
47 CFI judgment, para. 219.
48 Decision, paras 702–8.
49 Report for the Hearing, n. 45 above, para. 75.
50 Decision, para. 508 *et seq*. and para. 598 discussing Linux growth, disputed by Commission at para. 603.
51 Decision, paras 709–12.
52 Decision, para. 709.

information; the role of the Software Directive[53] and in particular its reverse-engineering exception,[54] the relevance of the value of the requested information compared with previous cases,[55] the use of other forms of IP like patents and trade secrets,[56] and the importance of earlier conduct in both previous supply and encouraging dependency by offering source code.[57] While the Microsoft case also addresses the important and interesting issue of tying,[58] space considerations take it beyond the scope of this discussion. The focus of this chapter is interoperability, its special relevance within the software industry, the role and consequences of standards, the interaction with IP and the impact and relevance of innovation. These issues are selected because of the unusual and interesting tensions arising with these particular facts.

As a result of alleged technical innovation by a super-dominant producer, further innovation by others in the industry could allegedly be restricted.[59] A party, itself a de facto standard owner and acknowledged user of various open industrial standards, appears to undermine emerging industrial standards, possibly with the aim of protecting its own monopolistic platform. Finally, the expansion of *Magill*'s new product test is both an interesting and arguably necessary development, and provides an exciting opportunity for the courts to address Article 82(b) EC's limiting 'technical development'. The scope for an IP 'justification' is interesting, with its role and scope still contentious in the world of software and interoperability standards.[60]

The rest of this chapter is structured as follows. The next section looks at interoperability, in an attempt to investigate the nature and extent of its requirements and implications. The following section on standardization looks at Microsoft's conduct with emerging standards, and the competition consequences resulting from de facto standardization of Windows. This is followed by an examination of the interaction between innovation

---

53 Decision, paras 32–3.

54 Decision, paras 292 and 687.

55 Case T-201/04 R *Microsoft* v *Commission* [2004] ECR II-4463, Interim Relief Order, paras 207–2.

56 Report for the Hearing, n. 45 above, paras 104–8, 148–50; P. Samuelson and S. Scotchmer, 'The Law and Economics of Reverse Engineering' (2002) *Yale Law Journal* 1575, 1619–20.

57 Decision, para. 211.

58 Microsoft had refused to sell a version of its PC operating system without WMP, its own media player.

59 Decision, paras 693–708.

60 T. Schoechle, 'Digital Enclosure: The Privatisation of Standards and Standardisation' (2003) *IEEE SIIT Conference Proceedings* 229, 231.

and IP. The chapter concludes by highlighting some of the critical issues presented by the Microsoft case.

3. INTEROPERABILITY

Introduction

Interoperability plays a considerable role in the market success and utility of software. Like a gatehouse controlling access to a program, it can bring serious antitrust concerns from its capability for leveraging, manipulating the homogeneity of software solutions[61] or offensively protecting monopolies.[62] The interoperability obligations of dominant software suppliers are riddled with considerable uncertainties, arising in part from legislative ambiguities and further exaggerated by the relative rarity of jurisprudence to assist in interpretation,[63] and the specific characteristics of the software sector. Given an ever-increasing reliance on software, arguably coupled with an increasing need for functioning multi-vendor componentized systems, it is likely that the interoperability issues posed by the Microsoft case will resonate into the future.

Like communication itself, the interoperability concept spans a vast range of meanings and terms,[64] all sharing a sense of connection and information-sharing between two or more entities. Like a series of bridges connecting separate islands, all interoperability mechanisms involve a number of interface connections at clearly defined places, where clearly defined material can be sent, received and handled. Computer systems are layered structured systems,[65] with the operating system at the bottom

---

[61] Decision, para. 613.

[62] CFI judgment, para. 1349 mentions interoperability's leveraging potential, quoting Bill Gates 'What we are trying to do is use our server control to do new protocols and lock out Sun and Oracle specifically . . . Now, I don't know if we'll get to that or not, but that's what we are trying to do'.

[63] The main EC case was *IBM Undertaking*, discussed in the Decision, para. 737. US cases include *Dell* and *EDI* mentioned in E. Derclaye, 'Software Copyright Protection: Can Europe Learn from American Case Law? Part 2' (2000) *European Intellectual Property Review* 56, 65.

[64] Including interface, communication, compatibility, applications programming interface (API), communication protocol, standardized access, see Decision, para. 32.

[65] M O'Rourke, 'Striking a Delicate Balance: Intellectual Property, Antitrust, Contract and Standardisation in the Computer Industry' (1998) *Harvard Journal of Law & Technology* 1, 5–6.

dealing directly with the hardware electronics, and one or more layers of applications programs built upon that.[66] Normally, software providers encourage interoperability,[67] with interfaces providing an important route into the program, bringing additional users, network benefits and often separate licensing revenue from the interface itself. At a basic level, the interoperability at issue in the Microsoft case concerns communication between external work group servers and the Windows PC operating system; though this has been contentiously extended to involve access to the Window's domain architecture at large and Window's server-server communication.[68] The initial reference point on interoperability, accepted by both parties, was the Software Directive which defines it in the Preamble and used it to circumscribe the Article 6 decompilation exception.[69]

Interoperability, the Software Directive and Article 82 EC

The Preamble to the Software Directive states that 'the function of a computer program is to communicate and work together with other components of a computer system and with users and, for this purpose, a logical and, where appropriate, physical interconnection and interaction is required to permit all elements of software and hardware to work with other software and hardware and with users in all the ways in which they are intended to function'.[70] This 'functional interconnection and interaction is generally known as 'interoperability', and can be defined as 'the ability to exchange information and mutually to use the information which has been exchanged'.[71] This simple view of being able to exchange and use information can mask a sometimes difficult delineation between access to data and access to functionality.

An important issue to be resolved was whether interoperability is one-way or two-way, notably whether one or both programs needs to work 'as intended', hinging on the precise meaning of 'they' above;[72] and whether it meant 'hardware and software elements of the program seeking interoperability', or 'both programs', argued respectively by Microsoft and the

---

66 Decision, para. 37.
67 Rotenberg, n. 40 above, 10–11.
68 CFI judgment, para. 374.
69 Decision, paras 755, 763.
70 Software Directive, Preamble, recital 10.
71 Software Directive, Preamble, recital 12.
72 R. Hart, 'Interoperability Information and the Microsoft Decision' (2006) *European Intellectual Property Review* 361, 362.

Commission. While Microsoft's arguments were rejected,[73] there are still uncertainties. What can be said about situations where it is not practical for all elements of both programs to work fully?[74] Could the word 'intended' also be ambiguous, potentially referring to either the interoperability seeker or both sets of developers? Could Microsoft argue that they actually 'intend' their products to work at best clumsily with external products, or even intend that they do not work at all with, for example, inferior external products potentially capable of tarnishing their image? Against this it could be argued that the relevant users have already licensed the Windows PC operating system, and should have a right to use it, functioning correctly, even potentially from within the wrapper of another program? Does the right to use a system imply a right to use its components?

Secondly, the primary purpose of defining interoperability in the Software Directive was arguably not to construct a detailed interoperability obligation on the program with which interoperability is sought, but rather to circumscribe the extent of the decompilation exception to copyright infringement in Article 6.[75] It merely makes explicit the extent of decompilation allowed for a programmer to achieve interoperability with another's program without having to seek permission or infringe copyright. It is essentially saying that the developer seeking interoperability is allowed to work as hard as he likes at decompiling interoperability information, so as to achieve as good a connection as he can. Arguably it amounts to permission for the seeker to extract rather than an obligation on the owner to provide.

However, as interoperability in the Software Directive applies to *every* program even the most minor or obscure, the Commission is keen to highlight[76] the Directive's clarification of the continuing application of Article 82 EC competition rules, when a 'dominant supplier refuses to make information available which is necessary for interoperability'.[77] This phrase 'to make information available' suggests an active rather than passive duty for the dominant.[78] As the CFI is also keen to highlight,[79] Article 82 EC is a provision of higher rank than the Software Directive.

---

73 CFI judgment, para. 226.
74 Decision, para. 757.
75 Decision, para. 747.
76 Decision, para. 748.
77 Software Directive, Preamble, recital 27.
78 Where supporting open industry standards or publishing APIs is active, and leaving external programmers to extract information by reverse-engineering is passive.
79 CFI judgment, para. 227.

The next issue concerned the degree of interoperability necessary to satisfy Article 82 EC. The threshold set by the Commission, and accepted by the CFI, was that of being necessary to allow rivals to remain viably in the market.[80] Before looking at this further, we will look in more detail at one of the specific problem areas, notably access to password information.

Passwords, Work Group Servers and Access

A primary task of work group server operating systems is to perform general office tasks like file, print and user/group administration services for small/medium PC networks.[81] Security is fundamental to this administration, both in authenticating or checking an entity is what it claims to be, by checking passwords, and in authorizing or checking the entity has the right to perform what it is trying to do.[82] Administration is fundamental to servers, and password data is essential for administration; this suggests that password data is essential for servers.

Prior to the transition from Windows NT to Windows 2000, server interoperability information like passwords had been actively available directly using standard techniques, protocols and even source code.[83] The Windows NT to 2000 transformation, partly in response to inadequacies of its own technologies in comparison with rivals, involved many radical changes. Along with infrastructure changes affecting how network data is managed and updated, there were changes in some basic protocols like LDAP and Kerberos.[84]

Among the consequence for users were enhanced flexibility and transparent access to Windows work group server services.[85] Having a server operate as domain controller (or 'switchboard operator') in a Windows domain, using two tools – Active Directory and multi-master replication mechanism, generally facilitated a single log-in system for users.[86] However, one consequence for rival server providers was that information previously available was now hidden and inaccessible. Microsoft argued that 'their system for replicating Active Directory is proprietary, and non-Microsoft servers cannot participate'.[87] The proprietary changes to

---

80 CFI judgment, para. 229.
81 Decision, para. 53; CFI judgment, para. 160.
82 Decision, para. 54.
83 Decision, paras 211, 578–84.
84 Decision, paras 244, 254.
85 CFI judgment, para. 186.
86 CFI judgment, paras 165–6.
87 Decision, para. 195.

otherwise open standards like LDAP and Kerberos[88] were also kept private to Microsoft.[89] In basic terms, these led to some information including password data being transferred only in these 'private' Microsoft-only channels. Unavailable to external servers directly, the passwords could not be checked, implying the authentication function could not be performed without looking to either indirect/unstable techniques like decompilation, or forcing users to log in twice.[90]

Ultimately this left users with a 'choice' between 'putting up with interoperability problems that render their business processes cumbersome, inefficient and costly, or embracing a homogeneous Windows solution'.[91] While Microsoft argued that external servers were still usable,[92] for many, particularly the less technically aware, such servers appear inadequate, and will not inspire confidence in users (or buyers), with neither program arguably working as 'intended', by users at least. Evidence was supplied indicating interoperability was the second most important factor (second to system reliability) when selecting servers.[93] This was supported by Microsoft's own use of interoperability as a key marketing argument for its Windows work group servers.[94] The two critical issues were first, identification of interoperability information, and secondly, the quality of access required to it.

What Information?

First, while interoperability information is usually restricted to documented specifications rather than source code or internal algorithms,[95] this case highlights how difficult it can be to distinguish between public interoperability information and private internals, especially in products like operating systems. Active Directory and Global Catalog replication, for example, are tools regularly used internally throughout Microsoft's

---

88 Decision, paras 244 and 254.

89 Report for the Hearing, n. 45 above, para. 113.

90 'For instance, if the work group server does not sufficiently interoperate with the security architecture of the Windows work group network, the user may have to log on twice if he wants to access both Windows-based resources and resources offered by the non-Microsoft work group servers': Decision, para. 183.

91 CFI judgment, para. 662.

92 CFI judgment, para. 340.

93 CFI judgment, para. 403.

94 CFI judgment, para. 394.

95 A specification is a description of what the software product must achieve, whereas the implementation relates to the actual code that will run on the computer. See CFI judgment, para. 199.

systems for propagating information, as part of its internal architecture or infrastructure.[96] Microsoft argues information on these goes beyond interoperability[97] into 'internal make-up of Windows server operating systems',[98] and has genuine fears that its systems' internal integrity could be compromised by allowing open access to this infrastructure.[99] A useful metaphor for interoperability information could be the implied right of access to the front entrance and door of a house, but beyond which amounts to trespass. Microsoft may fear that they are being ordered to open up a major interior staircase, risking untold damage to privacy and security. What protection does a dominant undertaking have against another firm using its internal and probably prized assets? Is there a limit on the information which can be demanded?[100] More contentiously, should a dominant undertaking *ever* be allowed to cite security risks as a justification for non-supply, when those risks may result from its *own* architectural design decisions?

This case also highlights one of the critical tensions in the underlying IP protection of software. Microsoft's fears of revealing internal information about its Blue Bubble or multi-master replication mechanism algorithms were dismissed by the Commission.[101] Emphasizing that source code and implementation details were not to be revealed, it was argued that rivals need only develop an algorithm achieving the same results as the Microsoft algorithm. Microsoft would not have to supply implementation details, merely a 'general description of that algorithm'.[102] Many in the software world may shiver at this, for it highlights one of the essential ironies of current software protection – very often it can be that 'general description' of an algorithm that is most valuable, yet ironically unprotected. Actually generating the implementation details, which are copyright protected, can often be a mere mechanical process, once the difficult work of designing the algorithm, or at least knowing what it must achieve, have been solved.

What Standard of Access?

Microsoft asserted the adequacy of its 'existing' interoperability methods including 'the use of open industry standards supported in Windows;

---

96 See e.g. CFI judgment, para. 181.
97 Judgment, para. 253.
98 Decision, para. 201.
99 Interim Relief Order, n. 55 above, para. 141.
100 Hart, n. 72 above, 365.
101 CFI judgment, para. 261.
102 CFI judgment, para. 265.

the distribution of client-side software on the client PC; and the reverse-engineering of Microsoft's products in order to gain access to the necessary interoperability information'.[103] An important distinction between these routes is that some allow direct access to information presented in a highly usable state, while the last method of reverse-engineering amounts to an indirect and painstaking extraction of low-level, hard-to-use information by decoding the executable/object code.[104] A prime example of this concerns the use of decompilation to extract the password data mentioned earlier which could not be accessed directly.

Microsoft disputed indispensability of direct access to password information by claiming that logging on twice was avoidable, as shown by the rival Samba server, which indirectly extracts some password information via painstaking decompilation of the object/executable code. Microsoft argued the presence of this potential (possibly precarious) route of reverse-engineering provides the less advantageous yet 'actual and potential alternative' described in *Bronner*[105] as adequate to effectively insulate them from the findings of indispensability necessary for finding the refusal to supply abusive. Fundamentally fragile, decompilation is slow, labour-intensive, sensitive to changes in code,[106] and largely unfeasible for large or complex programs[107] which change rapidly.[108] While Samba seems to avoid the ordeal of asking the user log in twice, its own documentation suggests they see their solution as partial and experimental, and its interoperability is said to be always at least one generation out of date.[109] The CFI estimated development time post-information acquisition at between three months and two years.[110] For many, software's short shelf-life effectively makes this route a non-starter. [111]

It is worth mentioning that the potential benefits of decompilation are further, and arguably unnecessarily, limited by the non-disclosure

[103] Decision, paras 666–7; Report for the Hearing, n. 45 above, paras 76–80.

[104] Decision, para. 685; Interim Relief Order, n. 55 above, para. 101.

[105] Case C-7/97 *Oscar Bronner*, para. 43; Case C-418/01 *IMS Health*, para. 28.

[106] Decision, paras 685–6.

[107] Samuelson and Scotchmer, n. 56 above, 1619–20.

[108] There is evidence that between 2000 and 2005, Windows has involved five versions, become increasingly complex and more than doubled in size from 15 to 35 million lines of code. M. Cusumano, 'What Road Ahead for Microsoft and Windows?' (2006) *Communications of the ACM* 21, 21–2.

[109] Decision, para. 685.

[110] Interim Relief Order, n. 55 above, para. 279.

[111] D. Flint, 'IP Rights and Wrongs' (2004) *Business Law Review* 142, 147.

requirement on any interoperability information obtained,[112] which effectively forces each vendor to repeat this painstaking decompilation for itself. Lifting the restriction requiring each company to reverse-engineer an executable for itself, at least for dominant products, could allow a market to develop for firms to specialize in providing interoperability information, freeing other vendors to focus on developing advanced features within their own specialist areas. Could this have provided an option enabling the dominant firm to preserve potential for some comparative advantage yet providing improved access for rivals? The Commission's remedy demanding interoperability protocols in a timely manner,[113] implies rival access well before new versions are shipped to customers, and probably prevents any significant comparative advantage.

As has been argued, while Microsoft's arguments about the adequacy of alternative interoperability approaches do not hold, it can also be argued that the Commission's decision that identical access is essential is itself disproportionate,[114] and may amount to the inappropriate intervention competition authorities are so keen to avoid.[115] It has been suggested that experts from standardization bodies could be used to help identify which interfaces need standardization,[116] and also to define the minimal core of information necessary to satisfy interoperability.[117] Arguably, such minimal interoperability information should be readily available for all de facto standards.

For a work group server this minimal core of information should include password data access, regardless of any difficulties resulting from Microsoft's chosen architecture. Importantly, is a debate needed on whether Microsoft should be free to make any information *beyond* this minimal core *temporarily* private for its own benefit, on the understanding that the information amounting to that competitive advantage should migrate back to the minimal core if it too becomes standard? The next section looks at the role of standards in more detail, and argues for them to play a more prominent role in the Commission's thinking.

---

112 Software Directive, Article 6(2)(b).

113 Decision, article 1(3).

114 Rejected by the CFI. See CFI judgment, para. 812.

115 Krechmer and Baskin, n. 14 above, 6.

116 Krechmer and Baskin, n. 14 above, 5–6, suggested ANSI involvement to declare what interfaces need standardization in Microsoft.

117 A. Chin, 'Decoding Microsoft: A First Principles Approach' (2005) *Wake Forest Law Review* 1, 14–15.

4. STANDARDS

Standards: An Introduction

Standards play a powerful role in shaping technologies and their use in society, by establishing an array of practices, procedures and processes addressing a range of diverse areas from communication protocols to manufacturing processes and quality assessment.[118] Standards have an interesting, even ironic relationship with competition. They arise at those junctions where one winner is better than a number of competitors, and subsequently create platforms from which further competition can develop within the precise parameters and constraints defined. Much like the significant chaos prevented by having a single nationwide dominant electrical domestic plug format,[119] many multi-vendor software systems function only because of well defined declared rules, templates or interfaces for compatibility or interoperability, usually relating to how information and instructions are passed between programs.[120] Examples include the http protocol which allows webpages to be accessed or displayed on almost any operating system platform regardless of how they were created.

Standards can be open or closed, public or proprietary, formal or informal. In contrast to formal committee standards, developed by agreement, de facto standards rely on the market for acceptance, by voluntary usage from customers and other producers. It is generally accepted that standards developed by formal standardization bodies benefit from consensus and being publicly accessible, but have their own disadvantages. These include being notoriously slow to develop,[121] due to the voting process; and more importantly, slow to change or improve in response to new advances; and may not always be as clear, focused[122] or useful as a standard which developed out of actual use. In contrast, proprietary standards, usually more unilateral, can respond to advances in technology at will, and may often be technically optimized for a very specific situation. The danger, however, is that accessibility can be controlled, as occurred in the Microsoft case.

Standards are particularly important in the Microsoft case for at least

---

118 T. Schoechle, n. 60 above, 230.

119 Lévéque, n. 24 above, 80; Krechmer and Baskin, n. 14 above, 3.

120 Krechmer and Baskin, n. 14 above, 5–6.

121 J. Farrell, 'Standardization and Intellectual Property' (1989) *Jurimetrics Journal* 35, 40–1.

122 Some standards can be too general in an attempt to be all things to all men.

two reasons. First, Windows 'is not only a dominant product . . . it is the de facto standard'.[123] There were fears Microsoft may have been trying to gain de facto standard status for its WMP by tying it to its PC operating system. Possibly Microsoft was similarly trying to augment its work group server into the role of de facto standard by limiting its rivals' interoperability access. The important role played by standards in opening up competition, and the increasing role of private power in significant parts of the standards arena, should raise some serious antitrust concerns about whether public interests are adequately represented and protected.[124] Secondly, standards' importances within computing are clear from the public and private efforts to develop standards for the benefit of all (for example Java).[125]

There is a fear that Microsoft's general conduct demonstrates a pattern of undermining emerging open standards.[126] This is worrying because it may hinder technical development, and mask the predatory conduct of a monopolist over-aggressively protecting its platform by what might be termed technical sabotage. The European Union is said to be committed to standardization,[127] but the extent of that commitment needs to be clarified

One really interesting issue highlighted by the Commission is that Microsoft originally encouraged interoperability; it even published some source code.[128] As a late entrant to the server market, this was arguably necessary to gain market access, where 'pledging support for already established technologies was important in gaining a foothold and the confidence of the customers'.[129] Then, after attaining a certain level of strength (30 per cent),[130] Microsoft restricted its interoperability information. Previous supply appeared less important in *Magill* and *Bronner*, than in the earlier *Commercial Solvents* and *Télémarketing*[131] cases.

It is interesting to ponder the true significance of this disruption of previous supply. Some have asked if similar demands could have been made

---

123 Decision, para. 472.
124 Schoechle, n. 60 above, 230.
125 See Decision, para. 43 for overview; para. 14 for details of the US Microsoft case concerning Sherman Act, s. 2 (unlawful maintenance of monopoly) in relation to Netscape and Java.
126 Decision, paras 243–72.
127 Software Directive, Preamble, recital 9.
128 Decision, para. 734.
129 Decision, para. 587.
130 Lévéque, n. 24 above, 83.
131 Decision, para. 556.

on an undertaking which always kept its interfaces closed, like Apple.[132] In reply it has been argued that it is unlikely that such dominance could have arisen with permanently closed interfaces, because the acquisition of dominance in software requires the realization of full network effects[133] and sufficient (compatible) applications to build an applications barrier to entry against rival platforms. It is unlikely that a sufficiently wide range of applications could be written without making interoperability information freely available. Closed interfaces offer a poor strategy for acquiring dominance but a good strategy for maintaining it post-acquisition.

Competition Consequences of Standards

The presence of standards, especially open standards, can bring many benefits to the market, consumers and producers. These result largely from the standard/interface effectively creating independent processes either side,[134] and providing the information necessary for componentization, specialization and differentiation.[135] This is especially beneficial for smaller undertakings unable to produce a complete system alone.[136] Accessible interfaces allow vendors to specialize on one particular component of the system, differentiate their product, add value to it, and sell it as an interchangeable part of a multi-supplier system, developing the market for everyone.[137] Benefits for consumers include additional choice, avoiding being locked-in to a single specific supplier,[138] and the confidence that their *system* could endure some suppliers leaving the market. Increased competition also brings potential for improved products. Essentially, standards, particularly open standards, create platforms upon which other producers have the confidence to innovate and interoperate, and consumers may have increased confidence to invest in.[139]

As suggested earlier, a product with closed interfaces is probably unlikely to achieve dominance, so most products which are dominant will probably have had open interfaces during their initial growth or

---

[132] Anderman, n. 36 above, 16.

[133] Farrell, n. 121 above, 47.

[134] Krechmer and Baskin, n. 14 above, 7.

[135] Schoechle, n. 60 above, 236.

[136] Farrell, n. 121 above, 36 and 38.

[137] Farrell, n. 121 above, 36.

[138] Decision, para. 613 highlights a Commission fear that uptake of new Windows 2000 features, particularly Active Directory, and decreased interoperability will contribute to further lock customers into Windows.

[139] M. Dolmans, 'Standards for Standards' (2002–2003) 26 *Fordham International Law and Journal*,163, 166.

market-acceptance stage. Farrell argues this is best achieved by accepting that areas like data-transmission, storage formats and user-interfaces are relatively arbitrary, but necessary for compatibility benefits. To satisfy the strong social need for standards usage and acceptance, some argue they should be devoid of IP protection.[140]

Once dominance is achieved, however, especially with something as hidden as software, new versions allow the possibility of changing the interface information,[141] leading to the situation where a standard has been born accessible to the public, nurtured to a level of maturity while inducing dependency by the market, and then modified and kept partially secret. Proprietary ownership of standards in general use can cause problems if access is restricted or insufficiently stable. Publishing less than adequate information, or modifying the interfaces frequently, especially with little notice, can also neutralize the benefits of standards, and consequently market development.[142]

Standards are usually good news for proprietary owners because of the licensing opportunities they bring.[143] In fact, one of the problems associated with public standards is hijacking or vested interests in the membership of standards bodies secretly influencing the standardization process a particular way, so that users of the standard are forced to license particular IP.[144] Of particular interest to our discussion is the opposite problem, however, namely where a firm with a proprietary standard which others actively want to license, refuses to deal. One possible explanation is a desire to protect the platform.[145]

Protecting the Platform

Microsoft was found to have refused to supply interoperability information, and the revenue that might have brought, with the effect of risking the elimination of competition in the server market. They were also found to have tied their streamed media player to the Windows PC operating system, with the effect of undermining competing players. It is interesting to speculate whether Microsoft's conduct and motivations can be

---

140 Farrell, n. 121 above, 47.
141 Farrell, n. 121 above, 47.
142 Farrell, n. 121 above, 39–40.
143 Farrell, n. 121 above, 47.
144 J. Killick, '*IMS* and *Microsoft* Judged in the Cold Light of *IMS*', (2004) 1(2) *Competition Law Review* 23, 32, describing ETSI in the EU and Dell in the United States.
145 See e.g. Rotenberg, n. 40 above, 10–11.

understood with help from the patterns predicted by Krechmer using Schumpeter's theories on monopolies.[146]

The advent of a monopoly is said often to involve the introduction of a paradigm shift in technology. The 'wave of creative destruction' sees the marginalization of existing technology, followed by market growth as the market accepts the new technology[147] and new consumers are brought in. What follows is a period of stability and possibly 'destructive creation' while the market awaits the next great paradigm shift (another wave of creative destruction) to render the current dominant technology itself marginalized.[148] During this stage, the monopolist may engage in market abuse and even sabotage to thwart any advancing paradigm shift in an attempt to protect its monopoly platform.[149] The swiftness with which rapid technological advances may render incumbent software products obsolete[150] and effectively valueless may help to explain this desire to control the arrival of any significant advances.

This may be easier in information-based network-effect industries like computing and open standards are one way to negate these effects.[151] It has been suggested that understanding Microsoft's rejection of the licensing income from its interoperability information requires a dynamic model where short-term profits are sacrificed for the long-term gain of protecting its platform.[152] Given the speed of technological progress in hi-tech computing, rendering products obsolete (and valueless) rapidly,[153] this approach is arguably quite rational.

A firm with a super-dominant position like Microsoft may want to continue encouraging the use of Windows by generally encouraging the development of compatible complementary applications (vertical interoperability), but they may wish to hinder the development of any competing platforms (horizontal compatibility).[154] It is interesting to consider how much of the conduct Microsoft has been recently criticized for involves programs which are potential platform rivals, including its dealings with

---

146 Krechmer and Baskin, n. 14 above, 3–4.

147 For example, canals took over from rivers, and were subsequently taken over by roads, Krechmer and Baskin, n. 141 above, 3–4.

148 Krechmer and Baskin, n. 14 above, 3–4.

149 Krechmer and Baskin, n. 14 above, 3–4.; S. Vezzoso, 'The Incentive Balance Test in the EU Microsoft Case: A Pro-innovation 'Economics-Based' Approach' (2006) *European Competition Law Review* 382, 388–9.

150 Lévéque,n. 24 above, 84.

151 Krechmer and Baskin, n. 14 above, 3–4.

152 Lévéque, n. 24 above, 84.

153 Lévéque, n. 24 above, 84.

154 Rotenberg, n. 40 above, 10–11.

Netscape,[155] the work group server and the Java Virtual Machine.[156] While some of these accusations focus on leveraging into adjacent markets, a common underlying aim may be an aggressive attempt to defend the Windows PC operating system platform itself from even potential rivals at all costs.

A work group server operating system, for example, while specifically in place to perform user and group administration, and facilitate the sharing of resources,[157] is also capable of running applications, and therefore in theory at least a potential platform, and importantly a threat to Windows PC operating system.[158] Limiting access to certain critical information, for example on authentication, reduces its potential in the market,[159] and its development into a competing platform.

While the focus of this chapter is on the interoperability side of this case, it is very interesting to contrast Microsoft's approaches to the server and the media player. With their server, Microsoft seems to try to reject their de facto standard status, and the view that alternative work group servers have been marginalized.[160] They assert their right to keep interoperability information proprietary and private, and claim that access to the detailed complete interoperability information is both unnecessary and unavailable. In contrast, with WMP, Microsoft assert the benefits of standardization, saying a standardized platform may 'spare the industry possible ambiguity as to the outcome of the competitive race among competing media players, thereby generating net efficiencies',[161] and actively provide access to useful libraries and APIs.

Probably conscious of this contrast, the Commission wisely may have been determined to make sure that if standardization does take place, it does so for the right reasons. There may be a bias towards the first strong player, like a homesteading effect,[162] sometimes coupled with a bandwagon effect,[163] as expectations about the winner become self-fulfilling prophecies

---

155 S Vezzoso, n. 149 above, 388–9.

156 K. Nikulainen, 'Open Source Software: Why is it Here and Will it Stick Around?' (2004) *SCRIPT-ed* 149, 160–1; Rotenberg, n. 40 above, 10–11.

157 Decision, para. 53.

158 A partial substitute.

159 Lévéque, n. 24 above, 83.

160 Decision, para. 90.

161 For example, by distorting statistics on Linux and presenting it as a single undertaking, rather than a format used by various smaller firms, Decision, para. 969.

162 D. Friedman, 'Standards as Intellectual Property: An Economic Approach' (1994) *University of Dayton Law Review* 1109.

163 Farrell, n. 121 above, 42.

as consumers gain confidence that the standard will endure (for example as happened with IBM PCs),[164] which may be hard to apply brakes to afterwards from tipping effects.[165] This can encourage a tendency for the market to standardize too early on immature technology.[166] Standards develop their own network effects, as acceptance brings increased value and usage.[167] Once momentum has gathered, standardization on a particular format can be difficult to reverse, even by superior technology. One example of this is the almost ubiquitous QWERTY keyboard.[168] First developed for early typewriters, designed to slow down typists and prevent certain keys hitting each other, its format continued even with electronic keyboards. Users familiar with it were reluctant to change,[169] even when the ergonomically designed Dvorak keyboard arrived on the market.[170] Against this, one could argue that at that time, a *universal* keyboard was needed, more than the *best* keyboard for the future. Worryingly though, both of Microsoft's two products at issue in this case, work group servers and Windows Media Player, were found to lag behind their competitors in terms of technology.[171]

In general, however, it seems that if standardization takes place, as far as possible, it should not favour immature or inferior technology. Probably for this reason, the Commission sought survey advice about technical opinions on WMP. They found it was rated highest by only two of fifteen.[172] As summarized by the CFI, it 'requires an examination of whether any positive effects associated with the increasing standardisation of certain products may constitute objective justification or whether, as the Commission contends, the positive effects of standardisation may be accepted *only* when they result from the operation of the competitive process in the market or from decisions taken by standardisation bodies'.[173] It is interesting to speculate what may provide the best judge or selector for standards to positively encourage, or at least avoid limiting, technical development.

---

[164] Farrell, n. 121 above, 39–40.

[165] I. Rahnasto, *Intellectual Property Rights, External Effects, and Anti-Trust Law* (Oxford: Oxford University Press, 2003), p. 183.

[166] M. Larvick, 'Questioning the Necessity of Copyright Protection for Software Interfaces' (1994) *University Illinois Law Review* 187, 211.

[167] Rotenberg, n. 40 above, 13.

[168] Farrell, n. 121 above, 46.

[169] Providing an example of switching effects.

[170] Farrell, n. 121 above, 37.

[171] Decision, paras 950, 669.

[172] Decision, para. 950.

[173] Interim Relief Order, n. 55 above, para. 401.

Curtailing Potential in Emerging Standards

A final method for protecting the platform is to try to undermine any new platforms developing in the public domain. One such innovation was Sun's 'Java experiment', which became an attempt to address the issue of platform independence, and so the applications barrier to entry for operating systems wishing to compete with Windows. The ubiquity of Windows implies most software, especially for the mass market, may never be ported to other operating systems, simply because the costs of porting are significant, UNIX[174] expertise is arguably rarer, and the gains can be quite low for marginal systems. The difference in markets could be compared to that between Fords and Ferraris.

Sun's idea was to bypass this need for porting by developing a platform which behaved like an operating system but actually was just an additional layer placed above it, with very clearly defined interfaces. Applications written in the Java programming language appeared to be compiled/interpreted just like other language, but actually ran on this 'Virtual Machine', enabling them to be written once, and run on any computer with a Virtual Machine installed.

Essentially the complicated porting process was encapsulated into the Java compiler/interpreter which needed to be set up for each machine. Two factors were critically important. First, this could be done once per operating system, rather than once per operating system per application program; and secondly, Sun made Java an open standard, with complete information freely available and openly accessible for programmers everywhere. Had it taken off, Java applications would work interchangeably on UNIX and Windows machines, without any additional effort from programmers. Some believe it could have provided the paradigm shift, that wave of creative destruction to undermine Windows' monopoly. It never got the opportunity.

Using an approach, regularly documented by critics as 'Embrace Extend Extinguish',[175] Microsoft appeared enthusiastic about Java, to the extent that it unilaterally added certain extensions to the Windows version. This robbed the virtual platform of identical behaviour across all platforms, and effectively extinguished its potential as a rival platform to Windows. A good language, it is still in use but, undermined by the lack

---

[174] UNIX, an open standard, is a primary competitor of Windows, described in the Decision, para. 42.

[175] Schoechle, n. 60 above, 238; Samuelson and Scotchmer, n. 56 above, 1619–20; FSFE in Report for the Hearing, n. 45 above, Supplement, para. 63.

of consistency across platforms it was designed to have, its full potential will not be realized.

Another example of this, briefly mentioned by the Commission and CFI, is Microsoft's extensions to various interoperability protocols. According to SIIA, 'Microsoft restricts its competitors' capacity to achieve interoperability . . . by failing to comply with industry standard protocols, by making minor (and unnecessary) additions to them and by then refusing to disclose information about those extended protocols to its competitors'.[176] Kerberos[177] is a security protocol originally developed by MIT in 1983, now maintained by IETF. Microsoft started to use Kerberos in Windows 2000, because it offered increased efficiency, security and flexibility over Microsoft's own proprietary system NT Lan Manager. We are told the extensions were useful but were not made available to rivals, and that using the un-extended Kerberos in a Windows domain led to authorization problems.[178]

It is undisputed that Microsoft has unilaterally extended open standards, and often kept the extent of those extensions secret, limiting others' interoperability.[179] While it can be seen as an attempt to undermine the foundations of any potential new platforms, there is always another side. As already mentioned, public standards are notoriously slow to modify and update due to the need to acquire consensus. Unilateral extensions may be the only way to achieve desired results *quickly*. The critical issues relate to the worth of these improvements,[180] whether they are subtle or significant, *essential* to achieve the goal, and above all, their need to be *private,* especially when relating to interoperability with something which is itself a de facto standard.

Intellectual property is important in the Microsoft case because ultimately both software and interoperability specifications are IP protected, and IP protection dictates the borders on which competition occurs.[181] The main tensions exist on two levels. First, on a philosophical level, there is the battle between the adherents of intellectual commons and free information, particularly for standards in the global digital

---

176 CFI judgment, para. 419.

177 Decision, paras 152–3; Kerberos is a security protocol originally developed by MIT in 1983, now maintained by IETF. Microsoft stated to use Kerberos in Windows 2000 because it offered increased efficiency, security and flexibility over their previous proprietary system.

178 CFI judgment para. 419.

179 Decision, para. 254.

180 Report for the Hearing, n. 45 above, Supplement, para. 63 *et seq.*

181 Farrell, n. 121 above, 48–9.

economy,[182] against followers of Locke, who believe that man should own the product of his intellectual labour, and that information ownership is necessary for innovation. Secondly, on a practical level, many believe IP protects inappropriately, in terms of explicitly protecting the trivial and only haphazardly the meriting. In fact cases like *Magill* and *IMS Health* have been described as the creation by competition law of solutions to address aberrations in some national copyright systems.[183] The next section explores the interaction between IP and innovation in the software sector.

5. INNOVATION

Innovation in the Software Industry

The Commission believed Microsoft's competitors innovated in the past, before the interoperability barriers associated with the Windows NT to 2000 transformation, and were currently innovating despite these problems.[184] While rivals built features users valued,[185] the market was ultimately deprived of them due to the interoperability barrier.[186] Instead of competing on the merits, rival products were artificially relegated to a secondary position.[187] Removal of the interoperability barrier would enhance competition and innovation, even within Microsoft itself. Against this, Microsoft argued that its competitors innovated merely to 'avoid being left behind', and that if Microsoft stopped innovating, its rivals probably would also.[188] While this argument might be undermined by the Commission's surveys which indicate Microsoft may in fact lag behind its rivals technologically, two interesting questions arise. First, as Microsoft alleged, would its competitors no longer innovate if Microsoft didn't?

182 T. Schoechle, *Re-examining Intellectual Property Rights in the Context of Standardization, Innovation and the Public Sphere* (Boulder: International Centre for Standards Research, University of Colorado, 2001).

183 Reimann, n. 29 above, 60–1.

184 Report for the Hearing, n. 49 above, para. 236.

185 Surveys showed that on certain important areas like reliability and security, Windows lagged behind UNIX, Linux and NetWare. See Decision, para. 699.

186 Report for the Hearing, n. 45 above, para. 239, claiming Microsoft lags behind its rivals in several characteristics important to consumers, but due to the interoperability barrier they must content themselves with Microsoft products.

187 Decision, para. 699.

188 Report for the Hearing, n. 45 above, para. 195.

Secondly, to what extent would Microsoft's own innovation be reduced by being forced to disclose interoperability information?

While both sides acknowledged the incentive to innovate arising from competition, it is difficult to accept Microsoft's perspective of its current rivals. The fact that Windows' dramatic transformation from NT to Windows 2000 was partly in response to the inadequacy of some of its own technology in comparison with its rivals[189] suggests its rivals were actually leading with innovative technology, rather than merely avoiding being left behind, as Microsoft alleged.

Against this, however, Microsoft's fears and the width of the disclosure order may merit concern. Microsoft was not ordered to disclose to Sun, Novell or other proven innovators, but rather 'any undertaking having an interest in developing and distributing work group server operating system products'.[190] Furthermore the disclosure is not for five years, as in the United States,[191] but rather indefinitely 'kept updated on an ongoing basis and in a timely manner'.[192] It may extend even to products not currently marketed.[193] What safeguards will protect Microsoft against mere reproduction of its functionality by less innovative rivals? What proportion of Microsoft's core products could be reproduced using the mandated access to Windows domain architecture and interoperability protocols by a person skilled in the art of programming? In which circumstances might the obligation cease? Is the remedy particularly wide because it relates to operating system interoperability – or could it be applied to any software?

It is submitted that Microsoft's incentives to innovate, particularly in the area of interoperability infrastructure, may indeed be affected. The Commission argue that Microsoft will still want to innovate in these for benefits internally, not least between Windows and its own servers,[194] and secondly because interoperability will improve its products' value in the eyes of consumers.[195] Against the first point, it is argued that Microsoft may not be aiming simply to *improve* their product as the Commission assumes, but rather at developing and maintaining a *comparative advantage over its rivals*. Against the second point is the crunch question. Does

189 For example, the move to Kerberos to address its security deficiencies compared with Novell. See Decision, para. 148.
190 Decision, article 5(1).
191 Report for the Hearing, n. 45 above, para. 197.
192 Decision, article 5(1b).
193 Lévéque, n. 24 above, 87–8.
194 Decision, para. 721.
195 Decision, para. 727.

the fact that the market has itself not chosen to protect interoperability, for example by consumers deciding to stay with older versions of Windows with fuller interoperability, demonstrate improved interoperability may not actually improve the value of Windows for its consumers *sufficiently* for it to be worthwhile?

The NT to 2000 transformation arguably brought two beneficial effects for Microsoft: it has regained ground lost to rivals who had been winning technology races for improved security and reliability, and secondly it has effectively disimproved those products in the eyes of consumers, by attacking the essential key of Windows' interoperability, and raised rival costs.[196] Interoperability gains may not be symmetrical between Windows and its external rivals. The essential question is whether Microsoft as a dominant undertaking is allowed to create a comparative advantage in an area as important as interoperability. While the net effect of disclosure will probably be beneficial overall, it is submitted that Microsoft at least may tend to avoid R&D in areas relating to interoperability, especially given that they do not appear to be motivated by licensing opportunities here, as suggested earlier.

Moving on from *Magill*

IP is important in the Microsoft case because it defines the underlying property rights that Article 82 EC restrains the use of. Ultimately, both software and interoperability specifications are protected by IP; and IP protection dictates the borders on which competition usually occurs.[197]

Satisfying Article 82 EC's exceptional circumstances, previously defined in *Magill/IMS Health*, required some flexibility in assessing indispensability and elimination of competition[198] as discussed earlier, but arguably the Microsoft case's two most significant contributions concerned objective justifications and incentives to innovate/the new product test.

Providing an opportunity to reflect on the increasing dependence on innovative computing in the post-Internet globalized world, the Microsoft case broke new ground by not focusing on the emergence of a new product, as in previous cases like *Magill*. Returning to the text of Article 82(b) EC, Microsoft stood accused not of preventing adequate interoperability per

---

196 J. Hogan, 'Competition Policy for Computer Software Markets' (2001) *Journal of Information, Law and Technology*, esp. p. 17, available at http://www2.warwick.ac/uk/fac/soc/law/elj/jlit/2001_2/hogan.html.

197 Farrell, n. 121 above, 48–9.

198 For example, in interpreting risk, likelihood and elimination of competition. See CFI judgment, para. 561.

se, but rather of 'limiting production, markets or technical development to the prejudice of consumers', raising questions about its precise meaning, limits and implications in the context of software.

New or Enhanced Products?

Microsoft argued that Sun's proposed innovations would not satisfy *Magill* because they do not apply to a 'new product' but an existing one.[199] Newness for software is especially difficult[200] due to the way it is constructed, often evolving organically from some earlier software rather than being built from scratch. It may be released regularly as a succession of versions, with each new version apparently more competent than the previous.[201] What is new software? Is the latest version *new*? Would or should one program be considered a 'duplicate' of another, or already 'existing' if they offered the same functionality options to the user?[202] What if the functionality looked similar to the user, but was achieved using different algorithms? Should it be relevant if one aspect of functionality (e.g. security) works more reliably in one program than another? If the suggestion that consumers attach their preferences to features rather than products is credible,[203] features may provide a more appropriate level of analysis than products. It is contentious and difficult to know exactly where the 'duplication' boundary can be drawn for software.[204] Many cases like *Apple*[205] have focused on user-interfaces which concern the 'look and feel' or visual display presented to the user. The work behind the user-interface is arguably still in need of adequate legal analysis. As Rotenberg has argued, the significance of computing has radically increased since the 1991 Software Directive, and the legal arsenal surrounding it needs to be updated accordingly.[206]

In many ways the precise boundaries of *Magill* were unfortunately ambiguous. Should the Court have rejected the case if both parties had been trying to produce the same type of TV guide,[207] for example, if hypotheti-

---

[199] Killick, n. 144 above, 43; see Report for the Hearing,Supplementary, n. 45 above, para. 95.

[200] Lévêque, n. 24 above, 75.

[201] Report for the Hearing, n. 45 above, para. 314.

[202] Derclaye, 'Software Copyright Protection: Can Europe Learn from American Case Law? Part 1' (2000) *European Intellectual Property Review* 7, 12.

[203] Lévêque, n. 24 above, 76.

[204] Derclaye, n. 63 above, 58.

[205] *Apple Computer, Inc* v *Microsoft Corp. and Hewlett-Packard Co.*, US Dist. Lexis 12216 (1992).

[206] Rotenberg, n. 40 above, 6–7.

[207] As with this case where both parties are producing work group servers.

cally RTE had itself produced a comprehensive TV guide, which was for argument's sake unpopular due to poor journalism and limited colour? Or equally if Magill's intention had not been to produce a new comprehensive multi-broadcaster guide but rather a more elaborate and colourful guide to RTE's own programmes? Given evidence of unmet consumer demand, how relevant should the precise type of the magazine be? This question is even more poignant given the CFI's focus on consumer harm in the Microsoft case, and the harm suffered by having desires unmet by existing products and artificially limited choices.[208] Does the critical distinction rely on differences in approach for different types of work – despite both being protected by copyright – and *Magill*'s lack of 'technical development?'

Genuine Technical Development

Microsoft tried to argue that unlike in *Magill*, its intellectual property was valuable and the result of expensive R&D.[209] Against this it could be argued that Microsoft's blocking of interoperability information was more serious than in *Magill* because it prevented the creation of valuable development and IP. The behaviour in *Magill* only limited production or markets – not technical development.

This is one of the primary distinctions between the Microsoft case and previous cases like *Magill, Ladbrokes* and *Bronner*, and brings a new scenario to competition law:[210] the potential for further genuine technical development. As discussed earlier, adequate interoperability information could potentially lead beyond a single end-product consumers may have an interest in; it could lead to a platform or whole family of potential advances. Blocking interoperability and interface standardization is serious because it prevents the benefits mentioned earlier like technical development, componentization, specialization and market development. The issue is how should regulators determine whether technical developments are being limited? The next section explores incentives for technical development.

Incentives, Innovation and Intellectual Property

Microsoft argued that losing the ability to control access to their interoperability information and code internals is a deprivation of the essence of

---

208 CFI judgment, para. 652.

209 Interim Relief Order, n. 55 above, para. 207.

210 Excluding *IBM Undertaking* (1984), arguably predating many current computing issues.

their core IP rights, and seriously hampers their incentives to innovate.[211] Because imitation brings higher gains than innovation, an economic goal of intellectual property is to limit copying to provide an incentive for innovative R&D, which may not otherwise exist.[212] While recognizing the complexities and uncertainties of innovation economics,[213] the obvious questions arise. First, could IP protection of software be considered inappropriate by protecting the wrong things in the wrong way? Secondly, in the real world of software, would that R&D happen anyway? And thirdly, could IP protection actually impede innovation and technical development in software?

Is Existing IP Protection of Software Appropriate?

Cases like *Magill* and *IMS Health* have been described as the creation by competition law of solutions to address aberrations in national copyright laws, where IP protection granted by national courts was inappropriate.[214] It has been suggested that this case highlights some deep problems in the use of copyright to protect software.[215] Software's copyright protection endures until 70 years after the programmer's death, which appears almost absurd compared with a shelf-life which is more suitably measured in months.[216] Arguably it may negate the traditional reluctance to interfere with competition, for fear of upsetting the delicate balance intrinsic in the temporary nature of intellectual property.[217] In practical terms the copyright protecting software may as well be permanent. It is aptly described as 'the cuckoo in the copyright nest'.[218]

Furthermore, the division of labour within intellectual property sees copyright protecting expressions and patents protecting ideas and the functional.[219] While software as source code could be seen as a literary work, it is difficult to see object code/executables as literary, and they are generally considered functional.

A fundamental problem with software is that arguably its most creative

---

211 Decision, paras 709–12.
212 Lévêque, n. 24 above, 77.
213 Vezzoso, n. 149 above, 387.
214 Reimann, n. 29 above, 60–1.
215 Farrell, n. 121 above, 47.
216 Flint, n. 111 above, 147.
217 Joined Cases C-241 and 242/91 P *Magill*.
218 S. Gordon, 'The Very Idea!: Why Copyright Law is an Inappropriate Way to Protect Computer Programs' (1998) *European Intellectual Property Review* 10.
219 Derclaye, n. 202 above, 9.

aspect is its algorithm, which is often devoid of protection in its own right. The literary source code and the object/executables are protected, but their creation can be relatively mechanical once the algorithm has been solved. A further complication highlighted by Farrell in 1989 is that interface information usually involves what starts off as merely *arbitrary* expressions.[220] For interfaces which go on to become gateways to de facto standards, that interface expression becomes more than arbitrary – it becomes *necessary* to compete in the marketplace. For Farrell it becomes effectively functional and inappropriate for copyright protection. He argues that IP protection of interface information is necessary only because of the absence of appropriate protection for the truly meriting aspects of the program.[221] A workable solution seems hard to find. While some advocate software patents for protecting software ideas, these too have their problems.[222] The difficulty in examining against the state of the art in software makes it especially difficult to know what is truly innovative, particularly as so much is effectively hidden from view.

Is IP Protection Essential for Software Innovation?

Economically, the software industry contains two opposing models, proprietary and open source.[223] The proprietary model is followed by companies like Microsoft and Sun, and is based on generally keeping source code secret, and licensing the use of executables and object code. Open source[224] seems to be based on more altruistic or cooperative desires like sharing ideas, information and most importantly source code. While financial gains from open source may have been relatively limited,[225] it is surprisingly popular among programmers, who generously give their time and ideas to a common pool for the public good, and among the many well-known examples in the market place are Linux and some brands of UNIX.[226] Potential negatives include navigation and selection, dependence on goodwill and a lack of indemnity,[227] but the fact remains that it

---

[220] Farrell, n. 121 above, 47.

[221] Farrell, n. 121 above, 47.

[222] L. Van Raden, 'Technology Dematerialised: Another Approach to Information-related Invention' (1996) *European Intellectual Property Review* 384, 384–9.

[223] Nikulainen, n. 156 above, 149 *et seq*.

[224] Open source is 'an established feature of the mainstream software market'. See Decision, para. 29.

[225] Nikulainen, n. 156 above, 160.

[226] Decision, para. 187.

[227] Nikulainen, n. 156 above, 172–3.

promotes open standards and can result in deeply significant innovation. The Internet itself developed out of the open sourced TCP/IP protocol.[228] Furthermore, some resulting code is often considered to be of higher quality than proprietary software,[229] with endorsements including the US government and the United Nations.[230] At its core may be a desire for programmers to display their talents to peers they admire, with open source like a large public gallery for software on the Web.

But it may be becoming an even stronger force. Hybrid forms of open source are emerging, many built on free source code but with the supplier earning fees for *services* like support, and Watson argues these hybrid forms will oust proprietary software to become the dominant software business model.[231] Offering advantages like increased accountability, increased talent base and software 'ecosystem', it offers gains for developers, businesses and consumers. Most importantly it asks whether the traditional need for IP to encourage R&D which would not otherwise happen is something that can simply go unchallenged in the current world.

Could IP Protection Impede Software Innovation?

While not arguing that all IP impedes innovation, it will be suggested that the converse is equally uncertain. Weaker protection is thought to allow more imitation and lead to competition on prices, costs and standardization.[232] Stronger protection may hinder imitation and impede standardization.[233] As we have already seen, standards can lead to both collaboration and platforms on which further innovation and development can take place; so limiting standardization could limit innovation. Farrell has suggested that strategies which try to neutralize the benefits of open systems by denying interoperability information would not stop innovation completely, but rather influence the direction it took.[234] Some thwarted innovators may put their efforts into building something completely new, potentially a paradigm shift to displace the incumbent monopolist, which may be very beneficial to the public. Alternatively their efforts may

---

228 Nikulainen, n. 156 above, 172–3.

229 Nikulainen, n. 156 above, 172–3.

230 L. Woodard, 'Open Source Software: How to Use it and Control it in the Corporate Environment' (2004) *Computer and Internet Law* 8.

231 R. Watson, M. Boudreau, P. York, M. Greiner and J. Donald, 'The Business of Open Source' (2008) *Communications of the ACM* 51(4), 41–6.

232 Farrell, n. 121 above, 48–9.

233 Farrell, n. 121 above, 48–9.

234 Farrell, n. 121 above, 48–9.

turn to incompatible products which may be of little overall value.[235] A further concern is the use of IP negatively, for simply fencing off the intellectual commons to defensively prevent use by another, rather than any constructive or positive goal, leading to unused technology which again is said to be of little or no value.[236]

It is impossible to discuss innovation, and incentives to encourage it, in isolation from issues like quality and quantity. Ranging from minor incremental improvements to more major paradigm shifts or Schumpeterian innovation, what really matters may not be simply the number of patents, new features or enhancements, but instead how much they are actually *valued* by consumers.[237] The Commission appears to see lack of choice as the manifestation of consumer harm. However, as Lévéque has argued, choice alone should not be as important as *useful* choices, or the decision may help to artificially maintain options which are neither valued nor required by the market.[238]

This raises interesting issues about the interaction between consumer harm, innovation and the impact of the Commission's intervention. Does the innovative profile of the industry need closer examination to see if most benefit could be achieved by a large number of serial, moderate, incremental improvements, or instead by encouraging the development of a smaller number of major paradigm shifts? What parameters should influence a regulator's decision on whether to intervene in the operation of the market, and the type of intervention required? Arguably, instead of focusing on disclosure of interoperability information, which may prevent Sun's construction of 'advanced server features', the Commission should have focused more on protecting emerging standards, possibly even Java, which may have become the next great paradigm shift to displace Microsoft as the dominant platform, with more widespread impact and benefits.

6. CONCLUSIONS

The aim of this chapter was to investigate some of the more unusual aspects of the Microsoft case, especially in relation to the interactions between interoperability, standardization and innovation. It attempted to

---

235 Farrell, n. 121 above, 48–9.
236 Vezzoso, n. 149 above, 387.
237 Lévéque, n. 24 above, 76.
238 Lévéque, n. 24 above, 76.

show this case is significant, despite its restriction to the CFI. Its significance relies on its expansion of previous boundaries and the introduction of a new focus for competition: the limiting of technical development.

Previous boundaries were expanded especially in satisfying indispensability, eliminating competition and the new product test. Various factors may have contributed to this development, and it is interesting to speculate on their relative importance as a means of predicting the impact of this judgment into the future.

How significant was Microsoft's unparalleled power and the modern world's dependence on computing? The Microsoft case involved interoperability information and operating systems. To what extent could it apply to interoperability information for application programs, e.g. CAD systems?[239] The European Union's various policy commitments on interoperability and standardization were mentioned. To what extent does the Microsoft case depend on these policy considerations? One of the Microsoft case's most powerful issues was arguably the blocking of more than a single product desired by consumers, but a whole family of advances. Will this become known as one of the Microsoft case tests?

Much was made of Microsoft's rivals' actual and successful innovations, past and present, to the extent that it was unclear who was lagging behind whom. How significant was this evidence? How would a situation be handled where a rival had *intentions* of technical development but without such a strong track history? This is unclear, particularly given the width of the remedy imposed.

How relevant was the disruption in previous supply, and that Microsoft had actively encouraged interoperability prior to the growth in its market share? As suggested by Rahnasto,[240] one of the goals of intellectual property rights should be to reward the creator not just for creating the work, but for bringing it to the public domain. Perhaps after bringing it there, and particularly after encouraging dependency on it, the creator may not then simply retract it. While all of Microsoft's protocols relating to server interoperability were ordered to be disclosed, regardless of their origin, some, like Kerberos, were originally open before Microsoft's proprietary extensions. Does the alleged 'Embrace, Extend, Extinguish' strategy amount to privatizing information which was previously public? Should it be significant for competition law? Should it become another Microsoft case test?

---

239 Software used widely in engineering and architecture to define and manipulate geometries for various simulation purposes.

240 Rahnasto, n. 165 above, 19.

While applauding the developments brought in this case, there are two sides to the judgment. The issues of measuring innovation and incentives for innovation, and the role played by IP, were explored. It is submitted that the CFI may have dismissed some arguments too quickly and that, particularly for the *merely* dominant, a far more detailed analysis is required.

While the Microsoft case's focus on limiting technical development recognizes the importance of protecting potential developments in the pre-production and marketing stages, there are also potential dangers, not least in protecting what ultimately the market itself has apparently not decided to value. Are there any guarantees that the innovative products it leads to will themselves be valued?

10. Tying, technological integration and Article 82 EC: where do we go after the Microsoft case?

Arianna Andreangeli*

1. INTRODUCTION

The CFI judgment in the Microsoft case[1] constitutes a high profile example of the impact of the EU antitrust rules on dominant undertakings operating in innovative industries and raises important questions on the suitability of the current legal framework governing cases of tying under Article 82 of the EC Treaty to examples of technological integration in the software market.[2] This chapter examines some of these issues and considers whether it would be feasible for the Commission and the EU courts to develop a different and perhaps more flexible approach to these practices.

After illustrating the EC rules governing 'classic' tying and analysing the position adopted by the Microsoft judgment, this chapter will consider the current approach of the US courts to technological integration in new economy markets and compare it with that applied by the CFI. It will argue that although this case dealt with the conduct of a 'super-dominant' company and its conclusions may not therefore be easily extended to other sets of facts, it could create uncertainty as to the suitability of the existing rules for tying in 'novel' industries. Thereafter, this chapter will speculate

* Many thanks are owed to Dr Amanda Warren-Jones for the many discussions on these issues and to Prof. Alison Jones of King's College, London, for her feedback. An earlier version of this chapter was presented at the Conference on The Next 50 Years: The Future of EU Law and Policy, hosted by the Institute of European Law of Birmingham Law School at the University of Birmingham, 3–4 July 2008. The author is grateful to the discussant, Dr Luca Rubini and to all participants. The usual disclaimer applies.

1 Case T-201/04 *Microsoft* v *Commission* [2007] ECR II-3601 ('CFI judgement'); see also Commission Decision COM (2004) 900, *Microsoft Core*, of 24 May 2004 [2007] OJ L32/23.

2 See Chapter 4, pp. 134 *et seq.*

on the possibility to develop an alternative approach to tying and suggest that the adoption of a more 'economics-based' test, especially in respect of the concepts of 'objective justification' and of the 'efficiency defence' may allow a more extensive examination of the efficiency gains and the consumers' benefits arising from the emergence of software 'common platforms'.

2. TYING, ECONOMICS AND ARTICLE 82 EC

Between Efficiency Enhancing Effects and the Threat of Foreclosure: Economic Approaches to Tying

Tying can be defined as an arrangement whereby the sale of the tying product is made conditional on the purchase of a distinct, otherwise economically unrelated, product or service.[3] It may be distinguished from the similar practice of 'bundling', i.e. the joint sale of two or more items that also remain available for purchase separately.[4] Both practices have recognized advantages, including economies of scale and of scope, lower production, distribution and advertising costs[5] and lower search costs for consumers wishing to satisfy 'complex economic needs'.[6]

Especially in industries characterized by 'non-linear' patterns of innovation where 'add-on' development constitutes a common expression of genuine technical progress,[7] tying is likely to be pro-competitive.[8] It enables suppliers to ensure adequate quality standards when allowing users to assemble different components could adversely affect the quality of the end-product,[9] can encourage research and development[10] and eventually result in a new product which benefits consumers 'above and beyond the individual components added together'.[11]

---

3 European Commission, DG Competition, *Discussion Paper on the Application of Article 82 of the Treaty to Exclusionary Abuses* (December 2005) (hereinafter 'Discussion Paper'), para. 177. For commentary, see, *inter alia*, D. Evans and J. Padilla, *The Law and Economics of Article 82* (Oxford: Hart Publishing, 2006), pp. 477–8.

4 Discussion Paper, para. 177.

5 Evans and Padilla, n. 3 above, 481.

6 Evans and Padilla, n. 3 above, 482.

7 *United States* v *Microsoft Corp.*, 147 F. 3d 935 (D.C.Cir. 1998).

8 *United States* v *Microsoft Corp.*, 147 F. 3d, 950.

9 *United States* v *Microsoft Corp.*, 147 F. 3d, 950.

10 D. Nalebuff, *Bundling, Tying and Portfolio Effects*, DTI Economics Paper No 1. (2000), pp. 60–1.

11 Nalebuff, n. 10 above.

However, traditional economic theory highlighted the danger that an undertaking that is already economically powerful on the tying product market may be encouraged to 'leverage' its economic strength, namely, to foreclose competition on the market for the tied product, through this practice.[12] As a result, competing suppliers, being deprived of sufficient demand, would eventually be forced out of the tied product market and the monopolist could extend its economic power onto it.[13]

More recent economic thinking, however, exposed the weaknesses of these traditional arguments, namely their failure to recognize that tying would only be profitable if entry in the market was not 'cost free' due to the presence of incumbent advantages[14] or to the monopolist's commitment to it as a means to differentiate its products.[15] The traditional theories also failed to examine the manner in which the tying and the tied product were priced[16] and especially to consider whether the price charged for the tied product as part of the combined sale was 'predatory', i.e. lower than the average running costs borne by the monopolist for its supply,[17] so that a 'hypothetical efficient competitor' could not 'match' the price for each individual product as stand-alone.[18]

However, it was also emphasized that pricing assessments should be conducted in the light of the features of each market, since especially in industries characterized by very high start-up investments and by a downward trend in the running costs,[19] a price appearing *prima facie* too low could still 'exceed the marginal costs of supply'.[20] The limited analysis conducted above illustrated that tying is an economic practice having a number of beneficial effects as well as raising several anti-competitive concerns. The next sections will consider the legal approaches to these arrangements adopted by EC law as well as under the US Sherman Act.

---

[12] Evans and Padilla, n. 3 above, 483–4.

[13] C. Ahlborn, D. Evans and J. Padilla, 'The Antitrust Economics of Tying: A Farewell to Per Se Illegality' (2004) *Antitrust Bulletin* 287, 323–4.

[14] Ahlborn, Evans and Padilla, n. 13 above, 485–6.

[15] *Inter alia*, Nalebuff, n. 10 above, 71–2.

[16] See, *inter alia*, E.M. Fox, 'Monopolisation, Abuse of Dominance and the Indeterminacy of Economics: The US/EU Divide' (2006) *Utah Law Review* 725, 735.

[17] See e.g. D. Crane, 'Mixed Bundling, Profit Sacrifice and Consumer Welfare' (2006) *Emory Law Journal* 423, 443–4; also Evans and Padilla, n. 3 above, 501–2.

[18] See Crane, n. 17 above, 449–50. Also Discussion Paper, paras 189–90.

[19] D. Ridyard, 'Exclusionary Pricing and Price Discrimination Abuse under Article 82: An Economic Analysis' (2002) *European Competition Law Review* 286, 288.

[20] Ridyard, n. 19 above, 291. See also Crane, n. 17 above, 469–70.

Tying and Article 82 EC: The Earlier Cases

After having outlined some of the economic arguments in favour and against tying, this section will examine the relevant EC antitrust rules. According to Article 82(d) EC, the subjecting in whatever form, on the part of a dominant undertaking, of 'the conclusion of contracts . . . to acceptances by the other parties of supplementary obligations which, by their nature or according to commercial usage, have no connection with the subject of such contracts' constitutes abusive conduct.[21]

Consequently, the European Court of Justice stated that tied sales should be prohibited by Article 82 unless it could be shown that they were consistent with 'commercial usage' or were otherwise 'objectively justified'.[22] The Commission added that, despite being often motivated by the need to enforce adequate standards of 'quality, reputation and good usage' of the products concerned,[23] tying could allow dominant companies to deprive competitors of their customers, thus excluding them from the market.[24] It would therefore be abusive if the undertaking responsible for it was dominant on the market for the supply of the tying product[25] and the tying and the tied products were 'separate',[26] so that individual customers wishing to obtain the former must be 'coerced' into purchasing the latter, either as a result of a contractual obligation or by less direct means of 'coercion', such as the promise of rebates applicable only to the sale of the 'package'.[27] In addition, the conduct must have 'market distorting foreclosing effects'[28] and not be 'objectively justified'.[29]

The assessment of the 'separate product' requirement focuses on the existence of distinct demand for each product so that, absent the tying,

---

21 Evans and Padilla, n. 3 above, 491.

22 See e.g. Case C-333/94 *Tetra Pak* v *Commission* [1996] ECR I-5951, paras 36–7; CFI judgment, paras 960–1.

23 Discussion Paper, para. 178.

24 Discussion Paper, para. 180.

25 See, *inter alia*, Commission Decision 88/138/EEC *Eurofix-Bauco/Hilti* [1988] OJ L65/19, paras 66–7.

26 See e.g. Case T-30/89 *Hilti AG* v *Commission* [1991] ECR II-1439, para. 66; also Commission Decision 92/163/EC *Tetra Pak II* [1992] OJ L72/1, para. 92.

27 Commission Decision 88/138/EC, *Eurofix-Bauco/Hilti* para. 75; Case T-30/89 *Hilti AG* v *Commission*, para. 68.

28 See e.g. Commission Decision 92/163/EC, *Tetra Pak II*, paras 119–20; see also Case C-333/94 P *Tetra Pak* v *Commission*, para. 37.

29 See e.g. Discussion Paper, para. 183; *inter alia*, Case C-333/94 *Tetra Pak* v *Commission*, paras 36–7.

they 'would be purchased separately'.[30] It can be based either on direct evidence that consumers, if given the choice, would acquire each product as a stand-alone or from the presence of independent suppliers of the tied goods or services.[31] Thus, in *Hilti*[32] the CFI held that consumers regarded the secondary products supplied by independent manufacturers to be used in Hilti's own nail guns as interchangeable vis-à-vis the consumable goods offered by Hilti itself.[33] It was added that an established practice of supply of those consumables by other producers existed and that, consequently, the primary good (i.e. the nail gun) and the secondary products (i.e. respectively, nails and cartridges) could be considered as separate.[34] The CFI rejected the applicant's claim that, due to its highly technical nature, the nail gun could be considered as a novel 'integrated product' together with its consumable products.[35]

The condition of coercion is fulfilled automatically in cases of contractual tying.[36] The CFI affirmed in the Microsoft judgment[37] that since 'in consequence of the impugned conduct, consumers are unable to acquire the Windows client PC operating system without simultaneously acquiring Windows Media Player',[38] the condition that 'the conclusion of contracts is made subject to acceptance of supplementary obligations' had been met.[39] However, when the obligation to purchase the products jointly arises from more 'covert' practices, it would also be necessary to assess whether it is 'rational' for the customer to buy each good or service separately due to the manner in which they are priced individually or jointly.[40]

Assessing whether tying results in market foreclosure requires an analysis of whether a 'hypothetical competitor' of the dominant company can attempt to attract demand from the 'tied' consumers and of whether

---

30 Discussion Paper, para. 185. See e.g. Commission Decision 88/138/EEC *Eurofix-Bauco/Hilti*, paras 55–6.

31 See e.g. Case T-30/89 *Hilti AG* v *Commission* [1991] ECR II-1439, para. 61.

32 Case T-30/89 *Hilti AG* v *Commission*.

33 *Hilti*, para. 66.

34 *Hilti*, para. 67.

35 *Hilti*, para. 68.

36 Discussion Paper, para. 183; see e.g. CFI judgement, paras 962–3.

37 CFI judgment.

38 CFI judgment, para. 960.

39 CFI judgment, para. 960.

40 Discussion Paper, para. 199; see, *inter alia*, Commission Decision 88/138/EEC *Eurofix-Bauco/Hilti*, para. 80. Also, for commentary, see M. Dolmans and T. Graf, 'Analysis of Tying under Article 82: The European Commission's Microsoft Decision in Perspective' (2004) *World Competition* 225, 231.

the latter constitute a significant part of the relevant market,[41] having regard to the features of the tie, the characteristics of the market, including any barriers to entry, the strength of the dominant position and the likelihood of countervailing strategies being adopted by competitors or customers.[42]

Prima facie abusive practice may still escape the prohibition enshrined in Article 82 EC if they are 'objectively justified'. The concept of 'objective justification' has been restricted by the EU courts to conduct motivated by purely objective factors[43] or by the need for a dominant undertaking to protect its commercial interests, subject to a requirement of proportionality.[44]

Also, although undertakings repeatedly attempted to challenge the Commission's findings of abuse on grounds of efficiency, the EU courts have so far been reluctant to accept these pleas.[45] Nonetheless, it is noteworthy that in its 2005 Discussion Paper, the Commission expressly called for a more 'economics-based' approach to exclusionary conduct and provided for an 'efficiency defence'.[46] To benefit from its application, the practice must improve the production or distribution of goods or services or promote technical or economic progress,[47] be indispensable to achieve the alleged benefits and constitute the least restrictive alternative among those capable of delivering the purported beneficial effects.[48] Also, its pro-competitive effects must outweigh its anti-competitive consequences,[49] be timely, significant, likely to be realized and to be passed on to consumers,[50] and the conduct must not eliminate competition from a substantial part of the affected market.[51]

The Commission emphasized that when it resulted in marketing previously separate goods in a 'new, innovative manner', tying could benefit

---

41 Discussion Paper, para. 195. See, *inter alia*, Case C-333/94 *Tetra Pak* v *Commission*, paras 27, 29–31.

42 Discussion Paper, paras 202–3.

43 See e.g., *mutatis mutandis*, Case 77/77 *Benzine en Petroleum Handelsmaatschappij BV* v *Commission* [1978] ECR 1513, paras 32–3.

44 See e.g. Case 27/76 *United Brands Company* v *Commission* [1978] ECR 276, paras 189–191.

45 See e.g. Case C-53/92 P *Hilti* v *Commission* [1994] ECR I-667, paras 15–16; Case C-333/94 *Tetra Pak* v *Commission*, paras 36–7.

46 Discussion Paper, paras 4, 85 *et seq.*

47 Discussion Paper, para. 85.

48 Discussion Paper, para. 86.

49 Discussion Paper, para. 87.

50 Discussion Paper, paras 88–90.

51 Discussion Paper, para. 91.

from the efficiency defence,[52] unless each product remained 'available to consumers on a regular basis . . . [and] on the same or better condition than those applicable by the dominant undertaking' or when the price charged for the 'package' did not reflect the cost savings arising from the combined sale.[53] Furthermore, for tying ensuring 'uniformity or quality standardization' the dominant undertaking should demonstrate that any efficiencies cannot be attained through less restrictive means, such as the independent supply of products meeting 'minimum quality standards'.[54]

Overall, it appears that the current interpretation of Article 82 EC, while it recognizes its efficiency-enhancing effects, could prove problematic for tying occurring in industries where the patterns of technological development are characterized by 'add-on' integration.[55] It is argued that the continuing reliance on the separate demand test and on a literal reading of the concept of 'coercion',[56] whilst remaining appropriate for tying in 'traditional', manufacturing industries, may not be suitable for markets characterized by the emergence of 'common platforms' incorporating a variety of functionalities.[57]

Having regard to the concept of market foreclosure, the 2005 Discussion Paper indicates that once it is shown that the dominant undertaking wields significant market power on a substantial part of the relevant market, the tie will be found to be 'likely to jeopardize competition'.[58] Although this view aims to avoid non-dominant suppliers being ousted from the relevant market, whether it may be appropriate to knowledge-based industries could be questioned.[59] It is suggested that since these markets are char-

---

[52] Discussion Paper, para. 205.

[53] Discussion Paper, para. 206.

[54] Discussion Paper, para. 206.

[55] See e.g. J. Lopatka and W. Page, '*Microsoft* and the Law and Economics of Exclusion' (1999) *Supreme Court Economic Review* 157, 187–8; also Evans and Padilla, n. 3 above, 491.

[56] See e.g. CFI judgment, para. 961. For commentary, see, *inter alia*, Ridyard, n. 19 above, 290–1.

[57] See e.g. *United States* v *Microsoft Corp.*, 147 F. 3d at 952, per curiam. For commentary, see, *inter alia*, M.L. Montagnani, 'Remedies to Exclusionary Innovation in the High-Tech Sector: Is there a Lesson from the Microsoft Saga?' (2007) *World Competition* 623, 641.

[58] Discussion paper, paras 198–9; see also Commission Decision 88/138/EEC *Eurofix-Bauco/Hilti*, paras 66–7; Case C-333/94 *Tetra Pak* v *Commission*, paras 119–120.

[59] See, *inter alia*, B. Ong, 'Building Brick Barricades and Other Barriers to Entry: Abusing a Dominant Position by Refusing to Licence Intellectual Property Rights' (2005) *European Competition Law Review* 215, 219–20; also, Ahlborn, Evans and Padilla, n. 13 above, 312–13.

acterized by a tendency on the part of the suppliers to compete 'for the market' by striving to supply the 'best' product which will become the industry standard for a generation, rather than to compete 'on the market', as in more 'traditional' economic sectors,[60] a 'broad-brush' application of Article 82 could penalize efficient conduct and jeopardize innovation.

Similar concerns could also arise for the concepts of 'commercial usage', 'objective justification' and 'efficiency defence'. The case law discussed above illustrated how the findings of 'coercion' and market foreclosure, resulting mainly from the applicant's dominance, 'trumped' any argument that the joint sale of the primary product and its consumables allowed the offer of a 'novel' integrated good.[61] In respect of 'objective justification', commentators argued that obliging a dominant company to prove that its tie was supported, e.g. by 'genuine motivations' to uphold 'product safety standards', amounted to imposing an 'almost impossible hurdle to overcome'[62] and could overlook significant efficiency gains.[63]

In the light of the above analysis, it may be concluded that, despite repeated calls for a more 'economics-based' approach to tying, the position adopted by the Commission and by the EU courts demonstrates extreme caution in its assessment.[64] The next section will instead briefly address the position adopted by the US courts.

Legal Approach to Tying under the US Sherman Act: From a 'Per Se Offence' to a More Flexible Standard

The position of the Commission and of the EU courts in respect to tying arrangements on the part of dominant companies may be usefully contrasted with the case law of some US courts. In *Jefferson Parish*,[65] the US

---

60 See, *inter alia*, Office of Fair Trading, *Innovation and Competition Policy*, Discussion Paper OFT377 (2002), paras 1.6 and 3.26–27; see also, *mutatis mutandis*, *United States* v *Microsoft Corp.*, 253 F.3d 34, 140 (DC.Cir. 2001). For commentary, see, *inter alia*, D. Evans, 'The Antitrust Economics of Multi-Sided Platform Markets' (2003) *Yale Journal on Regulation* 325; D. Evans and R. Schmalensee, *Some Economic Aspects of Antitrust Analysis in Dynamically Competitive Industries* NBER Working Paper No. 8268 (2001), pp. 42–3.

61 Case T-83/91 *Tetra Pak* v *Commission* [1994] ECR II-755, para. 119; see also, Ahlborn, Evans and Padilla, n. 13 above, 313.

62 A. Albors-Llorens, 'The Role of Objective Justification and Efficiencies in the Application of Article 82 EC' (2007) *Common Market Law Review* 1727, 1740.

63 Albors-Llorens, n. 62 above, 1746–7 and 1758–9.

64 Albors-Llorens, n. 62 above, 1759–60.

65 *Jefferson Parish Hospital District No. 2 et al.* v *Hyde*, 466 U.S. 2, 104 S. Ct. 1551 (1984).

Supreme Court held that tying arrangements created an 'unacceptable risk . . . of stifling competition' and thus were 'unreasonable per se'.[66] They would therefore be caught by section 1 of the Sherman Act, without the need for any further inquiry,[67] if they concerned two or more products that 'may be purchased separately in a competitive market' and, consequently, if competing suppliers were deprived of the freedom to sell 'either the entire package or its several parts'.[68] It must also be proved that the seller is exploiting 'its control over the tying product to force the buyer into the purchase of a tied product that the buyer either did not want at all or might have preferred to purchase elsewhere'[69] and that 'the existence of forcing is probable'.[70]

Nonetheless, later cases demonstrate the emergence of a more refined approach, taking into account the practice's pro-competitive effects vis-à-vis any negative implications[71] and limiting the remit of the 'per se' rule.[72] According to the Federal Court of Appeals in *Paladin*, tying would be unlawful if the seller could 'coerce a buyer to purchase the tied product . . . to obtain the tying product'[73] through 'economic pressure', making 'the assignment . . . so burdensome that customers would not have agreed to it' in the absence of the tie.[74]

This more flexible approach has also been applied to tying concerning software and hardware in the IT industry. In *IBM*,[75] the District Court of New Jersey, recognizing that these practices could ensure 'the practical and effective use of the tying product'[76] and thus reflect 'genuine innovation', held that even though the supplier enjoyed market power, the 'per se' condemnation would not always be justified.[77] Consequently,

---

66 *Jefferson Parish Hospital*, 466 U.S. 2 at 1556.

67 466 U.S. 2 at 1556.

68 466 U.S. 2 at 1558.

69 466 U.S. 2 at 1558.

70 466 U.S. 2 at 1560.

71 See e.g. *Independent Ink, Inc.* v *Illinois Tool Work, Inc.* 547 U.S. 28 S. Ct. 1281 (2006); see especially at 1289–91. For commentary, see A. Jones, 'Analysis of Agreements under US and EC Antitrust Law: Convergence or Divergence?' (2006) *Antitrust Bulletin* 691, 733–4.

72 *Independent Ink*, 547 U.S. 28 at 1287–88; see also Jones, n. 71 above, 734–5.

73 *Paladin Associates, Inc.* v *Montana Power Company*, 328 F.3d 1145, 1159 (9th Cir. 2003).

74 *Paladin*, 328 F.3d at 1160–1. For commentary, see e.g. Jones, n. 71 above, 738–9.

75 *Innovation Data Processing* v *IBM*, 585 F.Supp. 1470 (1984) ('*IBM*').

76 *IBM*, 585 F.Supp. at 1475.

77 *IBM*, 585 F.Supp. at 1476.

a tie allowing the supply of 'a system of technologically interrelated products'[78] should be assessed in the light of the consumers' preferences, the technical characteristics of the products and any benefits stemming from the sale of an 'integrated' version of the goods involved.[79] In the circumstances, the court concluded that the application of 'rule of reason' standards was necessary to foster innovation and that IBM, given the features of the software and its functional link with the tied hardware, had thus been justified in supplying them only 'as a single product and at a single price'.[80]

The above analysis, however brief, demonstrates that the US courts' approach to tying differs significantly from the cautious stance adopted by the EC Commission and by the EU courts. The next sections will address the issues arising from the application of the current standards to ties occurring in 'innovative' markets and consider whether the position applied in the Microsoft case may be suitable to the features of the IT market.

3. TYING IN THE NEW ECONOMY: 'VINTAGE WINE IN NEW BOTTLES'?

The EC case Against Microsoft

The previous section illustrated that the *IBM* case constituted an example of how to apply the US antitrust rules to joint sales' arrangements in the IT industry so as to reconcile the needs of effective competition with those of technical innovation.[81] In the EC legal system, the Microsoft case concerned the application of the legal standards developed for tying in 'traditional industries'[82] to the incorporation into 'common platforms' of software performing a variety of functions. In its 2004 Decision, the Commission found that Microsoft had abused its dominant position on the market for the supply of PC operating systems (OS), *inter alia*, by

---

78 *IBM*, 585 F.Supp. at 1476.

79 *IBM*, 585 F.Supp. at 1476.

80 See e.g. *United States* v *Microsoft*, 253 F.3d at 93–4.

81 *IBM*, 585 F. Supp. at 1476. For commentary see, *inter alia*, D. Evans and J. Padilla, 'Tying under Article 82 and the Microsoft Decision' (2004) *World Competition* 503, 510.

82 Case C-333/94 *Tetra Pak* v *Commission*, para. 37. For commentary, see Ahlborn, Evans and Padilla, n. 13 above, 315–16.

tying Windows to the media player software it produced, Windows Media Player (WMP).[83]

Microsoft challenged the Commission's findings that the integration of WMP into Windows did not constitute a unitary 'new product' or claimed that, in the alternative, the tie had such efficiency enhancing benefits that they countenanced its negative impact on competition.[84] It also claimed that since WMP was supplied at no extra charge and individual users could choose to employ a competing media player,[85] they had not been 'coerced' into adopting WMP 'at the expense of competing unbundled products'.[86] Microsoft also criticized the assessment of the 'market distorting foreclosing effects'[87] according to which, due to the tie, WMP would have become the 'standard of choice' for end-users and providers of media content[88] and thus lead to the 'entrenchment' of a homogenous Microsoft solution not only on the OS but also on the market for media players.[89]

Although in its 2004 Interim Order the CFI had expressed some scepticism,[90] its final judgment confirmed the Commission's conclusions. After reiterating the existing test for the legality of tying,[91] the Court held that it could not be excluded that the constant evolution characterizing high-tech markets could result in 'what initially appear to be separate products . . . being regarded as forming a single product, both from the technological aspect and from the aspect of the competition rules'.[92] However, this was not the case for WMP, since, despite being closely connected, the two programs fulfilled different consumers' needs[93] and there were a number of independent suppliers of media players competing with

---

83 Commission Decision COM (2004) 900, *Microsoft Corp*, of 24 May 2004 [2007] OJ C32/23 ('the Decision'). See also 'Commission opens proceedings against Microsoft's alleged discriminatory licensing and refusal to supply software information', Press Release IP/00/906, 3 August 2000.

84 Decision, para. 811.

85 Decision, paras 830–1.

86 Decision, para. 832.

87 Decision, paras 860–6.

88 Decision, para. 841.

89 Decision, para. 842.

90 Case T-201/04 R *Microsoft* v *Commission* [2004] ECR II-4463, paras 206–7, 212–13.

91 Case T-201/04, *Microsoft* v *Commission* [2007] ECR II-3601, paras 842, 859. See e.g. Case C-53/92 P *Hilti* v *Commission*; Case C-333/94 P *Tetra Pak* v *Commission* [1996] ECR I-5951.

92 CFI judgment, para. 913.

93 CFI judgment, paras 924–5.

Microsoft.[94] Accordingly, the reciprocal links would not suffice to make their combination a novel unitary product.[95]

In respect to 'coercion', the CFI, on the basis of a literal reading of Article 82(d) EC[96] held that this condition was fulfilled since Windows was not available to customers without WMP and it was impossible to remove the latter.[97] The circumstance that WMP was offered free of charge and the ability of customers to acquire alternative software were irrelevant since neither Article 82 EC nor the case law required compulsion to use the tied product or the imposition of charges for it.[98]

As regards the 'market distorting foreclosing effects', the CFI noted that by combining the supply of WMP with that of the OS, the applicant, which was already dominant on the market for operating systems, had achieved an unrivalled level of penetration of the neighbouring market for media players without engaging in any 'competition on the merits'.[99] Due to WMP being pre-installed, customers would be less likely to seek an alternative media player and more exposed to potential 'confusion' between different media functionalities,[100] and original equipment manufacturers (OEMs) would refrain from installing other media software through the costs involved and the resulting loss of hard disk space necessary for a program performing the same tasks as the pre-installed WMP.[101]

The CFI confirmed that other methods of distribution were not adequate alternatives to pre-installation[102] and discounted the circumstance that other media player software was available free of charge and could easily be installed on a Windows-run PC. Nor did it assess whether, in the light of the overall price of the Windows 'bundle', the 'zero price' on WMP was 'predatory'.[103] The Court thus accepted that due to the tie, Microsoft's share in the media-player market would increase along with the share in the OS market and result in WMP becoming the leading format.[104] It held that

---

94 CFI judgment, paras 926–7.

95 CFI judgment, para. 839; see also para. 921. For commentary see e.g. Chapter 4, section III.B.1.

96 CFI judgment, para. 961.

97 CFI judgment, paras 962–3.

98 CFI judgment, paras 962–3.

99 CFI judgment, paras 1038–39.

100 CFI judgment, paras 1041–2.

101 CFI judgment, paras 1044–5.

102 CFI judgment, para. 1053.

103 See also Discussion Paper, paras 189–91.

104 Decision, para. 882. See e.g., *mutatis mutandis*, *In re Microsoft Corporation Antitrust Litigation–Sun Microsystem, Inc.* v *Microsoft*, 333 F. 3d 517 at 521 (4th Cir. 2003), per curiam.

'the percentages of installation and use of media players' indicated a trend for media content providers to adopt WMP 'to reach the great majority of client PC users'[105] and against producing content in different standards.[106]

The CFI also rejected the claim that the tie could be 'objectively justified': although it could not be excluded that the 'de facto standardization' arising from the tying could benefit software developers and media content providers,[107] any advantage stemming from it could not counterbalance its 'market distorting foreclosing effects'[108] and could equally be secured by supplying the software as stand-alone.[109] It also rejected the arguments that the tie was consistent with 'commercial usage' or the expression of genuine innovation, since the applicant had failed to provide convincing evidence of 'technical constraints' preventing it from seeking an alternative way of distributing the product,[110] of the fact that this practice was common in the industry[111] or of any harm arising from the alleged 'fragmentation' of Windows.[112] The Court denied that by obliging it to offer a version of Windows without WMP, Microsoft's economic freedom to exploit its unique business model had been unduly restricted since the applicant could still offer an OS to which WMP was tied so long as it also supplied an 'unbundled' version of Windows.[113]

Overall, it appears that the conclusions of the CFI in the Microsoft case were consistent with the current interpretation of the conditions governing abusive tying and strongly motivated by the applicant's monopoly in the OS market.[114] However, significant questions remain as to the application of principles developed for conduct occurring in traditional industries to 'novel' markets. The CFI relied on the traditional 'separate demand' test to establish that WMP was distinct from the OS without considering whether integrating media functionality into the OS had resulted in a 'new', unitary product, offering 'advantages unavailable if the functionalities are bought separately and combined by the purchaser'.[115]

Having regard to 'coercion', the CFI emphasized the fact that Microsoft did

---

105 CFI judgment, para. 1062.
106 CFI judgment, paras 1061, 1066, 1069–70.
107 See CFI judgment, para. 1146.
108 CFI judgment, para. 1151.
109 CFI judgment, para. 1156.
110 CFI judgment, para. 936.
111 CFI judgment, para. 941.
112 CFI judgment, para. 1165.
113 CFI judgment, paras 1149–50.
114 See CFI judgment, para. 1062. See also Decision, para. 882.
115 *United States* v *Microsoft Corp*, 147 F3d at 948. See also, *mutatis mutandis*, *United States* v *Microsoft*, 253 F.3d at 90–2.

not offer a version of Windows without the media player facility as evidence of the inability of customers to obtain the two products separately[116] and declined to consider relevant the possibility for single users to install alternative media players on Microsoft-operated machines[117] without suffering any adverse economic effect from the tie.[118] These conclusions may be contrasted with cases in which the refusal to grant discounts to customers who had purchased complementary products separately from primary ones was found to be abusive because the concerned users, unlike customers willing to be 'tied' to it for the purchase of both products, were likely to suffer a significant economic disadvantage.[119] In the Microsoft case, however, the CFI refrained from examining whether Microsoft's policy allowed OEMs and end-users 'a meaningful commercial choice to buy the products separately'.[120]

With respect to the requirement of 'foreclosure', the CFI found that given the ubiquity of Windows, WMP would have enjoyed an unparalleled advantage over competing software and due to the 'network effects' characterizing the market would have eventually become the 'de facto standard' for users and media content providers through methods other than 'competition on the merits'.[121] However, it may be doubted whether the market would have actually 'tipped' in favour of WMP, due to the continuing presence of competing suppliers and of end-users willing to obtain competing software.[122]

It could also be doubted that the price applied by Microsoft on the bundle Windows-WMP was 'predatory', since making available media players free of charge for end-users is commonplace in the industry and allows users to obtain alternative software without suffering any disadvantage.[123] More generally, it could be questioned whether the dominant company should be held responsible for a breach of Article 82 EC when the foreclosing effects are mainly caused by the likely conduct of third parties, such as installers and end-users.[124]

---

116 CFI judgment, paras 961–3.

117 CFI judgment, paras 978–9.

118 CFI judgment, paras 951, 955, 960.

119 CFI judgment, para. 80. See also Chapter 4, section III.C.1–2.

120 Dolmans and Graf, n. 40 above, 231.

121 Case T-201/04, *Microsoft* v *Commission* [2007] ECR II-3601, para. 1054; see also paras 1057–8 and 1061. See also Case T-83/91 *Tetra Pak* v *Commission*, paras 137, 140; Discussion Paper, paras 188–9, 196–9.

122 See Chapter 4, section III.D.1.

123 See Discussion Paper, paras 189–91. For commentary see, *inter alia*, Ridyard, n. 19 above, 290–1.

124 See R. Pardolesi and A. Renda, 'The European Commission's Case Against Microsoft: Kill Bill?' (2004) *World Competition* 513, 561.

Finally, it is regrettable that the CFI declined to consider whether the obligation imposed on Microsoft to 'unbundle' WMP could jeopardize any gains brought to individual consumers by a 'unitary platform'[125] and instead held that any beneficial effects would have had been outweighed by WMP's unparalleled advantage in market penetration.[126] However, it is argued that this position, by not adequately taking into consideration the ability of tying to promote the growth of a popular common platform, appears inconsistent with the more 'economic-based' approach advocated by the Commission,[127] according to which 'combining two different products into a new, unitary product' would be more likely to be objectively justified than other forms of tying.[128] Consequently, despite the concerns for Microsoft's market power,[129] it is disappointing that the Court did not consider in more detail the applicant's claim of 'objective justification', especially due to its potential implications for the growth of the industry.[130]

Overall, it is concluded that the Microsoft case, while it can be read as the response of EC competition policy to the behaviour of a 'super-dominant' company in an industry characterized by peculiar competition dynamics, could have profound and as yet unpredictable implications for the interpretation of Article 82 EC. After examining the analysis of technological integration cases under the Sherman Act in the Microsoft litigation concerning Internet Explorer, the next sections will consider whether adopting a more 'benevolent' framework of analysis could accommodate the needs of innovative industries with those of genuine competition under Article 82 EC.

Technological Integration and US Antitrust Rules: the Internet Explorer Litigation

The section briefly discussed the approach of the US courts to tying and emphasized how the position under section 1 of the Sherman Act has

125 CFI judgment, para. 1110. See e.g. Evans and Padilla, n. 81 above, 510. See also, *mutatis mutandis*, Albors-Llorens, n. 62 above, 1759–60.

126 CFI judgment, para. 1151.

127 See Discussion Paper, paras 2, 84–95; also para. 205.

128 Discussion Paper, para. 205. See Chapter 4, section III.E.2, especially nn. 56 and 59 and accompanying text.

129 See CFI judgment, para. 1151.

130 See e.g. Case T-83/91 *Tetra Pak* v *Commission*, para. 119; also CFI judgement, paras 1038–39. For commentary see *inter alia*, Pardolesi and Renda, n. 124 above, 561; Cf. S. Vezzoso, 'The Incentive Balance Test in the EU Microsoft Case: A Pro-innovation "Economics-Based" Approach' (2006) *European Competition Law Review* 382, 388–90.

moved gradually from the 'per se' condemnation of this arrangement, subject to conditions of coercion and of market power enjoyed by the seller, to a 'rule of reason' analysis,[131] as in the *IBM* decision.[132] The US Court of Appeals for the District of Columbia had the opportunity to apply these standards to the case concerning the tied sale of Microsoft Internet Explorer and Windows.[133] Although the similarities with the facts at issue before the European Commission in 2004 should not be overplayed, it is nonetheless submitted that examining and comparing this case with the conclusions reached under the EC competition rules could be particularly helpful.

In its 2001 judgment the Court of Appeals for the District of Columbia considered the compatibility of the tied sales of Microsoft's PC OS together with its web-browser.[134] The claimant had alleged that Microsoft was seeking to marginalize its immediate competitors in the browser market and neutralize their ability to act as a threat to its leadership on the market for PC OS.[135] However, already at interim stage[136] the court took the different view that, far from doing 'nothing more than to metaphorically "bolt" two products together',[137] Microsoft had instead successfully proven the emergence of 'facially plausible benefits'[138] from its integrated design,[139] compared with leaving the same combination to the customer.[140] It was concluded that these positive effects should be subjected to a careful 'rule of reason' scrutiny vis-à-vis their anti-competitive implications.[141]

In its 2001 judgment the Third Circuit of the Court of Appeals reiterated that the application of the 'per se' rule established in the *Jefferson Parish Hospital* case[142] would not have been appropriate for tying arrangements in the computer software market,[143] since, especially due to the perceived inability of the judiciary to evaluate product design, there was a high risk

---

131 See n. 73 above and accompanying text. See e.g. *Jefferson Parish Hospital*, 466 U.S. 2 104 S. Ct. 1551; cf., *inter alia*, *Independent Ink Inc*, 547 U.S. 28 S. Ct. 1281 (2006).

132 *IBM*, 585 F.Supp. at 1475–6.

133 *United States* v *Microsoft Corp.*, 147 F. 3d at 935.

134 *United States* v *Microsoft*, 253 F.3d at 34.

135 *United States* v *Microsoft*, 253 F.3d at 69–71.

136 *United States* v *Microsoft*, 147 F.3d at 935.

137 147 F.3d at 949.

138 147 F.3d at 949.

139 147 F.3d at 952.

140 147 F.3d at 950.

141 147 F.3d at 951.

142 *Jefferson Parish Hospital*, 466 U.S. 2 at 1556.

143 *United States* v *Microsoft*, 253 F.3d at 90–1.

that it could 'stunt valuable innovation'.[144] The court recognized that the integration of new functionalities on an existing 'platform' was common in the software industry and led to hitherto novel efficiencies.[145] It therefore held that a 'per se' rule would not be suitable to 'technologically dynamic markets where product development is especially unlikely to follow an easily foreseen linear pattern', such as that for 'platform software'.[146] Instead, a 'rule of reason' approach would grant 'the first mover an opportunity to demonstrate that an efficiency gain'[147] could counterbalance any negative effects caused by the limitation on the freedom of choice enjoyed by its customers.[148]

The Court of Appeals acknowledged that the patterns of innovation of the software industry fostered the emergence of *prima facie* beneficial 'common platforms'[149] and that the 'addition of new functionalities to existing programs' responded to consumer demand and to the pressure from other competitors to develop attractive, innovative products.[150] Consequently, it held that any obligation to 'unbundle' software previously forming part of a unitary platform should be assessed carefully to avoid 'restraining functionalities of adjacent markets from being integrated in a sole', innovative product.[151] The appeal was allowed and the case remanded for decision on the merits in the light of this 'rule of reason' approach.[152]

Although the limited purview of this chapter does not allow any further comment on the outcome of the US proceedings against Microsoft, it is suggested that in assessing technological integration the US courts were concerned with securing the technical benefits arising from the creation of a common platform offering upgraded non-browsing features, which could not have been obtained only through a stand-alone browser.[153]

Another relevant factor was the lack of prejudice to the freedom of individual Windows users to deploy an alternative Internet browser and

---

144 253 F.3d at 92.

145 253 F.3d at 93.

146 253 F.3d at 94.

147 253 F.3d at 92.

148 253 F.3d at 92. See also at 94–5.

149 253 F.3d at 94.

150 C. Gastle and S. Boughs, '*Microsoft III* and the Metes and Bounds of Software Design and Technological Tying Doctrine' (2001) *Virginia Journal of Law and Technology* 7, 23–4.

151 *United States* v *Microsoft Corp.*, 147 F.3d at 952, per curiam. For commentary see, *inter alia*, Montagnani, n. 57 above, 641.

152 *United States* v *Microsoft*, 253 F.3d at 95–6.

153 Evans and Padilla, n. 3 above, 401.

the resulting lack of consumer harm.[154] Despite acknowledging that the consumers would have had fewer incentives to download competing software and that their 'inertia [could have worked] against a competitor',[155] it was argued that the requirement of 'coercion' had not been met and that, in any event, due to the combined sale, users had benefited from a 'free product . . . at zero research costs'[156] and therefore any anticompetitive effects would have been offset by the efficiencies generated by its integration into the operating system.[157]

Although the analogies between the two cases should not be exaggerated, it is clear that, just like Internet Explorer, WMP was available free of charge as part of the 'bundled' version of Windows and end-users remained free to obtain and use other competing software.[158] Consequently, it could be argued that the same degree of caution shown by the US courts toward choices of 'software design' could be justified for the integration of media functionalities into the OS.[159] The CFI instead declined to consider whether the availability of alternative software on similar conditions to those of WMP was compatible with the requirement of 'coercion'[160] or whether the consumer welfare-enhancing effects resulting from the expansion of Windows could have counterbalanced the adverse impact on competition from other media player software caused by the unavailability of a channel of distribution comparable to pre-installation. [161]

It is acknowledged that due to the costly and fact-intensive nature of a 'rule of reason' type of inquiry, the approach preferred by the CFI is undoubtedly attractive.[162] However, this position could eventually penalize pro-efficiency practices in 'non-linear' industries.[163] Accordingly, this prompts the question of how to frame an alternative test reflecting more accurately the realities of innovation-driven industries and reconcile the needs of technical development with the limits of the enforcement of

---

[154] J. Lopatka and W. Page, 'Monopolisation, Innovation and Consumer Welfare' (2000–2001) *George Washington Law Review* 368, 400–1.

[155] Lopatka and Page, n. 154 above, 404.

[156] Lopatka and Page, n. 154 above, 404.

[157] Lopatka and Page, n. 154 above, 404.

[158] Decision, paras 830–2.

[159] See *United States* v *Microsoft*, 253 F.3d at 94.

[160] CFI judgment, paras 961–3.

[161] CFI judgment, paras 1054, 1057–58, 1061.

[162] See, *mutatis mutandis*, *Independent Ink*, 547 U.S. 28 at 1289–91. For commentary, see Jones, n. 71 above, 734.

[163] Evans and Padilla, n. 81 above, 510. See also, *mutatis mutandis*, Albors-Llorens, n. 62 above, 1759–60.

the applicable antitrust rules. These issues will be addressed in the next sections.

4. TYING, TECHNOLOGICAL INTEGRATION AND THE NEW ECONOMY: GOING BEYOND THE MICROSOFT CASE?

In Search of an Alternative Approach to Technological Tying: the Requirements of 'Separate Product', 'Coercion' and 'Foreclosure'

The previous section illustrated how some US courts, conscious of the inherently pro-competitive effects of combined sales in the IT industry, prefer a 'rule of reason' approach to tying to assess whether the integration of two hitherto separate products results in a 'new product' characterized by functionalities which cannot be obtained if the 'assemblage' is left to the end-user.[164] By contrast, it is submitted that the position adopted by the Commission and the CFI may not adequately reflect the complexities of product design or the need to preserve the incentive to innovate in the software market.[165]

Despite acknowledging the constant and rapid evolution of this industry,[166] the CFI established 'separate demand' indirectly from the evidence of supply of competing media player software,[167] thus creating the risk that pro-efficiency arrangements may be outlawed and technical development jeopardized.[168] With respect to 'coercion', instead, this position, based on a literal interpretation of Article 82(d) EC,[169] does not appear entirely consistent with earlier decisions and with the views expressed in the 2005 Discussion Paper.

The Commission had already found in *Hilti* that the policy of reducing discounts to customers willing to purchase only the tying product

---

[164] *United States* v *Microsoft*, 147 F.3d at 948. For commentary see, *inter alia*, Lopatka and Page, n. 55 above, 199–200.

[165] Case C-333/94 P *Tetra Pak* v *Commission*, para. 37. See also CFI judgment, paras 939–41. For commentary see, *inter alia*, D. Evans and J. Padilla, 'Designing Antitrust Rules for Assessing Unilateral Practices: A Neo-Chicago Approach' (2005) 72 *University of Chicago Law Review* 73, 80–1; also, Lopatka and Page, n. 55 above, 200–1; see Chapter 4, section IV.

[166] CFI judgment, para. 913.

[167] CFI judgment, paras 922–4.

[168] CFI judgment, paras 940–1, 948. For commentary see, *inter alia*, Lopatka and Page, n. 55 above, 199–200.

[169] CFI judgment, paras 961, 967, 969–70.

amounted to an abuse of a dominant position,[170] because, although in principle 'cartridge-only orders' were possible, purchasers, unless they wanted to forgo the discounts, were de facto obliged to buy the products jointly.[171] Although on appeal the CFI and the Court of Justice did not comment on this point,[172] the Commission Decision appears to support the view that, to meet the 'coercion' requirement, the Commission would have to prove that by refusing the combined purchase, the customers would have suffered adverse financial consequences.[173]

Consequently, it could be argued that since WMP was available for free and end-users could use alternative media software without any disadvantage, the requirement of 'coercion' would not be satisfied.[174] It is also suggested that Microsoft's policy of offering WMP at no extra charge to all the purchasers of Windows, being consistent with that adopted by other suppliers, would be consistent with the industry patterns and thus not 'predatory'.[175]

The CFI's overall approach to the concept of coercion may be contrasted with the views adopted by some US courts. As was illustrated above, cases like *Jefferson Parish Hospital* and *Paladin* suggest that in the light of the 'rule of reason' scrutiny, this requirement would be met if the seller enjoyed significant market power and its customers would not have accepted the combined sale if they had not been threatened with a significant economic disadvantage resulting from their separate purchase.[176] It is therefore argued that the CFI should have opted for a less literal interpretation of coercion requiring proof that the customer is both under a contractual obligation to purchase two or more products together and that they would suffer a financial disadvantage from not using the tied product or seeking an alternative.[177]

As regards the requirement that the tie must have 'market distorting foreclosing effects', the theory that, due to the combined sale of WMP

---

170 Commission Decision 88/138/EC *Eurofix-Bauco/Hilti* [1988] OJ L65/19, para. 75.

171 Commission Decision 88/138/EC, para. 75. See also para. 80.

172 See Case T-30/89 *Hilti AG* v *Commission*, paras 100–1.

173 See e.g. Evans and Padilla, n. 3 above, 505.

174 See e.g. Dolmans and Graf, n. 40 above, 231.

175 Discussion Paper, paras 189–90; see also Evans and Padilla, n. 3 above, 505–6.

176 See e.g., *mutatis mutandis*, Evans and Padilla, n. 3 above, 504–5. See also, *mutatis mutandis*, *Independent Ink,* 547 U.S. 28 at 1289–91 See n. 67 above and accompanying text.

177 See e.g. *mutatis mutandis*, Evans and Padilla, n. 3 above, 504–5. Also Chapter 4, n. 61 and accompanying text.

with Windows, the media player market would have eventually 'tipped' in favour of Microsoft's software[178] was criticized as partly inconsistent with the available evidence proving that competing suppliers had remained active on the market, and as holding Microsoft responsible for the conduct of third parties.[179]

It is added that the CFI did not examine exhaustively whether the ability of media content providers to 'multi-home', that is, to supply their output in a variety of formats to reach the widest possible audience,[180] could have prevented Microsoft from squeezing competitors out the media player market. Commentators argued that multi-homing could have allowed Microsoft's competitors to maintain their 'audience' and thus minimize the 'lock-in effects' of the tie.[181]

More generally, it is submitted that the conclusions concerning market foreclosure do not appear to take into sufficient consideration the circumstance that in a market characterized by 'positive feedback externalities' a trend exists toward competition 'for the market', rather than 'on the market', as a result of which a de facto standard, which would dominate the market for a limited length of time, would emerge and become 'entrenched' until a 'better' alternative succeeds in displacing it.[182] It is thus suggested that while being innovative does not 'excuse' a powerful undertaking from respecting the competition rules or from not impairing competition,[183] targeting the 'generation leader' without assessing carefully whether the possibility remained for a new, 'future leader' to emerge, would not be entirely consistent with the market's innovation focus.[184] Accordingly, it is suggested that a rigorous, dynamic assessment of tying should always be undertaken.[185]

However, both the 2007 Microsoft judgment and the 2005 Commission Discussion Paper suggest that the existence of positive network

---

178 CFI judgment, paras 1038–39.

179 CFI judgment, paras 1054, 1057–58, 1061. See, *inter alia*, Pardolesi, and Renda, n. 124 above, 526–8 and 564–5; also Montagnani, n. 57 above, 625–6.

180 See e.g., *mutatis mutandis*, S. Bomse and S. Westrich, 'Both Sides Now: Buyer Damage Claims in Antitrust Actions Involving 'Two Sided' Markets' (2005) *Columbia Business Law Review* 643, 655–6.

181 See Evans, n. 60 above, 370–1.

182 See, *inter alia*, Office of Fair Trading, n. 60 above, paras 5.54–5.56. Cf. Discussion Paper, para. 199.

183 See e.g. Evans and Padilla, n. 165 above, 83–4. Also, Office of Fair Trading, n. 60 above, paras 5.68–5.69.

184 See, *inter alia*, Evans and Schmalensee, n. 60 above, 47–8.

185 See e.g. Evans and Schmalensee, n. 60 above, 23; also Lopatka and Page, n. 55 above, 187–8.

externalities is regarded by the CFI and the Commission as reinforcing a finding of abuse, rather than a circumstance to take into careful consideration to exclude this finding.[186] Despite the exceptional features of the Microsoft case, it could be doubted that the current approach to foreclosure adopted under Article 82 EC could be entirely compatible with the needs of new economy markets.[187] The CFI judgment also illustrated that strictly related to the consideration of the 'separate product' requirement is the assessment of the 'efficiency benefits' arising from the tied sale of the two programs.[188] These issues will be addressed in the next section.

Looking for Alternative Approaches: 'Objective Justification' and the 'Efficiency Defence'

It was illustrated earlier that the Commission and the CFI rejected Microsoft's claim that the technological integration of WMP into Windows could have any significant beneficial effects or constitute the outcome of innovative design choices.[189] Consequently, although it was characterized by exceptional circumstances and therefore would not be easily applicable to other cases, the Microsoft case may constitute a 'dangerous precedent' for the interpretation of the concept of 'objective justification' and of the requirements of the 'efficiency defence' since its emphasis on the finding of market power 'overshadows' the assessment of the pro- and the anti-competitive effects of 'novel' forms of product design. It is therefore suggested that a more flexible approach, perhaps similar to that adopted in the US Microsoft case, may be more suitable to assess the legality of the tying of new software functionalities to a common platform.

As was illustrated earlier, the Court of Appeals for the District of Columbia, conscious of the limits of the hitherto established 'separate demand test', took the view that 'backward looking enquiries' of separate consumer demand and 'direct industry custom' should be linked to the assessment of the efficiencies stemming from innovative integration[190] and

---

186 See Discussion Paper, para. 199; CFI judgement, para. 1151.

187 See, *mutatis mutandis*, Office of Fair Trading, n. 60 above, para. 1.6; also, Ahlborn, Evans and Padilla, n. 13 above, 323–4.

188 CFI judgment, paras 916; 960–1. See also Case C-333/94 P *Tetra Pak* v *Commission*, para. 37.

189 CFI judgment, paras 1152, 1155, 1159–60, 1165–6.

190 *United States* v *Microsoft Corp.*, 253 F.3d at 140. See Lopatka and Page, n. 55 above, 204.

that, therefore, there should be 'no presumption on the part of competition authorities that tying . . . [is] anti-competitive, even when undertaken by firms with monopoly power'.[191]

Although it is undeniable that this 'rule of reason' analysis[192] is very likely to prove complex and resource-intensive, its adoption would reconcile the needs of genuine competition with unhindered innovation. Consequently, some commentators suggested a 'simplified' rule of reason approach, addressing whether an anti-competitive effect is 'possible', whether it is 'plausible' and whether the arrangement has positive effects that offset any adverse impact on competition.[193]

The first condition assesses the overall anti-competitive effects of the practice, having regard especially to the likelihood that due to the technological integration competition would be foreclosed to the advantage of the dominant undertaking[194] and concentrates on whether the tying supplier enjoys market power and, if so, to what extent, whether the relevant market is competitive, whether the firm is 'committed' to the practice, whether any competitors are able to match it[195] and whether any buyer power exists.[196]

If the tie satisfies the criteria laid down by the first 'screen', it would have to fulfil the second 'tier' of this assessment,[197] i.e. whether the arrangement makes entry into the relevant market costly for potential competitors who, as a result, cannot supply existing customers with products of higher quality vis-à-vis the tied product, either because they do not find it profitable to enter the two markets simultaneously or because they would have found it more economically rational to enter the market for the complementary good first and, thereafter, that for the primary product,[198] or, finally, because customers who do not gain any utility from the tied product cannot refuse it.[199]

Finally, if it is established that the combined sale has anti-competitive effects that are both 'possible' and 'plausible', the antitrust authority will have to assess whether its pro-competitive effects offset the negative impact on the relevant market, having regard to its likely efficiencies, to any less

---

191 Ahlborn, Evans and Padilla, n. 13 above, 329.
192 *United States* v *Microsoft Corp.*, 253 F.3d at 140.
193 253 F.3d at 330.
194 253 F.3d at 334.
195 253 F.3d at 331–2.
196 253 F.3d at 332–3.
197 253 F.3d at 332–3.
198 253 F.3d at 334–5.
199 253 F.3d at 335–6.

restrictive alternatives and to whether these benefits can counterbalance any anti-competitive effects.[200]

It is submitted that this 'structured' test is likely to prove more reliable and flexible to assess technological integration. However, the unwillingness of the EU courts to allow arguments that a *prima facie* exclusionary practice could have beneficial effects for consumer welfare and product innovation[201] raises issues as to whether the proposed approach could be reconciled with the interpretation of Article 82 EC in tying cases.

It is suggested that the approach advocated by the Commission in its 2005 Discussion Paper could be interpreted as to incorporate a more flexible assessment of tying, at least in cases not involving super-dominant companies.[202] It could be argued that the assessment of whether the practice results in a substantial elimination of competition from the relevant market due to the degree of market power enjoyed by the dominant company and of the existence of barriers to entry is broadly consistent with the first prong of the 'structured rule of reason' test examined above, since it seeks to analyse whether it would be 'possible' for the practice to distort competition on the market for the supply of the tied product.[203]

The assessment of whether the tying arrangement is indispensable to achieve the efficiency benefits sought by the company, instead, appears similar to the 'plausibility' test advocated by the 'structured rule of reason'. It is suggested that by examining whether there are any less restrictive alternatives to the practice, this prong of the 'efficiency defence' focuses on whether the 'theory' that the practice has pro-competitive effects and is especially compatible with a substantial degree of competition is borne out by the facts of the individual case.[204]

The other requirement that any positive effects stemming from tying must outweigh its negative impact on competition appears consistent with the third element of the above approach since it requires the analysis of whether the dominant company has, due to the efficiency gains, an incentive 'to act pro-competitively for the benefit of consumers' by passing on any savings obtained from the practice.[205] According to the Commission's 2005 Discussion Paper, however, this incentive is strictly related to the degree of competitive pressure to which the dominant undertaking is

---

200 Evans and Padilla, n. 3 above, 516–17.
201 Discussion Paper, paras 88–9.
202 Discussion Paper, paras 86–7.
203 Discussion Paper, paras 91–2.
204 Discussion Paper, para. 86.
205 Discussion Paper, para. 87.

exposed and especially to its market power:[206] the greater its economic strength, the less likely the 'objective justification'.[207]

Although this view is consistent with the goal of Article 82 EC, namely protecting the competition process,[208] it should not be stretched as far as to 'overshadow' any welfare-enhancing effects and should be reconciled with the needs of the 'innovation fuelled' competition in the software industry and with the consumer benefits resulting from the 'race for the market'.[209] The Commission also appears to take into account only marginally the ability of end-users to 'react' to the negative effects of tying arrangements.[210] However, it is submitted that this assessment would be indispensable to examine whether, respectively, individual users are able to access and obtain alternatives to the tied product, and media content providers can counter the 'standardizing' effects of the tie by producing output that can be 'read' by a variety of formats.

In the light of these considerations, it can be concluded that the broadly framed prohibition of tying by dominant undertakings, adopted in the Microsoft case, does not allow a full reflection of the pro-competitive and welfare-enhancing effects of these practices in the IT industry. It is thus suggested that, at least in cases not involving super-dominant companies, a more flexible approach should be adopted, perhaps along the lines of the more 'economics-based' approach advocated by the Commission, which could be reframed to reconcile the objectives of Article 82 EC with the assessment of the characteristics of new economy markets.

5. TYING IN THE IT INDUSTRY: WHERE DO WE GO FROM THE MICROSOFT CASE? TENTATIVE CONCLUSIONS

The analysis conducted so far has attempted to address some of the issues arising from tying practices on the part of dominant undertakings in highly technological industries. It was argued that since tying can have clear economic benefits both for suppliers and for consumers, it should not in principle be prohibited without taking into account its impact on competition. Especially in 'innovation fuelled' markets, where the progressive integration of new functionalities on existing 'common platforms'

206 Discussion Paper, para. 90.
207 Discussion Paper, para. 90.
208 Discussion Paper, para. 91.
209 See, *inter alia*, Evans and Padilla, n. 81 above, 512.
210 Discussion Paper, para. 90.

characterizes technical progress, this practice, if undertaken by dominant companies, should not be 'presumed' to be illegal.

However, the recent Microsoft judgment demonstrated that the application of principles developed for 'classical' cases of tying to innovative forms of technical development may jeopardize progress in an industry where product design choices are often complex and unpredictable. Although this case dealt with extraordinary circumstances and therefore its conclusions may not be easily applicable to future cases, it illustrated the difficulties faced by the antitrust enforcement authorities in scrutinizing unilateral behaviour.

Accordingly, it was submitted that any competition analysis of tying in 'novel' industries should reconcile the protection and enhancement of the competitive process with the need to safeguard the drive toward technical development in 'knowledge based', R&D driven markets and should therefore fully analyse its pro- and anti-competitive effects. Therefore, it was suggested that to achieve these objectives, the existing standards, currently focused on a 'formal' assessment of what constitutes 'coercion', on a 'static analysis' of the 'separate product' requirement and on a restrictive reading of the notions of 'objective justification' and of the 'efficiency defence', should be replaced by a more flexible framework of scrutiny.

This chapter argued, also in the light of a comparison with the principles developed by the case law of some US courts, that the new test should concentrate on the actual impact of the practice on competition on the relevant market, on the likely harm to consumers and on whether anti-competitive impact can be counterbalanced by efficiency- and welfare-enhancing effects.

However, the continuing reliance on the concept of 'special responsibility' of dominant companies and the reluctance to read the concept of 'objective justification' more generously cast doubt on the possibility that an alternative approach could emerge. Despite its exceptional nature, the Microsoft case demonstrates the EU courts' reluctance to prefer more 'forward looking' frameworks of analysis of novel economic realities to 'tried and tested' approaches. It is therefore hoped that the call made by the Competition Commissioner, Neelie Kroes, for the adoption of a more 'open minded' approach to the assessment of *prima facie* exclusionary practices will be put in practice by DG Competition in its future activity.[211]

---

[211] See 'Exclusionary Abuses of Dominance: The European Commission's Enforcement Priorities', speech given at the Fordham University Symposium, 25 September 2008, SPEECH/08/47.

11. Economic aspects of the Microsoft case: networks, interoperability and competition

Maria J. Gil-Moltó

1. INTRODUCTION

Microsoft has been under scrutiny of both the Department of Justice in the United States and the European Competition Commission in the European Union in two complex cases that spanned over a number of years. These cases have been followed with great interest by economists, both academic economists and practitioners, all around the world. This is perhaps due to the fact that the computing industry is an industry in which a number of economic arguments such as network effects, complementarities and R&D incentives interplay and affect the effective level of competition. In fact, there is a feeling among economists that we can learn a lot about strategic behaviour in rapidly changing environments by understanding Microsoft's strategies.[1]

In the EC case, two of Microsoft's strategies were investigated: first, Microsoft's refusal to supply the essential information to make Sun Microsystems's work group server operating system, Solaris, compatible with Windows. This investigation followed the formal complaint by Sun Microsystems to the European Commission, in which it accused Microsoft of behaving anti-competitively by denying this necessary information. Microsoft was accused of trying to reduce the interoperability of Windows with other products produced by competitors in order to leverage its market power in the PC operating systems market onto the work group server operating systems market, a market in which Microsoft was also active.

The second issue involved in the case was Microsoft's practice of tying Windows Media Player (WMP) with Windows operating system, two

[1] D. Carlton, 'The Lessons from Microsoft' (2001) *Business Economics* (January) 47.

complementary products. Microsoft was accused of abusing its dominant position in the PC operating systems market to foreclose competition in the media player market. The investigation of this practice was initiated by the Commission on its own initiative, that is, without a third party filing a formal complaint against Microsoft. This second issue is reminiscent of the US case, in which Microsoft was under investigation for tying Windows with Internet Explorer. Although the two practices assessed by the Commission (denying the essential information to achieve compatibility and tying) are quite different, they also share some similarities, as both can be seen as ways to leverage market power onto a complementary market. Moreover, in both cases, the existence of network economies is at the core of the discussion.

The Commission's duty is to enforce the EC competition rules on anti-competitive business practices and abuses of monopoly power within the entire European Union when competition and the free market are affected. The Commission can require changes in the firm's behaviour (the so-called remedies) and also impose fines.

On 24 March 2004, the Commission published its Decision in the case,[2] concluding that Microsoft had breached EC law by leveraging its monopoly power in the PC operating systems market onto the work group server operating systems market and onto the market for media players. The remedies imposed on Microsoft were as follows. First, Microsoft was required to disclose to its competitors the necessary information to make their products interoperable with Windows operating system.[3] Secondly, Microsoft was ordered to untie Windows and WMP. In other words, Microsoft was ordered to offer to PC manufacturers a version of Windows without WMP. In addition to those remedies, a fine of €497,000,000 was imposed on Microsoft for abusing its dominant position in the European Union.[4]

Mario Monti, who was the European Competition Commissioner at

---

2 Commission Decision 2007/53/EC of 24 March 2004 [2007] OJ L32/23 ('the Decision').

3 It is important to clarify that Microsoft was not asked to disclose the source code of Windows but only 'complete and accurate specifications for the protocols' used by Windows work group servers in order to interoperate with Windows.

4 Microsoft appealed to the European Court of Justice without success. Microsoft was also fined for non-compliance, i.e., for not implementing the remedial measures, at later stages. The largest non-compliance fine imposed on Microsoft amounted €899,000,000. In May 2008, Microsoft appealed again (this time to the European Court of First Instance) with the objective of overturning the €899,000,000 fine.

that time, stated that the Decision would restore the conditions for fair competition in the markets concerned. The Commissioner also expressed the EU's concerns about Microsoft's general business model, which was thought to deter innovation and to reduce consumer choice. The Commissioner expressed his conviction that the Decision would establish clear principles for the future conduct of Microsoft.

Generally, we can say that competition policy aims at ensuring that competition in the marketplace is not restricted in a way that is detrimental to society.[5] The basic underlying principle is that a monopoly is allocatively inefficient. In other words, it leads to a loss in surplus (or deadweight loss). This constitutes the rationale behind policy-makers' interest in creating the conditions that make markets as competitive as possible, as the lower the degree of competition, the less (allocatively) efficient the market is. However, the usefulness of this argument in guiding competition policy is rather limited, especially in R&D intensive industries. Allocative efficiency is related to the market performance in 'static' terms. However, one should also consider the dynamic effects of competition in order to assess the welfare effects of monopolies or, by extension, of oligopolies. For example, it is far from clear that innovation rates and market power are negatively related, as firms will not have incentives to conduct R&D unless they can appropriate the returns to their investments.

The objective of this chapter is to provide a broad picture of what economics can say about competition in computer industries in general and about the EC Microsoft case in particular. To achieve this aim, we will review the academic contributions within the economics literature that are relevant to the case. Due to space constraints, we will focus on the first of the two practices, that is, Microsoft's refusal to supply competitors with the essential information to achieve interoperability with Windows.

To lay the foundations for the rest of the chapter, first we will describe the different elements in computer systems and how they give rise to separate but complementary markets. The definition of a market is a crucial step in the antitrust process and we will therefore discuss this definition in the case. Next, we will discuss the nature of competition in computer markets. It is relevant to note that although there are only a small number of firms in each of the computer markets, this does not necessary imply lack of competition. In fact, many analysts regard computer markets as highly dynamic and exposed to a great deal of competition. The type of competition in these markets can be defined as Schumpeterian. In this

---

[5] M. Motta, *Competition Policy: Theory and Practice* (Cambridge: Cambridge University Press, 2004).

chapter, we will describe the dynamics of competition in Schumpeterian markets.

Since one of the reasons why computer markets are Schumpeterian is the existence of network externalities, we will provide an overview of the literature on network economics and will use its main results to discuss the Microsoft case, paying particular attention to the (potential) reasons for Microsoft's actions. We will discuss the argument that the case can be seen as competition between systems with network externalities: The Microsoft system versus other systems based on servers. Typically in such cases, the incumbent firm (dominant platform) has incentives to deny interoperability in order to protect its market dominance. We will discuss the incentives to degrade interoperability as studied in the economics literature. Finally, we will consider the remedies imposed by the Commission and their implications in terms of innovation and welfare, which are far from univocal.

The structure of the chapter is as follows: in section 2, we will describe the elements integrating computer systems. In section 3, we will define what network economies are and the extent of their existence in computer markets. In section 4, we will analyse the market definition in the Microsoft case. In section 5, we will discuss the Schumpeterian nature of competition in computer markets. In section 6, we will discuss economic contributions regarding foreclosure and interoperability. Section 7 is devoted to the innovation and welfare implications of the remedies imposed on Microsoft. Section 8 summarizes the chapter and provides some final remarks.

2. COMPUTER SYSTEMS: DEFINITION AND ELEMENTS

A computer system is constituted by hardware and software. The hardware consists of the physical components of the system and the software is the computer programs. Software can be systems software or applications software. An application is a piece of software that targets a specific user's need, for example, word-processing or playing music. Two examples of Microsoft applications are Word and WMP for word-processing and playing music respectively. The purpose of systems software is to control the hardware of the computer and link the applications and the hardware. This link can only work if both the applications and the systems software use the same applications programming interface (API). Some examples of interfaces are UNIX API or Java APIs.

Users and sellers of hardware and software normally interact around 'platforms'. According to the definition in the Linux Information Project

(LINFO),[6] the term 'platform' refers to (i) the type of processor and/or other hardware on which a given operating system or applications program runs, (ii) the type of operating system or (iii) the combination of the type of hardware and the type of operating system running on it. Examples of platforms are IBM System 360, Apple Macintosh or Windows, the platform controlled by Microsoft. For the purpose of this chapter, we will use the second meaning of 'platform', i.e. the type of operating system.[7]

Systems software can also be called 'platform software', as it serves as a platform for all the applications that use the same interface as the operating system. For example, the interface needed to interact with Windows operating system is the Win 32 API, also property of Microsoft. To allow any software application to function in a computer using Windows, it would be necessary to make it compatible with the interface Win 32 API.

Typically, computer users will interact among themselves. In order to do so, their computers will have to be interconnected, constituting a network, typically through a server computer. In such a situation, a further piece of software is needed, the so-called 'work group server operating system', which enables the communication between (non-server) computers and servers. The 'non-server' computers connected to the server are often referred to as 'client' computers. As mentioned above, the first of the issues in the Microsoft case concerned Microsoft's refusal to supply to Sun, a work group server operating system producer, the necessary information to make its product, Solaris (which is UNIX based) interoperable with Windows.

It is obvious that the different elements of the systems described above are goods that are complements from the point of view of the consumer, as they have to be used in conjunction. Two goods are complements if their demands are positively related. For example, take Windows and

---

[6] See www.linfo.org/platform.html.

[7] Interestingly, different platforms are vertically integrated to different extents. See T. Bresnahan and S. Greenstein, 'Technological Competition and the Structure of the Computer Industry' (1999) *Journal of Industrial Economics* 1, and D.S. Evans, A. Hagiu and R. Schmalensee, *A Survey of the Economic Role of Software Platforms in Computer-Based Industries* RIETI Discussion Paper No. 04032 (2004). In the case of mainframe computers, there is a single platform offered by a single firm (IBM) with high levels of vertical integration (including hardware). In the case of PCs, the IBM PC platform was initially controlled by IBM, although later it became controlled by two other companies, one active in the (applications and operating systems) software market, Microsoft, and the other, Intel, in the microprocessors market. For an interesting discussion of the role played by the extent of vertical integration on the success of different platforms see Evans, Hagiu and Schmalensee, *ibid.*

the applications for Windows. If there is a decrease in the price of the operating system Windows, this would give rise not only to an increase in demand for windows but also to an increase in the demand for applications supported by Windows. The existence of complementarities between products has important implications for the market power that a firm dominant in one of the markets can extend into the complementary market. It is also relevant to note that, given the need that computer users have of interacting with other computer users, computer systems will be subject to network effects. In the next section we describe the nature of those effects.

3. NETWORK EFFECTS

Since computer users interact among themselves, computer systems or platforms are subject to network effects. The higher the number of users of one specific platform or system, the higher the demand for this platform is. This is a typical example of a network effect, because the utility the system provides to each individual user increases with the total number of users of the same platform. The intuition is clear: computer users frequently share documents created on their own computers with other users. Consumers therefore benefit from an increase in the number of users of their platform, as this reduces incompatibility risks and costs. In fact, the above is an example of 'direct' network effect.

Additionally, an 'indirect' network effect arises when a particular feature of a network is likely to be improved in a large network.[8] For example, the number of applications written for a given platform increases with the number of users of this platform; therefore a user of a given platform would benefit from an increase in the number of users of that platform through the wider range of available software.

It is worth mentioning that the wide availability of software is, in any case, a major determinant of the success of platforms. Interestingly, Apple and Microsoft have tried to encourage the writing of applications for their platforms. For example, in the late 1990s, Microsoft was spending over US$250,000,000 yearly on developer-related activities, such as training programs, marketing or research.[9] By helping developers, they were facilitating the creation of new software applications which, in turn,

---

[8] See S. Scotchmer, *Innovation and Incentives* (Cambridge, MA: MIT Press, 2004).

[9] Evans, Hagiu and Schmalensee, n. 7 above.

increased the likelihood of new users adopting Windows. In addition, the availability of applications available for a platform would constitute an entry barrier for other operating systems/platforms.

All in all, it is important to bear in mind that not only the existence of network economies but also the size of the networks (or in our case, the number of users in a platform) crucially affects the competitive environment in an industry. Further, there are interesting strategic implications of making a network or platform compatible or incompatible with another competing network. We will discuss this issue in more detail in section 6. Now we turn our attention to the definition of the relevant markets in the Microsoft case.

4. DEFINITION OF RELEVANT MARKETS

The first stage in the assessment of any antitrust case is the definition of the relevant market. A market comprises all the products or services that are substitutable by the consumer. In principle, based on the description of computer systems given above, the markets for the different elements of the computer system should be considered to be separate (although complementary) markets. The Commission identified two markets as relevant for the Microsoft case and separate from the point of view of the consumer: the market for (client) PC operating systems and the market for work group server operating systems. The Commission considered that the operating systems created for servers could not be used on PC hardware. Their argument was that such use would either not be technically viable or would deprive the user of hardware or software capabilities. Further, the Commission stated that the work group server operating systems fulfilled a specific demand need and neither other server operating systems nor PC operating systems were realistic substitutes for them.[10]

The definition of the relevant market made by the Commission was based on qualitative (mostly technical) judgements. As far as I am aware, no statistical or econometric study was conducted by or on behalf of the Commission to estimate the demand on the two identified markets. Such an analysis could have been used to test the validity of the qualitative analysis referred above. Interestingly, Van Reenen conducted an empirical study to estimate market level elasticities for servers, the results of

[10] The Commission conducted a market enquiry to study the substitutability between different types of servers. For more details on this and Microsoft's statements, see Decision, section 5.11.2.11.

which lend support to the Commission's view that work group servers and their operating systems are a separate market from other servers or other types of operating systems (such as PC operating systems).[11] Van Reenen's estimates of demand elasticities for work group server systems (hardware and software) are relatively low,[12] indicating that a price increase in the work group server operating systems would not affect dramatically the quantity demanded of work group servers. This implies that there are no good substitutes for work group servers from the consumers' point of view.

The empirical analysis of the work group server operating systems is more difficult as its demand is derived from the demand for the work group server hardware, as Van Reenen highlights. Further, hardware and software are often sold as bundles. This implies that it is difficult or impossible to collect good data on prices of server software. It can be argued, however, that given that the demand for work group server operating systems is derived from that of the work group server, if the latter is inelastic, the former has to be even more inelastic, therefore showing the existence of a market for work group server operating systems which is separate from those of other types of operating systems (server and client).

Apart from making any judgements about demand-side substitutability, it is also necessary to consider the separation from the point of view of the supply in order to reach any conclusions regarding the separation of the PC operating systems and the work group server software markets. Two markets are deemed to be separate from the point of view of the supply if a small but significant permanent price increase in one of the markets would not lead to entry into that market by firms active in the other market.[13] In the absence of entry barriers, such a price increase would attract entry. However, the need to incur high development costs or the existence of network externalities, either direct or indirect, may act as barriers to entry and make entry unprofitable. The Commission rejected the existence of supply-side substitutes for PC operating systems by concluding that software developers in adjacent markets would not be able to start producing PC operating systems without substantial costs and risks. Similar arguments were used to support the same conclusion regarding work group server operating systems.

---

[11] J. Van Reenen, *Is there a Market for Workgroup Servers?*', Centre for Economic Performance Discussion Paper No. 650 (2004).

[12] Often the work group servers are sold as a hardware and software bundle.

[13] Markets which are close either geographically or technologically.

5. NATURE OF COMPETITION IN THE COMPUTER INDUSTRY

The prominence of Microsoft in the computer industry is obvious. Their market share in the operating systems market was at the time of the antitrust case as high as 95 per cent according to the Commission. Was Microsoft therefore an unthreatened (quasi) monopoly at that time?

It is difficult to deny that there is competition in the industry, even in those segments where there are 'quasi-monopolies' such as the PC systems segment. The computing industry is a rapidly evolving, constantly changing technological sector. Often companies become dominant, but their dominance is contested by new entrants (normally, as a result of technological innovations). In some cases these new companies even manage to displace the former incumbents. Bresnahan[14] and Bresnahan and Greenstein[15] illustrate with examples how the computer industry has followed those dynamics. This type of competition dynamics can be labelled as 'Schumpeterian'.

The Schumpeterian paradigm describes competition in a dynamic fashion from an evolutionary perspective. An incumbent firm holds a dominant position until a firm enters the market with a successful innovation and displaces the former incumbent. This theory therefore explains progress and economic growth by means of 'creative destruction'.[16] Innovation, in Schumpeterian terms, is only a source of temporary market power. In the computing industry, there are only a small number of software platforms at any one time due to the existence of network economies. Further, sunk costs incurred by both consumers and software application developers imply that the incumbents in the platform markets will enjoy market dominance until a successful innovator appears in the market. The length of time during which an incumbent can hold its dominant position can be assimilated to a technological era.

This leads to a second question regarding the successful innovator: where can such a firm come from? An innovator may come from a neighbouring market, for example, the market for a complementary good. According to Bresnahan, technologies spend years without competing

---

14 T. Bresnahan, *The Right Remedy*, Stanford Law and Economics Olin Working Paper No. 233 (2002).

15 T. Bresnahan and S. Greenstein, 'Technological Competition and the Structure of the Computer Industry' (1999) *Journal of Industrial Economics* 1.

16 For more details see J. Schumpeter, *Capitalism, Socialism and Democracy* (New York: Harper, 1975; first published 1942).

with each other by serving different segments of the market.[17] These different technologies can become competitors by technological or market change – this is the so-called 'indirect entry'.

If we believe that competition in the computing industry takes place in a Schumpeterian way, Microsoft is so dominant because the nature of the industry leads to this type of outcome (large dominant firms). This does not mean that it is not facing any competitive threat.[18] In fact, some highly reputed scholars, such as Economides or Schmalensee, question the need or even usefulness of antitrust actions against Microsoft.

Economides[19] emphasizes that the fact that there are dominant firms in the market does not imply the existence of weak competition and claims that antitrust intervention in the computing industry is futile due to a number of reasons. In particular, given that the industry is a 'winner takes most' (due to the existence of network effects),[20] imposing a different market structure would generate inefficiencies. Further, even if antitrust authorities eliminate barriers to entry, once a few firms are established in the market, the addition of a new firm would not change dramatically market shares and prices.

Schmalensee indicates that traditional tests for monopoly should not be used in the computing industry.[21] Given that the industry is Schumpeterian, the leaders will necessarily have high market shares and the existence of network and scale economies will act as barriers to entry. Using traditional tests will lead to the conclusion that the software industry is highly monopolized (by different companies in different segments) and therefore should be under tight scrutiny of antitrust authorities. However, Schmalensee points out that this conclusion goes against the view of many analysts, who consider the computing industry as highly competitive, with aggressive innovation races and current monopolists being threatened and frequently overtaken by superior products.[22] This type of competitive threat is not accounted for in the traditional tests for monopoly power.

Further, if there can be only one survivor, the incumbent must exclude

---

17 Bresnahan, n. 14 above.

18 D. Evans and R. Schmalensee, *Some Economic Aspects of Antitrust Analysis in Dynamically Competitive Industries*, NBER Working Paper No 8268 (2001).

19 N. Economides, 'The Microsoft Antitrust Case' (2001) *Journal of Industry, Competition and Trade: From Theory to Policy* 7.

20 We will discuss in more detail the literature on network effects later in this chapter.

21 R. Schmalensee, 'Antitrust Issues in Schumpeterian Industries' (2000) *American Economic Review* 192.

22 Schmalensee, n. 21 above.

its competitors; otherwise, it will disappear from the marketplace. This poses the question whether strategies to survive can be labelled as 'anti-competitive'. Even more importantly, if the natural equilibrium is to have a monopoly, restraining competition can only harm welfare, especially if competition involves investments in innovation, product development or low prices. It follows from Schmalensee's argument that no antitrust action should be taken against Microsoft, as the corporation is simply trying to secure its survival.

In the upcoming sections we will discuss some relevant academic contributions regarding network effects that are helpful to understand the reasons that might exist behind Microsoft's actions as well as the consequences of them.

6. FORECLOSURE AND COMPETITION BETWEEN SYSTEMS

In this section we will provide a concise overview of the academic contributions dealing with network economies, paying special attention to the strategic issues derived from the choice of compatibility (or interoperability) between competing systems. Before starting, let us summarize the case, building on the basics discussed in the previous section.

Microsoft produced two goods, operating systems and work group server software, which are complementary products. Sun was also in the market for server software, therefore competing in that market with Microsoft. Microsoft was clearly the market leader in the operating systems market, with Windows installed on most PCs. As a consequence of the ubiquity of Windows and the existence of network effects, Sun needed to make its product compatible or interoperable with Windows; otherwise, Solaris would be of very little value to the vast majority of consumers. In fact, even evidence supplied by Microsoft to the Commission[23] highlighted the importance for work group servers of the degree of interoperability with PCs (and therefore with their operating systems). It is obvious therefore that Microsoft's refusal put Sun in a very difficult competitive situation in the work group server market.

All in all, as indicated in the introductory section, Microsoft was accused by the Commission of leveraging its market power onto the work group server operating systems market. However, according to the traditional views of economists, a monopolist in one market does not have incentives

---

[23] See Decision, para. 106.

to monopolize a complementary market. Furthermore, Microsoft's strategy changed over time. Interestingly, in the beginning of the development of the market for work group server operating systems, Microsoft did disclose all the necessary information to make Windows compatible with its competitors' products. To understand the reasons behind Microsoft's early and later strategy, let us turn our attention to the economic literature on complementary markets and competition between networks.

View of the Chicago School versus the Incentives to Foreclose Potential Competitors

The main line of defence of Microsoft is based around the Chicago School argument of 'one monopoly profit theory'.[24] According to this view, a monopolist does not have any incentives to monopolize a complementary market since it can extract all the profits from it by increasing the price in the monopolized market.

Illustrating this argument with the case, Microsoft could have raised the monopoly rents in the server software market by increasing the price of Windows operating system. Reducing the interoperability of Windows with the servers produced by the competitors would only lead to a reduction of the price consumers would be willing to pay for Windows.

Following the Chicago School's argument, we cannot find any reason to accuse Microsoft of behaving anti-competitively by degrading interoperability. In the Chicago School theory, the monopolist firm does not have any incentives to foreclose rivals in adjacent markets because of the lack of threat of entry. But is it very realistic to assume that Microsoft did not face any threat of entry?

On the one hand, entry into both the PC and work group server operating systems markets seemed to be expensive and time-consuming. In fact, the Commission stated these reasons to reject the existence of supply-side substitutability. Windows operating system is protected by the wide range of applications available in the Windows platform, which act as a short-run barrier. This, in principle, should preserve Microsoft's (quasi) monopoly of the operating systems market.

However, the Commission also stated that it could not be excluded that in the future there would be firms challenging Microsoft's dominant position in the PC operating systems market. Microsoft's actions could therefore aim at foreclosing potential competitors. By strengthening its position in the work group server market, Microsoft could reinforce

24 See Decision, recital 765.

the barriers to entry into the PC operating systems market: any future competitor in the PC operating systems market would have to produce a system which would need to be interoperable with Microsoft's work group server operating system.[25] It is important to note that there is evidence that Microsoft was worried about some competitors (Sun, Oracle and Netscape)[26] pushing for a model of centralized computing, with servers at the core of the systems.[27] Microsoft seemed to acknowledge the threat to the dominance of the Windows platform which this new computing model constituted.

Kuhn and Van Reenen explain very clearly how this new model threatened the dominance of the Windows platform: in the late 1990s, a larger number of applications could be delivered via servers, therefore putting users in less need of purchasing an expensive operating system such as Windows for their PCs, as they could simply use the applications through the servers. If users started using more frequently applications delivered by servers, software developers would increasingly write applications in the open standards which server operating systems typically use.[28]

It is worth a reminder here of the competitive dynamics of Schumpeterian industries. As discussed before, in Schumpeterian industries, competition derives from technological advances and competitors often come from neighbouring markets. In this case, although the server operating systems were not directly competing with the PC operating systems (as they constitute different markets), they were posing a threat due to the technological changes which were making Windows operating system less necessary for computer users.

Given this threat, Microsoft could have chosen to protect itself by monopolizing the server software market, consequently eliminating the potential competition of Windows. This would protect Microsoft's operating system in two ways. First, as indicated by the Commission, if Microsoft was dominant in the work group server operating systems market, any PC operating system producer would have to seek interoperability with Windows work group server operating system. This would constitute an additional barrier to entry into the operating systems market.

---

[25] See Decision, recital 769.

[26] See Decision, recital 771.

[27] It seems that Microsoft is also pushing for this model now, with the launching of Microsoft Azure cloud platform.

[28] K.U. Kühn and J. Van Reenen, 'Interoperability and Market Foreclosure In the European Microsoft Case', Centre for Economic Performance Special Paper No. 20 in B. Lyons, (ed.), *Cases in European Competition Policy: The Economic Analysis* (Cambride: Cambridge University Press, 2008).

Secondly, if Microsoft increased its market share in the work group server operating systems market, software developers would gradually shift away from writing software for other platforms, which would lead consumers to switch to Microsoft, reducing again the incentives of software developers to write software for other platforms.[29]

All in all, we have seen that Microsoft could have had incentives to foreclose competition in the complementary market of work group servers as a way to eliminate the potential threat of work group server software to PC operating systems. Essentially, the case can be interpreted as follows: Microsoft's operating system, Windows, is at the core of the dominating system. Potential competitors to this system arose in the late 1990s: the systems around work group server operating systems (and in particular, around Solaris). Naturally, Microsoft would want to foreclose the (potential) competing system. A way to do this is to degrade interoperability. In the next section, we review some contributions regarding competition between systems, so as to better understand the dynamics of competition between systems.

Basic Aspects of Competition Between Systems with Network Effects

As discussed above, computer systems are subject to network effects. It is therefore appropriate to discuss the literature on competition between networks to understand competition between computer systems. As each system has a network associated with it, the number of users of the system determines the size of its network.

Competition between systems has some distinctive features that separate it from competition between individual goods. Katz and Shapiro[30] or Scotchmer[31] highlight the fact that in many cases, the components for a system are bought in several stages. For example, at individual level, a consumer typically buys a computer, an operating system and some pieces of software at a given point in time, but will buy (at least she might consider

[29] In addition to this dynamic incentive to foreclose competition, Kühn and Van Reenen, n. 28 above, provide another static motivation: by dominating the server market, Microsoft could price discriminate more effectively in the operating systems market. Large firms would typically be less sensitive to the price of operating systems and therefore Microsoft would like to charge them a higher price than it would charge to small firms. Microsoft could identify large firms because they are willing to pay more for the complementary product (server systems).

[30] M. Katz and C. Shapiro, 'Systems Competition and Network Effects' (1994) *Journal of Economic Perspectives* 93.

[31] Scotchmer, n. 8 above.

buying) some other pieces of software or upgrades at a later stage. As a consequence of this, consumers will create some expectations about the availability of software for their purchased computer in the future. Other things being equal, software developers will write more applications for those platforms with a higher number of users.

Furthermore, different generations of consumers will be buying these goods in different periods of time. When buying goods in time 1, a consumer will consider her expectations about the future number of users of the network around each system and will adopt (other things being equal) the system that will have the highest number of users. In both cases, it can be clearly seen that competition between systems is not static. In fact, the market outcomes in one period will affect dramatically the competitive situation in upcoming periods. Therefore, we can say that competition between systems or networks is inherently dynamic.

According to Katz and Shapiro, another main feature of network competition is the coordination problem.[32] It is clear that consumers face a problem of coordination: when two competing goods affected by network economies are first introduced in the market, consumers would like to find a way to coordinate in choosing one of the two, as choosing different ones would result in inefficiencies. Firms also face a similar coordination problem. When developing new software, for example, a software creator would like the new application to be compatible with the main operating system platforms. Interestingly, given that consumers benefit from a network being as large as possible, these markets often end up being dominated by one of the firms initially present in the market. In other words, systems or network markets often tip towards one of the firms' goods. These are the so-called 'tipping equilibria', as labelled by Mahlueg and Schwarz.[33] If tipping occurs, the losing system will be progressively adopted by fewer and fewer consumers until effectively disappearing from the marketplace.[34]

Firms will try to use some strategies to make the market tip in their favour. For example, firms can opt to set heavily discounted prices in the early life of a good. This will secure a large number of consumers in those initial stages, which will consequently increase the probability of new con-

---

[32] Katz and Shapiro, n. 30 above.

[33] D. Mahlueg and M. Schwarz, 'Compatibility Incentives of a Large Network Facing Multiple Rivals' (2006) *Journal of Industrial Economics* 527.

[34] J. Farrell and G. Saloner, 'Installed Base and Compatibility: Innovation, Product Preannouncements, and Predation' (1986) *American Economic Review* 940; M. Katz and C. Shapiro, 'Product Introduction with Network Externalities' (1992) *Journal of Industrial Economics* 55.

sumers buying that good or system in later stages of the life of the good. The existence of a good in the marketplace that is perceived by firms to be superior to other goods could lead to the same result. Therefore, in those early stages, firms will frequently use aggressive advertising campaigns to promote the image of their goods.

Another key issue which requires our attention is the interoperability or compatibility properties of the system. Often computer users need to interact with others using a different system. It is therefore crucial from the point of view of users that a system is able to operate or communicate with another system. This property is called 'interoperability'. For two systems to be interoperable, they must be compatible and interconnected. From now on, we will use the terms compatibility, interoperability and interconnectivity interchangeably.

Katz and Shapiro cite a number of benefits of compatibility, such as lower marginal costs due to scale economies, technological spill-overs and learning effects, etc.[35]

Further, Matutes and Regibeau point out that compatibility also makes it possible for consumers to mix and match components from various systems.[36] This, in turn, should make competition between firms stronger. Taking the Microsoft case as an example, if Solaris and Windows were compatible, consumers could pick Windows as operating system and Solaris as work group server software. If they were incompatible, consumers using Windows would be almost bound to use Windows work group server. In principle, competition should be stronger in the first case than in the second. In fact, Katz and Shapiro[37] show that compatibility relaxes competition earlier in the product life-cycle but prevents one firm from gaining control of the market and therefore intensifies competition in later stages.[38]

It should be obvious that compatibility generates benefits for consumers (as it makes easier the communication between users of different systems) but it will not always be preferred by firms. Sun wanted Solaris to be compatible with Windows, as otherwise their market potentially would have been dramatically reduced. However, some firms might be interested in deliberately making their product incompatible with other products

---

35 Katz and Shapiro, n. 30 above.

36 C. Matutes and P. Regibeau, '"Mix and Match": Product Compatibility without Network Externalities' (1988) *RAND Journal of Economics* 221.

37 M. Katz and C. Shapiro, 'Technology Adoption in the Presence of Network Externalities' (1986) *Journal of Political Economy* 822.

38 This result seems to be in line with Microsoft's move from favouring interoperability to degrading it. We will discuss this change in more detail later.

in the market, even if they are complementary products, for a number of reasons. In the case of Microsoft, by denying compatibility to Solaris, Microsoft was strengthening the market position of its work group server software (as it would be perceived as superior to Sun's due to its perfect interoperability with Windows). Another reason behind the degradation of interoperability could be that Microsoft perceived work group servers and their operating systems as potential competitors to Windows and wanted to protect itself from this threat, as discussed above.

In the next section, we will review some seminal contributions from the economics literature on competition between networks in order to explain in detail the incentives of firms to grant or degrade interoperability.

Competition Between Networks: Dominance and Compatibility

A seminal paper in the literature on competition between networks is Katz and Shapiro,[39] who modelled a game between oligopolistic firms in a static framework in order to study firms' incentives to make their goods compatible with their competitors'. The authors highlight the importance of consumers' expectations: if consumers expect a firm to be dominant, then they will be willing to pay more for its good, and, as a consequence, the firm will in fact become dominant.[40] This means that in equilibrium there could be one dominant firm or many competing firms, depending on the consumers' expectations.[41] Regarding compatibility, it is shown that firms with good reputations or large networks will tend to degrade compatibility. Small firms, in contrast, will tend to be in favour of compatibility.

The limitation of Katz's and Shapiro's thesis is the lack of dynamics. As discussed above, competition between systems often takes place in a multi-period scenario. Therefore, it seems important to consider the implications of those dynamics.

Farrell and Saloner consider a game between consumers who take their purchasing decisions at different points in time.[42] Over time, new superior technologies appear. Each consumer decides which network to belong to

---

[39] M. Katz and C Shapiro, 'Network Externalities, Competition, and Compatibility' (1985) *American Economic Review* 424.

[40] The authors use a refined version of the Nash equilibrium, the 'fulfilled expectations equilibrium', which will be the recurrent equilibrium solution used in posterior contributions. This solution implies that consumers' expectations regarding the size of the competing networks are correct in equilibrium.

[41] They also show the existence of multiple equilibria for some sets of expectations.

[42] Farrell and Saloner, n. 34 above.

(i.e. to buy the old or the new good or technology) given what the other consumers have chosen. The equilibrium outcome depends therefore on the size of the installed base when a new good or technology is introduced, the difference in quality between the new good and the old one, and how quickly the network externalities around the new good are realized. Interestingly, one of the main results in Farrell and Saloner's paper is that network economies may actually inhibit innovation. This problem is referred to by the authors as 'excess inertia', a socially excessive reluctance to change to a new standard (i.e. the new good or technology becoming dominant) even when this new standard outperforms the old one (i.e. the old good or technology being dominant). For this effect to happen, there must be strong network externalities around the old standard. The authors also show that incumbent firms can use product pre-announcements and predatory pricing to deter entry. Both strategies would aim at protecting the differential in the sizes of the incumbent's and entrant's networks, which are the core of the competitive advantage of the incumbent.

Katz and Shapiro show that generally compatibility tends to be below socially optimal level and highlight the importance of technology sponsorship in determining which firm will become dominant (and therefore, which good or technology will become prevalent).[43] A firm is said to 'sponsor' a technology if it uses an aggressive pricing strategy in the early stages of the product life and recoups its investment in later stages when being already dominant. Naturally, this can only happen if the firm is the sole owner of the right to the production of a good (for example, through a patent). In the absence of sponsors, the firm which is dominant today will have an advantage due to the installed base and the derived network effects. If two technologies are sponsored, the one that will be superior tomorrow will have the advantage. It is worth commenting here that if there were scale economies, it would be difficult for a new entrant to sponsor the technology to the same extent as the incumbent, as its unit production costs would be higher.

More recently, Crémer, Rey and Tirole build on and extend the model presented by Katz and Shapiro in their 1985 paper to analyse connectivity in the Internet. In particular, they study the incentives of dominant backbones to provide interoperability with 'smaller' providers.[44] Their model can also be interpreted more generally as a model of competition between

---

[43] M. Katz and C. Shapiro, 'Product Compatibility Choice in a Market with Technological Progress' (1986) *Oxford Economic Papers* 146.

[44] J. Crémer, P. Rey and J. Tirole, 'Connectivity in the Commercial Internet' (2000) *Journal of Industrial Economics* 433.

systems. The authors assume a market for a network good and two firms which can endogenously determine the degree of interoperability of their products. Unlike Katz and Shapiro, where goods produced by each pair of firms can only be perfectly compatible or totally incompatible,[45] Crémer, Rey and Tirole contemplate also intermediate degrees of interoperability. The network around each of the two goods is constituted by the number of users that have already bought the good from the company in the past and are therefore users of the network around the good produced by the firm. For simplicity, we will refer to the firm with the larger installed base as the 'incumbent' and the firm with the smaller installed base as the 'entrant'. In our case, Microsoft would be the incumbent and Sun the entrant.

Apart from the current users of the network, there are also a number of new costumers who have to choose from which firm to buy – in other words, choose which network to join. Users benefit from network externalities, in the sense that their utility is higher the higher the number of consumers in the network. Further, this network externality extends on the number of users in the other network if the goods are interoperable, corrected by the degree of interoperability between the two networks. In other words, if the goods are fully incompatible, consumers would only benefit from an increase in the number of consumers using the same network as them; if goods were fully interoperable, consumers would benefit as much from an increase in the number of users in the other network as from an increase in their own network. If the goods were only partially interoperable, consumers would also benefit from the number of users in the other network but only to the extent of the degree of interoperability.

Motta discusses the 'tipping equilibria' in the Crémer, Rey and Tirole framework, that is when the market tips in favour of the incumbent or in favour of the entrant, and find the less compatible the goods are, the more likely the market will tip towards the incumbent.[46] Further, if goods are incompatible, tipping towards the entrant cannot occur. In other words, if the incumbent denies compatibility, it protects its market dominance. This can help us explain the incentives that Microsoft had to deny compatibility, as by doing so, it protected its competitive advantage. The competitive advantage the incumbent has derives from having a larger installed base, which will make a new consumer more likely to choose the incumbent's network instead of the new entrant's network.

---

[45] Katz and Shapiro, n. 39 above, also analyse the case of firms opting to become compatible with some other firms but incompatible with others. They refer to this case as 'partial compatibility'.

[46] Motta, n. 5 above.

However, Crémer, Rey and Tirole also show that in some circumstances, the incumbent might actually prefer full interoperability.[47] This can only happen when the installed base is small relative to the number of new consumers. Although full interoperability erodes the incumbent's competitive advantage, it also increases the demand of new consumers in the market.

All in all, the incumbent (or the firm with the larger installed base) will choose full or zero interoperability while the entrant (or firm with the smaller installed base) will always prefer full interoperability. More recently, Mahlueg and Schwarz extended Crémer, Rey and Tirole's model by allowing more than two firms.[48] Interestingly, according to their results, reducing interoperability may actually tip the market away from the incumbent. When facing multiple competitors, denying compatibility can (but does not necessarily need to) actually worsen the competitive position of the incumbent. In fact, this is more likely to happen the higher the number of rivals for a given size of the installed base. Further, the smaller the installed base, the lower the incentives to deny compatibility. Again, as in Crémer, Rey and Tirole, the incumbent faces a trade-off between increasing the demand and sacrificing its competitive advantage by making its product compatible with that of the entrants.[49]

To sum up, here we have turned our attention to the literature on competition between networks. This literature is highly relevant for the Microsoft case, as computer systems are subject to network effects. We have seen that the expectations of consumers regarding the future size of networks are crucial in explaining which systems become dominant. We have also seen that markets with network externalities often tip in favour of one of the firms. Firms will therefore try to implement strategies to tip the market in their interest.

According to the literature, if two competing networks are incompatible, tipping towards the smaller network cannot occur. Therefore, a dominant firm would have strong incentives to deny compatibility so as to protect its competitive advantage. Incompatibility will confer a competitive advantage on the firm with the largest network: if two systems cannot communicate with each other, a typical consumer will choose the system with the highest (expected) number of users, other things being equal. This could explain Microsoft's refusal to supply Sun with the necessary information to make their work group server operating system compatible with

47 Crémer, Rey and Tirole, n. 44 above.
48 Mahlueg and Schwarz, n. 33 above.
49 Crémer, Rey and Tirole, n. 44 above.

Windows. In contrast, the firm with the smallest network would prefer full interoperability so that the difference in the size of the networks does not impact consumers' decisions.

If the market is still growing, the dominant firm faces a trade-off: by favouring interoperability, it will increase its demand but it will erode its competitive advantage. Interestingly, Microsoft initially chose to disclose the information to make work group server operating systems compatible with Microsoft. In contrast, at a later stage, it chose the opposite strategy. We have seen some reasons which could explain this change of strategy: initially, when network computing was in its infancy, Microsoft could have chosen to achieve high degrees of interoperability to drive up its own demand. At that time, the market was still growing and the potential size of the market was still very large relative to the current number of users. When the market was mature and its own network was already large relative to the number of new consumers, it chose to deny compatibility presumably to protect its competitive advantage.

7. INTEROPERABILITY, INNOVATION AND WELFARE

In the previous section we analysed the motivations behind Microsoft's strategy. Here we discuss the implications of interoperability on innovation and welfare. Before starting this discussion, it is important to note that innovation rates and market power are not necessarily negatively related: although it is true that competition can stimulate innovation, it is also true that firms will not have incentives to conduct R&D unless they can appropriate the returns of their investments. Therefore, it is important to bear in mind that in some instances, excessive enforcement of competition law may damage the incentives to invest in R&D.[50]

As mentioned above, the Commission showed concerns about Microsoft's general business model, which was thought to deter innovation and reduce consumer choice. However, it is far from clear that forcing interoperability (as the remedy imposed) necessarily benefits investment in innovation. On the one hand, forcing Microsoft to disclose the necessary information so that the other software companies can make their products compatible with Microsoft's should result in cost savings for those firms. Furthermore, interoperability should increase the sales of

---

[50] R. Gilbert, 'Holding Innovation to an Antitrust Standard' (2007) *Competition Policy International* 3.

Microsoft's competitors, as now their products will be more valuable to consumers (due to the network economies described earlier). The increase in sales should in turn increase the incentives to innovate of Microsoft competitors.[51] However, in order to assess the effects of the remedy on the industry incentives to innovate, it is not enough to consider Microsoft's competitors in isolation; the impact on Microsoft is also relevant, especially when Microsoft is such a large firm relative to the other firms in the market.

The impact of the remedy on Microsoft's incentives to innovate is far less clear. On the one hand, if the measure would lead to a decrease in Microsoft's market share, naturally Microsoft's investment in innovation would decrease. Notwithstanding, one may also expect Microsoft to invest more intensively in innovation in order to protect its position from the new competitors rather than relying on foreclosing strategies such as tying or denying compatibility.

Interestingly, some analysts believe that Microsoft has never been particularly innovative and that its core products are essentially copies of already existing products. In fact, it seems that relevant people in the industry believe that innovation would be enhanced if Microsoft's monopoly position was removed.[52] A word of caution is needed here, as the industry association has an obvious interest in this matter.

The results in the economics literature with regard to the welfare implications of incompatibility in Schumpeterian markets are quite ambiguous. In particular, it has been shown that if a monopoly supplier of an essential systems component (in the Microsoft case, Windows operating system) is prevented from restricting interoperability, the market for the complementary market can tip in favour of a less efficient firm.[53] If that happened, welfare could be harmed by forcing interoperability.

There are some reasons to believe that, in computer markets, the best solution from the social point of view would be to have open interfaces, with hardware and software applications protected by intellectual property

---

51 Kühn and Van Reenen, n. 28, above. Typically, the R&D costs do not depend on the number of units of output actually produced. Therefore, the higher the quantity of output, the lower the R&D cost per unit of output and therefore the higher the profitability of the investment in R&D.

52 As Ed Black, President of the Computer and Communications Industry Association (CCIA) said, 'We're convinced that innovation will be greatly enhanced and improved if Microsoft's heavy hand of monopoly is removed from the industry'. See 'Has Microsoft stifled innovation?', BBC News, available at http://news.bbc.co.uk/1/hi/business/781765.stm.

53 R. Gilbert and M. Riordan, 'Product Improvement and Technological Tying in a Winner-Take-All Market' (2007) *Journal of Industrial Economics* 113.

rights (patents, etc.): if the interfaces were open, the prices for the different elements of the system would be determined by the extent of those rights rather than by the market power derived from the network effects around the platform.[54] From the policy point of view, unless there is a violation of competition law, in which case authorities may choose to force firms to disclose the interfaces as in the Microsoft case, it is typically difficult to find tools to make the interfaces open. Reverse-engineering could be one of those tools but might not work if the technologies are very complex.[55]

8. SUMMARY AND FINAL REMARKS

In this chapter, we have discussed the main economic aspects of the Microsoft case and, in particular, those related to the first of the practices assessed by the European Commission, that is, the refusal to supply the necessary information to make the competitors' work group server operating systems interoperable with Windows operating system. We have highlighted that network economies and complementarities between the different elements integrating computer systems are core issues in the case. We have paid particular attention to the rationale behind Microsoft's strategies according to the economics literature.

According to traditional theories, a (quasi) monopolist such as Microsoft would not have any incentives to monopolize a complementary market, as it could extract the monopolist rents in the complementary market (the work group server operating systems market) by raising the price of the monopoly good (Windows operating system). In order for the argument to be correct, a firm must hold an uncontested life-long monopoly position. However, Microsoft showed concerns about the birth of a new computer model based on servers, which some competitors were pushing at the time, which could pose a threat to Windows.

We have argued that the case can be viewed as a game between systems or platforms with network externalities: the Microsoft platform (centred on the Windows operating system) and the platform (or platforms) based on servers. Microsoft could have chosen to protect itself from the threat of other platforms by degrading the compatibility of Windows operating system with work group server operating systems. The literature on network economics has shown that those markets with network

---

54 Scotchmer, n. 8 above.

55 P. Samuelson and S. Scotchmer, 'The Law and Economics of Reverse Engineering' (2002) *Yale Law Journal* 1575.

externalities often tip in favour of one of the firms. According to the literature, if two competing systems are incompatible, tipping towards the one with a smaller network cannot occur. Therefore, a dominant firm, such as Microsoft, would have strong incentives to deny compatibility so as to protect its market position.

We have also discussed Microsoft's change of strategy regarding interoperability. The economics literature has shown that when a market is developing, the incumbent firm may choose to achieve high degrees of interoperability to drive up its own demand (as its installed base is small relative to the market potential). When the market is already mature and the firm's network already large relative to the number of new consumers, the incumbent firm would have incentives to protect its competitive advantage by degrading interoperability. This seems to fit well with Microsoft's change of strategy.

All in all, we have found support in the economics literature for the Commission's argument that Microsoft had incentives to leverage its market power onto the work group server systems market. Does this mean that taking action against Microsoft was justified? The advocates of the Schumpeterian paradigm would say it was not. In dynamic markets with network effects, any sort of intervention would be at best wasteful, and at worst distorting.

Interestingly, the Commission seemed to acknowledge that the computer markets are Schumpeterian: at least, the Decision on the case seems to indicate this, as the Commission explicitly states that software markets are subject to 'shifts in paradigm'.[56] However, the Commission did not take the Schumpeter argument as far as saying that intervention would be worthless or would lead to inefficiencies. In fact, the Commission was concerned about the fact that Microsoft was systematically eliminating potential competitors. The Commission believed that Microsoft was actually hampering dynamic competition by abusing its dominant position in the PC operating systems market. The refusal to supply the necessary information to achieve compatibility between work group server operating systems and Windows would be just another example of this general business model.

Furthermore, although the Commission seemed to recognize the threat of the new 'server centred' model to the Windows dominance, it considered the market for PC operating systems and the market for work group server operating systems as separate markets. One may wonder whether a wider definition of market could or should have been used, given this

---

[56] Decision, recital 770.

potential shift in paradigm. If so, perhaps the outcome of the case would have been more in line with Microsoft's interest.

There are other issues regarding the antitrust process in dynamic industries that I believe should be mentioned here. On the one hand, the antitrust process can take too long. In highly dynamic industries such as computing, two or three years might be an eternity. In the Microsoft case, the process spanned much longer than that. In fact, Microsoft only announced it would disclose interoperability information in 2008, four years after the initial decision was published and ten years after Sun filed its complaint. New technologies might 'die' in that time interval if they are not given a fair chance in the market.

Further, the computer industry is highly globalized, while antitrust laws and their enforcement are not. It would be more efficient and appropriate to assess cases in highly globalized industries with major international players on the basis of international antitrust standards and in international courts.

Finally, in highly dynamic industries, it is very difficult to evaluate the welfare effects of firms' actions. In a static setting, prices convey a lot of information regarding welfare. Moreover, competition law practitioners have at their disposal some econometric tools, such as the antitrust logit model, which can be used to estimate the impact of firms' actions in a number of situations. However, a welfare analysis in a dynamic setting is typically very complicated and can lead to ambiguous results, as it requires making a judgement on dynamic efficiency, especially if issues such as innovation incentives and uncertainty are taken into account.

12. *Microsoft* v *Commission*: a pricing perspective on non-price abuses

Derek Ridyard and Markus Baldauf

1. INTRODUCTION

This chapter discusses the economics of tying in the context of the Microsoft case. First, we consider the Microsoft tying practice in light of a broader economic framework that examines the relationship between tying and pricing abuses. We seek to explore the idea that it may be instructive to analyse tying, or 'non-price' abuses in general, within the framework that is normally used for the assessment of pricing abuses such as rebates and predation, and that there could be some insights from taking this non-standard perspective.

Secondly, we critically appraise the reasoning of the European Commission and Court of First Instance (CFI) when analysing the alleged abuses conducted by Microsoft. We conclude that, despite the in-depth analysis of both abuses relating to server software interoperability information and media players, there remains considerable uncertainty about the precise interpretation of the CFI's judgment. We question whether the Microsoft judgment has done much to clarify when tying practices by a dominant firm will be deemed to be in breach of Article 82 of the EC Treaty, and comment on the extent to which the CFI's approach can be consistent with a truly effects-based enforcement system such as is proposed in the recently published Guidance on the Commission's enforcement priorities under Article 82 EC ('the Commission's Article 82 Guidelines').[1]

The remainder of the text is organized as follows. Section 2 gives some case background and section 3 discusses the economic principles of tying. Section 4 comments on the CFI's analysis of tying in *Microsoft* v

[1] See Guidance on the Commission's Enforcement Priorities in Applying Article 82 EC Treaty to Abusive Exclusionary Conduct by Dominant Undertakings, 3 December 2008.

Commission. Section 5 analyses the implications of the judgment and of the remedies that have been put in place to deal with the abuse. Section 6 briefly concludes.

2. CASE BACKGROUND

The Commission's Article 82 case against Microsoft concerned the alleged leveraging of Microsoft's dominant position in client PC operating systems into two related markets, work group server operating systems and media players.

The Commission's investigation started following Sun's complaint about interoperability information in 1998. This interoperability information refers to the ability to link individual Windows PCs with a small server to enable file and printer sharing as well as administration of users and groups. In 2000 the investigation broadened to include a separate allegation of tying, this time of Windows Media Player (WMP) to the Windows PC operating system.

In March 2004 the Commission issued its Decision which found Microsoft guilty of (i) refusal to supply interoperability information, and (ii) anti-competitive tying of WMP to Windows.[2] As regards the first abuse, the Commission found that the refusal to supply interoperability information would foreclose competitors on the work group server market. Thereby, Microsoft would leverage its dominance in Windows into work group server operating systems.[3] Concerning the tying of WMP with Windows, the Commission held that this would provide a disincentive to use third party media players and would lead to a significant risk of weakening competition in media players in the near future.[4]

Microsoft appealed the Commission Decision and, in September 2007, the CFI upheld the Commission's views on the two Microsoft abuses in its Microsoft judgment.[5] Following the judgment, Microsoft agreed to comply with the CFI's ruling. Regarding the WMP abuse, Microsoft undertook to offer an unbundled version of Windows that did not contain WMP, alongside the bundled version. The second ruling regarding the availability of interoperability information turned out to be more difficult

---

2 Commission Decision 2007/53/EC of 24 March 2004 [2007] OJ L32/23 ('the Decision').

3 Decision, paras 779–84.

4 Decision, paras 978–84.

5 Case T-201/04 *Microsoft* v *Commission* [2007] ECR II-3601, para. 28 ('CFI judgment').

to comply with. Microsoft effectively engaged in access price negotiations with the Commission which ended with a non-compliance decision and a fine of €899,000,000.[6] Microsoft agreed in October 2007 to make available interoperability information for a one-off payment of €10,000.[7] Microsoft has not appealed the CFI judgment on the main case, but it has continued to contest the additional fine for non-compliance on the interoperability remedy.

3. ECONOMIC PRINCIPLES OF TYING

This section sets out the economic principles of tying and bundling. Starting from the principles as laid out in the Commission's Article 82 Guidelines, we explore the main economic views of the Chicago School and developments thereafter. We also describe the relationship between tying and pricing practices, both generally and in relation to the specific abuses alleged against Microsoft.

Introduction

Tying and bundling refer to sales strategies where firms offer a combination of distinct products. There are a number of ways in which products can be combined which can have different impacts on the affected markets.

It is useful to differentiate between (i) pure bundling, (ii) mixed bundling, and (iii) tying. If two products A and B are only sold as a bundle then the practice is referred to as pure bundling. Mixed bundling refers to a situation where A and B are available separately but are offered at a discount if bought together. Tying usually refers to a situation in which customers that purchase product A are also required to purchase product B.

The Commission's Article 82 Guidelines describe tying and bundling as 'common practices aiming at providing customers with better products or offerings in more cost effective ways' (para. 48). Indeed, any value-adding

---

6 Commission Decision C(2008)764 Final of 27 February 2008.

7 See 'Antitrust: Commission ensures compliance with 2004 Decision against Microsoft', Commission Press Release, 22 October 2007, available at http://europa.eu/rapid/pressReleasesAction.do?reference=IP/07/1567&format=HTML&aged=1&language=EN&guiLanguage=en. The flat fee of €10,000 applies to the so-called 'open source' software providers which, according to the Commission, provide the main surviving competitive constraint on Microsoft in this area. Microsoft also agreed a licence fee of 0.4 per cent for the use of the interoperability information by users who consider that relevant patents apply.

activity involves bundling of different components to create a product that is preferred by consumers to assembling the components themselves. Hence, it is useful that this benign explanation for bundling is recognized in the Commission's Guidelines.

A classic illustration of a bundle would be a car, which comprises a bundle of an engine, wheels, and many other components ranging from satellite navigation systems to cup-holders. The production process of mass market car assembly makes it prohibitively expensive for consumers to buy and assemble a car from individual components. In that particular case scale and scope economies make a centralized production process by the car manufacturer more efficient and the main reason for bundling in this case. Nalebuff[8] lists a number of other efficiency reasons why firms bundle, including cost reduction, quality improvement, as well as reducing pricing inefficiencies.[9]

However, a firm with market power in one product can also use bundling strategically to foreclose rivals or soften competition in the tied product. The Commission's Article 82 Guidelines note that (para. 48):

> an undertaking which is dominant in one product market (or more) of a tie or bundle (referred to as the tying market) can harm consumers through tying or bundling by foreclosing the market for the other products that are part of the tie or bundle (referred to as the tied market) and, indirectly, the tying market.

The competition concern in the context of bundling and tying is thus a theory of harm whereby a dominant firm can extend its dominance in one market to a related but separate market which would otherwise be competitive. As a result that second market would be less competitive and, in some theories, the firm's dominant position in the tying market would be protected to the ultimate detriment of consumers. Under a leverage theory of harm, a firm can combine two products and achieve higher profits from the bundle than the sum of the profits that can be earned by selling each product separately. In order to substantiate such a theory, however, a simple and powerful 'Chicago School' argument has to be overcome.

Chicago School argument

Any leverage of market power theory must address the question of whether a firm with a monopoly in one market can earn more than one monopoly

---

8 See D. Nalebuff, *Bundling, Tying and Portfolio Effects*, DTI Economics Paper No. 1 (2000), pp. 31–8, available at www.berr.gov.uk/files/file14774.pdf.

9 The pricing efficiencies that can be achieved via bundling parallel the efficiency arguments in vertical mergers where a double mark-up problem can be mitigated.

profit on that product by combining this product with a product that is sold competitively. The Chicago School response to this question is negative, as a monopoly can only earn a 'single monopoly profit'.

Consider the situation where only a monopolist supplies product A, which is used by consumers in combination with a complementary product B that is supplied competitively. By tying A and B, the monopoly supplier could easily 'extend' its monopoly position from A to A+B in that its share of sales of B could be increased. However, since a monopolist of A should already have set a price for A that maximized the profits from doing so, after imposing the A+B tie the monopolist should not be able to command more than the competitive margin on sales of B. Hence, the artificial 'monopoly' over B via the tie with A does not deliver an additional monopoly profit. Moreover, if there is a possibility that B can be supplied by a third party at a price below that which the monopolist could achieve, or if rivalry between suppliers of product B creates diversity and/or innovation that the monopolist would not have offered, then the monopolist of A would strictly prefer not to engage in tying. In that case, the demand for A increases if B is sold at a lower price, and therefore the value of the monopoly of A also increases. A tie which excludes a more efficient supplier of B would therefore lead to lower profits for A compared to a scenario without the tie.

According to the Chicago School argument, firms engage in tying and bundling behaviour for efficiency reasons but not for strategic reasons. Any market power that firms may have is, according to that argument, already fully exploited in the absence of tying and bundling.

Post-Chicago School arguments

The Chicago School argument that firms can only earn a single monopoly profit has an appealing simplicity. However, that argument relies on assumptions whose violation may lead to a break in the Chicago School reasoning. Two prominent modifications under which the traditional Chicago School view fails are (i) the protection of monopoly power over the tying product, and (ii) entry deterrence or exclusion in the tied product.[10]

Suppose there is a chance that a monopolist's position may erode over time, as competitors in an adjacent market B would find it easier to use their

[10] See e.g. M. Whinston, 'Tying, Foreclosure, and Exclusion' (1990) *American Economic Review, American Economic Association* 837, and D. Carlton and M. Waldman, 'The Strategic Use of Tying to Preserve and Create Market Power in Evolving Industries' (2002) *RAND Journal of Economics* 194.

position as suppliers of product B as a springboard from which to switch to the production of A at some point in the future. Then the dynamic incentives of the monopolist are changed. To apply this reasoning to the Microsoft case, according to the Chicago view a monopoly supplier of PC operating systems has an interest in the competitive provision of server operating systems (OS). This is due to the complementarity of the two products. If server operating systems are supplied efficiently, then this boosts demand for servers but also for PC operating systems. However, if at some point in the future one efficient supplier of server OS would be in a position to enter the PC OS market and compete against Microsoft, then a post-Chicago view would introduce the possibility that Microsoft might want to bundle Windows with the server OS and thereby fight competition in server software when it is still weak. This may not necessarily lead to higher profits in the server market, and indeed if Microsoft's server software is less innovative or less competitive than that of third parties, it carries a risk that it will reduce demand for Windows. But by delaying or foreclosing rivals' development in server software, Microsoft might be able to protect its Windows monopoly by strategically tying Windows with server OS.

A second post-Chicago view concerns the classic leverage of market power argument. According to that view, a monopolist of A can use a tie of A and B to force competitors in B out of the market. This could happen as a stand-alone provider of B now finds it more difficult to compete with the monopolist who can offer an integrated solution. In the Microsoft case, this theory might plausibly be illustrated by reference to the media player abuse. By integrating WMP into Windows, Microsoft would make it harder for stand-alone suppliers such as RealPlayer to compete. Tying could force competitors out of that market and Microsoft would be dominant in the adjacent market for media players as well. The consumer harm under this theory would arise only if a number of conditions are satisfied, including the condition that competitors would not re-enter the media player segment in the event of a subsequent price rise.

Such post-Chicago theories of harm essentially build on the simple Chicago School view by adding more complexity, including a dynamic perspective, to the analysis. Post-Chicago theories show that uncertainty about the future (e.g. erosion of monopoly power) or foreclosure of competitors by committing to compete fiercely in an adjacent market, can overturn the traditional view that there exists only a single monopoly profit in any one transaction.

However, it is one thing to describe a theory or model in which monopoly power protection or leverage could occur, and quite another to establish that one such welfare-reducing theory truly describes the motivation for (and effects of) tying in any particular case. Two factors are present here that greatly complicate the analysis of bundling allegations. First, if one accepts the proposition that 'bundling' is what all firms do when they seek to create added value products, there must be a general presumption that bundling itself is a normal commercial activity that should not generate suspicion in itself. That in turn means that there is a risk that intervention against bundling will harm efficiency and consumers by preventing firms from engaging in practices that are pro-competitive. Secondly, viewed from the perspective of a complainant firm that is an actual or potential supplier of the tied product or a bundled component, the commercial motivation to complain is the same irrespective of whether the practice is pro- or anti-competitive, since either scenario makes life harder for the complainant. This ought to magnify the caution one exercises when evaluating such complaints. We return to these issues in the discussion below.

Tying as a Pricing Concern

Although tying is often categorized as a 'non-price' abuse, in analytical terms it is possible to characterize tying and mixed bundling as pricing practices. Moreover, it is interesting to see how the treatment of tying fits with the approach that has been taken to competition enforcement against pricing abuses.

Consider the analysis of target rebates where a customer is granted a retroactive discount on all units purchased after a target is reached. To illustrate, let us consider a target rebate structure on a product with a list price of €1 and a cost per unit of €0.50. To incentivize higher levels of consumption, suppose that the supplier offers a rebate that reduces the price to €0.75 on all units if the total purchases of a customer in one period reach 100 units. A customer that purchases 100 units will then receive a rebate of €25 on the total list price payments of €100. Although a customer purchasing 100 units will be indifferent between this pricing structure and a list price of €0.75 without a rebate, the marginal incentives of the two schemes are very different. Specifically, a target rebate structure can be used to lock-in customers.[11]

Suppose a customer's total demand for the next period is 100 units, but that 75 units are 'must stock' sales that the customer feels obliged to buy from supplier M even under a standard list price. In other words, supplier M has a 'monopoly' over the first 75 units purchased by that customer. In the absence of a rebate structure the customer might wish to purchase 75 units from supplier M and then choose between M and rival supplier R

[11] See Commission's Article 82 Guidelines, para. 39.

for the remaining 25 units. However, once 75 units have been purchased from M, the customer has paid a total of €75. Under the discount scheme, the customer realizes that by purchasing the next 25 units from supplier M it will qualify for the rebate of €25. Effectively, therefore, supplier M's rebate structure has been set up such as to provide the last 25 units free of charge.

The Commission's Article 82 Guidelines suggest that this conduct should be analysed using what amounts to a predatory pricing standard.[12] The emphasis on marginal incentives matters as it is possible that the average price charged by supplier M (i.e. €0.75 in this example) is above the cost of supply but that the marginal price of the last 25 units which comprise the discretionary sales (i.e. zero in this example) lies below the cost benchmark (i.e. €12.50, comprising 25 times the unit cost of €0.50 in this example).

The figure below illustrates this example. Under a constant list price of €1 the customer's expenditure increases linearly up to 100 units (i.e. the line from A to B) where it jumps down to C (i.e. denoting the €25 customer reward once the target is reached). Although the average price per unit charged by the dominant firm exceeds the variable cost of €0.50 at whatever level of sales the customer chooses, as the customer's purchases increase, the marginal price of the 'discretionary' units purchased falls to below the cost of supply. Indeed, the illustration is constructed such that at any point beyond point Z (as shown in the Figure 12.1), the price charged by the dominant firm for the additional units between 75 and 100 units is effectively negative. Specifically, there does not seem to be any good reason why a customer would choose to buy between 75 and 100 units from this supplier, since at any point from Z to B the customer's total spend will exceed €75, and yet the discount structure shown here allows the customer to buy all 100 units from M for €75. If, as is depicted here, the first 75 units represent the 'must stock' level of purchases that the customer is bound to buy from firm M, it can readily be seen that there would be no scope for rival suppliers to compete for the additional 25 units of each customer's demand that lies in the 'discretionary sales' zone.

If we move away from the extreme case illustrated in Figure 12.1, it is evident that the potential for a roll-over rebate scheme to have exclusionary effects will depend on how much leverage the dominant supplier is able to exert through the 'must stock' or non-discretionary element of sales. This fact is summarized in the Commission's Article 82 Guidelines as follows (para. 41):

---

[12] See Commission's Article 82 Guidelines, para. 59.

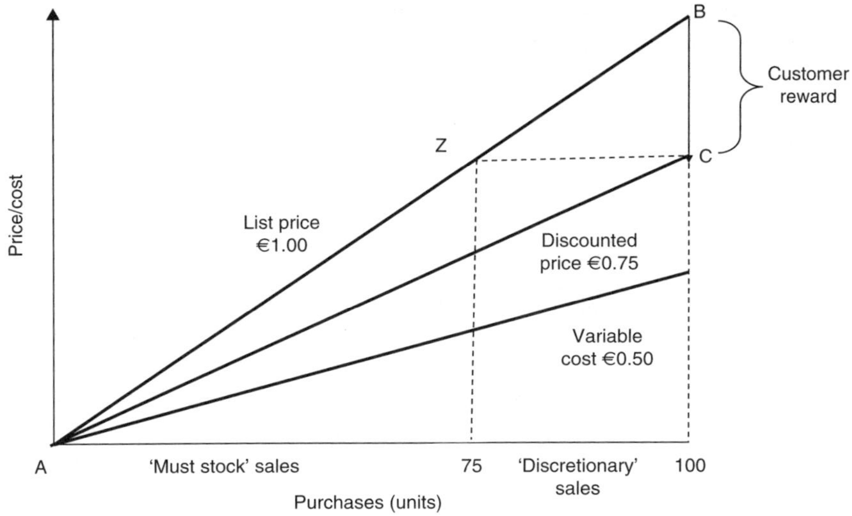

Figure 12.1 Illustration of foreclosure effects from a roll-over discount

> For retroactive rebates, it will generally be relevant to assess in the specific market context how much of a customer's purchase requirements can realistically be switched to a rival (the 'contestable share' or 'contestable portion'). If it is likely that customers would be willing and able to switch large amounts of demand to a (potential) rival relatively quickly, the relevant range is likely to be relatively large.

In the case where there is no 'must stock' element, i.e. where it is feasible for a competing supplier to win 100 per cent of a customer's purchases, the logical conclusion would be that this kind of roll-over discount scheme would lose its power to have exclusionary effects. In this scenario, each supplier could contest the right to supply all 100 units of supply to every customer, and the leverage effects that roll-over discounts can have would disappear. In terms of the illustration in Figure 12.1, a rival supplier would be able to win the business of the customer if it offered a proposition that beat the dominant firm's best offer of €75 for 100 units. That ought to be possible as long as the competing supplier has unit costs below €0.75.

In other words, the problematic effects of roll-over rebates arise from a form of leverage that is closely akin to the leverage exerted in tying cases. In the illustration in Figure 12.1, supplier M 'ties' its monopoly over must stock sales to the discretionary sales using the discount that is only applicable once the discretionary sales have been made. The 'stand-alone' suppliers of discretionary sales (i.e. suppliers without a brand loyal or locked-in customer base) are thus not in a position to compete solely for the discretionary sales but would need to offer a deal that competes across the entire bundle of must stock and discretionary sales. This leverage mechanism is acknowledged in the Commission's Article 82 Guidelines as follows (para. 38):

> A conditional rebate granted by a dominant undertaking may enable it to use the 'non contestable' portion of the demand of each customer (i.e. the amount that would anyhow be purchased by the customer from the dominant undertaking) as leverage to decrease the price to be paid for the 'contestable' portion of demand (i.e. the amount for which the customer may prefer and be able to find substitutes).

It should be clear from this discussion that tying can also be viewed and analysed as a pricing abuse using this rebates framework, with the tying product playing the role of the 'must stock' items and the tied product being represented by the discretionary sales.

Microsoft's Abuses in a Pricing Framework

In the Microsoft case, both of the abuses can be viewed as variants of tying. This is seen most clearly in the WMP abuse, where Windows (the tying product) is tied to WMP (tied product) to the detriment of stand-alone media player providers. Microsoft's supply of Windows corresponds to the 'must stock' sales and the supply of media players can be viewed as the contestable sales where Microsoft competes with stand-alone providers. A bundled version of Windows that includes WMP is then equivalent to a situation in which the price of the combination is no different from the price of Windows for the customer that intends to use an alternative media player. Therefore, the implicit price of WMP is zero.

In terms of Figure 12.1 above, the consequence of this pricing structure was that stand-alone providers of media players found themselves competing at a point similar to point Z, where it costs the consumer the same to buy just the 'must stock' items (in this case Windows) as buying the must stock item along with the discretionary item (in this case WMP). Indeed, since there was (prior to the CFI judgment) no unbundled version of Windows, there was no opportunity to avoid purchasing WMP.

In a classical assessment of the incentive effects of this kind of pricing structure, the focus would lie on what a rival media player supplier would need to do to make an attractive offer to the consumer, and on the incremental profitability to Microsoft of supplying WMP to a customer who bought Windows.

Clearly, it would not be possible in this case for a media player provider such as RealPlayer to compete 'bundle-to-bundle' with Microsoft, because to do so would require it to devise and market a rival operating system alongside its media player. The dominance of Windows and the network effects that protect that position ruled out any consideration of this counter-strategy.

This leads the focus to the incremental pricing incentives of supplying WMP. On the one hand, this assessment looks unpromising to Microsoft because the bundling of WMP in Windows meant that the 'price' of WMP was zero. So how could a stand-alone media player supplier compete against a free product? The complication in this case, however, was that the incremental cost to Microsoft of supplying a Windows product with WMP is plausibly zero, and that the established market price for the supply of stand-alone media players to consumers is also zero. Media players are provided free of charge to consumers in the hope that they will be taken up by PC users and hence encourage developers or creators of content to buy software licences from the media player supplier. This 'two-sided market' feature of media players does not make the standard framework redundant, but it does suggest that a zero price might not have the kind of market-foreclosing characteristics that it would create in other markets.

Turning to the interoperability abuse, the tying model does not describe Microsoft's conduct as neatly, but it could be seen as a practice whereby Microsoft made interoperability information (the tying product) available only to customers who bought the work group server OS (the tied product) to the detriment of rival stand-alone server OS providers. We can again consider what a stand-alone provider of such software (such as Sun Microsystems) would need to do to compete with Microsoft's offering.

The first question here is whether the interoperability information supplied by Microsoft is truly a 'must stock' item. Clearly, it is essential for servers to be able to work with Windows PCs, so some form of interface between the PC and the server is required, but it is perhaps less obvious that Microsoft is the only *possible* supplier of that interface. For example, it is arguably the case that server software suppliers themselves are able to achieve some degree of workable interoperability between their servers and Windows PCs even if that communication is not as good as can be achieved with access to Microsoft's own codes.[13]

For the sake of the argument in this chapter, let us assume that the

---

[13] This discussion has some parallels with the debate on essential facilities cases as to whether a third party supplier should have to show that it would be impossible or just inconvenient to have to compete without access to the alleged essential facility.

Microsoft interoperability information is so superior to any language that could be devised by an independent server supplier that it meets the 'must stock' status required for the application of leveraging analysis. In that case, the fact that such interoperability information could be obtained only by purchasing the Microsoft server software, and not as a stand-alone unbundled 'product', makes the analysis similar to that of the media player abuse.[14] If a customer can obtain the must stock item (the interoperability functionality) only by purchasing the discretionary (and potentially competitive) item (i.e. the Microsoft work group server software) then it seems obvious that stand-alone suppliers of work group server software face a big problem. Moreover, that problem appears more severe than in the media player case because suppliers of server software do not benefit from the kind of two-sided market benefits that allow media player suppliers to supply their products free of charge. This increases the likelihood that Microsoft's bundling of the server software with its own interoperability information had the effect of foreclosing rival server software suppliers from the work group server software market.

This description of the two Microsoft abuses illustrates that in any situation where a dominant firm chooses to tie products A and B together, it will be inherently difficult for stand-alone suppliers of product B to compete. The fact that consumers of product A in effect receive product B free of charge means that, within the pricing framework, any act of bundling is likely to fail the relevant price-cost test and to indicate a serious risk of foreclosure. If, in the pricing framework, the enforcement rule is that foreclosure concerns arise whenever the incremental price for the discretionary units lies below the costs of an efficient stand-alone rival supplier, then bundling will almost always attract such concern since the incremental price of the element that is tied to the primary good is by definition zero. We now turn to consider this issue in relation to the CFI judgment.

4. WHEN IS TYING AN ABUSE? THE CFI CRITERIA

In assessing the Commission's reasoning regarding Microsoft's tying abuse, the CFI confirmed the five conditions which need to be satisfied in order to demonstrate a tying abuse.[15] These conditions are:

---

[14] This description abstracts from many complex definitional issues regarding the technical status of the interoperability information and whether/to what extent it is protected by intellectual property rights.

[15] CFI judgment, paras 43–5.

(i) there must be dominance in the supply of the tying product;
(ii) the tying and tied good must be two separate products;
(iii) the tying product is not offered without the tied product;
(iv) the act of tying forecloses stand-alone competitors; and
(v) the tying conduct cannot be 'objectively justified'.

The following sections address each of these conditions in turn.

Dominance in Tying Product

The first condition to establish tying abuse is to find the undertaking dominant in the supply of the tying product. The case for finding Microsoft dominant in the provision of client PC operating systems seems largely uncontroversial in view of its sustained high market share in the supply of operating systems to PCs. The CFI held that Microsoft's market share was in excess of 95 per cent under stable market conditions and combined that with significant network effects which constituted barriers to entry into this market.[16]

As we note above, Microsoft's dominance in the tying product markets meant there was limited if any scope for bundle-to-bundle competition from rival suppliers of the two affected tied products, media players and work group server software suppliers. In the context of the previous discussion of 'discretionary' versus 'captive' sales, Microsoft enjoys a large 'captive' sales base from which to engage in market power leverage.

Separate Products

The second necessary condition of a tying abuse is that the tying and the tied product are 'separate products'. The CFI upheld the Commission reasoning in this regard.[17] The Commission essentially relied on existing case law where the criterion of independent stand-alone providers emerged to define separate products. Specifically, the Commission noted that in the previous *Hilti*[18] and *Tetra Pak II*[19] cases, the court:

---

16 Network effects exist when one user's demand for the product increases with the number of other users. In the case of operating systems, the case for network effects is yet stronger due to additional incentives for programmers to develop software for a popular platform.

17 CFI judgment, para. 44.

18 Case T-30/89 *Hilti* v *Commission* [1991] ECR II-1439.

19 Case C-333/94 P *Tetra Pak* v *Commission* [1996] ECR I-5951 ('*Tetra Pak II*').

> pointed out that there existed independent manufacturers who specialised in the manufacture of the tied product, a fact which indicated that there was separate consumer demand and hence a distinct market for the tied product.[20]

This might seem at first glance to be a simple 'common sense' approach. However, defining separate products is not a trivial matter and the focus on actual competitors (or stand-alone demand) in the tied product as part of the process of distinguishing tying from other value-added combinations raises many problems that are not fully appreciated by the CFI judgment.

Interestingly, the Commission's Article 82 Guidelines offer a slightly more circumspect definition, as follows (para. 50):

> Two products are distinct if, in the absence of tying or bundling, a substantial number of customers would purchase or would have purchased the tying product without also buying the tied product from the same supplier, thereby allowing stand-alone production for both the tying and the tied product.

As we note above, the problem here is that all value-adding activity involves a degree of 'bundling' of separate components, and virtually every product or service supplied by profit-seeking firms can be decomposed into various elements that have been 'bundled' together in the manufacturing or supplying process. However, no economic principles exist to determine where one product should end or another begins. This is problematic because it means that the line between tying (which is perceived as problematic) and normal value-adding economic activity (which is not) is hard to draw. This creates a 'fault line' in Article 82 EC enforcement that can only be addressed if a less per se and more effects-based approach is taken to identifying when tying is and is not harmful from an efficiency/welfare perspective.

The CFI's approach seeks to draw the necessary distinction by reference to the existence of a 'separate demand' for the tied product. However, it does not take much imagination to envisage situations where the existence of a thriving stand-alone market for the tied product can coexist with bundling by some suppliers. For example, it is possible to buy shoelaces as a stand-alone product in grocery stores and many shoe shops, but that does not make it suspicious that sellers of new shoes typically deliver their products bundled with shoelaces. Similarly, there exists an active and growing market for satellite navigation devices designed for in-car use,

20 Decision, para. 802.

yet a number of car manufacturers choose to supply certain models with integrated satellite navigation systems as standard equipment.

In practice, the use of the 'separate demand' criterion as a defining feature of bundling is likely to bias enforcement to focus on situations where a dominant firm chooses to bundle products that were previously sold in unbundled format, and to rule out of considerations those situations where the added functions have always been supplied in integrated form. This in turn is likely to pick up cases where a stand-alone provider feels aggrieved or threatened with foreclosure when a dominant firm chooses to introduce a new variant that bundles the formerly stand-alone product. As such, it is an approach that will be friendly to would-be complainants. But it is far from clear that this distinction will be an efficient way to distinguish bundling that has anti-competitive effects from that which is benign or pro-competitive.

The debate on this point mirrors a wider debate that can be seen in the enforcement of Article 82 against refusal to supply and essential facilities cases. Some of the most heavily criticized Article 82 decisions are those in which firms have chosen to integrate their services to some related activity and in the process locked out a third party provider who was previously a customer of the dominant firm in question. Examples include *Commercial Solvents,*[21] in which the firm cut off supplies to a downstream processor and decided to engage in that processing on its own account, and *Hugin,*[22] in which a far from dominant cash till machine producer decided to conduct its own after-sales servicing and in the process ceased supply of spare parts to Lipton, a third party repairer.

These cases arose because the actions of the allegedly dominant firm cut off supplies to a third party which then had a clear incentive to complain. However, as we note above in the context of post-Chicago theories of harm, there is no necessary correlation between the incentive of a disadvantaged rival to complain, and a likely effect on consumer welfare. Hugin, for example, did not increase or meaningfully extend its market power by cutting Lipton out of third party repairs, and it is highly plausible that Hugin would have a higher incentive to ensure smooth and competitively priced after-market service for its brand than Lipton would have had. More tellingly, it seems extremely unlikely that, had Hugin always adopted a policy of controlling its own after-market servicing, the decision to do so would have attracted any competition law scrutiny, or that

---

21 Joined Cases 6 and 7-73 *Commercial Solvents and others* v *Commission* [1974] ECR 223.

22 Case 22/78 *Hugin Kassaregister* v *Commission* [1979] ECR 1869.

a complaint by a prospective third party servicing supplier that demanded Hugin unbundle its unified service offering would have succeeded in persuading the Commission to take up its case.

In the context of essential facility and refusal to supply cases, the Commission's Article 82 Guidelines state that it can be abusive to refuse to unbundle a previously bundled product as well as to bundle a previously unbundled product (para. 78):

> The Commission does not regard it as necessary for the refused product to have been already traded: it is sufficient that there is demand from potential purchasers and that a potential market for the input at stake can be identified.

However, they go on to suggest that there is more likelihood of a case being taken up if the third party was previously supplied (para. 83):

> The criteria set out in paragraph 80 apply both to cases of disruption of previous supply, and to refusals to supply a good or service which the dominant company has not previously supplied to others (de novo refusals to supply). However, *it is more likely that the termination of an existing supply arrangement is found to be abusive than a de novo refusal to supply*. (Emphasis added)

This greater risk in the assessment of the same conduct depending on the existence of actual competitors is highly relevant to the Microsoft case. An operating system such as Windows contains literally thousands of different attributes and functions that have been bundled together in a single product, yet the two aspects that led to the Article 82 case both arose from situations where Microsoft chose to change the nature of its product, offering to incorporate aspects that had not previously been included. That in turn led stand-alone suppliers of media players and work group server software to complain about this change to the viability of their business models. Whilst such complaints are entirely understandable from the commercial perspective of the firms involved, a broader question is whether consumer welfare is any less well served because Microsoft chose to incorporate an extra functionality (say WMP) into Windows. How, apart from the historical accident that media players had previously not been included as part of Windows, is that different from the bundling of any other attribute that has always been included in Windows?

The debate on Chicago and post-Chicago School theories seeks to answer such questions by reference to specific theories of competitive harm relating to dynamic theories of monopoly power protection and/or extension. Such theories need to do more than simply identify that Microsoft managed to extend the scope of its dominant Windows product (or, equivalently, that a previously independent supplier has now lost its opportunity to compete). Yet, although the post-Chicago arguments were advanced by the complainants in the case (indeed, a number of such theories were invented – and certainly sponsored – by complainants looking to gain traction for their concerns), there is no clear record in the Commission Decision or the CFI judgment of these theories being fully tested and of their consequences being used to justify the eventual remedies. Instead, one gains the impression that the allegations of abuse were upheld because the Commission and the CFI felt sympathy for the complainants' predicament. But that is not the same as identifying a net loss to consumer welfare or economic efficiency.

Tying Product Not Offered Separately

The third criterion applied by the CFI concerned whether the tying and tied products are offered separately. The Commission noted that Microsoft's licensing model required that WMP is pre-installed within the Windows operating system.[23] Moreover, it was also impossible to uninstall the WMP from Windows due to the high degree of integration with other components of the operating system.[24]

With respect to the media player abuse, Microsoft's main defence was that since media players were (and remain) in any event available to consumers to download free of charge, the bundling in question did not preclude rivals from continuing to offer their media players in competition. Hence, the act of integrating WMP into Windows simply provided an extra convenience to PC producers and consumers in not having to undertake this task themselves. Moreover, since the marginal cost to Microsoft of supplying an extra unit of software is plausibly zero, it was by no means clear what form an unbundled solution to this problem should take. The problem for rival media player suppliers was not that the bundling of WMP into Windows put them at a price disadvantage, but rather that it increased the convenience to consumers of opting for WMP, and that this added convenience could tip the market towards WMP and against competing products.

With respect to the server software abuse, it was clearer that Microsoft did not offer the interoperability information as a stand-alone option, separate from the supply of the server software itself. Moreover, it does seem clearer that the terms of supply of the unbundled interoperability

---

23 Decision, para. 827.
24 Decision, para. 828.

information would need to be significantly better than the terms on which the bundled Microsoft work group server software should be supplied. But the exact terms on which this unbundling should take place proved to be a source of additional problems (and additional fines) for Microsoft.

We discuss some of the economic issues raised in the design and implementation of remedies in the following section. For now, however, the key point is that, on its own, a requirement to offer the tied and tying products separately is not a sufficient solution to any abuse caused by bundling. It is also necessary to consider the terms on which the unbundled elements are priced. This insight is made obvious by the analogy between bundling and rebates cases that we have discussed above, yet it has seldom been addressed in the non-price abuse cases.

Foreclosure

The fourth criterion to assess anti-competitive tying is concerned with foreclosure of stand-alone providers. In the context of the WMP tie, the question at hand was whether the practice would force third party products (for instance, the RealPlayer or QuickTime players) from the market. The Commission's argument rests on the fear that tying would prevent third party competitors from reaching the necessary level of market penetration of users.[25] A small user base would mean that developers would stop using their format, which would ultimately force them to leave the market.[26]

The Commission Decision does discuss the possibility of competing media players gaining market access through alternative distribution channels (e.g. OEM pre-installation and end-user media player downloads). If there are sufficient users who would install a third party product in addition to WMP then competitors offering a better product might not be foreclosed. Clearly, integration of WMP with the operating system 'guarantees' a larger user base, and the assumption seems to be that the huge convenience of an integrated media player within the ubiquitous Windows system would provide an impetus to grow the use of WMP and shrink the opportunities for rival media players.

With respect to the server software market, there is also a lack of precise information on the effects of Microsoft's conduct on third party server software providers, but the Commission's 2007 Press Release announcing

---

[25] Decision, sections 5.3.2.1.4.1.1 and 5.3.2.1.4.1.2.
[26] Decision, para. 863.

the final resolution of the access terms dispute does indicate that Microsoft enjoys a 70 per cent share in this market, and that open source products are 'virtually the only alternative for users' to the Microsoft product.[27]

'Objective Justification'

The final criterion to consider when evaluating tying practices is the existence of an 'objective justification'. The precise meaning of this criterion remains obscure. It appears to incorporate a diverse series of possible factors such as safety considerations (none of which apply in the Microsoft case) and maybe some efficiency arguments in defence of tying.

As regards compelling objective reasons to justify tying, Microsoft argued that integrating WMP into Windows would lead to efficiencies in distribution as consumers did not have to spend time and effort to assemble the required software.[28] It also argued that tying WMP into Windows had pro-competitive effects in making it easier for application developers to make available media which ultimately benefits end-users.[29] However, as is often the case with such efficiencies, the factors which increased the convenience of using WMP were also the very features that made it (relatively) inconvenient for consumers to choose rival media players, and hence contributed directly to the foreclosure effects that define the abuse. This underlines the fact that it seems almost impossible to devise a satisfactory efficiency defence for conduct that has market-foreclosing effects under EC competition law.

With respect to the server software abuse, Microsoft argued that unbundling the interoperability information from Microsoft's own server software would create adverse incentive effects, reducing the rewards to innovation. However, the Commission and the CFI were scathing about Microsoft's inability to justify such dynamic efficiency arguments and they remained unconvinced that adequate rewards for innovation could not be achieved through an unbundled solution. This point, however, is virtually indistinguishable from the wider question of what price Microsoft should be permitted to charge for the information, since that price will determine the rewards it will receive.

---

[27] See 'Antitrust: Commission secures compliance with 2004 Decision against Microsoft', Commission Press Release, 22 October 2007.

[28] This argument is in essence related to the discussion of value-added activities in section 2 above.

[29] Decision, para. 962.

5. IMPLICATIONS OF THE MICROSOFT REMEDIES

Although the CFI judgment upheld the Commission Decision and is explicit about Microsoft's duty to offer both the interoperability information and a version of Windows without WMP, there remains considerable ambiguity about the terms of the unbundling. Indeed, due to a lack of guidance on the price that should be charged for the stand-alone products, the unbundling remedy is, by design, incomplete. A brief discussion of the remedies serves to underline some of the broader issues we have identified above regarding the conclusions on abuse.

Access to the Interoperability Information

Regarding the interoperability information, the CFI referred to Article 5(a) of the Commission Decision whereby: 'Microsoft . . . shall, on reasonable and non-discriminatory terms, allow the use of the Interoperability Information'.[30] However, before an agreeable access tariff could be defined, the Commission engaged in a lengthy dialogue with Microsoft following the CFI ruling. It was Microsoft's failure to find an acceptable level for the access fee that led the Commission to impose a further €899,000,000 in fines. A significant portion of the Commission's non-compliance Decision argues that the royalty rates suggested by Microsoft were unreasonably high, without defining a competitive price benchmark.[31] However, there is a wide variety of candidates for what constitutes a 'reasonable' price level in the absence of any guidance on this in the Decision.

At one extreme, a dominant firm will invariably argue that it is reasonable to set licence fees at such a level as to provide compensation for the losses in profits it will suffer by allowing third party suppliers into the previously foreclosed market. That desire for compensation may well seem reasonable to the dominant firm, but if the Decision has been justified in mandating third party access, that ought to reflect a conclusion (often an implicit one) that the state of the world in which access is denied will generate monopoly profits to the dominant firm. In this context, it is understandable that an approach to access charges that compensates the dominant firm for lost monopoly profits will be deemed unreasonable.[32]

30 Decision, article 5(a) and CFI judgment, para. 266.

31 Commission Decision C(2008)764 Final of 27 February 2008.

32 More pertinently, charges set at this level are likely to be too high to make entry viable. The reasoning is that if the dominant firm's profit-maximizing choice

A more competitor-friendly principle would be to set access terms at levels that allowed rivals to compete viably, irrespective of how great the loss of profit would be to the dominant firm from doing so. It appears that this was ultimately the standard that the Commission required Microsoft to meet, but imposing this test is highly problematic for a dominant firm. As a matter of principle, the approach is likely to involve a significant degree of expropriation of the dominant firm's property rights. At a practical level, the identification of an access price that allows third parties to compete will be difficult because it requires the dominant firm to observe the internal business conditions of the potential rivals.

The Commission's October 2007 Press Release provides some feel for just how far apart contested views can be on what constitutes a reasonable solution. Microsoft originally offered a patent licence of 5.95 per cent, but this was eventually beaten down to 0.4 per cent in the final settlement. Microsoft was also forced to retreat from its original strong contention that the information was protected by intellectual property rights, to an obligation to offer a flat fee of just €10,000 for open source code competitors who believed that such intellectual property rights did not apply.

One would need to know more about the interaction between Microsoft and the Commission following the Decision to assess why it took so long to find a solution that was deemed to bring Microsoft's conduct in line with legal compliance. From the outside, it appears that the Decision itself (and indeed the CFI judgment) fell well short of prescribing the level at which Microsoft should make the interoperability information available. Judging from the eventual outcome, one infers that the Commission's actual view was that any fee above a nominal level would be abusive, and had the Decision itself stated this it would have clarified where the Commission saw the line between reasonable and abusively high prices for access to the information. This episode illustrates that unbundling remedies are meaningless without defining an applicable price benchmark for the individual elements of the bundle.

Now that an access pricing remedy is in place, however, it does seem to have provided a safeguard against the competitive harm that was identified in the server software abuse. To the extent that the abuse finding was based on the concern that foreclosure of rival work group server software suppliers would protect Microsoft's dominance in Windows, the remedies now provide for the continued existence of open source server software providers who can offer a product that works seamlessly with Windows.

---

was to exclude downstream entry, it must be less remunerative to allow access on terms that would make entry viable.

Under the post-Chicago theories of monopoly power protection, this remedy will be judged a success if the existence of such suppliers provides a foundation for software providers that have some power to constrain Microsoft's position in the PC operating systems market.

Unbundling WMP

The remedies for unbundling WMP leave many more questions unanswered. The CFI referred to Article 6(a) of the Commission Decision stating that Microsoft shall 'offer a full-functioning version of the Windows Client PC Operating System which does not incorporate Windows Media Player'.[33] Microsoft responded by offering an unbundled version of Windows (excluding WMP) alongside the conventional bundled version. However, it was permitted to offer the two versions at the same price, and so it is perhaps unsurprising that the vast majority of consumers and PC manufacturers have opted to buy the bundled version. Microsoft has reported that the unbundled version, Windows XP N, accounts for 0.005 per cent of overall Windows XP sales in Europe.[34]

If one accepts the premise of the guilty verdict on WMP – that offering a bundled version of Windows harmed competition and consumers because it foreclosed stand-alone media player suppliers – it is very hard to see how this remedy could put right the competitive wrong on which the ruling of abuse was founded. Any such remedy would have needed to counteract the competitive advantage that Microsoft gained by bundling WMP with Windows, and that would have needed to take the form of either a price discount for the unbundled version to discourage consumers from buying the bundled version of Windows, or an outright ban on bundling WMP within the Windows product so as to enable Microsoft and its rivals to compete on a level playing field in the supply of media players.

Since the main barrier to rival media player providers is the sheer convenience to the consumer of having WMP already integrated and installed on every Windows PC, the more logical remedy would have involved the enforced unbundling of the Windows product so as to level the playing field 'down' in a way to make media player installation opportunities accessible

---

[33] Decision, article 6(a).

[34] See Microsoft, Fact Sheet: Windows XP N Sales, April 2006, available at www.microsoft.com/presspass/legal/european/04-24-06windowsxpnsalesfs.mspx. Microsoft further notes that OEMs were not interested 'in installing and selling computers with a less than fully functioning version of Windows XP' and that OEMs had more than doubled the average number of pre-installed media players in addition to WMP in Europe between 2004 and 2006.

to other suppliers. That would have been a controversial move, however, since it would have constituted a conscious decision to eradicate the clear efficiency that arises from the convenience of integrating the media player functionality into the operating system. However, if the Commission was truly satisfied that Microsoft's WMP abuse would have an adverse effect on competition and consumers, such tough choices might be required. In contrast, the actual remedy imposed suggests that either the alleged abuse was not serious after all, or that the Commission for some reason lacked the courage of its convictions in identifying a remedy that would right the perceived harm to competition.

6. CONCLUSIONS

After lengthy proceedings into the two Microsoft abuses, there is still considerable uncertainty as to when tying (i.e. the combination of separate attributes into a single product) constitutes an abuse. The five pronged test outlined by the CFI as a way to assess tying practices provides no clear principles that offer practical guidance to dominant suppliers, or indeed to Microsoft in particular.

On one reading, the Microsoft judgment leaves the impression that dominant firms face a general duty to unbundle separate elements of their products wherever a third party supplier of a stand-alone element complains. The single biggest problem is that, as discussed above, there is no clarity on where any such obligation to unbundle should start or end, and no operational rule exists to draw the distinction between a value-adding 'component' and a separate product.[35]

In reality, it seems likely that decisions by dominant firms to extend existing products in such a way as to offer additional features that were previously provided by third party providers are much more likely to attract Article 82 scrutiny than decisions to continue to offer a historically bundled product. That distinction has more to do with the development of an enforcement policy that is responsive to complainants who fear

---

[35] This impression that the CFI judgment has not clarified the definition of abusive bundling seems to be confirmed by the fact that the Commission has now opened a further formal case against bundling by Microsoft, this time involving the bundling of the Internet Explorer browser into the Windows operating system. On 15 January 2009, the Commission confirmed it had sent a Statement of Objections to Microsoft on this latest case. See http://europa.eu/rapid/pressReleasesAction.do?reference=MEMO/09/15&format=HTML&aged=0&language=EN&guiLanguage=en.

foreclosure, than to the identification of scenarios where a valid post-Chicago theory of harm has identified a significant detrimental effect to consumers or economic efficiency.

Given the multifaceted nature of Microsoft's products, there is an almost endless range of possible tying 'abuses' of which Microsoft could be accused. And since product improvements in the software industry (as with many other sectors) generally take the form of adding increased functions to the previous version of the product, there is an acute risk that any new version of Microsoft's products will generate complaints from suppliers of software that perceive themselves threatened by any added scope of Microsoft's Windows operating system. We would therefore question what the Microsoft Article 82 case has done to clarify a more predictable or effects-based approach to Article 82 enforcement against anti-competitive tying.

13. The quest for appropriate remedies in the EC Microsoft cases: a comparative appraisal

Nicholas Economides and Ioannis Lianos

1. INTRODUCTION

The Microsoft cases in the United States and in Europe have been influential in determining the contours of the substantive liability standards for dominant firms in US antitrust law and in EC competition law. The competition law remedies that were adopted, following the finding of liability, seem, however, to constitute the main measure for the 'success' of the case(s). An important disagreement exists between those arguing that the remedies put in place failed to address the roots of the competition law violation identified in the liability decision and others who advance the view that the remedies were far-reaching and that their alleged failure demonstrates the weakness of the liability claim. This study evaluates these claims by examining the variety of remedies that were finally imposed in the EC Microsoft cases, from a comparative perspective. The study begins with a discussion of the roots of the Microsoft issues in Europe and the consequent choice of a remedial approach by the European Commission and the European Court of First Instance (CFI). It then explores the effectiveness of the remedies in achieving the aims that were set. The non-consideration of the structural remedy in the European case and the pros and cons of developing such a remedy in the future are briefly discussed before more emphasis is put on alternative remedies (competition and non-competition law ones) that have been suggested in the literature. The study concludes by discussing the fit between the remedy and the theory of consumer harm that led to the finding of liability and questions a total dissociation between the two. We believe that it is important to think seriously about potential remedies before litigation begins. However, we do not require an *ex ante* identification of an appropriate remedy by the plaintiffs, since this could lead to underenforcement or overenforcement.

In 2004, the European Commission adopted a Decision declaring that

Microsoft had violated Article 82 EC[1] by committing two abuses of its dominant position on the market for PC operating systems (the first EC Microsoft case).[2] Microsoft was held to have abused its dominant position by refusing to supply competitors with certain interoperability information and to allow them to use it for the purpose of developing and distributing competing products on the market for work group server operating systems. It also found that Microsoft had infringed Article 82 EC by making supply of its client PC operating system Windows conditional on the simultaneous acquisition of its Windows Media Player (WMP). The CFI affirmed the Decision of the Commission in 2007.[3]

Following complaints by Opera, the Norwegian web-browser developer, in December 2007 the Commission initiated investigations and sent a Statement of Objection (SO) in January 2009[4] alleging a violation by Microsoft of Article 82 EC for tying its web-browser Internet Explorer to its dominant client PC operating system Windows. On 16 December 2009 the Commission gave its approval to the choice screen proposal suggested by Microsoft and adopted an Article 9 of Reg. 1/2003 commitment decision.[5]

This study will focus on the remedies that were adopted by the Commission and confirmed by the CFI in the first EC Microsoft case, as well as those accepted by the Commission in the second EC Microsoft case, and will *not* examine the liability issue or the specific substantive standards for the finding of an abuse of dominant position in EC competition law.[6] Although there will be some references to the remedial strategy adopted

---

[1] Article 82 of the EC Treaty prohibits the abuse of a dominant position that one or more undertakings have in a relevant market when there is an affect on trade between Member States.

[2] Commission Decision 2007/53/EC of 24 March 2004 [2007] OJ L32/23 ('the Decision').

[3] Case T-201/04 *Microsoft Corp.* v *Commission* [2007] ECR II-3601 ('CFI judgment').

[4] European Commission, MEMO 09/15, 17 January 2009, available at Europa Press Release.

[5] See European Commission at http://europa.edu/rapid/pressReleases-Action.do?reference=IP/091941 and http://ec.europa.eu/competition/antitrust/cases/decisions/39530/final_decision_en.pdf (full version). In the final settlement, Microsoft made additional commitments on interoperability between rivals' software and its own, including Windows, Windows server, Office, Exchange and SharePoint.

[6] On the tying part of the case, see Nicholas Economides and Ioannis Lianos, 'The Elusive Antitrust Standard on Bundling in Europe and in the United States in the Aftermath of the Microsoft Cases' (2009) 76(2) *Antitrust Law Journal* 483 available at http://papers.ssrn.com/sol3/papers.cfm?abstract_id=1078932.

in the United States for practices that were closely related to those condemned in the EC Microsoft case, this study will also not systematically compare the US remedy with the EC remedy, for the simple reason that each remedy addressed a different competition law problem, and therefore required the adoption of different measures to address that problem.

Competition law remedies are adopted with the aim to restore competition in the market: this includes the 'micro' goal of putting the infringement to an end, compensating the victims,[7] and curing the particular problem to competition, but also the 'macro' goal of putting incentives in place 'so as to minimize the recurrence of just such anti-competitive conduct'.[8] This study embraces a broader view of the concept of remedies than Council Regulation 1/2003 on the implementation of the rules on competition laid down in Articles 81 and 82 of the EC Treaty.[9] Competition law remedies seek generally to restore 'the plaintiff's rightful position, that is, to the position that the plaintiff would have occupied

---

[7] Taking illegal gains away from the law violators and 'restoring the monies to the victims' constitutes a principal goal of competition law remedies: see Robert Pitofsky, 'Antitrust at the Turn of the Twenty-First Century: The Matter of Remedies' (2002) 91 *Georgia Law Journal* 169, 170.

[8] Eleanor Fox, 'Remedies and the Courage of Convictions in a Globalized World: How Globalization Corrupts Relief' (2005) 80 *Tulane Law Review* 571, 573.

[9] Council Regulation 1/2003 [2003] OJ L1/1. According to Article 7 of Regulation 1/2003, the aim of competition law remedies is 'to bring the infringement effectively to an end'. Remedies should therefore be distinguished from sanctions against undertakings, as the latter have the aim to punish the infringer and to provide compensation to victims or society in general. See also, on the distinction between remedies and sanctions, OECD, *Remedies and Sanctions in Abuse of Dominance Cases*, DAF/COMP(2006) (May 2007), p. 18, available at www.oecd.org/dataoecd/20/17/38623413.pdf: '(t)ypically, remedies aim to stop a violator's unlawful conduct, its anticompetitive effects, and their recurrence, as well as to restore competition. Sanctions are usually meant to deter unlawful conduct in the future, to compensate victims, and to force violators to disgorge their illegal gains'. This distinction does not adequately take into account that sanctions and damages often affect the incentives of the wrongdoers in their future behaviour on the market. This study adopts a broader view of remedies, which includes different aims, allegedly also those performed by sanctions, such as stopping the illegal conduct and preventing its recurrence, restoring competition, deterrence, just compensation, disgorgement of illicit profits. This overall approach may provide a more useful analytical framework for analysing the effect of competition law on the specific market. Furthermore, the restrictive position adopted by Regulation 1/2003 concerns public enforcement and does not take into account the emerging role of private enforcement in EC competition law, following the publication of the White Paper on Damages Actions for Breach of the EC Antitrust rules, COM(2008)165.

if defendant had never violated the law' or 'to restore the defendant to the defendant's rightful position, that is, the position that the defendant would have occupied absent the violation'.[10] In other words, remedies are a cure to a 'wrong' the defendant committed, 'in contravention of some legally-recognised right of the plaintiff's'[11] or of the category of right-recipients that the legislator aimed to protect. The wrong of the defendant gives rise to the enforceable right of the plaintiff (or the protected category) to impose on the defendant a correlative duty of stopping the illegal behaviour, paying damages, making restitution, or adopting a specific behaviour. An important aspect in the definition of remedies is therefore to determine who would be the beneficiary of this right, in other words the protected category that retains the right to impose a correlative duty to the defendant. We will assume that the protected category is the consumers of the relevant market harmed by the 'wrong' committed by the defendant.[12] A wider perspective would be to consider that the protected category consists of the 'broader public' who derive benefits from the principle of competition, allegedly jeopardized by the practices of the dominant firm.[13]

Whichever perspective is chosen, 'restoring competition' should not be interpreted as reaching perfect competition (or free competition if one takes a deontological perspective), which is practically unattainable, and in some cases normatively an undesirable objective from a public policy perspective.[14] The remedy aims to restore the market that would

---

10 Douglas Laycock, *Modern American Remedies: Cases and Materials* (Little, Brown, 1994), p. 2.

11 Michael Tilbury, Michael Noone and Bruce Kercher, *Remedies: Commentary and Materials* (3rd edn, LBC Information Services, 2000), p. 1.

12 In this case, consumer welfare or consumer sovereignty will be proxies of consumer harm.

13 See the Opinion of Advocate General Kokott in Case C-8/08 *T-Mobile Netherlands BV and others*, 19 February 2009, paras 58 and 71, defending the view that the objective of EC competition law is to 'protect competition as such' because this is of benefit, not only for consumers but for 'the public at large'. In Case C-8/08 *T-Mobile Netherlands BV and others*, 4 June 2009, para. 38, the European Court of Justice accepted that 'Article 81 EC, like the other competition rules of the Treaty, is designed to protect not only the immediate interests of individual competitors or consumers but also to protect the structure of the market and thus competition as such' but did not adopt the position of Advocate General Kokott with regard to the ultimate beneficiaries of the principle of competition, thus suggesting that a possible interpretation of the aims of EC competition law is the avoidance of a long-term consumer harm.

14 In industries with significant network effects, even in the absence of anti-competitive actions, the natural equilibrium is neither perfect competition nor an egalitarian market structure. Markets with strong network effects, such as the

have existed in the absence of the conduct found illegal, that is, what is commonly called the 'but for' market conditions.

Competition law remedies list also a prophylactic objective: 'ensure that there remain no practices likely to result in monopolization in the future'.[15] This is certainly a difficult enterprise that requires from the courts a guessing exercise linked to a counterfactual analysis of the situation in the market with and without the specific competition law violations. This is particularly true in complex and dynamically evolving markets, where static models cannot easily predict the situation that would have existed absent the restraint. It also requires a difficult decision on the appropriate remedy enforcement mechanism, as the judge should decide on the degree of her involvement (as opposed to market forces or regulatory institutions) in the operation. One could indeed perceive the operation of designing appropriate remedies as being, first of all, a decision over the need for regulatory interference in order to bring the self-correcting forces of the market back to their usual operation, as the default mechanism that would adjust the incentives of market actors and therefore the interaction between supply and demand in the specific sector of the economy. Thus, remedies could be (i) setting up conditions for the market to work, or (ii) directly influencing or guiding the market.

There are, of course, different choices that can be made and combined in order to affect the incentives of market actors and restore 'competition', defined as the best possible outcome for the consumers of the specific relevant market in terms of price, quality, variety, innovation etc., if one assumes (as does this study) a consumer-driven competition law and policy. First, it is possible to contract out the remedy to other affected market participants by enabling them to sue for the recuperation of the

---

market for operating systems of PCs, are 'winner takes most' markets with significant market share and profits inequality as well as high concentration. Thus, the 'but for' world that would have existed in the absence of anti-competitive actions is one of very significant inequality. Attempting to impose the perfectly competitive egalitarian environment of a non-network industry can lead to lower social benefits. *See* Nicholas Economides, 'The Economics of Networks' (1996) 14 *International Journal of Industrial Organization* 675, available at www.stern.nyu.edu/networks/Economides_Economics_of_Networks.pdf; Nicholas Economides and Fredrick Flyer, *Compatibility and Market Structure for Network Goods*, Discussion Paper EC-98-02 (Stern School of Business, New York University), available at www.stern.nyu.edu/networks/98-02.pdf; and Nicholas Economides, 'Competition Policy in Network Industries: An Introduction' in Dennis Jansen (ed.), *The New Economy and Beyond: Past, Present and Future* (Cheltenham: Edward Elgar, 2006), available at www.stern.nyu.edu/networks/Economides_Competition_Policy.pdf.

[15] See *United States* v *Microsoft Corp.*, 253 F.3d 34, 103 (D.C. Cir. 2001).

damages suffered because of the conduct found illegal or for more than the damages incurred in order to deter market participants from adopting a similar anti-competitive conduct in the future. Secondly, it is possible to develop remedies that would affect the discretion of market participants to run their business, in other words affect their autonomy as market participants and consequently their incentives. The latter could be conceived as a continuum ranging from preserving some degree of discretion for market participants (in the case of contractual remedies, such as commitments) to purely non-voluntary schemes, unilaterally imposed by the public authorities. One could also distinguish remedies that relate to the conduct of the market participants and attempt to affect their incentives to adopt a specific form of conduct (by creating disincentives such as fines, or, more brutally, by imposing injunctions, interdictions, conduct remedies) from more intrusive remedies that affect the infringing company's or management's status (criminal sanctions, structural remedies).

The next section will briefly discuss the roots of the Microsoft issues in Europe and the consequent choice of a remedial approach by the Commission and the CFI. The third section will critically assess the effectiveness of these remedies. Time has been relatively short since these remedies were adopted to be able to proffer a well-substantiated judgement on the success of the remedial strategy adopted in Europe. Two sources of wisdom will, however, be employed in order to make a relatively informed assessment of the remedial part of the EC Microsoft case so far. First, we will refer to the example of the US Microsoft cases and the effectiveness of the remedial strategy employed, not only in order to add a comparative law perspective to this study but because the EC remedial strategy has been influenced by the US remedial experience in the US Microsoft case. Secondly, we will incorporate in our analysis the recent business history of this specific sector and the emergence of new market characteristics, new products and competitors, as is usually the case in the rapidly evolving high-tech markets. The fourth section will discuss the non-consideration of the structural remedy in the EC case and will reflect on the prospects of developing such a remedy in the future. The fifth part will conclude by discussing alternative remedies (competition and non-competition law ones) that have been suggested in the literature and that could provide the adequate incentives to market participants. The final section will conclude.[16]

---

[16] The important issue of the proportionality of the remedies imposed to Microsoft will be the object of another study: Nicholas Economides and Ioannis Lianos, 'A Critical Appraisal of Remedies in the EU Microsoft Cases', forthcoming (2010) 2 *Columbia Business Law Review*.

2. DESIGNING OPTIMAL REMEDIES AND THE ROOTS OF THE MICROSOFT PROBLEM IN EUROPE

The design of optimal remedies requires a clear identification of the competition law problem that the antitrust remedy is attempting to address. It may be that competition authorities and courts develop different remedial strategies for precisely similar or analogous fact patterns, because the competition law problems that were identified as the source of consumer harm in the liability phase of the decision are different. This study builds on the assumption that consumers should be at the centre of the attention of competition law enforcers, not only at the liability phase of the decision, but also at the remedy phase.

In the background of the finding of a competition law violation there is always a consumer harm story, in other words a narrative of consumer harm that is built on specific inferences from the facts of the case and that is established by different types of evidence: circumstantial, empirical or theoretical, quantitative or qualitative. In order to understand and assess the remedies adopted in the Microsoft case, we need to briefly unravel the dominant narrative of consumer harm that led to the adoption of these specific remedies. Additionally, often actions can be identified as anti-competitive and their likely effect can be determined, but the quantification of their effect is much more difficult. Thus, a full restoration of the market to the 'but for' world may be unfeasible. Often all that can be done is to eliminate the impediments to competition that resulted from anti-competitive actions.

In Europe, the dominant narratives of consumer harm in the first Microsoft EC case were two: first, an issue of lack of interoperability and compatibility that allegedly harmed consumers; secondly, a story of leveraging. Both stories are different from the dominant narrative of the US Microsoft case, although they also relate to the business strategy of Microsoft to integrate different applications in its Windows platform, the source of Microsoft troubles in the United States. However, there are different views on the anti-competitive effects of this strategy of integration. While in the United States, the main story of anti-competitive harm was that Microsoft was essentially attempting to preserve the dominance of the Windows' platform,[17] in Europe the Commission and the CFI perceived

[17] The leveraging attempted monopolization part of the browser market claim was not successful. See *United States* v *Microsoft Corp.*, 253 F.3d at 80–1, although an undertone of leveraging theory existed in some other claims. See e.g. the integration of Internet Explorer and Windows (253 F.3d at 65–6).

Microsoft's strategy as essentially being focused on the applications part of the business, where it attempted to extend its dominant position through the network effects of its platform.[18] The different narratives of consumer harm justified the choice of a different remedial strategy.

Institutional differences with the United States, such as the unavailability of civil remedies (fines) for infringements of sections 1 and 2 of the Sherman Act, while fines are frequently imposed in Europe, may also explain the different remedy mixture in each jurisdiction. Private enforcement and damages actions are also less frequent in Europe than in the United States. Frederic Jenny rightly observes the close relation between civil sanctions and damages, from a deterrence perspective, even if the beneficiaries of the compensation are different in each case:

> (i)t makes no difference whether payments are made to the state budget or to consumers. Thus the current discussion in the EU on private enforcement should take into account the fact that even if the purpose of private enforcement is to compensate victims rather than to punish violators, the possibility of adding compensatory damages to administrative (or criminal) sanctions increases the overall cost of being caught for violators and therefore increases the deterrent effect of the enforcement system. This means that when considering whether an enforcement system is over deterrent or under deterrent (and when considering whether more or less resources should be devoted to public enforcement), one should take into account the effect of the interaction between public and private enforcement. For example in jurisdictions (such as the US) where it is relatively easy for victims to bring civil suits against antitrust violators that have inflicted harm on them, there is, *ceteris paribus*, less need for public enforcement than in countries where it is more difficult to bring such actions (such as in the EC Member States). Cross-Atlantic comparisons of fining policies between the US Department of Justice and the EC Commission sometimes seem to suggest antitrust enforcement is as vigorous in the EC as in the US because the level of sanctions meted out by the Commission tends to be nearly as high (or sometimes higher) as penalties obtained by the US Department of Justice. But if such comparisons do not take into account civil enforcement as well as public enforcement, they can be highly misleading.[19]

---

[18] The Commission also argued that Microsoft had a maintenance of monopoly/defensive leveraging objective for the interoperability part of the Decision: Decision, paras 768–70, but the extension of monopoly power was the primary concern in both the interoperability and the tying parts of the case. See also, CFI judgment, paras 1288, 1327, 1344 ('it must be borne in mind at the outset that the two abuses at issue form part of a leveraging infringement, consisting in Microsoft's use of its dominant position on the client PC operating systems market to extend that dominant position to two adjacent markets, namely the market for work group server operating systems and the market for streaming media players').

[19] Frederic Jenny, 'Optimal Antitrust Enforcement: From Theory to Policy

The alleged consumer harm narrative is intrinsically related to the imposition of a specific duty on the defendant to cure the wrong committed. It therefore affects the mixture of the different types of remedies adopted. In some cases, that will require the adoption of a specific duty to act (conduct remedies). In other cases, it will entail a substitutionary (pecuniary) remedy, often when it is difficult or impossible to cure all the negative effects of the practice on the protected category with conduct remedies. It is therefore important to understand the mixture of all types of remedies, specific and substitutionary, adopted by different jurisdictions in order to form an idea on their comparative effectiveness. We will first discuss the conduct remedies imposed on Microsoft in Europe before examining the substitutionary remedies (fines, damages).

Specific (Conduct) Remedies

The Commission adopted conduct remedies for both anti-competitive practices of Microsoft. These remedies should respect the usual requirements of proportionality[20] and the existence of a relation between the remedy and the infringement that has been established.[21] The first remedy addressed the interoperability/compatibility issue, the second the tying/leveraging issue.

Interoperability/compatibility

The Commission found that Microsoft had refused to provide Sun with information enabling it to design work group server operating systems which could seamlessly integrate in the 'Active Directory' domain architecture, a web of interrelated client PC-to-server and server-to-server protocols that organize Windows work group networks. Microsoft's refusal to provide interoperability to Sun was found to be part of a broader pattern of conduct of refusing the relevant information to any vendor of work group server operating systems. Microsoft developed this strategy after it had, for a certain period of time, provided analogous information for previous versions of Microsoft's products to Sun and to the industry at large. The Commission found that this disruption of previous

---

Options' in I. Lianos and I. Kokkoris, *The Reform of European Competition Law: New Challenges* (The Hague: Kluwer, 2009).

20 Case 15/83 *Denkavit* [1984] ECR 2171, para. 25 and Case C-354/95 *R* v *Minister for Agriculture, Fisheries and Food, ex parte National Farmers' Union and others* [1997] ECR I-4559, paras 49 and 50.

21 Joined Cases 6/73 and 7/73 *Commercial Solvents and others* v *Commission* [1974] ECR 223, para. 45

levels of supply eliminated competition in the relevant market for work group server operating systems, as this information was indispensable for competitors operating in that market.[22]

The objective pursued by Microsoft was to leverage the quasi-monopoly power it had in the operating systems market to the work group server systems market. Due to network effects, Windows is an indispensable platform for most applications. In reaching this conclusion, the Commission relied on evidence that there was a link between the enhanced interoperability from which Microsoft's work group server operating systems benefited, in comparison to competing work group server operating systems, and the rapid rise to dominance of Microsoft's applications in the work group server operating systems market. The Commission proceeded even further and attempted to show consumer harm, as in the absence of Microsoft's refusal to provide interoperability, the competitors would have been able to provide new and enhanced products to consumers. The Decision of the Commission did not include any evidence of the existence of projects for new products or investments that were not carried on because of Microsoft's conduct. Rather, it emphasized the indirect nature of consumer harm provoked by Microsoft, which put interoperability at the centre stage of the competitive struggle. Consumers seemed, however, to attach greater importance to other product characteristics, such as reliability and security. The Commission rejected the objective justifications advanced by Microsoft. The Commission did not make a full market inquiry on whether the free provision of software and the expansion of functionality of Windows create benefits to consumers. Such potential benefits should have been balanced with the losses to consumers from the alleged anti-competitive actions.

The European Court of Justice's case law recognizes that in exceptional circumstances a refusal to license may constitute an abuse under Article 82 EC.[23] This was found to be the case, after the Commission proceeded to a

---

[22] The exact market definition for interoperable systems was contested between Microsoft and the Commission. Here we take the liability verdict as given.

[23] For an analysis, see Ioannis Lianos, 'Competition Law and Intellectual Property Rights: Is the Property Rights' Approach Right?' in John Bell and Claire Kilpatrick (eds), *Cambridge Yearbook of European Legal Studies* (Oxford: Hart Publishing, 2006), pp. 153–86. The CFI gave a broad interpretation of the 'new product rule' in comparison to the previous case law: '(t)he circumstance relating to the appearance of a new product as envisaged in *Magill* and *IMS Health* . . . cannot be the only parameter which determines whether a refusal to license an intellectual property right is capable of causing prejudice to consumers within the meaning of Article 82(b). As the provision states, such prejudice may arise where

qualitative balancing of the incentives of Microsoft and its competitors to innovate in the marketplace. Imposing a duty to provide interoperability would not reduce Microsoft's incentives to innovate, because, from the Commission's point of view, this is the way competition takes place in this industry. It will also preserve the incentives to innovate of Microsoft's competitors. This finding was based on three implicit assumptions: first, competition constitutes the most adequate market structure to promote innovation in the software market;[24] secondly, Microsoft's competitors would have the incentive to provide new products and functionalities to consumers in order to be able to compete and would not clone Microsoft's products; and thirdly, that the Commission-imposed disclosures on interoperability among Microsoft servers would not diminish Microsoft's incentives to innovate in systems of servers. Further direct evidence of exclusionary intent, such as company internal documents, carried the conviction of the Commission that Microsoft's objective was to restrict competition in the work group server operating systems market.

In adopting the conclusion on Microsoft's liability, the Commission was indirectly influenced by the existence of a previous remedial strategy addressing problems of interoperability in the software sector.[25] In fact, although the decision of the Commission targeted the refusal of interoperability by Microsoft to Sun, it is clear from the general description of the competition law problem with which the Commission was confronted in this case that it envisioned the issue of interoperability more broadly and therefore not strictly confined to the facts of the specific case. For example, the Commission referred to the strong network effects that existed in this market, thus reducing considerably the contestability of Microsoft's

---

there is a limitation not only of production or markets, but also of technical development': CFI judgment, para. 647. The focus on the limitation of technical development to the detriment of consumers widens the scope of application of Article 82 EC in comparison to the position of the European Court of Justice in Joined Case C-241 and 242/91 P, *RTE and ITP* v *Commission* [1995] ECR I-743, para. 50 ('*Magill*') and Case C-418/01 *IMS Health* v *NDC Health* [2004] ECR I-5039, paras 34–5, which found that except in exceptional circumstances, a refusal to license intellectual property rights cannot by itself constitute an abuse of a dominant position. Such cumulative exceptional circumstances exist when the refusal to license is unjustified, prevents the emergence of a new product for which there is a potential consumer demand and excludes 'any' or 'all' competition on a secondary market.

24 In reaching this conclusion, the Commission did not fully consider innovation by new companies that might be bought by the dominant company or with whom it might create strategic alliances, and then their products would be sold or marketed by the dominant company.

25 Commission Decision IV/29.479, *IBM*.

dominance in the platform and applications parts of its business. The Commission also emphasized, when it examined the issue of Microsoft's dominant position, the 'strong commercial and technical associative links' between the PC operating systems market and the work group server operating systems market, with the result that 'Microsoft's dominance over the PC operating systems market has a significant impact on the adjacent market for operating systems for work group servers'.[26] This observation communicates the idea that the competition law problem with which the Commission was confronted was of a structural nature (relating to the nature of the market and not necessarily linked to the specific characteristics of the excluded rivals) and therefore required the development of a set of remedies that would address the problem of interoperability at its core.

The Commission referred to previous industry practice, in particular the licence agreement with AT&T relating to the disclosure of portions of the Windows source code,[27] to previous decisional practice, such as the *IBM* precedent, and to the existing regulatory framework, in order to emphasize the need to establish interoperability in the software market. Furthermore, the EC Software Directive adopted in 1991[28] restricted the exercise of copyright over software (including exercise by non-dominant undertakings) for interoperability reasons and explicitly provided that its provisions were without prejudice to the application of Article 82 EC, in particular if a dominant undertaking refused to make available information which is necessary for interoperability.[29]

The main objective of the remedy was thus to restore interoperability, at least to the same degree that existed on the market before the alleged disruption by Microsoft of the previous supply of information. This raised two difficulties.

First, the Commission had to define the requisite degree of interoperability. This is an issue linked to both the liability and the remedy parts of the decision. Microsoft argued that it already provided some form of interoperability, which was allegedly found insufficient by the Commission, as this degree of interoperability was still providing an advantage to Microsoft's work group server operating systems. The issue could be framed as a platform neutrality problem: where a platform owner also provides complementary goods or services (applications), which rely on the platform and which compete with other applications. Had Microsoft

[26] Decision, para. 526.
[27] Decision, para. 212.
[28] Council Directive 91/250/EEC of 14 May 1991 on the legal protection of computer programs [1991] OJ L122/42 ('Software Directive').
[29] Decision, para. 763.

not provided full (or native) interoperability to its own work group server operating systems, after providing the same degree of interoperability in the past with competing applications, most likely the Commission would not have found a violation of Article 82 EC. In other words, the Commission understood interoperability in relative (not absolute) terms, requiring in systems composed of components of different companies the same level of interoperability achieved between the dominant platform's components. This created a paradox as the Active Directory did not exist in the past (before Windows 2000) and Microsoft had not provided interoperability information in the past. Rather, what Microsoft provided was a licence to the source code of Windows itself, for others (mainly AT&T) to use to build bridges between UNIX and Windows. But providing Windows source code was not what the Commission wanted Microsoft to do. Secondly, the Commission had to decide the institutional arrangement that would have achieved most effectively the required degree of interoperability. This issue relates to the implementation mechanism for the remedy, which raised important difficulties.

Defining the Requisite Degree of Interoperability

One could attempt a comparison between the EC interoperability remedy and the interoperability remedy imposed in the US Microsoft case: contrary to the EC case, interoperability was a minor point of the liability claims of the US Department of Justice and the 19 states against Microsoft. Of course, incompatibility between different operating systems (OS) created an inequality in market shares, with Microsoft ending with a lion's share of the OS market for PCs.[30] Thus, it could be argued that the lack of technical compatibility in operating systems (the fact that Windows applications do not run on Linux or Apple in native mode and vice versa) resulted in dominance by Microsoft in the market for OS for PCs, and in turn this was the foundation of Microsoft's distributional advantage for any type of application or middleware that could be added to the Windows platform.

---

30 In industries with strong network effects, lack of compatibility leads to a natural equilibrium of severe market share and profit inequality even in the absence of anti-competitive acts. See, Nicholas Economides, 'Public Policy in Network Industries' in Paolo Buccirossi (ed.), *Handbook of Antitrust Economics* (Cambridge: MIT Press, 2008), available at www.stern.nyu.edu/networks/Economides_Public_Policy_In_Network_Industries.pdf. When anti-competitive acts are proven, the appropriate remedy should not be to restore perfect competition with egalitarian market shares and profits but rather the natural oligopoly equilibrium that has severe market share and profits inequality.

The US case The issues in the US case were mainly the contractual and technological integration of Internet Explorer and Windows, along with a number of measures adopted with relation to Internet Explorer (IE), and a number of acts adopted with the aim to undermine Sun's cross-platform Java. In order to build a stronger integration between IE and Windows, Microsoft had adopted a number of practices, such as (i) imposing licence restrictions barring original equipment manufacturers (OEMs) from a number of activities, such as removing IE icons, causing a new interface to load in place of Windows, altering the appearance of the Windows desktop; (ii) designing Windows to exclude IE from the Add/Remove Programs utility or to commingle IE only and shell code in the same files and otherwise technologically tying IE with Windows; (iii) entering agreements with Internet access and content providers to promote and favour IE and IE technologies; (iv) contractually tying IE with Windows.

The theory behind the case, accepted by Judge Thomas Penfield Jackson of the District Court in his liability decision,[31] was mainly that Microsoft's aim was to protect its monopoly in the operating systems market (platform) from the threat of middleware such as Sun's Java technologies and Netscape, which could have evolved into a rival platform for applications. Microsoft engaged in a strategy of annihilation of that threat,[32] through a series of measures, such as withholding technical information, contractual and design measures, etc. The District of Columbia Circuit unanimously affirmed some of Judge Jackson's liability findings with regard to IE, including most notably monopolization of the OS market for PCs.[33] Judge Jackson also found liability of tying IE with Windows as a per se tying claim, but this was reversed by the District of Columbia Circuit on appeal. The US Department of Justice declined to pursue the tying claim under the rule of reason approach suggested by the District of Columbia Circuit.

Crucially, however, the District of Columbia Circuit did not address the claim that Microsoft withheld valuable technical information from Netscape in the liability part of the decision. William Page and Seldon Childers note that 'nothing in the opinion supports the propositions that a monopolist has a general obligation to make its products compatible with those of its rivals or to help its rivals develop products that can inter-

---

31 *United States* v *Microsoft Corp.*, 87 F.Supp.2d 30 (D.D.C. 2000).

32 87 F.Supp.2d at 46. The District of Columbia Circuit found that the plaintiffs did not establish a high probability of success of the attempted monopolization claim, in particular, but demonstrated that substantial barriers to entry protected that market: *United States* v *Microsoft Corp.,* 253 F.3d 34, 81 (D.C. Cir. 2001).

33 253 F.3d 34.

operate with its own'.[34] Interoperability became, however, an important concern in the remedial part of the US Microsoft case. Judge Jackson's 2000 remedial order called for a variety of conduct orders, in addition to the structural vertical separation of Microsoft, including a requirement that Microsoft disclose applications programming interfaces (APIs), communications interfaces and technical information necessary for developers to ensure that their software was compatible with Windows and therefore to 'interoperate effectively with Microsoft platform software'.[35]

The District of Columbia Circuit vacated the remedial order for a number of reasons, including the fact that Judge Jackson failed to offer an explanation of how the remedy would restore competitive conditions and that, following the reversal of most of the liability holdings, it was necessary to remand the case to the trial court in order to establish appropriate remedies. Interestingly, the District of Columbia Circuit linked the design of an appropriate remedy with the issue of causation, by mentioning that the courts must base their remedies on 'some clear indication of a significant causal connection between the conduct enjoined or mandated and the violation found directed toward the remedial goal intended'.[36] The remedy should also be carefully 'tailored to fit the wrong creating the occasion for the remedy'.[37] It is interesting to note that on remand, after a further trial, the district court rejected the divestiture remedy for IE and Microsoft Office, suggested by the plaintiffs, because '(n)either the evidentiary record from the liability phase, nor the record in this portion of the proceeding, establishes that the present success of IE is attributable entirely, or even in predominant part, to Microsoft's illegal conduct'.[38] Following the referral to the district court, the United States and nine states (the New York group) entered a settlement with Microsoft and agreed to a proposed final

---

34 William H. Page and Seldon J. Childers, 'Software Development as an Antitrust Remedy: Lessons from the Enforcement of the Microsoft Communications Protocol Licensing Requirement' (2007) 14 *Michigan Telecommunications and Technology Law Review* 77, 86 available at www.mttlr.org/volfourteen/page&childers.pdf.

35 *United States* v *Microsoft Corp.*, 97 F.Supp.2d 59, 67 (D.D.C. 2000).

36 97 F.Supp.2d at 105. The court also indicated when remanding the case to the district court that '(i)n devising an appropriate remedy, the District Court also should consider whether plaintiffs have established a sufficient causal connection between Microsoft's anticompetitive conduct and its dominant position in the OS market', the court noting that 'we have found a causal connection between Microsoft's exclusionary conduct and its continuing position in the operating systems market only through inference'.

37 97 F.Supp.2d at 107.

38 *New York* v *Microsoft Corp.*, 224 F.Supp.2d 76, 185 n. 81 (D.D.C. 2002).

judgment. Judge Kollar-Kotelly reviewed the settlement under the Tunney Act in order to determine if it was in the public interest[39] and confirmed the consent decree with only minor modifications.[40] A group of states (the California group) pursued a more extensive relief[41] but they were finally granted a similar relief to the New York group.[42] The District of Columbia Court of Appeals affirmed both final judgments.[43] Judge Kollar-Kotelly, the district court judge, supervised the enforcement of the remedy.

The District of Columbia District Court's decision included some 'forward-looking' remedies that attempted to guarantee a degree of interoperability between Microsoft's operating system and middleware applications, as well as between Microsoft's PC operating system products and third party server operating systems. It was thought that such interoperation 'will play an integral role in the successful emergence of new software products and platforms and that fostering such interoperation is an appropriate remedial objective in this case'.[44] This remedy was allegedly demanded by the states and included in the consent decree without any particular thought as to the extent of the obligation imposed on Microsoft and the difficulties of its enforcement.[45] Middleware was defined more broadly than the browser and the Java applications that were the main subjects of the decision, and also included WMP, Windows Messenger, Outlook Express 'and their successors in a Windows Operating System Product',[46] although it was contended that these 'forward looking provisions' aimed to 'foster competition in the monopolized market in a manner

---

39 *United States* v *Microsoft Corp.*, 215 F.Supp.2d 1 (D.D.C. 2002).

40 *U.S.* v *Microsoft*, 231 F. Supp 2d. 144 (D.D.C. 2002)

41 *New York* v *Microsoft Corp.*, 209 F.Supp.2d 132 (D.D.C. 2002).

42 *New York.* v *Microsoft Corp.*, 224 F.Supp.2d 76 (D.D.C. 2002), final judgment.

43 *Massachusetts* v *Microsoft Corp.*, 373 F.3d 1199 (D.C. Cir. 2004).

44 *New York* v *Microsoft Corp.*, 224 F.Supp.2d at 171.

45 As is explained by Page and Childers, n. 34, above, at 97, the idea of requiring Microsoft to disclose protocols for interoperation of server-based applications and Windows had arisen during the settlement negotiations mediated by Judge Posner and were not mentioned in the liability phase of the decision. The negotiations did not focus on the web-browser as it had become clear by that time that Microsoft had won the 'browser war'. The US Department of Justice and the states were instead worried that Microsoft could leverage its monopoly power onto the server operating systems market and thus 'maintain its dominance by retarding the ability of non-Microsoft servers—servers being the vital, digitized, data-filled libraries that served corporate networks and the Internet—to hook onto PCs powered by Windows'.

46 *New York* v *Microsoft Corp.*, 224 F.Supp.2d at 275.

consistent with the theory of liability in this case'.[47] The consent decree required Microsoft to disclose not only APIs that were used by Microsoft middleware to interoperate with a Windows operating system product in order to place rival middleware suppliers on an equal footing with Microsoft in developing applications for Windows, but also 'any communications protocol', which is 'implemented in a Windows Operating System Product installed on a client computer' that is 'used to interoperate, or communicate natively (i.e., without the addition of software code to the client operating system product) with a Microsoft server operating system product'.[48]

Communication protocols constitute the rules for the transmission of information between servers and clients or between servers and other servers. Communication protocols may 'perform a function akin to that performed by traditional middleware because they provide a platform for applications running "for" use on a PC', thus enhancing the ability of these non-Microsoft server operating systems to provide a platform which competes with Windows itself.[49] The district court limited its disclosure requirement for protocols that had a sufficient nexus to the theory of the liability of the case, maintenance of monopoly: only communication protocols implemented in a Windows operating system product installed on a client (PC) computer used to interoperate or communicate natively with the Microsoft server operating system product were covered.[50] This followed the rejection, by the district court, of the attempt of the plaintiffs to link interoperability as a general concept to the findings of liability and, consequently, the 'overbroad' disclosures that these were requesting. Such overbroad disclosure would have led to the cloning of Windows without violating Microsoft's intellectual property rights (IPRs). The court defined cloning as 'the creation of a piece of software which replicates the functions of another piece of software, even if the replication is accomplished by some means (e.g. reverse-engineering) other than the literal repetition of the same source code'.[51]

The district court rejected the states' definition of interoperable, as it equated this concept to interchangeable.[52] That would have denied Microsoft returns from its investment in innovation and divested Microsoft's IPRs of their value, as well as decreasing the incentives of

---

47 224 F.Supp.2d at 193.
48 224 F.Supp.2d, final judgment, part III.E.
49 224 F.Supp.2d at 172–3.
50 224 F.Supp.2d at 173.
51 224 F.Supp.2d at 176.
52 224 F.Supp.2d at 227.

software developers to innovate since they would have created clones of Microsoft's product.[53] The district court assumed that a greater degree of interoperability would have increased the risk of cloning and therefore led to greater homogeneity in the market. Additional difficulties for an extensive disclosure related to the need for Microsoft to maintain product flexibility, but again the indirect connection of the interoperability remedy with the liability findings in this case limited the court's activism. The district court also rejected the plaintiff's demand to require Microsoft to provide this information without being permitted to charge a reasonable royalty in exchange for the licence of its intellectual property.

The State of Massachusetts challenged the remedy decision of the district court to the Court of Appeal arguing, among other claims, that the district court had imposed a restrictive disclosure obligation on Microsoft. With regard to communication protocols, it was argued that native interoperability was only one out of five possible approaches to achieving interoperability between Windows client (PC) operating systems and non-Microsoft server operating systems. The Court of Appeal found that complete interoperability would have been imprudent and that the objective of the court should be to 'advance the ability of non-Microsoft server operating systems to serve as platforms for applications', in conformity with the liability theory of the case.[54] The court ruled that 'full' or 'seamless' interoperability was not appropriate in this case. Pursuant to section III.E of the remedies judgment, Microsoft put in place a protocol licensing programme in September 2002.[55]

The EC case The broader scope of the consumer harm theory followed in the EC Microsoft case had an impact on the degree of interoperability required. Contrary to the US Microsoft case, the leveraging of Microsoft's quasi-monopoly power in the Windows operating system (platform) to the applications was the principal theory of harm in the EC Microsoft case. The two forms of conduct sanctioned by the European Commission, refusal to interoperate and tying, were intrinsically linked to this specific theory of consumer harm. Certainly, defensive leveraging was mentioned as an additional concern but the core of the case was leveraging.[56] It was thus possible for the Commission to impose stricter and more extensive

---

53 224 F.Supp.2d.

54 *Massachusetts* v *Microsoft Corp*, 373 F.3d at 1224.

55 For additional information on the monitoring process of the protocol licensing programme, see the Joint Status Reports on Microsoft's Compliance with the Final Judgment, available at www.usdoj.gov/atr/cases/ms_index.htm.

56 See our analysis, n. 18 above.

requirements on Microsoft. Furthermore, contrary to the US case, the existence of consumer harm was not inferred by the possibility of middleware to operate as a competing platform to Windows in the future. There was some evidence in the Decision that supported the contention that consumers were harmed by the exclusion of competing work group servers, as it was 'diminishing consumers' choices by locking them into a homogenous Microsoft solution'.[57] This causal link between the theory of harm and the anti-competitive practice can be explained by the emphasis put in EC competition law on the special responsibility of dominant firms to preserve competition[58] and the importance the Commission gave to network effects as significant barriers to entry reducing the contestability of the operating systems and the work group server markets.[59]

Sun was therefore able to extend the interoperability requirement to server-to-server communication protocols that were non-native. According to the Commission, this was linked to the perception that compatibility should extend beyond the Windows domain architecture or computer system as, in order to benefit from the upgrade from Windows to Windows 2000 and profit from the advanced features of the Windows 2000 domain, the work group servers should be Windows 2000-compatible.[60] This was possible partly because Microsoft had integrated Active Directory support directly into the Windows server which guaranteed interoperability 'within a computer *system* encompassing several Windows client PCs and several Windows work group servers linked together in a network', therefore implying 'both client-to-server and server to-server interoperability' in a seamless way.[61] As the Commission noted in the Decision:

---

57 Decision, para. 782.

58 Case C-322/81 *NV Nederlandsche Banden Industrie Michelin* v *Commission* [1983] ECR 3461 ('*Michelin I*'), para. 57; CFI judgment, para. 775; Case T-203/01 *Michelin* v *Commission* [2003] ECR II-4071 (*Michelin II*), para. 97. See also, Opinion of Advocate General Kokott in Case C-95/04 P *British Airways plc* v *Commission* [2007] ECR I-2331, para. 23: '(w)ithin the scope of the application of Article 82 EC, a dominant undertaking is subject to certain limitations that do not apply to other undertakings in the same form. Because of the presence of the dominant undertaking, competition on the market in question is weakened. Therefore – whatever the causes of its dominant position – that undertaking has a particular responsibility to ensure that its conduct does not undermine effective and undistorted competition in the common market. A practice which would be unobjectionable under normal circumstances can be an abuse if applied by an undertaking in a dominant position'.

59 Decision, para. 448.

60 Decision, para. 169.

61 Decision, para.178.

> The common ability to be part of that architecture is *an element of compatibility* between Windows client PCs and Windows work group servers. This compatibility can be described in terms of interoperability with the Windows domain architecture.[62]

The Commission found that the degree of interoperability of a non-Microsoft work group server affects the 'efficiency with which that work group server delivers its services to the users of the network', as 'other work group server operating system vendors that want to compete for customers having an existing investment in Windows need access to information relating to interoperability with the Windows domain architecture'.[63] Sun was indeed requesting Microsoft to provide full (native) interoperability information for its server Solaris, including server-to-server native interoperability, the type and degree of interoperability that was explicitly rejected by Judge Kollar-Kottely in the US Microsoft case. Sun requested specifications that would enable the company to implement in its products this ability for native interoperability. In comparison, the fact that this information was proprietary was mentioned in the US case as a factor limiting disclosure.

The scope of the interoperability requirement was also broader than in the US case. The US Microsoft Communications Protocols Licensing programme was limited to client-server communication[64] but did not extend to the interoperability between server-to-server protocols that are functionally related to the client PC, as was requested in the Commission's Decision.[65] Other interoperability solutions were not considered to be equivalent. The interoperability requirement imposed by the Commission was not open-ended, however, but concerned precisely the core work group server tasks of file, print and group and user administration, which were essential for rivals to compete in the work group server operating systems market.[66] The refusal that was at stake in the Decision was that to provide a full specification of the protocols underlying the Windows domain architecture, which organizes the way in which Windows work group servers deliver work group server services to Windows client PCs.[67] The Commission insisted that while Sun's requests involved both client-

62 Decision, para. 182.
63 Decision, paras 183–4.
64 Microsoft's Communications Protocol License Agreements, section 2.2.(e) License Scope, Reservation of Rights. Available at www.microsoft.com/protocols/mcpp.mspx.
65 Decision, paras 287, 289, 688–91.
66 Decision, para. 566.
67 Decision, para. 567.

to-server and server-to-server interoperability, the latter interconnections and interactions were functionally related to the client PC, noting that 'the link back to the client PC operating system market implies that the competitive value of the information refused derives from Microsoft's market strength in the client PC operating system market', thus building the necessary causal link between the dominant position and the abuse.[68]

The Commission found that Microsoft's refusal to supply full specification of the protocols used by Windows work group servers to deliver work group server services to Windows group networks aimed to allow the use of that specification to build interoperable products and distinguished that from the implementation of these specifications, which were not to be disclosed.[69] The Commission noted that it was common industry practice to provide interface specifications without giving access to all implementation details (e.g. standard–setting organizations on best practices in software specification).[70]

Microsoft's work group server operating system products had also enjoyed a rapid rise to dominance in the market.[71] The Commission linked Microsoft's growth to the launch of Microsoft's Windows 2000 generation of products, for which Microsoft had disclosed less interoperability information than for previous generations.[72] Microsoft's competitors have been unsuccessful in challenging Microsoft's position: Novell's market shares decreased considerably and Linux and UNIX products had only a marginal presence in the market[73] and did not represent a significant threat to Microsoft. The lack of interoperability locked-in customers in a 'homogeneous Windows solution for work group networks'.[74] According to the Commission, which based its findings on consumer surveys, interoperability was 'the key factor driving the uptake of Microsoft's work group server operating systems'.[75] The Commission

---

68 Decision, para. 567.

69 Decision, para. 570. 'The specification is descriptive in nature and describes what an implementation must achieve, not how it achieves it. The implementation is, on the contrary, algorithmic as it has to provide a process or set of rules to be followed in calculations or problem-solving operations that will run on a computer': Decision, para. 65. In other words, contrary to implementations, specifications do not have to be executable (run on a computer).

70 Decision, para. 571.

71 Decision, para. 590.

72 Decision, para. 592.

73 Decision, para. 597.

74 Decision, para. 613.

75 Decision, paras 637, 665. It is not entirely clear, however, if the specific consumer surveys were as conclusive as the Commission concludes in the Decision.

emphasized server to server interoperability as it viewed client-to-server and server-to-server interoperability as 'tightly linked to one another',[76] a consequence of the new integrated architecture of Windows to function as a system.[77] As long as server-to-server communication was necessary in order to perform a server-to-client communication, Microsoft had to provide specifications for these communication protocols in order to enable Novell's products to compete.

The linkage with the quasi-monopolistic position of Microsoft on the client PC operating systems market is more indirect and in essence weaker than in the case of server-to-client communications. The Commission found nevertheless that server-to-server interoperability was an 'indispensable input' for Microsoft's competitors to be able to compete and did not distinguish between the different degrees of indispensability of a server-to-client or server-to-server interoperability and the various degrees of interoperability that could have influenced the remedy imposed. Additionally, the Commission did not clearly show that the high degree of interoperability among servers that it demanded was sufficiently influenced by Microsoft's dominant position as regards Windows clients.

Microsoft's conduct was found to produce consumer harm: first, consumer harm came in the form of reduced consumer choice as non-disclosure would have eliminated or marginalized products that could provide interoperability in 'heterogeneous computing environments';[78] secondly, Microsoft has been able to impair 'the effective competitive structure in the market' by gaining a dominant position in the market for work group server operating systems.[79] The Commission did not believe that enhanced interoperability would lead to cloning.[80] The definition of cloning by the Commission was not, however, similar to the definition of cloning in the

---

The surveys did not fully assess the value that consumers would place on interoperability compared to other features of Microsoft and non-Microsoft servers. Additionally, it is unclear whether the surveys were filled only by server buyers in the relevant antitrust market as defined by the Commission.

76 Decision, para. 689.

77 The Commission noted that 'the proper functioning of a Windows work group network relies on an architecture of client-to-server and server-to-server interconnections and interactions, which ensures a transparent access to the core work group server services', known as 'Active Directory domain architecture'.

78 Decision, para. 703. Locking-in consumers into a homogenous Microsoft solution and therefore diminishing consumer choice indicated, according to the Commission, the existence of important consumer harm. Decision, para. 782.

79 Decision, para. 704.

80 Decision, paras 713–29.

US case given by Judge Kollar-Kotelly, for whom cloning was precisely what the European Commission called functional equivalence.[81] The Commission rejected the definition of cloning as functional equivalence and implied that cloning would exist only if Sun was authorized to copy Microsoft's source code.[82] The existence of functional equivalence would not lead to a similar product, as the Commission assumed that 'Microsoft's competitors will have to provide additional value to the customer, beyond mere interoperability of their products with the Windows domain architecture, if such products are to be commercially viable'.[83] The Commission found that there was no qualitative difference, from the point of view of innovation, between the protocols on client-to-server communication that Microsoft had agreed to provide under the US consent decree with the Communications Protocols Licensing programme, and the protocols required for server-to-server interoperability, as these 'involve the same type of protocols—sometimes the very same protocols' and that therefore any disclosure would not affect Microsoft's incentives to innovate.[84]

Microsoft was ordered 'to disclose complete and accurate specifications for the protocols used by Windows work group servers in order to provide file, print and group and user administration services to Windows work group networks'[85] as well as to authorize the implementation of these specifications in work group server operating system products.[86] As it was previously noted, this disclosure covered 'both direct interconnection and interaction between a Windows work group server and a Windows client PC, as well as interconnection and interaction between a Windows work group server and a Windows client PC that is indirect and passes through another Windows work group server'.[87] It also applied prospectively

---

81 *New York* v *Microsoft Corp.*, 224 F.Supp.2d at 175–6, cited by William H. Page, *Mandatory Contracting Remedies in the American and European Microsoft Cases*, University of Florida Levin College of Law Research Paper No. 2009-22 (5 May 2009), pp. 29–30, available at SSRN at http://ssrn.com/abstract=1073103. According to Judge Kollar-Kotelly, 'the clone emerges from a process of reverse engineering, which consists of the study of functionality in the original product and the attempt to produce a product which accomplishes the same end. The process of cloning the functionality of a competitor's product is usually an expensive and time-consuming undertaking which, if successful, will enable the cloned product to function as a replacement for the original product.'

82 Decision, paras 718–19.

83 Decision, para. 722.

84 Decision, para. 728.

85 Decision, para. 999.

86 Decision, para. 1003.

87 Decision, para. 1003.

to future generations of Microsoft's products, implying that Microsoft should update the disclosed information, each time it brought to market new versions of its products.[88] The aim set for the remedy was 'to ensure that Microsoft's competitors can develop products that interoperate with the Windows domain architecture *natively supported* in the dominant Windows client PC operating system and hence viably compete with Microsoft's work group server operating system'.[89] The disclosure did not cover the source code but the Commission also added that 'to the extent that this Decision might require Microsoft to refrain from fully enforcing any of its intellectual property rights, this would be justified by the need to put an end to the abuse'.[90]

Article 5 of the Decision required that any disclosure should be made on 'reasonable and non discriminatory terms'. This implied: first, that 'the disclosures should be made to *any* undertaking having an interest in offering work group server operating system products' and in a timely manner;[91] secondly, that any remuneration that Microsoft might charge for supply should not reflect the strategic value stemming from Microsoft's market power in the client PC operating system market or in the work group server operating system market, allowing its recipients to 'viably compete with Microsoft's work group server operating system';[92] and thirdly, that the terms 'under which they can make use of the disclosed specifications will remain reasonably stable'.[93] We will examine in a subsequent section how these conditions, in particular the second one, led to substantive litigation. However, it was the design of an implementation mechanism for the remedies that raised the most important difficulties.

Difficulties of the Implementation Mechanism

The period after the European Commission's decision: slow progress
Article 7 of the Commission's liability Decision required Microsoft to submit a proposal to the Commission 'for the establishment of a suitable mechanism assisting the Commission in monitoring Microsoft Corporation's compliance'. The Commission retained the right to impose such a mechanism by Decision, if Microsoft's proposal was not found 'suitable'. The Commission followed the example of the US Microsoft

88 Decision, para. 1002.
89 Decision, para. 1003.
90 Decision, para. 1004.
91 Decision, para. 1006.
92 Decision, para. 1008(ii).
93 Decision, para. 1008(iv).

antitrust case, where a technical committee was appointed with the aim to ensure compliance, thus rejecting the option of a simple reporting mechanism. The complexity of the Decision, and in particular the need to constantly verify the accuracy and completeness of the information provided by Microsoft, as well as the need to provide adequate information on specifications, would have indeed required, in some circumstances, the inspection of Microsoft's source code in order to resolve any issue of accuracy and completeness of the specifications disclosed, thus requiring a more institutionalized structure, such as a Monitoring Trustee. The Monitoring Trustee was urged to adopt a proactive, rather than reactive, role in enforcing the interoperability, as well as the tying, part of the Decision.

Microsoft was required to propose a mandate for the Monitoring Trustee. This mandate was subject to a number of principles, among others, the designation of the Monitoring Trustee by the Commission, the independence of the Trustee from Microsoft, the guarantee that 'the Monitoring Trustee would have access to Microsoft's assistance, information, documents, premises and employees to the extent that he may reasonably require such access in carrying out his mandate' and 'full access to the source code of the relevant Microsoft products'.[94] The Monitoring Trustee had the possibility to hire experts to carry out certain precisely defined tasks on his behalf and it was specified that all costs of establishment of the Monitoring Trustee, including a fair remuneration, should be borne by Microsoft.[95]

Microsoft submitted the first proposal for the establishment of a monitoring mechanism in April 2004 and followed up with the submission of two draft agreements that it intended to offer as part of a Work Group Server Protocol programme (the 2004 WSPP agreement).[96] The experience of the US Communications Protocol programme (MCPP)[97] and

---

[94] Decision, para. 1048.

[95] Decision, para. 1048(v).

[96] These included the licence agreement that Microsoft 'planned to use in order to make available the intellectual property in its protocols' ('the 2004 WSPP Development and Distribution Agreement'), and 'a draft form of evaluation agreement that Microsoft planned to use in order to enable prospective licensees to evaluate the protocols we would be making available before entering into a license for such protocols' ('the 2004 WSPP Evaluation Agreement'). For a corporate description of Microsoft's Intellectual Property Licensing programme, see Eve Psalti and Keith Hageman, 'Microsoft's Intellectual Property Licensing Program Boosts Customer Choice', available at http://download.microsoft.com/download/3/a/6/3a601f1b-ab32-486b-83de-dff660162125/MPP_IP_White_Paper.pdf.

[97] See www.microsoft.com/protocols/mcpp.mspx.

the monitoring of the remedy by the US Technical Committee were, in a way, instructive of the difficulties the implementation of the Commission Decision would also face.[98]

Most difficulties related, as in the US case, to the scope and the quality of the documentation provided by Microsoft in order to fully comply with the Decision. William Page and Seldon Childers detail the compliance efforts undertaken by Microsoft and the Technical Committee in the US Microsoft case as an ongoing project readjusted according to the market results it was achieving: these were not those anticipated, as after the first year of the programme and the initial release of the documentation, only four companies had agreed to a MCPP licence.[99] Under the instigation of the monitoring Judge Kollar-Kotelly, Microsoft was required to make significant changes to the MCPP licences, to reduce the royalties required and to perform a number of promotional activities in order to attract new licensees.[100] The Technical Committee had also extended the degree of disclosure of the protocols by requiring Microsoft to show licensees how to use the protocols and created 'an ancillary software development that would field test the protocols in order to check if the information provided by Microsoft would enable the Technical Committee's engineers to write implementations; this amounted to test Microsoft's compliance by using the information provided'.[101] Microsoft went as far as to create an 'interoperability lab', in order to test MCPP protocol implementations for MCPP licensees and to offer 'direct access to Microsoft product development teams and in-person support from experienced engineering staff during testing'.[102] As it is reported by Page and Childers, 'these efforts led to substantial increases in staffing for both Microsoft and the Technical Committee', as more than 210 Microsoft employees and 40 Committee staff were involved in the operation.[103]

The 'one at a time' method of fixing problems in the communication of the protocols was replaced in 2006 by a more comprehensive approach and a 'new overarching specification' for the technical documentation, put under the supervision of Robert Muglia, an experienced Microsoft executive. This new programme was based on 'the specification agreed

---

[98] For an excellent account, see William H. Page and Seldon J. Childers, n 34 above, 108.

[99] Page and Childers, n. 34 above, 114. To date, only SAMBA has worked in any significant way with the information provided through the MCPP licence.

[100] Page and Childers, n. 34 above.

[101] Page and Childers, n. 34 above, 117.

[102] See www.microsoft.com/protocols/mcpp.mspx.

[103] Page and Childers, n. 34 above, 120.

upon between Microsoft and the European Monitoring Trustee'.[104] According to Page and Childers, this new specification was the result of a formal collaboration between the Technical Committee and the European Commission's Monitoring Trustee and involved the rewriting of the technical documentation, 'eventually replacing the bulk of the work performed to date, while incorporating everything Microsoft has learned while trying to meet the prior standards, as well as complementary requirements from the EU documentation standards'.[105] The importance of this project required the extension of the programme until November 2009, with a possibility of further extension until November 2012.[106]

The European Commission's Decision had the advantage of intervening at a later stage when the US experience could have been very instructive for the design of the interoperability remedy. It also requested, however, disclosure of information that was never before the subject of a disclosure programme. The result of the Commission's Decision was therefore not only to oblige Microsoft to adopt the Work Group Server Protocol programme, but also to extend the scope of the US MCPP to the extent that this would have made possible compliance with both US and EC requirements. It is clear that in a global market where products are marketed at the global level, it is very difficult and costly to maintain two different compliance or communications protocols programmes: the programme that imposes the strictest disclosure obligations ends up setting the standard of disclosure.

Microsoft lodged an application for suspension of the Decision with the CFI[107] and also applied for an annulment of the Commission's Decision.[108] However, it decided on its own initiative not to enforce articles 5(a), 5(b), 5(c), 5(e), 6(a) and 6(b) of the Decision, pending the outcome of the interim measures proceedings before the CFI. The President of the CFI rejected

---

[104] Joint Status Report on Microsoft's Compliance with the Final Judgments, *United States* v *Microsoft Corp*., No. 98-1232 (CKK) (D.D.C. 30 August 2006) (hereinafter 'JSR August 2006'), at 3, available at www.usdoj.gov/atr/cases/f218000/218096.pdf.

[105] Page and Childers, n. 34 above, 122.

[106] Joint Status Report on Microsoft's Compliance with the Final Judgments *US* v *Microsoft*, 22 April 2009, available at www.usdoj.gov/atr/cases/f244900/244920.htm.

[107] Application for Suspension of the Commission Decision of 24 March 2004 (COMP/C-3/37.792 Microsoft), Case T-201/04 R *Microsoft* v *Commission* [2004] ECR II-4463.

[108] See CFI judgment.

Microsoft's application for a suspension order in December 2004.[109] Following an exchange of views between Microsoft and the European Commission on different draft decisions, the Commission adopted a Decision in July 2005, setting a detailed framework for the Monitoring Trustee's functions, determining the procedure of appointment of the trustee and describing the rights and obligations of each party.[110] The Commission appointed as Monitoring Trustee, Professor Neil Barrett, a computer scientist, from a shortlist of four experts submitted by Microsoft in October 2005.[111] In the meantime, the European Commission had received from Microsoft a proposal on the technical documentation to be disclosed, as well as suggestions as to the non-discriminatory and reasonable conditions under which the information would be disclosed.[112]

The compliance process for the interoperability part of the Decision faced two difficulties that led to a number of exchanges between the Commission and Microsoft and eventually a number of penalty decisions under Article 24 of Regulation 1/2003.[113] The first series of difficulties concerned the extent to which Microsoft provided the European Commission with complete and accurate technical documentation. There is an inherent ambiguity in this kind of exercise. Since the subject matter was intensely technical, it was hard for the lawyers on each side to communicate effectively with one another and to find a consensus on which aspects of Windows the Commission wanted Microsoft to document and share with competitors. The second series of difficulties related to the imposition of reasonable and non-discriminatory terms, and in particular the establishment of royalties for the WSPP licences.

OTR, the external technical experts of the Commission prior to the appointment of the Monitoring Trustee, found the proposals sent by Microsoft to be insufficiently complete, in particular as there was missing information and a lack of introductory and explanatory materials, making the technical information virtually unusable for developers without prior knowledge of the Microsoft environment. The Commission found that the WSPP remuneration scheme also presented several problems as it did not

---

109 Case T-201/04R *Microsoft* v *Commission*.

110 Commission Decision, *Microsoft* 28 July 2005, c(2005) 2988 final.

111 IP/05/1215.

112 IP/05/673.

113 Article 24 of Regulation 1/2003 entitles the Commission to impose such penalty payments not exceeding 5 per cent of average daily turnover in the preceding business year per calendar day to compel companies to put an end to infringements of EC Treaty antitrust rules, where an infringement has been established by a previous Commission antitrust Decision.

comply with the three conditions for the remuneration to be declared reasonable and non-discriminatory: i.e. that the protocols were Microsoft's own creation, the protocols were innovative, and the remuneration should be in line with a market valuation for technologies deemed comparable to any innovations identified by Microsoft.

Microsoft was indeed offering two separate licensing agreements to companies: a 'No-Patent Agreement', which allowed licensees to use the protocols without taking a licence for some disputed (by third parties) patents that Microsoft considered as being necessary, and an 'All IP Agreement' which included a patent licence for these disputed patents. For both licensees, Microsoft divided the protocols into Gold, Silver, Bronze price categories, from the most to the least innovative information or not necessarily innovative category, for which Microsoft imposed no royalty. The Commission found that the WSPP agreements offered by Microsoft were lacking in all three conditions.[114]

In light of these failings, the Commission issued a Decision in November 2005 pursuant to Article 24(1) of Regulation 1/2003 which warned Microsoft that if it did not comply with its obligations to supply complete and accurate information and to make the information available on reasonable terms, it would face a daily fine of up to €2,000,000.[115]

Following this Article 24(1) Decision, Microsoft provided, some days after the expiry of the deadline, a new version of technical documents and announced in January 2005 that it was offering a source code licence to all potential licensees. The Commission found that this documentation was not 'substantially different' from the earlier documentation and did not seem impressed by the source code announcements as this did not necessarily respond to the need to provide some active support to third party developers if these were to understand the specifications described

---

[114] In particular, the Commission noted that Microsoft's maximum royalty pricing levels would place the potential recipient of the interoperability information at a significant competitive disadvantage vis-á-vis Microsoft 'if the royalty that it has to pay is the same as the stand-alone price of Microsoft's work group server operating system product' (Decision, para. 118) and that even the minimum pricing levels would create 'a significant constraint on the ability of the work group server operating system vendor to compete if the cost of interoperating (which is necessary to be able to viably compete) is one fifth of the value of the dominant vendor's entire work group server operating system product' (Decision, para. 120). This issue is reminiscent of a margin squeeze claim.

[115] Commission Decision imposing a periodic penalty payment pursuant to Article 24(1), available at http://ec.europa.eu/competition/antitrust/cases/decisions/37792/art24_1_decision.pdf.

by Microsoft in the technical documentation provided.[116] Following consultation with the Advisory Committee of Member State Competition Authorities,[117] and supporting reports from the Monitoring Trustee and other external consultants, the Commission sent a new Statement of Objection for non-compliance with the obligation to provide complete and accurate technical documentation (the first step in an Article 24(1) Decision),[118] and later issued a decision for non-compliance pursuant to Article 24(2) of Regulation 1/2003 imposing on Microsoft a further €280,5 million for continued non-compliance with the March 2004 Decision and (this time acting on the basis of Article 24(1)) raised the periodic penalties to €3,000,000 for non-compliance.[119] Microsoft introduced an action for annulment of this decision at the CFI in October 2006, requesting the annulment or reduction of the amount of the periodic penalty imposed.[120]

But this was not the end of Microsoft's troubles. The Commission had raised in the first Article 24(2) Decision the possibility of also fixing periodic penalty payments for non-compliance with the second aspect of the Decision: charging reasonable remuneration for access to or use of the interoperability information. Both the Monitoring Trustee and the Commission's external advisor submitted reports which concluded that the remuneration levels proposed by Microsoft as a starting point for negotiation with licensees were not reasonable.[121] Following this consultation, the Commission sent Microsoft a Statement of Objection on 1 March 2007 indicating that there was no significant innovation in the interoperability information and concluded that the prices suggested by Microsoft were unreasonable.[122] In response, Microsoft submitted revised

116 MEMO/06/76.

117 2008/C 138/04 [2008] OJ C138/3.

118 IP/06/298.

119 Commission Decision fixing the definitive amount of the periodic penalty payment of 12 July 2006, available at http://ec.europa.eu/competition/antitrust/cases/decisions/37792/art24_2_decision.pdf; Summary of Commission Decision, 12 July 2006, Case COMP/C-3/37.792 *Microsoft* [2008] OJ C138/1. According to Article 24(2) of Regulation 1/2003, '(w)here the undertakings or associations of undertakings have satisfied the obligation which the periodic penalty payment was intended to enforce, the Commission may fix the definitive amount of the periodic penalty payment at a figure lower than that which would arise under the original decision'.

120 Case T-271/06 *Microsoft* v *Commission*, later removed from the register of the Court as Microsoft decided to discontinue the proceedings.

121 For a more detailed description, see Final Report of the Hearing Officer in Case COMP/C-3/37.792 *Microsoft*, available at http://ec.europa.eu/competition/antitrust/cases/decisions/37792/ho_report_2008.pdf.

122 IP/07/269. The Commission found that, regarding the 'No-Patents Agreement', there was no innovation in any protocol in the Gold and Silver

WSPP agreements that included a revised royalty table providing for a new remuneration scheme, to be assessed by the Commission.

The period after the CFI's judgment: acceleration At this stage of the proceedings, the CFI rendered its judgment, which annulled Article 7 of the Decision insofar as it ordered Microsoft to submit a proposal for the establishment of a mechanism involving a Monitoring Trustee independent from the Commission.[123] The Commission asked Microsoft to provide all documents and information Microsoft had provided to the Trustee or his team to the Commission from the date of the appointment of the Trustee.[124] The judgment of the Court on the liability issue strengthened the Commission's position in the negotiation process and finished by convincing Microsoft to agree to alter a certain number of the conditions in the WSPP licence regarding the provision of interoperability information ('the Neelie Kroes–Steve Ballmer agreement').[125] These included the alteration of the terms of the licence in order to render it compatible with the open source software model, the reduction of the royalty to a flat fee of €10,000 and the reduction of royalties for a worldwide licence including patents from 5.95 per cent to 0.4 per cent. The initial royalty claimed by Microsoft was of the range of 7 per cent. In comparison, the royalty rates of the standard MCPP agreement between Microsoft and the US government were 4 per cent of the net revenue of the licensee.[126] This figure was modified as a consequence of the European Decision and it is now 0.4 per cent.[127]

More concretely, Microsoft will now offer two agreements: a 'No-Patent Agreement' which would allow access to the interoperability information,

---

categories and that only four minor Bronze protocols represented a limited degree of innovation. As regards the 'All IP Agreement' category, the Commission also found that these were unreasonable, but this time not because of the absence of innovation, as the Commission indicated that the existence of patents indicates the existence of innovation, although it is possible to challenge the patents or to implement software which, in their view, does not infringe the patented technology.

[123] See our analysis below.

[124] Final Report of the Hearing Officer, at 5, available at http://ec.europa.eu/competition/antitrust/cases/decisions/37792/ho_report_2008.pdf.

[125] William H. Page and Seldon J. Childers, 'Bargaining in the Shadow of the European Microsoft Decision: The Microsoft-SAMBA Protocol License' (2008) 102 *Northwestern University Law Review* 332.

[126] See Commission Decision C(2008)764 final fixing the definitive amount of the periodic penalty payment imposed on Microsoft, para. 246, available at http://ec.europa.eu/competition/antitrust/cases/decisions/37792/decision2008.pdf.

[127] See www.microsoft.com/interop/FAQ.aspx.

but without taking a licence for patents which Microsoft claims necessary, with the flat royalty fee, and a 'Patent Agreement' for patents which Microsoft considers relevant, where the royalty fee would be limited to 0.4 per cent of licensees' product revenues.[128] In addition to these two licences, Microsoft took an 'irrevocable pledge not to sue open source developers (whether they are individuals, nonprofit organizations or commercial entities, such as companies and their employees, working in an open source development project) for development and noncommercial distribution of implementations of these Open Protocols'.[129]

The Neelie Kroes–Steve Ballmer agreement was not greeted overwhelmingly by the members of the open source software community,[130] essentially for two reasons: first, 'the terms were still incompatible with the GPLv3 (General Public License),[131] the standard open source license employed by open source software',[132] and secondly, the €10,000 flat royalty fee could 'discourage use by small free and open source development teams, which typically have no operating budget'.[133]

It had nevertheless a direct impact on the marketplace, as the Commission supported in December 2007 the conclusion of a licensing agreement between Microsoft and Samba ('the PFIF agreement')[134] for the covered protocols. Samba is an open source/free software package that gives administrators flexibility and freedom in terms of set-up, configuration and choice of systems and equipment for work group servers and which provides interoperability to a number of platforms, such as UNIX, Linux, IBM System 390, Open VMS and other operating systems. The involvement of Samba in the EC Microsoft litigation has been well explained elsewhere,[135] but it is interesting here to note the following points: Samba decided to intervene in 2003, when its existence was portrayed by Microsoft as a proof that there was no need to provide interoperability information to competitors and that reverse-engineering techniques were already in

---

128 IP/07/1567.

129 Page and Childers, n. 125 above, 343.

130 See www.samba.org/samba/PFIF/PFIF_history.html at 6.

131 See www.gnu.org/copyleft/gpl.html.

132 An important characteristic of Samba is that it is free and that it offers, according to GPL, permissive licensing terms, the possibility to change Samba software, which is available to download for free from the Samba website, and a copyright licence that requires derived works to be available under the same copyright.

133 Page and Childers, n. 125 above, 344.

134 The Protocol Freedom Information Foundation Agreement. PFIF was a non-profit corporation created by the Software Freedom Law Center (SFLC) in order to license the documentation to free or open source developers.

135 See www.samba.org/samba/PFIF/PFIF_history.html.

use and sufficient.[136] Samba's role became more prominent when the companies that initiated the complaint, in particular Sun and Novell, settled the case with Microsoft. This prevented these companies from playing an active part at the appeal stage and therefore sharing their important technical experience with the Commission and the Monitoring Trustee. The SFLC (representing SAMBA) had stepped into the procedure as an intervener in order to provide the Commission with technical support if needed in the appeal, and a SFLC representative participated to the CFI's hearings. Samba's role in the litigation became particularly prominent as it is now 'the most important non-Microsoft technology in the server market . . . which emulates the behavior of Windows server products, but runs on Linux' and 'the de facto standard for most non-Microsoft network enabled products' used by work group server companies such as IBM, Apple, Sun and Novell for their engines.[137]

The licence agreement between Samba and Microsoft was made possible with the mediation of the European Monitoring Trustee, who was still in place at the time, as the Commission had not formally repealed Article 7 of the 2004 Commission Decision.[138] The Monitoring Trustee put Samba's and Microsoft's engineers directly in contact to try and fix the most problematic parts of the agreement. In particular, Microsoft was willing to provide, as an annex to the agreement, an indication of all the patents it claimed in its licensed information and agreed not to sue Samba for infringement of an unlisted patent.[139] These 'patent maps', which have also become a prominent feature of Microsoft's interoperability policy,[140] provide developers with an opportunity to attempt to successfully design around Windows, without risk of patent infringement. Microsoft has only included patents on the patent map that it believes are necessarily infringed by any implementation of the protocol. The Samba licence constitutes by far the most important development of the EC Microsoft Decision's remedial phase.

In February 2008, the Commission adopted a second Article 24(2) Decision which imposed an additional €899,000,000 penalty for charging unreasonable prices for access to interface documentation for work group servers.[141] The Decision made clear that in order to be reasonable

---

136 Decision, paras 293–7. The Commission rejected this argument as Samba could not function as an Active Directory primary domain controller.

137 Page and Childers, n. 125 above, 335, 336.

138 See www.samba.org/samba/PFIF/PFIF_history.html, at 6.

139 Page and Childers, n. 125 above, 347.

140 See www.microsoft.com/protocols/default.mspx#patent%20maps.

141 Decision C(2008)764, n. 126 above.

the remuneration charged by Microsoft should exclude the strategic value stemming from Microsoft's market power in the client PC and work group server operating systems markets.[142] The Commission decided that the WSPP pricing principles to which Microsoft had agreed could serve as a point of reference for the assessment of the reasonableness of the prices. In particular, the Commission assessed the innovative character of the interoperability information provided by Microsoft, which forms the second WSPP pricing principles criterion, by examining the prior art for each claimed specification, and arrived at the conclusion that a very large part of the unpatented information (merely trade secrets) lacked innovation.[143] The Commission referred to the usual criteria of patentability (novelty, non-obviousness) in order to define the innovative nature of the information as 'an operational proxy', mainly for the reason that these are 'settled concepts' in the area of intellectual property.[144]

An action for annulment against this Decision was brought at the CFI, arguing, among other pleas, that the Commission committed a manifest error of assessment 'by requiring Microsoft to establish that trade secrets were innovative under a heightened patentability test in order to justify the imposition of royalties for a license to such trade secrets'.[145] The Commission then examined the third condition for the remuneration to be declared reasonable and non-discriminatory. It noted that Microsoft had provided similar technical documentation of protocols royalty-free in the past, a conduct that it discontinued when it acquired a dominant position in the work group server operating systems market; that the royalties charged in the MCPP licence agreements should not be considered as concrete evidence of market valuation, in particular as they did not bring the requisite results; and finally that remuneration charged in the context of standard setting organizations (SSOs) should be considered as comparable, thus indicating that Microsoft charged unreasonable prices. The Commission noted that 'Article 5 of the Decision does not prevent Microsoft from submitting its WSPP protocols to an SSO, thereby possibly reaping alleged 'non-royalty benefits' in the form of cross licenses or services provided by the SSOs'.[146] This aspect will be examined in the last section of this chapter.

In a recent press release, the Commission reaffirmed Microsoft's 'ongoing

---

142 Decision C(2008)764, para. 107.

143 Decision C(2008)764, paras 130–8. See also, http://ec.europa.eu/competition/antitrust/cases/decisions/37792/decision2008_annex.pdf.

144 Decision C(2008)764, para. 138.

145 Action brought on 13 May 2008, [2008] OJ C171/42.

146 Decision C(2008)764, n. 126 above, para. 271.

obligation to supply complete and accurate interoperability information' but took notice of the Court's judgment on Article 7 of the 2004 Decision, removed the Trustee provision from the 2004 Decision and repealed the 2005 Trustee Decision, which provided for the modalities of the monitoring mechanism and the appointment of a Monitoring Trustee.[147] The changes in Microsoft's behaviour, the possibility for third parties to exercise their rights directly before national courts, with the operation of private enforcement provisions in Microsoft's licence agreements, as well as the experience gained since the process of compliance started in 2004, convinced the Commission that the need for technical assistance should now be of an ad hoc character.

Tying

In comparison to the complex and long-running compliance procedures with the interoperability part of the Decision, the conduct remedy imposed with regard to the tying of Windows Media Player to Windows was relatively straightforward. The 2004 Commission Decision took the view that Microsoft had violated Article 82 EC, in particular because of the possible leveraging of its quasi-monopolistic position in the PC operating systems market to the media-player market. As it is explained in the Commission's Decision, the US judgments did not solve that particular anti-competitive problem. First, the US proceedings focused only on the maintenance of monopoly argument and the leveraging argument was abandoned at the appeal level. The plaintiffs abandoned the tying claim after the Court of Appeal ruled that technological tying should be examined under a rule of reason. Secondly, as a consequence of the narrow focus of the US liability decision, there was no specific remedy included for tying:[148] the US judgment did not provide means enabling OEMs and end-users to remove WMP code from the PC operating system (as it was technically unfeasible to remove the WMP code without running the risk that other parts of the operating system and third party products relying on WMP would not function properly),[149] but only requested Microsoft to provide OEMs and end-users the means to remove access (including icons) to the WMP application or to disable automatic launches.[150]

The effectiveness of this remedy was limited, as only few OEMs

[147] IP/09/349.

[148] However, bundling also formed part of the maintenance of monopoly claim: *United States* v *Microsoft Corp.*, 253 F.3d at 65.

[149] Decision, para. 829.

[150] *New York* v *Microsoft Corp.*, 224 F.Supp.2d at 153–5.

took advantage of this possibility.[151] The alleged lack of success of the remedy[152] could be explained by the fact that the final remedial order did not require Microsoft to charge a lower licence fee to OEMs that deleted access to Microsoft middleware, although this eventuality was included in Judge Jackson's remedial order.[153] In addition, the Commission may have found this remedy inadequate 'because it reinforced the applications barrier to entry from which Microsoft benefited by encouraging content providers to encode their products in Microsoft's standards'.[154]

The importance of the leveraging argument and network effects in the EC case and the insistence of the Commission on the need to restore the freedom of choice of the consumers that were coerced by Microsoft's conduct to use WMP as a default media-player led to a more intrusive remedy than in the US Microsoft case. The fact that WMP was offered for free, that there were other ways to reach consumers for competing products, and that the consumers were not forced but simply likely to use WMP, did not influence the conclusion of the Commission that there was coercion. The extent of the competition problem was of a structural nature: the ubiquity of Windows undermined because of the network effects competition in media-players.[155] This was thought to deter innovation and reduce consumer choice as competing media-players that consumers preferred were excluded from the market.[156]

The extent of the competition problem identified, Microsoft's distributional advantage, led to a more intrusive competition law remedy than in the US case, affecting Microsoft's freedom to design its products. Article 6 of the Decision requested Microsoft to offer a version of Windows for

---

151 William H. Page and John E. Lopatka, *The Microsoft Case* (Chicago: University of Chicago Press, 2007), p. 215.

152 One could, however, also argue that taking into account the liability claim, which was that OEMs were forced to carry Internet Explorer because they could not exclusively promote other browsers, the remedy was fully 'successful' in providing them with that option. The fact that they may or may not choose to take advantage of that right may not necessarily mean the remedy was unsuccessful, unless a 'successful' remedy is defined as a socially desirable market outcome, which could blur the distinction between competition law intervention and regulatory alternatives.

153 Page and Lopatka, n. 151 above, 216.

154 Page and Lopatka, n. 151 above, 218.

155 Decision, para. 979. As the Commission put it, 'through tying with Windows, Microsoft uses Windows as a distribution channel to anti-competitively ensure for itself a significant competition advantage in the media player market. Competitors, due to Microsoft's tying, are *a priori* at a disadvantage irrespective of whether their products are potentially more attractive on the merits'.

156 Decision, paras 978–84.

client PCs which does not include WMP media files,[157] the new version being equally performing. The remedy applied to licences for both end-users and OEMs. Microsoft was also asked to refrain from using 'any technological, commercial, contractual or any other means which would have the equivalent effect of tying WMP to Windows', for example by selling the new version at a higher price than the Windows with WMP version.[158] This did not include directly an obligation for Microsoft to offer the Windows without WMP version for a lower price than for the Windows with WMP version, since most competing media-players were offered for free. In addition, the Decision included an indication of activities having an effect equivalent to tying to which Microsoft should not resort, such as privileged interoperability between WMP and Windows or any other favourable treatment for Windows, conditional discounts, punishing or threatening OEMs who obtained Windows without WMP, tying WMP to other products that 'would exhibit a similar ubiquity as Windows', such as Microsoft Office.[159] The Commission rejected Microsoft's arguments that removing the WMP would undermine the integrity of the operating system, as for the Commission any interdependencies between the two products were the result of 'deliberate choice by Microsoft' and the integration of WMP was not a precondition for the multimedia capabilities of Windows.[160] In other words, the remedy imposed attempted to unravel the various links that tied WMP and Windows. Microsoft was given 90 days to implement the remedy. The Commission rejected Microsoft's proposal to include other media-players in Windows (the must carry remedy). This aspect will be examined more extensively below.

As was the case for the interoperability remedy, Microsoft invoked its right to seek a suspension of the Decision, which was refused by order of the President of the CFI. The CFI upheld the liability and the remedial part of the decision. The Monitoring Trustee supervised Microsoft's compliance with the remedy. Microsoft launched Windows XP N (for 'not with media functionality') to European Union countries in mid-June

---

157 According to the Commission, 'these files contain the technologies which have been identified as bringing about the foreclosure effect by virtue of WMP being tied to Windows, namely the files that support the proprietary Microsoft codecs, file formats and DRM formats and the WMP user interface': Decision, para. 1019.

158 Decision, para. 1012.

159 Decision, para. 1013(v).

160 Decision, paras 1027, 1031. The Commission distinguished between two sorts of dependencies: 'technical' which would by definition lead to the non-functioning of the operating system, and functional dependencies which can be dealt with 'gracefully': Decision, para. 1033.

2005. Almost 200 ancillary or support files were removed from XP Home and Professional Editions. According to a Microsoft press release in April 2006, there has been virtually no demand from PC manufacturers, retailers and consumers for Windows XP N, and only 1,787 copies of Windows XP N have been sold to retailers and distributors in Europe; more importantly, no OEM was interested in installing and selling computers with a less than fully functional version of Windows XP.[161]

Measured in terms of the number of sales for the Windows XP N edition, the effectiveness of the remedy can certainly be questioned.[162] The Commission's hope of widespread adoption of Windows XP N and the emergence of new powerful competitors did not materialize.[163] One could compare the situation of the media-player market with that of web-browser market, which was the subject of the US Microsoft case. As was previously explained, after the Court of Appeal's judgment, the tying case was dropped. By the time of the Court of Appeal's decision, Microsoft commanded an impressive share of the web-browser market (almost 90 per cent). It is only recently that Mozilla Firefox, a competing web-browser developed by Netscape in the form of open source software in 2004, after Netscape's defeat in the 'first browser war',[164] has been able to challenge Internet Explorer's dominant position, with Internet Explorer's usage share reducing to 66.1 per cent in the second quarter of 2009.[165] The situation is somewhat different in the media-player market, where a number of competing programs developed during the same period. One could suggest that one of the reasons for the faster development of competing products in the media-player market than in the web-browser market was the relatively important constraint and distraction that litigation in Europe

---

161 See www.microsoft.com/presspass/legal/european/04-24-06windowsxpn salesfs.mspx.

162 The alleged ineffectiveness of the remedies may raise questions as to the validity of the liability theory of harm in the first place. One could claim that Microsoft was essentially found liable for failing to produce a product – Windows without media functionality – that no one wanted.

163 There is no doubt that powerful competition existed in media-players before the introduction of Windows XP N, as evidenced by the huge successes of the iPod and the associated media format, as well as the Adobe Flash Player.

164 See http://en.wikipedia.org/wiki/Browser_wars.

165 See http://en.wikipedia.org/wiki/Usage_share_of_web_browsers. Mozilla Firefox had 22.47 per cent of usage share. According to other reports, the Internet Explorer versions had a total of 54.4 per cent market share in July 2009, a significant decline from 65.8 per cent in March 2009. See www.techcrunch.com/2009/07/05/since-march-internet-explorer-lost-114-percent-share-to-firefox-safari-and-chrome/?awesm=tcrn.ch.Furthermore, Apple Safari 4 and Google Chrome have done well since their releases, too.

caused to Microsoft's management, and the effect the Decision had on Microsoft's aggressive competitive ethos.[166]

Substitutionary Remedies

Substitutionary remedies may take different forms, e.g. fines, damages, disgorgement of illegally acquired gains. As is the case for remedies in kind, the objective of substitutionary remedies is to place the plaintiff or the protected category of rightholders in the situation that would have existed absent the infringement. This could be achieved through compensation of the rightholders and/or by restoring competition. For example, the objective of fines is to raise the costs of the violation of competition law and therefore affect the incentive for undertakings to adopt a similar conduct in the future. In that sense, pecuniary sanctions such as fines aim to restore competition. This deterrence effect will also affect the incentives for all other undertakings likely to adopt similar conduct in the future. This assumes, as Frederic Jenny observes, 'that persons engaging in illegal practices are rational individuals who (implicitly) consider the expected cost and the expected benefit to them of violating a law and will engage in such a violation only if it pays (that is, if the expected benefit outweighs the expected cost to them) when they are risk neutral or if the expected net gain is sufficiently large, if they are risk averse'.[167] It follows that '(i)n order to achieve . . . optimality, the basic framework on penalties should be a quantitative one, rather than qualitative. In other words, the quantity of the penalty has to be linked to the measure of the effect that the infringement provoked, rather than on the quality of the action undertaken'.[168] The monetary transfers involved may have different addresses. Indeed, substitutionary remedies may consist in fines, which is a monetary transfer to the tax-payer, or damages, which is a monetary transfer to the 'victims' of the anti-competitive practice. The choice of one over the other, or of a

---

166 Gary L. Reback, *Free the Market!* (New York: Portfolio, 2009). See also the remarks of William E. Kovacic, 'Designing Antitrust Remedies for Dominant Firm Misconduct' (1999) 31 *Connecticut Law Review* 1285, 1288–92, arguing that the existence of an antitrust lawsuit may inhibit aggressive commercial behaviour by the defendant as well as distract the defendant's employees from more productive functions, thus imposing formidable costs on the company. One could, however, remark that Microsoft continued to introduce new products in the market, such as Zune (media-player hardware) and Silverlight (for Internet media playback, like Adobe Flash Player).

167 Jenny, n. 19 above.

168 Enrico Leonardo Camilli, 'Optimal Fines in Cartel Cases and the Actual EU Policy' (2006) 29(4) *World Competition* 575.

combination of both, depends on the emphasis given by each legal system to deterrence or compensation. For example, fines serve merely a deterrence aim, although it is possible that they could also be conceptualized as a compensation mechanism, if one adopts the position that the restoring of competition will benefit the 'public at large'. In any case, setting an optimal level for civil sanctions and damages should take into account the interaction of these two forms of substitutionary remedies.

Fines

Article 3 of the Commission's Decision imposed on Microsoft what appeared at the time as a record fine in an abuse of dominance case.[169] The Commission calculated the amount of the fines according to the method set in the Guidelines on Setting Fines of 1998, revised in 2006.[170] This includes two steps: first, determine the basic amount of the fine, and secondly examine the existence of aggravating or attenuating circumstances. The Commission took into consideration in order to set the basic amount of the fine the gravity of Microsoft's infringement, a leveraging strategy which comprised two separate abuses: a refusal to supply and a tying abuse. The Commission found that Microsoft had engaged in a 'general pattern of conduct', which could produce 'significant effects on the competition landscape', in particular as it would have given Microsoft the ability to erect further barriers to entry in the client PC operating systems market and thus 'to limit the risk of a change of paradigm that could strip Microsoft's overwhelming dominance on the client PC operating system market of its competitive importance'.[171] Microsoft would thus be able to extend its quasi-monopolistic position into the server industry or the market for the delivery of content over the Internet and on multimedia software. The fact that Microsoft had already achieved a dominant or leading position in these industries was found a sufficient indication of the gravity of the infringement.

The initial amount for gravity was set at €162,732,101, without distinguishing which amount represented the fine for the refusal to supply interoperability infringement and which the one for the tying infringement. This starting amount was doubled in order to ensure 'a sufficient deterrent effect on Microsoft', in light of the undertaking's significant economic capacity.[172] The duration of the infringement was also particularly long: the refusal to supply abuse lasted six years and it was still ongoing at the time of

169 The latest record is held by the fine imposed on Intel. See IP/09/745.

170 Guidelines on the Method of Setting Fines [1998] OJ C9/3; Guidelines on the Method of Setting Fines [2006] OJ C210/2.

171 Decision, paras 1061–8.

172 Decision, para. 1076.

the decision; the tying abuse lasted more than five years. The Commission set the overall duration of the infringement at five years and five months, thus increasing the basic amount of the fine by 50 per cent to €497,196,204, taking into account an increase of 10 per cent for each year of participation in the infringement. The fine represented 7.5 per cent of Microsoft's turnover on the market for client PC and work group server operating systems in Europe,[173] thus below the threshold of 10 per cent set by the Guidelines. No aggravating or attenuating circumstances were found.

The CFI affirmed the fine imposed by the Commission and rejected Microsoft's arguments that no fine should be imposed, as the infringements resulted from 'novel theories of law' or that Microsoft had already taken measures, following the US settlement, to provide the necessary degree of interoperability.[174] The Court also acknowledged that 'the obligation to state reasons does not require the Commission to indicate in its decision the figures relating to the method of calculating the fines'.[175] Finally, the CFI found that the doubling of the basic amount of the fine by the Commission was justified for deterrence reasons: in a prescient (given recent developments) paragraph, the Court noted that 'since Microsoft is very likely to maintain its dominant position on the client PC operating systems market, at least over the coming years, it cannot be precluded that it will have other opportunities to use leveraging vis-á-vis other adjacent markets'.[176]

Although the fine imposed on Microsoft seems particularly important, its deterrent effect may be questioned. In the high technology sector, where network effects may tip the market for some time towards a particular technological standard, incurring the costs of civil penalties may still be a profitable strategy for monopolists. The effectiveness of this part of the EC remedy should be examined in comparison with the pecuniary sanctions imposed in the US Microsoft case. There is no provision for civil penalties, such as fines, under the Sherman Act and their adoption may not be possible, at least in the near future.[177] In US antitrust law, pecuniary

---

173 CFI judgment, para. 1319.

174 CFI judgment, para. 1324.

175 CFI judgment, para. 1361.

176 CFI judgment, para. 1363.

177 The proposal to make the necessary amendments to permit the imposition of civil fines has been rejected by the recent Antitrust Modernization Commission, *Report and Recommendations* (April 2007), pp. 285–91. For a critical analysis, see Stephen Calkins, 'Civil Monetary Remedies Available to Antitrust Enforcers' (2006) 40 *University of San Francisco Law Review* 567; Harry First, 'The Case for Antitrust Civil Penalties' *Antitrust Law Journal* (forthcoming); New York Law and Economics Research Paper No. 08-38, available at SSRN at http://ssrn.com/abstract=1162353.

sanctions take the form of wealth transfers to the victims of the exclusionary practice, which may engage a private action to collect damages. Most often, this leads to settlements entered between the monopolist and the claimants. The next section will discuss the availability of damages and settlements as an effective 'pecuniary' remedy. These remedies, to which one could add restitution/disgorgement, rarely ordered in the United States and unavailable in Europe, provide compensation/restitution to the victims of the competition law infringement, as well as deter the monopolist or dominant firm from adopting similar practices in the future by acting indirectly on their incentives.

Damages

In comparison to the amount of the fines imposed by the European Commission, the monetary transfers to consumers and competitors affected by Microsoft's antitrust law infringement in the US case seem particularly important. According to Harry First, more than 220 private cases have been filed against Microsoft, from consumers and rivals.[178] Consumer class actions represent the largest group of claims (more than 80 per cent), with individuals having filed 30 cases and state Attorneys General having filed two cases on behalf of their non-business citizens.[179] This category of private plaintiffs had an important hurdle to overcome, as they had to prove that they were overcharged, following Microsoft's maintenance of monopoly in the operating systems market. As indirect purchasers, they were barred from bringing a federal antitrust private damages claim,[180] with the exception of some states that provide the possibility for state antitrust actions filed in state courts. All class actions had also to pass the procedure of class certification, which was in this case overly complicated by the fact that it was not clear how much of the alleged overcharge the direct purchasers had passed on to indirect purchasers. This required individualized determinations which made class certification particularly difficult.[181]

Important difficulties also arose with regard to the existence of an overcharge for Windows, as Microsoft was allegedly able to maintain its monopoly power by excluding potential competing platforms in the

---

178 Harry First, *Netscape is Dead: Remedy Lessons from the Microsoft Litigation*, NYU Law and Economics Research Paper No. 08-49 (29 August 2008), available at SSRN at http://ssrn.com/abstract=1260803.

179 First, n. 178 above, 6.

180 *Illinois Brick Co.* v *Illinois*, 431 U.S. 720 (1977).

181 The majority of the courts adopted, however, a liberal standard for class certification. See Page and Lopatka, n. 151 above, 235.

operating systems market.[182] The issue revolved on the question of what would have been the price of Windows, had Netscape and Java been able to challenge Microsoft's dominant position and develop a competing platform. Judge Jackson's judgment contained some indications that Microsoft was able to charge higher prices for Windows 98 upgrades, while lower prices would have also been profitable. However, Judge Jackson also recognized that it might be in Microsoft's interest to 'keep the price of Windows low today' in order to support the growth of the operating systems market.[183] These elements offered the possibility to OEMs, such as IBM and Gateway, which did not accept Microsoft's offer to distribute and promote Internet Explorer and therefore did not receive any compensation in the form of rebates, to enter significant settlements with Microsoft.

Additional private damages suits in the US Microsoft case included the two competitors that brought the case against Microsoft in the European Union, Netscape/AOL and Sun. Netscape settled in 2003, while Sun settled a few days after the publication of the Decision of the European Commission in 2004 and consequently retreated as a third party intervener in the EC litigation. This had the effect of pushing SAMBA and the open source community to step in as the main opponent of Microsoft in the post-decision 2004 period, until they settled in the aftermath of the CFI's judgment. As for Microsoft's other opponents in the EC antitrust case, both RealNetworks and Novell settled, with the exception of Novell's pending lawsuit against Microsoft relating to the damage suffered by WordPerfect (for lack of interoperability information), which because of its cross-platform capacity posed a potential threat to Microsoft's

---

182 Whether Netscape together with Java could have been a real threat to Windows was not clear and definitely not proved. Netscape's CEO Jim Barksdale completely dismissed that likelihood at trial, stating that Netscape never planned such entry into operating systems. However, Microsoft had taken this potential threat very seriously as internal Microsoft emails presented at trial revealed. But if Netscape's success was very unlikely in the absence of anti-competitive actions, the remedy should be limited to erasing the anti-competitive hurdle and should not involve a restructuring of the market.

183 *United States* v *Microsoft*, 84 F.Supp.2d 9, 27 (D.D.C. 1999), Finding of Fact, para. 66). However, this argument is not credible given that Microsoft already had over 90 per cent market share in the OS market. In fact, it is likely that potential competition in the OS market drove Microsoft to charge a significantly lower price than the unconstrained monopoly price. For a detailed analysis of pricing of Windows, see Nicholas Economides, 'The Microsoft Antitrust Case' (2001) 1 *Journal of Industry, Competition and Trade: From Theory to Policy* 7, 16–19, available at www.stern.nyu.edu/networks/Microsoft_Antitrust.final.pdf.

monopoly in the operating systems market.[184] In total, the settlements in the United States appear to have exceeded US$3.5 billion.[185]

In comparison, the fine imposed by the European Commission, which represents only a fraction of the total amount of settlements, seems to lead to underdeterrence, absent private enforcement. This conclusion is reinforced by the absence of any private action brought against Microsoft for damages in the European Union. There are two cumulative explanations for this: first, private enforcement of EC competition law is only nascent and does not include a system of treble damages or other incentives for private actions.[186] Secondly, the heart of the EC case was not maintenance of monopoly, and therefore a possible overcharge for Windows, but the extension of the monopoly power of Microsoft to the work group server and media-player markets. Concerning the work group server market, it is not clear if consumer harm took a different form than just a slower pace of innovation because of the exclusion of competitors, or whether it led also to an increase in the prices charged by Microsoft. In the media-player market, the product was given away for free, so the harm to consumers was not relating to higher prices but to possibly lower quality, as allegedly better quality media-players were excluded from the market. It would, however, be extremely difficult and costly to quantify this reduction in quality.[187] Because of the limited access of European consumers to damages and the difficulties in obtaining damages in the United States as a result of comity concerns, in particular after *Empagran*,[188] European consumers will remain without compensation and, consequently, there will be less deterrence. The weakness of private enforcement of competition law in Europe indicates that fines should be set at a higher level in order to ensure more effective deterrence.[189]

---

184 First, n. 178 above, 9.

185 First, n. 178 above, 27.

186 See the recent discussion of possible options in European Commission, White Paper on Damages Actions for Breach of the EC Antitrust Rules, COM (2008)165.

187 However, during the infringement period there was significant innovation and entry of new products, such as the iPod and the Adobe Flash Player.

188 *F. Hoffmann-La Roche Lt.* v *Empagran SA*, 542 U.S. 155 (2004).

189 This supposes, however, a clarification of the liability standard under Article 82 EC. The European Commission has recently adopted guidance on Article 82 EC: DG Competition, Communication from the Commission, Guidance on the Commission's Enforcement Priorities in Applying Article 82 EC Treaty to Abusive Exclusionary Conduct by Dominant Undertakings, 864(2009)final. Note the guidance on enforcement priorities is a softer law instrument than guidelines: it

3. CRITICAL ASSESSMENT OF THE REMEDIES

The success of the interoperability remedy required a sustained and continuing effort of setting and monitoring compliance standards, which was particularly difficult in the absence of a regulatory authority that could supervise its enforcement. The European Commission initiated the mechanism of the Monitoring Trustee, which proved particularly useful in the promotion of the SAMBA-Microsoft settlement, the only positive outcome so far of the Commission's Decision. However, the CFI annulled this part of the Decision. The crafting of remedies involves the consideration of an adequate institutional mechanism for their enforcement. The design of the remedy for the tying part of the Decision was also particularly problematic, as the Commission took a quasi-regulatory role by imposing on Microsoft a particular product design which, however, produced very poor results in the marketplace.

Enforcement Difficulties of the Interoperability Remedy: Institutional Aspects

The appointment of a Monitoring Trustee was the primary mechanism of enforcement of the remedy imposed by the Commission for both the interoperability and tying parts. The Monitoring Trustee was required to assess whether the information made available by Microsoft was complete and accurate, and to ensure that Windows XP N was of no less performance than any bundled version of Windows which Microsoft would continue to provide on the market. The Monitoring Trustee was independent from Microsoft, although on its payroll. Article 4 of the Decision imposed on Microsoft an obligation to refrain from repeating any act or practice which would have the same or equivalent object or effect as the anti-competitive conduct. This exemplified the forward-looking role of the Monitoring Trustee, as it was clear that 'the obligation to disclose interoperability information must apply 'in a prospective manner' to future generations

---

is complementary to the Commission's specific enforcement Decisions. The choice of the instrument of guidance on enforcement priorities offers to the Commission more leeway in presenting its approach on Article 82 EC. The Commission could not have adopted guidelines contrary to the rulings of the EU courts (see the most recent reminder by Advocate General Kokott in Case C-8/08 *T-Mobile Netherlands BV and others*, para. 29). The Commission maintains the ability to reject a complaint when it considers that a case lacks priority for other reasons (e.g. lack of Community interest).

of Microsoft's products'.[190] Microsoft successfully challenged this part of the Decision at the CFI for lack of legal basis.

The CFI found that Regulation 17/62, in force at the time of the Decision, did not provide the Commission with the authority to compel Microsoft to grant to an independent monitoring trustee powers which the Commission itself was not authorized to confer to a third party.[191] The Court questioned the independence that the Monitoring Trustee would have had from both the Commission and Microsoft and the broad scope of his powers and mission. It also noted that no limit in time was envisaged for his continuing intervention in monitoring Microsoft's compliance. Furthermore, the principle of proportionality required that the costs associated with the enforcement of the remedy and compliance should not be borne by the undertaking but by the Commission, in fulfilling its own investigation and enforcement responsibilities.[192]

The conservatism showed by the CFI in envisioning an effective compliance mechanism seems misplaced. First, the independence of the Monitoring Trustee from Microsoft, but also from the Commission, ensured his impartiality, which was an essential characteristic in order to enhance compliance and cooperation from Microsoft. This was crucial for the success of the remedy (providing adequate information on specifications). After all, it was because the Monitoring Trustee had developed a relation of trust with Microsoft's technical staff that he had been able to mediate successfully between Microsoft and SAMBA, ironically during the period following the Court's judgment and before the Commission formally replaced him with a system of ad hoc external experts.[193] It may have not been possible to achieve the same degree of cooperation from Microsoft had the Commission employed internal or external experts for the enforcement of the Decision, as in this case no direct relation (without the intermediation of lawyers) would have existed between Microsoft's technical staff and the technical staff of the parties requiring interoperability. It is true that the Commission's Decision should have included a realistic time horizon for the monitoring of the Decision and should have quantified the costs. However, as became clear in the compliance procedure under the US antitrust decision, the extent and time scale of monitoring was an unknown factor depending on the clear articulation of what the government wanted Microsoft to produce and on the will-

190 CFI judgment, para. 1270.
191 CFI judgment, para. 1271, 1278.
192 CFI judgment, para. 1277.
193 Page and Childers, n. 125 above, 346.

ingness and ability of Microsoft to provide detailed specifications for its interoperability information. Sharing the costs of the enforcement mechanism would have limited the exorbitant costs for Microsoft, which may seem out of proportion, but at the same time it would have reduced to a minor extent Microsoft's incentives to comply with the Decision. The Commission could nevertheless have taken in charge a larger proportion of the expenses during the first period of the operation of the enforcement mechanism, Microsoft's share progressively increasing in order to incur the costs of delayed compliance.

The appointment of the Monitoring Trustee illustrates the blurring of the distinction between competition law and regulation, when it comes to the enforcement of far-reaching and forward looking remedies, with regard to the scope of the obligations imposed and the time-horizon of the remedy. The European Monitoring Trustee intervened three years after the Technical Committee in the US antitrust case began to monitor Microsoft's compliance. The US Technical Committee had become at that time a quasi-regulatory entity with 40 experts employed and with the ability to persuade the US Department of Justice and the states that additional obligations and burdens should be imposed in order to ensure effective interoperability. The Technical Committee could receive complaints, interview Microsoft's staff and examine the Windows' source code, subject to confidentiality; the expenses of the Committee, including the salaries, being covered by Microsoft.[194] The Monitoring Trustee was able to build on these efforts to ensure interoperability and to benefit from the US experience but he also contributed to the compliance effort in the United States. Indeed, in 2006 the US Technical Committee started working closely with Microsoft's experts in order to improve the technical documentation provided to licensees, using 'as a starting point the specification agreed upon between Microsoft and the Monitoring Trustee' in the EC case.[195]

One could envision a higher degree of cooperation at the remedial stage of multi-jurisdictional cases, such as Microsoft, if compliance is ensured by an independent entity, like a Monitoring Trustee or a Technical Committee, including the sharing of the costs of the compliance mechanism between jurisdictions. It is clear that despite the different theories of antitrust liability in Europe and in the United States, in the end, the remedies imposed with regard to the interoperability part of the Decision

---

194 *State of New York* v *Microsoft Corp.*, 224 F. Supp 2d 76, 273–274 (D.D.C. 2002).

195 Joint Status Report on Microsoft's Compliance with the Final Judgments, *United States* v *Microsoft Corp.*, 2006 WL 5154418 (D.D.C. Aug. 30, 2006) (CCiv. Nos 98–1232, 98–1233).

it the end converged. This type of international cooperation at the remedial stage of antitrust cases could be enhanced if the Commission had the ability to appoint independent compliance officers/experts. The procedure has been used in the context of commitment Decisions under Article 9 of Regulation 1/2003, such as the *Deutsche Bundesliga*[196] and *FA Premier League*[197] cases concerning the collective selling of media rights to football matches, where the Commission appointed a monitoring trustee to monitor the auctions of the Premier League rights, and in *Repsol*,[198] where the monitoring trustee had the task of monitoring the opening up of the fuel distribution system in Spain. Monitoring trustees have also been used in merger cases cleared with obligations and commitments, where the trustees enjoy important powers, such as the supervision and management of the divested business, the exercise of shareholder rights or the appointment of board members.[199] The CFI's decision in the Microsoft case raises questions as to the legality of this practice, in particular as the company giving the commitment is usually required to incur the trustee's costs. Regulation 1/2003 does not grant the Commission any power to establish such monitoring mechanisms and this is certainly an issue that has to be tackled in the recent review process of Regulation 1/2003.[200]

'Failure' of the Windows N Remedy and the 'Must Carry' Proposal

As discussed above, the Commission Decision, upheld by the CFI, found Microsoft liable for tying WMP with Windows. WMP participates in a market where it and its substitute media-players are distributed without charge. Since there are always costs of developing such software, both Microsoft and its competitors sell below the production and distribution cost of media-players. Of course, as part of Windows, WMP forms part of the Windows revenue.

Companies such as Microsoft and its competitors (for example,

---

196 Commission Decision 2005/396/EC, *Bundesliga* [2005] OJ L134/46.

197 Commission Notice published pursuant to Article 19(3) of Council Regulation No 17 concerning case COMP/C.2/38.173 and 38.453, *FA Premier League* [2004] OJ C115/3.

198 Commission Decision 2006/446/EC, *Repsol* [2006] OJ L176/104.

199 See e.g. Commission Decisions COMP/M.5406 *IPIC/MAN Ferrostaal AG* [2009] OJ C114/8; COMP/M.5253 *Sanofi-Aventis/Zentiva*, 4 February 2009; COMP/M.5224 *EDF/British Energy*, 22 December 2008. Commission Notice on remedies acceptable under Council Regulation 139/2004 and under Commission Regulation 802/2004 [2008] OJ C267/1.

200 Although nothing is included on this topic in European Commission, *Report on the Functioning of Regulation 1/2003*, COM(2009)206 final.

RealAudio) distribute their media-players for free with the hope that their software development costs will be recouped if (i) in the future the product is sold at a positive price, or (ii) the firm will be able to sell upgraded versions of the software (with more features) at a positive price, or (iii) the firm will be able to sell products or services complementary to the free product (for example, music or video downloads at a positive price or software that produces audio or video in a compatible format). Although media-players have been distributed for free for almost a decade and have experienced significant technological advances, there is no evidence that their basic versions will ever be sold at a positive price. Additionally, with the exception of Apple's iTunes, there is no evidence of substantial revenues from sales of complementary products,[201] and iTunes profits come almost exclusively from sales of the complementary hardware (iTunes players). Thus, there are no damages arising from higher prices because of restriction of competition, since no company charges a positive price. The only possible damages could arise from a restriction of the full extent of varieties and qualities of media-players that might be available in the absence of the tying behaviour of Microsoft.

The variety issue is further complicated by the fact that a number of companies distribute media-players that each have a 'favoured' format but can also play content in a number of other formats, to the extent that the other format owners allow it. So, for example, WMP plays WMA (the Microsoft-favoured format) as well as MP3 (based on a public standard) but does not play the RealAudio format because its specifications have not been made public. Similarly, RealAudio plays its proprietary format, as well as WMA, MP3, and others. Thus, wide distribution of WMP does not necessarily imply dominance of the WMA *format* since WMP can play many formats. It is possible, however, to argue that even dual encoding (i.e. encoding in a number of different formats) may confer a distributional advantage to Microsoft. Ian Ayres and Barry Nalebuff noted that 'Microsoft would still have the unique ability to ensure that its media player would be on all new machines—and thus eventually on all machines' and that 'in turn, would mean that a content provider that encoded its content in the WMP format would be ensured nearly 100% reach in the market' and would have therefore little incentive to engage

---

[201] Of course there are attempts to get revenue from complementary goods. For example, RealNetworks offers an upgraded version at a positive price as well as subscription services for content. However, these revenues are not substantial and have led to the decline of companies that are essentially only in the software media-player business, such as RealNetworks.

in dual encoding.[202] The conclusion that WMP will eventually be on *all* PCs is true only under restrictive modelling assumptions, and empirical evidence attests that it is certainly not true today. Additionally, the fact that WMP plays a number of other formats, including some based on open standards, makes the exclusivity argument of including WMP with Windows weak. In the aftermath of the US case settlement, any consumer as well as any computer manufacturer can set up any media-player as the default one, thereby severely limiting any distributional advantage of the joint distribution of WMP with Windows. However, they do not benefit from the same distributional opportunities as WMP, precisely because dual encoding may not be materially equivalent to ubiquitous encoding. Finally, one could argue that the distribution advantage that any player enjoys is also limited because any rival media-player can be downloaded and installed in a few minutes. If consumers do not think it is worth spending a couple of minutes to download and install rival players, clearly consumers do not see significant value in the variety and quality that rival players may add. Thus, the damages that can be ascertained from Microsoft's distributional advantage cannot be substantial. The Commission and the CFI may have overestimated the distributional advantage conferred on WMP by its joint distribution with Windows.

The Commission imposed as a remedy on Microsoft the requirement to produce and distribute in the European Union a version of Windows without WMP, which became known as Windows XP N. The Commission's remedy allowed Microsoft to continue producing and distributing in the EU the US version of Windows that included WMP but was subject to the requirements of the consent decree that resolved the US case The CFI did not mandate a specific price difference between Windows and Windows XP N.[203] The two versions of Windows were sold

---

202 See Ian Ayres and Barry Nalebuff, 'Going Soft on Microsoft? The EU's Antitrust Case and Remedy' (2005) 2 *The Economist's Voice* 1, 5.

203 The lack of a price difference requirement is in sharp contrast to the proposal to the district court by the nine states ('litigating states') which did not agree with the US Department of Justice Microsoft settlement that was also signed by nine other states. The litigating states proposed to 'freeze Windows' in its pre-1998 condition and impose on Microsoft the requirement to sell any additional functionality at an additional price. It is interesting, however, that the CFI noted in its judgment that '[s]hould Microsoft now decide to sell the unbundled version of Windows at the same price as the bundled version, the Commission would examine that price by reference to the present market situation and in the light of Microsoft's obligations to refrain from any measure having an equivalent effect to tying and, if necessary, adopt a new decision pursuant to Art. 82 EC'. CFI judgment, para. 908.

in the EU at the same price, and practically no OEM bought and adopted Windows XP N.[204] Thus, the remedy imposed by the Commission had no noticeable effect in the marketplace. At the same time, the dire predictions of expanded dominance of WMP never materialized in the long period between the beginning of the EC case and the Commission's Decision, or even later. In contrast, a new, until recently proprietary, format promoted by Apple (tied to hardware also produced by Apple!) has become the dominant format in the market for song downloads, a key market for goods that are complementary to media-players. Additionally, Flash Player, a new player from Adobe, has become the standard video-player in web-browsers.

We are at a loss to understand why the European Commission thought that requiring Microsoft to produce and distribute Windows without WMP was going to change significantly competition in media-players. It was almost mathematically certain that Windows XP N (without WMP), sold at the same price as Windows (with WMP), would not sell well, and therefore would have little impact on the market share of WMP. It is also hard to imagine how depriving consumers of WMP in Windows XP N in the post-US settlement environment, where both the OEM and the final consumer can designate any media-player as the default one, would have enhanced consumers' choice. The Commission rather considered that consumers expected a media-player but argued that the OEMs should be free to build PCs that feature a non-Microsoft media-player.

In negotiations before the Commission's Decision was announced, the Commission rejected a reported Microsoft proposed remedy to include in the distribution of Windows three rival media-players besides WMP and let the consumer designate the default player.[205] This proposal, which would have guaranteed as wide a distribution of RealAudio and other players as WMP, would have erased any distributional advantage of WMP, would have dispelled any tying concerns, and would have given full decision power to consumers. Such a remedy would have addressed the competition law concerns raised by Microsoft's abuse much more effectively than the proposed remedy.[206] At the same time, its adoption would

---

[204] Windows XP N sold less than 2,000 copies.

[205] See Byron Acohido and Noelle Knox, 'Regulators Want Microsoft to Pull Media Player Out', *USA Today*, 25 March 2004, available at www.usatoday.com/money/industries/technology/2004-03-25-msoft-cover_x.htm.

[206] Indeed, the issue in this case was 'not that Microsoft integrates [WMP] in Windows, but that it offers on the market only a version of Windows in which [WMP] is integrated, that is to say, that it does not allow OEMs or consumers to obtain Windows without [WMP] or, at least, to remove [WMP] from the system

have at least guaranteed the ability of even a dominant firm (Microsoft) in the complementary good (Windows) to innovate and distribute in the way it finds most appropriate. The benefits of this proposal both for consumers and innovation are obvious and substantial in comparison to the imposed remedy.[207] It provides consumers with the best of both worlds: the benefits of stand-alone media-players and the benefits of an integrated solution.

We argue that the requirement that a dominant firm 'must carry' the competitors products should, however, only be imposed when (i) there are substantial distributional advantages for the dominant firm, and (ii) there are substantial consumer losses arising from the lack of distribution through the dominant firm. Because of the US case settlement, computer manufacturers can install any media-player they want without facing any penalties or retaliation from Microsoft. To the extent that computer manufacturers install what consumers desire, the present extent of distribution of WMP with Windows seems more a reflection of consumers' choice than a decision by Microsoft. Of course, consumers are likely to be better off if they receive more free software delivered with their new computer. This, however, does not mean that the dominant firm should have the obligation to distribute this software, and additionally to do so without collecting practically any revenue from competitors whose software it is forced to distribute, unless the operating system is considered as an essential facility. But in this case the standards of liability are different (allegedly stricter) than those required for tying.[208] It seems to us that, if a

---

consisting of Windows and [WMP]'. CFI judgment, para. 1149. The remedy could have identified a number of media-players from those existing at the time of the commitment of the abuse that could have been integrated into Windows. It is in this respect different from a common carrier obligation, as it would not necessarily have extended to media-players that would have been commercialized after the termination of the abuse.

207 This is particularly surprising since Prof. Mario Monti, head of the Commission at the time, was quoted as saying as regards the objectives of the Commission in the Decision: 'In the end, we decided to do what's best for innovation and European consumers.' Acohido and Knox, n. 205 above.

208 The Court of Justice took a restrictive view of the obligation of a dominant undertaking to grant access to its facilities by imposing a number of conditions in Case C-7/97 *Oscar Bronner GmbH & Co. KG* v *Mediaprint* [1998] ECR I-7791, paras 41, 45–6. The refusal 'must be likely to eliminate all competition' on the part of the competitor requesting access, such access should be indispensable and not only make it harder for the requesting undertaking to compete, and it should not be capable of being objectively justified. With regard to the indispensability condition, the Court held that access would have been indispensable only if it was not economically viable to create a home-delivery system for a newspaper with a comparable circulation to the dominant firm's. One could argue that the conditions in

competition authority decides to impose a 'must carry' remedy, it should bring a proper essential facilities case, rather than rely on the more favourable liability standards of tying (as regards standard of proof) and then ask for a 'must carry' remedy.

The 'must carry' obligation is of special interest because it has been considered by the European Commission as a remedy in its current investigation of Microsoft for bundling Internet Explorer with Windows, as discussed in detail below.[209] Clearly, the Commission could not require that Windows be distributed without a web-browser and the ability to download a browser because that would severely cripple the ability of the typical user to reach the Internet. But does it make sense for Microsoft to be required to distribute rival browsers?

It could be argued that requiring Microsoft to distribute rival browsers may not provide an appropriate remedy, in the presence of weak anticipative effects. As with media-players, competing web-browsers can be downloaded and installed in a few minutes, so the reluctance of consumers to do so might show that they do not find it sufficiently desirable. To this claim it is possible to respond that consumers may have a status quo bias favouring Internet Explorer, particularly because, having used only Internet Explorer, the user has no real way of knowing what it might mean for a web-browser to be superior.[210] One could also advance a natural reluctance to take on additional learning costs associated with using a different browser. OEMs may also refrain from the additional support costs that are associated with offering another browser. It could be argued, nevertheless, that the damage that consumers may incur from the joint distribution of Internet Explorer with Windows is very limited. In the particular

---

Bronner set the outer boundaries of the special responsibility of a dominant firm and consequently of the corresponding duty, under Article 82 EC, to abstain from any action that would be likely to exclude rivals from the market. The excluded rival would be granted access only if it is impossible for an undertaking with a comparable output to the dominant firm to develop such facility, which indicates that the Court applies a 'not yet as efficient' as test.

209 MEMO/08/19, available at http://europa.eu/rapid/pressReleasesAction.do?reference=MEMO/08/19 (awaiting the publication of the final decision of the Commission).

210 Behavioural law and economics have emphasized the consideration of status quo bias in envisioning consumer behaviour. See William Samuelson and Richard Zeckhauser, 'Status Quo Bias in Decision Making' (1988) 1(1) *Journal of Risk and Uncertainty* 7. On the importance of heuristics and biases in analysing behaviour, see Daniel Kahneman, Paul Slovic and Amos Tversky (eds), *Judgment under Uncertainty: Heuristics and Biases* (Cambridge: Cambridge University Press, 1982).

case of the browser, as contrasted with the media-player, there is almost full compatibility between the various browsers. Additionally, Firefox provides a plug-in that emulates Internet Explorer and can even be used for live updates from Microsoft that require Internet Explorer. As with the media-player analysis, there are no damages because of price competition, since all the browsers are distributed for free. Additionally, the almost full compatibility of browsers implies that the benefits of variety and quality will be smaller than in the media-player market. Thus, it seems likely that imposition of the 'must carry' remedy might be out of proportion in this case.

If the effects on consumers are considered to be more substantial, the 'must carry' remedy might be an appropriate remedy, although it could face some practical difficulties. The issue of the mandatory Java distribution was raised in the US Microsoft case.[211] The court found that a 'must carry' requirement would have not provided a substantial benefit to competition, once Microsoft's anti-competitive restraints on other channels of Java distribution were lifted by the other parts of the court's remedy (exclusivity arrangements).[212] The reason for the court's reluctance was, however, its uneasiness in granting a specific competitor, Sun Microsystems, an advantage in its efforts to compete with Microsoft, not accorded to other competitors in the industry. The court noted that 'favoritism of one market participant over another in a remedy provision places the Court in the improper position of exerting too much control over the market'.[213] An adequate remedy would provide equal treatment to third parties, in order to restore competition. For example, complainants should not be the only ones receiving the benefits of a 'must carry' obligation: any firm that is capable of challenging the dominant firm should be included in the design of this obligation. It follows that for the must carry obligation to function equitably, new products should also be periodically included. This could raise some practical difficulties, such as which browsers (from the five main ones and/or browsers from niche players) to include, and on what licence terms, as well as how to align the release schedule of these browsers with the release schedule of Windows, to be solved by further negotiation between the parties.

Negotiations between the Commission and Microsoft on whether to implement a version of a must carry rule gave rise to important recent developments. As previously explained, the Commission opened formal

---

211 *New York* v *Microsoft*, 224 F.Supp.2d at 188–90.
212 224 F.Supp.2d at 189.
213 224 F.Supp.2d at 189.

proceedings on Opera's complaint in December 2007 and issued a Statement of Objections to Microsoft in January 2009. To terminate the Commission's current investigation in the Internet Explorer case, Microsoft initially announced[214] that it would not distribute the standard Windows 7 in Europe. Instead, it intended to produce and distribute in Europe a special edition of Windows 7 called Windows 7 E which would not have Internet Explorer or any other browser pre-installed, adopting the removal approach of the Windows XP N remedy imposed by the Commission in the WMP case, as the sole version of Windows in Europe. OEMs would have the option to install a web-browser of their choice as the default as well as include other browsers before the PC reached the final consumers.

As part of the initial proposal of Microsoft, European consumers who would buy an upgrade to Windows 7 for Windows Vista or XP, as well as those consumers who would buy Windows 7 and install it themselves from scratch on a 'naked' computer (which comes from the manufacturer without an operating system) would be given a version of Windows 7 E that would include a file transfer protocol (FTP) link to a website from which they could download and install Internet Explorer 8. The Commission applauded Microsoft's steps to provide OEMs more flexibility, but was critical of Microsoft's decision on the distribution of the retail upgrade or retail clean install.[215]

Based on that public feedback, as well as on private discussions, Microsoft withdrew its unilateral plan of distributing Windows 7 E[216] and proposed a final resolution that would commit[217] it to (i) distribute a 'ballot screen' through software update[218] to European users of Windows XP,

---

214 See www.bloomberg.com/apps/news?pid=newsarchive&sid=abzAzMCoi 3Rw.

215 See Memo/09/272, 12 June 2009, available at http://europa.eu/rapid/pressReleasesAction.do?reference=MEMO/09/272&format=HTML&aged=0&language=EN&guiLanguage=en.

216 See http://microsoftontheissues.com/cs/blogs/mscorp/archive/2009/07/31/windows-7-and-browser-choice-in-europe.aspx.

217 Microsoft's Commitment to address the competition concerns identified by the European Commission in Case No. COMP/C-3/39.530, available at www.microsoft.com/presspass/presskits/eu-msft/docs/07-24-09Commitment.doc ('Commitment').

218 The words 'ballot screen' were used inappropriately in the preliminary design of the remedy; the appropriate words are 'choice screen'. There is no ballot here and there is no decision by majority or any other rule that will be imposed on all participants. The screen will allow each consumer to set the default browser for him or herself, and allow the consumer to uninstall Internet Explorer.

Windows Vista, Windows 7, and Windows client PC operating systems, by means of Windows update; and (ii) allow both OEMs and users to turn on or off Internet Explorer.[219] Thus, the remedy does not only concern Windows 7. The European Commission received comments from third parties and finally accepted Microsoft's commitments by adopting an Article 9 Regulation 1/2003 decision on 16 December 2009.[220]

This remedy may have far-reaching consequences on the structure of the web-browser industry and the distributional advantage of Internet Explorer. The choice screen will give those users who have set Internet Explorer as their default web-browser an opportunity to choose whether to install (and which) competing web-browser(s) in addition to the one(s) they already have.[221] Users will be able to select one or more of the web-browsers offered through the choice screen. Microsoft commits to distribute and install the choice screen software update 'in a manner that is designed to bring about installation of this update at a rate that is as least as high as that for the most recent version of Internet Explorer offered via Windows Update'.[222] It is also emphasized that 'nothing in the design and implementation of the Choice Screen and the presentation of competing web browsers will express a bias for a Microsoft web browser or any other web browser or discourage the user from downloading and installing additional web browsers via the Choice Screen and making a web browser competing with a Microsoft web browser the default'.[223]

The design of the choice screen attempts to represent as best as possible actual consumer preferences. At the same time, it avoids providing an excessively large choice that would have occupied a lot of disk space. The choice screen will be populated with the 12 most widely-used web-browsers that run on Windows 7 as measured semi-annually by averaging monthly usage share data for the previous six months for which data is available, with only one browser per vendor listed and shares for different released versions of the same vendor's browsers added together to determine the browser's total usage share.[224] That will not include Internet

---

219 See www.microsoft.com/presspass/presskits/eu-msft/docs/ANNEX_A.doc for a detailed description of how this will be implemented in Windows 7.

220 Commission Decision, Case COMP/C-3/39.530 – *Microsoft*, available at http://ec.europa.eu/competition/antitrust/cases/decisions/39530/final_decision_en.pdf (hereinafter EU Microsoft II decision), Microsoft's commitments are included in the Annex of the Commission's decision (hereinafter Commitments).

221 Commitment above, para. 8.

222 Commitment, para. 9.

223 Commitment, para. 10.

224 Commitment, para. 11 and 14.

Explorer 'or any other browser which is based on Internet Explorer's rendering engine and the development or distribution of which is funded in whole or in substantial part by Microsoft'.[225] The choice screen will display icons of the basic identifying information on the web browsers in a horizontal line and in an unbiased way. In addition, the choice screen will prominently display the final releases of the five web-browsers with the highest usage share in the EEA, the remaining seven being displayed if the user scrolls sideways and in a random order.[226] In order to ensure a higher degree of transparency, only those web browsers included in at last two of the three data sources for usage share information for web browsers (ComScore, NetApplications and StatCounter) would be considered for the choice screen. These will be ranked according to the arithmetic means of their numerical ranks in the data sources, taking into account their best ranking in two data sources.[227] It is also specified that 'Microsoft will bear the costs of the technical implementation of the remedy in Windows and may not charge for the inclusion of a third party web browser in the Ballot Screen'.[228]

The 'must carry' remedy is limited to web-browsers and any web-browser vendor eligible to appear on the choice screen should refrain from installing additional software in the same download. This is an interesting hybrid. Microsoft has to include the promotion of competing browsers, but does not have to distribute the code of third parties' browsers. The duration of the commitment is five years, leaving a wide window of opportunity to Microsoft's rivals, and in particular Google, to take hold of a significant part of the web-browser market.

On turning Internet Explorer on or off, 'Microsoft will ensure that if Internet Explorer is turned off, then (i) it can only be turned on through user action specifically aimed at turning on Internet Explorer; (ii) the user interface cannot be called upon by applications; and (iii) no icons, links or shortcuts or any other means will appear within Windows to start a download or installation of Internet Explorer'.[229] A website will provide all necessary information about turning on or off Internet Explorer. In addition, Microsoft 'will maintain that page so that other browser vendors can link to it if they wish'.[230] In essence, the 'OEMs will be free to pre-install any web browser (or browsers) of their choice on PCs they ship and to set any

---

225 Commitment, para. 14.
226 Commitment, para. 13.
227 Commitment, para. 14.
228 Commitment, para. 14.
229 Commitment, n. 217 above, para. 1.
230 Commitment, para. 1.

browser as the default web browser'.[231] Microsoft has also committed 'not to retaliate against any OEM refraining from developing, using, distributing, promoting or supporting any software that competes with Microsoft web browsers' through an alteration of commercial relations with that OEM, or by withholding the application of preferential terms, or finally by entering into any agreement with an OEM that conditions the grant of any monetary payment, discount or the provision of preferential licensing terms or any other preferential treatment on the choice of Internet Explorer.[232]

In many ways, the European Commission's proposed outcome is similar to that of the US consent decree. The US consent decree allowed OEMs and final consumers to choose the default browser; similarly, OEMs and final consumers will choose the default browser in Europe. But there are also important differences.

First, the US consent decree was broader since it applied to all middleware, while the proposed EC outcome covers only browsers. Besides browsers, middleware includes email clients, audio-players, instant messengers, Java, and other software that functions between the operating system and applications.

Second, unlike in the United States, where all final consumers are given the opportunity to choose a default browser (and other middleware) through a 'set defaults' screen, Microsoft's commitment in Europe will give a choice of browser to final consumers *only* if their computer has Internet Explorer set as the default browser.[233] If the computer manufacturer has set up a browser other than Internet Explorer as the default, the final consumer will not be presented with the EC ballot screen or the 'set defaults' screen available to US consumers. Thus, the mechanism is tilted (i) against Microsoft since computers with a non-Internet Explorer default will not have the same choice (that might have resulted in Internet Explorer); and (ii) in favour of non-Microsoft *commercial* browser vendors (Chrome, Opera, Safari, etc.) who can compensate OEMs to set up their

---

[231] Commitment, para. 2

[232] Commitment, paras 4–5.

[233] Also note that in the European Union, final users will be *automatically* prompted to choose a browser, if their computer came with Internet Explorer as the default, while in the United States they are not automatically prompted but just have the option of choosing defaults. See http://microsoftontheissues.com/cs/blogs/mscorp/archive/2009/07/31/windows-7-and-browser-choice-in-europe.aspx: 'Shortly after new Windows PCs are set up by the user, Microsoft will update them over the Internet with a consumer ballot software program. If IE is the default browser, the user will be presented with a list of other leading browsers and invited to select one or more for installation.' No choice screen will appear to users if Internet Explorer is not the default browser.

browser as a default (and then will not have the ballot screen appear to final consumers). This may favour non-Microsoft browser vendors that have the deepest pockets.

Third, in the proposed EC outcome, Microsoft is obligated to line up many competitors' browsers for the final consumer to choose from. Thus, the Commission's proposed outcome is a 'must carry' rule imposed on Microsoft, especially since it applies only to computers where the OEM has installed Internet Explorer as the default. In the US middleware default set-up screen, the consumer is faced with a list of browsers chosen by his computer's manufacturer. Depending on the computer manufacturer's choices, this list could be extensive, but could also be limited to a single browser (Internet Explorer or another one) and the consumer would need to take extra steps to download other choices.

Fourth, the proposed EC outcome allows OEMs and consumers to uninstall more layers of Internet Explorer, if they wish, than just the front end of Internet Explorer that the US decree allows. In the proposed EC outcome, an OEM may choose never to show the existence of Internet Explorer to the final customer. Even so, deeper layers of the Internet Explorer API will remain in Windows when Internet Explorer is 'off' and an applications manufacturer will be able to call and utilize the Internet Explorer API for both the 'on' and 'off' Internet Explorer functions. Additionally, users can always 'turn on' Internet Explorer even if the OEM has turned it off. OEMs cannot permanently disable Internet Explorer.

Fifth, for an OEM that has chosen a default browser other than Internet Explorer in Europe, the operating system and security updates will not appear to be carried out through Internet Explorer. That is, even if Internet Explorer does the updates in the background, the consumer will see an interface that does not mention Internet Explorer.[234]

4. A CRITICAL DISCUSSION OF THE STRUCTURAL REMEDY OPTION

In thinking about a potential structural remedy in the EC case, it is worth discussing its imposition in the US case. This is because, in both cases, the issue was also leveraging monopoly power to a market of a complementary good.

In the US case, Judge Jackson adopted the plaintiff's remedies proposal

---

[234] This means that the Windows updates will be provided in the same way they are provided today in Vista and in Windows 7 Release Candidate.

word-for-word and imposed a break-up of Microsoft into two 'Baby Bills',[235] an operating systems company which would inherit all the operating systems software, and an 'applications' company with all the remaining software assets. Cash and securities holdings of other companies held by Microsoft would be split between the resulting entities. Bill Gates and other officers of the company would not be allowed to hold executive and ownership positions in both of the resulting companies.[236]

In arguing for the break-up, the government put forward a number of reasons. But since there was only an extremely short formal hearing on remedies, there was no chance for both the government's and Microsoft's cases on remedies to be discussed and evaluated. The government and the judge have stated (formally and informally) the following arguments for a break-up:

(i) that they considered the repeated violations of antitrust law by Microsoft as an indication that Microsoft would not follow any conduct or contractual restrictions; in fact, in some informal remarks, government officials believe that they were 'tricked' by Microsoft in settling the 1995 case with terms that Microsoft was able to exploit;
(ii) that the lack of remorse by Microsoft's executives was a clear indication that Microsoft 'could not be trusted' to implement any other remedy;
(iii) that the break-up was a 'surgical cut' that would create the least interference with business;
(iv) AT&T and the rest of the telecommunications industry benefited from AT&T's break-up, and so should Microsoft and the software industry—after all both industries have network effects;
(v) the break-up would eliminate the incentive for vertical foreclosure; and
(vi) the break-up would reduce the 'applications barrier to entry' since now the applications company might write popular Microsoft applications (such as MS Office) for other platforms.

The government failed to show that the proposed (and later abandoned) break-up was the appropriate remedy. The US Department of Justice did

---

[235] This is a word-play on 'Baby Bells' that was used in referring to *AT&T* and the first name of the co-founder and then CEO of Microsoft, Bill Gates.

[236] For a more detailed evaluation of the final US remedy, see Nicholas Economides, 'Comment of Nicholas S. Economides on the Revised Proposed Final Judgment in United States v. Microsoft', 22 January 2002, available at www.usdoj.gov/atr/cases/ms_tuncom/major/mtc-00022465.htm#comments.

not perform the appropriate cost-benefit analysis to show that conduct remedies were not sufficient and that a break-up was necessary. None of the affidavits in the remedies phase even approached a discussion on evaluating alternatives. Additionally, a few weeks before Judge Jackson's decision, under the supervision of Judge Posner, the government and Microsoft had reached a compromise that imposed only conduct remedies.[237] The government failed to justify why it was ready to compromise a few weeks earlier (in the settlement negotiated by Judge Richard Posner who was asked to try to find a settlement by Judge Jackson) on behavioural remedies, but later claimed that structural remedies were necessary. Harry First notes that the plaintiffs would probably have been more successful 'had they clearly had such a remedy in mind at an earlier stage in the proceeding'.[238]

The first argument of the government in support of a break-up does not stand to reason. The 1995 case was settled with a decree that explicitly stated that Microsoft could include in its operating system any additional functionality. It is reasonable that Microsoft (or any observer, including the US Department of Justice) would believe, given the 1995 consent decree, that adding browser functionality to Windows did not violate the consent decree.[239] This, of course, does not mean that adding such functionality would not violate antitrust law in general, but it lays to rest the idea that the government was tricked by Microsoft. The fact that companies and antitrust enforcers often have an asymmetry of information is very common and expected, and cannot be considered a 'trick', or a reason not to enter into agreements between antitrust authorities and companies.

The second argument of the plaintiffs in support of the break-up seems excessive. Antitrust enforcement is not an emotional tug of war in which the egos of either the plaintiffs or the defendants need to be satisfied. The show of remorse or lack thereof by Microsoft executives could not possibly define the remedy. We find it hard to believe that the judge would be correct in finding a different remedy appropriate if enough Microsoft executives simply showed public remorse. Moreover, Microsoft, like any other defendant, had a right to appeal (and it did so). A defendant's belief that he will prevail on appeal should not result in punishment.

---

237 The settlement was rejected by the states.

238 First, n. 178 above, 32.

239 The dispute regarding the application of the 1995 consent decree ended with a District of Columbia Circuit ruling in favour of Microsoft's understanding of the meaning of the decree. *United States* v *Microsoft,* 147 F.3d 935 (D.C. Cir 1998).

The third argument, that the break-up would be a surgical cut and therefore would disrupt the industry the least, is countered by the facts. A break-up of Microsoft would eliminate Microsoft as a flexible and formidable competitor. The wholehearted endorsement of a break-up by Microsoft's competitors in servers and back office (who were not found in the US case to have incurred damages through the Windows monopoly but would greatly benefit from the confusion and disruption created by a Microsoft break-up) is evidence that the break-up would be one of the most disruptive possible outcomes. Generally, break-ups of large companies are complicated and drawn-out affairs that disrupt the company that is broken up, the producers of complementary goods to its products, and its customers.

The fourth argument, that since AT&T's 1982 break-up was successful, so would Microsoft's, is incorrect. AT&T was divided into the long-distance company (AT&T), and seven regional operating companies, each of which remained a regulated local telecommunications monopoly until 1996. The destruction of AT&T's long-distance monopoly encouraged competition, which brought sharply lower prices and immense consumer benefits. However, there are a number of key differences between the two companies and their competitive situations, and these differences make it very likely that a Microsoft break-up, besides harming Microsoft, would harm consumers and the computer industry.

In 1981, AT&T was a 100-year-old regulated monopoly with many layers of management. For historical reasons, the local phone companies within the old AT&T, such as New York Telephone, were managed separately from the 'long lines' division. Thus, it was not difficult to separate the divisions since they functioned on many levels as separate companies. AT&T also had an abundance of managers to help cope with the break-up. By contrast, Microsoft is a young, entrepreneurial company run by few top executives, and its divisions are fluid. While this has made Microsoft an efficient and successful company, it also means that a break-up would have posed significant managerial problems and severely reduced the company's flexibility. Finally, AT&T was a regulated utility, and regulation guaranteed that the companies emerging from the break-up stayed interconnected. In contrast, the Microsoft break-up would likely to lead to incompatibilities and further loss of efficiency.

The US Department of Justice's two-way break-up plan was premised on the hope that an autonomous applications company would create a new operating system to compete with Windows. But at trial it was stipulated that more than 70,000 applications run on Windows, creating what the government called 'the applications barrier to entry' in the operating systems market. The new applications company, however capable, would be unlikely to be able single-handedly to create a successful rival operating system in short order.

The break-up of Microsoft, first proposed by the government, imposed by Judge Jackson, and, after the District of Columbia Court of Appeal's decision not pursued by the government, would have had detrimental effects. First, the break-up would probably have resulted in higher prices. If the US Department of Justice was correct and Microsoft kept its OS prices low so that it could exercise its monopoly power in the adjacent browser market, the post-break-up 'Baby Bill' that would inherit the operating system would have no incentive to keep the price low. The OS Baby Bill would no longer have the incentive to disadvantage any applications companies. Thus, if the US Department of Justice's theories are correct, the OS Baby Bill would exercise its monopoly power and raise the price of the operating system to the detriment of consumers. If the US Department of Justice was correct and Microsoft has significant monopoly power because of the 'applications barrier to entry', higher prices would be the direct result of the break-up. Second, as explained earlier, the break-up would likely eliminate the efficiencies that make Microsoft a flexible and formidable competitor.

A break-up would likely temporarily eliminate the incentive for interference from operating systems to applications and vice versa. Of course, the same can and has been accomplished by conduct restrictions without the cost and the disruption of a break-up. Moreover, the district court's break-up proposal did not impose permanent restrictions on the post-break-up functions of the resulting companies. The OS and the applications Baby Bills would have been able to enter into each other's business soon after the break-up. It is very likely that a few years after such a break-up, one of the resulting companies would dominate both markets.

5. ALTERNATIVE REMEDIES

The difficulty of devising adequate remedies that address the applications entry barrier issue as well as the distributional advantage of Windows, and the alleged 'failure' of the traditional conduct remedies employed in this case,[240] led some commentators to suggest alternative and unconventional remedies, including non-antitrust alternatives.

---

240 Carl Shapiro, 'Microsoft: A Remedial Failure' (2009) 75 *Antitrust Law Journal* 739.

Public Procurement Procedures as an Antitrust Remedy: Reducing the Applications Barrier

Regulation is not the only way states can intervene in the marketplace. Increasingly, state ownership and/or state contracting/spending are employed in order to achieve specific public policy objectives.[241] Competition in the marketplace might be one of those objectives. Professor Herbert Hovenkamp raised the possibility of public contracting being used as a tool to reduce Microsoft's applications barrier to entry, and gave the example of Alcoa, where the government sold the productive capacity of aluminum it owned under the conditions of the Surplus Property Act, which 'required the government to consider the impact on competition whenever it sold a significant piece of private property to a private firm' and excluded Alcoa from participating to the bid for government plants.[242] According to Hovenkamp, '(t)oday the government could do something similar by requiring its departments and agencies to use open-source software as an alternative to Microsoft's products'.[243]

This would increase the open source software installed base, as governments are among the principal purchasers of software products, and would help the economy move from a monopolized to a competitive computer platform network. The benefits for innovation would be particularly important, as recent studies have showed that innovative incentives (investments in applications) are sometimes greater for open source than for proprietary software platforms.[244] Microsoft would be able to participate in the government bidding process, under the condition that it submits its own open source products, either by developing new products or by making public the source code of Windows. This may improve allocative efficiency, as the government would also be able to purchase software products at a lower price (not including remuneration for intellectual property rights), and dynamic efficiency with increased competition between different products (assuming that a competitive market is better

---

241 See Christopher McCrudden, *Buying Social Justice* (Oxford: Oxford University Press, 2007).

242 Herbert Hovenkamp, *The Antitrust Enterprise* (Cambridge, MA: Harvard University Press, 2005), p. 302.

243 Hovenkamp, n. 242 above.

244 Nicholas Economides and Evangelos Katsamakas, 'Linux v. Windows: A Comparison of Application and Platform Innovation Incentives for Open Source and Proprietary Software Platforms' in Juergen Bitzer and Philip J.H. Schroeder (eds), *The Economics of Open Source Software Development* (Elsevier Publishers, 2006), available at www.stern.nyu.edu/networks/Economides_Katsamakas_Linux_vs._Windows.pdf.

suited for innovation than a monopolistic market for software products). One could also envision as a condition for Microsoft's participation in a call for tenders the unbundling of its applications from the operating system so as to guarantee an installed base to competing formats, or a wide interoperability with all existing or new formats. Of course, any imposed restriction of software choice would also precipitate reductions in utility of government users, at least in the short run. These utility losses of the Hovenkamp proposal have to be considered and balanced with the potential benefits outlined above.[245]

The decision of the Brazilian government to switch from Microsoft proprietary software to open source software and to pass legislation making the use of open source software mandatory for governmental departments was reportedly aiming to force Microsoft to rethink its business model.[246] The German government has also adopted guidelines for federal, state and local governments, as well as other public sector agencies, interested to migrate from Microsoft proprietary technology to open source software and signed contracts with IBM for computer systems based on Linux operating systems.[247]

These initiatives may have influenced Microsoft's progressive commitment with interoperability, and probably led to the publication of the 'interoperability principles.[248] An example may be the interoperability of Microsoft's former proprietary OOXML (Office Open XML file format), now a formal ISO standard,[249] with the OpenDocument Format (ODF)

---

245 Additionally, there would be far-reaching effects into the realm of industrial policy if the government specified a particular model of software development, predicting what finished software products would provide the greatest value per dollar spent. If Microsoft is forced to make the Windows source code public, this would reduce Microsoft's incentives to drive that product forward with new innovations, as others could then offer essentially the same product for free, possibly only subject to risk of patent infringement suits. Also, there is no significant evidence that the open source model can become a replacement for for-profit software. See Nicholas Economides and Evangelos Katsamakas, 'Two-sided Competition of Proprietary vs. Open Source Technology Platforms and the Implications for the Software Industry' (2006) 52 *Management Science* 1057, available at www.stern.nyu.edu/networks/Economides_Katsamakas_Two-sided.pdf; Economides and Katsamakas, n. 244 above.

246 See Steve Kingstone, 'Brazil adopts open-source software', BBC News, 2 June 2005, available at http://news.bbc.co.uk/2/hi/business/4602325.stm.

247 See 'IBM signs Linux deal with Germany', BBC News, 3 June 2002, available at http://news.bbc.co.uk/2/hi/business/2023127.stm.

248 See www.microsoft.com/interop/principles/default.mspx.

249 See http://en.wikipedia.org/wiki/Standardization_of_Office_Open_XML#cite_note-0.

standard, which is supported by Sun Microsystems, IBM, Novell, Nokia, Intel and Red Hat. This led to the release of Microsoft Office 2007 service pack 2, a product that, according to Microsoft, 'provides built-in support for more file formats than any other productivity suite on the market' and which comes with a 'new programming interface that will make it easy for developers to make any other document format show up in the drop down menu and be selected by users as their default, putting it on a par with the major formats already supported in Office 2007'.[250] This business culture evolution may have been provoked by the recent competition law challenges on interoperability and the use of public procurement as a way to increase competition in the marketplace. The cumulative impact of these combined antitrust and non-antitrust remedies is outside the scope of this study and should be empirically examined.

Standard Setting Organization and De Facto Versus De Jure Standardization

The alleged de facto standardization of the Windows architecture work group computing environment or the Windows media-player platform through the leveraging of Microsoft's dominant position in the operating systems market was a development that both the European Commission and the CFI abhorred.[251] The CFI was particularly clear that its reservations did not concern the process of standardization, which may provide benefits to consumers, but the way this de facto standardization took place in this particular case. The Court noted that '(a)lthough, generally, standardization may effectively present certain advantages, it cannot be allowed to be imposed unilaterally by an undertaking in a dominant position by means of tying'.[252]

A possible alternative is to delegate the task of developing interoperable standards to an SSO, which will assist the competition law authority or court with a burdensome monitoring mechanism in implementing interoperability requirements. In this case, the standard will not emerge

---

250 See http://microsoftontheissues.com/cs/blogs/mscorp/archive/2009/04/28/following-through-on-our-commitment-to-interoperability.aspx.

251 See Decision, para. 779, where the Commission noted that the position of Microsoft on the client PC operating systems market will enable it to 'determine to a large extent and independently of its competitors the set of coherent communications rules that will govern the de facto standard for interoperability in work group networks'. But note that standardization to WMA and WMV never occurred, but was assumed by the Commission to be later disproved in actuality. Today, as well as before the imposition of the Windows XP N remedy, WMA and WMV are not dominant media formats.

252 CFI judgment, para. 1152.

by a process of de facto standardization by a dominant firm but will be the outcome of negotiations. The SSO's activity will be closely monitored in order to avoid cartel-like behaviour or deceptive conduct, and to guarantee transparent and open procedures.[253] However, different problems with this specific solution are the imbalance of power between Microsoft and its competitors in the SSO and the subsequent risk that the standard approved will not be 'sufficiently' interoperable with competitors' products.[254] Additionally, the standard setting process is slow and could thus retard innovation in some dimensions while accelerating it in others. Furthermore, an agreement by competitors on a standard tends to restrict competition because competitors are limited largely to competing within the specific narrow confines of the standard, that is, just the best implementation of it. It follows that breakthrough innovation with alternative approaches tends not to occur because everyone is focused on implementation of the standard.

6. CONCLUSION

The success or the failure of the remedial action in the US and the EC Microsoft cases is still, five years after the District of Columbia Circuit decision on remedies in the United States and the same period since the Commission's Decision, a matter of controversy.[255] Some tend to link

---

[253] See Philip J. Weiser, 'Regulating Interoperability: Lessons from *AT&T*, *Microsoft*, and Beyond' (2009) 76 *Antitrust Law Journal* 271. See, however, the rejection of the 'truth-in-standards' provisions suggested to the non-settling states by the District of Columbia Circuit on the ground that these were unrelated to the violation found. The non-settling states would have required Microsoft to continue supporting any industry standard it has publicly claimed to support until it publicly disclaims such support, or the standard expires or is rescinded by the standard setting body, and to continue to support an industry standard any time it makes a proprietary alteration.

[254] See the recent investigation by the European Commission of the interoperability of OOXML, which was approved as an ISO-recognized international standard in April 2008. However, there have been allegations (currently being investigated by the European Commission) that there have been irregularities or attempts to influence the vote at the European Committee for Standardization and the International Organization for Standardization, thus illustrating the difficulties of guaranteeing the transparency of the process. See www.pcworld.com/article/144036/microsofts_iso_win_may_raise_antitrust_issues.html.

[255] See, most recently, the exchange between Shapiro, n. 240 above and Keith N. Hylton, 'Remedies, Antitrust Law and Microsoft: Comment of Shapiro' (2009) 75 *Antitrust Law Journal* 773.

the alleged failure of the remedy, or its unexpected costs and scope, with the issue of liability, professing the notion of what has become known as 'if you cannot fix it, it isn't broken'. Although it is clear that, in principle, the costs of remedies should not outweigh the consumer benefit they achieve, it is also contended that plaintiffs employ a sequential information model that addresses one issue at a time. It would be therefore inappropriate to dismiss a case simply because the plaintiff did not identify an adequate remedy. Harry First rightly observes that 'it seems inevitable that plaintiffs will refine their case as they learn more in the course of the litigation process', in particular in high-tech industries where technological change is so complex and so rapid that there is a need for quick action.[256]

At the same time, the litigation process is cheap compared to competition in price or product development. Thus, rivals have significant incentives to sue global dominant firms on multiple grounds and in multiple jurisdictions with the expectation that some suit will ultimately be successful in some jurisdiction. And, sometimes, one or more of these cases is picked up and pursued by an antitrust authority, as happened with the two cases against Microsoft, one in the United States and one in the European Union. To some extent, the lack of fully-thought-out remedies in both of these cases is a consequence of the history of the cases, i.e., how they were started by allegations of rivals who were primarily interested in improving their competitive position vis-à-vis the dominant firm rather than remedying all the consequences of anti-competitive behaviour.

The anti-competitive effects of these practices were clearly identified and a dominant narrative emerged as a retrospective rationalization of different practices and strategies adopted by Microsoft that harmed consumers: the maintenance of monopoly story in the US case and the leveraging story in the EC case. The identification of a specific consumer harm story could operate as a limit to the identification of adequate remedies. Antitrust liability stories transcend the different stages of a case, including the issue of remedies that need to address the specific consumer harm. The US Microsoft case was problematic in this respect as there was no a direct link between the antitrust liability story of maintenance of monopoly and the forward-looking remedies adopted. It is clear that Microsoft executives were concerned by the potential (but unlikely) erosion of the Windows platform's ubiquity from the joint actions of Sun and Java. The competitive threat to Windows did not materialize but Microsoft raised the walls of its fortress preventively in order to defend its position from Java's and

[256] First, n. 178 above, 31.

Sun's naval attack (if one employs Carl Schapiro's fortress metaphor).[257] But is it legitimate to require dominant firms to bring down the walls of their fortress or to keep them at the same level they were before, when they identify, perhaps wrongly, the existence of a potential threat of attack? There is a fine conceptual line between an illegitimate preventive wall-raising exercise and a legitimate meeting of competition defence. Lowering the wall some centimetres will certainly be an option, but the question will then be of how much lower and for what reason.

In comparison, the narrative of the first EC Microsoft case fits better with the remedies imposed. The issue here was that the dominant firm was using an existing fort to attack a new area and extend its fortification. The dominant firm would have thus been able to reinforce the defences of its existing fort and to increase the risks for those attacking it. The remedy in this case seems more straightforward in comparison with the previous setting: terminating the extension of the fortification will bring the end of both the ambition to reinforce the existing fortifications and to occupy a new area.

What this metaphor shows is that the choice of the adequate narrative among different consumer harm stories should correspond to the remedy sought. This was certainly the case with the EC Microsoft case but not with the US Microsoft case, where the difficulty for the leveraging argument to be accepted by the courts, as well as a change in the administration and possibly the reframing of the government's claim,[258] led to the development of a narrative (maintenance of monopoly) that had only an indirect link with the bulk of the forward-looking remedies that were finally imposed.

This mismatch between the consumer harm story/narrative and the remedy sought is also manifest in the second EC Microsoft case. Although the Commission seemed to advance a consumer harm story based on the relatively favourable (for its position) case law on tying, establishing some form of quasi per se illegality of tying if a company has a dominant position, the 'must carry' commitment accepted by the Commission as an adequate remedy for the competition problem does not address this particular issue. Unbundling would have certainly looked like the most adequate remedy for a leveraging concern. However, the Commission reacted negatively when Microsoft decided to unbundle Internet Explorer from Windows 7 E. The 'must carry' remedy adopted fits better with an essential facilities case, where Windows would have been considered

---

257 Shapiro, n. 240 above, 747.

258 Harry First and Andrew I. Gavil, 'Re-framing Windows: The Durable Meaning of the Microsoft Antitrust Litigation' (2006) *Utah Law Review* 679, 682.

indispensable for the distribution of a web-browser. We do not criticize the remedy as such, which could perhaps prove to be effective, in terms of reinvigorating competition in the web-browser market, but rather the apparent mismatch between the consumer harm story and the remedy. It would be particularly damaging for the development of competition law and economic growth in general if plaintiffs could employ the less demanding (in terms of standard of proof) theory of consumer harm in order to achieve the most far-reaching (in terms of commitments from a dominant firm) remedies. The problem cannot be solved by the characterization of the Microsoft case as strictly a 'tying' case. The classification of abuses under Article 82 EC is not a clear-cut exercise and there is always a fine conceptual line that distinguishes different categories of abuses, if one takes an effects-based approach.[259]

[259] See Ioannis Lianos, 'Categorical Thinking in Competition Law and the "Effects-based" Approach in Article 82 EC' in Ariel Ezrachi (ed.), *Article 82 EC: Reflections on its Recent Evolution* (Oxford: Hart, 2009), pp. 19–49.

14. Beyond Microsoft: an international agreement on abuse of market power?

Carlo Petrucci

1. INTRODUCTION

Competition law of the United States, European Union and numerous other countries, applies to firms operating outside their territory. By relying on the distinction between conduct and effect, states and countries may assert jurisdiction to apply their competition law when the effects of business conduct materialize within their territory, regardless of where a firm is incorporated and/or operates.

In the United States, the extraterritorial application of domestic competition law is called 'effect doctrine' (*United States* v *Aluminium Co. of America*),[1] and in the European Union 'implementation doctrine' (*Wood Pulp*).[2] In both cases the parties' conduct took place outside the US and EU territory, but since the effects materialized in their territory, the US and EU courts asserted jurisdiction to apply domestic antitrust laws. Both cases concerned cartels, in the first case a quota system for imports among aluminium producers and in the second an agreement in the wood pulp market entered into by producers and trade associations. Although the foundational cases of extraterritorial application of competition law are cartels, there has been little doubt that all competition rules apply to international transactions such as regulation of mergers and unilateral conduct.

Internationalization of competition law is not a new matter. In the past, initiatives towards common antitrust rules were promoted, but they have always been unsuccessful.[3] The issues related to extraterritoriality of com-

---

1 148 F.2d 416 (2d Cir. 1945).

2 Joined Cases 89, 104, 116-117 and 125–129/85 *Ahlstrom Oy* v *Commission* [1988] ECR 5193, para. 16 ('*Wood Pulp I*').

3 The Draft Havana Charter (1948) aimed at establishing the International Trade Organisation (ITO), which included some competition rules (V, Article

petition law and the initiatives carried out to put in place an international antitrust regime have promoted considerable debate among scholars and legal practitioners.

In broad terms, it can be summarized into two opposite stances: at one extreme of the spectrum, it is advocated that extraterritorial application of antitrust no longer provides adequate solutions to the problems posed by international business. Thus, international substantive antitrust rules are desirable. International substantive antitrust rules (also, common international antitrust rules, international antitrust, and similar terms) refer to a single set of competition rules that would be applicable to international transactions.

At the other end of the spectrum, it is argued that the current status of extraterritorial application of competition law should be preserved. It is acknowledged that the current situation is not optimal, however, this is better than having uniform competition law.

The Microsoft[4] case is an opportunity to revamp the debate as to whether uniform competition rules applicable to international businesses are desirable, and to examine the costs and benefits arising from the lack of such rules, as well as costs and benefits that would derive from them.

The debate is particularly interesting since Microsoft operates in the information technology industry characterized by high degree of innovation. Here, the antitrust laws have an impact on the structure and competitiveness of this market. In addition, Microsoft was subject to antitrust investigation in both the United States and European Union; in particular, it was accused of violating section 2 of the Sherman Act and Article 82 of

---

46) applying to: 'Business practices affecting international trade which restrain competition, limit access to markets, or foster monopolistic control, whenever such practices have harmful effects on the expansion of production or trade and interfere with the achievement of any of other objectives set forth in Article 1'.

In 1976, the Organisation for Economic Co-operation and Development (OECD) made recommendations to outlaw restrictive business practices adopted by multinational firms. Similar initiatives were undertaken by the United Nations Conference on Trade and Development (UNCTAD), where some rules on restrictive business practices were drafted.

In 1996, the Singapore Ministerial Conference of the WTO (World Trade Organization) created the Working Group on the Interaction between Trade and Competition Policy'. At the Doha Ministerial Conference of the WTO in 2001, a working group was instructed to clarify the core principles of international competition policy, including transparency, non-discrimination, procedural fairness and hardcore cartels. However, after the deadlock of the Cancún Ministerial Conference, in 2004 the General Council decided that competition policy matters would not be included in the WTO's work. See www.wto.org/english/tratop_e/dda_e/dda_package_july04_e.htm.

4 T-201/04 *Microsoft* v *Commission* [2007] ECR II-3601 ('CFI judgement').

the EC Treaty, two provisions that regulate conduct of entrepreneurs with market power. However, the outcomes have been different: in the Unites States the case was settled, whereas in the EU, Microsoft was found liable of abusing its dominant position.

This chapter is concerned with the problems of uniform rules regulating unilateral practices carried out by entrepreneurs with market power. This area of antitrust is particularly troublesome since it reflects different ideas of how to treat entrepreneurs which, due to their market success, have acquired considerable market power, and the extent to which competitors should be protected against monopolistic practices conducive to market exclusion. This is not to say that other areas of competition law are uncontroversial, thus making an international agreement feasible. For example, some international mergers have been assessed differently, the reason being that they change the market structure and the conditions in which competition occurs.[5] Even in the area of anti-competitive agreements, disagreement might arise with respect to vertical agreements. However, the rules on how to curb single firm's market power go to the heart of the debate as to what we mean by legitimate competition and the limits to be imposed on economic freedom.

This chapter is structured as follows. The second section summarizes the rationale behind the extraterritorial application of competition law. The third section outlines the problems and limits of the extraterritoriality of antitrust. Section 4 considers some objections raised against uniform international rules and analyses the problems with the adoption of a common standard for dominant entrepreneurs' unilateral practices. Section 5 examines the market approach to unilateral practices and the theory of regulatory competition in competition law. Finally, the chapter concludes by comparing costs and benefits arising from uniform/diversity of competition law and questions whether the market approach to the problem of conflicting competition laws always works.

2. RATIONALE FOR THE EXTRATERRITORIAL APPLICATION OF COMPETITION LAW

The application of national competition law to firms incorporated and/or operating abroad enables states to curb anti-competitive conduct

[5] Commission Decision 2004/134/EC *GE/Honeywell* [2004] OJ L48/1. For a comment, E.M. Fox, 'Mergers in Global Markets: GE/Honeywell and the Future of Merger Control' (2002) *University of Pennsylvania Law Review* 457.

originating abroad that causes adverse effects in their jurisdiction. This is desirable for the following reasons.

First, the state of origin (i.e. where the conduct is put in place) lacks competition law. From the state of origin perspective, the conduct is lawful, therefore if the target state did not apply its competition law, its consumers or firms would be left harmed and unprotected.

Secondly, the state of origin has competition law, which applies to any anti-competitive conduct originated in its territory, but whose effects may also materialize abroad, however it enforces it poorly. This might be due to lack of resources, which induces the state of origin to prioritize the punishment of conduct affecting its consumers or firms. Again, the extraterritorial application of competition law remedies such lack of enforcement.

Thirdly, the state of origin has competition law, but it does not apply to anti-competitive conduct occurring in its territory, either because its harm materializes abroad, or because an express antitrust exemption is provided to firms engaged in anti-competitive conduct that affects other states. In other words, a conduct that in normal circumstances would be punished is exempted since its effects materialize in foreign jurisdictions.[6] From a pure national and economic perspective, this is beneficial since firms operating in that state enrich themselves at the expense of foreign consumers or firms. Thus, the extraterritorial application of competition law counters the effects of outbound competition restraints not enforced by the state of origin.

The above examples are not exhaustive, as other situations might occur. In general, firms might exploit different regulation to enhance their welfare at the expense of national consumers or producers. Clearly, exploitation of different regulations is not necessarily negative, indeed choice of law shows that they can accommodate firms' interest without harming third parties. However, there is the fear that consumers and national firms may be easily exploited by foreign firms by using competition law gaps. Extraterritoriality is supposed to prevent this outcome.

---

[6] This is the case of 'export cartels', such as firms that fix prices, decide quotas and allocate markets when exporting their products abroad.

3. DRAWBACKS AND LIMITS OF THE EXTRATERRITORIAL APPLICATION OF COMPETITION LAW

The extraterritorial application of antitrust is not uncontroversial. First, it might be incompatible with the international law principle of territorial sovereignty. Here it should be noted that uncertainty exists as to the reach of international law.[7] With regard to competition law, the Advocate General, in the *Wood Pulp* case, distinguished between prescriptive jurisdiction and enforcement jurisdiction, and affirmed that the imposition of a sanction against foreigners concerns prescriptive jurisdiction, whereas enforcement jurisdiction consists of the 'power of a state to give effect to a general rule or an individual decision by means of substantive implementing measures which may include even coercion by the authorities'.[8] He concluded that the latter violates international law, whereas the former does not. On this basis, extraterritoriality of antitrust is lawful. However, this solution has clear limits: if a judgment or administrative decision cannot be enforced in a foreign state, foreign firms might not be deterred from carrying out anti-competitive conduct.

Secondly, the extraterritorial application of antitrust often generates tensions between the countries involved, with the risk of triggering trade wars, retaliatory measures or revamping protectionism or nationalism.[9] National competition law tends to reflect the economic reality of a certain state. It reveals its attitude on how to regulate markets, and is the result of a balance between different economic interests. When foreign competition law is invoked, such balance is disrupted. What is a gap of regulation for the law of state A, might be a deliberate choice not to regulate a certain matter by state B.

Thirdly, the extraterritorial application of competition law causes overregulation, which occurs when domestic antitrust laws apply simultaneously to the same conduct. In turn, this causes higher compliance costs (e.g. merging firms have to file in each jurisdiction in which the merger produces effects) and legal uncertainty (difficulty in making the

---

7 An important case concerning extraterritoriality in international law is *Lotus* (*France* v *Turkey*) (1927) PCIJ, Ser.A, No. 10, 23.

8 *Wood Pulp I*, Opinion of Advocate General Darmon, para. 28.

9 E.M. Fox, 'Antitrust and Regulatory Federalism: Races up, Down, and Sideways' (2000) *New York University Law Review* 1781, 1803. See e.g. the *GE/Honeywell* case in which a merger between two US multinationals was cleared by the US antitrust agencies, but prohibited by the European Commission.

conduct comply with two different laws).[10] In theory, impossibility in legal compliance cannot be ruled out (e.g. different laws provide for incompatible requirements, a firm either complies with one law, thus violating the other, or vice versa). Connected to the problem of overregulation, it has been noted that when two or more laws apply simultaneously and one provides for stricter requirements than others, the stricter law prevails over the others.[11] The Microsoft case confirms this point, as the remedy imposed by the European Commission[12] and upheld by the Court of First Instance (CFI) is more pervasive than that provided by the consent decree between the US enforcement agency and Microsoft. Overregulation might also jeopardize the level playing field among firms operating in the international context since some are subject to fewer requirements than others.

Finally, the extraterritorial application of competition law corrects the lack of enforcement by the foreign state, but cannot evidently deal with all anti-competitive conduct: the intervening state asserts jurisdiction only when its economic interests are at stake.[13] An additional limit concerns its effectiveness. States' territory is far from the anti-competitive conduct; as antitrust violations are difficult to detect, states might not be in a position to assess whether adverse economic effects are the result of foreign anti-competitive conduct or not. Even when the anti-competitive conduct is apparent, problems remain about the collection of evidence from foreign countries.[14]

4. OBJECTIONS AGAINST THE ADOPTION OF COMMON INTERNATIONAL COMPETITION RULES

One of the reasons for the failed adoption of international antitrust common rules was the United States' fear of losing sovereignty in antitrust

---

[10] This concern has also been voiced by the US Department of Justice in its 2008 report, *Competition and Monopoly: Single-Firm Conduct under Section 2 of the Sherman Act* (2008), p. 167, available at www.usdoj.gov/atr/public/reports/236681.htm.

[11] When one law imposes stricter requirements than other(s), the most prohibitory law wins. E.M. Fox, 'Global Problems in a World of National Law' (1999) *New England Law Review* 11, 12. See also US Department of Justice report, n. 10 above 169.

[12] Commission Decision 2007/53/EC of 24 March 2004 [2007] OJ L32/23.

[13] M. Taylor, *International Competition Law: A New Dimension for the WTO?* (Cambridge: Cambridge University Press, 2005), p. 66.

[14] Taylor, n. 13 above.

policy. In addition, many multinationals are American and thus they would be the main target of such international rules, which would be a threat to US interests.[15] Therefore, it was argued that national law and cooperation among antitrust agencies are sufficient to resolve the issues arising in the international context.[16] At first glance, such an attitude seems surprising since the United States has applied its law outside its jurisdiction and shaped the competition laws of other countries.[17] Thus, international antitrust law should be the final accomplishment of US interest in exporting and supporting acceptance of the market economy. However, national antitrust laws differ from each other: they may have similar structure or wording, but also may pursue different goals. The next sections deal with the policy goals underpinning dominant entrepreneur's unilateral conduct. However, before proceeding, it is worthwhile setting out some general considerations.

First, the economic reality of a country poses different regulatory needs. The competition law of an *advanced* economy tends to be consistent with the needs of large businesses and to pursue efficiency goals. On the other hand, the competition law of a *developing* state inevitably takes into account the needs of its young industry and the wish to protect it from foreign competitors.[18] As an economy evolves, the economic framework changes. As a result, competition law changes in the course of time. Conduct that used to be considered anti-competitive might receive a different treatment later.

Secondly, competition law plays a crucial role in ensuring the competitiveness of the market. However, additional non-economic goals may enter the antitrust discourse. Social concerns may be included when devising economic regulation.[19]

Thirdly, the meaning of the core concepts of competition law (e.g. competitive market, restriction of competition) may be supported by

---

[15] D.J. Gerber, 'Competition Law and the WTO: Rethinking the Relationship' (2007) *Journal of International Economic Law* 707, 710.

[16] For an outline of the US responses to such initiatives, see E.M. Fox, 'Competition Law and the Millennium Round' (1999) *Journal of International Economic Law* 665, 669.

[17] For example, after the Second World War, EC competition law was strongly influenced by the United States, see D.J. Gerber, *Law and Competition in Twentieth Century Europe: Protecting Prometheus* (Oxford: Oxford University Press, 1998).

[18] E.M. Fox, 'We Protect Competition, You Protect Competitors' (2003) *World Competition* 149.

[19] E.M. Fox and L. Sullivan, 'Antitrust – Retrospective and Prospective: Where are We Coming From? Where Are we Going?' (1987) *New York University Law Review* 936.

economics, but there is no scientific and universally accepted definition of the optimal competitive market. A definition of a competitive market is inevitably influenced by the history and culture of a certain country.[20]

5. UNILATERAL PRACTICES AND THE PROBLEM OF DIFFERENT POLICY GOALS

The treatment of unilateral conduct is the area where consensus is more difficult to achieve since the underlying policy goals may differ greatly. The prohibition of abusive unilateral practices presupposes that the firm has market power; and the central concern is to avoid the *abuse* of market power. This is expressed by section 2 of the Sherman Act, which provides for the monopolization offence, and Article 82 EC, which provides for the prohibition of dominant position. It is generally said that abuse of market power consists of exploitative practices (i.e. practices that exploit consumers) or exclusionary practices (i.e. practices implemented to drive out competitors and that do not serve to compete on the 'merits'). Traditionally, the second category has received more attention than the first. There are numerous problems concerning exclusionary practices, and the main one is the policy goal underlying the prohibition of such practices. In particular, two stances contend for providing its rationale.[21]

The first one lies in the need to defend the competitive process. Although there is no conclusive definition of the meaning of 'competitive process', it refers to a type of market organization which is open, in which small entrepreneurs have the right to compete on the merits, and their ability to compete is not impaired by dominant entrepreneurs. Protecting the competitive process requires that dominant entrepreneur's conduct not related to competition on the merits, and which prevents other entrepreneurs from competing, has to be constrained.

The criticism of this goal is that protecting the competitive process might result in the protection of inefficient competitors. It is often difficult to distinguish between practices that increase, or are the result of, efficiency and those purely aimed at driving out competitors. Competition is a rivalry between competitors, but eventually such rivalry might come to an end, and as a result, a few firms acquire market power whilst the others are forced to exit the market. Competition results in the exclusion of some competitors, but this is precisely what the market entails. Market

---

20 Fox, n. 18 above.
21 Fox, n. 18 above.

power acquired as a result of victorious and meritorious competition is desirable since it is an incentive to behave efficiently and, ultimately, the reward for meeting consumer demand. Seen in this light, protecting the competitive process might send out the wrong signal: firms would not have an incentive to behave efficiently as they would be deprived of their success, whereas inefficient firms would be protected even though they did not strive to offer better deals to their customers.

On the other hand, entrepreneurs with significant market power may impair the workings of the market by preventing existing entrepreneurs from competing effectively. Indeed, dominant entrepreneurs might put in place conduct that does not serve consumers, nor does it have any business justification, and that is designed to prevent competitors from carrying out their economic activity efficiently. This gives the wrong signal to small firms as they are not encouraged to keep on competing despite the presence of a dominant firm; it also sends the wrong signal to dominant entrepreneurs as they no longer have to strive to serve consumers better.

The goal of protection of the competitive process means that market power must be the outcome of meritorious competition and not used to drive out competitors. By prohibiting exclusionary practices, dominant firms have to compete by using means that would be used 'as if' other competitors exerted competitive pressure.

The second policy objective of the prohibition of exclusionary practices focuses on efficiency and is narrower than the defence of the competitive process. According to this approach, exclusionary conduct is not related to the effect on the market mechanism (foreclosure of the market, impairment of rivals to compete, and so forth), but is based on the effect on the output of the dominant entrepreneur and to consumer welfare.[22] According to this view, a unilateral conduct should be prohibited if it results in a restriction of output of the firm.[23] Conversely, when a conduct does not result in an output restriction, it can be presumed to be efficient.[24] Such a view derives from the broader paradigm advocated

---

[22] Fox, n. 18 above.

[23] This view is drawn from basic microeconomics, which shows that when firms reduce their output, prices rise.

[24] R.H. Bork, *The Antitrust Paradox* (New York: Basic Books, 1978, reprinted with a new introduction and epilogue, Free Press, 1993). He divided business conduct into three categories: conduct aimed at creating efficiency (beneficial), conduct aimed at creating monopoly power and restricting output (detrimental) and other conduct not related to efficiency (neutral). 'The task of antitrust is to identify and prohibit those forms of behaviour whose net effect is output restricting and hence detrimental' (at 122).

by the Law and Economics movement whereby law should be devised in such a way as to enhance efficiency. This view, applied to antitrust, means that non-economic values as well as economic values such as openness of markets and equal opportunities for economic actors should be removed from the antitrust discourse.[25]

6. EVOLUTION OF THE POLICY OBJECTIVES IN THE UNITED STATES AND EUROPEAN UNION

In the United States, the defence of the competitive process was a policy goal followed during the Warren era,[26] which resulted in considerable antitrust intervention.[27] The Reagan administration abandoned such an interventionist policy since it was deemed to hamper US firms' ability to compete. In this context, the Chicago School offered the theoretical support in favour of antitrust retrenchment by placing trust in the virtues of self-correction of the markets and by offering a model of antitrust exclusively oriented to efficiency/consumer welfare.[28] Whilst the post-Chicago School rejected some of the most radical tenets of the Chicago School, US antitrust is nowadays oriented to the goals of consumer welfare and efficiency. The US Department of Justice states that the law on unilateral treatment should achieve 'the objectives of maximizing economic growth by protecting the competitive process and consumer welfare',[29] the difficult issue being which goal should be preferred when these two goals conflict with each other. While it is accepted that consumer welfare is also enhanced by protecting the competitive process, the reverse is not necessarily true. In this case, the efficiency/consumer welfare goal seems to be preferred.

By contrast, nowadays, the EC treatment of unilateral practices is sympathetic to the defence of the competitive process. Its roots date back to the German ordoliberal tradition which conceived of competition law as a

---

25 Bork, n. 24 above, 422–3. He complained that an egalitarian ideology pervaded antitrust.

26 For example, the Supreme Court held that 'Antitrust laws in general, and the Sherman Act in particular, are the Magna Carta of free enterprise. They are as important to the preservation of economic freedom and our free-enterprise system as the Bill of Rights is to the protection of our fundamental personal freedoms'. *United States* v *Topco Associate*, 405 U.S. 596, 610 (1972).

27 Fox and Sullivan, n. 19 above, 945.

28 See below for a discussion on consumer welfare.

29 US Department of Justice report, n. 10 above, 169, 2.

means to give individuals the right to compete in the market and as a constraint on economic power. This stance is reflected by the European Court of Justice, which established that 'the undertaking concerned has a special responsibility not to allow its conduct to impair genuine undistorted competition on the common market'.[30] This approach has been confirmed in the Microsoft case, as the CFI pointed out that consumers may be harmed directly or indirectly, i.e. by impairing an effective competitive structure.[31] However, there has been debate as to whether this policy is still appropriate, and in the future the objective of Article 82 EC could be construed in such a way as to enhance consumer welfare and ensure an efficient allocation of resources.[32] This approach might result in placing less emphasis on maintaining a competitive structure favourable to small businesses if a dominant undertaking's conduct increases consumer welfare.

7. EUROPEAN MARKET INTEGRATION AS A COMPETITION POLICY

Protection of the competitive process or enhancement of efficiency are not the only goals; indeed, EC competition law shows that other goals may be assigned to competition law. Historically, the main objective of the European Community has been the fulfilment of the internal market, the accomplishment of which required the four freedoms of movement of the EC Treaty: freedom of movement of people, goods, services and capital. Integration of markets enhances welfare by removing barriers and technical and legal obstacles, and allowing production factors to move freely within the European Union. Therefore, the achievement of the internal market requires the prohibition of Member States putting in place measures that prevent or restrict such freedoms. However (and herein lies the relationship between the internal market and competition law), restrictions and obstacles to such freedoms can be put in place not only by the Member States, but also by private parties. For example, private

---

30 Case 322/81 *NV Nederlandsche Banden Industrie Michelin* v *Commission* [1983] ECR 3461, para. 57.

31 CFI judgement, para. 664.

32 See the European Commission, DG Competition, Discussion Paper on the Application of Article 82 of the Treaty to Exclusionary Abuses, December 2005, available at the European Commission website. See also, Communication from the Commission, Guidance on the Commission's Enforcement Priorities in Applying Article 82 EC Treaty to Abusive Conduct by Dominant Undertakings, 3 December 2008, COM(2008) 8 and 25.

parties may agree to share between themselves the markets of the Member States. If the EC Treaty forbids the Member States from limiting such freedoms, such prohibition may be more complicated to enforce among private parties. Thus, competition law has served the purpose of preventing private parties from jeopardizing the internal market. The Court of Justice adopted the policy integration goal, indeed it underpinned competition law with the EC Treaty provision providing that the activity of the European Community shall include a 'system ensuring that competition in the internal market is not distorted'[33] in such a way as to ensure that the competition rules are enforced with a view to achieving the internal market.[34] However, the relationship between the internal market and competition law may be problematic. In particular, problems arose when the economic freedom of the parties to arrange their transactions was in conflict with the achievement of the internal market. This was evident in the context of vertical agreements,[35] where territorial protection of the distributor was felt necessary to enable him to recoup distribution costs, but it also resulted in the fragmentation of the internal market. Also some unilateral practices have been found to be an abuse of dominant position on the grounds that they resulted in the division of the internal market.[36] It cannot be ruled out that the accomplishment of the internal market will ease the prohibition of agreements or conduct that causes, to a certain extent, the division of the internal market. However, recent EU membership by Eastern European countries suggests that it is still too early to abandon the policy objective of the internal market. Consequently, from the European perspective, it would be difficult to accept an international agreement providing entrepreneurs' right to implement practices that restrict the four European freedoms.

---

[33] Article 3(1)(g) EC.

[34] See e.g. Case C-56/65 *Société La Technique Miniere* [1966] ECR 234 and Case C-26/76 *Metro* v *Commission (No. 1)* [1977] ECR 1875.

[35] Joined Cases C-56 and 58/64 *Etablissements Consten SA and Grundig-Verkaufs GmbH* v *Commission* [1966] ECR 299. The case concerned the granting of exclusive distribution rights from a German producer to a French distributor. Such exclusive rights provided that the distributor was the only one in the French territory, with the consequence that the producer could not appoint other French distributors and had to prevent other European distributors from importing its products in France. Such restraints aimed at enabling the French distributor to recoup the investment made for the distribution of the German products, but they also resulted in the fragmentation of the European market. As a result such restraints were found to be contrary to Article 81 EC.

[36] Case 27/76 *United Brands Co.* v *Commission* [1978] ECR 207, para 183. For a recent case confirming this approach, see Joined Cases C-468–478/06, *Sot. Lelos kai Sia EE and others* v *GlaxoSmithKline* [2008] ECR I-7139.

8. CONSUMER WELFARE AS A BASIS FOR INTERNATIONAL AGREEMENT

It has been seen that consumer welfare is becoming a recurrent theme in the European competition policy discourse. Thus, it may be argued that its adoption as a benchmark for the treatment of exclusionary practices could be the basis for international antitrust.[37]

However, consumer welfare has often been used in ambiguous way[38] and it does not necessarily solve the problems of how to distinguish between desirable and undesirable unilateral practices. Originally, the notion of consumer welfare dates back to the neo-classical economist Marshall, and refers to the difference between the consumer's willingness to pay for a product and the price paid for it. Its central role in antitrust enforcement was advocated by the Chicago School,[39] even though its scholars were referring to the total welfare, i.e. the sum of producer and consumer welfare, without distinguishing among two such categories.[40] Nowadays, divergence exists between those who prefer the total welfare standard, i.e. the sum of the consumer and producer welfare, and those who advocate the consumer welfare standard. However, even if it were accepted that international antitrust rules should be based on consumer welfare, this would not solve all problems. This is because a competition policy exclusively oriented to enhance consumer welfare would be undesirable. Protecting consumer welfare in absolute terms would require eliminating market power; but it has been seen that market power is an important incentive to behave efficiently and to reward the risks taken when making investments on innovation or infrastructures. This was reiterated in the *Trinko*[41] case which stated that '[t]he mere possession of monopoly power, and the concomitant charging of monopoly prices, is not only not unlawful; it is an important element of the free-market system'.[42] High prices attract other firms, which will also have to invest, and the resulting competition will drive prices down to the competitive

---

[37] US Department of Justice report, n. 10 above, 169, 176.

[38] J.F. Brodley, 'The Economic Goals of Antitrust: Efficiency, Consumer Welfare, and Technological Progress' (1987) *New York University Law Review* 1020, 1032: 'The term consumer welfare is the most abused term in modern antitrust analysis'.

[39] See e.g. Bork, 'the only legitimate goal of American antitrust law is the maximization of consumer welfare': n. 24 above, 51.

[40] See e.g. Bork, n. 24 above, 91.

[41] *Verizon Communications, Inc.* v *Law Offices of Curtis V. Trinko, LLP*, 540 U.S. 398 (2004).

[42] 540 U.S. at 407.

level. When this mechanism works (for example, there are no or low barriers to entry), the central problem is to strike a balance between desirable market power and consumer welfare.

If protection of consumer welfare, on the one hand, cannot be pursued in the absolute, on the other hand, it cannot be assumed that market power always results in investments and innovations. In the context of an international agreement on exclusionary practices, it should also be noted that consumers of a certain country might be more tolerant than others to unilateral practices that lessen their welfare. Clearly, no definitive answer can be given and any solution inevitably embeds value judgements. In addition to this, exclusionary practices may harm consumers of different countries to different degrees, or even exclusively harm consumers of other countries and not domestic ones. In this case, the traditional economic approach whereby business conduct is permitted if producer's gain outweighs consumer's loss cannot realistically work at the international level. Thus, an international agreement should either prevent such imbalance in consumers' loss, or provide for compensatory mechanisms.[43]

A second problem is the definition of consumer welfare: it may consist of price only or additional elements that consumers appreciate (quality, choice, and so forth). The former makes antitrust more manageable as it does not have to take into account aspects whose assessment is inevitably subjective. Nevertheless, the inclusion of choice as an element of consumer welfare is a more realistic model of what consumers expect from the market economy.[44] In addition, in some sectors, choice of products, particularly among products of different quality, is deemed more worthwhile than a uniform cheap product. The US antitrust agencies, when defining the anti-competitive harm resulting from competitors' collaboration, consider that consumers may be harmed not only by higher prices, but also by detriment to competition in quality, service or innovation.[45] Although choice is not mentioned, it is clear that price is not the only element constituting consumer welfare.

The European Commission is more explicit as it states that one of the negative effects of market power is the 'ability to maintain product quality and *variety* or innovation below competitive levels for a significant period

---

[43] See below.

[44] For a comprehensive analysis of the consumer choice paradigm, see N. Averitt and R. Lande, 'Using the "Consumer Choice" Approach to Antitrust Law' (2007) *Antitrust Law Journal* 175.

[45] US Department of Justice and Federal Trade Commission, Antitrust Guidelines for Collaborations Among Competitors, 64 Fed Reg. 54483 (1999), available at www.ftc.gov/os/2000/04/index.htm #7.

of time'.[46] With respect to unilateral conduct, the European Commission reiterated that consumer welfare includes both price and choice.[47] With regard to EC case law on Article 82 EC, the Microsoft case confirms that consumers' choice is an important criterion when assessing the impact of a certain practice on consumers.[48] The importance of choice is also reflected in other EC cases on refusal to deal. For example, in the *Magill* case[49] the CFI upheld the Commission Decision and confirmed that conduct preventing the production and marketing of a new product for which there is potential consumer demand amounted to an abuse of dominant position. Although offering a new product belongs to the phenomenon of innovation, ultimately, it results in more choice for consumers. Nevertheless, choice of product cannot be pursued in absolute terms, since this could result in excessive protection for inefficient firms which supply the market with a unique product, even if most consumers prefer alternative and cheaper products.

Increasing consumer choice may also be critical in 'refusal to deal' cases. It has been seen that unsatisfied demand for a new product is one of the requirements for compelling a dominant entrepreneur to deal with other entrepreneurs. However, compulsory dealing lessens the incentive to innovate, and/or innovate with respect to the monopolist and its competitors: the dominant entrepreneur knows that it will earn less profit, thus reducing its incentive to invest, and its competitors will not invest since they know they can rely on the dominant entrepreneur's assets.[50]

---

[46] Guidelines on the Application of Article 81(3) of the Treaty [2004] OJ C101/97, para. 26.

[47] Communication from the Commission, Guidance on the Commission's Enforcement Priorities in applying Article 82 EC Treaty to Abusive Conduct by Dominant Undertakings, 3 December 2008, COM(2008)8.

[48] CFI judgement, para. 652. The Commission and the CFI took into consideration consumers' opinion that non-Microsoft work group server operating systems were better than Windows ones.

[49] Case T-69/89 *Radio Telefis Eireann* v *Commission* [1991] ECR II-485 ('*Mag: II*'), para. 73. This judgment was confirmed by the Court of Justice in Joined Cases C-241 and 242/91 *Radio Telefis Eireann (RTE) and Independent Television Publications Ltd (ITP)* v *Commission* [1991] ECR II-485. See also Case C-418/01 *IMS Health GmbH* v *NDC Health GmbH & Co. KG* [2004] ECR I-5039.

[50] However, the argument that denial of access to the dominant entrepreneur's assets is an incentive for its competitors to carry out their own innovation and develop their infrastructure also has some limits: in the Microsoft case the CFI, in upholding the Commission's argument, noted (para. 636) that allowing access to protocols by Microsoft's competitors was not a disincentive for them to develop their innovative products, on the contrary it allowed consumers to take advantage of Microsoft's competitors' innovation. Indeed, one may also question whether Microsoft's innovation is better that that of its competitors.

There is no definitive answer as to what extent antitrust should protect consumer choice as this depends on a variety of factors that inevitably reflect cultural preferences. This may add further scepticism about the feasibility of an international antitrust agreement on unilateral conduct. However, the problems of where to strike the balance between market power and consumer welfare, and the content of consumer welfare, exist in any jurisdiction. It will be seen that in the international context the real issue is how the adverse effects of market power and increases of consumer welfare are distributed.[51]

9. SELF-DESTRUCTING MONOPOLY AND *LAISSEZ FAIRE* IN GLOBAL MARKETS

A general objection against international antitrust and, in particular, against common rules on exclusionary practices, rests in the belief that self-correction of the market is better, quicker, and more effective than antitrust intervention. This is the Chicago School stance, which advocated minimum public intervention in the economy and, consequently, little antitrust enforcement. Even though it was accepted that market failures occur, it was argued that public intervention does not necessarily improve or correct such failures; and even if public intervention may remedy such failures, the market corrects them more quickly and more efficiently.[52]

This attitude particularly fits exclusionary practices. Market power acquired after the exclusion of competitors means high prices. This attracts other firms, thus forcing the dominant entrepreneur to lower prices. Even if such an adjustment requires time, losses caused by market power are smaller than losses resulting from beneficial practice wrongly condemned. This is because some beneficial practices may lower production costs; consequently prohibiting such practices prevents all businesses from carrying out conduct that lowers costs.[53] In addition, antitrust analysis requires a great deal of market information and sometimes information is not available or accurate. This makes antitrust enforcement prone to fail. Finally, some conduct is complex to evaluate and therefore it is believed that the market decides better than the courts.[54]

---

51 See below.

52 See e.g. F. Easterbrook, 'The Limits of Antitrust' (1984) *Texas Law Review* 1.

53 Easterbrook, n. 2 above, 16.

54 H. Hovenkamp, *The Antitrust Enterprise* (Cambridge, MA: Harvard University Press, 2005), p. 47. Hovenkamp, unlike most of the Chicago School, recognizes the existence of strategic behaviour (behaviour that may result in a

Scepticism about antitrust intervention may be replicated in the international context with regard both to substantive rules and to enforcement. International rules on exclusionary practices would be a compromise between a purist efficiency approach and an approach that takes into account wider economic values. This would result in a vague standard that would provide little guidance to firms. The problem is aggravated by the fact that such rules would be difficult to change, since they would be based on an international treaty, and any reform requires unanimity.[55]

The vagueness of the standard would have repercussions for enforcement: indefinite rules would confer discretion on the enforcer, which might fail to pursue the right policy: states, through their representatives in the international enforcing authority, would try to maximize their national welfare, and in particular that of national producers.[56] However, against this argument, it could be responded that the European experience shows that supra-national governance has been successful. Whilst it is true that some EU Member States exert pressure to protect their national producers (especially the so-called national champions), it is equally true that the European Commission has achieved sufficient independence in carrying out its competition policy.

With regard to the efficacy of the market in giving a better response than antitrust enforcement (either public or private), it can be said that this is not always the case. Cartels may last a long time.[57] Likewise, the Microsoft case shows that Microsoft's market power in the operating systems market has not been eroded over the years. Dominant entrepreneurs may prolong their market power through strategic conduct that considerably delays the entry of new competitors. If it is true that some conduct may be very difficult to evaluate, it is equally true that some exclusionary conduct is plainly anti-competitive and may not be deterred by the extraterritorial application of the competition law of the target state.

---

competitor's exclusion), but he is sceptical that antitrust enforcement is able to give an appropriate response (at 9).

55 P.B. Stephan, 'Global Governance, Antitrust, and the Limits of International Cooperation' (2005) *Cornell International Law Journal* 173.

56 Stephan, n. 55 above, 202–17.

57 A recent report commissioned by the European Commission shows that the average cartel duration is five years. Final Report, *Making Antitrust Damages Actions More Effective in the EU: Welfare Impact and Potential Scenarios*, p 98, available at http://ec.europa.eu/comm/competition/antitrust/actionsdamages/documents.html.

10. INTERNATIONAL REGULATORY COMPETITION IN COMPETITION LAW

A second argument against uniform international antitrust relies on the regulatory competition theory. This theory holds that when individuals and factors of production can move freely, regulators endeavour to attract businesses by providing for regulation favourable to businesses' interests. These regulatory changes trigger a process of competition among regulators in creating the best set of incentives to accommodate business interests. As a result, the best regulatory regime (i.e. the regime that most enhances economic welfare) will emerge at the expense of other regimes that maintain costly and unnecessary legal requirements. In this case, the theory holds that competition amongst regulators triggers a 'race to the top' and therefore common rules applicable to all jurisdictions are undesirable since they prevent such a race. This process is also beneficial since it weakens particular interest group influence over regulation.[58]

However, regulatory competition may not lead to optimal outcomes, as third parties might be adversely affected by low legal standards. In this case, it is said that competition among regulators triggers a 'race to the bottom' and therefore common rules are necessary to avoid such an outcome.

The regulatory competition paradigm has been applied, among other things, to the US regulation of corporate law.[59] It has also been questioned whether regulatory competition applies to competition law.[60] If this is the case, it must be seen whether competition among competition laws leads to a race to the 'top' or to the 'bottom'. The implication is clear: if there is a race to the top, not only is international antitrust unnecessary, but it is also detrimental, since it would prevent the emergence of the best domestic competition law regime. Conversely, if there is a race to the bottom, international antitrust is desirable since it could prevent pernicious competition among states.

Before proceeding, it is necessary to define what we mean by 'bottom'

---

58 W. Bratton, J. McCahery, S. Picciotto and C. Scott, *International Regulatory Competition and Coordination* (Oxford: Clarendon Press, 1996). Indeed, the theoretical basis of regulatory competition can be traced into public choice theory.

59 L.A. Bebchuk, 'Federalism and the Corporation: The Desirable Limits of Competition in Corporate Law' (1992) *Harvard Law Review* 1435.

60 E.M. Fox, 'Antitrust and Regulatory Federalism: Races Up, Down, and Sideways' (2000) *New York University Law Review* 1781. Also, A.T. Guzman, 'Antitrust and International Regulatory Federalism' (2001) *New York University Law Review* 1142.

and 'top' in competition law. In general, 'bottom' has a negative connotation: the law has been changed (e.g. it provides for fewer legal requirements, and consequently firms have fewer constraints), but it results in a decrease of economic welfare. Conversely, 'top' refers to a situation where the law has been changed, and results in an increase in economic welfare. Here the problem lies in applying such categories to antitrust. Any antitrust rule bears different consequences for consumers, producers and distributors, thus any change in antitrust alters the economic relationship between these subjects. This poses the problem of which perspective (consumers, producers, etc.) should be adopted when defining 'top'. Economists would answer that 'top' is when antitrust maximizes economic welfare (i.e. the sum of producer and consumer welfare) regardless of how such welfare is distributed between them. This view corresponds to an efficiency-oriented antitrust. However, this view is questionable, as there is no normative basis for holding that if producers' gains outweigh consumers' losses, efficiency is achieved and thus consumers have to bear their losses.

In addition, efficiency is not a neutral concept and should be interpreted according to the economic context in which firms operate. Business environment dictates the conditions by which conduct can be said to be efficient. For example, the type of efficiency pursued by a country with large corporations is different from that of a country with young industries[61] or with a large number of small and medium-sized enterprises.

Although 'top' and 'bottom' are ambiguous terms, it is worth investigating whether the existence of different national antitrust regimes is a factor that firms take into account when deciding where to conduct their business. If so, states might have an incentive to change their competition law to attract business. In this respect, it has been noted that firms establish businesses in a state in order to serve a particular market and competition law is only a part of the entire regulatory environment. Consequently, it is doubtful that states compete by changing their competition law to attract foreign business.[62] Competition law might affect firms' decisions differently depending on the circumstances. A lax regulation of unilateral conduct would benefit a prospective foreign firm in a dominant position, but not a small foreign firm that wants to compete against a dominant national firm. Similarly, a strict regulation of unilateral conduct would force a prospective foreign dominant firm to change its commercial policy implemented in a certain country, but it would not deter it from entering a profitable market. Competition law is a marginal incentive in the decision

61 Fox, n. 60 above, 1793.
62 Fox, n. 60 above, 1789.

to enter a market.[63] Other factors such as market profitability, consumers' attitude, competitors and barriers to entry, tax law and the whole regulatory environment play a more important role in such a decision.

In addition, even assuming that states lowered their competition law standard to attract international companies, the extraterritoriality application of competition law would frustrate such an attempt, since the stricter regime would apply to a foreign firm. When competition law has an international reach, either a company ceases to do business in a state with strict competition law or, if the company wants to do business in that state, it will have to comply with the competition law of the host state. It follows that regulatory competition of antitrust laws is unlikely.[64] However, it has been noted that an indirect form of regulatory competition might occur where states compete for capital and innovation-producing firms. In this case, competition law is devised in such a way as to protect innovation and investments.[65]

Although states do not change competition law with a view to attracting firms, the existence of competition law regimes may influence a state in its type of competition policy. When a state has a competition law oriented to efficiency, its firms may be in a better position to compete against foreign firms operating in a state whose competition law incorporates various goals (i.e. fairness, distributors' freedom of trade, etc.). In this case, the latter state might want to change its competition law to enable its firms to be more efficient and to compete better.[66] Although it is difficult to draw a comprehensive conclusion, it is clear that states do not compete by offering attractive competition laws and therefore there is no race to the bottom or to the top. Rather, states tend to configure their competition law in such a way as to accommodate their industry and the characteristics of their economy. Clearly, this can be done by putting in place inefficient policies (e.g., protectionism, tolerance of domestic cartels, etc.), but also by combining policies pursuing efficiency, protection of small domestic producers or distributors, etc. In conclusion, no argument in favour of or against the adoption of international competition rules can be drawn from the theory of regulatory competition.

---

[63] Fox, n. 60 above, 1789.

[64] A.T. Guzman, 'Antitrust and International Regulatory Federalism' (2001) *New York University Law Review* 1142, 1149.

[65] Stephan, n. 55 above, 215.

[66] Fox, n. 60 above, 1792.

11. BENEFITS OF UNIFORM INTERNATIONAL RULES

The existence of competition law regimes is likely to encourage forum shopping by competitors.[67] International business operating in the European Union may choose to lodge an antitrust complaint in this jurisdiction as they know that Article 82 EC has a lower standard than its US counterpart. In the Microsoft case, some complainants were also US firms (e.g. Novell) and the remedy of disclosure of interoperability information for work group servers would enable Microsoft's competitors to develop better products and to foster competition. Here, positive effects for consumers are evident, both to EU and US consumers. This situation gives rise to a paradox; the European Union supported international antitrust rules, but pluralism of competition law has benefited EU consumers (though it might also benefit US consumers who prefer Microsoft's competitors' products), and also some US firms. By contrast, the United States rejected proposals to unify international antitrust rules, specifically to protect its multinational corporations, but they would have benefited more from a single international standard that, presumably, would have been a compromise between the US and EC regimes.

This also shows that the idea that states use their domestic competition law to benefit their national producers at the expense of global welfare is at least an oversimplification.[68] Extraterritorial application of antitrust bears a number of economic effects that affect different economic subjects, regardless of where they are located (domestic consumers, domestic and foreign producers, etc.). Where foreign antitrust has credible enforcement, its effects diffuse across jurisdictions. Common international rules would reduce the costs of different antitrust laws, since once a single standard is set, firms would be able to comply with it, with resulting lower compliance costs and litigation risks. However, adopting a single standard has a cost: lack of experimentation.[69] Once a decision is made, it binds all; and, as is mentioned above, some decisions might not suit the economic context of a certain country.

---

[67] This concern has also been raised in the US Department of Justice report, n. 10 above, 169.

[68] For example, Stephan, n. 55 above.

[69] Experimentation is a benefit highlighted by the adherents of the theory of regulatory competition. S.G. Calabresi, '"A Government of Limited and Enumerated Powers": In Defense of *United States v. Lopez*' (1995) *Michigan Law Review* 752.

12. ADVANCING THE UNDERSTANDING OF GLOBAL TRADE

International antitrust would bring an important benefit: the achievement of an international vision in the understanding of global trade problems.[70] National law has clear limits in the appreciation of such problems, limits deriving, by way of example, from partial market information and lack of incentives of antitrust enforcers to take into account all interests concerned by anti-competitive conduct. National enforcement authorities may deliberately pursue policies increasing national welfare or, simply, they may not be aware of the background from which anti-competitive conduct originates. EU history shows that it would have not been possible to build the internal market without an underlying EC law. It also shows that the Member States managed to overcome pursuance of national interest in favour of a more general interest.

International vision would allow the identification economic effects caused by business conduct. Rules in general, and antitrust laws in particular, have welfare distributive consequences.[71] Scholarly argument for a large part of law and economics maintains that legal rules should be devised in order to maximize efficiency and they should not intervene in order to redistribute the wealth created by economic transactions since this would result in inefficient redistribution and inefficient legal rules.[72] According to this view, redistribution would be best accomplished directly by income tax and welfare transfer programmes.[73] However, the argument that efficiency is the only goal of antitrust rules, and it is irrelevant how such efficiency gains are distributed, is contentious. Replicating such an argument in the international context is even more contentious. Let us suppose that exclusionary practices harm consumers of different states to a different degree. In this case, it is difficult to argue that the nationality of harmed consumers should be irrelevant. It is equally difficult to think that states affected by anti-competitive conduct would not endeavour to remedy this situation on the grounds that the conduct in question, overall, advances economic welfare. In theory, the extraterritorial application of competition law by the adversely affected states could remedy such a situation. However, this would be the sub-optimal solution, as extrater-

---

[70] Fox, n. 60 above, 1802.

[71] H. Hovenkamp, 'Distributive Justice and the Antitrust Laws' (1982) *George Washington Law Review* 1, 2.

[72] See e.g. L. Kaplow and S. Shavell, *Fairness versus Welfare* (Cambridge, MA: Harvard University Press, 2002), pp. 33–4.

[73] Kaplow and Shavell, n. 72 above, 33.

ritoriality has many drawbacks. On the contrary, more benefits could be achieved if international antitrust rules could take into account how economic effects impact on different consumers. This means that antitrust analysis should be carried on in conditions allowing the identification of all 'winners and losers' of business conduct, which requires comprehensive vision.[74] When adverse effects materialize mainly in a certain country, international antitrust should also remedy such an imbalance. This could be the basis for an international agreement acceptable by all countries. It is doubtful that the extraterritoriality of competition law is producing better results.[75]

13. CONCLUDING CONSIDERATIONS

In this chapter the arguments for and against international rules on unilateral conduct, and specifically on exclusionary practices, have been examined. Arguably, the treatment of exclusionary practices is one of the most controversial areas of competition law, which makes an international agreement more difficult to achieve. Difficulties in defining unlawful conduct and controversies as to how to assess whether it is lawful or not would be reflected in an international agreement. However, complying with various national requirements is costly. These costs are greater when it is difficult to comply with two or more laws. The greatest cost arises when, due to the impossibility of complying with two or more laws, an overall beneficial transaction is not carried out. International rules would eliminate such costs.

The costs of common international antitrust rules are more difficult to assess, due to lack of empirical evidence. The main objection can be summarized as being that international antitrust rules would not suit the economic needs of all countries. The US variant of this argument is that antitrust law that does not pursue efficient transactions results in welfare losses. Here it can be replied that efficiency is not a unique concept, but varies according to the business environment. In addition, it has been seen that, due to the extraterritorial application of competition law, jurisdictions

---

74 As Fox puts it: 'Proper analysis requires a vision from the top'. See Fox, n. 60 above, 1803.

75 It could be argued that a tax system designed to compensate consumers of a foreign country adversely affected by anti-competitive conduct originating in another country could be an alternative to the introduction of common substantive antitrust rules. However, realistically, this prospect would be even more difficult than achieving common international rules.

with efficiency oriented antirust cannot be isolated from foreign antitrust enforcement. Another objection lies in the fact that common international rules would prevent experimentation with new rules. However, such rules would apply to international transactions, whereas national laws would still apply within their scope of application. Thus, diversity of laws would still remain, which may provide arguments and evidence to change unsuitable international rules.

It is difficult to measure the costs and benefits of international antitrust. There is, however, a benefit even more difficult to assess, that justifies international antitrust: the achievement of a better position from which to assess the effects of international business conduct. In turn, this would be an important contribution to global economic governance.

Epilogue

Bo Vesterdorf

At a first reading, Article 82 EC would seem a rather clear and simple rule of law. Quite simply, dominant undertakings may not abuse their position and the Article even indicates in a non-exhaustive way some types of conduct which may be abusive. At a closer look, things, however, become more complicated. On which market and when is the particular undertaking dominant? And, if dominant, what kind of conduct is abusive? And is this specific kind of conduct only abusive under specific circumstances? And even if one may have an instinctive, immediate reaction of finding of abuse in certain situations, it is not at all always easy to explain and give legal reasons in detail why.

When discussing such issues it must, at the same time, be kept in mind that it appears indirectly from Article 82 EC, and very directly from the case law of the European Court of Justice and the Court of First Instance (CFI), that dominant undertakings are also entitled to compete, even vigorously, as long as they compete on the merits of their products or services. They are therefore also entitled to acquire intellectual property rights (IPRs) and benefit from the protection accorded by such rights under the law, and exercise and defend these rights vis-a-vis their competitors or others. They are evidently also entitled, and should be encouraged, to innovate and in that connection have the right to defend against free-riding.

However, they are indeed also obliged to respect and abide by the competition rules in order to avoid the harmful effects their conduct may entail for consumers, directly or indirectly. It is often said that dominant undertakings have a special obligation not to prevent or distort competition. That is correct to the extent that the market power they enjoy means that the effects of their market conduct will be more important and may be more destructive for competition than that of non-dominant undertakings. This is why Article 82 EC prohibits abusive behaviour, i.e. behaviour where the dominant undertaking uses its specific market power in a way that cannot be called normal competition and which either prevents or distorts competition.

Article 82 EC is a difficult rule of law which is, unfortunately, neither clear nor simple to apply in practice. Dominant undertakings must, however, abide by the rule but cannot seek much guidance from the text of that provision in order to know where the limit between legal and illegal conduct may be drawn, except what can be learned from the relatively few Article 82 decisions in the case law.

The Microsoft case which ended with the judgment by the CFI on 17 September 2007, has in a particularly clear way highlighted (i) the very difficult line between competition law and IPRs, as well as (ii) the difficulty in finding a reasonable balance between the right to develop/innovate and the obligation not to hinder or distort competition in doing so.

The first bone of contention in the Microsoft case stemmed from the refusal by Microsoft to give some competitors access to interoperability information; the second matter in question arose from the decision by Microsoft to integrate its Windows Media Player into its Windows operating system software.

The very complex technical, factual and legal problems of the case which were examined and decided by the European Commission and confirmed by the CFI have not surprisingly inspired much legal debate and writing on the merits of the Commission's Decision and, in particular, the judgment by the CFI. It has also become very clear that the debate has divided the waters, in the sense that those in favour of strong protection of IPRs have criticized both the Decision and the judgment, claiming that they will lead to an undesirable weakening of IPRs, while others deny this to be the case. As regards the tying part of the Microsoft case, it is claimed by many that the Decision may hamper the incentive for dominating undertakings to innovate by way of developing existing products, while others disagree, simply suggesting that it was unnecessary for Microsoft to tie the media player to Windows since leaving a free choice to the consumer might very well have led to the same result for Microsoft but at least given its competitors a more level playing field.

Having read the interesting papers collected here, regarding both the US case and the EC case, I think that it can safely be said that all of the issues raised by the 'refusal to license problem' and the 'tying problem' have been thoroughly examined and discussed. It is, however, not surprising – at least to me – to see that views on these problems and the solution given to them in the United States and in Europe by the Commission and the CFI are very different and clearly illustrate the schism that the two different issues give rise to.

In recent years, it has more and more become generally accepted that competition law issues cannot reasonably be discussed and solved without looking into the economics of the market and the effect of certain conduct on the market. It is increasingly claimed that alleged breaches of Article 81 EC and, in particular, Article 82 EC should be examined not only from a legal point of view but even more importantly from an effects point of view, taking into consideration what consumer harm the examined conduct really may have had or may have in the future. There is no doubt that this is important to bear in mind, both during the administrative examination of the case and at the judicial level. This kind of approach, which has long been accepted in the United States by the authorities and the courts, is now an approach also confirmed and adopted in the Commission Guidance on Article 82 EC, as an important part of examining cases of exclusionary conduct. That any examination of exploitative conduct also needs to examine the economics of the market seems to be similarly justified.

This collection of papers on the US Microsoft case and on the EC Microsoft case also covers this kind of approach, with some very interesting contributions by economists, taking issue in particular with the CFI judgment, in part criticizing it for a lack of sufficient examination of the economics of the case.

There seems to be more or less general agreement among the contributors to this work that, first, the EC Microsoft case was a very special case, concerning an undertaking holding a worldwide dominance of some 90–95 per cent of the market for operating systems software for personal computers; and, secondly, that one therefore needs to be careful about drawing too far-reaching conclusions from the judgment. There also seems to be more or less general agreement that the 'exceptional' circumstances which according to the case law may oblige a dominant undertaking holding IPRs to accord a licence to a competitor have been somewhat expanded. Some of the contributors agree with this approach, while others rather reject it.

With regard to the tying part of the case, there is the same divide, some of the contributors claiming that the approach of the judgment may have a stifling effect on innovation or product development, while others claim that precisely because of the obligation to unbundle, Microsoft will need to innovate or improve its media player because of the increased competition from other media player producers. There is, I think, some merit to both points of view, as has been explained very well in the chapters on that part of the case in this collection.

Since the difficulty of finding the right balance between, on the one hand, respect for IPRs and, on the other hand, maintaining effective competition is bound to continue and there will be future cases dealing with these problems, there can be little doubt that the debate on the Microsoft case and its merits will carry on into the future; and this will also apply in respect of the problems posed by the tying element. This collection of papers represents a valuable contribution to the ongoing debate.

Bibliography

Acohido, B. and Knox, N., 'Regulators Want Microsoft to Pull Media Player Out', *USA Today*, 25 March 2004

Ahlborn, C., Evans D. and Padilla J., 'The Antitrust Economics of Tying: A Farewell to Per Se Illegality' (2004) *Antitrust Bulletin* 287

Albors-Llorens, A., 'The Role of Objective Justification and Efficiencies in the Application of Article 82 EC' (2007) *Common Market Law Review* 1727

Anderman, S.D., 'Does the Microsoft Case Offer a New Paradigm for the "Exceptional Circumstances" Test and Compulsory Licenses under EC Competition Law' (2004) *Competition Law Review* 7

Anderman, S.D. and Kallaugher, J., *Technology Transfers and the New EU Competition Rules: IP Licensing after Modernisation* (Oxford: Oxford University Press, 2006)

Andreangeli, A., 'Case Note on T-201/04, Microsoft v Commission, Judgment of 17 September 2007' (2008) *Common Market Law Review* 863

Areeda, P. and Hovenkamp, H., *Antitrust Law* (New York: Aspen Publishers, 1995)

Arhel, P., 'L'affaire Microsoft: à propos de la decision du TPICE de 17 septembre 2007' (2007) *Les Petites Affiches, Doctrine* (21 November 2007) 3

Averitt, N. and Lande, R., 'Using the "Consumer Choice" Approach to Antitrust Law' (2007) *Antitrust Law Journal* 175

Ayres, I. and Nalebuff, B., 'Going Soft on Microsoft? The EU's Antitrust Case and Remedy' (2005) *The Economist's Voice* 1

Bebchuk, L.A., 'Federalism and the Corporation: The Desirable Limits of Competition in Corporate Law' (1992) *Harvard Law Review* 1435

Bergqvist, C., 'Konkurrencesagen mod Microsoft' (2008) *Ugeskrift for Retsvaesen* 103

Bomse, S. and Westrich, S., 'Both Sides Now: Buyer Damage Claims in Antitrust Actions Involving "Two Sided" Markets' (2005) *Columbia Business Law Review* 643

Bork, R.H., *The Antitrust Paradox* (New York: Basic Books, 1978, reprinted with a new introduction and epilogue, Free Press, 1993)

Bowman, W., 'Tying Arrangements and the Leverage Problem' (1957) *Yale Law Journal* 19

Bowman, W., *Patent and Antitrust Law: Legal and Economic Appraisal* (Chicago and London: Chicago University Press, 1973)

Bratton, W., McCahery, J., Picciotto, S. and Scott, C., *International Regulatory Competition and Coordination* (Clarendon Press: Oxford, 1996)

Bresnahan, T., *The Right Remedy*, Stanford Law and Economics Olin Working Paper No. 233 (2002)

Bresnahan, T. and Greenstein, S., 'Technological Competition and the Structure of the Computer Industry' (1999) *Journal of Industrial Economics* 1

Brodley, J.F., 'The Economic Goals of Antitrust: Efficiency, Consumer Welfare, and Technological Progress' (1987) *New York University Law Review* 1020

Calabresi, S.G., '"A Government of Limited and Enumerated Powers": In Defense of *United States v. Lopez*' (1995) *Michigan Law Review* 752

Calkins, S., 'Civil Monetary Remedies Available to Antitrust Enforcers' (2006) *University of San Francisco Law Review* 567

Camilli, E.L., 'Optimal Fines in Cartel Cases and the Actual EU Policy' (2006) *World Competition* 575

Carlton, D., 'The Lessons from Microsoft' (2001) *Business Economics* (January) 47

Carlton, D. and Waldman, M., 'The Strategic Use of Tying to Preserve and Create Market Power in Evolving Industries' (2002) *RAND Journal of Economics* 194

Chin, A., 'Decoding Microsoft: A First Principles Approach' (2005) *Wake Forest Law Review* 1

Crane D., 'Mixed Bundling, Profit Sacrifice and Consumer Welfare' (2006) *Emory Law Journal* 423

Crémer, J., Rey, P. and Tirole, J., 'Connectivity in the Commercial Internet' (2000) *Journal of Industrial Economics* 433

Cusumano, M., 'What Road Ahead for Microsoft and Windows?' (2006) *Communications of the ACM* 21

Debroux, M., 'Vers une Banalisation de la Propriété Intellectuelle dans l'analyse d'abus de Dominance?' (2007) *Contrats Concurrence Consommation, Focus* (October) 2

Derclaye, E., 'Software Copyright Protection: Can Europe Learn from American Case Law? Part 1' (2000) *European Intellectual Property Review* 7

Derclaye, E., 'Software Copyright Protection: Can Europe Learn from American Case Law? Part 2' (2000) *European Intellectual Property Review* 56

Derclaye, E., 'Abuse of a Dominant Position and Intellectual Property

Rights: A Suggestion to Reconcile the Community Courts' Case Law' (2003) *World Competition* 685

Dolmans, M., 'Standards for Standards' (2002–2003) *Fordham International Law Journal* 63

Dolmans, M. and Graf, T., 'Analysis of Tying under Article 82: The European Commission's Microsoft Decision in Perspective' (2004) *World Competition* 225

Drexl, J., 'Intellectual Property and Antitrust Law, *IMS Health* and *Trinko*: Antitrust Placebo for Consumers instead of Sound Economics in Refusal-to-Deal Cases' (2004) *International Review of Intellectual Property and Competition Law* 788

Easterbrook, F., 'The Limits of Antitrust' (1984) *Texas Law Review* 1

Economides, N., 'The Economics of Networks' (1996) 14 *International Journal of Industrial Organization* 675

Economides, N., 'The Microsoft Antitrust Case' (2001) *Journal of Industry, Competition and Trade: From Theory to Policy* 7

Economides, N., 'Competition Policy in Network Industries: An Introduction', in Jansen, D. (ed.), *The New Economy and Beyond: Past, Present and Future* (Cheltenham, Edward Elgar, 2006)

Economides, N., 'Public Policy in Network Industries', in Buccirossi, P. (ed.), *Handbook of Antitrust Economics* (Cambridge, MA: MIT Press, 2008)

Economides, N. and Katsamakas, E., 'Linux v. Windows: A Comparison of Application and Platform Innovation Incentives for Open Source and Proprietary Software Platforms' in Bitzer, J. and Schroeder, P. (eds), *The Economics of Open Source Software Development* (Amsterdam: Elsevier Publishers, 2006)

Economides, N. and Katsamakas, E., 'Two-sided Competition of Proprietary vs. Open Source Technology Platforms and the Implications for the Software Industry' (2006) 52 *Management Science* 1057

Economides, N. and Lianos, I., 'The Elusive Antitrust Standard on Bundling in Europe and the United States in the Aftermath of the Microsoft cases' (2009) 76(2) *Antitrust Law Journal* 483

Economides, N. and Lianos, I., 'A Critical Appraisal of Remedies in the EU Microsoft Cases', forthcoming (2010) 2 *Columbia Business Law Review*

Economides, N. and Flyer, P., *Compatibility and Market Structure for Network Goods*, Discussion Paper EC-98-02 (Stern School of Business, New York University)

Eklöf, D., 'Microsofts Licensvägran i Skottlinjen' (2007–2008) *Juridisk Tidsskrift* 681

Evans, D., 'The Antitrust Economics of Multi-Sided Platform Markets' (2003) *Yale Journal on Regulation* 325

Evans D., Hagiu, A. and Schmalensee, R., *A Survey of the Economic Role of Software Platforms in Computer-Based Industries*, RIETI Discussion paper No. 04032 (2004)

Evans, D., Nichols, A. and Schmalensee, R., 'United States v. Microsoft: Did Consumers Win?' (2005) *Journal of Competition Law and Economics* 497

Evans, D. and Padilla, J., 'Tying under Article 82 and the Microsoft Decision' (2004) *World Competition* 503

Evans, D. and Padilla, J., 'Designing Antitrust Rules for Assessing Unilateral Practices: A Neo-Chicago Approach' (2005) *University of Chicago Law Review* 73

Evans, D. and Padilla, J., *The Law and Economics of Article 82* (Oxford: Hart Publishing, 2006)

Evans, D. and Schmalensee, R., *Some Economic Aspects of Antitrust Analysis in Dynamically Competitive Industries*, (2001) NBER Working Paper No. 8268 (2001)

Farrell, J., 'Standardization and Intellectual Property' (1989) *Jurimetrics Journal* 35

Farrell, J. and Saloner, G., 'Installed Base and Compatibility: Innovation, Product Preannouncements, and Predation' (1986) *American Economic Review* 940

First, H., *The Case for Antitrust Civil Penalties*, NYU Law and Economics Research Paper No. 08-38, NYU School of Law, Public Law Research Paper No. 08-43 (2008)

First, H., *Netscape is Dead: Remedy Lessons from the Microsoft Litigation*, NYU Law and Economics Research Paper No. 08-49 (2008)

First, H. and Gavil, A.I., 'Re-framing Windows: The Durable Meaning of the Microsoft Antitrust Litigation' (2006) *Utah Law Review* 679, 682

Flint, D., 'IP Rights and Wrongs' (2004) *Business Law Review* 142

Forrester, I., 'Compulsory Licensing in Europe: A Rare Cure to Aberrant National Intellectual Property', Presentation at the US Department of Justice/Federal Trade Commission Hearings on Competition and Intellectual Property Law and Policy in the Knowledge-Based Economy: Comparative Law Topics, Washington, DC, 22 May 2002

Forrester, I., 'Article 82: Remedies in Search of Theories?' (2004) *Fordham Corporate Law Institute* 167

Forrester, I., 'EC Competition Law as a Limitation on the Use of IP Rights in Europe: Is there a Reason to Panic?' in Claus-Dieter Ehlermann and Isabela Atanasiu (eds), *European Competition Law Annual 2005: What is an Abuse of a Dominant Position?* (Oxford: Hart Publishing, 2006)

Forrester, I., 'The Server Technology Issues' (2007) *Contribution to the 11th Annual Competition Conference of the International Bar Association* 9

Fox, E.M., 'Competition Law and the Millennium Round' (1999) *Journal of International Economic Law* 665

Fox, E.M., 'Global Problems in a World of National Law' (1999) *New England Law Review* 11

Fox, E.M., 'Antitrust and Regulatory Federalism: Races up, Down, and Sideways' (2000) *New York University Law Review* 1781

Fox, E.M., 'Mergers in Global Markets: GE/Honeywell and the Future of Merger control' (2002) *University of Pennsylvania Law Review* 457

Fox, E.M., 'We Protect Competition, You Protect Competitors' (2003) *World Competition* 149

Fox, E.M., 'Is there Life in *Aspen* after *Trinko*? The Silent Revolution of Section 2 of the Sherman Act' (2005) *Antitrust Law Journal* 153

Fox, E.M., 'Remedies and the Courage of Convictions in a Globalized World: How Globalization Corrupts Relief' (2005) 80 *Tulane Law Review* 571, 573

Fox, E.M., 'Monopolization, Abuse of Dominance, and Refusal to License Intellectual Property to Competitors: Do Antitrust Duties Help or Hurt Competition and Innovation? How Do We Know?' in Claus-Dieter Ehlermann and Isabela Atanasiu (eds), *European Competition Law Annual 2005: What is an Abuse of a Dominant Position?* (Oxford: Hart Publishing, 2006)

Fox, E.M., 'Monopolisation, Abuse of Dominance and the Indeterminacy of Economics: The US/EU Divide' (2006) *Utah Law Review* 725

Fox, E.M., 'The Efficiency Paradox' in Robert Pitofsky (ed.), *How the Chicago School Overshot the Mark: The Effect of Conservative Economic Analysis on US Antitrust* (Oxford: Oxford University Press, 2008)

Fox, E.M. and Sullivan, L., 'Antitrust, Retrospective and Prospective: Where are We Coming From? Where are We Going?' (1987) *New York University Law Review* 936

Friedman, D., 'Standards as Intellectual Property: An Economic Approach' (1994) *University of Dayton Law Review* 1109

Gastle, C. and Boughs, S., '*Microsoft III* and the Metes and Bounds of Software Design and Technological Tying Doctrine' (2001) *Virginia Journal of Law and Technology* 7

Geradin, D., 'Limiting the Scope of Article 82 EC: What Can the EU Learn from the U.S. Supreme Court's Judgment in *Trinko* in the Wake of *Microsoft*, *IMS*, and *Deutsche Telekom*?' (2005) *Common Market Law Review* 1519

Gerber, D.J., *Law and Competition in the Twentieth Century Europe: Protecting Prometheus* (Oxford: Oxford University Press, 1998)

Gerber, D.J., 'Competition Law and the WTO: Rethinking the Relationship' (2007) *Journal of International Economic Law* 707

Gilbert, R., 'Holding Innovation to an Antitrust Standard' (2007) *Competition Policy International* 3

Gilbert, R. and Riordan, M., 'Product Improvement and Technological Tying in a Winner-Take-All Market' (2007) *Journal of Industrial Economics* 113

Gordon, S., 'The Very Idea!: Why Copyright Law is an Inappropriate Way to Protect Computer Programs' (1998) *European Intellectual Property Review* 10

Gstalter, J., 'L'arrêt Microsoft et la mise en œuvre de l'article 82 CE. Quels enseignements pour l'analyse fondée sur les effets?' (2007) *Revue Trimesterielle de Droit Européen* 742

Guzman, A.T., 'Antitrust and International Regulatory Federalism' (2001) *New York University Law Review* 1142

Hart, R., 'Interoperability Information and the Microsoft Decision' (2006) *European Intellectual Property Review* 361

Hausmann, H.C., 'Das Microsoft-Urteil: Zwischen Kartellrecht und Gewerblichen Schutzrechten' (2008) *Multimedia und Recht* 381

Hawk, B. and Denaeijer, N., 'The Development of Articles 81 and 82 EC Treaty: Legal Certainty' in Claus-Dieter Ehlermann and Isabela Atanasiu (eds), *European Competition Law Annual 2000: The Modernisation of EC Antitrust Policy* (Oxford: Hart Publishing, 2001)

Hogan, J., 'Competition Policy for Computer Software Markets' (2001) *Journal of Information, Law and Technology*

Hovenkamp, H., 'Distributive Justice and the Antitrust Laws' (1982) *George Washington Law Review* 1

Hovenkamp, H., *The Antitrust Enterprise* (Cambridge, MA: Harvard University Press, 2005)

Howarth, D. and McMahon, K., '"Windows has Performed an Illegal Operation": The Court of First Instance's Judgment in Microsoft v Commission' (2008) *European Competition Law Review* 117

Hylton, K., 'Remedies, Antitrust Law and Microsoft: Comment of Shapiro' (2009) *Antitrust Law Journal* 773

Idot, L., 'Comment Mettre Fin à une Superdominance?' (2007) *Europe, Focus* (October) 2

Jenny, F., 'Optimal Antitrust Enforcement: From Theory to Policy Options' in Ioannis Lianos and Ioannis Kokkoris (eds), *The Reform of European Competition Law: New Challenges* (The Hague: Kluwer International, 2009)

Jones, A., 'Analysis of Agreements under US and EC Antitrust Law: Convergence or Divergence?' (2006) *Antitrust Bulletin* 691

Kahneman, D., Slovic, P. and Tversky, A. (eds), *Judgment under Uncertainty: Heuristics and Biases* (Cambridge: Cambridge University Press, 1982)

Kaplow, L., 'Extension of Monopoly Power through Leverage' (1985) *Columbia Law Review* 515

Kaplow, L. and Shavell, S., *Fairness versus Welfare* (Cambridge, MA: Harvard University Press, 2002)

Katz, M. and Shapiro, C., 'Network Externalities, Competition, and Compatibility' (1985) *American Economic Review* 424

Katz, M. and Shapiro, C., 'Technology Adoption in the Presence of Network Externalities' (1986) *Journal of Political Economy* 822

Katz, M. and Shapiro, C., 'Product Compatibility Choice in a Market with Technological Progress' (1986) *Oxford Economic Papers* 146

Katz, M. and Shapiro, C., 'Product Introduction with Network Externalities' (1992) *Journal of Industrial Economics* 55

Katz, M. and Shapiro, C., 'Systems Competition and Network Effects' (1994) *Journal of Economic Perspectives* 93

Killick, J., '*IMS* and *Microsoft* Judged in the Cold Light of *IMS*' (2004) *Competition Law Review* 23

Korah, V., *An Introduction to EC Competition Law and Practice* (Oxford: Hart Publishing, 2004)

Korah, V., 'Refusals to License Contrary to Article 82 EC: *IMS* – When are the Circumstances Special?' (2005) *Fordham IP Conference Papers* (forthcoming)

Körber, T., 'Geistiges Eigentum, essential facilities und "Innovationsmissbrauch": Überlegungen zum *Microsoft*-Fall im Lichte der EuGH-Entscheidung *IMS Health GmbH*' (2004) *RIW* 881

Körber, T., 'Wettbewerb in dynamischen Märkten zwischen Innovationsschutz und Machtmissbrauch' (2007) *Wirtschaft und Wettbewerb* 1209

Kovacic, W.E.,'Designing Antitrust Remedies for Dominant Firm Misconduct' (1999) 31 *Connecticut Law Review* 1285, 1288–92

Krechmer, K. and Baskin E., *Microsoft Anti-Trust Litigation – The Case for Standards* (Boulder: University of Colorado, 2000)

Kühn, K.U. and Van Reenen, J., 'Interoperability and Market Foreclosure in the European Microsoft Case', Centre for Economic Performance, Special Paper No. 20 in B. Lyons (ed.), *Cases in European Competition Policy: The Economic Analysis* (Cambridge: Cambridge University Press, 2008)

Langer, J., 'The Court of First Instance's Microsoft Decision: Just an Orthodox Ruling in an Un-Orthodox Case' (2008) *Legal Issues of Economic Integration* 183

Larvick, M., 'Questioning the Necessity of Copyright Protection for Software Interfaces' (1994) *University Illinois Law Review* 187

Laycock, D., *Modern American Remedies: Cases and Materials* (Little, Brown, 1994)

Leupold, H. and Pautke, S., '*IMS Health* vs. *Microsoft*: Befindet sich die Kommission bei Kartellrechtlichen Zwangslizenzen (erneut) auf Konfrontationskurs mit dem EuGH?' (2005) *EWS* 108

Lévéque, F., 'Innovation, Leveraging and Essential Facilities: Interoperability Licensing in the EU Microsoft Case' (2005) *World Competition* 71

Lianos, I., 'Competition Law and Intellectual Property Rights: Is the Property Rights Approach Right?', in Bell, J. and Kilpatrick, C. (eds), *Cambridge Yearbook of European Legal Studies* (Oxford: Hart Publishing, 2006)

Lianos, I., 'Categorical Thinking in Competition Law and the "Effects-based" Approach in Article 82 EC', in Ezrachi, A. (ed.), *Article 82 EC: Reflections on its Recent Evolution* (Oxford: Hart, 2009)

Lopatka, J. and Page, W., '*Microsoft* and the Law and Economics of Exclusion' (1999) *Supreme Court Economic Review* 157

Lopatka, J. and Page, W., 'Monopolisation, Innovation and Consumer Welfare' (2000–2001) *George Washington Law Review* 368

Mahlueg, D. and Schwarz, M., 'Compatibility Incentives of a Large Network Facing Multiple Rivals' (2006) *Journal of Industrial Economics* 527

Mariotti, R., 'Note: Rethinking Software Tying' (2000) *Yale Journal on Regulation* 367

Matutes, C. and Regibeau, P., '"Mix and Match": Product Compatibility without Network Externalities' (1988) *RAND Journal of Economics* 221

McCrudden, C., *Buying Social Justice* (Oxford: Oxford University Press, 2007)

McGowan, D., 'Between Logic and Experience, Error Costs and the U.S. v. Microsoft Corp.' (2005) *Berkeley Technology Law Journal* 1185

Milgrim, R., 'Commission Proposed Capital Punishment – by Definition – for Trade Secrets, a Uniquely Valuable IP Right' (2006) *Journal of Patent and Trademark Office Society* 911

Moldén, R., 'Mandatory Supply of Interoperability Information: The *Microsoft* Judgment' (2008) *European Business Organization Law Review* 305

Montagnani, M.L., 'Remedies to Exclusionary Innovation in the High-Tech Sector: Is there a Lesson from the Microsoft Saga?' (2007) *World Competition* 623

Motta, M., *Competition Policy: Theory and Practice* (Cambridge: Cambridge University Press, 2004)

Nalebuff, D., *Bundling, Tying and Portfolio Effects*, DTI Economics Paper No. 1 (2000)

Nikulainen, K., 'Open Source Software: Why is it Here and Will it Stick Around?' (2004) *SCRIPT-ed* 149

O'Donoghue, R. and Padilla, J., *The Law and Economics of Article 82* (Oxford: Hart Publishing, 2006)

O'Rourke, M., 'Striking a Delicate Balance: Intellectual Property, Antitrust, Contract and Standardisation in the Computer Industry' (1998) *Harvard Journal of Law & Technology* 1

Ong, B., 'Building Brick Barricades and Other Barriers to Entry: Abusing a Dominant Position by Refusing to Licence Intellectual Property Rights' (2005) *European Competition Law Review* 215

Page, W.H., *Mandatory Contracting Remedies in the American and European Microsoft Cases*, University of Florida Levin College of Law Research Paper No. 2009-22 (2009)

Page, W.H. and Childers, S.J., 'Software Development as an Antitrust Remedy: Lessons from the Enforcement of the Microsoft Communications Protocol Licensing Requirement' (2007) *Michigan Telecommunications and Technology Law Review* 77

Page, W.H. and Childers, S.J., 'Bargaining in the Shadow of the European Microsoft Decision: The Microsoft-SAMBA Protocol License' (2008) *Northwestern University Law Review* 332

Page, W.H. and Childers, S.J., 'Measuring Compliance with Compulsory Licensing Remedies in the American Microsoft Case', 6 November 2008

Page, W.H. and Lopatka, J., *The Microsoft Case* (Chicago: Chicago University Press, 2007)

Pardolesi, R. and Renda, A., 'The European Commission's Case Against Microsoft: Kill Bill?' (2004) *World Competition* 513

Peeperkorn, L., 'IP Licences and Competition Rules: Striking the Right Balance' (2003) *World Competition* 527

Peritz, R.J.R., 'The "Rule of Reason" in Antitrust Law: Property Logic in Restraint of Competition' (1989) *Hastings Law Journal* 285

Peritz, R.J.R., 'Antitrust Policy and Aggressive Business Strategy: A Historical Perspective on Understanding Commercial Purposes and Effects' in *Workshop and Conference on Marketing, Competitive Conduct and Antitrust Policy* in (2002) *Journal of Public Policy and Marketing* 237

Peritz, R.J.R., 'Tipping and Network Effects' in D Moss (ed.), *Network Access: Lessons Learned in Regulation and Antitrust* (New York: Routledge Press, 2004)

Peritz, R.J.R., 'Competition Policy and its Implications for Intellectual Property Rights in the United States' in S.D. Anderman (eds), *The Interface Between Intellectual Property Rights and Competition Policy* (Cambridge: Cambridge University Press, 2007)

Peritz, R.J.R., 'Freedom to Experiment: Toward a Concept of Inventor Welfare' (2008) *Journal of the Patent and Trademark Office Society* 245

Peritz, R.J.R., 'Patents and Progress: The Incentive Conundrum', ATRIP Annual Conference, Max-Planck Institute, Munich, Germany, 21 July 2008

Peritz, R.J.R., 'The Roberts Court after Two Years: Antitrust, Intellectual Property Rights, and Competition Policy' (2008) *Antitrust Bulletin* 153

Pitofsky, R., 'Antitrust at the Turn of the Twenty-First Century: The Matter of Remedies' (2002) 91 *Georgia Law Journal* 169, 170

Rahnasto, I., *Intellectual Property Rights, External Effects, and Anti-Trust Law* (Oxford: Oxford University Press, 2003)

Reback, G.L., *Free the Market!* (New York: Portfolio, 2009)

Reimann, C., 'Essential Function vs Essential Facility: Defining the Amount of R&D Protection in High-tech Industries after *IMS* and *Microsoft*' (2004) *Competition Law Review* 49

Ridyard, D., 'Essential Facilities and the Obligation to Supply Competitors' (1996) *European Competition Law Review* 438

Ridyard, D., 'Exclusionary Pricing and Price Discrimination Abuse under Article 82: An Economic Analysis' (2002) *European Competition Law Review* 286

Ridyard, D., 'Compulsory Access under EC Competition Law: A New Doctrine of "Convenient Facilities" and the Case for Price Regulation' (2004) *European Competition Law Review* 669

Ritter, C., 'Refusal to Deal and Essential Facilities: Does Intellectual Property Require Special Deference Compared to Tangible Property?' (2005) *World Competition* 281

Rochet, J.C. and Tirole, J., 'Two-Sided Markets: A Progress Report', 12 March 2004

Rotenberg, B., *The Legal Regulation of Software Interoperability in the EU*, NYU Law School Jean Monnet Working Paper No. 7 (2005)

Samuelson, P. and Scotchmer, S., 'The Law and Economics of Reverse Engineering' (2002) *Yale Law Journal* 1575

Samuelson, W. and Zeckhauser, R., 'Status Quo Bias in Decision Making' (1998) 1(1) *Journal of Risk and Uncertainty* 7

Schmalensee, R., 'Antitrust Issues in Schumpeterian Industries' (2000) *American Economic Review* 192

Schoechle, T., *Re-examining Intellectual Property Rights in the Context of Standardization, Innovation and the Public Sphere* (Boulder: International Centre for Standards Research, University of Colorado, 2001)

Schoechle, T., 'Digital Enclosure: The Privatisation of Standards and Standardisation' (2003) *IEEE SIIT Conference Proceedings* 229

Schumpeter, J, *Capitalism, Socialism and Democracy* (New York: Harper, 1975; first published 1942)

Scotchmer, S., 'Standing on the Shoulders of Giants: Cumulative Research and the Patent Law' (1991) *Journal of Economic Perspectives* 29

Scotchmer, S., *Innovation and Incentives* (Cambridge, MA: MIT Press, 2004)

Shapiro, C., 'Microsoft: A Remedial Failure' (2009) 75 *Antitrust Law Journal* 739

Stephan, P.B., 'Global Governance, Antitrust, and the Limits of International Cooperation' (2005) *Cornell International Law Journal* 173

Taylor, M., *International Competition Law: A New Dimension for the WTO?* (Cambridge: Cambridge University Press, 2005)

Temple Lang, J., 'Defining Legitimate Competition: Companies Duties to Supply Competitors and Access to Essential Facilities' (1994) *Fordham International Law Journal* 437

Temple Lang, J., 'Anti-Competitive Non-Pricing Abuses under European and National Antitrust Law' (2003) *Fordham Corporate Law Institute* 235

Temple Lang, J., 'European Community Competition Policy: How Far Does It Benefit Consumers?' (2004) *Boletín Latinoamericano de competencia* (February) 128

Thyri, P., 'Immaterialgüterrechte und Zugang zur wesentlichen Einrichtund: Der Fall Microsoft im Licht von IMS-Health' (2005) *Wirtschaft und Wettbewerb* 388

Tilbury, M., Noone, M. and Kercher, B., *Remedies: Commentary and Materials* (3rd edn, LBC Information Services, 2000)

Van Raden, L., 'Technology Dematerialised: Another Approach to Information-related Invention' (1996) *European Intellectual Property Review* 384

Van Reenen, J., *Is there a Market for Workgroup Servers*? Centre for Economic Performance Discussion Paper No. 650 (2004)

Vesterdorf, B., 'Article 82 EC: Where Do We Stand after the *Microsoft* Judgment?' (2008) *Global Antitrust Review* 1

Vezzoso, S., 'The Incentive Balance Test in the EU Microsoft Case: A Pro-innovation "Economics-Based" Approach' (2006) *European Competition Law Review* 382

Watson, R., Boudreau, M., York, P., Greiner, M. and Donald, J., 'The Business of Open Source' (2008) *Communications of the ACM* 41

Weiser, P., 'Regulating Interoperability: Lessons from *AT&T*, *Microsoft*, and Beyond' (2009) 76 *Antitrust Law Journal* 271

Whinston, M., 'Tying, Foreclosure, and Exclusion' (1990) *American Economic Review* 837

Whish, R., *Competition Law* (5th edn, London: Butterworths, 2003)
Winterscheid, J., 'The EC Decision Against Microsoft: Windows on the World, Glass Houses, or Through the Looking Glass?' (2004) *The Antitrust Source* (September) 1
Woodard, L., 'Open Source Software: How to Use It and Control It in the Corporate Environment' (2004) *Computer and Internet Law* 8

Index